The Brazos Introduction to
<u>Christian Spirituality</u>

The Brazos Introduction to
Christian Spirituality

Evan B. Howard

BrazosPress
a division of Baker Publishing Group
Grand Rapids, Michigan

Published by Brazos Press
a division of Baker Publishing Group
P.O. Box 6287, Grand Rapids, MI 49516–6287
www.brazospress.com

Printed in the United States of America

Library of Congress Cataloging-in-Publication Data
Howard, Evan B., 1955–
    The Brazos introduction to Christian spirituality / Evan B. Howard.
        p.   cm.
    Includes bibliographical references and index.
    ISBN 978-1-58743-038-1 (cloth)
    1. Spirituality. I. Title. II. Title: Introduction to Christian spirituality.
    BV4501.3.H693 2008
    248—dc22   2008020471

Unless otherwise indicated Scripture is taken from the New Revised Standard Version of the Bible, copyright © 1989, by the Division of Christian Education of the
National Council of the Churches of Christ in the United States of America. Used
by permission. All rights reserved.

Scripture labeled KJV is taken from the King James Version of the Bible.

Scripture labeled NEV is taken from the New Century Version® Copyright © 1987,
1988, 1991 by Word Publishing, a division of Thomas Nelson, Inc. Used by permission. All rights reserved.

Scripture labeled NIV is taken from the HOLY BIBLE, NEW INTERNATIONAL
VERSION®. NIV®. Copyright © 1973, 1978, 1984 by International Bible Society.
Used by permission of Zondervan. All rights reserved.

"A Sequential Stage Model" (fig. 7.1); "Contours of Crisis" (fig. 7.2); "Modes of Re-
sponse" (fig. 7.3); and Prescriptions and Proscriptions of the Advocate" (fig. 7.4) by
Lewis Rambo in *Understanding Religious Conversion*. Used with permission of Yale
University Press.

Contents

Acknowledgments

It is difficult to know how to express thanks to those who have participated in a book that has been in the making for over thirty years. I remember sitting with Gregg Goyins in a restaurant in 1976, sketching, on my napkin, a first draft of what was to become the summary chart in chapter three. I called it my "napkin doctrine of the changed life." Though its shape has altered some, essentially it's still the same napkin doctrine. Yes, Greg? It was, however, Jody Dillow—who visited to discuss things theological and spiritual—that was the stimulus for me to write this down. Thank you, Jody. After many years, here is my response to your questions.

Many have contributed to the shape of this book. I have loved my years at school, where ideas have grown in dialogue with my professors at Whitworth College (Norman Krebbs, Ron White, Dale Bruner), Trinity Evangelical Divinity School (Walter Liefeld, Grant Osborne, Wayne Grudem), Gonzaga University (Bernard Tyrrell, Michael Rende, Joy Milos), and Graduate Theological Union (Sandra Schneiders, Beth Liebert, Joel Green, Eleanor Rosch). As the footnotes in the text will reveal, I owe a special debt to Donald L. Gelpi, whose intellectual vision and guidance helped me to fit together many pieces that had been lying scattered on the table of my mind.

A number of pastors welcomed me as participant-observer in the practice of Christian spirituality. I have appreciated sharing in the dreams of Keel Dresback, William Leslie, Rob Sheild, Michael Brodeur, Tom Belt, and Larry Day. Each have made a contribution to this book. Ongoing conversations with the folks at Renovaré (Richard Foster, Linda Graybeal, Lyle Smith-Graybeal, Dallas Willard) and with the crew of the Diploma in the Art of Spiritual Direction (DASD) at San Francisco Theological Seminary (especially Mary Rose Bumpus, Susan Phillips, Beth Liebert, Tom Glenn, Nancy Wiens) have clarified particular issues or ideas in this book.

And then there are the students (at the Vineyard Internship Program in San Francisco, DASD, Salt Lake Theological Seminary, St. Paul's Episcopal Church, Mesa State College, and at seminars with various groups) and directees who have offered valuable insights and corrections. For example, one student at a two-week DASD class, on the way out of worship, offered the word "Integrating" for the sixth stage of human experience. Another student, Ted Scott, guided me to the material on transition in chapter ten.

As my daughters have grown older, they too have contributed to the shape of this book. The idea for a textbook of this type arose in the context of working with them through David Myers's model textbook, *Exploring Psychology*. Claire insisted that I provide chapter summaries in my book. Terese's contribution is present in my last-minute changes of wording that give ever-increasing respect to ambiguity.

It was not always easy to acquire the resources I needed to prepare for this book. I am especially grateful to Valley Books and Coffee, Genesis Christian Marketplace, the Upper Room Bookstore, the library at Graduate Theological Union, my own public library (especially Dorothy Patton in interlibrary loans), and to Sam Metcalf, Steve Parish, and Nick Parish. I am especially grateful to those who have supported Spirituality Shoppe over the years, making this kind of research and writing possible.

A number of people read part or all of this book along the way. I am grateful for their suggestions. In addition to students, Jeff Benson, Jody Dillow, Paul Parsons, Greg Zuschlag, Don Gelpi (and the other members of the Murray Group), Tom Adams, John Handley, and Ian Wrisley are to be thanked. Brazos Press invited me to write this book with Protestant, Catholic, and Orthodox Christians in mind, which became a delightful challenge. David Pertz offered himself to me by carefully reading the entire text from the viewpoint of the Orthodox tradition. Each summer I have gathered with a few evangelical scholars in Christian spirituality to pray, play, and read together. These men have offered suggestions, support, and stimulus all the way through this project. Many thanks to Jim Wilhoit, Paul Bramer, Dan Albrecht, Lelan Harris, Tom Schwanda, Michael Glerup, Klaus Issler, and Ken Collins.

The editorial staff at Brazos have been patient, supportive, and exceptionally helpful (I have learned that textbooks are not easy to construct). Rodney Clapp believed in this book from the start and gave me important advice at the half-way point and at the end of the first full manuscript. Rebecca Cooper has endured many phone calls when I did not know proper procedure for things. Lisa Ann Cockrel navigated the book through difficult transitions. At my request, Jennifer Conrad Seidel served as copyeditor for this book. Thank you for your generosity and your usual magic. Paula Gibson, Dan Malda, and Brian Brunsting have done a superb job with the interior and exterior design of the book. Jeremy Wells was a help early on with marketing requests.

The process of acquiring images for the book was new (and complicated) for me. Thanks to Tania Hajjar and Logan Macdonald at the public library, Joey Montoya and Becky Wolford at Mesa State College, and Jonathan Phillips who all helped with computer search-and-storage procedures. Sally Barto, Krystan Bruce, and Terese Howard created rubber stamps for many of the historical portraits. Zina Lahr created drawings to communicate things I had in mind. Nick and Jennifer Parish combined photographic and computer graphic skills to represent ideas in the text. If a picture is worth a thousand words, you all said more than the text!

Finally, two others must be mentioned. First there is Carlton ("Coky") Hartman. His regular support and prayers and wisdom have contributed a great deal to my staying the course through this project. And then, there is my wife, Cheri. She was a special friend before the napkin doctrine was written. She has shared all my conversions, has read every page (most of them more than once), has confirmed every picture, and has provided the "home" (meant in the deepest possible sense) in which a book like this could be written. I love you.

Introduction

Christian spirituality is *in*. Christian colleges and seminaries are now regularly offering courses on spiritual formation, spiritual direction, and related topics. Students are practicing spiritual disciplines, reading devotional classics, and listening to others' stories of faith. Some will have questions about the conceptual frameworks within which the disciplines have been practiced or within which the dynamics of relationship with God have been understood. What is all this talk about "dark nights of the soul"? How do I relate the spirituality of Teresa of Avila to that of Jonathan Edwards or Maximus the Confessor? Others may wonder how the diverse practices of lived spirituality square with fundamental Christian beliefs. How does the practice of charismatic prayer or common Eucharist relate to our justification with Christ? Some may have valuable exposure to Christian spirituality in *part* but are interested in seeing a vision of the *whole*. It is with a view to these kinds of people and these kinds of questions that *The Brazos Introduction to Christian Spirituality* is written. I have designed this book to fill the need for a topical survey text in Christian spirituality. My hope, therefore, in writing this text is to provide an illuminating and interesting topical survey of Christian spirituality.

Perspectives

As a survey of *Christian* spirituality, this book aims to present the characteristics of spirituality as seen through the Christian faith, generally speaking. The question we ask in this book is, simply, What does relationship with God look like for Christians? For this reason I draw from and write to Christians from the three major traditions (Eastern Orthodox, Roman Catholic, and Protestant). (Unfortunately, I am unequipped to speak from the variety of forms of Christianity currently flowering in Africa, Asia, and South America. For more on these forms see, for example, Philip Jenkins, *The Next Christendom: The Coming of Global Christianity*, and Lamin Sanneh, *Whose Religion is Christianity?*) I summarize the main features of Christian spirituality by pulling together those elements that are common to Christians from various traditions. I illustrate the variety of form in Christian spirituality by giving examples from particular traditions. I have neither space to nor interest in arguing for the superiority of one tradition over another. Where appropriate I have discussed strengths and weaknesses inherent in different approaches to relationship with God. Finally, the history of Christian spirituality reveals a rich mixture of truth and ambiguity, and I have tried to honor this mixture in my presentation.

As a topical *survey* of Christian spirituality, this book provides an understandable summary of the diversity of Christian thought and practice regarding the main topics of the field. This book does not treat, for example, comparative or apologetic spirituality. Rather than viewing Christian prayer in comparison with Buddhist meditation, this text will simply summarize how Christianity itself—in its common and diverse aspects—prays. Similarly, while I try to present Christian spirituality in a coherent framework, I do not spend time defending the reasonability of the framework. Furthermore, with regard to references and endnotes, this text simply points to the wisdom of the family of God insofar as our brothers or sisters contribute to the topic at hand. I do not take the time to indicate where and how I may disagree with other aspects of someone's approach. My reference to another simply means that I affirm at least *this aspect* of his or her thought. Once again, neither space nor my own interests permit the dialectic necessary to differentiate myself from others in every point.

As a *topical* survey, the text is weighted somewhat in favor of the general rather than the particular. The trend in many introductions to Christian spirituality has been to lean toward the particular, surveying the field from a historical perspective and offering summaries of major themes at points along the way. Indeed, this trend has been necessary in order to free the study of spirituality from ties to dogmatics, which became burdensome when trying to forge an authentically interdenominational and interdisciplinary field of study. Nonetheless, I believe that now we can offer a sense of the whole that points to the general (recognizing that even this assigns the author a dangerous "perimeter-drawing" task) while respecting the particular. The text interfaces the particular into the general by means of illustrative examples, historical portraits, and what I have called "issue essays."

How to Use this Book

I tend to be a "big picture" kind of guy. My students tell me that they get the most out of my teaching when I show how a number of different things fit together. And while I constantly face the dangers of a distorting totalization, I find that my preoccupation with big pictures often helps students see things in a new light. I hope to accomplish something of the same in this text. So, in order to make this book *illuminating*, I have incorporated a couple of elements characteristic of my own study and teaching of Christian spirituality.

First, this text draws from a variety of different resources. As we will see in chapter 2, the study of Christian spirituality—as an exploration of the relationship between *God* and *human persons*—necessarily involves both theological categories (requiring biblical, dogmatic, and historical study) and categories from the human sciences (requiring psychological and sociological study). Furthermore, the exploration of Christian spirituality involves both formal academic research and informal personal experience. Prayer, for example, has been explored not only by the saints and mystics of history, but also by medical researchers, cognitive psychologists, anthropologists, and philosophers of religion, as well as by people like you and me. What insights might these diverse resources bring to our understanding of Christian prayer? My aim is not to provide a comprehensive coverage of any single discipline (for example, I tend to draw more from cognitive psychology than other branches of psychology due to my own background and interests), but rather to point to the key questions, figures, and ideas that shed light on the general survey of Christian spirituality and to illustrate how an interdisciplinary approach to Christian spirituality might look.

Second, this text provides a survey of Christian spirituality within a single coherent framework (the "big picture"). My goal is to give some insight concerning how various traditions, practices, and perspectives can be comprehended as a whole. To this end the text will develop, though not defend, a way of looking at the God-human relationship that helps make sense of a number of details regarding the spiritual life. The chapters are designed to present this framework piece by piece and then to apply this framework to the practical dimensions of Christian spirituality as the book progresses. For this reason the book moves from the more difficult material to the easier, progressing from method to theology to dynamics to practice. Pay careful attention to the charts and diagrams presented in the text. Pay attention to the structure of chapters 3 through 7. These charts and chapters provide the basic framework within which the practical aspects of relationship with God are explored. This introduction to Christian spirituality might seem tough in the beginning, but I believe it will be well worth the effort in the end.

But I hope this text is not only illuminating, but *interesting* as well. To this end the following features have been included:

- *Chapter outlines* and *chapter objectives* at the start of each chapter provide a general orientation to the flow of the chapter and to the tasks you should be able to perform upon completion of the chapter—encouraging you to begin with the end in mind.
- *Sidebars* summarize materials in the text or provide brief quotes from primary sources.
- *Focus boxes* provide you with portraits of historical figures and movements, or

with essays on key issues in Christian spirituality.

- *Charts, pictures, cartoons*, and such provide helpful visual illustrations and highlight key information.
- A *glossary* at the end of the book defines unfamiliar terms or terms that are used distinctively in this text. These terms are displayed in bold in the text at their first significant appearance. It is recommended that you look up the term in the glossary when you first encounter it. At times the glossary will direct you to a fuller discussion of the term later in the text than its first significant appearance. See index for further details.
- Near the chapter summary in each chapter, you will find a section entitled *Practicing Christian Spirituality*. In these sections I have offered personal exercises or "soul projects" appropriate to each chapter. These exercises require personal application of the material presented. I believe that if a student were to complete each of these exercises, the study would become not an assignment but a retreat, and the text would be not merely illuminating or interesting but *transforming*.
- At the end of each chapter, you will find a *chapter summary*, *questions* for consideration, and a list of works titled *Looking Further* to help you identify resources for further exploration.

Introducing
Christian Spirituality

OBJECTIVES

In this chapter you will gain a preliminary acquaintance with Christian spirituality. You will get an inspiring feel for the classics of Christian spirituality by reading a sample of Bernard of Clairvaux's essay on loving God. You will also be introduced to some of the main trends and issues facing the study of Christian spirituality. After reading this chapter you should be able to

- distinguish some of the differences between spirituality and other related terms;
- explain something of the diversity of Christian spirituality as well as something of the unity of Christian spirituality.

Finally, you will spend some time reflecting on what it might mean for you to love God with all your heart, soul, strength, and mind.

Let's begin by listening to a couple of sample expressions of Christian spirituality. Our first expression is taken from William Faulkner's *The Sound and the Fury*, published in 1929.[1] In this story, Faulkner paints a picture of life in the southern United States, and, more particularly, in this scene we catch the tail end of an African-American church service in the old South. Let's join young Ben, little Frony, their mother Dilsey, and the rest of the congregation as they listen to the sermon. What does Christian spirituality look like for the characters of Faulkner's story?

The preacher fumbled in his coat and took out a handkerchief and mopped his face. A low concerted sound rose from the congregation: "Mmmmmmmmmmmmmm!" The woman's voice said, "Yes, Jesus! Jesus!"

"Breddren! Look at dem little chillen settin dar. Jesus wus like dat once. He mammy suffered de glory en de pangs. Sometime maybe she helt him at de nightfall, whilst de angels singin him to sleep; maybe she look out de do' en see de Roman po-lice passin." He tramped back and forth, mopping his face. "Listen breddren! I sees de day. Ma'y settin in de do' wid Jesus on her lap, de little Jesus. Like dem chillen dar, de little Jesus."

"Mmmmmmmmmmmmmmmmmmm! Jesus! Little Jesus!" and another voice, rising:

"I sees, O Jesus! Oh I sees!" and still another, without words, like bubbles rising in water.

"I sees hit, breddren! I sees hit! I sees Calvary, wid de sacred trees, sees de thief en de murderer en de least of dese; I hears de boasting en de braggin: Ef you be Jesus, lif up yo tree en walk! I hears de wailin of women en de evenin lamentations; Den, lo! Breddren! Yes, breddren! Whut I see? Whut I see, O sinner? I sees de resurrection en de light; sees de meek Jesus sayin Dey kilt Me dat ye shall live again; I died dat dem whut sees en believes shall never die. Breddren, O breddren! I sees de doom crack en hears de golden horns shoutin down

de glory, en de arisen dead whut got de blood en de ricklickshun of de Lamb!"

In the midst of the voices and the hands Ben sat, rapt in his sweet blue gaze. Dilsey sat bolt upright beside, crying rigidly and quietly in the annealment and the blood of the remembered Lamb.

As they walked through the bright noon, up the sandy road with the dispersing congregation talking easily again group to group, she continued to weep, unmindful of the talk.

"He sho a preacher, mon! He didn't look like much at first, but hush!"

"He seed de power en de glory."

"Yes, suh. He seed hit. Face to face he seed hit."

Dilsey made no sound, her face did not quiver as the tears took their sunken and devious courses, walking with her head up, making no effort to dry them away even.

"Whyn't you quit dat, mammy?" Frony said. "Wid all dese people lookin. We be passin white folks soon."

"I've seen de first en de last," Dilsey said. "Never you mind me."

"First en last whut?" Frony said.

"Never you mind," Dilsey said. "I seed de beginnin, en now I sees de endin."

In our second (also fictional) sample, we listen in to a conversation at a coffee shop after a poetry reading. Where do you see Christian spirituality here?

"You know, I think I'm getting tired of this scene."

"Really?" Sarah said. "You've got to be kidding. Your reading tonight was fresh. You had them hanging on every word. And that part about the entertainment industry being cyber-puppets in the hands of the system—you really broke it down."

"Yea, exactly," Jason chimed in. "And look at this crowd. Kailee, you've been here long enough. It's really starting to happen."

"Thanks guys, you're sweet." Kailee hesitated, taking a sip.

"There's really something on your mind," Sarah probed.

"I'm not sure how to talk about it, if I can even put it into words. Funny, me the poet, with no words."

"Go ahead. Take your time." Sarah invited, "We'll wait."

"You see," Kailee began after a brief pause, "maybe that's the whole point. Its just so easy to critique this and deconstruct that. I can find words anywhere and everywhere to show how superficial things are. Nobody's real and we all know that. And so here we are, the 'enlightened' ones proclaiming everybody else's non-reality. And yet . . ."

"And yet," Jason repeated.

Again Kailee hesitated. "Yesterday I was taking the sub home from school, and you know when you go around the turn in the North tunnel how the wheels screech and the cars shake a little this way and that, and then you come out by that little park?"

Jason and Sarah nodded.

"Well, I came out, and saw the park, and someone had planted a few petunias there. It wasn't much, but they were so nice. And I thought how there they were, so still and quiet, and so pretty right there just outside all the noise and the commotion."

"Uh huh," responded Jason.

"I wanted to stop. To just sit with those petunias, just to *be* there, *with* them, you know? But really, as I thought about it, and I imagined myself actually *doing* it—now don't think I'm crazy—I was actually kind of afraid."

"Afraid?" Sarah asked.

"Afraid of petunias?"

"No, not afraid of petunias," Kailee retorted. "Listen to me . . . Ever since I left home I've been making noise. I've been shaking people around. I've been racing here and there telling the world that it's all a farce, that there's no meaning, that the powers have duped us all into a blind and mindless bliss. I question authority, I question God, I question everything . . . And there, just outside there are these petunias, . . . these answers, . . . in absolute stillness. Not the kind of answers we show off in our poetic fashion shows every week here, but *real* answers. I mean the real thing. This

could change everything for me. But I'm not sure I want to go there."

When we are confronted with "de beginnin and de endin" or when we look beneath our shallow cynicism into a mysterious stillness, whether we hear in a shout or in a whisper, we come face to face with the world of spirituality.

What Is Christian Spirituality?

In the past two decades, there has been a virtual explosion of published literature associated with **spirituality**. One can readily find discussion of the spirituality of sports, twelve-step spirituality, new age spirituality, as well as the spiritualities of every possible religious movement. Bernard McGinn, in his contribution to the first volume of the *Christian Spirituality Bulletin*, notes that he turned up some thirty-five different definitions of *spirituality*.[2] One wonders whether contemporary Western culture hasn't followed the example of Humpty Dumpty, who, when confronted about his use of language replied, "When *I* use a word, it means just what I choose it to

> Christian spirituality refers to a relationship with God as lived in practice, as dynamics are formulated, as explored through formal study.

mean—neither more nor less." Associations between the term *spirituality* and widely different sectors of religious culture have caused some Christians to look with caution at participation in spirituality. Yet, however vague the current use of the word may be, the term *spirituality*, and the phenomena associated with it, have been around for some time, and are likely to attract attention for some time to come.

The term *spirituality* was introduced to the West by the use of the Latin *spiritualitas*

What Is Christian Spirituality?

At the level of practice, Christian spirituality is a lived relationship with God. We actually live out, in practice, a relationship with God. ("My spirituality has been nourished by worship music lately.")

At the level of dynamics, Christian spirituality is the formulation of a teaching. We synthesize a way of understanding the dynamics of how relationship with God works. ("My spirituality, just like Lutheran spirituality, emphasizes the role of faith in God's finished work on the cross.")

At the level of academic discipline, Christian spirituality is a formal "field" of study. We engage in systematic investigation of the lived relationship or formulated teachings of the Christian church. ("My research in spirituality aimed at exploring the ways in which 'darkness' and 'light' were used in ancient Christian texts to describe Christian growth.")

to translate the Greek adjective *pneumatikos* (spiritual; from *pneuma*, "spirit"). In early Greek and Latin Christian writings, spirituality referred to one's appropriation of the Spirit of Jesus in life and ministry. The term was also used philosophically for that which pertains to the immaterial soul (spirit, as opposed to body). At times these two meanings were linked in an unfortunate rejection of bodily and material existence in favor of the pursuit of the spiritual life. The term was also used more narrowly to refer to the inner states or dispositions of the soul (referring, for example, to an uneasiness of one's spirit). In the seventeenth and eighteenth centuries, *spirituality* came to be used synonymously with *devotion*, *piety*, and *religion*. More recently, however, the latter two have gained a negative

connotation—consider how we now look with disdain on the empty formalism of one who is pious or religious. Other comparable terms (*spiritualité* in French, *Geistigkeit* in German, *spirituality* in English) carried these various nuances through the nineteenth and into the twentieth centuries. As spirituality was introduced to an increasingly pluralist and secular Western culture, it received still broader meanings: meanings that were decreasingly associated with distinctly religious life.

In spite of the variety of nuance, however, the dominant meaning of *spiritual* or spirituality refers to human interaction with the transcendent or divine. Within the Christian tradition, it refers specifically to relationship with God through Jesus Christ. Thus, at least in a general sense, Christian spirituality says something about the character of an individual's or a group's relationship with God through Jesus Christ. Both the cultivation of relationship with God and the experience of that relationship are contained and emphasized within the current use of the term. Nearly all of the literature published on Christian spirituality addresses, to some degree, this general sense of the term.

Scholars have explored a more precise definition of spirituality in a few key articles.[3] Walter Principe distinguishes between three levels of meaning of the term with reference to the Christian tradition. At the practical or existential level spirituality is "life in the Spirit as brothers and sisters of Jesus Christ and daughters and sons of the Father." Thus we can speak of spirituality as describing the character of our *actual, lived relationship* with God through the Spirit of Christ, as describing our **practice** of relationship with Christ. Second, there is the level of the *formulation of a teaching about* the lived reality. At this level one might speak of Ignatian or Lutheran spiritualities—referring not to Ignatius's or Luther's own lived experience, but rather to the teachings, the examples, and the encouragements that dominated their approaches to the spiritual life and that have become patterns for their followers.

The exploration of this level often involves the development of models of understanding the **dynamics** of relationship with God. Principe's third level identifies the use of the term to refer to the formal study of the first and second levels. Hence we may speak of the *academic field* of Christian spirituality, which reflects systematically on lived experience of Christ and the formulations surrounding that experience. Literature on Christian spirituality tends to focus on one or another of these levels, though rarely does the literature address only one of these areas exclusively.[4]

Principe's threefold categorization of meanings provides a helpful structure within which to approach spirituality. This text will blend aspects of all three. At times (and especially in the first two chapters) we will focus attention on Christian spirituality as an academic field. At times (and especially in chapters 5 through 7) we will explore models of the dynamics of the divine-human relationship—formulations by which we understand the Christian spiritual life in general. At other times (and especially chapters 8 through 11) we will review approaches to the practical cultivation of our lived relationship with God. By integrating these three elements—practical lived experience, wisdom about the dynamics of relationship with God, and intelligent methods of scholarship as students of Christian spirituality—we will be introduced to Christian spirituality in all its dimensions.

One thing that is common to all dimensions of Christian spirituality—practice, dynamics, and study—is ongoing dialogue with the classic spiritual texts of the Christian faith. Indeed, the flowering of interest in spirituality in recent decades has developed predominantly through a recovery of the wisdom of the past. Central to this development has been the republishing of many of the spiritual classics of the Christian faith.[5] Similarly, a number of popular anthologies of spiritual literature aimed at stimulating devotional practice have been published.[6] Studies of historical models have explored diverse ways of understanding divine-human dynamics.[7] Along with these, scholarly investigations of aspects of the history of Christian spirituality[8] have also contributed to the effort of this generation of Christians to reappropriate the spiritual heritage of the Christian faith.

One of the most delightful ways of diving into Christian spirituality is through the reading of these classics. By ruminating on the writings of these masters of the spiritual life, we allow ourselves to be instructed and inspired in the deep things of relationship with God. One of the best-loved of these classics is the little treatise "On Loving God," written by Cistercian mystic Bernard of Clairvaux (1090–1153). We have provided a few excerpts from this treatise for your refreshment. As you read, ask yourself, What makes this a classic piece of spiritual literature? How does reading this make me feel—guilty? full of longing? embarrassed? whole? How do *I* love God? Have I ever thought about the reward I receive in loving God? Spend some time with Bernard of Clairvaux's "drop of water" illustration. Imagine what it might be like to be dissolved fully into Christ and yet not lose any of your self in the process. Stay just for a moment with your reading after you are finished, and savor what may have been gained.

Distinguishing Terms

Having introduced Christian spirituality, we can begin to clarify how the word *spirituality* is to be distinguished from other related terms. Religious terminology is notoriously ambiguous, and terms like *spirituality, mysticism, spiritual formation,* and *religion* are certainly no exception. Needless to say, imprecisely using terms like *spirituality* and *mysticism* results in an unavoidable overlap of communication. Some understand mysticism as others might understand spirituality. Some speak of spirituality as others might speak of spiritual theology or spiritual formation, and so on. Therefore it may serve us well to review the history and use of some

Historical Portrait: Bernard of Clairvaux

Excerpts from Bernard of Clairvaux's "On Loving God"[9]

First see in what measure God deserves to be loved by us, and how he deserves to be loved without measure. For (to repeat briefly what I have said) "he first loved us" (1 John 4:10). He loved—with such love, and so much so generously—us who are so insignificant and who are what we are. I remember that I said at the beginning that the way to love God was without measure. Now since the love which is directed to God is directed to something immense, something infinite (for God is both immense and infinite)—who, I ask, ought to draw a line to our love or measure it out? God loves, whose greatness knows no bounds (Psalm 114:3), whose wisdom cannot be counted (Psalm 146:5), whose peace passes all understanding (Philippians 4:7), and do we measure out our response? It is clear, I think, how much God ought to be loved, and for what merit in him. For his own merit, I say, but to whom is it really clear how great that is? Who can say? Who can feel it? . . .

Lord, you are good to the soul which seeks you. What are you then to the soul which finds? But this is the most wonderful thing, that no one can seek you who has not already found you. You therefore seek to be found so that you may be sought for, sought so that you may be found. . . .

But since the Scripture says that God made everything for himself (Proverbs 16:4; Revelation 4:11) there will be a time when he will cause everything to conform to its Maker and be in harmony with him. In the meantime, we must make this our desire: that as God himself willed that everything should be for himself, so we, too, will that nothing, not even ourselves, may be or have been except for him, that is according to his will, not ours. The satisfaction of our needs will not bring us happiness, not chance delights, as does the sight of his will being fulfilled in us and in everything which concerns us. This is what we ask every day in prayer when we say, "Your will be done, on earth as it is in heaven" (Matthew 6:10). O holy and chaste love! O sweet and tender affection! O pure and sinless intention of the will—the more pure and sinless in that there is no mixture of self-will in it, the more sweet and tender in that everything it feels is divine.

To love in this way is to become like God. As a drop of water seems to disappear completely in a quantity of wine, taking the wine's flavor and color; as red-hot iron becomes indistinguishable from the glow of fire and its own original form disappears; as air suffused with the light of the sun seems transformed into the brightness of the light, as if it were light itself rather than merely lit up; so in those who are holy, it is necessary for human affection to dissolve in some ineffable way, and be poured into the will of God.

of these terms as a way of clarifying our definition of Christian spirituality and of introducing a few issues that will appear here and there throughout our encounter with Christian spirituality.

Mysticism: The Conscious Experience of the Presence of God

The term **mysticism** has roots in the Greek term *mystikos,* generally meaning secret or hidden. For the early Christians, what was hidden is now made known through Christ: hidden meanings of Scripture are now revealed, the mysteries of the sacraments are now available to those who participate. The phrase *mystical theology* expresses the character of the Christian's relationship with God now revealed through Christ and the Spirit in the church.[10] The emphasis in the early, or patristic, period of the church was on the Christian's participation in the objective work of Christ, and early mystical writings, such as those of Origen (ca. 185–ca. 284), Gregory of Nyssa (ca. 330–ca. 395), and Evagrius Ponticus (346–99), maintained this emphasis.[11] The homilies of Pseudo-Macarius (ca. 400) and the writings of Pseudo-Dionysius (ca. 500) also contributed significantly to the early Christian mystical consciousness.

During the Middle Ages, mystical interest began to shift toward the subjective experience of those who were united with Christ, and especially toward the experience of that union in the prayers of certain individuals, often referred to as contemplatives or mystics. While many Protestants subjected the notion of mystical union to a thorough reconceptualization, the focus on subjective experience in Roman Catholicism became especially prominent following the influence of the Carmelite mystics, especially Teresa of Avila (1515–82) and John of the Cross (ca. 1505–ca. 1560).

In the nineteenth and twentieth centuries, mysticism became a focus of attention not only among theologians and religious devotees, but also among philosophers and students of religion.[12] Likewise, the fields of psychology and comparative religion brought to the exploration of mysticism new questions, new approaches, and a new level of sophistication. Much of this research in mysticism brought with it a fascination with special experiences and states of consciousness.

Currently *mysticism* and *mystic* are used with all of the nuances mentioned above. Historian Bernard McGinn offers a mature summary of Western Christian understanding of mysticism centered around the notion of presence. He writes, "Thus

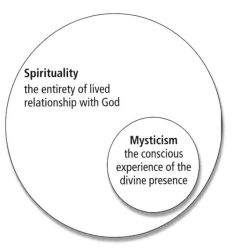

FIGURE **1.1**
Spirituality and Mysticism

Spirituality
the entirety of lived
relationship with God

Mysticism
the conscious
experience of the
divine presence

we can say that the mystical element in Christianity is that part of its belief and practices that concerns the preparation for, the consciousness of, and the reaction to what can be described as the immediate or direct presence of God."[13]

How then are we to distinguish mysticism from spirituality? Both emphasize the experiential aspect of faith. Both mysticism and spirituality give special attention to the life of the spirit. But whereas mysticism finds its center in the consciousness of God's presence, spirituality refers to a broader reality—as Principe put it, "life in the Spirit." Mysticism, unlike spirituality, is focally concerned with the human consciousness of the direct presence of God. Spirituality, on the other hand, is concerned with the entirety of the lived experience of an individual or group in relationship with God. The present work will use *spirituality* as the more encompassing term and will use *mystics* and *mysticism* primarily in reference to the consciousness of God's immediate presence. We will explore the nature of mysticism in greater detail in chapter 9.

Spiritual Theology: The Science of the Development of Christian Maturity

The phrase **spiritual theology** has its origins in the religious and academic climate of the Roman Catholic Church during the eighteenth and nineteenth centuries, especially in France. Distinctions between the study of doctrine and the study of ethics, along with the development of a "science" of the spiritual life, though not unknown in the Middle Ages, were aggressively explored in the sixteenth and seventeenth centuries. An interest in theological specification combined with an interest in the life of Christian perfection, creating two new theological specializations: ascetical theology, which addressed progress in Christian life in its earlier stages, and mystical theology, which explored the further stages of spiritual maturity.

Pursuit of this new science led to the production of standard manuals of Christian spiritual life, detailing the steps of progress from the onset of the spiritual life to the peak of Christian perfection. (This period or style of Catholic spirituality is sometimes referred to as "manual spirituality.") Ultimately, in the wake of disputes, new terminology was developed to minimize the distinction between ascetical and mystical stages. The term *spiritualité* in French was used to speak of the whole of the Christian's progress in perfection, and in English, *spiritual theology* became the term used to identify the science of this phenomena as a whole. Thus a recent manual by Jordan Aumann defines *spiritual theology* as "that part of theology that, proceeding from the truths of divine revelation and the religious experiences of individuals, defines the nature of the supernatural life, formulates

the directives for its growth and development, and explains the process by which souls advance from the beginning of the spiritual life to its full perfection."[14]

Other scholars of Christian spirituality distinguish spiritual theology from academic theology (whether dogmatic theology, systematic theology, biblical theology, or the like); and in so doing, they emphasize an approach to theological studies that respects the personal engagement of the theologian.[15]

There are a couple of important similarities between spiritual theology and the discipline of Christian spirituality. First, they both involve the student personally as well as academically. Christian spirituality is a "self-implicating discipline."[16] Christian spirituality involves not simply exploration of the character of relationship with the divine (a **descriptive** element), but also an interest in the improvement of that relationship (necessitating a **normative** element). Furthermore, spiritual theology and spirituality use both theological and experiential data. The development of a separate science of the spiritual life (spiritual theology) originally involved an intentional integration of both theological truths and psychological truths, a tendency that persists in current treatments of spiritual theology. Similarly, current thinking of spirituality as relationship with the divine demands an **interdisciplinary** synthesis of insights regarding the divine, the human, and the nature of relationship.

How then should we distinguish between spiritual theology and spirituality? First, they differ subtly in subject matter. We have seen clearly that the subject matter of spiritual theology is *growth toward perfection*. The literature on *spiritual theology* is often preoccupied with stages and grades of development to perfection: as Charles André Bernard lists, "the degrees of charity, the grades of prayer, the degrees of humility."[17] Some, however, find an exclusive interest in growth toward perfection to be insufficient. Scholars of Christian *spirituality* suggest that the subject matter to be explored is, rather, the entirety

Well, I haven't actually died to sin, but I did feel kind of faint once!

of the divine human relationship itself. As Philip Sheldrake writes of spirituality as it developed from spiritual theology, "it does not so much concern itself with defining 'perfection as with surveying the complex mystery of human growth in the context of a living relationship with the Absolute."[18]

Second, spiritual theology and the discipline of Christian spirituality differ in their understanding of the relationship between the theological disciplines. Spiritual theology frequently assumes a hierarchical approach to the theological disciplines: dogmatic theology teaches us what to believe, ethical theology instructs us concerning how to act according to the demands of strict obligation, and ascetical or mystical theology (spiritual theology) shows us how we might progress beyond the requirements of obligation to the heights of spiritual perfection.[19] Just as ethical theology possesses a subordinate relationship to dogmatic theology, so ascetical and mystical theology are subordinate to ethical and dogmatic theology. For many scholars of Christian spirituality, however, the shift to spirituality involves a breaking from this hierarchical relationship of doctrine and life. Many found that the manuals of spiritual theology presumed an exclusivity of thought and practice that was not conducive to fruitful dialogue among Christians of various groups or to a renewed appropriation of biblical theology and other related disciplines.

Finally, spiritual theology and the discipline of Christian spirituality differ in their perspective of the field. Spiritual theology emphasizes the individual: the growth to perfection of the individual believer. The field of Christian spirituality, however, is interested in drawing attention to the broader concerns and connections involved in the Christian's relationship with the Creator of the earth and the people on the earth.[20] Christian spirituality is concerned with all human relationships, it is argued. In the field of spirituality, one makes an effort to integrate the personal, spiritual, social, and ecological dimensions into a single cohesive approach to relationship with God.

This book is a text in Christian *spirituality*, not spiritual theology. The aim of this text, therefore, is to explore relationship with God with a broad subject matter, a broad range of methods, and a broad perspective. Nonetheless, we will address spiritual growth toward Christlikeness in a variety of ways, especially in chapters 7 and 8.

Sanctification: The Doctrine Concerning God's Action in Bringing Christians into Holiness

We also must distinguish between the consideration of spirituality and that of **sanctification**. The term *sanctification* derives from the Latin *sanctus* (holy) and was also used to translate the biblical Greek *hagiazo*, "to make holy." The term was eventually identified with the theological consideration of the work of God by which Christians grow in holiness— thus we speak of the doctrine of sanctification or sanctifying grace. (In the Eastern Church one considers also the doctrine of deification.) For example, the Reformed tradition's *Westminster Shorter Catechism*, originally written in 1646, defines *sanctification* (in question 35) as "the work of God's free grace, whereby we are renewed in the whole man after the image of God, and are enabled more and more to die unto sin and live unto righteousness." In the seventeenth century, the notion of sanctification was theologically important especially in placement alongside the notion of justification, which referred to the work of God in bringing people into the family of Christians.

Spirituality, as we have learned, addresses more than the growth of the believer, though that is certainly an important element. The scope of spirituality is the entirety of the lived and experienced relationship with God, as mentioned above. Thus the purview of humiliation, justification, regeneration, sanctification, glorification, and more are all potentially within the scope of spirituality. Insofar as sanctification is viewed as a segment of the whole of the divine-human relationship, it must be seen as a subcategory of spirituality.

Though never entirely separated, the study of sanctification and the study of spirituality may also be distinguished by method. Within reflection on sanctification, primary attention is paid to the *normative* dimension, the clarification of how relationship with God *ought* to be understood and pursued within the context of the faith. Scripture, church tradition, and theological reasoning have played the leading roles in the development of an understanding of sanctification. When discussing spirituality, however, greater (though not exclusive) attention is paid to the *experiential* dimension. What is foremost to a student of Christian spirituality is the believer's real, actual, existential, experienced relationship with God (how relationship with God is actually understood and lived). Thus, while students of sanctification might spend much of their time reading the sermons of John Wesley (1703–91), founder of the Methodist movement, students of spirituality might be found reading the journals of John Wesley. Christian spirituality ultimately mediates between the descriptive and the normative. Christian *spirituality*, as lived relationship with God, simply *is* and therefore deserves to be described honestly from a phenomenological perspective. Yet as authentic *Christian* spirituality, it cannot be entirely removed from the desire for the cultivation of or improvement of relationship with God within the context of a tradition of faith. Therefore it will draw from and feed into discussion of the normative. As a text addressing Christian *spirituality*, this book will not merely present the doctrine of God's work in bringing Christians into holiness; rather, it will cover the whole of relationship with God. We will address the issues of Christian spirituality bearing on the doctrine of sanctification more closely in chapters 7 and 8.

Religion: A Culture's Transcendent Synthesis of Myth, Doctrine, Ritual, Experience, and Ethics

By now you may be wondering, as the portrait of spirituality gets broader and broader, whether the term might not eventually engulf the whole of religion itself. Indeed, as one looks at the flood of publications, seminars, retreats, organizations, centers, programs, and whatnot that identify themselves in some form with the word *spirituality*, one begins to wonder.

Let us take as our point of reference an approach to defining **religion** that is used by many scholars in the study of religion: Ninian Smart's six-dimensional analysis of religion.[21] Smart suggests that we look at religion and religions in terms of a family resemblance among sacred narrative (or myth), doctrine, ritual, institution, experience, and ethics. How might we find spirituality in this model? On the one hand, it might appear that spirituality would simply fit into the "experience" segment of religion: whereas dogmatic theology addresses the doctrine of the Christian religion, spirituality addresses Christian experiences. Yet it is not as simple as that. The subject matter of spirituality is not the experiences of the faith, but the lived, experienced relationship as such—as a whole. Doctrine may not be the focus of spirituality, yet insofar as our view of God affects our actual relationship with God, doctrine begins to enter into the field of spirituality. Likewise, the structures and patterns of ritual are not spirituality, yet the way ritual fosters or hinders actual experienced relationship with God does bear on spirituality. Thus spirituality may indeed touch on each of the dimensions of religion, yet it does so only insofar as it is centrally involved in a person's or group's actual lived relationship with God.

Nevertheless, although there may be overlap between religious studies and spirituality in terms of content, there is an important difference in terms of scholarly method. The study of religion—at least as many promote the field of religious studies—differs significantly from spirituality in terms of the position of the scholar or student. There is, among many in religious studies, an effort to limit the attention of the field to "neutral" descriptions of religious phenomena. In order to prevent the degeneration of religious studies to cheap proselytism, it is argued that the scholar must be (or at least must present the appearance of being) personally disengaged from the material being studied. Christian spirituality, however, does not pretend to approach, nor does it desire, such neutrality. As mentioned above, spirituality is a self-implicating discipline, involving not only careful study of the subject matter, but a real desire to cultivate relationship with God through Christ. In this sense Christian spirituality involves a methodology for insiders, an approach to lived relationship with God that is concerned not simply with phenomenal description but also with improvement—an approach that mediates not simply the descriptive but also the normative.

Spiritual Formation: Exploring the Means by Which Believers Are Fostered toward Growth in Christ

Emphasis on the improvement of relationship, on the normative (and formative), brings us to the final term being considered: **spiritual formation**. The roots of spiritual formation lie in the history of the training of priests and religious, especially within the Roman Catholic church. One finds spiritual formation mentioned in such places as the documents of Vatican II that address the formation of priests and the Constitutions of the Society of Jesus that address the development of young Jesuits. Interest in spiritual formation spread from Roman Catholic training to Protestant circles in the past few decades. Protestant psychiatrist and scholar of Christian spirituality Gerald May distinguishes between spiritual formation, spiritual guidance, and spiritual direction as follows:

The Language of "Spiritual" Studies

- Mysticism: exploring the conscious experience of the divine presence
- Spiritual theology: the science of the development of Christian maturity
- Sanctification: the doctrine of growth in Christian holiness
- Religion: exploring the confluence of myths, institutions, doctrines, and experiences regarding matters of ultimacy within human civilization
- Spiritual formation: exploring the means by which growth is fostered in Christian life
- Christian spirituality: systematic reflection on the character of lived relationship with God through Christ

---

Spiritual formation is a rather general term referring to all attempts, means, instructions, and disciplines intended towards deepening of faith and furtherance of spiritual growth. It includes educational endeavors as well as the more intimate and in-depth processes of spiritual direction.

Spiritual guidance can apply to any situation in which people receive help, assistance, attention, or facilitation in the process of their spiritual formation. This applies not only to deepening one's personal realization of relationship to God, but also to the dynamic living-out of that realization in the actions of daily life. Spiritual guidance can come through almost any conceivable channel. Certainly it can occur in church or other religious community settings, but it can also come from friends, family, coworkers, scripture, nature, art, and a multitude of other sources.

When spiritual guidance occurs in a formal one-to-one relationship with another individual, it can be called *spiritual direction.*[22]

May's distinctions point to an important feature of spiritual formation: while spiritual theology and the doctrine of sanctification approach growth in maturity from the reflective side—the side of "science"—spiritual formation approaches the same topic from the practical side, exploring the relationships and means by which believers are fostered toward growth in Christ.

This brings us to the point of asking about the distinctions between spiritual formation and spirituality. Once again, while there are similarities between these two ideas—for example, both have ties to the practical and both attend to personal growth in Christ—spirituality appears to be the broader idea, embracing spiritual formation as a vital part of its horizon. In the present text, therefore, we will survey the broader question of relationship with God in general, and will explore the specifics of spiritual formation in a separate chapter (chapter 8).

Forms of Christian Spirituality

We encounter Christian spirituality at three levels: the level of *practice,* which refers to our actual cultivation and experience of relationship with God; the level of *dynamics,* which refers to our formulation of the patterns of lived divine-human relationship; and the level of *academic discipline,* which refers to the formal field of study that explores the first two levels in a systematic manner. As we all know, people differ in a variety of ways. Because people differ, spiritualities differ. Thus we can expect to find a diversity of approaches to spiritual practice, a diversity of formulations or models of the dynamics of divine-human relationship, and a diversity of schools of thought related to the methods and content of the academic discipline of Christian spirituality. Thus we can speak of a variety of types, or **forms**, of Christian spirituality. Indeed, at times it seems wiser to speak not of Christian spirituality, but rather of Christian spiritualities. These differences can be illustrated by a few examples, though you will gain a

fuller understanding of this as you explore each of the chapters of this book.

The Level of Practice

At the level of *practice,* it is easy to comprehend that different individuals and groups tend to approach and experience God differently. Theologian Alister McGrath, for example, presents a range of variables that give rise to different types of spirituality.[23] Some differences are due to differences in personality—for instance, one person may be more or less emotional than another. Thus we can speak of affective spiritualities (those that focus on our felt sense of God's presence) or speculative spiritualities (those that reflect on the great truths of the Christian faith). Some differences are a result of one's geographic location. Thus Celtic spirituality expresses a different character than Rhineland mysticism. Some differences are due to our location in time. Thus late-medieval spirituality is somewhat different from the patristic spirituality of the first five or so centuries of Christian history. Each of these differences, and each type of differences, highlights some aspects of our relationship with God and minimizes others. For this reason there are inherent strengths and weaknesses of each type of spirituality.

The Level of Dynamics

At the level of *dynamics,* the level of formulating a "teaching about" relationship with God or an "approach to" relationship with God, we can see again that differences will affect the models of relationship with God we develop and enact. Dutch scholar Kees Waaijman identifies three basic forms of spirituality—lay spirituality, schools of spirituality, and countermovements—the latter two of which identify groups that have formulated established teachings about the dynamics of relationship with God.[24] Some differences in our understanding of the dynamics of relationship with God are attributable to our religious traditions (and subtraditions). Thus we can speak of

Our worship architecture both reflects and shapes our "forms" of spirituality. What form do *you* have?

Orthodox, Jesuit, or Lutheran spiritualities. Some may see relationship with God as a journey (as in Gregory of Nyssa's *Life of Moses*), others as a marriage (as in Bernard of Clairvaux's sermons on the Song of Songs). Some approaches will be rooted in Catholic Scholasticism (such as John of the Cross's *Ascent of Mount Carmel*), and others will be rooted in Protestant Calvinism (such as Lewis Bayly's *The Practice of Piety*). Some formulations of spiritual experience might reflect debates concerning the role of prayer in the Christian life (as does *Hesychast* spirituality) or issues surrounding sixteenth century Spanish Catholicism (as does Ignatian spirituality), while others might originate from issues addressing twentieth-century ecumenical questions (as does the spirituality of Taizé). More recently, Geoffrey Wainwright and others have used attitudes of the church toward culture to outline some of the differences between spiritualities.[25]

The Level of Academic Discipline

Christian spirituality also exhibits diversity at the level of *academic discipline*. This diversity can be seen first of all with regard to the subject matter under consideration. For example, since relationship with God involves both beginners and those who are more mature, the standard historical divisions between ascetical and mystical theology become relevant. Scholars of spirituality also exhibit diversity with regard to their method of approach to the subject matter. Some view relationship with God more descriptively (thus giving rise to historical, psychological, and phenomenological analyses of spirituality), others more normatively (thus giving rise to theological, philosophical, and application-oriented approaches to spirituality). Michael Downey divides methodological approaches to studying Christian spirituality into four primary groups: the theological method, the historical method, the anthropological method, and the appropriative method.[26] Those who write and teach about Christian spirituality also differ with regard to a sense of openness to the variety of understandings, practices, and experiences associated with Christian spirituality. Bruce Demarest recognizes these differences as he divides the "leading voices" in Christian spirituality into three camps: progressives (those most open to input from a variety of fields and viewpoints), moderates, and conservatives (those least open).[27]

Christian spirituality comes in a variety of forms. We experience God as unique individuals and communities. We collect together in groups with common understandings of the dynamics of relationship with God. We investigate that relationship with different methods and perspectives. Try this exercise. Think of your own personality, your background, your community, your style of study. What form of spirituality do you have?

Trends in Christian Spirituality

In each century, believers explore relationship with God in the context of their own perspectives, interests, and concerns. Contemporary scholars and practitioners of Christian spirituality are no exception to this rule. Indeed, as we sought to distinguish *spirituality* from other similar terms, a few features characteristic of current approaches to Christian spirituality were introduced. Highlighting a few trends characteristic of the academic study of Christian spirituality (which in turn reflects broader trends in lived spirituality), and noting a few of the possibilities and dangers along the way, will give us a still clearer picture of Christian spirituality.

Descriptive

First, people today are inclined to approach relationship with God more from a descriptive or experiential approach and less from a prescriptive or normative approach. People today are interested in what people actually think, experience, or do, not merely in what their church or scriptures say relationship with God is or ought to be like. The current study of Christian spirituality has a tendency to emphasize the particular case as opposed to the universal principle. The strength of this trend has been to facilitate an appreciation for the diversity of Christian life. The danger is that we can lose sight of the forest for the trees. We may forget the normative in the midst of interest in the descriptive. The present text will blend the descriptive with the prescriptive by paying special attention to the dynamics of relationship with God: patterns of relating that are outlined in the norms of scripture and tradition but that are more thoroughly developed by a descriptive exploration.

Emphasis on Experience

The second trend in spirituality, related to the first, is an emphasis on experience.

If there is one feature on which scholars of the academic field of Christian spirituality universally agree, it may be the idea that Christian spirituality addresses experience. This emphasis on and discussion of experience has opened up new pathways and perspectives for understanding relationship with God. *Experience*, however, is a notoriously vague term, at times bringing confusion rather than clarity. The present text will address the nature of experience with as much precision as a textbook allows. In chapters 3 and 5 we will explore a specific model of human experience rooted in theology, philosophy, and the human sciences. This model will then serve as a framework within which the rest of the material in the book will be comprehended. By paying careful attention to the model of divine and human experience presented in these early chapters, you will discover a sense of the whole within which all the details of conversion, prayer, spiritual formation, and so on can be more easily recognized and comprehended.

Room for the Corporate

Third, the field of Christian spirituality has increasingly made room for the corporate. The spiritual manuals of a century ago considered relationship with God almost exclusively in terms of the interior life of an individual believer. This is not the case now. Today students of spirituality also study the spiritual life of local *communities*. Scholars are careful to understand spiritual life within the context of larger traditional and corporate structures, the body of Christ as lived and living. People think of the aims of spiritual maturity not only in terms of the intimacy of personal devotion, but also in terms of expressions of worship and love in congregational and political life. The field of spirituality is beginning to consider community as a *means* of mediating relationship with God. One student asks, "Although I still value the depth and quality of the traditional (one-on-one) approach to spiritual direction, I am increasingly considering this question: how do faithful communities become spiritual companions or directors for one another in the twenty-first century?" While an earlier generation may have focused on private spiritual disciplines, contemporary students increasingly desire to explore the role of public life in the divine-human relationship. Many aspects of Christian spirituality are being explored from a corporate perspective. This new focus on the communal is restoring a much-neglected aspect of gospel spirituality. Nonetheless, one faces the danger of community *replacing* authentic relationship with God. The present text will include both individual and corporate dimensions of Christian spirituality throughout the book, paying special attention to the life of care in chapter 10.

Somewhat Engaged

Fourth, the contemporary exploration of spirituality is perhaps best understood as a "somewhat engaged" field of study. It is not as detached as religious studies, yet it is not as narrowly practical as the subdiscipline of spiritual formation. There is permission, if not encouragement, to be moved, affected, even transformed by one's studies and to let that transformation influence the process and conclusions of the study itself. Scholars in Christian spirituality do want to help people grow in authentic relationship with God, yet they take great care not to let the field of spirituality degenerate to a shallow devotionalism. Our aim is not simply the cultivation of popular devotion; it is the well-researched reflection on the nature of relationship with God. And for this reason there is a serious academic side to the field of spirituality. The present text will respect this tension between the theoretical and practical. It begins with the theoretical, setting the notion of relationship with God within a carefully considered understanding of each of the parties. Nevertheless, it will offer more practical wisdom and

especially as we progress through the text. It will treat at length some of the nuances of relationship with God that are of special value to pastors and spiritual caregivers. It will, on occasion, offer suggestions for spiritual growth. This practical wisdom will, however, be set within a survey of the studied reflections of scholars of Christian spirituality.

Interdisciplinary

Finally, the trend in Christian spirituality appears to be a move toward greater interdisciplinarity. One need only review the articles in *Spirituality Today*, *Christian Spirituality Bulletin* (now *Spiritus*), and other related journals to see this trend. As scholars explore both the divine and human dimensions of Christian spirituality, as they pursue an understanding of

> What is called for in a Christian theology of spirituality is a dialectical understanding of community and individuality. In this understanding, neither term is thought without the other. . . . The embodied practices of the Christian life are inseparable from their setting in the Christian community—there is no community without these embodied practices and there can be no authentic practices without a sound and supporting community.
>
> —theologian Samuel M. Powell[28]

what relationship with God is all about, they seek dialogue partners in the arts and sciences alike. The strength of this approach is, again, its value in opening up new ways of looking at the divine-human relationship. The danger, however (especially as the field of Christian spirituality is a young discipline), is that fascination with novelty may either lure us from our moorings in the Christian tradition or make the field so diffuse that there is little to hold it together. The present text will draw from a variety of disciplines—especially biblical studies, philosophy, theology, history, and the human sciences. We will examine the interdisciplinary approach to Christian spirituality in greater detail in chapter 2.

The Foundations of Christian Spirituality

While the forms and trends in Christian spirituality point us to the diversity of relationship with God, we must, at the same time, attend to the unity of Christian spirituality. Because each individual is human and each group comprises humans, and because God is the same God in every relationship, there will be a certain sameness in the character of relationship with God throughout Christian history. Thus we can speak of a fundamental pattern or "**foundations**" characterizing Christian relationship with God in general, foundations that support our practice, our understanding of the dynamics of the divine-human relationship, and our formal study of Christian spirituality. The foundations of Christian spirituality arise primarily from "questions posed specifically by the Christian tradition of revelation about the nature of God, human nature and the relationship between the two."[29] Yet they also arise as we reflect on certain patterns of human existence as specifically human as well as from scientific and philosophical reflections on the nature of relationship itself and from the situations and questions of life in general. These foundations clarify the definition not simply of Christian *spirituality*, but also of the nature of an authentic *Christian* spirituality.

Christian Revelation

The primary foundation of Christian spirituality is the revelation of God—in Jesus Christ, in the scriptures, and in the Spirit through the church. Christian spirituality is grounded in Christian revelation. While we respect the mystery of God, aware that all our theologizings are meager attempts to comprehend the incomprehensible, we must affirm at the same time that authentic Christian relationship with God grows in dialogue with the fundamental texts and truths of the Christian faith. Therefore, approach to relationship with God must be rooted in the revelation of God through Christ and the scriptures, as interpreted through the historic body of Christ. The sacred character of Christian revelation will be assumed in this text.

The Living God

The second foundational principle of authentic Christian spirituality is the reality of the spiritual world. Spirituality implies *Spirit*. If Christian spirituality addresses the actual lived relationship between people and God, then the actual living reality of God must be understood from the start. It may be possible to present a religious studies approach to Christian spirituality in which one prescinds from presuppositions regarding the reality or character of the divine and chooses rather to explore Christian spirituality by speaking strictly of the *human's* response to a "perceived transcendent." In the present text (which is a text for "insiders"), we will simply assume the being and activity of the Christian God. Thus we will speak not simply of how the human perceives and relates to the divine, but also of how God relates to us. In so doing we are not exercising sectarian presumption; rather, we are summarizing the wisdom of revealed scriptures, the wise observations of two millennia of Christian history, and our own experience of Spirit. How we understand God affects how we cultivate relationship with God and, frequently, our very experience of the relationship with God.

Human Experience

But just as spirituality is about Spirit, it is also about the *human* relationship with Spirit. Therefore, in order to comprehend Christian spirituality, not only must we address the dynamics of the Spirit's work, but we must also explore the nature and dynamics of human experience. We must speak of the ways of God with people, but we must also speak of the ways of people with God. Hence, our third foundational principle of Christian spirituality is that human experience, in all its richness, is related to God. Christian spirituality sees God in relationship with humans—heart, mind, soul, and strength—and it acknowledges the full multidimensionality of human experience. Thus our approach to relationship with God must account for our active and contemplative sides. Thus we must consider the ways in which all our faculties and operations (imagination, perception, emotions, intellect, volition, and so on) serve to help or hinder relationship with God. Thus we must comprehend spirituality in the context of all our relationships as humans: with ourselves, with God, with others, and with the ecosphere.

Relationship with God

Next, we move from reflecting on each of the participants to reflecting on the dynamics of the divine-human relationship itself. Christians believe not only in the existence of the divine and the human, but also in the fact of their joining. A real God and real human without real connection (as in, perhaps, an extreme deist position) offers no foundation for spirituality. Christian spirituality assumes the mutual self-communication of two parties (divine and human), where one reveals and shares something of one's experience to the other and with the other. This is our fourth principle of Christian spirituality. Christian spirituality expresses the transformation of one by means of another. Social psychological terms such as approach, symbolic interaction, and entrustment, then, all have their place in the understanding of Christian spirituality. Christian spirituality involves the sharing of selves. Thus, as an exploration of the fullness of God (insofar as this can be known or experienced) encountering

the fullness of human experience, authentic Christian spirituality must attempt to embrace the whole of the gospel. (Shall we call it the "full gospel"?) It aims at being Christ-centered, Spirit-led, and love-expressive. It will seek to reconcile faith and works, evangelism and social action, attending to all those arenas of life where God and human share life together.

A Relationship of Love

The final foundational principle of the basic framework of Christian spirituality is this: the fundamental character of the relationship between the divine and human is love. Love is at the center of God's own Trinitarian life. The movement of God toward humanity is a movement of love, a love to the death. The greatest commandments concern our love for God and for one another. Thus, for example, an authentic approach to Christian spirituality begins from a place of rest in the loving acceptance God gives us through Christ. Likewise, authentic Christian spirituality, as a spirituality of love, will not be neutral. Jesus exercised his relationship with God from a stance of active, compassionate identification with those in need around him. If Christian spirituality has anything to do with becoming like Christ, it must seek to operate from this same identification. Though the practices and politics of spirituality may vary, authentic spirituality will not be able to avoid involvement with suffering and need. Christian spirituality embraces the virtues of Christ: justice, chastity, patience, contentment, mercy, and especially love.

Christian spirituality, as the actual relationship of a person or group with God through Jesus Christ—either existentially cultivated and experienced, formulated into a model for understanding and practice, or explored systematically within the academic community—exhibits not only a wide diversity of types but also a unity of foundational principles. The framework of our understanding of relationship with

29

The Foundations of Christian Spirituality

- Christian spirituality is grounded in Christian *revelation*.
- Christian spirituality assumes the living reality of the Christian *God*.
- Christian spirituality involves *human experience*, in all its richness.
- Christian spirituality explores the *relationship* of divine and human, in all its complexity.
- The fundamental character of Christian spirituality is a relationship of *love*.

God in Christ is founded on Christian revelation, the character of God, of the human, and of the nature of their relationship. It is the task of Christian spirituality as an academic discipline, and of the present text, to illumine this blend of unity and diversity in holy love.

Christian Spirituality's Big Issues

Any field of study has its own set of big issues—questions or topics that shape the character of that field and that often organize the contents of introductory textbooks in the field. Psychology textbooks address personality, development, perception, cognition, and so on. Textbooks in philosophy discuss knowledge, cosmology, metaphysics, ethics, logic, and the like. It is the same in Christian spirituality. The big issues that have been raised over the centuries with regard to our relationship with God will form the major divisions of this book, again gradually progressing from the more theoretical to the more practical.

How Do We Explore Relationship with God?

The first issue to be discussed is the issue of *methodology*. Just how are we to ask questions about the relationship between humans and God? What do scholars of Chris-

tian spirituality *do* when they explore the divine-human relationship? How can the mysteries of the divine-human relationship be explored such that we remain faithful to both our Christian heritage and the actual lived experience of Christians, past and present? We have already seen that there are a variety of scholarly methodologies of approaching reflection on our relationship with God. We will survey the questions regarding the relationship between Christian spirituality and a variety of disciplines relevant to its study in chapter 2.

Who Are We as Humans?

Having addressed the question of methodology, we will be ready to explore the nature of the persons or parties that form the relationship of Christian spirituality. In chapter 3 we will explore the nature of human experience: What does it mean to be human? What is it about us that makes it possible for us to relate to God? How do we experience or express relationship with God? Chapter 3 will present the more philosophical model of human experience, describing something of the operations, processes, and relationships involved in human experience.

Who Is God?

In chapter 4 we will shift attention from the human to the divine. In what sense is God knowable or unknowable? What is it about God that makes relationship with God possible? What is God like? How does God communicate with humans? How does God express or experience relationship? How do people develop an understanding of who God is for them? These may seem like sophisticated theological questions, yet the nuts and bolts of our spiritual formation are frequently attached, either consciously or unconsciously, to just such questions.

Nevertheless, human experience cannot be really understood apart from its place in the *plan* of God, especially with reference to Christ. What is humanity about in the

A Few Questions of Christian Spirituality

- What do scholars of Christian spirituality *do* when they explore the divine-human relationship?
- What is it about humans that makes it possible for us to relate to God?
- How does God communicate with humans?
- How does God experience relationship?
- How does relationship with God fit into God's plan for the universe?
- How is a relationship with God similar or different from a relationship with other humans?
- How does relationship with God affect us?
- How are Christians conformed into the likeness of Christ?
- What does it mean to "speak" or to "listen" to God in prayer?
- How does relationship with God affect family, ecology, evangelism, politics, or other forms of care?
- How can we "know God's will" for us in the particulars of life?
- What facilitates (or kills) "revival"?

what might relationship with God look like? How does what we know of human relationships help us understand relationship with God? What do we see when we look at the experienced relationship of a believer to Christ? We will first survey the wide range of diversity in lived experience of God. Then we will look more closely at some fundamental dynamics underneath that diversity.

How Are People Transformed in Christ?

Chapter 7, then, takes the outline of relationship with God presented above and develops it into an exploration of transformation. How does relationship with God affect us? What kinds of change happen through relationship with God? How long does transformation take? Are some changes better than others? We will consider Christian transformation as the Godward reorientation of human experience. We observe the work of God and humans in Christian transformation; then we explore the length, breadth, and depth of transformation.

How Are Christians Formed into the Likeness of Christ?

By this time we will have grasped a few of the basic dynamics of Christian relationship with God, and we will be ready to address some of the more practical topics related to Christian spirituality. Chapter 8 addresses the fundamental question of spiritual formation: How is it that Christians are conformed increasingly into the likeness of Christ? Who is involved? What kinds of disciplines are appropriate? Should Christians be ascetics? And what is all this formation *for*? We will first look at a few biblical principles that shape our understanding of spiritual formation. Then we will explore the contexts, agents, aims, tasks, and means of spiritual formation. Our aim in this chapter is to survey the factors involved in an intentional pursuit of relationship with God, such that sense

ultimate scheme of things? Who are we in the light of God's work? Therefore, in chapter 5, we will develop our model of human experience beyond the philosophical to the theological. We will explore three fundamental aspects of human existence: the greatness of human experience as an image of God, the tragedy of human experience due to sin and Satan, and the restoration of human experience in Christ. Here we will touch on a few important theological questions insofar as they are relevant to Christian spirituality.

What Is Relationship with God?

By the time we reach chapter 6 we will really begin to examine relationship with God. Given what we know of human experience and our restoration in Christ,

Pursuing Spirituality: A Dangerous Practice?

The pursuit of Christian spirituality might seem at first to be a perfectly safe, if not a positively sanctified, enterprise. What harm could come from cultivating one's relationship with God? What danger could there be in the disciplined exploration of our relationship with God?

Much harm, indeed, some have said. While some Christians are practicing spiritual disciplines, attending retreat centers, joining spiritual direction workshops, and pursuing advanced degrees in spirituality, others are concerned that such pursuits place believers into unwitting cooperation with diabolic strategies, non-Christian worldviews, and practices that do not reflect the authentic Christian faith. They are concerned that, through involvement in the practices and people associated with Christian spirituality, Christians are being seduced into an apostasy of eschatological proportions. Dave Hunt and T. A. McMahon, for example, critique current interest in spirituality, stating, "It is our conviction, based upon years of research and mountains of evidence, that the secular world is in the late stages of succumbing to the very deception that Jesus and the apostles predicted would immediately precede the Second Coming. We are gravely concerned that millions of Christians are falling victim to the same delusion."[30] Some, like Hunt and McMahon, label this current interest in Christian spirituality as a New Age seduction. Others warn of Christianity's decay into gnosticism, an approach to the divine-human relationship that denies fundamental Christian beliefs. But the root of their concern with relationship to spirituality is the same. Some are persuaded that the pursuit of spirituality as practiced today often promotes an approach to relationship with God that distorts the Christian faith. For this reason, they argue,

the leaders, the institutions, the literature, and the influences associated with Christian spirituality ought to be avoided.

This concern deserves careful attention. I have personally known Christians who abandoned their faith, and whose lives were shipwrecked, in the context of exploring spirituality. Nonetheless, the fact that I write an introduction to Christian spirituality should indicate that I believe avoidance is not the best response. How are we to chart the course of our relationship with God in contemporary life so that Christ, and not culture, is primary? At what point does authentic Christian faith become compromised? When does sincere pursuit of God become an illicit dabbling in the demonic? The New Testament epistles are full of warnings and rebukes regarding these matters. The epistle of 1 Timothy, for example, warns that "some will renounce the faith by paying attention to deceitful spirits and teachings of demons" (1 Timothy 4:1). Our beliefs, our actions, and our associations may all contribute to the character of our relationship with God. For this reason, an introduction to *Christian* spirituality must be attentive to the boundary lines of thought, practice, and community that are essential to the Christian faith—as difficult as they may be to identify at times.

The issue of the boundary lines of authentic Christian spirituality is well acknowledged by students of Christian spirituality, both ancient and contemporary.[31] Desert elders ("fathers" and "mothers" from around the fourth century who sought to pursue devoted relationship with God in the deserts of the Middle East), Puritan divines (who articulated the dynamics of the divine-human relationship in the English-speaking world of the sixteenth and seventeenth centuries), and contemporary sages all present guidelines, characteristics, and criteria in hopes of giving a general indication of the boundary lines of authentic Christian spirituality. My suspicion is that we are best served, in this regard, by following a simple thesis: the pursuit of Christian spirituality remains authentically Christian to the degree that it consciously embodies the foundational principles of Christian spirituality. Likewise, spirituality distorts the Christian faith as it is no longer upheld by this foundation. Let us explore this thesis further.

Is the pursuit of Christian spirituality a dangerous practice? Well, it all depends. Are we reaching into the revealed texts and traditions of historic Christianity? Is our exploration of the dynamics of the divine-human relationship founded on the fundamental truths of the Christian faith? If so, then Christian spirituality is not only safe, but saving. When we release our moorings from the sacred texts and traditions, or when we fail to pursue increase in knowledge and love because we are so tightly tied to these moorings, Christian spirituality begins to flounder. Do we acknowledge the personal God of Christianity? When we consider spirituality simply as a human enterprise, or when we misrepresent God as a mere force or as a deity that contains no mystery, our spirituality enters into the danger zone. Are we seeking to love God with all our heart, mind, soul, and strength? Are we recognizing the fullness of human experience as we relate to God? To the degree that a form of spirituality isolates itself in fascination with one dimension of life (for example, in felt experiences of the Spirit), our approach to relationship with God has lost authenticity and has become a dangerous affair. What about our assumption of the richness of the divine-human *relationship*? Are we embracing the "full gospel"? Do we acknowledge the range of contributions to our understanding of this full gospel from a variety of Christian traditions? Are we living in a relationship of love with God and others? Is our interest in devotion an escape from relationships or a way into relationships? Are we doing, as well as believing, the truth? Let us be watchful, lest Christian spirituality become a dangerous practice.

Here are some additional questions to ponder: It is one thing to evaluate the danger of pursuing Christian spirituality, but what about the danger of *not* pursuing Christian spirituality? Should we be concerned if our pursuit of relationship with God is *not* dangerous? Could Christ's call to follow perhaps be a call into the danger zones?

can be made of the variety of practices and approaches to spiritual disciplines.

What Is Prayer?

One cannot speak of Christian spirituality without, sooner or later, speaking of prayer. We will survey reflection on prayer in chapter 9. My aim is not to create a guidebook to personal prayer; rather we will explore the dynamics of prayer in light of a variety of different perspectives and in the context of our model of human experience. How are mind and emotions involved in prayer? What particular means have been used to facilitate corporate or personal communication with God? What is it like to "listen" to God how do the ordinary dynamics of relationship affect the life of prayer? What happens when we pray? What happens when God "answers" prayer? What kinds of effects might prayer have on those who pray, or on the world?

What Does It Mean to Care?

In chapter 10, we shift our attention from the life of prayer to the life of care.

Christian spirituality is not just about our relationship with God as individuals. It is fostered and expressed in relationship with others. Yet while there has been much systematic reflection on the life of prayer, there has been little of this with regard to the life of care. For this reason chapter 10 will be somewhat exploratory. What is Christian care all about? Who are the "others" for whom we care? What do we give them when we care? From what contexts do we offer care? What kinds of issues will we have to face when we offer care? Are there particular ways of offering care, like there are ways of prayer? These are the kinds of questions to be explored as we look into the life of care.

How Do We Know What Is from God?

We treat the topic of discernment in chapter 11. Christian discernment deals with issues involved in the question, How do I know what is or is not from God? Questions regarding the discernment of God's presence or God's will arise when we explore our vocation, when we act as a community, when we evaluate our experience, or when we assess the trends of our times. What kinds of virtues best make us ready to recognize the presence and will of God? How do communities get ready to meet together to decide direction for the group? How can we tell whether a "move of God" is really from God or not? This chapter will present the process and dynamics involved in getting to the place where we can say with confidence, "*This* is God."

Where Does Real Renewal Come From?

Our final chapter, chapter 12, will draw things together around the theme of renewal. Renewal, revival, revitalization, reform, and the like have been at the heart of Christian spirituality since ancient times, and they are also relevant today. Once again, using the model of Christian spirituality developed in the previous chapters, we will consider just how Christian renewal might be comprehended. We will look at the dynamics of development and decay of renewal. We will explore the cultivation and correction of revival. We will explore the renewal of our selves, of our communities, and of our world.

"This is my fourth sermon on the transforming power of the gospel. Why do you look like the same old bunch?"

Practicing Christian Spirituality

An Exercise in Loving God with Heart, Soul, Strength, and Mind

The first great commandment is that we would "love the Lord your God with all your heart, and with all your soul, and with all your strength, and with all your mind; and your neighbor as yourself" (Luke 10:27). While it would be wrong to be too exacting about just what each of these terms means here, it is clear that the passage encourages us toward a spirituality of wholehearted devotion to God. The present exercise is a way of enabling and inspiring us to dream of what that kind of devotion might look like.

First, find your sacred place and time, a place and time to be with God. They should be free of distractions. Remember, Christ himself is with us in the Spirit. Settle down and set your mind on the things of God. This may take some time. That's OK.

Now, let's begin with the *heart*. Think about your heart for a moment. When you think about your heart, or the Bible's understanding of heart, what do you think of? Think of any key "heart" moments in your life. What were they like? Have you loved anyone with your heart? What was that like? What might it be like to love the Lord with your heart? With *all* your heart? How would you feel if you loved the Lord with all your heart? How might life be different for you than it is now?

Then move on to the *soul*. Reflect on the soul—the biblical portrait of the soul, your own understanding of it. Just what *is* a soul? What is *your* soul? Have you had any "soul" moments in your history? What might it mean to love from the soul (or to love with soul)? Spend some time thinking about loving God with soul, with *all* your soul. Allow yourself to get excited about just what it might look like to love God with all your soul.

Then the *mind*. First spend a little time just thinking about the mind, about what it means to have a mind. Again, review your history: Have you ever had any significant "mind" moments in your past? Have you ever thought about loving someone with your mind? What might it mean to love God with your mind? With *all* your mind? What might you be thinking if you loved God with all your mind?

Finally turn your thoughts to *strength*. Take your time. What, in this passage, might be meant by strength? Where is your own strength? Has your own strength ever been of importance to you? What does it mean to love someone with strength? What might it mean to love the Lord your God with strength? What would you be doing if you loved God with *all* your strength?

When you have finished, bring each of the elements together in a wholehearted expression of devotion to God. Offer your love to God. Offer him wholehearted love—with all your heart, your soul, your mind, your strength, to the best of your ability. Perhaps you would like to symbolize this offering with a song, a liturgical prayer, a posture of devotion. Allow God the Spirit to respond to you. Perhaps you might like to jot a few notes down from your time with God for future reference.

Lord God, we desire to pursue relationship with you. We cannot pretend spirituality, but we simply come honestly before you. Take our hearts, our souls, our minds, our strength, and enable us to love you more and more. In Jesus's name. Amen.

CHAPTER SUMMARY

1. Christian spirituality refers to relationship with God as lived in practice, as people formulate an understanding about the dynamics of lived relationship with God, and as a formal discipline of academic study that investigates that relationship.

2. Christian spirituality is distinct from mysticism in that mysticism addresses special experiences of the presence of God, whereas spirituality addresses the entirety of the relationship. Spirituality is distinct from spiritual theology in that spiritual theology tends to focus on the individual's growth toward perfection. It differs from sanctification in that it is not the investigation of a doctrine, but of a lived relationship. Spirituality differs from religious studies in that it does not attempt a scholarly neutrality; spirituality is somewhat engaged. Finally, Christian spirituality differs from spiritual formation in that spiritual formation looks toward the means of maturity, whereas spirituality explores the whole of the life.

3. Christian spirituality appears in a variety of forms. There are different forms of lived spiritual practice based on differences in personality, geography, situation, and the like. Spirituality takes on different forms of formulation when groups of people collect around ways of understanding the dynamics of relationship with God (for example, the Lutheran approach to spirituality). The academic discipline of Christian spirituality can take on different forms as distinct expressions of the aims and methods of the discipline are expressed.

4. Scholars and practitioners of Christian spirituality currently have a tendency to approach relationship with God from the perspective of describing actual life, to emphasize experience, to explore the corporate aspects of relationship with God, to permit careful study and personal transformation to influence one another, and to use a variety of disciplines in the exploration.

5. Although we may see a wide range of diversity in Christian spirituality, this diversity is built upon a few foundational principles. Christian spirituality is rooted in the sacred texts and teachings of the Christian faith. It assumes the reality of God and Spirit. It acknowledges the fullness of human experience. Our understanding of Christian spirituality is constructed in terms of the real relationship between God and humans, the possibility and actuality of God and humans sharing lives. It brings us to the recognition that the God-human relationship is ordered to be a relationship of love.

Questions

1. Why would anyone want to study Christian spirituality rather than that which is identified by mysticism, spiritual theology, or any of the other terms discussed in the chapter? To what do you personally look forward in encountering the world of Christian spirituality?

2. What kinds of literature do you think a scholar in Christian spirituality might read, as distinct from that read by a scholar in Christian theology or Christian history? What kinds of methods of study might be unique to Christian spirituality?

3. Toward which form of Christian spirituality are you inclined? Why?

4. What would you have to do, as a student of Christian spirituality, to maximize the possibilities and avoid the problems that arise from the current trends in Christian spirituality?

5. What are the foundational principles of Christian spirituality? How would big differences regarding one of these principles create differences in how a person practiced lived spirituality? Give examples.

6. What are Christian spirituality's big issues? Which of these issues are most interesting to you? Why?

LOOKING FURTHER

Practice

Richard Foster's *Celebration of Discipline: The Path to Spiritual Growth*, twentieth anniversary ed. (San Francisco: HarperSanFrancisco, 1998), an introduction to spiritual disciplines, has become a classic of Christian spirituality in its own right. *Orthodox Spirituality: An Outline of the Orthodox Ascetical and Mystical Tradition: A Monk of the Eastern Church*, 2nd ed. (Crestwood, NY: St. Vladimir's Press, 1978), is a nice, simple outline of spirituality from the Orthodox tradition.

Dynamics and Historical Models

The Study of Spirituality, edited by Cheslyn Jones, Geoffrey Wainwright, and Edward Yarnold (New York: Oxford University Press, 1986), is a standard review of most of the primary historical figures and groups and the key themes in Christian spirituality. The Classics of Western Spirituality (Paulist Press) is not a single book but rather an entire library of classics. Check out the entire selection. See also the three-volume series *Christian Spirituality* (published by Crossroad), which covers in greater depth and detail the history and themes of Christian spirituality. (These three volumes are also volumes 16–18 of the series *World Spirituality: An Encyclopedic History of the Religious Quest*.)

Study

Exploring Christian Spirituality: An Ecumenical Reader, ed. Ken Collins (Grand Rapids: Baker, 2000), is an excellent sampling of writings in the academic field of Christian spirituality. Michael Downey's *Understanding Christian Spirituality* (New York: Paulist Press, 1997) is a fine brief overview of the issues and perspectives of the discipline of Christian spirituality. *Spiritus* (previously published as *Christian Spirituality Bulletin*) is the journal of the Society for the Study of Christian Spirituality.

Exploring Christian Spirituality

2

OBJECTIVES

In this chapter you will learn about the study of Christian spirituality, how we explore the nature of relationship with God. You will be introduced to six realms of experience which provide us information about what relationship with God is like. You will get a feel for the ancient practice of *lectio divina* (holy reading). By the end of the chapter you should be able to

- list significant resources for exploring Christian spirituality;
- identify the unique contributions each provides to the study of Christian spirituality;
- describe the dangers that attend the use of each realm of experience and suggest means of avoiding them;
- strategize the integration of different realms of experience for the use of exploring relationship with God.

Finally, you will have a chance to consider your own approach to exploring relationship with God in a contemplative exercise.

The notion of exploring often brings up images of caravans of people with pith helmets hacking their way through the jungle, or perhaps early American trappers fording wild rivers, searching for passage to the Pacific. Exploring is venturing into unknown territory: seeing what may have never been seen, mapping what may have never been mapped, "boldly going where no one has gone before." Or if we are not the first to explore an area, we can use someone else's map and explore for ourselves territory new to us. Exploring usually involves the use of tools: maps, shoes, boats, guides, and so on. Different tools are needed for different kinds of explorations. The aim of exploration is to discover, to gain some kind of knowledge. Perhaps there is something in particular we are looking for, or perhaps we just want to see what we will find. Such is the nature of exploring.

We have defined Christian spirituality in terms of a three-fold division. Christian spirituality is the lived relationship between a community or a person and God. It also is a way of approaching that relationship, a formulation of the dynamics that characterize life with God. Finally, Christian spirituality is also the academic discipline within which relationship with God is systematically studied. *This* is our "unknown territory." We are venturing into the universe of the Christian's relationship with God to see what we might find. How do Christians live out relationship with God? How do they formulate their understanding of the dynamics of relationship with God? How is relationship with God in the Christian faith approached in terms of formal study?

Our interest in the present chapter is to examine *how* the unknown territory of Christian spirituality is to be explored: what tools we must bring with us into the journey, what guides we may find along the way, what strategies we must keep in mind so as to avoid the various dangers that attend the exploration of Christian spirituality (and there *are* dangers). While, as we shall see, the practice of lived relationship with God is itself a means of learning

what Christian spirituality is all about, there are also formal means of exploring the territory. This is the world of Christian spirituality as an academic discipline. And since our focus here will be on *how* to explore—on methodology—this chapter will primarily address Christian spirituality as an academic discipline. Having situated our approach to learning about Christian spirituality in the present chapter, we then will be free, in the following chapters, to plunge into the exploration itself, applying the tools, guides, and strategies identified in this chapter.

The Study of Christian Spirituality as Interdisciplinary Exploration

As we discovered in the previous chapter, Christian spirituality can be explored from a number of approaches: theological, historical, practical, and so on. We also learned that Christian spirituality is increasingly studied from an *interdisciplinary* perspective, bringing together the insights of different resources and approaches in a single exploration. This is because the guides, tools, and strategies for exploring relationship with God are to be found in a variety of "places," including both formal academic disciplines and less formal means of learning. But just what *is* interdisciplinary study? What does it accomplish? Why pursue interdisciplinary study? And how are we to go about it?

What Is Interdisciplinary Study?

Interdisciplinary study brings together a number of "disciplines" into a coherent exploration. We employ both physiology and physics to explore the world of sports. We employ chemistry and economics to explore agriculture. But in this text, we will use the term *interdisciplinary study* to refer not only to the integration of various formal, academic disciplines, but also to the integration of these with less formal realms of experience into our exploration of relationship with God.

On the one hand, interdisciplinary study simply makes official what we do in everyday life. When we move to a new town, for example, we read the paper, we look at statistics about the town offered by the chamber of commerce, we visit with the locals, we walk the streets. Perhaps we buy a book of local history. Written texts, formal research, informal relationships, and personal experience all contribute to our exploration of this town. Thus through a variety of formal and informal means (an "interdisciplinary" approach), we get to know the town. We do this kind of thing—mixing insights from formal and informal sources—all the time in our daily lives. Our intuitions are compared with facts presented on paper. Facts presented in one field are compared with others. Intentional interdisciplinary study—integrating both formal and informal sources of insight—simply makes explicit the operations we use all the time. And in the present text, we will explore the ins and outs of relationship with God in this manner.

Why Do Interdisciplinary Study?

Interdisciplinary study is valuable in that it not only makes formal our ways of ordinary knowing, but also addresses the needs of contemporary academic concerns. These are unique times in the halls of learning. Issues regarding philosophy, literature, history, linguistics, and other disciplines have forced a rethinking of the foundations and methods of Western thought. By openly welcoming both formal and informal reflection concerning relationship with God, we bring to our study of Christian spirituality multiple levels of accountability. By looking at relationship with God from the viewpoints of a variety of different disciplines, we invite the participation of a number of different communities of discourse, thereby intentionally structuring checks and balances into our own fallible pursuits. By being intentionally interdisciplinary, we can speak of relationship with God as "insiders" without sacrificing the intellectual integrity necessary to address important issues introduced by "outsiders."[1]

How Do We Do Interdisciplinary Study?

Interdisciplinary study in Christian spirituality seeks to summarize the range of thought in various academic fields and realms of experience in an effort to bring it all to bear on one's understanding of relationship with God. Different questions related to spirituality will suggest different disciplines to pull together. For example, if I were exploring the different experiences people have in mystical prayer, I might pull together insights from the writings of the classic mystical writers, from the wisdom of Christian theologians, and from psychological research on states of consciousness. On the other hand, if I were exploring the stages of spiritual maturity of local congregations, I might draw from the Pauline epistles, from philosophers of community, and from sociological studies of group dynamics. In each case there is a pulling together of insights from various fields to illumine our understanding of relationship with God. This pulling together requires "**coordinating**" the fields employed. To coordinate one kind of learning with another is to comprehend each in such a way that the insights of both viewpoints are in meaningful relationship. Information from different realms of experience or academic disciplines can be coordinated with each other by thinking in terms of *agreement, compatibility,* or *opposition*.[2]

Information from different sources **agree** when they say the same thing about the same reality. For example, both experimental psychology and literature affirm that human emotion has an important social dimension. Data are **compatible** either when they say different but true things about the same reality or when they say true things about two different but interrelated realities. The historical statement "God's love has been experienced variously in various periods of history" is different from but compatible with the theological statement "Love is a primary attribute of God." Likewise, a sociological theory of corporate unity may speak of a different topic from that of personal piety, but they can both be integrated within a larger understanding of communal and personal spiritual formation. Where we find agreement or compatibility (or when opposition has been resolved), we can receive from the contributions that one discipline gives to another. Social sciences may tell us something about the nature of community ritual behavior present in corporate worship; psychoneurology may have something to tell us about the workings of the brain involved in mystical experiences. Each discipline, each realm of experience (whether formal or informal) is familiar with its own range of topics, possesses its own set of internal criteria for acceptance, and provides both insights for and constraints on other realms of experience with which it is related. Thus, by encouraging the interplay of realms of experience in our exploration of Christian spirituality, we allow the strengths of different ways of thinking to enrich our understanding of the relationship with God while encouraging the weaknesses of these same kinds of thinking to be corrected by interaction with each other.

Finally data are in **opposition** when they contradict one another. In such a case, the data appear to demand a resolution. It would be very difficult both to accept the philosophical claim that God does not speak today and simultaneously to develop a spirituality that seeks to account for experiences of divine prophetic utterance. When information from different resources seem to be in opposition, we must resolve the opposition as best we can. This is not always easy. Each academic discipline or informal means of experience offers insights unavailable to the rest, and therefore it has within itself the possibility of correcting a theory not attuned to its insights. The art is to identify the precise contribution or correction provided by one discipline or informal area of study to another.

Ultimately we achieve resolution to opposition by choosing one of the following, depending on the specific situation:

- *rejecting inadequate insights* when false testimony or insufficient evidence is superceded by those sources providing clearer testimony or evidence. This happens, for example, when we evaluate a claim that Christians did not speak in tongues after the establishing of the canon of scripture by collecting samples from historical documents of Christians speaking in tongues.

- *revising less adequate frames of reference* when a certain way of interpreting testimony or evidence is rejected in the face of a better framework of interpreting information. This happened, for example, when the data of Christian growth and maturity were found to be better explained within a single process (spiritual theology) than in two thoroughly distinct processes (ascetical and mystical theologies).

- *developing a more comprehensive frame of reference.* Here we show apparent opposition to be *merely* apparent when examined through a more comprehensive perspective. This happens when, for example, we embrace both the contributions of liberationist emphases on action and contemplative emphases on inaction within a more comprehensive understanding of human experience.

- *resting in ambiguity or renouncing any attempt to reconcile opposition.* There are times when we realize that our attempts at flawless coherence are insufficient to the topic. This is especially true when we finite humans attempt to comprehend relationship with an infinite God. Sometimes it is better to admit the limits of our understanding, to release our grip on knowing, and to yield to unknowing. Indeed, there are times when our obsession with certainty or absolute consistency inhibits

FIGURE 2.1
**Coordinating Information from Different
Realms of Experience**

Realm One	Realm Two

—Do they agree? Do they say the same thing about the same reality?
- Welcome common insights and confirmations.

—Are they compatible? Do they say different but true things about the same reality? Do they say true things about different but interrelated realities?
- Interrelate insights, terms, and concepts together in common language(s) and incorporate contributions into single perspective.

—Are they in opposition (apparent contradiction)?
  —Reject inadequate insights.
  —Revise less adequate frames of reference.
  —Develop a more comprehensive frame of reference.
  —Rest in ambiguity or renounce any attempt to reconcile opposition.

our discovery of relationship with God, and we must then positively renounce our grasping attachment to our own comprehension and abandon ourselves to the One who is incomprehensible.

This text will explore Christian spirituality by integrating six realms of experience, or disciplines (four formal and two informal), into a single presentation. Each of these realms—personal experience, biblical studies, informal relationships, history, theology and philosophy (here treated as a single discipline),[3] the human sciences, along with many other possible resources[4]—has a set of distinctive contributions to make to our understanding of relationship with God. Each has its own possibilities and problems. Nonetheless, these six realms will be the equipment we shall take with us on our exploration of Christian spirituality.

Personal Experience: Living Faith, Hearing Truth

We begin with personal experience because this is where most of us begin our exploration of relationship with God: with our own spiritual lives. While we are concerned to submit our experience to the closest possible scrutiny, we acknowledge—and even welcome—the limits and insights that come with being embedded in our own personal spiritual experiences. To examine the role of personal experience in our exploration of Christian spirituality is to consider the ways in which lived experience shapes inquiry and vice versa. What does attention to our own experience bring to our exploration of spirituality? In what ways does personal experience foster (or hinder) our understanding of—as we have defined Christian spirituality—"the actual relationship of persons or groups with God through Jesus Christ: as existentially cultivated and experienced, as formulated into a model for understanding or practice, or as explored systematically within the academic community." In responding to such questions, it is helpful to think in terms of two phrases: living faith and hearing truth.

Living Faith

Personal experience is where our faith is lived. This lived-ness of faith generally arises prior to detailed intellectual exploration regarding the nature of faith (though certainly some categories are necessarily present even in order to comprehend experience *as* experience). Yet the lived-ness of faith also follows from our explorations regarding the nature of faith as insights affect the ways in which we perceive and relate to God. This lived-faith aspect of personal experience both inhibits and fosters exploration of relationship with God. Personal experience as lived faith inhibits exploration of Christian spirituality when we assume that relationship with God always looks like *our* relationship with God. If we come to the exploration of Christian spirituality aware of this danger, however, we can adopt a discipline of academic **self-examen** that softens the harmful effects of our own biases. First we expose ourselves to the experiences, perspectives, and practices of others through informal relationships and formal study. Then we attend to the motives and movements of our own soul even as we consider others'. We ask, why is *this* not interesting to me? What feelings and inclinations arise as I pursue this topic or this text? What do these feelings reveal about my own background and concerns? We adopt an **asceticism** of scholarship that fasts from the gluttony of simply feeding our own pet ideas, that castigates our intellectual and spiritual self-assurance by listening carefully and respectfully to the experiences and ideas of others different from ourselves, and that submits to the authority of the checks and balances provided by quality interdisciplinary scholarship.[5] By using the spiritual disciplines of self-examen and asceticism, we embody an approach to personal experience that is likely to minimize the dangers inherent in listening to our own experience as we explore relationship with God.

But while personal experience can, at times, inhibit our exploration of Christian spirituality, we also, for the same reasons, have cause for celebration. *Our very limitations,* the very particular lived-ness of our experience, give to certain features of that experience a unique salience. And thanks to this limited salience, aspects of Christian spirituality uniquely available to an individual or a group can be noticed and experienced by that individual or group. Thus, for example, certain aspects of Christian discernment were uniquely mediated to Christendom through the experience of Jesuit founder Ignatius of Loyola (1491–1556) as he recuperated from a leg wound. Here, in this one experience, core insights of a spiritual classic were born. The personal experience and particular historical situations of Carmelite **nun** Therese of Liseaux (1873–97), of Russian scholar and **monk** Theophan the Recluse (1815–94), and founder of the American Holiness movement Phoebe Palmer (1807–74) all play an essential part in mediating the wisdom of God to the community of God's people. Likewise,

we can assume that as explorers of Christian spirituality, our own embeddedness in history and experience will serve not simply to inhibit, but also to enhance our exploration and understanding of the relationship of humans with God through Christ.[6]

Hearing Truth

This brings us to our next point: personal experience is not only a context of lived faith from within which exploration of Christian spirituality is conducted; personal experience is also our context for hearing the truth. The insights of our exploration into Christian spirituality come *to us*. For this reason, there is a certain advantage of an ever-deepening personal experience of relationship with God for the sake of an increasing clarity of understanding of the nature of that relationship in general. Writers in the first few centuries of the church insisted on the need for theologians to pursue the practice of the spiritual life. For example, Athanasius (295–373), the fourth-century bishop of Alexandria, writes,

> Anyone who wants to look at sunlight naturally wipes his eye clear first, in order to make, at any rate, some approximation to the purity of that on which he looks; and a person wishing to see a city or country goes to the place in order to do so. Similarly, anyone who wishes to understand the mind of the sacred writers must first cleanse his own life, and approach the saints by copying their deeds. Thus united to them in the fellowship of life, he will both understand the things revealed to them by God and, thenceforth escaping the peril that threatens sinners in the judgment, will receive that which is laid up for the saints in the kingdom of heaven.[7]

There is a certain personal acquaintance and conformity with the subject matter of Christian spirituality—a "**connaturality**," as the medievals put it—that is gained from a life lived intentionally with reference to the Spirit of the living God. Living life in response to God gives one a unique familiarity with the things of Christian spirituality that cannot be gained otherwise, much as participating in the act of golfing gives one a familiarity with golfing that cannot be gained by reading books.

Using Personal Experience

How do we foster the use of personal experience as a guide to help us as students of Christian spirituality? A few suggestions may be considered. First, plunge deep but be in relationship with others. Exploration at times demands taking risks, venturing into unknown territory, facing your fears. This is particularly true of the exploration of relationship with God. You must go where you must go. If you are not willing to risk the uncertainties involved in encountering the presence of Almighty God, perhaps serious exploration of Christian spirituality is not for you. Because of these risks, however, it is always good to have a friend nearby. Just as deep sea explorers often have a line connected to help above, to people who will pull them up in case of emergency, so also you might think of establishing a relationship with someone who might be there to "pull you up" when you need it or simply to sit around and listen to the stories of what you discovered down below.

Second, don't be afraid of imitating others, yet be yourself. This may sound like a contradiction, but it's not. We begin to become ourselves through imitation. This is true of virtually every kind of learning. Apprentice painters often go through seasons of learning to paint "like" Pierre-Auguste Renoir, "like" Rembrandt van Rijn, "in the style of" Vincent van Gogh. Similarly, scholarship is learning to think "in the style of" those whom we incorporate. Yet in time, one can discover one's self—distinct from all the imitations. A stroke of the brush, an independent idea, and we *find ourselves*, never wholly independent from those we have imitated yet with a unique contribution to offer. It is the same in the spiritual

---

Using Personal Experience

- Plunge deep, but be in relationship with others.
- Don't be afraid of imitating others, but be yourself.
- Pay attention.

---

life. In exploring the spiritual life, we travel down roads others have traveled before. "I would like to try on the mantle of the **desert elder** for a while." "Just for fun, let's experiment with Methodist class meetings for one year." And so on. Of course, with this kind of exploration, one faces the danger of "dabbling," where personal spirituality begins to look more like a shopping trip than an authentic relationship with God. There is also the danger of turning personal spiritual formation into an attempt to become the next Francis or Clare of Assisi. But at the same time, exploration of relationship with God needs the freedom to find itself through imitation.

Finally, pay attention. If your personal experience is going to be a tool in exploring Christian spirituality, you will have to be aware of what goes on in your relationship with God. Keeping a journal, or some system of notes, may be helpful in order to record the goings on of your own spiritual life. You can integrate this information with that gained from the other resources for exploring Christian spirituality. Once again, in the practice of paying attention, another danger arises—namely, that personal spirituality will become an exercise in analysis rather than a delightful, spontaneous relationship with God. Watch out for this! It is easy to discuss all manner of spiritual dynamics, complete with personal illustrations, and all the while avoid the real work of authentic relationship with God. Nonetheless, personal experience can play the vitally integral role in exploration of Christian spirituality that it should play as the context of living faith and hearing Truth.

Let's consider Samantha, for example. What might it mean for Sam, a student of Christian spirituality, to incorporate her own experience of Christ into her study of relationship with God? Let's say she is exploring the themes of darkness and light as images of Christian growth. She has chosen to read a few classic writings from church history, to examine these themes in the scriptures, and to keep a journal for two years exploring these themes in her own life. As time progresses she begins to compare the insights from her journal with those she has discovered in scripture and history. She finds that both darkness and light are found in scripture and in history as places of God's dwelling. Yet in her own experience she is nervous about darkness. Even in her dreams, darkness is only a theme of fear. Is this due to something in her? Do others feel the same at times? What factors could be considered to bring a full integration of the data of Sam's experience with the material from formal study? She realizes that while scripture and history mention darkness as a place of God's dwelling, her religious training has never mentioned this. Spirituality was always about light, about ever-increasing clarity. Perhaps she has found a new insight.

The question of personal experience's relationship to the exploration of Christian spirituality is of special concern to those teaching and writing about Christian spirituality. With regards to teaching, the issue comes up in the context of deciding whether to include an experiential component in a class on Christian spirituality. Does the inclusion of "soul projects" or "classroom experiences" in courses on Christian spirituality make the courses less "scholarly," too subjective, or perhaps even manipulative? It is possible that spiritual "practice" can hinder the fair understanding of the character of relationship with God. But it is also possible that practice can enhance that understanding.[8] With regard to writing about Christian spirituality, writers of academic spirituality have been given greater freedom for expressing the personal side of things, for better and for worse. The challenge is to be honest about what one may as an individual bring to the exploration of Christian spirituality (strengths and weaknesses) but at the same time to allow personal experience to be informed by careful interdisciplinary scholarship and self-examination.[9]

Personal experience can be a valuable guide in our exploration of relationship with God. It is the vehicle through which faith is lived and truth is heard. Yes, there are problems in listening to the guidance of personal experience, but if we use our guide carefully these dangers become the very possibilities of unique discoveries.

Holy Scripture: Mediating Faith, Speaking Truth

Our second guide in the exploration of Christian spirituality is Christian scripture. As *Christian* spirituality, we explore a relationship with God that is normatively influenced by the texts and traditions of the Christian faith. Thus Sandra M. Schneiders, one of the founders of the contemporary academic field of Christian spirituality, writes, "Christian spirituality is constitutively *biblical* and how the Bible functions in the lived spirituality of the Christian as well as how it is studied and for what purpose in the field of spirituality are questions which cannot be avoided."[10] While the three great traditions of the Christian faith (Eastern Orthodoxy, Roman Catholicism, and Protestantism) have disagreed about the precise relationship of scripture to tradition, all are in agreement that "in Sacred Scripture, the Church constantly finds her nourishment and her strength, for she welcomes it not as a human word, 'but as what it really is, the word of God.'"[11] How does the Bible function in our life and study? Take a moment and ask yourself, "When I pick up my Bible, why am I doing it? What do I hope to get from the scriptures?"

We use scripture for common liturgy and personal comfort. It functions as a kind of worldview map, presenting a perspective on reality and values within which we can comprehend our experience. We find ourselves singing the poetry of scripture, imagining the stories of scripture, and wrestling over the teachings of scripture. We use scripture to critique both ourselves and our culture. It is used as a means of speaking and listening to God. Scripture is also *used* for less honorable ends: to bolster one social position, to berate others, or to justify our own sinful biases. Passages about the descendants of Ham were *used* to justify the mistreatment of black slaves. Passages about human dominion over the earth are *used* to justify mistreatment of the environment. Scriptures are *used* and twisted again and again to found and maintain cult groups of every kind. Even the devil *used* scripture to tempt our Lord Jesus to abandon his calling (Matthew 4:5–7). Recognizing the various uses of scripture (positive and negative), our aim here is to consider how the scripture can function as a resource for opening up something of the nature of the relationship we have with God through Christ. We can summarize the roles that scripture plays in this venture by use of the phrases *mediating faith* and *speaking truth*.

Mediating Faith

When I say that scripture "mediates" faith, I mean that scripture functions as a primary vehicle through which we receive the transforming grace of Christ in our lives or through which our faith is interpreted and expressed. The Bible is *the* sacred book of the Christian religion. Scripture arose *from* spirituality, from the encounter of people with their God, and it also *shapes* that spirituality such that our encounter with God itself is comprehended and even "experienced" within the perspective of biblical language and worldview.[12] As such, the Bible is birthed from, expresses, and interprets the lived spirituality of Christian believers. Our stories are understood within the Story (and the stories) of the Bible. Our prayers are biblically shaped and our failures are biblically diagnosed.

Our homilies are (hopefully) grounded in scripture and our missions are inspired by scripture. Scripture mediates faith.

Speaking Truth

Furthermore, scripture speaks truth. The Holy Bible is not merely sacred text, but also revealed Word. We do not go far enough simply to speak of the scriptures as a "witness" to revelation or as the written expression of the "human response" to revelation. God not only encounters people within biblical events, disclosing his character and purposes; God also gives interpretations of these events, interpretations that are revelation in their own right. One form of God's revealing encounter and interpretation is the writing, collecting, and formation of the biblical canon. The sacred text of Christianity is revealed by God and recognized by the community of God's people. Therefore, as a canon of revealed Word, scripture bears a special kind of authority in our exploration of Christian spirituality. In both our lived relationship with God and our account of the nature of the divine-human relationship, our thoughts, feelings, and actions are obliged to "fit" the revelation of God displayed in and through the texts of holy scripture. Our respectful treatment of scripture includes the historical or propositional dimension of scripture (facts, concepts, doctrines, statements *about* things), but it is not exhausted by that dimension. Be aware! On the one side is the danger of neglecting the historical and doctrinal matrix within which the divine is communicated. On the other is the danger of missing God's "commune-ication" out of preoccupation with the history or doctrine.[13]

Using Holy Scripture

Having suggested the kinds of roles scripture plays in our exploration of Christian spirituality, we must now ask how we might best approach scripture such that it is able to mediate faith and speak truth, especially with regard to our exploring and embodying relationship with God. As our interpretation of scripture—in devotion, in preaching, in doctrine, in cultural evaluation—is pivotal to our approach to relationship with God, this is no minor question. Unfortunately, there is no solid agreement on how we are to approach the scriptures. Christian interpreters have struggled with this question and are struggling still.[14] Perhaps, by way of summary, it is best to include a variety of methods of interpretation (drawing both from the history of Christian spirituality and the history of biblical interpretation), allowing each method to constrain the others. We can, therefore, think of coming to a text of scripture by means of a kind of chiasm divided into two primary tasks: getting you into the text and getting the text into you.[15]

Part One: Getting You into the Text

1. *Pray for Understanding*
   It is the Spirit who gives light to the text and brings understanding to the heart and mind. While trust in God's power to reveal is no excuse for careless study, still we realize that God's enlightenment stands behind and beyond all our efforts at understanding. Ask God to grant that understanding.

2. *Initial Reading and Outline*
   Read the text you are studying a few times. Use different translations. Perhaps you can read the whole book in which your passage is located just to get a feel for the book. Write out an outline of the section of scripture that surrounds your passage in question.

3. *Identify with the Early Setting*
   Examine the setting of the passage to give you a feel for the times that are reflected in the text before you. Investigate any historical developments leading up to the context your passage reflects. Examine any social or cultural habits that may illumine the passage, such as the religious background of the regions in view.

Address questions of authorship, date, setting, and such if necessary. Exercise your imagination to place yourself in the setting and context of the times, to feel what it may have been like to be there.

4. *Notice Literary Form*
   Determine what kinds of literature your passage contains. Is it poetry, prophecy, story, legal material, letter, or something else? If you are in a story (as in the Gospels), identify the development of the plot and the characterization. Look for poetic verses if appropriate; explore imagery, metaphor, and the like. How are these structured and why are they structured that way? Look at your passage as a piece of good literature. Begin to write out a more detailed outline of the literary structure of the passage. Explore in order to understand the flow of the passage. You may want to write the passage out in its entirety in a different graphic layout, such as an "outline format," so you can see the development of what is said.

5. *Define Unclear Words*
   You may find words, phrases, and concepts that you do not understand. Use dictionaries, concordances, and lexicons to come to greater clarity on what these particular words and phrases may have meant and might mean now. Identify the points of analogy in metaphors. Be careful not to be over picky about precise words; sometimes the authors of scripture were picky about definitions, sometimes they weren't. The context of a word will often be the best guide to its meaning.

6. *Comment on, Question, and Clarify the Meaning of the Text*
   Write out your own ideas about the passage and, if necessary, for each phrase of the passage. Make a list of questions and related comments. Research the questions through the standard resources for biblical stud-

ies. Ask, Why is this passage, this book here in the Bible? and What is the enduring message? Try to identify not only with the *teachings*, but also with the *emotional content* represented in the text. Take all of your data concerning this passage and let it inform your imaginative reconstruction of what it might have been like when it was written. Allow your imagination to raise new questions or to clarify your understanding of the passage thus far.

7. *Summarize*

Ask, What have I gained thus far? and How is it changing me?

PART TWO: GETTING THE TEXT INTO YOU

6'. *Comment on, Question, and Clarify Yourself*

Ask yourself, What questions, issues, doubts, and such am I bringing to this study? Consider what opinions you bring concerning the text as you start. How did you feel about the text when you first read it? Why? How does your own background, socioeconomic level, history, gender, and such affect how you approach the text? What situations are influencing you personally at this time? What does your denomination say about this text? What biases might you need to be aware of as you look at the text? Be honest about yourself and about what you bring to the study of the text.

5'. *Define Emerging Patterns*

Look for appropriate similarities between the structure, words, and images of your passage and the primary themes of human relationship with God in general. Are there patterns or dynamics that can be characteristic of the way God works with all people or in certain conditions? Look for the ways in which God and a person or a community relate. How do the images and metaphors evoke our

consideration of God's work in this passage and in our lives?

4'. *Notice Literary Purposes*

Establish what the text was trying to *do* (not just what it was trying to *say*). Ask, How might this text (or author) want the reader to respond? Look for the purposes of the literature—is it pedagogical, expressive, presentative, affective, relational? Ask, How would I look, act, feel, think, if I really "got" this text? You can rewrite the passage in your own language, considering how this passage might be expressed if it were written here and now. You might also begin to make a list of applications appropriate for yourself or others.

3'. *Identify with the Contemporary Setting*

Identify any continuity or discontinuity between the setting of your passage and the present setting. Look at historical development, geography, religious background, and culture. In what ways is your situation parallel to that of the text? How might the sense

OF COURSE, THERE MAY BE OTHER INTERPRETATIONS.

Figure 2.2 Biblical Method and Biblical Spirituality: A Chiasm

(Interpretive techniques and spiritual traditions *in italics*)

Getting You into the Text	Getting the Text into You
1. Pray for Understanding	(*All traditions and techniques*)
2. Initial Reading and Outline	
3. Identify with the Early Setting	(*Historical, social, source, tradition, redaction techniques*)
	(*Ignatian and Pietist traditions*)
4. Notice Literary Form	(*Form, new literary techniques*)
5. Define Unclear Words	(*Lexical, semantic techniques*)
6. Comment on, Question, and Clarify the Meaning of the Text	(*Exegetical, theological, canon critical techniques*)
7. Summarize	
6'. Comment on, Question, and Clarify Yourself	(*Traditions of historical spirituality, foundational theological techniques*)
5'. Define Emerging Patterns	(*Typological, metaphorical traditions and techniques*)
4'. Notice Literary Purposes	(*Rhetorical critical techniques*)
3'. Identify with the Contemporary Setting	(*Ideology critical techniques*)
	(*Traditions of consciousness examen*)
2'. Slow Reading	(*Benedictine, Orthodox traditions*)
1'. Pray for Action	(*Desert traditions*)

of the text, in view of its setting, be *inappropriate* to your current setting or to that of others? (Remember that there is always the issue of right text, wrong time. Pay attention to the condition of your heart or the hearts of those who are under your consideration.) How can the concerns of God, as expressed in the text, be translated into today's culture without doing injustice to the text? Make good use of current reading, listening, discussion, and reflection for this. Here is another opportunity for picturing, for drama, and the like.

2'. *Slow Reading*
Use meditation, exploration of the dissonance or harmony of yourself and the passage, or other similar methods to simply "waste time" in the passage. Allow yourself to play with the words and themes. Use free association to see what connections come up. See the passage as if it were addressing you. Picture the metaphors as if you were directly involved. Initiate a dialogue with the passage. What does the passage say to you? What do you say to it? What do you find the passage doing *to* you? Allow the Spirit free reign with the passage in your heart.

1'. *Pray for Action*
This prayer moves from approach to response. As you encounter the text, do you experience comfort, worship, repentance, boldness, grief, or praise? Allow yourself, and those with whom you relate, to give back to God just what God is doing in you through your passage. Ask the Lord to enable you to do what the text asks of you, however radical.

How might Samantha pursue the themes of darkness and light with scripture as a source of Christian spirituality? She would come to the scriptures with respect, acknowledging that what is found therein is sacred wisdom. That is, she is coming to learn what *God* thinks about darkness and light and Christian growth. She waits before the text, ready to be confronted by the Spirit who inspired the text. Then she dives in, reading and reading, looking up this passage and that image. She investigates historical settings so that she can reimagine, as best she can, certain phrases in the context in which they were originally given. She finds herself surprised by passages that describe God as dwelling in darkness, and she must look at her own heart to see what colors her reactions. She explores metaphorical patterns and rhetorical devices, exploring what the scriptures are trying to *do* with this theme. Ultimately she finds herself facing a God who dwells in deep darkness, ready to go there herself.

Informal Relationships: Discovering Perspectives and Models Close at Hand

What should be obvious, but is too frequently left unsaid, is that our family, friends, peers, colleagues—our communities of informal relationships—are sources of spirituality for us. This is true at an existential level; we find support and nourishment spiritually from those around us. But it is also true in terms of our exploration of relationship with God: our informal relationships shape how we understand relationship with God. We can see this influence as a problem for Christian spirituality. For example, our relationships could potentially bias or pollute our "neutral" approach to understanding Christian spirituality. But we can also see this as a source of possibility. That is, our informal relationships provide us with unique resources for exploring relationship with God that, when used wisely, can be valuable to our growth in understanding Christian spirituality. More specifically, *informal relationships provide for us, close at hand, perspectives and models of what relationship with God is all about.*

Perspectives and Models

Our earliest exposure to religion is usually facilitated by those closest to us. Parents' influence is especially strong. Ralph Hood and his associates, summarizing their research on influences on religiosity in childhood and adolescence, write,

"There is copious evidence that parents have considerable impact on the religiosity of their children, both when their offspring are younger and also when they are adolescents and young adults."[16] Even a parent's antagonism or indifference to religion will communicate impressions of how one should relate to "god." Seemingly insignificant gestures, tone of voice, and offhand comments reveal to a child much about the significance of relationship with God. But whether influenced by parents, grandparents, neighbors or the like, our earliest sense of what relationship with God involves is developed within the context of informal relationships. Our nascent understanding of spirituality is formed in response to the messages we get from those around us.

And this understanding develops from within these same contexts of informal relationships. As we grow older, the circle of those who influence us grows wider. Teachers, friends, church, and media all offer **perspectives** on religion or **models** of how relationship with God is lived out. A friend from school goes to a Pentecostal church where they speak in tongues. A science fiction movie speaks not of God, but of a Force that pervades everything. Grandmother's church might celebrate a special holiday for Our Lady of Guadalupe. From these sources we begin to collect religious stories, impressions, and feelings that inform our developing understanding of relationship with God—whether or not you may be aware of it, whether or not you would say you even *have* any experience of relationship with God. And as time goes along, this collection of models can get to be pretty large and somewhat confusing.

As we grow older, our informal relationships shape the range of religious options and ideas surrounding us. Our closest relationships are with those people we *trust*. While we may ignore most of the options seen on the news or mentioned in a class at school, we will risk seeing what our closest friend sees, experiencing something of what our sister experi-

Historical Portrait:
An Introduction to *Lectio Divina*

Lectio Divina, a very old means of bridging scripture and spirituality, is seeing something of a revival these days. The term *lectio divina* literally means "divine reading." It was used to refer to the material read as well as to the act of reading holy books. John Cassian (c. 360–430), who visited the deserts of the East and carried their wisdom to the Western monasteries, refers to the practice in his works.[17] It is Saint Benedict (the patriarch of western monasticism, c. 480–550), however, who explicitly encourages the practice, making it a standard part of monastic life for centuries to follow. In his *Rule*, or guide for monastic living, Benedict instructs that "the brothers should have specified times for manual labor as well as for prayerful reading (*lectio divina*)."[18]

The practice of prayerful reading developed within the context of Western monastic life, in a somewhat predictable schedule of prayer, work, and reading. The times of prayer (known as the Divine Office) were dominated by common worship gatherings, where psalms and scriptures are chanted, intercessions are made, times of silence are kept, and faith is affirmed. Times of work involved diligent, but not frantic, activity. Times of reading, of *lectio*, enabled one to bring it all together. Reading, study, imagination, prayer, reflection, and silence were all combined in *lectio*. As Jean Leclercq writes, "*Lectio* provided calm and relaxed meditation, a loving disposition, and a fervent interest in exegesis or at least in its results. It created a spiritual atmosphere within which the problems dealt with by biblical science remained religious problems—an atmosphere of faith in which one learned, in a manner always mysterious, to enter into the experience of the inspired authors, and especially of Christ."[19]

While *lectio divina* developed as a single, integrative practice, it tends to be discussed in terms of four separate elements. The first element of *lectio divina* is simply reading (*lectio*). In the early monastic culture, reading was usually done out loud, with the consequence that a reading was also a hearing of the text. In oral reading, already the mouth, the ears, and the mind are involved in the internalization of the passage. Slow reading naturally shades into the second element: meditation (*meditatio*). The root idea of scriptural meditation is still that of a wholehearted, prayerful reflection on the text, making use of mind, feelings, imagination, and intention. The third element of *lectio divina* is that of prayer (*oratio*). The prayer of *lectio* expresses the sincere movement of the heart to God, stimulated by the reading of and meditation on scripture. In reading God offers himself to us. In prayer we offer ourselves to God. The final element of *lectio divina* is contemplation (*contemplatio*). Contemplation points "to those moments in prayer when some form of more direct contact with God is attained."[20]

Whether our approach to prayerful reading employs well-defined techniques for interacting with the text or whether we simply sit down and relax with our Bible, present with God as we read, *lectio divina* can be a helpful means of integrating biblical studies and Christian spirituality. A number of introductions to the practice are available today.[21] *Lectio divina* is one monastic practice that is as relevant today as it was in the fifth century.

ences. Our closest relationships invite us outside ourselves, such that we end up bringing something new into ourselves. This is true of experimenting with food. (Ever tried a new dish at a restaurant at a friend's encouragement?) It is also true of our spiritual lives. Our trust in our closest relationships permits us to risk and to explore how relationship with God might be understood from the other's perspective, how it might be lived out as the other lives it out. As Cistercian writer Aelred of Rievaulx (1109–67) writes in his classic *Spiritual Friendship,* "Whatever counsel is to be given is more easily received from a friend and is more steadfastly retained, for a friend's power in counseling must needs be great, since there can neither be doubt of his loyalty nor suspicion of flattery."[22] A friend's encouragement to try something will not be taken as religious manipulation. A sister's encouragement to share her perspective will not be received as authoritarian control. Consequently, our exploration of Christian spirituality is conducted within a network of informal relationships that have already invited and continue to invite us into new ways of experiencing and understanding that relationship. They show us models of living and perspectives of understanding our faith. This is as true for the scholar of Christian spirituality as it is for the average person on the street, and it is true for groups as well as for individuals. A group's fundamental sense of its relationship with God (say, that of a congregation) is provided by those who establish that congregation. Later, associations with others (visiting leaders, new priests, other congregations) further shape the character of a congregation's relationship with God. A congregation may take a distinct shift in its own sense of what its relationship with God is about in the wake of a spring renewal meeting. Yet for both groups and individuals, the influence a relationship has is usually a matter of trust between the parties.

Close at Hand

These relationships provide perspectives and models of relationship with God *close at hand.* It is one thing to read a book about a relationship with God lived out in the context of intentional identification with the poor. We can read about Mother Theresa of Calcutta and appreciate—at a distance—her sense of seeing Christ in the poor with whom she relates day by day. It is another thing entirely to share the life of a close friend who lives intentionally among the poor and who is learning to see Christ in the poor. We open ourselves to participate in our friend's experience. Perhaps we visit our friend and, through the friend, we visit the poor. The notion of relationship with God as seeing Christ in the poor becomes perhaps no longer a distant idea. Through relationship with our friend it becomes a real possibility, an invitation. Thus our conception of spirituality—our understanding of what relationship with God looks like—is shaped by this perspective, which is brought close at hand through an informal relationship. Likewise, our sense of how relationship with God may be lived is often "caught" in a similar way. Perhaps, after watching our children receiving such wonderful graces through contemporary worship music, for example, we might open ourselves to buying some music and inviting God to touch us through it.

Using Informal Relationships

We have defined spirituality in terms of a relationship with God as lived in practice, as dynamics are formulated through reflection, and as explored through formal study. We "use" informal relationships for the exploration of Christian spirituality insofar as we give these relationships permission to serve as a resource for each of these dimensions. Your practical understanding of Christian spirituality benefits from informal relationships, for example, as you allow your friend to show you how he or she prays. Your understanding of the dynamics of relationship with God is illumined through informal relationships, for example, as you let a friend (or a spiritual director) describe to you his discernment between the conviction of God and the accusation of the enemy. Your understanding of the formal study of Christian spirituality is advanced through informal relationships through colleague-ship, for example, as you receive the comments of your peers in the discipline—as they tell you (and show through their work) how they are exploring relationship with God.

> Whoever is in possession of a true friend sees the exact counterpart of his own soul. . . . They can scarcely, indeed, be considered in any respect as separate individuals, and wherever the one appears the other is virtually present.
>
> —Cicero (104–43 BC)[23]

Our trusted relationships encourage us to experiment in our practice of relationship with God, to refine our formulations about the dynamics of relationship with God, and to perfect our formal inquiry in Christian spirituality.

While there are benefits to be gained from using informal relationships in Christian spirituality, there are also dangers involved. Informal relationships are subject to the same finiteness and limitations mentioned earlier with regard to personal experience. Our breadth of understanding will only be as large as the spectrum of those whom we allow to affect us, though to include the influence of others takes us beyond simply personal experience. Nevertheless, if we intentionally cultivate a wider trust, we are further stretched and have the potential for a broader understanding of relationship with God.[24] At the same time we must be careful to use the other resources available to us (scripture, history, theology and philosophy, human

sciences) to inform, correct, and confirm the data received from personal experience and informal relationships. Each and every resource provides a unique, but uniquely fallible, resource for our understanding of Christian spirituality. That is why we use them together.

Let's consider a different example. Miguel, a Guatemalan, desires to know more about this Christian spirituality thing. His personal background has been in Pentecostal Christianity, but recently he has found some friends that attend *both* Protestant and Catholic services. In the Catholic Bible study, they talk about "spirituality." "What does this mean?" he asks his friends. "What is *spirituality*? How do *you* relate to God? What do you get out of Catholic Christianity that you don't in Pentecostal?" Perhaps he begins to explore the ideas and the practices of his friends. He investigates scripture, talks with his pastor at the Pentecostal church. He decides to remain in the Pentecostal church, but gains a greater appreciation for his brothers and sisters in the Catholic church. Through his trust in a few informal relationships, Miguel was introduced to new models and perspectives close at hand.

Informal relationships shape our practice, our reflections about the dynamics of relationship with God, and the formal study of Christian spirituality. While we look on this influence as a blessing, we must also recognize that the influences from our informal relationships also can be problematic. There is a danger of relationships fostering unhealthy biases toward relationship with God. Some people, however, are more private or introverted in their ways of exploring, and the dangers of bias from informal relationships might not be as strong. In any case, this danger may be addressed by cultivating a wide range of informal relationships, allowing yourself to be influenced by different perspectives as well as by intentionally making use of the other resources of Christian spirituality to refine or correct bias when needed.

Christian History: Discovering Perspectives and Models at a Distance

As mentioned in the previous chapter, the rediscovery of the classics of Christian devotion has been a central element in the development of Christian spirituality in the past few decades. One reason for this is that church history provides us with a unique kind of mentorship in Christian spirituality by exhibiting models and perspectives at a distance. Archbishop Rowan Williams, in his *The Wound of Knowledge: A Theological History from the New Testament to Luther and St. John of the Cross*, writes,

> If "spirituality" can be given any coherent meaning, perhaps it is to be understood in terms of this task: each believer making his or her own that engagement with the questioning at the heart of faith which is so evident in the classical documents of Christian belief. The questioning involved here is not our interrogation of the data, but its interrogation of us. It is the intractable *strangeness* of the ground of belief that must constantly be allowed to challenge the fixed assumptions of religiosity; it is a *given*, whose question to each succeeding age is fundamentally one and the same. And the greatness of the great Christian saints lies in their readiness to be questioned, judged, stripped naked and left speechless by that which lies at the centre of their faith.[25]

The culture shock of visiting the worlds and the people of Christian history makes this history a powerful resource. The cutting edge of Christian spirituality lies in allowing ourselves to be addressed by the core truths and realities of the faith, truths and realities that have addressed believers for two millennia. By opening ourselves to the history of the church, we make ourselves vulnerable to the same truths and realities as they have touched others. And at times they touch us, as well.

Perspectives and Models

The history of the church, like our informal relationships, provides us with perspectives and models. By looking back to our sisters and brothers who lived long ago, we can see how they lived out their relationship with God, and our understanding of the nature of relationship with God is enriched. Through the sources of church history (books, architecture, artifacts, and such), we "become friends" with prophetic visionary Birgitta of Sweden (1303–73) or with Japanese social reformer Toyohiko Kagawa (1888–1960). By "playing with" their ideas and practices (for example, by following Kagawa's lead in opening one's home to the homeless), we begin to share something of their own relationship with God. Furthermore, by looking through the ups *and downs* of church history we can become equally aware of the pitfalls and traps along the journey of relationship with God as we learn from others' mistakes.

Ideas for prayer and spiritual formation are there to be collected along the path of church history. Wise interpretations of the dynamics of the spiritual life, useful for discerning and responding to the situations in the lives of ourselves and others, are there for the taking. Finally, for those interested in the formal study of Christian spirituality, church history is a virtual treasure-house of case studies in relationship with God, both for the descriptive task of learning how people actually carry on relationship with God and for constructing a framework by which we can determine how relationship with God might be fostered or improved (the normative task). The literature of Christian history (both primary sources and studies of historical figures and movements) is increasingly available in translation (see Looking Further). A chart listing some of the key figures, movements, and issues in the history of Christian spirituality is found in figure 2.3.

At a Distance

Still there are differences between our friendships with the ancients and our own informal relationships. Whereas informal relationships provide us with perspectives and models *close at hand*, church history

Figure 2.3
The History of Christian Spirituality: Select Figures, Movements, Issues

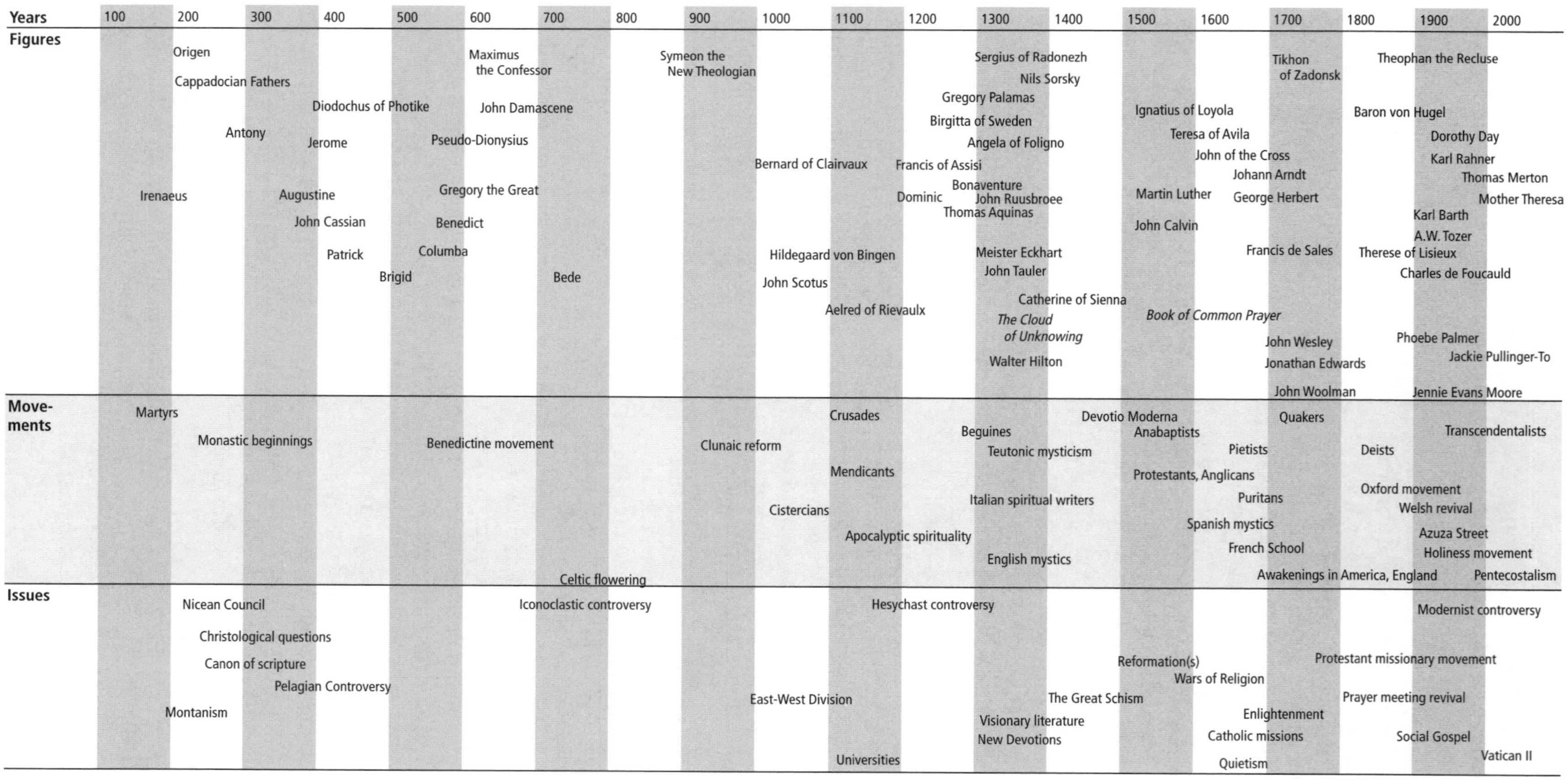

Years: 100 · 200 · 300 · 400 · 500 · 600 · 700 · 800 · 900 · 1000 · 1100 · 1200 · 1300 · 1400 · 1500 · 1600 · 1700 · 1800 · 1900 · 2000

Figures

- Origen (~200)
- Cappadocian Fathers (~300)
- Irenaeus (~200)
- Antony (~300)
- Diodochus of Photike (~400)
- Jerome (~400)
- Augustine (~400)
- John Cassian (~400)
- Patrick (~400)
- Pseudo-Dionysius (~500)
- Benedict (~500)
- Columba (~500)
- Brigid (~500)
- Maximus the Confessor (~600)
- Gregory the Great (~600)
- John Damascene (~700)
- Bede (~700)
- Symeon the New Theologian (~900)
- Bernard of Clairvaux (~1100)
- Hildegaard von Bingen (~1100)
- John Scotus (~1100)
- Aelred of Rievaulx (~1100)
- Francis of Assisi (~1200)
- Gregory Palamas (~1300)
- Birgitta of Sweden (~1300)
- Angela of Foligno (~1300)
- Bonaventure (~1300)
- Dominic (~1300)
- John Ruusbroec (~1300)
- Thomas Aquinas (~1300)
- Meister Eckhart (~1300)
- John Tauler (~1300)
- Sergius of Radonezh (~1400)
- Nils Sorsky (~1400)
- Catherine of Sienna (~1400)
- The Cloud of Unknowing (~1400)
- Walter Hilton (~1400)
- Ignatius of Loyola (~1500)
- Martin Luther (~1500)
- Teresa of Avila (~1600)
- John of the Cross (~1600)
- Johann Arndt (~1600)
- George Herbert (~1600)
- John Calvin (~1600)
- Francis de Sales (~1600)
- Book of Common Prayer (~1600)
- Tikhon of Zadonsk (~1700)
- John Wesley (~1700)
- Jonathan Edwards (~1700)
- John Woolman (~1700–1800)
- Theophan the Recluse (~1800)
- Baron von Hugel (~1900)
- Dorothy Day (~1900)
- Karl Rahner (~1900)
- Thomas Merton (~1900)
- Mother Theresa (~1900–2000)
- Therese of Lisieux (~1900)
- Karl Barth (~1900)
- A.W. Tozer (~1900)
- Charles de Foucauld (~1900)
- Phoebe Palmer (~1900)
- Jackie Pullinger-To (~1900–2000)
- Jennie Evans Moore (~1900)

Movements

- Martyrs (~100–200)
- Monastic beginnings (~300–400)
- Benedictine movement (~600)
- Clunaic reform (~900–1000)
- Crusades (~1100)
- Cistercians (~1100)
- Mendicants (~1200)
- Apocalyptic spirituality (~1200)
- Beguines (~1300)
- Teutonic mysticism (~1300)
- Italian spiritual writers (~1300)
- English mystics (~1300)
- Devotio Moderna (~1400)
- Anabaptists (~1500)
- Protestants, Anglicans (~1500)
- Spanish mystics (~1600)
- Puritans (~1600)
- French School (~1600)
- Quakers (~1700)
- Pietists (~1700)
- Deists (~1700)
- Awakenings in America, England (~1700–1800)
- Oxford movement (~1800)
- Transcendentalists (~1800)
- Welsh revival (~1900)
- Azuza Street (~1900)
- Holiness movement (~1900)
- Pentecostalism (~1900–2000)

Issues

- Montanism (~200)
- Nicean Council (~300)
- Christological questions (~300)
- Canon of scripture (~300)
- Pelagian Controversy (~400)
- Iconoclastic controversy (~700)
- Celtic flowering (~800)
- East-West Division (~1000)
- Universities (~1100)
- Hesychast controversy (~1300)
- The Great Schism (~1400–1500)
- Visionary literature (~1400)
- New Devotions (~1400)
- Reformation(s) (~1500)
- Wars of Religion (~1500–1600)
- Enlightenment (~1700)
- Catholic missions (~1700)
- Quietism (~1700)
- Protestant missionary movement (~1800)
- Prayer meeting revival (~1800)
- Social Gospel (~1900)
- Modernist controversy (~1900)
- Vatican II (~2000)

provides us with the same resources *at a distance*. I can trust my best friends to know me. When they suggest that I experiment with a certain approach to prayer, I know that they are making their suggestions for my own good, directed at my own specific circumstances. Things are not necessarily the same, however, with regard to saints Barsanuphius and John (desert fathers of sixth-century Palestine whose answers to the questions of disciples became a classic of Orthodox spirituality).[26] The at-a-distance-ness of saints Barsanuphius and John brings both possibilities and difficulties into our exploration of relationship with God. Barsanuphius and John, as revealed in their texts, do not know me and my situation. I cannot be as certain that their suggestions are given with *my* best interest in mind. Perhaps their circumstances bear no relevant parallel to mine. This could be a problem.

And yet, here are two people whose wisdom has gained the respect of Christians for centuries. I have no personal friends who are desert fathers or mothers. But by reading the guidance of Barsanuphius and John I can get a vague feeling for what that life might be like. And perhaps there are elements of that life, different as it is from mine, that are intriguing enough to experiment with. The very distance of church history enables us to play with it in our minds and in our lives.

Also, the distance of history enables us to play with perspectives and models apart from the intensity of the dynamics of close relationships. Barsanuphius and John are not necessarily nearby, telling me whether I've gotten something right. I can just experiment and see how it works for me, without the pressure of the relationship. At times there is nothing like a close friend or family member to offer the resources we need to understand our relationship with God. At other times, we need the freedom to explore ideas and models far from our own context in time and place.

Using Christian History

As we have seen, each resource for exploring Christian spirituality provides not only a unique set of benefits, but also a unique set of issues that must be faced when using that resource. It is no different with church history. The resources of church history can be used to distort or to avoid authentic relationship with God, just as they can be used to cultivate the same. It all depends on how we "do history," on how we examine the past in relationship to our present.[27]

Picking through the past. Have you ever picked out the chocolate chips from your cookies in order to eat them all at once or picked through your chicken casserole for the peas in order to set them aside? We do the same with church history. We pick a hero (like Saint Francis of Assisi, founder of the Franciscan Order, 1181–1226) out of church history and highlight an aspect of his life (like his critique of avarice) setting him up as a poster child for this one issue. (We do this with our anti-heroes as well.) We excerpt sound bites from church history, without being careful to understand the life and thought of others in the context of their own time and place.

Argument history. A second, but related, way we do history can be called "argument history." In argument history, figures and movements, models and perspectives offer support (or ammunition) for our way of looking at relationship with God, for our paradigm of faith. (This is not simply a matter of doctrine. Paradigms of faith exist for how prayer is experienced as much as for our concept of the Trinity.) Thus we read John of the Cross in order to defend the validity of our particular approach to **contemplative** prayer. In this kind of reading, the need to have the upper hand in the argument (or the need to protect our paradigms of faith) fosters an overconfidence in "what really happened" with regard to certain figures or movements in church history, and an insensitivity to the difficulties and details of historical research can distort our understanding of the past (and, consequently, our understanding of relationship with God in the present).

Big-picture history. In big picture history we are interested in the flow of it all. Big picture history presents history as a grand progression: German philosopher G. F. Hegel's (1770–1831) grand dialectic of Spirit, American theologian Jonathan Edwards's (1703–58) history of the work of redemption, and so on. At times these grand presentations of history highlight or neglect theological or spiritual models in such a way as to distort the complexity of the past in the service of presenting a cohesive big picture.[28] For example, big-picture histories of Christian spirituality have tended to communicate a clerical or monastic elitism that has opened perspectives and models for some and closed perspectives and models for others.[29] Again, we must be careful to check these big pictures of relationship with God against the details of history. By attending to the real dynamics of history, our understanding of relationship with God is placed face-to-face with the messy realities of the people who actually related to God.

Microhistory. A final way of approaching the history of Christian spirituality can be called "microhistory." This approach despairs of reclaiming the past in any "true" form, questions the possibility or benefit of any big picture, and doubts our efforts to identify relevant models and perspectives. Microhistory retreats into the details of figures and movements in an effort simply to rehearse the stories of others. The danger, however, is in seeing history *merely* as different stories apart from any wider viewpoint. Bernard McGinn, a historian of mysticism, writes that "historical reconstruction, when well done, is more than mere description: it is always guided and informed by explanatory perspectives that are at least implicitly constructive."[30] We dare not abandon our goal of grasping something of the character and dynamics of actual lived relationship with God simply because of the dangers of historical research. The fact of the "history" of history—that history constantly revises itself and *develops* on some basis of intersubjective observation and interpretation—indicates that there is hope for historical reflection not simply on the diverse spiritualities of history, but also on the character of *spirituality* as such.

What does this mean practically for the explorer of spirituality today? First, *be open, yet careful* in interpreting ancient texts. Become sensitive to the contexts from which and within which history arises. Remember your distance from the past. Learn to ask the kinds of questions that help you to understand relationship with God in the terms and world of the people of the past.

Second, *allow yourself to appreciate, to resonate with, and to be shocked, challenged, and moved by the figures and movements of history.* Yet at the same time, beware of idealizing or demonizing history. History provides a wide range of valuable resources. You have a gold mine within reach. But to safely receive these resources, you must be attentive to the interests, questions, and agendas you yourself bring to the interpretation of history. Philip Yancey, a popular Christian author, illustrates this point, writing about his own reading of the history of Christian spirituality:

> Church history yields many examples of people who took spiritual discipline to an unhealthy extreme, mortifying their bodies and shunning all pleasures. We rightly recoil from such extremes. Yet as I read their accounts now I note that these "spiritual athletes" were acting voluntarily, and few looked back on their experiences with much regret. We live in a society that cannot comprehend those who fast or carve out two hours for a quiet time, and yet honors professional football players who work out with weights five hours a day and undergo a dozen knee and shoulder surgeries to repair the damage they inflict on themselves in the sport. Our aversion to spiritual discipline may reveal more about ourselves than about the "saints" we criticize.[31]

Third, *drink deeply from your own tradition.* Something lies between the "close-at-hand-ness" of informal relationships and the "at-a-distance-ness" of church history. It is the assimilation of our own specific Christian tradition. We are likely to be more familiar with resources from our own tradition, even if we may not be close to a given individual within the tradition. We are more keenly aware of the kinds of benefits (and pitfalls) our traditions provide. To receive (and be received by) a given tradition is a little bit like making a friend. It is learning to live with another's strengths and weaknesses and to allow yourself to be invited into a deeper relationship with God in and through the realities of who this friend is and may become.

Fourth, *set your focus toward understanding both spiritualities and spirituality*. With regard to *spiritualities*, history provides case study after case study to help you learn something of what actual lived relationship with God through Jesus Christ is. Relationship with God is not to be understood apart from the particularities of real people's experience. Yet human beings are commonly *human* beings. And the God worshiped by Christians is One—through all time and space. Hence it is possible to explore not simply *spiritualities*, but *spirituality*—the tendencies, patterns, and dynamics of the divine-human relationship as such. Here, your job is not simply to collect and comprehend individual stories from the past, but to comprehend the whole in light of the parts, all the while respecting the contexts of the parts.

Finally, what I have said regarding history can be equally applied to learning from contemporary communities of indigenous Christianity throughout the world. While we generally recognize three main traditions of Christianity (Roman Catholic, Protestant, Orthodox), the fact is that there have been (and still are) a variety of forms of Christianity that do not neatly fit into these models. Syrian, Ethiopian, and Indian forms of Christianity have thrived for centuries. Growing communities of believers in Asia, Africa, and South America exhibit a unique character independent of the hegemony of any of the three primary Christian traditions. To explore the character of relationship with God lived out in these indigenous Christian communities is, once again, to explore models and perspectives *at a distance*—perhaps the distance of space rather than time.[32]

Let us return to Samantha once again, who is eager to learn about the themes of darkness and light. How will she incorporate the wisdom of the past? She investigates the "two ways" language—the way of darkness and the way of light—of the *Didache* (first or second century). She selects a few well-known representatives of the theme of darkness, perhaps Gregory of Nyssa's *Life of Moses, The Cloud of Unknowing* (fourteenth century), or John of the Cross's *Dark Night of the Soul*. She learns that part of the concerns surrounding the fourteenth-century Hesychast controversy in the East had to do with a claim to behold the Divine Light, so she looks into the works of Gregory of Palamas (1296–1359), who defended the Hesychasts. And so on. Some of the literature is very strange to her as she reads it. Both the Hesychast vision of Divine Light and the idea of God dwelling in a "cloud of unknowing" are new. She must explore their context further. John of the Cross's distinction between different "dark nights" (somewhat connected to stages of Christian growth) and his description of the darkness of the final night as being a blindness due to light add insight to her exploration. Her study of the details keeps her faithful to the people of history, but her question— What can I learn about Christian growth from these themes?—keeps her faithful to the project of history, comprehending relationship with God as a whole.

History provides an exploration of relationship with God and a host of resources. Our practice is enriched as we appropriate the wisdom of the past (and the distant present) into our own lived relationship with God. Our reflection on the dynamics of relationship with God is illumined as we see how others have understood the character of relationship with God. The formal academic discipline of Christian spirituality is grounded in historical reflection, for in the history of the church lies the vast majority of concrete data of people's experience of relationship with God.

Theology and Philosophy: Unified Viewpoints Related to Traditional Communities

If we are to explore spirituality, the relationship of humans with God, sooner or later we will have to do some serious thinking about *God*. We will have to face some of the big questions of life, such as Who is God? Who are we? and What is life about? And we will have to do this thinking in a disciplined manner so as to avoid promoting fallacies, contradictions, or falsehoods. And for many of us, this thinking is done in the context of a tradition, an ongoing relationship with a community of believers who have thought about these things long before we came along. And so we are led into the worlds of theology and philosophy. While personal experience, informal relationships, and history provide us with a host of particulars (experiences, insights, perspectives, models, and the like), the fields of theology and philosophy foster understanding of relationship with God by helping us to tie these particulars into a coherent whole.

It is virtually impossible to neatly summarize "the relationship of theology (or philosophy) to Christian spirituality." The Orthodox tradition has tended to shy from formal systemization, preferring to express the Truth through practices of liturgy and prayer. With the development of scholastic theology in the medieval period, the Roman West gradually experienced a separation of spirituality from theology and philosophy, a separation that has only recently begun to be healed.[33] The origins of many Protestant movements are not simply in theological disputes, but in concerns with the means through which people accessed relationship with God. Some movements were particularly concerned with matters of the integration of theology and spirituality. Others maintained their separation. Our task is to consider the uses of theology and philosophy specifically for the exploration of relationship with God. We shall do so by considering three questions: What is spirituality? What is theology? How do we coordinate the categories, the fruits, and the activities of these two, especially in terms of exploring relationship with God? Then we will briefly look at the field of philosophy.

What Is Spirituality?

We have considered the definition of spirituality as dealing with the lived relationship with God in the previous chapter. We also learned that one can approach Christian spirituality with a view to the aims of relationship with God (prescriptively) or with a view to the actual lived experience of those who have relationship with God (descriptively). If one approaches spirituality more from the *prescriptive* side (for example, as "spiritual theology"), then theology will play a central role in defining the task and the conclusions of the exploration of spirituality. If, however, one approaches Christian spirituality *descriptively*, then theology will tend to serve as one component helping the interpreter to comprehend the character of a person's or group's experience, much as the analysis of worldview functions in the field of anthropology. Thus, depending on how we see spirituality, we will find ourselves using the resources of theology in a variety of different ways.

What Is Theology?

Just as the roles that theology performs in our exploration of spirituality shift when our understanding of *spirituality* shifts, they do so also when our understanding of *theology* shifts. And our understanding of theology has experienced some serious shifts. The term *theology* itself refers to the discourse or study (*logos*) about God (*theos*), but long ago theology expanded from reflection on God to support a wide range of images. Some imagine theology as a *transmission of tradition*. In this image, theology is the faithful handing down of "the faith," or "the Great Tradition," which has passed from apostle to disciple to bishop to each generation. A second image is a *confessional* image, wherein official rulings or statements (papal utterances, conciliar statements, confessions of faith) are used as standards against which individual "cases" of belief and practice can be assessed. Theology can also be viewed as a matter of textual interpretation and synthesis. Here, in this *exegetical* image, the aim is not the re-presentation of the tradition or propositional truth, but rather a clearer reading of the text of scripture seen both within the original contexts and in the contexts of today. Theology has been viewed as a *community thinking* about its god together, as a study of the "Christian" contribution to the *history of ideas*, and as the designation of religious *identity markers*, whereby those in power label who is in and who is out of the club.[34]

The past century has witnessed not only the birth of the academic discipline of Christian spirituality, but also a radical reconfiguring of theology that has brought it closer to the tasks of spirituality. Thus, while some may conceive of or "do" theology much as it was done during the Enlightenment (divorced from spirituality), others see the task of theology as necessarily involved with the lived experience of relationship with God. It is clear to most that it is time for the separation of theology and spirituality to end. Theologians from all traditions are writing with an increased sensitivity to spirituality.[35] The question is, what does this mean? What might a reconciliation of theology and spirituality look like? Historical theologian Andrew Louth, bringing in the spiritual dimension of the theological task, speaks of theology as a "fascination of a lover with

the beloved."[36] Similarly, theologian Ellen Charry speaks of the "pastoral function of doctrine," arguing that doctrine is not merely informative, but also performative, that doctrine is presented not simply to instruct our minds, but to move our hearts and transform our lives.[37] It is clear that we define theology variously, and with good reason. The tasks and emphases of theology change somewhat with time, place, and person. Yet both theologians and scholars of spirituality are seeing the need of the one for the other.

Using Theology

Having looked at the nature of spirituality and theology, we are left with the question of coordinating the two with the art of using theology for spirituality. How do we take the terms, categories, tasks, and fruits of theology and relate them meaningfully to those of spirituality so that theology serves as a valuable resource for our exploration of relationship with God?[38] Since the function of theology is to *provide a somewhat unifying view related to a traditional community*, our

> If you are a theologian, you truly pray. And if you truly pray, you are a theologian.
>
> —Evagrius Ponticus[39]

job is to appropriate this function within the context of our own community. Below are four specific ways that you can do this.

First, because theology reflects deeply and carefully on themes that are especially relevant to our understanding of relationship with God, we are wise to reflect on the big themes of Christian spirituality in dialogue with theologians. Understanding of the sense of closeness or distance to God in prayer, for example, will draw on not only knowledge of psychology, but also the doctrine of God as both transcendent and immanent. And how we view God's transcendence and immanence will significantly shape not only our academic theories of spirituality, but also our personal and congregational habits of drawing close to God.

Second, because theology presents general frameworks for interpreting relationship with God as a whole, we are wise to evaluate those theological frameworks within which we see relationship with God. Whether we admit it or not, we are all theologians to a certain extent. At whatever level of sophistication, our history in the faith provides us with a set of control beliefs—an integrating factor that serves to make sense of our spiritual world.[40] By doing theologically informed spirituality, insights from history, psychology, personal experience, and so on can be placed into dialogue with a big picture presented and corrected by those who have gone before.[41]

Third, theology nourishes and sustains spirituality. Theology, by addressing the hard questions of God and by presenting the big picture of God, constantly inspires, feeds, and challenges relationship with God. This is true whether we are thinking of spirituality as lived relationship, reflected dynamics, or formal study. Theology confronts us with aspects of the things of God we have not considered. Think of theology as a formal way of acting out your fascination with the Beloved. Allow theology to

"Actually, nobody considers that to be a significant theological issue anymore . . . although it was the reason our denomination was first formed."

pull you into God. One who never studies theology can conveniently avoid facing what it may mean to live in the presence of God as God really is.

Finally, theology functions as a critic of spirituality. We have already discovered this in the previous chapter in our discussion of authentically *Christian* spirituality. Theological categories are used to determine an approach to relationship with God that is or is not authentically *Christian*. Theology is also frequently employed to help evaluate religious experience: for example, repeated visions of a powerful being who acts cruelly or who encourages self-destruction would be rightfully questioned concerning their divine origin. This picture of God simply does not fit with traditional theology.[42]

Philosophy and Spirituality

Philosophy, like theology, confronts the big questions of life: what is real, true, beautiful, right, important, and so on. Philosophy, like theology, aims at the synthesis of the particulars into a somewhat coherent whole. But while theology seeks to unify insights and ideas within the context of a faith tradition, philosophy seeks unification within a more general understanding of reality as such. While theology evaluates an account of human-divine relationship by the plumb lines of scripture and tradition, philosophy evaluates our relationship with God according to the rules of logical reasoning. Theologian Donald L. Gelpi has nicely summarized a few of the roles that philosophy serves with relationship to theological and scientific reasoning:

Philosophical categories seek to criticize, interpret, and contextualize the categories of theology and of the non-philosophical sciences which deal with human experience. Critical philosophy passes judgment on the truth or falsity, adequacy or inadequacy of the more or less tacit philosophical presuppositions which shape theological and scientific thinking. Philosophical categories interpret the results of theology and the other sciences when they apply to them in the sense in which philosophy defines them. Constructive philosophy seeks to create a theory of the whole which contextualizes the results of detailed scientific and theological investigations into reality. This constructive philosophy does first by specifying the realms of experience which different theological and scientific disciplines address and by showing their relationship to one another.[43]

It is interesting to note that while philosophical terms, tasks, and frameworks played significant roles in the development of spirituality throughout the patristic and medieval periods of Christian history, philosophy is rarely discussed today in the context of exploration of relationship with God.[44] Philosophers are beginning to discover the spiritual dimension of the work of philosophy,[45] and they have struggled with questions of the meaning of mystical experience.[46] We are only beginning to consider what roles philosophy might play in the exploration of relationship with God.[47]

Let us consider another example. Ian, a pastor, is interested in exploring the ways in which congregations *as communities* carry on relationship with God. In his pastoral work he finds himself not only addressing individuals, but also the congregation as a living unit. And, since he has an academic bent, he wants to use the insights of theology and philosophy to help him explore this dimension of relationship with God. What theologians give insights regarding community life? He looks to the early development of the idea of church, to Cyprian, bishop of Carthage (d. 258), and to those in his own tradition, the early Anabaptists (sixteenth century). He explores the idea of community in the monastic theology of Bernard of Clairvaux. By this investigation, Ian considers the ideas of community and spiritual life within a larger context of meaning. He peeks into the philosophical works of Josiah Royce (1855–1916), Edmund Husserl (1859–1939), John Macmurray (1891–1976),

and Emmanuel Levinas (1906–95), whose integrations of logic, philosophy, and community serve as a check on his own thought. His study both confirms and challenges his suspicions about leading a community into deeper relationship with God. Perhaps his study leads him to the concept of the Trinity as a foundational principle for communitarian identity: God is community, One in Three. Thus, through the integration of theological and philosophical resources, Ian's big picture, and his practice of spirituality, grows.

Theology and philosophy have much to offer our exploration of relationship with God. Theology and philosophy reflect on the themes, the big questions that are before us when we ask about relationship with God. Theology and philosophy offer basic frameworks within which the details of personal experience, interpersonal relationships, and historical and scientific investigations can be comprehended. Theology provides grounding with a faith tradition. Philosophy provides grounding within the overall frameworks of reasonability. Theology and philosophy can also nourish and sustain spirituality, pointing us to new ideas, expressing our fascination with the Beloved, opening our minds and hearts to God.

The Human Sciences: Insights and Specificity

The last realm of experience for exploring Christian spirituality to be examined in this text is the human sciences. The human sciences (psychology, sociology, and the like) have an obvious relevance to spirituality as a divine-*human* relationship. The human sciences offer spirituality means of paying special attention to relationship with God as lived by real human persons. They suggest insights, terms, perspectives, and such concerning how humans *as humans* relate to God. Furthermore, while theology and philosophy often provide us with large general interpretive frameworks within which the particulars are unified, the

63

human sciences ground both the perspectives and the particulars in greater empirical specificity. Unfortunately, defining the human sciences is no easier than defining theology. Psychology and sociology *are*, currently, a loosely affiliated collection of subdisciplines, each with their own topics of interest, methodologies, societies, journals, and so on. There is a world of difference between clinical and cognitive psychologies, between participant observation and strict statistical social research, between the study of the experience of love in different cultures and the analysis of neurological networks coordinating emotion in the human brain. There is no single human science (or even a single psychology) whose word is the last word on human nature. For better and for worse, what we have before us in the human sciences are a collection of diverse research communities and programs, each with their own resources for understanding relationship with God.

Psychology

The communities and subdisciplines encompassed by the term *psychology* have much to offer our exploration of relationship with God, and students of Christian spirituality are beginning to make use of these resources in a variety of ways.[48]

1. Psychology offers to Christian spirituality terms, insights, and perspec-

"It has been said that the church today is too reliant upon psychology. How does that make you feel?"

tives especially with regard to the *human* side of the divine-human relationship. We can think of the human dynamics of prayer, for example, in terms of psychological research associated with object-relations theory. We might explore connections between developmental psychology's interest in stages of personal growth and the interest of some saints in stages of spiritual development. With this kind of approach, some have discovered particular insights concerning specific aspects of spirituality, while others have developed larger conceptual frameworks for looking at relationship with God that are inspired by influential psychological schools or theories.[49]

2. As a field that studies the person, psychology might offer insights in an analogical way to consider who God, as personal, might be. There are problems and possibilities here. It is very easy—and very dangerous—to attribute to God specific dynamics of thinking, feeling, willing, or acting that are derived from studies on human persons and have nothing to do with God's real experience. Yet at the same time, reflection on the nature of person does seem to offer suggestions for our contemplation of a personal God. We will explore this further in chapter 4.

3. Psychology can also stimulate insights concerning our understanding of classical spiritual writings and figures. Erik Erikson's psychoanalytic analysis of the life of Protestant reformer Martin Luther (1483–1546), for example, is well known. There has also been since William James (1842–1910) an interest in exploring the "psychology of the mystics": describing the character of mystical experience, exploring how the mystics understood the nature of the human person, and exploring

early Christian spiritual disciplines (asceticism) through the lens of psychology.[50]

4. Psychology can also bring an increased specificity to our understanding of the definition of spirituality. The experimental psychological sciences are designed to define things such that they can be examined through repeated observations. The use of operational definitions of spirituality and recovery, for example, might facilitate an investigation regarding the rate and quality of improvement from particular diseases by a segment of the population. Thus, through the ongoing refinement of empirical specificity, our idea of what spirituality *is* is itself clarified and refined.[51]

5. Another function of psychology for our understanding of relationship with God is to bring an increased specificity regarding the human psychological operations involved in relationship with God. For example, when we say, in the process of discerning God's work, that the vision I had last night was not God, but rather a consequence of my eating pizza too late, we are placing things in categories (God, not God). This process of categorization is an ordinary human process, a process examined in great detail by cognitive psychology. Thus, to learn something about ordinary human categorization, we might learn something about Christian discernment. Likewise, developmental psychology informs our understanding of relationship with God in various stages of life. This use of psychological research functions as a kind of constraint on our theorizing in Christian spirituality.[52]

6. In a similar manner, psychology can provide increased specificity regarding the dynamics of the divine-human relationship. Psychology does not only study the operations of the human mind; it also investigates the situations and basic relationships of human life. Trust, surrender, and love—key themes in Christian spirituality—are all explored in interpersonal psychology. One can use insights from environmental psychology to explore relationship with God in urban settings (is there an urban spirituality?) or in situations of trauma.[53]

Finally, psychology can serve the therapeutic dimensions of Christian spirituality. Relationship with God involves, to one extent or another, growth in holiness and in wholeness. It is not only a life of prayer, but also a life of care. Hence, at times our growth in relationship with God will bring us face-to-face with problems or issues that are generally addressed in the context of helping relationships. At times we face our problems and issues and are drawn into relationship with God in new ways. These kinds of questions are most often discussed as psychological dimensions of spiritual guidance.[54]

Social Sciences

The social sciences offer similar resources to our exploration of relationship with God. Only whereas psychology tends to offer insights concerning *individual* spirituality, the social sciences offer insights regarding *corporate* spirituality (and corporate aspects of individual spirituality). Like psychology, the social sciences tend to be divided into specialized subdisciplines, each with its own set of methods and topics of interest. There is a great deal of difference between functionalist, symbolic interactionist, and communitarian approaches to society. There is a great deal of difference between doing ethnographic summaries, analyzing suicide statistics, and conducting surveys. Consequently, as with psychology, there is no room for glibly proclaiming what the social sciences have to say about spirituality. We are forced to carefully synthesize, to search for the most generally accepted conclusions, and to admit diversity of approach and opinion.

1. The social sciences can bring clarity to our understanding of the nature of corporate spirituality as *corporate*. Have you ever been in a gathering where something happened to the whole group, where you might say that it was not just a matter of this or that *person's* relationship with God, but of a work of God with the entire *gathering*? The New Testament contains letters written not only to individuals, but also to churches, to *corporate bodies*. What does it mean to convert to God not simply as an individual, but also as a *community*? Just as the psychological investigation of habit informs our knowledge of spiritual discipline, of ascetical practice, so too the sociological study of ritual brings us insights regarding corporate means of grace.[55]

2. The social sciences can also bring increasing specificity to our understanding of the forms of Christian spirituality insofar as they are associated with social roles. The care of a young believer by a more mature believer, for example, has taken various forms throughout the history of the church due in part to shifts in the ways leader-follower or teacher-disciple roles have been understood. We speak of clerical or lay spirituality, ways of conducting relationship with God that are related to one's place in the church institution. We mention privatized and ecclesial spiritualities, solitaries and communities, emphasizing the personal or social sides of relationship with God. Social sciences explore the ways we group ourselves

(or isolate ourselves). Because of this the social sciences may offer much to our understanding of the forms of spirituality.[56]

3. Social science can also bring an increased specificity regarding the character of spirituality in terms of social subgroups and trends. How might women, for example, carry on relationship with God *as women* in ways that are distinct from how men do so (given their differences in perceptions, orientations, experiences, and so on)? What about different social classes, ethnicities, and such? The social sciences can offer insights concerning the changing habits of spiritual life in light of larger social groups and trends.[57]

Finally, the social sciences can provide assistance in directing the outward social thrust of relationship with God. As mentioned in the previous chapter, authentic Christian spirituality is not neutral. It reaches to areas of need. These are *social* values expressed in the realities of the social climate of today. Poverty, oppression, and injustice are not simply subjects for a sociology or economics textbook or for political science speeches. These are matters of God's heart. But they *are* also subjects discussed in the social sciences. As author Ron Sider puts it (regarding economics), "Since economics is central to our world, non-economists like you and me will have to just do our best to understand without being intimidated by the fact that our understanding is only partial."[58]

Using the Human Sciences

Having reviewed the psychological and social sciences, a few observations are in order regarding the use of the human sciences for exploring Christian spirituality. First, the use of human sciences to inform spirituality may be more or less familiar to you, depending on what specific Christian tradition you are connected with. Protestant denominations have made more use of these resources in the past, though they are increasingly mined by the Roman Catholic and Orthodox traditions. Some traditions tend to be more cautious about employing psychological terms and ideas in the context of theological thinking than others.[59]

Second, remember that we are not simply speaking of the use of the human sciences to facilitate the *academic discipline* of spirituality. The insights of the human sciences are offered here as resources for the *exploration of relationship with God*: living practice, reflections on dynamics, and formal study. You can use the insights of developmental psychology not only to understand the nature of the human-divine relationship. You can also gain insights from developmental psychology, for example, as to why your six-year-old does not pray like you do.

One danger to watch out for in the use of human sciences is what Malcolm Jeeves calls the fallacy of "nothing buttery." This is the logical step from saying (correctly), for example, that human beings possess complex neurological networks that organize responses to the environment, to making the (invalid) conclusion that humans are "nothing but" complex stimulus-response mechanisms. Or the step from saying (correctly) that our social setting shapes the ways in which humans think to making the (invalid) conclusion that humans are "nothing but" reflections of their social construction.[60] We must train ourselves to look through the eyes of "insofar as we are social and psychological," without surrendering our awareness that we are "also more" than these dimensions, or more than what can be measured by the sciences that study these dimensions.

Another trap is the false dichotomy between contemplative and scientific psychology (or sociology). Some writers reveal a tendency to dismiss academic psychological research in favor of a "contemplative psychology" drawn from the writings of the saints—or created from theological and philosophical reflection. Others, however, will complain about the lack of psychological sophistication of Christian history (favoring a more developed scientific psychology or a psychological framework drawn from non-Christian sources). We must learn to listen to everybody with an open mind and heart. History provides insights and perspectives at a distance. Science provides empirical grounding for theories we develop from the insights of the divine-human relationship of the past. We dare not promote an account of relationship with God that ignores the most generally accepted empirically substantiated insights of the human sciences regarding how humans think, feel, and act or an account that fails to listen to the wisdom of the ages.

We have seen in our review of the use of the human sciences for the exploration of Christian spirituality that they accomplish a number of helpful functions.[61] They have the potential of grounding our insights with greater empirical specificity. They can suggest ideas about God analogically. They can guide our active living-out of relationship with God in the context of others. With care, the human sciences can be valuable assets toward our exploration of relationship with God. The focus box on the following page explores an example of the integration of human science information within Christian spirituality.

Other Resources for Exploration

This list of six resources is by no means exhaustive. The dynamics of the human-divine relationship are revealed in virtually every aspect of life, and for this reason the possibilities for interdisciplinary collaboration (including both formal and informal means) are endless.

Certainly the humanities can be explored as windows on the divine-human relationship. We could explore nineteenth-century European spirituality through the window of the novel. And what better source of reflections on hope for heaven in Christian spirituality than the spirituals of American slave culture? Likewise, to study Orthodox

Is it OK to imagine things when I pray?

One question that comes up when we talk about relationship with God is the question of how to pray. And when we talk about how to pray, sometimes this further question comes up: what do we do with images that pop up in our mind when we are praying? Perhaps it is not a matter of images spontaneously "popping up in our minds," but rather a matter of whether we ought to cultivate the use of these images: picturing Christ on the cross, picturing ourselves in the middle of a Gospel story, or something similar. The role of imagery in Christian devotion has been discussed throughout the history of the church. Some declare it a key to experiencing relationship with God. Others condemn the use of imagery as idolatry or as dangerous association with occultist practices. What's the good Christian to do? In addition to the careful exposition of scripture regarding this topic, perhaps the insights of cognitive psychology could come to our aid. By exploring just what goes on when people imagine, perhaps we can learn something about the roles that imagination plays (or ought to play) in Christian devotion.

Mental imagery has been explored for centuries. Hundreds of studies have been conducted on mental imagery in recent decades, most of them quite fascinating to read.[62] In spite of some continuing debates, psychologists have made significant progress in understanding what our imagination is all about. It is fair to say that, thanks to this research, we can accept with a high degree of probability a number of propositions:

1. Imagery plays a much more significant role in human cognition than we had previously thought.

2. The primary functions of mental imagery involve the presentation, conservation, and manipulation of information extracted from the environment.

3. Imagery is similar to perception.

4. Yet whereas perception is predominantly a retrieval operation, mental imagery is also a constructive operation, integrating data into a coherent whole.

5. Reason is necessary to clarify mental imagery.

6. People differ in predisposition toward imagery; just as there are logical geniuses, so there exist those individuals who are especially adept and given to image.

7. Image holds a special connection with emotion.

What implications might such empirical findings have on our understanding of the role of imagination in Christian devotion?

First, if mental imagery is really such a central element in human life, a life created by God, we might expect that mental imagery might play a valuable role in our relationship with God. The communication of God to humans is a communication to whole persons, including thought, feeling, and imagination.

Second, if mental imagery grasps, evaluates, and responds to what is before us, functioning more clearly in areas where other functions are weak, then we might expect imagination to facilitate elements of knowing God that are less available through the use of discursive reason or other operations. Thus, we can expect that some aspects of God's communication will be better grasped or expressed in image, although ultimately God transcends our reason or image.

Third, if mental imagery is constructive in part, we can expect that Christian imagery will also be mixed in character, as constructions of human mental process. Many spiritual masters have written about the need for discernment, acknowledging that while God does at times communicate through the medium of the imagery arising in our minds, we have no guarantee that any given image will be a pure expression of God.

Finally, if mental imagery and emotion are tied closely together, especially in the context of interpersonal relationship, we might expect that mental imagery might play a powerful role in facilitating deeply emotional aspects of our relationship with God. Indeed, it is precisely with regard to this connection with emotions that mental imagery has played a key role in Christian spiritual practice.

Psychology helps us to know what it means to be human. To be human is to imagine: to picture and re-picture; to re-hear, to re-experience our world within as from without. Just as God became flesh, condescending to our ways of apprehending, so too it seems God has seen fit to communicate to the human imagination in scripture and in experience. Of course, like all human operations, imagination is partial in its perception. Just as we can be deceived in our thinking, so also we can be led astray by false images. Nonetheless, just as we apply thinking and feeling with care in our relationship with God, so it seems justifiable, given the insights of psychology, to recommend the cultivated and uncultivated use of imagery in relationship with God when that use is appropriate to the setting and when it is under the careful discernment of a wise and caring community.

iconography is not simply to explore a genre of art. Rather it is to explore a vehicle of encounter with God.

Again, the study of religions other than Christianity can illumine the dynamics of Christian spirituality. Just as with the six resources listed above, we find areas of agreement, complimentarity, and opposition as we explore Christian spirituality in light of the study of the world's religions. For example, how are the Christian monastery, the Buddhist sangha, the Hindu ashram alike or different? How might you compare Celtic Christian prayers of protection to Navajo healing rites? What can we learn about Christian devotion by exploring the notion of submission in Islam?

One can even use the natural sciences as resources for exploration of Christian spirituality. For instance, for centuries human relationship with God has been lived out in the context of relationship with the land.

What might that look like now, in light of our ecological studies? Quantum physics is beginning to reveal a world that includes a measure of relativity, of indeterminism, of freedom. What might these insights contribute to a Christian understanding of relationship with God? Studies of ants converge with studies of the human brain to suggest that mind might have a greater social dimension than we had previously conceived. What might this research have to say about Trinitarian spirituality?

As I mentioned, the possibilities are endless. Each area of study, formal or informal, provides its own unique contribution to our understanding of relationship with God. Each offers its own kinds of correction and critique to the others. Each can be corrected and critiqued uniquely by the others. By using a variety of resources together we gain an increasingly full and clear picture of what relationship with God might look like.

Figure 2.4
Exploring Christian Spirituality

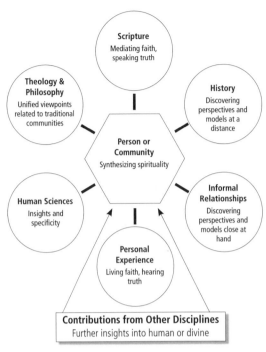

Scripture
Mediating faith, speaking truth

Theology & Philosophy
Unified viewpoints related to traditional communities

History
Discovering perspectives and models at a distance

Person or Community
Synthesizing spirituality

Human Sciences
Insights and specificity

Informal Relationships
Discovering perspectives and models close at hand

Personal Experience
Living faith, hearing truth

Contributions from Other Disciplines
Further insights into human or divine

Putting It All Together

We began the chapter by playing with the idea of exploration, considering what exploration involves and what one needs in order to explore. We have discovered that the exploration of relationship with God is best accomplished as an *interdisciplinary* exploration, using the resources of both formal academic disciplines and informal means of learning about things. Let us return to that image as we close this chapter. You have found a few guides, tools, and strategies for the exploration of the somewhat unknown territory of Christian spirituality. These are a few things to take with you as you go out to investigate just what relationship with God is all about. You will find a summary in figure 2.4.

But now that we know what to take with us, what do we do when we explore relationship with God? Simply put, we explore! We wander, looking here and there, noticing this or that, venturing into valleys and over mountains. Our resources are not the exploration. Rather they are the *tools*

we use to assist our exploration. We simply journey into relationship with God, using these tools to help navigate and understand what we see along the way. We wander and wonder, just like any explorer. Might there be a refreshing stream down there? Isn't that view just gorgeous? I wonder, could you grow potatoes in that soil? And likewise, as we explore relationship with God, would it be good to advise many to use imagination for devotional practice? For whom would it be beneficial and for whom not and why? Might there be a refreshing stream in the charismatic practice of speaking in tongues? Look at the way my friend Jane lives out her relationship with God. Isn't that beautiful? I wonder if Christians today could grow in holiness from the use of a kind of monastic rule of life? And so on. You just explore.

Part of the art involved in the study of Christian spirituality is selecting which tools to use for different explorations. As mentioned above, different questions of Christian spirituality might suggest the use of the insights from different realms of experience. We guard ourselves as we explore, asking ourselves, Am I reading these historical texts merely from the perspective of my own interests and agendas? Am I avoiding the challenge of what my friend has been trying to show me about God? Then, when the resources have been selected and studied, we face the task of coordinating insights. At times, insights from these different areas of study will express agreement. The study of history and the study of scripture and theology may point, for example, to the paradoxical presence of both the greatness and sinfulness of humankind. At other times, insights from areas of study will express compatibility, though not agreement. While sociology, for example, does not weigh in on the valuation of the greatness or sinfulness of humankind, it can offer many insights regarding the ways in which human greatness or sinfulness is acted out in the context of the dynamics of human societies. These insights of sociology may be fully compatible with the insights of theology or history. In situations of agreement or compatibility, we have freedom to explore further and see what insights one resource may provide another. At other times, however, insights from different resources may be opposed and therefore must be reconciled. In these cases, we must (as outlined above) choose from the following: reject the information from one source as incorrect or as based on insufficient evidence; reject a frame of reference used to interpret information as inadequate; construct a more comprehensive frame of reference capable of embracing the best insights of the resources; or either rest in ambiguity or renounce the prospect of reconciliation altogether.

But generally, to get started, you simply start exploring, just like in the jungle. You compare, analyze, ask questions, develop hunches, imagine things, and develop ideas. You play. Speaking of *playing*, it might help to think of interdisciplinary work as akin to playing in a jazz band. There *is* structure to jazz, but it is not always that clearly defined. Each instrument—bass, drums, saxophone, keyboards, and so on—makes a unique contribution to the band.

At times each instrument actually takes the lead and dominates the others. The whole, however, is actually held together by something greater than each of the instruments: the "groove" grasped by the band together. Sometimes a player gets to using an instrument for his or her own egocentric ends and leaves the band far behind. (This player has thus left the "groove.") But it is by playing itself that the reality of music is discovered. So it is with our interdisciplinary approach to Christian spirituality. Each area of study makes its own contribution. Each takes the lead at times and has the potential of leading the others by virtue of its own unique contribution. It is not any one discipline that holds the whole together, but something more (the Spirit) that is grasped by the whole. I can overplay one area of study and leave the Spirit far behind. And it is only actually in playing, in sincere exploration, that the music of relationship between God and humans is discovered. And by playing, looking at this and that, making sure to keep your tools and instruments always by your side, you will discover treasure you never thought you would find.

Questions

1. What are the key resources for exploring Christian spirituality? What are some of the strengths and weaknesses of employing each of them for the study of relationship with God?

2. Are there any other realms of experience that you might add to the list of resources discussed in this chapter? What would you add and why? What problems and possibilities might the use of your additional resources involve?

3. How do you bring together insights from different fields to bear on a question of Christian spirituality? Describe one example.

4. How is the exploration of Christian spirituality as a formal academic discipline different or similar to the exploration of relationship with God personally or corporately? How would you as a leader of a group (or as an individual believer) adjust the process of exploration outlined in this chapter for the purposes of practical (nonsystematic) exploration of aspects of relationship with God?

5. Design for yourself a study in Christian spirituality. What questions about relationship with God (what big issues) are you interested in? What realms of experience, formal or informal, might be appropriate to use in this exploration? How would you coordinate the insights of these realms? What problems and possibilities might you need to be aware of?

Practicing Christian Spirituality

A Journey into the Land of God

Get quiet and comfortable. Think about each sentence carefully as you read. Allow your imagination to help you in this exercise. You are about to go on a journey into the land of God. You have been planning on this journey for some time. Ask yourself, What do I think about this journey? How do I feel about exploring relationship with God? Think about how you got here, about who encouraged you to make the journey. Spend some time thinking about what you hope to find on this journey. What are you looking for in this land of God? What have you heard about this land from others? What do you think it might look like? What might you confront as you go there? What are you afraid of in this journey?

Now it is time to pack for the trip. What will you take with you? One by one, pick up those resources that are most important to you or those that you just want to take along. Look at each one as you put it into the pack: special relationships, books, ideas, academic disciplines. What do you want to take on this journey into the land of God? Why? Consider carefully each item. How have you related to this item in the past? How do you hope it will help you on your trip now? What will you need right here and now in order to explore relationship with God? Then place it in your pack and go on to the next.

When you are through packing, spend some time just thinking about your trip to the land of God. How do you feel about trips when you are ready to go? Are there good-byes to say, anticipations of hellos in the future? What kinds of attitudes do you usually have on journeys? What kind will you need on this journey?

When you are finished, take some time and write down any valuable insights in your journal. Knowing how you start a journey sometimes helps you later when the going gets tough.

God, our Guide and our Goal, we step out into relationship with you. We take what we have to bring, but we also need your protection. We both fear and celebrate the adventure of getting to know you. Thank you for all the resources to help us. We look forward to your presence on the way and at the end. In Jesus's name. Amen.

CHAPTER SUMMARY

1. Christian spirituality is beneficially studied through an interdisciplinary approach, drawing together wisdom from a variety of realms of experience, both formal and informal. Each realm of experience brings to our exploration of relationship with God distinct insights and distinct means of checking the insights from other realms of experience.

2. Our own personal experience provides the place from which our faith is lived and the world within which truth is heard. Our background, personality, and such enable us, for better and worse, to notice and focus on things in ways that are from our own unique perspective.

3. The sacred texts of Christian scripture are the primary vehicle of the communication of the Christian faith. The transmission of relationship with God throughout the centuries is also a history of biblical interpretation. Lived faith is a process of biblical appropriation. The language of relationship with God is a scriptural language. Christian spirituality involves a faithful hearing of the truth from the revealed Word of God, both in Christ and in scripture.

4. Through informal relationships we are brought in touch with different perspectives on relationship with God and models of relationship with God. Through our ordinary relations with others we see *close at hand* ways of thinking, of praying, and of being that confirm or challenge our own patterns of relating to God.

5. Through familiarity with Christian history we are brought in touch with an even wider range of perspectives and models of relationship with God. Because the figures, movements, and issues of Christian history are seen *at a distance*, however, we can explore them more at our leisure. We must be careful, though, to understand the wisdom of history in the context of its own setting—at a distance.

6. Theology and philosophy offer ways of seeing insights about relationship with God in terms of big pictures that make sense to the communities of faith within which we live. Theology draws together the primary questions of faith into a comprehensive perspective. Philosophy addresses the primary questions of life itself and keeps our thinking clear and logical.

7. The human sciences offer new insights, especially about the human aspects of relationship with God. They tell us about the patterns of personal and corporate life that are not provided from the other fields. They provide a kind of empirically grounded specificity that can put an appropriate check on reflection from other realms of experience.

8. We study the nature of relationship with God by putting together these realms of experience (along with others that might be used). We discover the insights that each brings to the specific question of spirituality we may have. Then we coordinate the insights of the fields together, looking for areas of agreement, complimentarity, or opposition.

LOOKING FURTHER

General

Bruce Demarest's book *Satisfy Your Soul: Restoring the Heart of Christian Spirituality* (Colorado Springs: NavPress, 1999) provides a balanced biblical-theological approach to many of the first questions we ask when venturing into the exploration of Christian spirituality. For an encyclopedic introduction to the academic field of Christian spirituality, see Kees Waaijman, *Spirituality: Forms, Foundations, Methods*, trans. John Vriend (Leuven, Belgium: Peeters, 2002).

Personal Experience

The Solace of Fierce Landscapes: Exploring Desert and Mountain Spirituality, by Belden Lane (New York: Oxford University Press, 1998), is a classic example of reflecting academically on Christian spirituality intentionally involving the experiences of one's own personal life. The journals of John Wesley (available in many editions), a cofounder of Methodism, show the integration of mind and heart in the work of one of the church's Protestant pioneers.

Biblical

Here are three separate approaches to integrating text and spirituality. The first is the most practical and the last is the most theoretical: Evan B. Howard, *Praying the Scriptures: A Field Guide for Your Spiritual Journey* (Downers Grove, IL: InterVarsity Press, 1999); Robert J. Mulholland Jr., *Shaped by the Word: The Power of Scripture in Spiritual Formation* (Nashville: Upper Room, 1985); and Sandra M. Schneiders, *The Revelatory Text: Interpreting the New Testament as Sacred Scripture*, 2nd ed. (Collegeville, MN: Liturgical Press, 1999).

Informal Relationships

Aelred of Rievaulx's classic *Spiritual Friendship*, trans. Mary Eugene Laker (Kalamazoo, MI: Cistercian Publications, 1977) addresses the development of friendship in Christ.

History

The Story of Christian Spirituality, ed. Gordon Mursell (Minneapolis: Fortress, 2001), is another historical survey of Christian spirituality, filled with color pictures. For an excellent discussion of a variety of methodological issues related to the integration of history and spirituality, see Philip Sheldrake, *Spirituality and History: Questions of Interpretation and Method* (Maryknoll, NY: Orbis, 1998).

Theology, Philosophy

Vladimir Lossky's *The Mystical Theology of the Eastern Church* (Crestwood, NY: St. Vladimir's Press, 1998) is a classic introduction to mystical theology from the Orthodox perspective. Like his book on history, Philip Sheldrake's *Spirituality and Theology: Christian Living and the Doctrine of God* (Maryknoll, NY: Orbis, 1998) discusses the relationship between spirituality and theology.

Human Sciences

Elizabeth Liebert, *Changing Life Patterns: Adult Development in Spiritual Direction* (New York: Paulist Press, 1992), is an insightful work that uses the findings of one aspect of experimental psychology (developmental psychology) to enhance our understanding of relationship with God. For a good example of an influential model of contemplative psychology, see Gerald May, *Will and Spirit: A Contemplative Psychology* (San Francisco: Harper and Row, 1983).

Human Experience

OBJECTIVES

In this chapter you will be introduced to human experience, what it means to be human. You will learn about what experience is and the kinds of things that make up any experience. You will explore the nature of human experience: the operations, stages, and relationships that characterize human experience and that help to define who we are as individuals and communities. You will get a chance to explore your own experience.

This is not an easy chapter. You will be introduced to many new terms and concepts. You will get the most out of this chapter if you are prepared to spend some time just thinking—in a relaxed kind of way—about the concepts introduced. Allow yourself the freedom to muse over each of the terms, each of the concepts, playing with the ideas. You need not have everything mastered after reading this chapter. We will return to these themes again and again throughout the text.[1] After reading this chapter you should begin to be able to

- list the elements present in any experience;
- identify the primary operational systems of human experience and give examples of their use;
- show how human experience progresses through a number of recognizable stages;
- name the key spheres of relationships in human experience, showing how each sphere shapes who we are;
- describe how corporate experience is similar to individual experience;
- list the main principles that assist in understanding corporate experience, giving examples from a community with which you are familiar;
- explain what is meant by depth when talking of human experience.

In Christian spirituality the richness of God encounters real human people. Some of us are morning people. We wake up first thing in the morning full of thoughts and ideas and energy. But when the evening drags on we find ourselves fighting to focus in conversation. Others of us are night people. We drag ourselves out of bed, lucky if we can think clearly enough to make a cup of coffee. Nonetheless, we are the life of the party at night. Does this affect our spirituality? You bet it does! Think of your own relationship with God. When do you find quality time with God? Have you ever struggled with your sleep patterns and their effect on your spiritual life? We relate to God as real, flesh-and-blood humans.

The basic framework of Christian spirituality brings the realities of human experience together with the Christian God. We have seen the emphasis given to experience in our discussion of the trends and foundations of Christian spirituality in chapter 1. Especially in the light of these foundations and trends, clarity with regard to what we mean by *experience*—and in particular *human experience*—is vital to the task of exploring Christian spirituality.[2] In the present chapter we will look at human experience from the viewpoints of philosophy and the human sciences. In the following chapter we will inquire about God. Then, in chapter 5, we will return once again to human experience from the viewpoints of biblical studies and Christian theology. Our aim in the present chapter, then, is to present the beginnings of a working model of human experience that will illumine our understanding of the divine-human *relationship* in the chapters to follow. But first we must clarify just what we mean by *experience*.

Understanding Experience

The term **experience** is used in a variety of ways. We often use *experience* to indicate practical wisdom gained through long-term exposure to some aspect of life. We say of some woman, for example, that she is an "experienced" pianist. In a similar way we say that some situation corresponds with "my experience" ("*My experience* is that there have always been long lines in that department store."). Some philosophers use *experience* to refer to the source of human knowledge: our observation of external, sensible objects or of internal mental operations. Others use *experience* to refer to a particular stage in the human process; one has an experience about which one later reflects and responds. The broadest approach to experience employs the term as a fundamental metaphysical category, a way of describing the very nature of reality. In this approach all reality is seen within experience and as experience: atoms are regarded not as static things, but rather as momentary configurations of a more dynamic experience.[3] By considering experience—and particularly human experience—as a fundamental category, we facilitate a unique comprehension of both the stability and dynamism in reality and we highlight the essential relatedness of things. Such an approach to experience facilitates the kind of clarity necessary to comprehend Christian spirituality as human relationship with God. In this textbook, therefore, we will use the term *experience* in two different ways.[4] We will use *Experiencing* to refer to a stage of human process involving sensation (inner and outer), perception, and such. Yet we will also explore the use of "experience" in a broader sense. Thus, for example, rather than speaking about a human *being*, we will speak of human *experience*. Let us begin with this broad understanding of experience.

What is present in *any* experience: any experience whatever, real or imaginary? What is manifest most basically, for example, in atomic experience, in the experience of a sunflower, in the experience of a lover? The most basic elements of experience divide into three groups.

First, there is a sense of *Quality*—of *Evaluation*—or adaptive response. At any level of reality one can identify adaptive, evaluative responses to certain qualities.

Atoms react to, adapt to, evaluate the presence of other atoms (reacting to polarity, exchanging particles, communication of energy, and the like). Sunflowers are aware of the presence of the sun. There is a certain quality that is communicated by the presence or absence of sunlight, a quality (light) that is being assessed constantly by the sunflower, and to which the sunflower responds or adapts. When a newlywed looks into the eyes of the beloved, the newlywed is aware (more or less) of a set of qualities and evaluative responses: feelings, hopes, thoughts, sensations, and so on. Even one's imaginative experience of a unicorn arises as the presence of certain qualities (shape, size). Thus, whether we are talking about the adaptations of colliding atoms, of a flower's response to the sun, of one newlywed's gaze toward the other, or even the imaginary experience of a unicorn, a sense of quality, or evaluation, attends every experience, every moment of experience.

Some philosophers approach this element by speaking of the "subject" of experience, and with regard to *human* experience they sometimes think of this in terms of consciousness. But in order to explore our broader approach to experience, let us try not to think in terms of a subject as *having* an experience, but rather of phenomena arising to *become* an experience. This way of thinking is not easy to grasp. Allow yourself to muse. What would it be like if we weren't things but experiences? What makes up experience anyway? Think, for example, of the powers of attraction and resistance at the atomic level, of the chemical reactions in sunflowers, of the mental and physiological responses of human emotion—how they change and develop as each experience develops. Those responses are the experience(s) that, together with the elements we will describe below, *become* the atom, the plant, the person. Thus **Quality** or **Evaluation** is the first primary element in any experience. The precise type of a given experience (whether it is atomic, botanic, human, imaginary, or so on) can

---

What Do We Mean by "Experience"?

1. Experience is practical wisdom gained through life.
   - "She is an *experienced* pianist."
   - "In my *experience*, there are long lines in department stores."
2. Experience is a source, process, or stage of human knowledge.
   - "What I *experience* with my senses, I then consider with my intellect."
   - Experiencing, Understanding, and so on (stages of human experience defined herein).
3. Experience is a way of speaking about reality; we speak not of *things* or *beings* but of *experiences*.
   - "Our *experience* as humans usually involves a social dimension."

---

be determined in part by an examination of the nature of the *evaluative* elements present in the experience.

The second basic element of any experience is a sense of **Force**, of **Act**, of confronting, of the *necessity* to evaluate. In any experience the sense of quality arises along with a sense of presence. One atomic experience (one atom) is what it is, in part by virtue of its sense of other impinging forces. Hydrogen atoms are what they are because of their unique configuration of interacting subatomic particles. The sunflower is what it is in part by virtue of its unique relational configuration to other forces (light, soil, water), other acts forcing reaction. The lover's experience is what it is in part simply because of the presence of the other insofar as that other appears to the lover. Being is relationship, and Force constitutes that relatedness. Consciousness is ordinarily consciousness *of* something. There is, in the confrontation with that which arises in all experience, a self-negating identification of other (this is not me) which, in turn, continually re-

FIGURE **3.1**
The Basic Elements of Experience (in the broad sense)

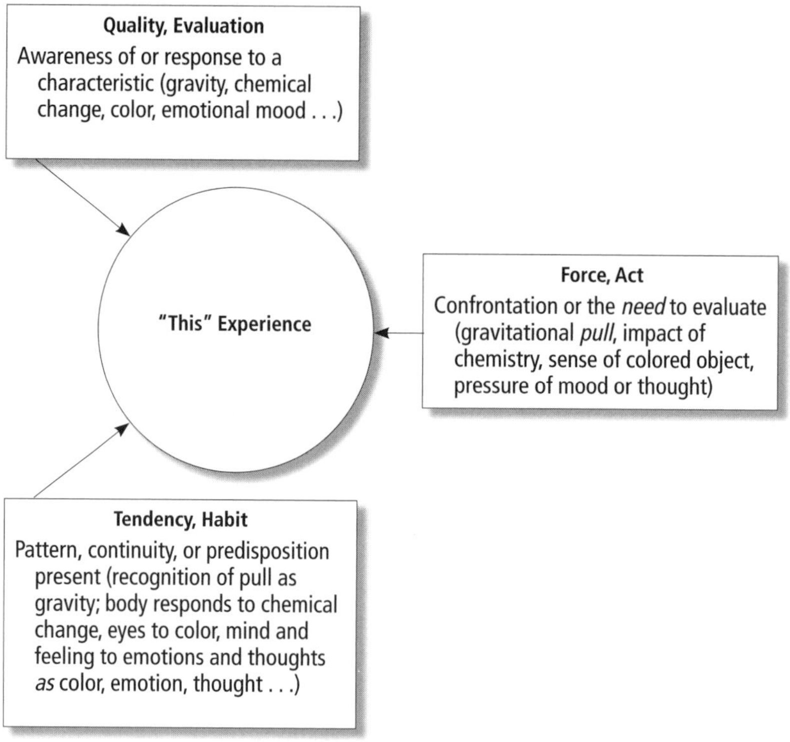

constitutes the self. This is true of atoms, plants, and humans.

The sense of that to which we must respond can be either physical or nonphysical. We step on a nail and the sensation of sharpness arises as a force demanding response. Thoughts also arise in our minds in a similar manner. We are constantly flooded by a stream of feelings, intentions, thoughts, and decisions to which we respond on a moment-by-moment basis. *This* thought arises and we either go with it or choose not to. If (to speak in terms of consciousness again) the first element of human experience might be looked at as the flow, the *stream*, of consciousness itself, then the second element of experience might be looked at as the *contents* of consciousness. Again, philosophers sometimes refer to this second element by speaking of the objects of experience. Yet in a broader approach to experience, however, things do not face objects. Rather both *evaluations* and *forces*

join to help create the experience that is present.

While some philosophers speak of the two elements above as the whole of reality (subjects and objects; acts and interpretations), our approach speaks of *three* primary elements in experience.[5] The third basic element in any experience whatever is a sense of *Tendency*, of **Habit**, of pattern, of continuity. There is a pattern, a continuity, to Quality and Force and their interaction. Think of the atom again. The experience of the atom is what it is in part because the impinging forces are recognized. Atoms are built to respond in certain ways to certain charges. Indeed, it is this very patterning of evaluation and response and presenting forces that *makes* atoms what they are. Likewise, the sunflower senses the presence of the sun *as* the sun. It naturally evaluatively responds accordingly. There is a tendency for plants to respond to the sun in certain ways and to respond to the presence of water in other ways. It is the presence of Quality, Force, and Tendency together that constitute the sunflower's experience as a sunflower. In our lovers, we can see that the gaze means something to both. Human experience involves not only act and evaluation. It also involves meaning, and meaning comes from tendencies: tendencies in expression and in recognition. While some might think of this element in terms of law or rule, it is best to see this element as a bit more flexible. Novelty in itself is a pattern. Rules change slightly over time and in different contexts, and the sense of evaluative options differs slightly as experience develops.

The arising together of these three elements (Quality/Evaluation, Force/Act, Tendency/Habit) constitutes an experience in the broad sense. What that experience is—whether atom, sunflower, or human—depends on the configuration of these elements. It depends especially on the third element, for it is the element of Tendency that identifies the stable pattern or trajectory (some say the "essence") that gives experience meaning and being. Again, it is the uniting of these elements that constitutes experience. The presence of a sense of Force (perhaps due to some chemical in the soil) might seriously alter the way the sunflower responds evaluatively to the action of the sun. But neither the chemical nor the sun are to be considered merely objects. Nor is the sunflower to be considered merely a subject. Rather the presence of these patterns at this time with these Tendencies creates the "sunflower experience" that is. The lover's experience involves a rich complex of Tendencies within and without. The lover does not simply *have* a set of feelings, sensations, intuitions, and such. Rather these Tendencies, as they arise, constitute the lover at that time. In a very deep sense, they *are* the lover. As we shall see in the chapters ahead, who I *am* cannot be separated from my relationships, my relationship with God, and my Habits of relating with God. Again, this way of looking at things is not easy to get. Keep playing with it. We will come back to these

notions at various times in the book. Over time it will become clearer.

Having explored the broad understanding of any experience, we will now proceed by considering the following thesis regarding specifically human experience:

Human experience arises as embodied soul/mind/self/spirit, constituted by the somewhat integrated arising of various mental-biological operations or systems of operations, which ordinarily proceed in generally definable stages and develop in time and space, within the context of a web of relationships and at various levels of depth, while maintaining its own unique being.

Embodied Soul/Mind/Self/Spirit

First, human experience *arises as embodied soul/mind/self/spirit*. By saying this, we affirm something quite obvious. We intuitively know ourselves as body; we intuitively know ourselves as soul/mind/self/spirit (any of these words can be used at this point). Think of what it is like when you pick up a hammer to strike the next roofing nail into the shingle, when you feel the pain of a cramp in your body, when you sense the tender touch of another (or the horrifying touch of violence). In these moments, we existentially grasp the identification of our self as *embodied*. At the same time we also know human experience as soul/mind/self/spirit. There are other times (like dreaming) when life appears to be little connected to our bodies. We also receive the flow of experience itself as possessing meaning, a kind of integration transcending bodily existence. We experience our experience as both body and soul.

While we can point to moments when one or the other dimension is prominent, most often they are experienced together. I remember learning how to use a spray machine to paint houses. I had used sprayers when I attempted my own paint business, but it wasn't until I was working side

81

by side with journeymen painters that I actually "caught it." They kept telling me about the feel of the motion from side to side that characterizes the proper spray stroke. I would watch them and listen to their instructions: how to hold my wrist, when to press and release the trigger, how far to overlap in each stroke, the angle of the gun, the distance from the wall. But again and again, I could not produce the quality of work my foremen did. Over time, however, I began to catch on. It was not a classroom learning, however. I would just do something right and notice (yet a just barely conscious noticing) that it was right. Gradually this aspect and that aspect of the skill fell into place until, like my mentors, I too knew what the proper spray stroke "meant." It was a knowledge that involved an entire system of meaning: customers, dollars, films of paint thickness, color, reflected light, and on and on—all of which were assumed and expressed in this single bodily motion. But it wasn't a knowledge remembered in the mind. It was a knowledge learned, expressed, and lived in the body, in the feel of the movement of my arm from one side to another.[6]

Humankind has struggled throughout history to comprehend intellectually what our embodied existence might mean. Some of the viewpoints have significantly influenced the history of Christian spirituality. Ancient Greece debated whether the soul was a substance and whether it was immortal. Some Greeks and Romans were suspicious of bodily experience (like sexual expression), promoting instead a spirituality that emphasized the place of the mind (*nous*). Modern European philosophers discussed the mind-body problem, inquiring whether our spiritual search could be distinguished from our biochemistry. In the East, Hindus and Jains argued for *Atman* (the enduring self or soul), while Buddhists argued for *Anatman* (denying the existence of an enduring soul or self), advocating radically different approaches to spiritual life. Psychologists have offered models of the ego, the organism, and the actualized self.

More recently we have talked about "socially constructed models of the self," the "central executive," and the postmodern "death of the self."[7] This very struggle points to our need to comprehend *something*, however vague. Whether we conceive it in terms of an enlivening principle, an integrative center, or even simply as "a convenient way of referring to a series of mental and bodily events and formations that have a degree of causal coherence and integrity through time,"[8] we are trying to come to grips with a reality common to nearly all of us, nearly all of our waking lives. *Embodied soul.* Suzanne Noffke, in her article on soul in the *New Dictionary of Catholic Spirituality*, sums up the matter nicely. After reviewing the variety of terms used to refer to soul, she writes,

> Whatever the term, what is agreed is that human beings are spirit as well as flesh. Yet we have no experience at all of this spiritual aspect of ourselves except as rooted in our physicality, in our bodies. The theory of how soul and body, the spiritual and the physical, are joined in the human person has fascinated philosophers and religious thinkers for at least as long as history and literature have been recorded. The practical implications of the question are pivotal to an integrated spirituality.[9]

Literate or developed society is currently in the midst of a rediscovery of the body. Philosophers, historians, social critics, and writers in Christian spirituality are all calling us to a renewed appreciation for our embodied existence and for the positive relationship of body to soul.[10] We identify only literate or developed society here because much of the world—those who scrape out their living and who witness the ravages on the human body of manual labor, violence, or diseases that will not be treated—does not need a rediscovery of the body. For these, the appreciation of embodiment has never waned. Many farmers and laborers, people with disabilities, and athletes have an edge on the academics when it comes to intuition of the soul's embodiment. Nonetheless, it might be helpful, in introducing human experience, to draw attention to a few aspects of the soul-body connection that have been noted by literates in developed societies of late.

First, *the body structures the soul*. Whereas Aristotle thought of the soul as the form of the body—the pattern or principle that organizes the material stuff of the human body into a living being—it might also be possible to conceive of the body as the form of the soul. One's presence in *this* body, in *this* place and time, organizes our selves to experience the world the way we do. Thus, our experience of both self and world—our thoughts, feelings, and actions—fit the way our bodies and brains are built to receive information. Consider the housefly. Due to the structure of its eyes, the Tendencies of visually perceived Qualities and Forces are quite different than for a human. Flies have a radically different visual experience than humans.[11] One can also identify other subtendencies of evaluative response contained within the more general tendency of visual perception: retinal recording, synaptic transfer, image coding, memory comparison, and so on, each of which have corresponding physiological structures and which produce unique effects on one's experience of the world and on one's self as "one who sees." Body structures self.

One delightful story illustrating this phenomena is "The Dog Beneath the Skin," recorded in neurologist Oliver Sacks's *The Man Who Mistook His Wife for a Hat and Other Clinical Tales*. A medical student had been using amphetamines. One night he dreamt of being a dog. When he awoke, and for the next three weeks, his sense of smell was greatly enhanced, probably due to an excitation of a particular part of the brain. He could recognize people by their smell. He could smell their emotions. "He could recognize every street, every shop, by smell—he could find his way around New York, infallibly, by smell."[12] How did this change in physiology affect this man's *soul*, change the man him*self*? "Somewhat intellectual before, and inclined to reflection and abstraction, he now found thought, abstraction and categorization, somewhat difficult and unreal, in view of the compelling immediacy of each experience."[13] Human experience is what it is because our bodies are what they are. If we had dog bodies (and dog brains) *we ourselves* would be different. While few of us have enhanced olfactory perception, some have greater sensitivity to adrenaline than others. Some are oriented more toward auditory or kinesthetic perception than others. Some of us are brain-injured, disabled, or genius. Our spirits take form in our bodies.

A second way the body and soul are connected is that *the soul constitutes itself through the body*. It is not just that we *have* a body, or that we *use* a body, but also that we *are* bodies (at least for the present). One tendency of human experience recognized by many is the tendency to *initiate*: to move our own experience to some extent from one moment to the next, to attend to this and not that, a capacity to generate response to that which confronts (again, the junction of Evaluation, Force, and Tendency). From a broad approach to experience, human initiation is not merely a *reflection* of some essential self created long ago, but rather the very *constitution* of the self by the self (*as* an experience). Hence, what we are is the sum total of the Tendencies established up to and including the absolute present. The point here is that this constitution of the self is executed *bodily*. The stereotypical teenage decision to take up smoking in order to fit in is the choice of a self through bodily patterns and habits. This is also what posture and pose are all about. (Have you ever thought about what postures you use in prayer and how your self is embodied through these postures?) Yet not only our decisions regarding concrete actions, but even our attention to emotions or thoughts reflect certain physiological (even synaptic) patterns.

Third, just as mind is structured by body, so also body is structured by mind. The French philosopher Maurice Merleau-Ponty makes this point with regard to human ar-

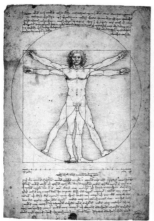  

How does one's body structure one's soul?
How is one's soul constituted through one's body?

tistic expression: "The obvious fact is, however, that the colours of the palette or the crude sounds of instruments, as presented to us in natural perception, are insufficient to provide the musical sense of music, or the pictorial sense of a painting."[14] Psychologists are beginning to discover that the same environmental stimulus will produce different electro-physiological responses in the brain depending on the context of the stimulus and the state of the organism at the time the stimulus is delivered. Perception is experienced only in terms of a framework of meaning, a meaning given to and by the self. Likewise, emotions are experienced and expressed quite differently in one culture than another. Consider the religious notion of an ecstatic experience in various cultures. How does it appear? How is it experienced bodily? Body and mind thus mutually structure each other such that one has meaning in the context of the other.

Finally, actions taken with regard to our physical body involve the body politic as well. This matter comes up with respect to spirituality, for example, in the studies of bodily renunciation (regarding food, sex, and the like) in history. The decision not to marry is made within a network of social meanings as well as personal meanings and physical processes. Those of us whose bodies do not fit the models of beauty assigned by our current time and place are well aware of how the situatedness of our bodies in the body politic structures the very frameworks of the soul. Anorexia is not only a personal or physical issue; it is a social issue, as behaviors are often precipitated by social pressures regarding one's body. Body, culture, self—all are implicated one with the other.[15]

Human experience arises as embodied soul/mind/self/spirit. One dimension cannot be fully understood without the other (at least in terms of the majority of human experience). We shall now explore how this body-self gives rise to the thoughts, feelings, and volitions that form the contours of human experience. In the chapters that follow we shall explore in greater detail the significance of the integration of body and mind for our relationship with God.

The Operations and Systems of Human Experience

Human experience is also *constituted by the somewhat integrated arising of various mental-biological operations or systems of operations.* As we learned above, Habits and Tendencies that we usually perceive as mental or as having to do with an encompassing self are encountered *in, through,* and *by* human bodies. We will use the term ***operations*** to identify the particular physiological or mental tendencies to evaluate, respond, and adapt to that which confronts us, indicating by this word all particular tendencies of evaluation and response, both those that perform a very specific function (such as image-retrieval, concept recognition, event appraisal, or hormonal activation) and those that combine specific functions to form larger activities (such as perception, choice, desire, and disgust).

There are at least two, and possibly three, primary sets of operations in human experience: integrative patterns in mental-physical process through which the human Evaluates, adapts, and responds. Some have referred to these sets of basic integrative tendencies as "faculties," but it might be most helpful to think, with the human sciences, in terms of **operational** *systems* (think of the circulatory system or the digestive system). Our aim, in identifying fundamental *systems* of evaluative response (operational systems), is not only to identify particular operations characteristic of human experience, but also to class the special relationships that these operations have with each other such that they can be recognized as wholes.

Cognitive

Cognitive or conceptual operations (the intellect) exhibit a special sensitivity to the structure of the environment, of that which confronts. Inquiry, insight, deduction, comparison, synthesis, and other similar particular operations fall into this category. Many of the individual components of category formation and retrieval, language production and recognition, and theoretical and practical judgment are to be comprehended here. Both verbal and spatial processing fall into the general category of cognitive operations. As a number of discrete operations cooperate to enable a particular way of acting that highlights verbal or spatial process with this sensitivity to the structure of the environment, one can recognize a cognitive *system*. We shall see, however, that the cognitive system employs

a variety of particular operations, within and without its own system.[16]

Affective

Affective operations (the emotions) are especially sensitive to the meaning of environment-person relationship (what happens when something confronts someone) and more heavily involve physiological processes (hormonal activity, heart rate, galvanized skin responses, and the like). Feeling, attraction, action tendency, excitement, mood, reaction, along with the host of labels for individual emotions (fear, anger, joy, and so on) fall into this category. Affective operations function by means of changes in what psychologists call "heat": action readiness ("I'm so happy I could sing"), phenomenological tone ("I just *feel* happy"), physiological processes (increased heart rate), appraisals of situation significance ("This is the best day of my life"), mental preoccupation ("I just can't stop thinking of her smile"), and other tendencies. Affective operations evaluate the environment with relationship to concerns that govern our sense of the significance of our relationship to that which confronts us. The *affective system* incorporates both affective and cognitive operations within a unique means of adapting to the confronting environment distinct from the cognitive system.[17]

Volitional

One can also posit a third system: the **volitional** *system* (the will). This system appears to be more sensitive to intentionality, deliberative action or self-control. Whereas affectivity and cognition respond to the confronting "out there" (even when the "out there" is an interesting thought), the sole object on which the volitional system acts appears to be the process of human experience itself—the choice to attend to this perception, the decision to take this action, the election to cultivate this desire. Volitional operations are involved in the cognitive system at such points as, for example, choosing to adopt a theory. Volitional operations are involved in the affective system in such events as nursing a grudge. Thus volition functions, along with the forces of the environment, to move the self from one moment to the next, as the autonomous contribution to the motion of affective or cognitive process. As such, volition may be less an independent system itself; rather, it arises as the development of affect or cognition insofar as they fall under the autonomy or deliberation of the human person.[18]

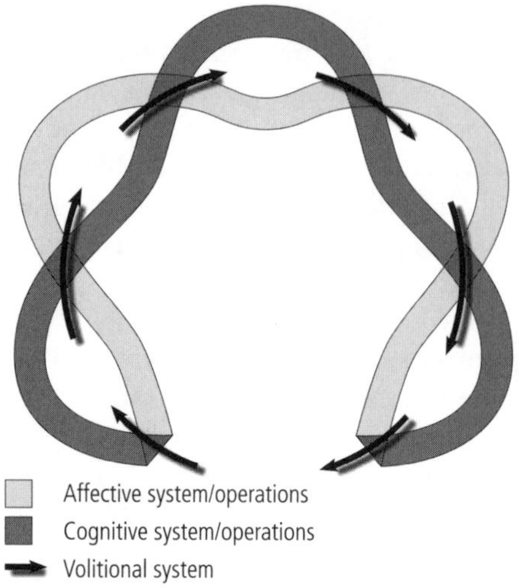

Cooperation among Operations and Systems

Operations from these three basic systems work together to evaluate, adapt, and respond to our environment. This working together includes various patterns of operational integration. Very specific operations (such as retinal recording, synaptic transfer) can be integrated within a single operation (perception) within one basic system (cognitive). Furthermore, entire operational systems use operations from other systems. The affective system is dependent on cognitive operations for proper affective functioning. For example,

> So once again: what we have before us in our study of spiritual formation is the whole person, and the various basic dimensions of the human self are not separable parts. They are aspects thoroughly intermingled with each other in their natures and actions.
> —Dallas Willard[19]

emotional activation involves the appraisal of both the character and the significance of situations for the person involved (for example, a person's evaluation that snakes are dangerous). Likewise affective operations are necessary for cognitive processing. Think, for example, of how it feels to raise

FIGURE 3.2
Operations and Systems

☐ Affective system/operations
■ Cognitive system/operations
➤ Volitional system

an important question. Now think of how it feels to get a hunch about that question, but then the hunch doesn't pan out, and then a new idea brings you closer to an answer. Finally you solve the problem. How does this solution feel?

The phrase *somewhat integrated* is included in our definition of human experience to account for the ambiguities of human experience. Aside from the various dis-integrations labeled in the *Diagnostic and Statistical Manual of Mental Disorders,* there are a host of more subtle ways in which affect, cognition, and volition may be working disharmoniously. We humans have been known to "jump to conclusions" or to be "all head and no heart." At times, thoughts and feelings arise with little relationship to one another, and human experience can appear to be a random presentation of mental events.

Needless to say, different people are oriented toward these operations and systems variously. Some people are more sensitive to the affective system (feelers) and others to the cognitive (thinkers). Some are more attuned to spatial processing (artists) and others to verbal processing (writers). Still others are sensitive to volition and action (doers).

Spiritual writers throughout the ages have explored relationship with God in terms of our operations and operational systems. John of the Cross, for example, divides the progression of purification, in his famous *Ascent of Mount Carmel*, into sections addressing appetites, intellect, memory, and will. Likewise Lutheran spiritual writer Johann Arndt (1555–1621) writes of the new birth as a work of God "by which our heart, thoughts, mind, understanding, will, and affections are made holy, renewed, and enlightened as a new creature." Theophan the Recluse speaks of our enslavement prior to God's sanctifying work of grace in terms of the lack of attunement of the mind, will, heart, and body to the new way of life.[20] Likewise, more recent integrations of human experience and Christian spirituality make reference to similar systems of operations. The followers of Adrian Van Kamm speak of inner- and intraformation, including remembering, imagining, knowing, feeling, and so on. Elizabeth Liebert and Nancy Wiens speak of "non-thematic," "affective-imaginative," and "interpretive" dimensions of human experience. Dallas Willard divides mind (thought and feeling) and spirit (heart or will).[21] The comprehension of discrete but interrelated operations within identifiable systems enables us to make sense of the workings of human experience and then to see how these patterns of human experience are involved in relationship with God. We will explore the connections between our operational systems and our relationship with God in greater detail in the chapters ahead.

Figure 3.2 illustrates the integration of these operations and systems. The two separate bands of lines represent the cognitive and affective systems. They weave in and out of each other, illustrating the interconnectedness of cognitive and affective operations. The arrows moving around the whole represent the volitional system, the motion of human experience itself, from one moment to another.

The Process and Stages of Human Experience

While human experience is not wholly predictable (for example, we jump to conclusions), on the whole it tends to follow a general pattern. Human experience *ordinarily proceeds in generally definable stages.* The configuration and the character of the operations involved in human experience are identifiably different at different stages of human experience. Human experience flows in a particular direction. Medieval psychological models (borrowing from Aristotle and Augustine) spoke of a movement from the sensitive to the intellectual to the volitional. Empiricist philosophers spoke of a movement from impressions to simple ideas to compound ideas. Some philosophers speak of an "evaluative continuum" involving a development of different types of "feelings." Buddhist traditions speak of *aggregates* developing from form, to sensation, to perception, to mental formation, to consciousness. Behaviorist psychology speaks of a development from stimulus to response (or later a development from stimulus through organism to response). Cognitive psychological textbooks tend to order tables of contents from perception, to memory, to inquiry and categorization, to language, to problem solving and decision making. Even scientific descriptions of the process of emotions reveal a similar development. When these schema are compared, a basic structure emerges. The synthesis in this text identifies six separate stages.[22]

Being Aware

The first stage of experiential process is associated with bare consciousness, or **Being Aware** itself. Human experience arises from a living or real *capacity* to evaluate, and at its most basic level this capacity involves the possibility and initial experience of mere awareness. Humans are unaware of the range of sounds that are available and present to a rabbit. Some humans (musicians) are trained to be aware of a wider range of sounds than others. They hear the sounds differently than nonmusicians do. Human experience begins to develop as phenomena (Quality) appear (Force) within our range of awareness. When I walk into a grocery store to shop for some flour for supper, I am immediately confronted by a wide range of sights, smells, sounds, and even emotive moods arising from my experience with stores. These may or may not be strongly present to me at the time, but all enter into my simple Being Aware stage of the experience at the grocery store.

Being Aware is often called consciousness. Consciousness—at least ordinary consciousness—involves a few variables, each of which operates on a continuum: range (open to restricted), intensity (dull to alert), energy (relaxed to tense), and level (conscious to unconscious).[23] By taking account of these variables we can begin to talk about states of consciousness. Our state of consciousness, changing constantly with the movements of the predisposing variables (for example, whether focused and intense or open and relaxed) constrains the possibilities of what can be sensed and perceived. When I enter a store to shop for flour, my awareness is usually in a fairly restricted frame: I am looking to get the item and leave. Intensity could be somewhat dull or alert, depending on my day; so also with the energy of my consciousness.

The stage of bare awareness also involves the real presence of the forms that structure experience, thus affecting not only *what* is experienced, but *how* it is experienced. As I enter the store, my physiological, mental, and cultural givens affect not only the content of that bare awareness, but also the Quality that particular Being Aware itself possesses. Range, intensity, energy, and level differ from human to human, from moment to moment.

Finally, it is possible to understand Being Aware, especially at its beginning moment, as more fundamental than simply a stage of human experience. From this perspective, the stages of human experience might be pictured as waves on the ocean of consciousness. Thus Being Aware can be viewed as the raw material on which all of human experience arises. Being Aware, as stage or state, is the point or the frame *from which* all that is experienced is experienced. It is the character of the emptiness on which all somethingness arises.

Experiencing

The second stage is characterized by **Experiencing**. We include in this stage all that is discussed in the psychological literature as stimulus, sensation, perception, and initial memory processing. Philosophers refer to this stage when they speak of the development of experience from sense experience through perception and the production of imagery.

From a general field of awareness, a sense of Force arises toward certain elements of that general field. When I walk into the store I am more or less aware of a vast range of sensations, feelings, and thoughts. Yet my perceptual Experiencing of the store usually tends to focus on a few central matters that are presented to me with greater force: a particular advertisement, the voice of an acquaintance, the smell of fresh bread. Affective operations at this stage begin to identify elements of concern in a vague way, highlighting particular elements for attention. Likewise, conceptual operations will structure—from the mass of sights, smells, feelings, and such—a sense of *what* I am dealing with. Items are recognized (their Tendency identified), earlier plans are ordered in light of current perceptual input, and feelings guide me to my proposed end. If I am set on my shopping task (volition), the aisle down which I usually find the flour will probably carry more perceptive Force than the other aisles. I will notice characteristics about this aisle more than the others.

Contrary to earlier empirical philosophies, the process of human Experiencing is not simply a passive reception of sensations and the transformation of them into perceptions and memories or images. Not only have the givens of awareness already structured what and how impinging forces can be evaluated, but also the process of Experiencing itself is an active process. Perceptual selection from the mass of sensitive phenomena, recognition of patterns *as* this or that, the appearance of initial affective energy signaling concern (necessary for perception), and many other operations demonstrate the dynamic and interactive character of human Experiencing.[24] It may be, for example, that as I approach the aisle down which I usually find the flour, the aisle appears quite different. The flour and other baking items are not there and the other products shelved there are shelved in an order never seen before in this store. I am somewhat surprised because I expected to perceive the flour within a certain schema of meaning (the way shelves are usually organized). Now something is different.

Understanding

From Experiencing, one moves to **Understanding**. Thinking and feeling, in their various types, are to be included in this stage. Philosophers speak of this stage in terms of inquiry, hypothesis, insight, and the like. Inquiry might begin in my experience with regards to shopping as I confront the rearranged baking items aisle. What has happened? Where is the flour I was looking for? The affective and conceptual operations triggered into functioning from this inquiry will begin to offer possible ideas until insight leads to a reasonable and satisfactory (affective) hypothesis. The stage of Understanding also includes much of what cognitive psychology discusses under conceptual processing, general knowledge, and language processing. At this stage concepts are explored in light of various theories. Here we look at the various aisles of the store, comparing one to another, incorporating ideas from other parts of our experience to formulate an idea of why flour is not on the usual shelf and where I might find it now. We attend to features of the situation. I notice the holiday foods shelved in the usual baking items aisle and wonder whether the upcoming holiday has something to do with the reorganization of the store.

Emotions research discusses the same stage in terms of appraisal and regulation. Perhaps by now I am greatly concerned that I have not found the flour. I may have checked in three or four aisles. What if the store is out of flour? I have to bake a pie for my boss, who is coming soon for supper. Affective appraisal operations begin to signal the significance of this situation for my concerns. Nonetheless, I do not totally freak out, because affective regulative operations remind me that I am in a public place and that excessive emotional expression is not really appreciated here. (By the way, much of this is barely conscious unless we attend to it.) Thus Understanding begins to grasp and respond to that which confronts us.

Human experience is noetic-adaptive. It adapts to the environment by "knowing" it. We seek to adapt ourselves to that which confronts us; and in so doing, that which confronts us is, to some extent, mediated to us. This noetic mediation receives a heightened focus at the stage of Understanding as humans make sense of their world. For example, as I search the various aisles for the flour, I pick up a large amount of information about the situation confronting me. I notice products, patterns of shelving, holiday music, decorations, and more as possible sources of information about my inquiry. I recognize and order facts about "the way things are" insofar as they are needed for the task at hand. Finally, I notice the sugar on a large shelf far to one side of the store. Perhaps the flour is with the sugar. Perhaps the store is not simply out of flour, but the employees have moved the baking items to make special room for the holiday items. And at this point I have linked insight to inquiry and have suggested a real hypothesis. Needless to say, affective operations adjust accordingly.[25]

Judging

The fourth stage is associated with **Judging**. At this stage, human experience moves from the question, What is the case? to Is it really the case? Wonder, inquiry, hypothesis, and abduction are primary in Understanding, whereas verification, demonstration, deduction and induction take center stage in Judging.[26] Psychological literature often addresses patterns of human judgment in terms of language processing, learning, or decision making.[27] Yet judgment involves not only judgments of reason, but judgments of feeling. In lyric, in art, in intuition, and in empathy, human feelings bring a sense of clarity into experience. Affective experience at the Judging stage completes the processing of concern and appraisal and moves toward definite emotion formation, although the character of emotional experience changes as human experience itself develops.

In terms of our shopping example, at the stage of Judging I begin to look and see whether the flour is with the sugar. I check to see whether other aisles are affected by the holiday interest, verifying my "moved because of the holidays" hypothesis. Sure enough, many other aisles have been slightly reorganized and holiday goods of one sort or another are shelved where other products had been present. And sure enough, there, near the sugar, is the flour.

Deciding/Acting

Judging moves toward **Deciding** and **Acting**. Psychological research involves an entire spectrum of studies on decision making. Likewise, philosophers of various schools of thought emphasize decision and action as a kind of termination of the evaluative continuum.[28] Deliberation leads to decision and concrete action. At this stage there is an investment, an entrustment, of the person in the judgment previously made, either through the formation of a thought, belief, or feeling or in the taking of a concrete action, affecting the confronting environment. In a similar manner, affec- tive experience may achieve an expressive stage at this point of affective process, giving rise to action tendency, phenomenal feelings, mental preoccupation, physiological changes, and the like. Thus after evaluating (very briefly) various courses of action in light of my knowledge of the whereabouts of the flour, I decide to pick up the flour and head on to the checkout counter. I also decide that I have enough information to form a belief that the flour was unusually shelved because of the shelving requirements of the holiday items.

Integrating

Finally, the fruits of decision and action, in turn, bring the person to a stage of **Integrating**. Philosophies of various types recognize that the process of experience ultimately serves to transform us, creating paradigm shifts, changes of horizon, worldview adjustments, conversions, and revolutions.[29] Psychological literature is beginning to emphasize this aspect as well, speaking of gestalts, feedback, perspective, constructivism, and reintegration. Some of the literature addressing conditioning, reinforcement, and theory revision bears on this stage. In terms of our example, my shopping encounters, for example, give me a host of information and feelings that provide feedback for further experience. While these encounters may not serve to trigger a major paradigm shift in my life, my sense of store arrangement may be expanded, my understanding of what happens to stores in a holiday season may be more thoroughly informed, and my understanding of emotional tendencies under time constraints may be more developed. Integration involves both adjustments in worldview and the shaping of affective predispositions.

Integrations of one kind or another finally cycle back to shape the character of Being Aware itself through interaction with preexisting accumulated knowledge or habits and sociohistorical conditioning. Both *of what* I am Aware and *how* I may Be

Aware in the next moment of awareness (at least the next time I enter the store) are shaped by the transformations taking place at the stage of Integrating. The interaction of transformation and reintegration at the last moment of Integrating joins with the preexisting conditions at the first moment of Being Aware to form new possibilities for evaluation and action in the face of the confronting environment. This interaction, in turn, creates a new person-to-environment relationship (and indeed, it re-forms the person himself or herself), and thus the cycle of human experience begins again.

As we learned with relation to the operational systems of human experience, so here with the stages of human experience we find that people are variously predisposed. Some people tend to have special abilities at the level of Being Aware. They are able to attend to the range, intensity, energy, and level of awareness as others around them cannot. Consequently, they are able to see (and live) as others don't. Others are all about Experiencing. They sense every detail of the world. They might be upset at Understanding or Judging types for not noticing these details. Still others live in a world of Decision and Action, where life is about making decisions and getting things done. Finally, there are those people who are especially sensitive to Integrating, those big-picture people who consciously see life in terms of a whole and who are very conscious of the wholes within which others experience life.

Again, our thesis states that human experience ordinarily occurs within this process or pattern. By "ordinarily occurs" I simply mean that there is a general tendency of human experience to flow in a predictable direction, frequently passing through recognizable stages on its way. Empirical analysis of human categorization alone—not to mention studies of other aspects of human experience—gives ample evidence that ordinary human cognition does not necessarily always follow the ideal logical structure. Often human experience func-

tions more efficiently within a finite universe by taking shortcuts. As mentioned above, we frequently jump to conclusions, bypassing Understanding and moving directly to Judging. Likewise we leap without looking, moving directly from Experiencing to Acting without Understanding or Judging. Many of the heuristics and biases discussed in the psychological literature on judgment and decision making involve neglecting the use of particular operations or entire stages of experiential process due to the prominence of some salient feature of the environment or of the experience as developing.

Much of the time, the neglect or misuse of an operation is simply a result of normal patterns of experiential organization. But, in addition, operations at each stage can be dysfunctional. Being Aware may be mindful or repressive; we may be attentive or closed in our Experiencing; our Understanding may be intelligent or biased; our Judgments may be reasonable or invalid; our Decisions may be responsible or irresponsible; our Integration may reflect a yieldedness to reality or a hardening toward reality. We may live wisely or foolishly. It is precisely at these junctures where the possibility of volition or self-control has central relevance. At any stage in human experience, there may be a need for the volitional system to initiate patterns within the process, thus shaping the development of human experience itself. Yet this action of human volition is itself achieved within the context of a variety of constraints from within and beyond us. Furthermore, in addition to breaks in the process due to finitude or *dys*-function, there are times where process is interrupted due to *supreme* function. To adapt a phrase, truth happens. In this way constraint, autonomous volition, and the forces of reality interact, giving rise to the mysteries of human life. Once again we shall discuss the implications of the stages of the process of human experience for Christian spirituality in the chapters to follow.

Figure 3.3 illustrates this cycle of stages in human experience. Being Aware is not

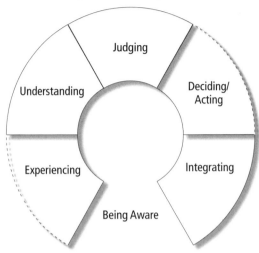

FIGURE 3.3
Stages of Human Experience

bounded, reflecting the empty or open character of this stage or state. The dotted lines at Experiencing and Deciding and Acting represent the room for interplay with what confronts us at these two stages: at Experiencing, when we are sensing and perceiving that which confronts us, and at Deciding/Acting, when we are effecting change on that which confronts us.

The Web of Relationships

Human experience is made up of operations: Tendencies of mind and body that Evaluate that which arises with Force. These evaluative operations can be grouped into three main systems: cognitive, affective, and volitional. These operations, furthermore, arise in a process generally involving six stages (Being Aware, Experiencing, Understanding, Judging, Deciding and Acting, and Integrating). By looking at the systems and process of human experience, we explore the Tendencies of Quality/Evaluation present in human experience. Yet, as we have learned, experience is a joining of Tendency with both Quality/Evaluation and Force/Act. To say that our evaluations arise in response to that which confronts, or to that which arises with Force, or to that which Acts on us (as in the examples

of stepping on a nail or realizing you have forgotten something) is to say that we are essentially relational. Human experience *develops within the context of a web of relationships.*

While some philosophers speak of a variety of "dimensions" of human experience (biological, psychological, social, spiritual), here we will emphasize the relatedness of human experience.[30] Human experience apart from multiform relatedness simply does not exist. Without relatedness there is no source of impinging Force. No impinging Force, no experience. In this sense interrelatedness is a necessary, though not sufficient, condition for human experience. Furthermore, the character of our relationships (the kinds of impinging Forces) help to make us who we are. Our thoughts, feelings, and choices only arise within the context of a complex network of others to which we relate. These others, to which we are necessarily related, affect us at the Experiencing stage, serving as perceived causes of our experiencing such and such. They provide the contents—the objects, the environment, the world—of our experience. Having entered through Experiencing, these others serve to form the material from which our memories, thoughts, images, feelings, decisions, and such are formed (Understanding and Judging). As one moves to Deciding and Acting, these others of our relatedness are once again confronted as the world, the objects, the environment *on which* we act.

The precise impact of relationship on human experience involves the combination of (1) the introduction of a kind of configuration of experience (my encounter with a grove of aspen trees or with a liturgical gathering configures my experience in unique ways) and (2) the activity of cognitive and affective operations developing in particular patterns, resulting in (3) images, feelings, and the like, which in turn reorganize belief formation and personal transformation. The others of our relatedness can be grouped variously. We will explore five separate spheres of human relatedness, which have no necessary hierarchy. They are simply separate kinds of relatedness.

Nature

Humans exist in relationship to *nature*. The forces of nature confront us at every side. Human experience is physical, chemical, biological, zoological, ecological. The force of gravity, the composition of soils, the presence of bacteria, the sounds and feel of plant and animal life—these and more shape our existence. This is simply part of what it means to be an embodied soul. For example, one's family medical history presents certain predispositions of relationship with nature which shape that self. A person with a physiological predisposition toward alcoholism might be presented with a very different set of choices and feelings in life than someone who has no alcoholic history or predisposition. Similarly, one's geographic and historical location enable particular relationships with various natural forces. A person who lives in a teepee during the thirteenth century and a person who dwells in the concrete jungle of a twenty-first-century urban ghetto are exposed to different diseases, possess different hopes, raise their families differently, and express worship to God differently in part because

of the differences in their relationship to nature.

Self

Second, humans experience a relationship with a *self*. Human experience is deeply psychological and personal. Our own thoughts, feelings, and choices can become the objects of our own thoughts, feelings, and choices, confronting us at times with intense Force. (Do you ever experience thoughts you can't get rid of?) As our developing experience is comprehended as a somewhat unified whole, there arises within our experience a perceived "self" with which we have to do (for example, in the adolescent's question, Who am I?). The dynamics of self-relationship are often the stuff of clinical psychology, although there are a variety of approaches to self-understanding and relationship with the self in both psychological and philosophical reflection. Thus self-appropriation or self-improvement arises as persons take fundamental responsibility for their operations—for thoughts, feelings, and choices such that the relationship with the self is transformed. (Have you ever known someone who chose to lose a great deal of weight and found his or her sense of self transformed?) We can also attend and address our own evaluative responses: for

> Human experience, apart from multiform relatedness, simply does not exist.

example, a particular event in one's experience (say, a near-fatal auto accident) may initiate a significant sensitivity to one's Being Aware; or another set of events (a sermon at church) may awaken a sense of one's own lack of sincere, intelligent inquiry. In these ways (and many more) we reflect on this developed and developing integration of operations and stages called a self. Our own sense of who we are, the projections of possible action into the imagined future, the processing of both joy and pain—all are shaped by this relationship with self.

Other Humans

Third, humans experience relationship with *other humans*. Human experience is interpersonal, social, economic, political, and fraternal. At times, the deepest elements of our experience arise from relationships with other people. Philosophical reflection in the past century has tended to stress the social embeddedness of human experience. Recent research in emotions emphasizes the fundamentally social aspect of human experience. An entire spectrum of social sciences addresses the nature of interpersonal relationships.[31]

As we learned in our discussion of informal relationships in chapter 2, relationships provide us with a range of opportunities for being (models and perspectives). Indeed, we can take a step further. Our network of relationships (history, culture, family, close friends, and so on) forms for us a framework within which, for the most part, we exist. Our language shapes the ways in which we can describe or even experience life. Our patterns of emotional expression have meaning within the cultural norms of expression that surround us. Our tendencies of Being Aware (for example, our capacity to attend to this or that, or our predisposi-

tions regarding the range, intensity, and energy of consciousness) are shaped by our relationships with others. Thus, while we have the capacity to transcend social influence, who a given individual *is* cannot be understood apart from a grasp of the configuration of relationships that form that individual.

Spiritual Realities

Human experience also involves relationship with *spiritual realities*. While not greatly emphasized in philosophical or psychological literature outside of transpersonal psychology and indigenous philosophies,[32] religious literature has long affirmed this sphere of relatedness, whether speaking of various spirits, angels, or other inhabitants of a spiritual sphere. The spiritual world appears to us as something with which we are confronted, whether in a vision or merely as an inclination of the emotions—for example, when a woman walking home to her village from the fields at night encounters a powerful spirit who attacks her. Whether we are a simple Scottish farmer, or an Australian Aborigine, or an American businesswoman, the realm of spiritual realities is not simply something we believe in. It is something we face, something to which we are related.

The shape of human experience is constrained by our own predispositions with relation to the spiritual world and by our history of encounters with it. Just as some people are more social or more attuned to nature than others, so too some are more predisposed to spiritual forces than others: they see or sense spirits, or perhaps angels, more easily than do others. Some, Christian or not, are more drawn to the things of the spiritual realm more readily. For this reason, while Christian spirituality has to do with relationship with God, our understanding and practice of this relationship with God cannot be separated from our interaction with other spiritual forces. This is why spirituality and what is often called "spiritual warfare" are learned together.[33]

"Pastor Billingsley thought it might be best if I told you what I told him last night . . ."

Divine

Finally, humans live in relationship with God, who ultimately transcends all nature, self, others, and the world of spiritual beings (in the sense that God is fundamentally different from other spiritual beings, as addressed in chapter 4). It is ultimately *this* relationship that spirituality is all about. And once again we differ with regard to our experiences of the divine. One person may have a history of intense divine encounters, while another may grow up in an atmosphere of quiet, subtle, but nonetheless real regard for the God who is the source of all creation. The human experience of each person arises in the context of relationship with God, whether attended or not. But we shall address all this in the chapters ahead.

Corporate Experience

So far in this chapter, we have been speaking of human experience as if it is the experience of an individual. An individual has (or is) a body, uses cognitive operations, makes decisions, and is shaped by relationships with others. Yet in raising the subject of our relatedness, we are brought to consider another facet of human experience: human experience is not only individual; it is also *corporate*. We live before God not only as individuals, but also as *communities*. Indeed, perhaps, as American philosopher Josiah Royce (1855–1916) suggests, "our social experience is our principal source of religious insight."[34] A number of features characterize interpersonal relationships and human corporate experience. These features ground our understanding of the experience of a community. We will return to these features again throughout the text, especially in our discussion of relationship and in our exploration of care.

Self-disclosure. First, corporate experience is built on *self-disclosure*. However inadequate self-disclosure may be, without some form of manifesting ourselves, interpersonal relationships would be impossible. At times we are not even aware

> For with us they [the angels] make one City of God, which is addressed in the words of the psalm, 'Most glorious things have been said about you, City of God.' Part of this City, the part which consists of us, is on pilgrimage; part of it, the part which consists of the angels, helps us on our way.
>
> —Augustine[35]

that we have disclosed ourselves to another: our eyes dilate and our interest is revealed; a twitch of our lips uncovers an otherwise hidden sadness; our style of walk and gesture manifest our own particular way of being. Yet also consciously, through gesture, expression, language, and act, we disclose ourselves to others. Self-disclosure involves every aspect of human experience. Thus, I may disclose to you through conversation my Experience of the curry I ate for supper last night. I might express my affections for Latin jazz, or my cognitive analysis of the rhythms, or my will to explore them further on a hand drum. I may share something of my pattern of Integrating by giving my perspective on things. I might also reveal my relationships: for example, by speaking about—or by introducing you to—my cat. I can express the most trivial concerns ("I'm a little chilly") or the depths of my heart ("I love you"). We disclose all of who we are.

Symbolic expression. Second, disclosing something to another (*dis-close*, to make open or public what was closed) involves a system of *symbolic* expression, presentation, and representation. Even the unconscious dilation of the eyes discloses interest, for example, to the savvy jewelry salesperson, because that dilation is comprehended within a framework of embodied meaning. The dilation probably means that the customer looking at wedding rings is especially interested in *this* ring, the ring that was the object of the dilated glance. When self-disclosure is mediated through gesture and especially through language, the forms of symbolic meaning become much more refined. Self-disclosure is expression in that it takes something of ourselves and brings it out. Self-disclosure is presentation in that it is an action of the self, an embodiment of the self in time. Self-disclosure is representation in that this action of the self is given and received within a context of symbolic meaning. Whether crude or refined, whether consciously or unconsciously revealed (or interpreted), self-disclosure is always given in the context of symbolic meaning. Relationship is mediated through symbolically meaningful self-disclosure.[36]

Communication. As self-disclosure is expressed within symbolically meaningful frameworks, we begin to communicate with others. And, at the root of community (*commune*-ity) is communication (*commune*-ication). Communication involves a number of aspects. It is *semi-intentional*, a blend of unconscious and conscious self-disclosure. However trivial—and however much is unconsciously disclosed in the moment—any communication requires at least the commitment (intention) to remain for the duration of some level of interaction and to say something (again intention). It also involves *encounter*, the confrontation of the one by the other. In encounter you become a significant element within my experience (Force).[37] Communication involves *interaction*, the sharing of meaningful verbal and nonverbal symbols. Relationship is not just action, wherein I act on you, but inter-action, wherein we act toward each other and with each other. Finally it involves *reception*, or at least the hope that what I say will enter another's experience, just as what is communicated to me enters my experience.

Comparison and imitation. Meaningful self-disclosure not only opens up the possibility of communication. It also enables comparison and imitation. We hear the report of another person who went out to the wilderness for three days of silence. Our curiosity is piqued and we decide to try it

ourselves. We look at the body of another and we compare it to our own. We desire the kinds of objects another has, so we do the things the other does. We are enraptured by the beauty of a song and we practice music ourselves. Sometimes we compare and imitate others randomly. (Maybe you have found yourself imitating another's accent to yourself after that person has left.) Comparison and imitation are characteristic of human experience (and of other forms of life). Experience that is truly corporate (that is, the experience of a body of individuals and not just of a random collection of individuals) requires a significant level of comparison and imitation.[38]

Common and shared. Communication and imitation both lead to the possibility of having something in *common*, of people *sharing* a single experience. You and I went to school together as children. We have lived in the same town all our lives. We have a *common* history. When we communicate, this common history is grasped between us through a *common* memory. A few of us support the same political party. We *share* a *common* hope for our future, a hope that is communicated between us. Social psychologist Steve Duck, speaking of close relationships, writes, "Friends and intimates develop their own sets of shared concerns, common interests and collective problems, as well as shared meanings, common responses to life and common emotions. Friends are often appreciated exactly because they share private understandings, private jokes or private language."[39]

Relationship involves the *mutual experience* of one another. We ride the same rollercoaster and share the thrill of the loop. My thrill and your thrill shape the experience of the other and form a single experience we share. We talk late into the night about war and peace and I get the sense that you understand (and respect, or even agree) with my views and values. My feelings affect you and yours affect me—and so on, as every aspect of human experience is shared (operations, stages, relationships, depths, and such). "Relation is reciprocity," Jewish philosopher Martin Buber (1878–1965) proclaims.[40]

Community (*commune*-ity, formed through a network of relationships) is constituted by the common. Diversity brought together through the common equals community. What we have in common—what we share, those aspects of experience that mutually penetrate each other—define the type and the degree of community of a given group of people. Josiah Royce draws attention to a number of features essential to community: the sharing of past history, present events, future hope; the mutuality of common events, common actions, common love, common interpretation. The presence of all these constitutes (creates and gives the essential character of) community in any given place and time.[41] We share parentage or home and form families. We all like square dancing or progressive politics or urban gardening, and we regularly meet together to facilitate these activities. We form collectives or "lifestyle enclaves."[42] We live in a shared geography, and because of that we share the work or life that comes from that piece of geography.[43] We share faith and form churches. We share geography and form towns and cities. We share government and geography and form nations. And so on.

Identity and roles. Furthermore, within this context of communication, imitation, and common experience, individuals develop *identities* and *roles*. As we mentioned above, relationships provide the individual with his or her self-defining context. George Herbert Mead (1863–1931), founder of the field of social psychology, addressing the relationship of social control to individuality, writes that social control is "actually constitutive of and inextricably associated with that individuality; for the individual is what he is, as a conscious and individual personality just in as far as he is a member of society, involved in the social process of experience and activity."[44] The individual cannot be grasped apart from the matrix of relationships that participate in the individual's experience.

Corporate Experience

Corporate experience
begins with simple self-disclosure,
made clearer to others by means of symbolic expression,
which leads to communication.
Comparison and imitation are always part of corporate experience.
Communication and imitation lead to the development of common and shared experience,
which leads, in turn, to mutual experience.
Within this context of mutual experience, we take on identity, roles, and corporate self-identity.
Most visibly, we express this experience in community and culture.

The way this functions is that we Integrate our experience in terms of identities. We share the vocational training and kinds of activities of other people in the construction industry and so we identify ourselves as in the trades or as a laborer. We appreciate the music, the clothes, and the values of those who spend lots of time skateboarding, and so we identify ourselves as a skater. We share the sufferings of those who do not have material necessities and we identify ourselves as poor. We are model-train builders, Hispanics, Gen-Y'ers, charismatics, Canadians, and so on. This process of claiming identities is necessarily both embracing and excluding. Through claiming identity we recognize our sharedness with others and allow our experience to be shaped by others of like experience. Yet, at the same time, claiming identity is also identifying that which we are *not*. To be poor can also mean to be not rich. To be Serbian can also mean to be not Croatian. To be charismatic can also mean to be not dispensational.[45]

The establishing of identities leads to the predisposing of our experience in terms of roles. Sociologist Robert Ezra Park

(1864–1944) writes that "the conceptions which men form of themselves seem to depend upon their vocations, and in general upon the role that they seek to play in the communities and social groups in which they live, as well as upon the recognition and status which society accords them in these roles."[46] Communities, as the blending of diversity around commonness, create places for people to fit in each grouping. Indeed, each place to fit forms an identity within a larger grouping of identity. One may find a place to fit within one's identity as an American by taking the role of a loyal critic, identifying with those Americans who appreciate their country but who at the same time consider it important to draw the country to account on given issues. Similarly, families provide roles for enablers, caretakers, problem children, and so on.

Corporate self, corporate identity. Shared experience and shared identities lead ultimately to the development of *corporate identities* or corporate selves. This is not just a matter of individuals finding their identity in the context of groups, but rather of the *group itself* possessing a single identity. Plato speaks in this way when he speaks of the ideal State in his *Republic*, comparing the structure of a State to the structure of human experience.[47] Just as individuals feel and think (operations), Experience and Decide (stages), relate to nature and God (web of relationships), and so on, so also corporate entities *as corporate entities* think (the mind of the group) and Decide ("*we* chose to . . ."). Corporate identity also makes possible not only relationship between individuals (as in a simple friendship), but also *corporate relationships*: those between individuals and groups (such as my relationship with my hometown or neighborhood) or relationships between groups and groups (such as the relationship between my hometown and the Hispanic community). Likewise we can speak of the relationship that a local congregation, as a single self, might have with the Trinitarian God.

The strength of corporate identities is a function of the leadership structure of the community, the depth and degree of sharedness involved, and the quality of diversity and integration of the parts included in the whole. And, like individual identities, corporate identities necessarily involve both exclusion and embrace toward others outside the community as identified. Thus not only do individuals identify themselves as black as opposed to white, but a community of people (say, a town) might identify itself as white as opposed to black. Furthermore, with the identification of corporate identity, we can also recognize the reality of corporate *responsibility*. The prophets bring the judgment of God not only on individuals, but also on nations. The mind or will of a given community is formed from the interplay of formal leadership and informal consent or consensus. Those in power, at different levels for different communities, and to a lesser extent the community as a whole share the responsibility for corporate life (whether for good or for ill).

There is a mutual shaping between individual self and corporate self. Just as individual self is shaped in context of social realities, so also social realities are formed in the context of the lives of the individual people that form the community. Chinese philosopher Confucius (ca. 551–479 BC) insisted on the importance of fundamental values being embodied in the individual leaders and members of a community. American sociologist Robert Bellah and his associates, in the 1980s, drew particular attention to the decay of values (the biblical and Republican strands) held by key individuals that helped ground American culture. The corporate self is formed, in part, by the character of the individuals identifying with that corporate reality.[48]

Community and culture. As a number of elements of corporate self blend together, a culture forms. Shared activities, values, aesthetics, and so on combine to shape the character of cultures. In one sense, culture is the embodiment of community—the

Now that you have read about corporate experience, ask yourself, what does *corporate* relationship with God or *community* spirituality look like?

patterns or Tendencies that characterize a community as self. Cultures, in turn, are embodied in concrete *institutions*. Thus Europe has its own intellectual institutions (like the University system), economic institutions (like the Euro), political institutions (like the separate governments of the individual nations), aesthetic institutions (like a museum), and so on. Cultures, as large integrations of community life, are held together by ambiguous forms of symbolization, practice, and order. (Consider, for example, the ambiguity retained in the various definitions of *culture* in the English language.) There is no such thing as a pure culture in any community. There are simply formed and informing networks shaping the developing experience of the community. Furthermore, since culture is embodied in institutions, the kind of relationship a person or group has with the institutions of a community expresses the kind of relationship one has with the culture. Thus, by our interactions with the institutions of a given culture or community, we interact with the community as corporate entity. Christian spirituality, which sees humans "in relationship," addresses not only our inner experience with God, but also our relationships with the institutions of culture—for we are both individuals and members of communities belonging to the King.

Thus, human experience is not only individual; it is also corporate. Individuals think. Corporations think. Persons Integrate. Culture Integrates. Individuals relate to others. Communities relate to nature. People relate to God. The Trinitarian God relates to communities of believers *as communities*. Christian spirituality addresses not only the relationship of individuals and God, but the dynamics of corporate relationship with God as well. The web of relationships that characterize human experience thus broadens our understanding of the character of human experience itself.

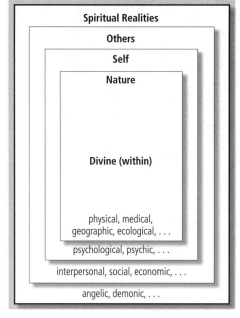

FIGURE 3.4
The Web of Relationships

Just as there are gaps and glitches in the stages and *operations* of human experience, so also the *web of relationships* is constantly subject to function and dysfunction, to the awkward finiteness of human relationability, and to worse. Social bigotry, ecological neglect and abuse, personal woundedness, and spiritual rebellion are all byproducts of this inherent human relatedness. And just as humans can take intentional steps toward self-appropriation, so also can we take steps toward re-relating to nature (ecological responsibility), to others (social responsibility), to spiritual entities (for example, in spiritual warfare), and to God. And just as recent integrations of human experience and Christian spirituality make reference to something akin to our operational systems, so also they refer to something akin to what we are calling the web of relationships. Van Kamm, for example, speaks of innerformation (self), interformation (others), the formation of "outer immediate circumstances" (events and such close at hand), and the formation mediated through the wider world (nature

and other forces outside our purview). Elizabeth Liebert and Nancy Wiens speak of the intrapersonal arena (self), the interpersonal arena (ordinary relationships with others), the systems and structures arena (more corporate relationships), and the arena of nature. Dallas Willard speaks of humans as possessing (or relating to) a soul, a mind, a will, a heart or spirit, a body, and a social dimension.[49] Though the terms may differ here and there, there is a growing consensus that we are, and that we relate to God, in the context of a variety of dimensions and relationships.

Human experience arises in the contexts of a web of relatedness: to nature, to ourselves, to others, to the spiritual world, and to God. We are not ourselves apart from these relationships. Our relationship with God is lived out in the midst of this web. Figure 3.4 illustrates the spheres of relatedness that form the contexts of human experience. Again, there is no necessary hierarchy between these types of relationship, no reason why they are ordered as presented in the chart. They are simply separate spheres of influence.

The Depth Dimension of Human Experience

We talk about it all the time. "That movie cut me *to the heart*." "God touched me *in my deepest places*." "These decisions are not just New Year's resolutions. I am changing my life *at the core*." "That lecture was truly *deep* and profound. I have to rethink everything now." Human experience arises *at various levels of* **depth**. We use "depth" language to describe levels of significance within human experience or degrees of influence on the whole of human experience. Things that are *deep* affect us with greater significance (Force) than do ordinary, superficial, or shallow things. Just as human experience is formed by operations arising by stages within the context of relationships, so also human experience is formed by the levels of depth at which our thoughts, feelings, and choices arise. We might have a particularly deep experience that lasts only a few moments. Or we might go through an entire season of life where we are almost constantly challenged to the depths. But who we are at any given time is formed, in part, by the levels of depth at which we are living.

Level One

Perhaps this dimension of human experience can be illustrated by speaking in terms of the three operational systems (cognitive, affective, volitional). At the most shallow level, cognition operates with just *thoughts*: "Here is the pen." "What does he mean by that statement?" "This dress is not like that dress." Affectivity operates at this level with simple *feelings*: cold, hot, grumpy, excited, afraid, worried. Volition operates at this level in terms of simple *choices* and *actions*: We choose to look this way. We are actively involved in washing the dishes. We engage in conversation.

Level Two

At the next deepest level, cognition moves from thoughts to *beliefs*, from individual thoughts to thoughts contained within patterns of thinking. Here, my thoughts regarding the dresses are not just simply comparisons. Indeed, perhaps my evaluation of the dresses now introduces a serious doubt regarding my previously held belief that the best dresses were the most expensive. My question about the meaning of a friend's statement is, at this level, not merely a question about semantics. Perhaps it is a question about my estimation of his character. Affectivity operates at level two as patterns of *emotions*. Once again, we are dealing not with simple individual feelings, but rather with established tendencies of feeling. Perhaps feeling grumpy is part of a predisposition toward late-afternoon irritation. On the other hand, perhaps grumpiness is a subcomponent of depression. Likewise perhaps feeling excited is connected with a thrilling skydiving adventure, a habit enjoyed on a regular basis. Similarly, volition at this level operates in

terms of *habit* (Tendency). Here we are not talking about simple choices and actions; we are talking about patterns of choices and actions. Someone interrupts me, and my habit of rinsing off the dishes before washing is endangered. Habits of relating with another are established (or broken) by conversation.

The strength with which a pattern is established, the significance of the issues related to a pattern, and the length of time over which a pattern is established all factor into the perceived *depth* of aspects of human experience. At the upper levels of experience, we can alter thoughts, feelings, and choices without affecting the other operational systems significantly. We can choose to wash this glass before that glass without being much affected emotionally or cognitively. But at deeper levels, change at one operational system will influence the other operational systems. Changing a well-established habit will involve emotions. Rethinking an important belief will often result in changes in how we choose to live. (Perhaps we will look for dresses elsewhere.)

Level Three

At a still deeper level, cognition operates at the level of *worldview*. Here we are talking not simply about patterns of thinking, but about the framework within which the patterns of thinking fit. At level three, the question, What does he mean by that statement? is not just a matter of understanding what my friend is saying or even of my beliefs regarding his character. It is, rather, that his comments are forcing me to rethink my whole perspective on life and reality. At this level, it is a question of how I make sense of experience in general. Thinking goes to the structures of our thought-life itself. Likewise, affectivity operates here with regard to *nuclear concerns*. Nuclear concerns are those concerns that drive, that structure, the overall pattern of our emotional experience in general. For instance, our anger takes us to the hurts that have driven us to the

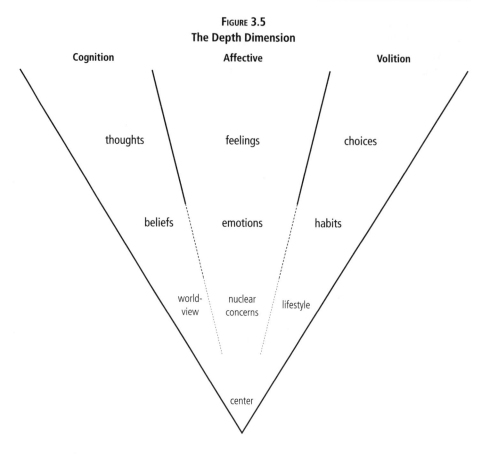

FIGURE 3.5
The Depth Dimension

patterns of anger for much of our life. Or our excitement reveals a fundamental physiological predisposition toward adrenaline rush, a nuclear concern. Volition at this level addresses issues of *lifestyle*. Perhaps washing dishes by hand (rather than loading them into a dishwasher) is part of a much larger lifestyle choice. When my spouse brings up the question of buying a dishwasher, the whole issue of lifestyle choice comes up front and center. Perhaps I have established my whole life around this particular person with whom I am now conversing. What began as a simple discussion about washing dishes is now challenging that relationship.

At level three—the level of worldview, nuclear concern, and lifestyle—it is almost impossible to effect serious change in one operational system without serious investment from the rest. Making changes in our fundamental lifestyle can determine the kinds of things that we get emotional *about*. Experiencing fundamental shifts in our core emotional concerns (as might happen through counseling or healing) is bound to affect the way we see the world, the way we lead our lives. Reworking our worldview cannot but have consequences on our feelings, on our lifestyle. This is what it means to be challenged to the depths. Everything about who we are is up for grabs. Indeed, at times, it may seem like the deeper we go, the less distinguished our work with this or that specific area becomes. To address our worldview *is* to address our nuclear emotional concerns. To address our lifestyle *is* to address our worldview.

Level Four

Finally, perhaps we could posit a level still deeper where cognition, affectivity, and volition are entirely joined at the deepest point. At this point the absolute center of the self is reached, and individual operations and systems are transcended.

Needless to say, these levels of depth appear in the experience of corporate entities as well as in the experience of individuals. There is a difference between the times in a congregation's life when its members are making decisions about the color of the carpet and those times when they are forced to rethink what they, as a congregation, are all about. There is a difference between the moment of grace that comes to a community through the way a song is presented and the season when the Holy Spirit shakes the community to its foundations through a sweeping revival.

Figure 3.5 illustrates the depth dimensions within which human experience arises. The dotted lines indicate the increasing permeability of the operational systems as human experience descends to deeper levels.

Developing and Unique

Finally, human experience *develops in space and time yet maintains its own unique being*. Human experience is not a static reality. Persons and corporate entities are developing selves, identifiable by virtue of the real Tendencies inherent in each experience but developing in time and space insofar as they are Tendencies and not mere things.

The insights of developmental psychology offer much at this point. By acknowledging the collective insights of this field, we realize that our thoughts, feelings, choices, Experiencing, Awareness, relatedness to different spheres, and so on are framed, experienced, and structured differently at different points in our development.[50] Psychologists suggest various stages of development for each of our areas of personal development. A child at an early stage of cognitive development generally will not be able to think (or feel) like someone much older does. Someone who has not worked through the issues of adolescence will have difficulties seeing

the world from the perspective of middle adulthood (no matter how old she or he is). The character of human experience, who we are, is constrained by the forces of our own development.

The same is true of corporate entities. There are commonly acknowledged patterns of change and development in communities. Groups move from charismatic

> There is a level of mystery to human experience that simply cannot be penetrated by academic reflection.

to institutional leadership, from decay to renewal, and so on. Ambiguity in the wider environment leads to a state of anomie in societies, just as certain developments lead to identity crises for individuals. And as communities face confusion or feel threatened, members may respond by detachment (escape) or by engagement (warrior), with the accompanying dangers, just as change in individuals can lead to dangerous periods of reintegration.

Consequently, not only are we different individuals and communities because of our temporal and historical location, but we are different also because of our *developmental* location. I am not the man I was thirty years ago (and not just because I have less hair). The Roman Catholic Church is not what it was a hundred years ago. The very structuring of our experience is accomplished within the frameworks of human development.

Nonetheless, in the midst of all these contexts, and relationships, and shaping, and such, we must never forget that each human, each community, is a *unique* experience and that it maintains that uniqueness throughout its life. There is a level of mystery to human experience that simply cannot be penetrated by academic reflection. And we must simply admit it. It is easy to reduce human experience to a few simple categories and to then use these categories as easy-to-understand handles by which one's spiritual life can be mastered. But this is not the reality of human experience. There is, within human experience, a kind of irreducible complexity that must never be denied. No matter how much or how carefully philosophy and human science penetrate the nature of human experience, something always seems to be left unsaid. And at times, it feels like what is unsaid may be more significant than what is said. Perhaps this is what drives us to *theological* reflection about human experience (the topic of chapter 5). Or perhaps it just drives us to be silent before the unique mystery that we are as humans.

Conclusions

Now that we have covered this ground in detail, let us repeat again our working definition of human experience as a whole:

Human experience arises as embodied soul/mind/self/spirit, constituted by the somewhat integrated arising of various mental-biological operations or systems of operations, which ordinarily proceed in generally definable stages and develop in time and space, within the context of a web of relationships and at various levels of depth, while maintaining its own unique being.

A summary of all of these elements of human experience is illustrated by figure 3.6. You can see now how the dotted lines of Experiencing and Deciding open out to input from the spheres of our relatedness. Tendencies of evaluation and action called

operations (affective, cognitive, volitional) arise in phenomenal appearance, ordinarily within a process (involving six stages), in the context of a variety of relationships (to nature, self, others, the spiritual world, and God) and at a variety of degrees of depth and development.

Changes in one element of human experience foster changes in the others. If my emotional sensitivity (affective operations) is transformed such that I become much more affectively aware, for example, this, in turn may affect my process of inquiry (Understanding), because I will be more sensitive to the affective cues guiding the process of inquiry. Similarly, transformations with regard to a neighborhood's relationship to nature may foster entire new ways of thinking (cognitive system) as this transformation makes the neighborhood more aware of ecological concerns. Significant improvements in logic (Judging) may affect, for instance, my relationship with social groupings: as I see through the logical fallacies underlying the presentations of various social groupings, I will become less susceptible to media manipulation.

As mentioned above, human experience is somewhat predictable yet somewhat mysterious. This predictability and mystery can be grasped together within the model presented. While each individual (and each community) is unique, it still remains that each is *human* and thereby can be understood and related to as such. We have now integrated insights from philosophy and the human sciences into a single cohesive system of understanding. What remains is to consider human experience from the standpoint of Christian theology. We will return to this in chapter 5.

Figure 3.6
A Model of Human Experience

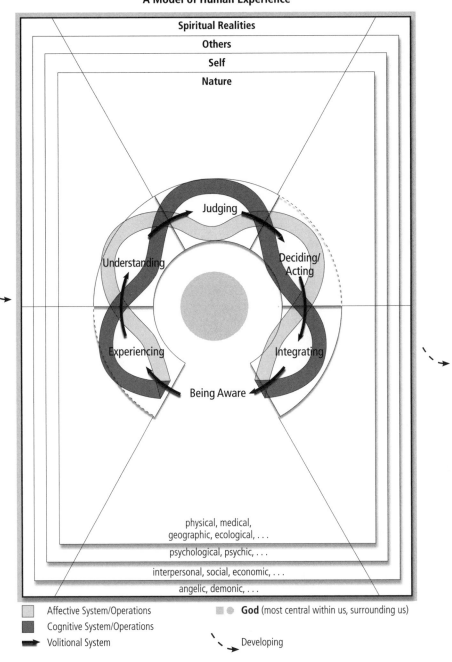

A Prayer of Human Experience

O God, Three in One—
  You who are gathered together in unity,
  You who dwell within—
  I consent to Your presence this day,
  My complexity in Your Unity.
O God, Son and Lord and Savior,
  I yield to You this day
        my mind, ready to think the thoughts of Christ;
        my emotions, ready to feel the feelings of Christ;
        my will, ready to intend the acts of Christ;
        my body, ready to embody the life of Christ;
              insofar as I am able.
O God, Source of all Life,
  I entrust to You this day
        my Being Aware, open to the presence of God;
        my Experiencing, open to the encounters from God;
        my Understanding, open to the inquiry of God;
        my Judging, open to the logic of God;
        my Deciding and Acting, open to the wisdom of God,
        my Integrating, open to the logos of God.
O God, Holy Spirit who breathes on the church,
  I am here with You this day,
  connected, even as You are connected,
        with myself, connected in authenticity,
              denying the flesh, following the Spirit;
        with others, connected in solidarity,
              renouncing the world, embracing community;
        with nature, connected in harmony,
              groaning for restoration, celebrating creaturehood;
        with spiritual forces, connected in spirit,
              resisting the devil, joining with angels;
        obedient to God.
O God, One in Three,
  I am Yours
  from the shallows to the depth,
  growing in time,
        in love.

CHAPTER SUMMARY

1. Understanding human experience begins with understanding experience. From a broad perspective, an experience exists when there is an Evaluation or a sense of Quality that joins to a Force or Act with a degree of Habit or Tendency.

2. *Human* experience appears when certain characteristic Tendencies of Evaluation, called *operations*, arise. These operations divide into three main systems: a cognitive system (intellect), an affective system (emotions), and a volitional system (will). The function of the volitional system is simply to govern the movement of the other two systems.

3. The operations of human experience tend to arise in distinct *stages*, creating a sense of process in the flow of human experience. Being Aware provides the room for Experiencing. Experiencing, in turn, stimulates Understanding, which leads to Judging. Judging is embodied in Deciding and Acting. Deciding and Acting, in turn, feed back into human experience providing a sense of Integrating, which in turn shapes our Being Aware. And from there the cycle continues.

4. Human experience grows in the context of a *web of relationships*. Our relationships shape the kind of experience that we are. The key spheres of relationship—to nature, self, others, spiritual realities, and the divine—enter our experience at the stage of Experiencing and form the objects that inform our memories, reflections, feelings, and so on. We act on these objects at the stage of Deciding.

5. Human experience is not only individual but also corporate. Through such dynamics as self-disclosure, symbolic expression, communication, comparison, and imitation, humans have the potential to have aspects of experience in common, to share experience together. We take on identities and roles in the context of others. These lead to the creation of *corporate selves* or *corporate identities* that are unique (or "single") experiences, just as individuals are: they have the potential for feeling, deciding, and relating as a unit.

6. Human experience has *depth*. At a first level of depth we live in a world of thoughts, feelings, choices, and actions. At a deeper level we find beliefs, emotions, and habits. At a still deeper level we discover our worldviews, nuclear concerns, and lifestyle. Beneath this there is perhaps a still deeper core.

7. Human experience *develops*. The Tendencies of our operations, stages, and ways of relating change over time as individuals and communities grow and change.

8. Human experience is *unique*, to each individual, to each community.

Practicing Christian Spirituality

Getting to Know Your Own Experience

Having learned about human experience in general, let's now take the opportunity to ask the perennial question, Who am I? You can review this assignment as an individual, or you can complete this assignment together as a corporate entity, such as a small group.

First, spend some time thinking about your self-embodiment. What is your body like? How do you get along with your body? Think about eating, rest, manual labor, exercise, illness or injury, sexual life, hygiene. How do these aspects of your experience inform your identity? Now think about soul, self, mind. What do these words say to you about who you are?

Next, take some time to think about your own operational systems—your thinking, feeling, and choosing. Toward which of these are you more oriented? How do you tend to think about things? Do you visualize in your head a lot? Do you carry on conversations in your head with yourself or imagined others? How do you feel? Do you experience emotion with physical changes (an elevated heart rate, sweating, and such), with tendencies to action ("I wish I could just do it"), or with mental preoccupation (you can't stop thinking about it)? How much control do you have over your feelings (or how much control do you exercise)? What kinds of feelings are easy (or hard) for you? Why? Now explore your own volition. Try to examine how your own experience moves from moment to moment. How do your own choices play a part in this movement? What have been your important choices? How did you make these? How are you formed by your own choices?

Next, look at the stages of your experience—how thought, feeling, and choice cycle around the process of human experience. Become aware of your own Being Aware. When is your awareness more open or more restricted? When are you most alert or least alert? How do these affect who you are at any given moment? Consider your Experiencing: your sensations, perceptions, image production, and such. Are you an experiencing kind of person? What do you tend to notice? Why? How about your Understanding? Are you often focused on some question? How do you resolve inquiry? What kinds of Judgments do you make about reality? On what basis do you make them? How do you make Decisions? Are you an acting kind of person? Are you threatened by decisions, or are they exciting to you? Do you pay much conscious attention to Integration? Are you a big-picture person, or do you just let life move from here to there, attending to the details? Are there any areas of dysfunction in your experience? Can you guess what influences these?

Then explore your relationships. Think about your relationship with nature. Think about yourself as a biological self, as an animal, as part of an ecosystem. What comes to your mind when you think about yourself that way? How do these factors shape who you are in particular? Think about your relationship with yourself. Are you very attentive to this? Are you an introvert or an extrovert? How has your understanding of yourself changed over the years? What about relationships with others? What social groups are you a part of—what race, what gender, what social class? How might these affect who you are today? How do you relate to others? Who are you? Think about your relationship with other spiritual forces. What do you think about angels, demons, or other spiritual realities? What experiences, environments, and people have shaped your understanding and experience of *God*? How do you relate to God now? How might this affect your own experience as a human person?

Now consider what is deep to you. Explore the different levels of depth in your own life. Descend from thoughts to beliefs to worldview. Descend from feelings to emotions to nuclear concerns. Descend from choices to habits to lifestyle. What is confronted at each level for you? When are you touched to the core? Why?

Reflect on your own development. See yourself as a baby, as a child, as an adolescent, as a young adult, and so on. What are the key changes you have experienced? Which key experiences have fostered developmental growth? Which have hindered that growth?

Finally, rest in your own uniqueness. Become aware of the mystery of your own self. Forget trying to figure yourself out and just enjoy you.

Questions

1. What is the difference between *having* an experience and *being* an experience?

2. What might life be like for someone who has a cognitive disorder or an affective disorder? How would this disorder affect the rest of her or his experience?

3. How do feeling and thinking behave differently at the different stages of human experience? What specific operations may be emphasized in one stage that are not in another? How might thinking and feeling influence each other at each stage of experiential process? How does the volitional system function to move experience along?

4. What difference does all this make for understanding and practicing our relationship with God?

5. What might characterize the healthy experience of a corporate entity? What would characterize an unhealthy community experience?

6. How do the different spheres of relationships affect one another? Give an example of how different contexts of nature, self, others, spiritual realities, and the divine might give rise to different experiences.

LOOKING FURTHER

General

For other similar treatments of human experience used for the sake of exploring Christian spirituality, see Elizabeth Liebert, "Supervision as Widening the Horizons," in *Supervision of Spiritual Directors: Engaging in Holy Mystery*, ed. Mary Rose Bumpus and Rebecca Bradburn Langer (Harrisburg, PA: Morehouse, 2005), 125–45; Susan Muto, "Formative Spirituality," *Epiphany International* 6, no. 1 (Spring 2000): 8–16; and Dallas Willard, *Renovation of the Heart: Putting on the Character of Christ* (Colorado Springs: NavPress, 2002).

Experience

For the centrality of our understanding of experience for our understanding of Christian spirituality, see Michael Downey, *Understanding Christian Spirituality* (New York: Paulist Press, 1997), 118–31; Mary Frohlich, "Spiritual Discipline, Discipline of Spirituality: Revisiting Questions of Definition and Method," *Spiritus* 1, no. 1 (Spring 2001): 69–70; and Edward Howells, "Review of *Minding the Spirit: The Study of Christian Spirituality*," *Spiritus* 5, no. 2 (Fall 2005): 223–27. For a more in-depth analysis of experience similar to that presented in this text, see Donald L. Gelpi, *The Turn to Experience in Contemporary Theology* (Mahwah, NJ: Paulist Press, 1994), 1–8, and Donald L. Gelpi, *The Gracing of Human Experience: Rethinking the Relationship Between Nature and Grace* (Collegeville, MN: Liturgical Press, 2001), 263–314.

Operations

A number of philosophical works treat the "faculties," or operations, of human experience, from Aristotle's *On the Soul*, to Thomas Aquinas's *Summa Theologica*, to Thomas Hobbes's *Leviathan* and David Hume's *A Treatise of Human Nature*, and beyond. Standard introductory texts to the field of cognitive psychology (such as Margaret Matlin's *Cognition*, 3rd ed. [Forth Worth: Harcourt Brace, 1994]) cover the basic issues of the cognitive system. For a survey of empirical theories of emotion, see Randolph R. Cornelius, *The Science of Emotion: Research and Tradition in the Psychology of Emotion* (Upper Saddle River, NJ: Prentice Hall, 1996). A fascinating treatment of the phenomena of vision—from an analysis of the physics of light through the perceptual process to discussion of consciousness—can be found in Stephen Palmer, *Vision Science: Photons to Phenomenology* (Cambridge, MA: MIT Press, 1999).

Stages

For a treatment of stages from Experiencing through Deciding and Acting, see Bernard Lonergan, *Insight: A Study of Human Understanding* (New York: Harper and Row, 1958). For a compatible treatment of the evaluative continuum, see Donald L. Gelpi, *The Gracing of Human Experience: Rethinking the Relationship Between Nature and Grace* (Collegeville, MN: Liturgical Press, 2001). I have presented an earlier version of these stages in dialogue with Lonergan and Gelpi (and in dialogue with the psychology of categorization and emotion) in Evan B. Howard, *Affirming the Touch of God: A Psychological and Philosophical Exploration of Christian Discernment* (Lanham, NJ: University Press of America, 2000).

Relationships

A treatment of the "dimensions of experience" that parallels our treatment of the web of relationships can be found in William Barry, *Spiritual Direction and the Encounter with God: A Theological Inquiry* (Mahwah, NJ: Paulist Press, 1992), 28–41. See also the treatments of human experience listed above under "General."

The God
of Christian Spirituality

OBJECTIVES

In this chapter you will be introduced to the God with whom Christians have relationship. While this is not a chapter on theology, it is a theological chapter in that you will consider some of the terms and issues regarding the Christian understanding of God. Nevertheless, the aim here is to help you see how your view of God affects your lived relationship with God. You will get to know a bit *about* God, in order to help you get to *know* God better. You will also explore both how we develop our images of God and how to recognize when fostering change in our "God-image" is appropriate. By the end of the chapter you should be able to

- identify different ways of speaking about God;
- describe the significance of a spirituality that is rooted in a God who is self-existent, personal, and Trinitarian;
- explain how the spiritual discussions of the presence of God are connected with our understanding of God's transcendence and immanence;
- show how placing emphasis on different aspects of God's activity fosters different types of spirituality;
- summarize key features of God's primary operations and how they affect our view of the God-human relationship;
- present the strengths and weaknesses of relating to God through names and images;
- distinguish between kataphatic and apophatic spiritualities;
- give direction to someone who is struggling with his or her understanding of God.

Introducing the Christian God

It was the Sunday worship celebration on the last day of a five-day conference. "Come to the table!" the program read. Members of an ecumenical missionary community living and working among the poor of the world, along with their guests, had sung songs, shared stories, and heard messages about inviting the world's outcasts to the banquet of God's love. And now, in closing, we were all gathered around a table decorated with napkins and plates, flowers, baskets of fruit, communion bread, goblets of juice, and other instruments of celebration.

As a prelude to Holy Communion we were instructed to step up to the table, lift one of the goblets up to the air, and "toast" the Lord of the feast. After a brief pause one man stepped up, lifted up the cup and said, "Cheers to Jehovah, the one who restores all things." Others followed. "To the one who sits with us in our pain and says, 'I know you, my child.'" "To the giver of new beginnings." One young man who had adopted two refugee children lifted his cup "to the one who adopted us." Another young man who had struggled for years on the streets toasted "the one who makes us strong through our weaknesses." There were few dry eyes, as nearly all of those in attendance lifted a cup to God. Finally, we celebrated Holy Communion together and left for our homes all over the globe.

To speak of spirituality is to speak of relationship with God. And to speak of relationship with God, we must speak of *God*: not simply of the concept of God, but of the *living* God who exists apart from our conceptions—the God who meets us in concrete relationship. "The one *who* _____ [fill in the blank]." Assuming that God is indeed alive, our aim is to discover something about the character of the Christian God with whom we relate. In the previous chapter, we were introduced to ourselves. In this chapter we will be introduced to God.

There has recently been something of a renewal of interest in the "topic" of God

among theologians. Furthermore, this interest in God bears a distinct relevance to Christian spirituality: talk of a "practical Trinity" seeks to recover the origins of reflection about God in the spiritual experience of the early church; "models of God" are offered as images through which an authentic spirituality can be lived in the context of our unique situation; debates about the "openness of God" call us to reconsider the significance of God's character for our practice of prayer, our search for guidance, our experience of suffering, and our social and evangelistic responsibilities.[1] Exploration of spirituality and discussion of God are now intimately connected.

Challenges to Our Concept of God

This return to thinking about God has been fueled in part by challenges to the Christian concept of God. Some claim that traditional portraits of the Christian God are overly patriarchal, imperialist, racist, capitalist, hierarchical, or militaristic. Others suggest that the world may give greater evidence of a self-organizing existence rather than of an existence imposed by an outside creator. Of special concern to many is the notion (present not only in Christianity, but in many religions) that one's god is *the* God, exclusively and savingly experienced only within the confines of a single religious system.[2] These are not insignificant challenges; they poke at the very heart of Christian self-understanding. And we must face these challenges, exploring the Christian understanding and experience of God in the context of a sincere struggle with the questions of the day and in humble submission to the sources from which knowledge of God is to be found.

Humility is especially necessary when we attempt to speak of God, and all the more so when we attempt to speak of the *living* God and not merely of our God-concept or God-image. We must recognize at the start that God "is known through knowledge and through unknowing."[3] Part

The Ways of Speaking of God

1. The Way of Affirmation	What can be said of God positively from Scripture and tradition	God is one, God is the source of all there is, and so on.
2. The Way of Causality	What we can know and say by virtue of God's reality as cause of what is	By looking at the design, we learn about God, the designer; by looking at goodness, we learn about the Good One; and so on.
3. The Way of Analogy	What we can know and say through illustrations from our experience	God is like a rock (he is stable, yet we assume God is not material), God is like a shepherd (he provides care, yet he does not wear sandals), and so on.
4. The Way of Eminence	What we may know and say by seeing God as the perfection of a given reality	For example, God is the *heavenly* father, the image of what fatherhood ought to be.
5. The Way of Negation	What we can know and say by exploring those things we should not or cannot say of God; what we know supremely but cannot speak of God	God is not human, God is not physical, God is not identical with our concepts of God, and so on.

of this blend of knowing and unknowing is a result of the juxtaposition of (a) the supreme otherness of the character of God and (b) God's choice to condescend or to accommodate himself to our forms of perception: we know "through knowledge" because God has condescended in self-giving communication through means by which we might perceive God; we know "through unknowing" because the God so communicated *is* much more than our perception can grasp. This blend of knowing and unknowing in exploring God is due not only to the presence of our own finitude, but also to our own sinfulness. At times, we fail to know God because we (for a variety of reasons) avoid God. Indeed, perhaps the personal challenges involved in recognizing and speaking of God are greater even than the academic challenges.

Thankfully, Christians have a helpful framework for navigating this blend of knowing and unknowing in the "ways of speaking of God" common to Western medieval theology.[4] In the present chapter we will organize our introduction to the Christian God by means of this basic medieval framework. In the following chapter we will approach our understanding of God (and human experience) in terms of the gospel of Jesus Christ. In the present chapter we will first address a few points by the "way of **affirmation**," considering what we can say of God using the most assured statements

of Christian biblical and theological studies. We will look at illustrations of God's active presence by the "way of **causality**," which explores what might be known and said of God by exploring signs of God's activity in the world. The "way of **analogy**" explores God in terms of how God may be similar to (yet different from) things we are familiar with: God is like a rock, a wind, a father, and so on. The "way of **eminence**" explores God in terms of how God may be the supreme example of things we are familiar with: God is the supreme light, the supreme Father, the supreme good, and so on. We will use the way of analogy and the way of eminence to speak of the operations, names, and images of God. Finally, as we struggle with the adequacy of these ways to fully comprehend God, we will shift to the "way of **negation**," exploring God by a discussion of what God is *not*, and by a peek into the inexpressible perception of God through the revelation of uncreated Light. As a further means of organizing our exploration, we will consider, point by point, the following thesis:

The God with whom Christians relate is a self-existent Trinity who, though transcending time and space, accommodates to and is immanently present within time and space; who is actively present; who is experienced in terms of operations bearing similarity to those of humans; to whom we attribute a variety of names and images; with whom we struggle; and who ultimately transcends all attempts to fully comprehend God in concept, language, act, or feeling.

The Process of Coming to Know God

Let us begin, however, by saying a few words about how human beings actually develop an understanding of God. By identifying a few factors that shape our knowing of God, and by showing how the influence of these factors can be refined by means of the interdisciplinary methodology in spirituality outlined in chapter 2, we will be better prepared to enter into an exploration of the Christian God.

Our knowledge of God is not simply passively received, but also personally constructed. From our earliest years, we develop an image of God, a "sense of who God is," shaped consciously and subconsciously by habits of parental care, exposure to religious traditions and teachings, and significant religious experiences.[5] And this exposure itself arises in the context of a much larger, developing sociocultural God-image,[6] a context that can be complex at times. We find ourselves developing not in the context of a single dominant culture, but rather in the contexts of conflicting schools of thought, even of competing worldviews. Each individual, and each community, must navigate its own God-image in the context of the specific forces acting on it. Thus, as we move from the work of "assimilation" to the work of "accommodation,"[7] our names, teachings, and experiences of God are interwoven—not without difficulty—with our personal histories, parental models, and cultural frameworks to forge a working God-image.

Nevertheless, we are not trapped by this process. Our God-images are *working* images and hence *revisable* images. I can attend to my own God-image and even to my image-construction process. I can become mindful of my own misrepresentations and my own shallow portraits of God. I can awaken to and acknowledge the selfish motives that may have guided the constructions of my God-image in the past.[8] I can press beyond the structures of culture and training to realize aspects of God's character undeveloped within my environment. I can allow my thoughts and feelings to be re-formed in the light and the leading of Truth.

This refinement of our knowledge of God is experienced to some extent through thoughtfully and prayerfully exposing our existing God-image to ideas, images, questions, and feelings from a variety of sources. By applying an interdisciplinary methodology to the topic of God, we can be introduced to God in a manner appropriate to the study and practice of Christian spirituality. We draw on texts, themes, images, and issues of scripture to illumine aspects of the Christian teaching concerning God. We draw from the history of theology and spirituality and discover how other Christians have described God's character and experience. While the sciences are inadequate to present God as measurable, one can suggest, from the characteristics of the measurable world, something of the active presence of the creator. We draw from informal relationships and personal experience to bring a sense of concreteness to our exploration. We address theological issues, attempting to synthesize biblical and historical material into a coherent unity. We use philosophical categories in an effort to interpret, critique, and synthesize our understanding of God.

Self-Existent Trinity

Self-Existent

The early Christian creeds affirm God as **self-existent** Trinity: as the maker of heaven and earth, as Father, Son, and Holy Spirit. By affirming God's self-existence Christians recognized that the experience of the God with whom they dealt bore less similarity to the experience of the multiple deities of the surrounding cultures and

Historical Portrait:
Excerpts from A. W. Tozer's *Pursuit of God*[9]

A. W. Tozer (1897–1963) was a compassionate pastor, compelling convention speaker, and prophetic writer. He carried forward the vision of the Christian Missionary and Alliance Church and, through his speaking and writing, drew segments of American Christianity ever closer to God.

God wills that we should push on into His Presence and live our whole life there. This is to be known to us in conscious experience. It is more than a doctrine to be held, it is a life to be enjoyed every moment of every day. This Flame of the Presence was the beating heart of the Levitical order. Without it all the appointments of the tabernacle were characters of some unknown language; they had no meaning for Israel or for us. The greatest fact of the tabernacle was that *Jehovah was there*; a Presence was waiting within the veil. Similarly the Presence of God is the central fact of Christianity. At the heart of the Christian message is God Himself waiting for His redeemed children to push in to conscious awareness of His Presence. . . .

Who is this within the veil who dwells in fiery manifestations? It is none other than God Himself, "One God the Father Almighty, Maker of heaven and earth, and of all things visible and invisible," and "One Lord Jesus Christ, the only begotten Son of God; begotten of His Father before all worlds, God of God, Light of Light, Very God of Very God; begotten, not made; being of one substance with the Father," and "the Holy Ghost, the Lord and Giver of life, Who proceedeth from the Father and the Son, Who with the Father and the Son together is worshipped and glorified." Yet this Trinity is one God, for "we worship one God in Trinity, and Trinity in Unity; neither confounding the Persons, nor dividing the Substance. For there is one Person of the Father, another of the Son, and another of the Holy Ghost. But the Godhead of the Father, of the Son, and of the Holy Ghost, is all one: the glory equal and the majesty coeternal." So in part run the ancient creeds, and so the inspired Word declares.

Behind the veil is God, that God after Whom the world, with strange inconsistency, has felt, "if haply they might find Him." He has discovered Himself to some extent in nature, but more perfectly in the Incarnation; now He waits to show Himself in ravishing fullness to the humble of soul and the pure in heart.

The world is perishing for lack of the knowledge of God and the Church is famishing for want of His Presence. The instant cure of most of our religious ills would be to enter the Presence in spiritual experience, to become suddenly aware that we are in God and that God is in us. That would lift us out of our pitiful narrowness and cause our hearts to be enlarged. This would burn away the impurities from our lives as the bugs and fungi were burned away by the fire that dwelt in the bush.

greater similarity to the experience of the God of the Hebrews.[10] By affirming God's Trinitarian existence, the earliest Christians distinguished themselves from both the philosophical and the Jewish circles of the day. By affirming God as a self-existent Trinity today, we affirm the most distinctive elements of the God to whom we relate as Christians. Other statements about the Christian God are rooted in this one.

To acknowledge God as self-existent is to recognize that our experience, and that of our world, does not arise merely from itself, but rather arises ultimately from a Source that has no source. "You have been our dwelling place in all generations," the psalmist declares. "Before the mountains were brought forth, or ever you had formed the earth and the world, from everlasting to everlasting you are God" (Psalm 90:1–2). Likewise, the apostle Paul, in agreement with some of the poets of his time, states that "in him we live and move and have our being" (Acts 17:28). The God of the scriptures is the creator of all and is dependent on no one. "To whom then will you liken God[?]" "Who taught him knowledge, and showed him the way of understanding?" "Have you not known? Have you not heard? The LORD is the everlasting God, the Creator of the ends of the earth" (Isaiah 40:18, 14, 28). Our existence is a derived existence. God's existence is underived.

This God who is the source of all must be distinguished from the deities of polytheism. Unlike the gods of the surrounding nations—which were known to experience birth and death, who acted from their own needs, and who were only seldom and capriciously involved in the matters of the world—Yahweh was "from everlasting to everlasting" (Psalm 90:2), "the Alpha and the Omega" (Revelation 22:13), caring for his creation.[11] The "high eternal Father" speaks of this care for the world in the following manner: "O my dearest daughter, as I have told you so often, I want to be merciful to the world and provide for my reasoning creatures' every need. . . . I always provide, and I want you to know that

what I have given humankind is supreme providence. It was with providence that I created you, and when I contemplated my creature in myself I fell in love with the beauty of my creation."[12] Unlike the Graeco-Roman relationship to the gods of polytheism, therefore, Christian spirituality is not characteristically a spirituality of anxious placation but rather one of worshipful submission.

The self-existent God of Christianity must also be distinguished from pantheist or monist formulations of deity. There is a tendency for European philosophies to see the world in terms of "Being," that which is in the foreground. There is an awareness in Asian philosophies of the background of "Nothing." There is a certain sensitivity in American philosophies to "Becoming," to the movement between Nothing and Being. Each of these tendencies has led to different expressions that identify "god" with the universe: God as All-Being, God as Absolute Nothingness, God as Process.[13] Yet, the Christian God is ultimately none of these. God is *independent* from Being, Process, and Nothingness. Self-existence implies an existence *independent* from the world. While some Christians have described creation as a necessary emanation of God's fullness or have approached creation as arising from within the being or experience of God, the church has always believed that the Lord God is the creator of all things, distinguished from (though not distant from) his creation.[14] Therefore, whereas the spirituality of pantheistic or monist systems involves facilitating the consciousness of an ontological identity with Reality, relationship with the Christian God involves an experience of unity with distinction, harmony through dependence, worship with relationship.

Perhaps the central biblical passage concerning God's self-existence—and the one which best indicates the type of spirituality that flows from an acknowledgement of God's self-existence—is God's revelation of his name in Exodus 3:14. Here, when asked for a name, God simply says "I AM

WHO I AM. . . . Thus you shall say to the Israelites, 'I AM has sent me to you.'"[15] There is, in the I AM, a recognition of the active prior-ness, the ambiguous Source-ness and self-existence of God beneath all that is or will come to be. God's Is-ness is the most fundamental reality of all. Our being, our experience, is vague, unclear, uncertain. It vacillates, it is confused, it exhibits irreconcilable multiplicity. God's Being, however is total, single, ultimate.

A student of mine wrote of a time when "I went through a 'dark night of the soul.' It was a time when God shed light and truth into my secret places. Memories haunted me and fear gripped me. I questioned God about a particular incident that I could not forget: a time when I felt powerless. With anger and hurt I called out, 'Where are you, God?' Suddenly my emotions were stilled and peace flooded my mind and heart. God's Spirit spoke only two words, though they began the long journey to healing. 'I AM' was all He said."

It is this supremeness of God—this realness that stands above our realness, this entire set-apartness—that lies behind our understanding of God as *holy*. Consequently, Christian spirituality rests on the acknowledgement of God's self-existent holiness: ontologically, aesthetically, and morally.

Trinity

Christians have consistently found themselves worshiping a God who is distinct from the world, who is the source of the world, and who is *singularly* distinct from, yet also the Source of, the world. Yet at the same time Christianity was born with the discovery that this singular Source, and God, was experienced in relationship with Jesus and within the experience of the Holy Spirit. Christian spirituality is Trinitarian spirituality. Thus Bernard McGinn writes, "Faith in the three-personed God—Father, Son, and Holy Spirit—has marked Christianity from the start, however much this belief can be shown to have evolved in clar-

ity and expression. For Christians . . . faith in the Trinity was not a piece of mere speculation but an intensely real part of Christian life, especially in prayer and liturgy."[16]

To introduce the Trinity, then, is not simply to clarify a difficult point of doctrine. As theologian Catherine Mowry LaCugna argues, "The doctrine of the Trinity is ultimately not a teaching about the abstract nature of God, nor about God in isolation from everything other than God, but a teaching about God's life with us and our life with each other."[17] To know the God of Christian spirituality is to know a three-personed God, a God with whom we relate as Father, Son, and Holy Spirit. Hence it is perfectly appropriate for a follower of theologian Karl Barth, for example, to point us directly to Jesus Christ as the place to learn about God and, likewise, for a Pentecostal, for example, to point us to the church's experience of the Spirit as the place to learn about God.

While there are intimations of the plurality of God's character in the Hebrew scriptures, it was through reflection on Jesus that Trinitarian thought and spirituality was born. Jesus's followers recognized the deity of Christ as they heard his teachings, saw his works, encountered him as a person, and witnessed his death and resurrection. Every aspect of their experience of Jesus pointed to the fact that this man was no mere human, but was indeed "one with the Father."[18] Similarly, the only conclusion that they could affirm concerning their experience of the enlightening, empowering, unifying Spirit of God was that indeed the Spirit was equal in divinity with the Father and the Son.[19] Clues of the full Trinitarian worship of the earliest community of believers can be found within the pages of the New Testament.[20] Thus the church from its earliest history felt itself to be confronted with God as Father, Son, and Spirit.

In time, different models of the Trinity developed by which the simultaneous unity and plurality of the Trinity could be comprehended.[21] Two of these are the "**social model**" of the Cappadocian fathers and

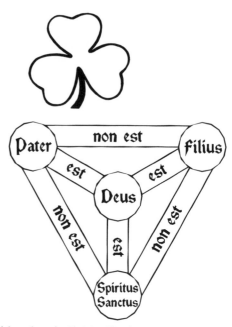

The triniatrian god, worshipped and symbolized throughout the Christian Church.

the "**cognitive model**" of Augustine of Hippo. The Cappadocian fathers—Greek theologians Basil the Great of Caesarea (d. 397), Gregory of Nazianzus (d. 390), and Basil's younger brother Gregory of Nyssa—together formulated the distinction between the *persons* (*hypostasis* or *prosopon*) of the Father, Son, and Spirit and the *essence* (*ousia*), or nature, of their identical divine being. "The Cappadocians," summarizes Thomas Hopko, "identified Jesus the incarnate Son of God with God's Word and Wisdom witnessed to in the Hebrew Scriptures, as they identified the Spirit of Christ with God's Spirit who inspired the law and the prophets."[22] The Cappadocians suggested that we think of the Trinity somewhat like we might think of three persons (Peter, James, John) sharing a single human nature. However, where bodily distinction separates human persons sharing the same finite human nature, no distinction can be found for the members of the divine Trinity. Just as one person might give herself or himself to another in love, so each member of the Trinity is in a relationship of giving and receiving in love with the others.

The Latin divine Augustine of Hippo (354–430) suggested a different analogy in order to picture the relationship of the Trinity, or perhaps to point to a sign of the Trinity that he felt was present inherent in human experience. He began with the singularity of the divine worshiped by Christians and Jews alike. He then drew attention to the intrinsic unity between different operations within the human mind: memory, intellection, and will (or mind, knowledge, and love). Just as there is a sense in which the mind, in the integration of its operations, "loves" itself in a kind of supportive unity in plurality, so we can think of the unity of the Trinity as the harmony of one mind expressing itself to itself and through itself to others in love.

These two models of the Trinity have tended to fuel different forms of Trinitarian spirituality. Social models of the Trinity tend to give emphasis to the interpersonal nature of the Godhead and therefore to encourage a relationship with God discovered in community. The Cappadocians themselves believed that humans are, like their creator, made to be persons in community. Models of the Trinity based on psychological analogies tend to encourage a spirituality of interiority as wisdom and love are joined in contemplative union with the soul, just as the Word (Son) and Love (Spirit) are joined with the Father in the Trinitarian unity.[23]

Seeing God as a Tri-*unity*, we acknowledge the single heart and mind expressed in every form of our relationship with God. The Father who forms, the Son who redeems, and the Spirit who renews express the same self-existence of the Christian God. The operations, names, and images of God equally apply to each of the persons of the Godhead (though functionally speaking, some are more appropriate than others). Seeing God as a *Tri*-unity, we encounter a God who is experienced as Father, Son, and Holy Spirit, each with distinct roles in the economy of salvation. Attending to each of the persons of the Godhead introduces fresh elements to one's spirituality. A spirituality of the *Father* relates to God as creator and source (as in some Celtic or Amish spiritualities) or perhaps as lawgiver (as in early Jewish Christian or contemporary theonomist spiritualities). A number of distinct Christocentric or *"Son"* spiritualities have arisen through the centuries. Some give special devotion to Jesus as the child, others to the imitation of the life of Christ. Some see their relationship with God in light of Christ's sacrificial death for their sins, others see life in consequence of the victory won by that same death, resurrection, or exaltation. Finally, attention to the wind of the *Spirit* stimulates the Pentecostal and charismatic spiritualities of East and West. Each of these various Trinitarian spiritualities carries its own character, emphasizing certain exercises and certain experiences. Furthermore, as can be imagined, each particular emphasis, each spirituality, facilitates certain strengths and weaknesses in our relationship with God.[24]

Most importantly for distinguishing the character of the Christian God, and the type of relationships that develop from such

a God, is that the Triune Christian God (and, consequently, Christian spirituality) is *personal* and *interpersonal*. Thus Ewert Cousins, editor of the multivolume *World Spirituality: An Encyclopedic History of the Religious Quest*, states that the distinguishing characteristic of Christian spirituality is "that Christian spirituality is personal and interpersonal." "The Christian path," he asserts, "consists of the awakening of the personal center of the human being, by God's personal grace and Christ's compassionate, redemptive personal love within the Christian community, in a journey that leads to personal union with the tripersonal God."[25] The personal, relational images of God in the Scriptures (God and people, lord and servant, parent and child, husband and wife, friend and friend) are not simply random metaphors. While less personal images are used of God (like light, food, fire, rain), the personal are more frequent and more central. They are found in the "landmark" passages of scripture, such as Genesis 1–3; 17; Exodus 3; 2 Samuel 7; Jeremiah 31; Ezekiel 38; Hosea 2; Luke 2; Romans 8; Revelation 21. Other images of God are illustrative; the personal images are paradigmatic. While some consider a personalist interpretation of God as anthropomorphism, "it is more theologically precise to say that the fullness of personhood exists in God alone, and that our limited understandings of personality and personalization are inadequate reflections of the genuine freedom and responsible self-determination that we find incomparably in God and only inadequately in ourselves."[26]

The God to whom Christians relate is the three-personed God, and a Trinitarian spirituality pushes the Christian beyond the "how" questions of spirituality into the "who" questions of spirituality. "Who is the Father to whom we pray in the name of Christ? Who is the Christ in whose mission we go forth to all the nations? Who is the Holy Spirit who draws us together into a life of wonderful communion? Only as we know who this triune God of Grace is, and what he has done once and for all and is continuing to do for us and with us and in us, can we truly know how to serve."[27]

The One Who Transcends and Is Present in Time and Space

This God we know and enjoy and who knows and enjoys us, this self-existent Trinity, both transcends and is present to us in time and space. God is both infinitely apart from us and deepest within us. From these aspects of God's character, we gain a sense of the **transcendence** and **immanence** of God—and of the presence of God.

Transcendence and Immanence

The one whose existence is from himself, whose experience is derived from none and who gives being to all, transcends even the frameworks of space and time within which we have being.

> Long ago you laid the foundation of the earth,
>   and the heavens are the work of your hands.
> They will perish, but you endure;
>   they will all wear out like a garment.
> You change them like clothing, and they pass away;
>   but you are the same, and your years have no end. (Psalm 102:25–27)

> Where can I go from your spirit?
>   Or where can I flee from your presence?
> If I ascend to heaven, you are there;
>   if I make my bed in Sheol, you are there.
> If I take the wings of the morning
>   and settle at the farthest limits of the sea,
> even there your hand shall lead me,
>   and your right hand shall hold me fast. (Psalm 139:7–10)

In such imagery the children of God try to express the infinite transcendence of the God with whom they relate. Similarly, the epistle of Jude closes with a blessing to "the only God our Savior, through Jesus Christ our Lord, be glory, majesty, power, and authority, before all time and now and forever" (Jude 25). Solomon's prayer at the dedication of the first Israelite temple communicates the tension of God's transcendent and immanent presence: "But will God indeed reside with mortals on earth? Even heaven and the highest heaven cannot contain you, how much less this house that I have built!" (2 Chronicles 6:18). The epistle to the Ephesians speaks of God choosing the elect "before the foundation of the world" (Ephesians 1:4), as the first epistle to Timothy calls God "King of the ages, immortal, invisible, the only God" (1 Timothy 1:17). Speaking of God creating before the world and of there being no locality that can hold God were the means used by the writers of scripture to express that their experience of God was the experience of a God who was not limited or confined in space and time. Prayers in one location may be answered in another. Promises given in one time may be fulfilled years, even centuries, later. The same Savior who was intimate friends with Mary and Martha in first-century Palestine can rescue us in twenty-first century New Zealand.

One point must be made in order to clarify the spirituality of the God who transcends time and space. It will be obvious by now that God must not be conceived of simply as a thing. God is no thing. That is what is most clear about God. To conceive of God simply as a great thing or man up in the sky is to neglect the infinitude of the one who, not being a thing, is the source of all things—not simply a person, but the source of all that is personal. Yet at the same time we must not conceive of God as a kind of force. Conceiving of God as some kind of force or principle present in the world falls prey to the same mistake as thinking of God as a thing, for it too brings the infinite down to the level of the finite. Just as God is beyond all things, is no thing, so God is beyond all force, is no force. Thus God comprehends both force and being within himself who is the source, sustenance, and end of all that is. God simply *is* in a much different way than all else. God is not to be thought of simply as existing in all spaces—as if God were really big, or as existing in all times, as if God were really old. The transcendence of God demands not that God simply be big or old, but that space and time themselves be principles of which God is the source. Likewise, God is not time*less* or space*less*; rather God simply transcends time and space. The God we know is not limited to our perspectives, confined to our places, restricted by our schedules. God is Beyond.[28]

Yet even while we speak of God as transcending time and space, we must also, with equal insistence, acknowledge that God also dwells *within* space and time as we know it. First, the very transcendence of God demands that God also be supremely immanent. If God is not subject to any time or space and is the source of both, this also means that *all* time and space are available to God and that God is present to all. Once again, this is not to identify God with all that is, in some kind of pantheism. But just as God must not be identified with the finite, so God must not be considered as simply "away" from it either. *Because* God is transcendent, God is also immanent. God is fully present in every space and time, simply because God is not bounded by either. Secondly, not only does logic demand that we accept the presence of God within time, but consideration of the scriptures demands the same conclusion. The Bible is fundamentally the record of God's dealings with humankind in time and space. A spirituality that, through overemphasis on God's transcendence, fails to regard God's dynamic interplay with humanity within time will fail to relate to the God of the scriptures. God parts the sea in real space. God called his people to obey in real time.

The exile happened in time and place. In the fullness of time God sent his Son to a particular place. The sending of the Spirit of God was experienced in time and space. There is no indication in scripture that God's interactions with humanity within time and space are some kind of illusion to be distinguished from the "real" world of God's infinity. Rather our time and space are presented in scripture as equally real to that of God's (though ours are somewhat shadowy and temporary by comparison).

One way of looking at this is to think of an analogy between the in-carnation of the Son and what we might call the "in-temporalization" of the Godhead. Just as Christ truly experiences life in the flesh in-

> For if God is beyond everything, he is also in everything.
>
> —Jean Daniélou[29]

sofar as he relates to us as Son, even though as eternal Logos he dwells with the Father from eternity, so also the Godhead experiences temporal succession and all that goes with this insofar as God relates to us within time even though God also exists from eternity. This in-temporalization of God should be seen as part of God's self-giving accommodation or condescension to human experience. While God is not limited to time and space, God chooses to relate to us within the frameworks of time and space.[30]

The Presence of God

Having gained a sense of the God who both transcends and accommodates himself to space and time, we are now in a position to consider the notion of the presence of God, a much-used notion in Christian spirituality.[31] The first thing to notice is that there are a number of ways of thinking of the presence of God. Theologian Thomas Oden summarizes the thought of the first few centuries of Christian history concerning the presence of God in the following list:

- God is *naturally* present in every aspect of the natural order.
- God is *actively* present in a different way in every event of history.
- God is in a special way *attentively* present to those who call upon his name.
- God is *judicially* present in moral awareness, through conscience.
- God is *bodily* present in the incarnation of his Son.
- God is *mystically* present in the Eucharist.
- God is *sacredly* present and becomes known in special places where God chooses to meet us.[32]

In addition to this list, as we mentioned in chapter 1, mysticism is defined in terms of one's consciousness of the immediate presence of God. A. W. Tozer and others speak of the experience of the *manifest* presence of God, those moments or seasons when God's presence in any of the other ways is vivid to someone's experience.[33] We often speak of a personal presence of God with us while we are aware of God's ontological presence, a presence that involves a sharing of experience. One can also think of God's presence in terms of God's embodiment: in the law, in the temple, in the monarchy of Israel, in Jesus, in the church, in the poor. Examining this list, we can see that there is more to the notion of God's presence than simply the fact that God participates in time and space. God's participation in time and space is expressed in a different manner with each type of presence. What is involved in God's incarnational presence in Christ is quite different from God's attentive presence to those who pray. Thus God may be present to us in a number of ways at the same time.

The "practice of the presence of God," well known through the life and writings of French lay brother Brother Lawrence (1614–91), involved the recognition of God's constant nearness. Practicing the presence of God tunes one's awareness to God's personal attentive presence with believers through the Spirit. By the constant turn of attention to that presence of God, and by yielding one's spirit to God's Spirit, one learns to live continually in intersubjective union with God. A similar notion is understood by French spiritual writer Jean-Pierre de Caussade's (1675–1761) "sacrament of the present moment" and by the Eastern Orthodox concept of "watchfulness" or "attentiveness."[34]

One can see by the various uses of the term *presence* that both the character of God's real participation in time and the character of our awareness of that participation are involved in the various ways of speaking about and experiencing God's presence. Part of spirituality is the sovereign work of God, when God seems to just *manifest* his presence, whether we are consciously attending to God or not. Yet part of spirituality is the learning to attend to God's presence. As we learn to attend to those special places and times—or to attend to God's presence in every place and time—where God communicates himself, we grow in the practice of the presence of God.

The One Who Is Actively Present

In the Christian God we are confronted with the one who is not only present, but *actively* present. Indeed, God's way of being toward us is acting. The consequence of this for Christian spirituality is that the most primary fact of our relationship with God is not our movement toward God (though that might be what we are most conscious of), but God's movement toward us. By applying the "way of causation" to our knowing and speaking of God, we may be drawn to notice the signs of God's active presence all around us. Attention to the signs and manners of God's active presence gives rise to different forms of spirituality. Finally, by attending to common tendencies exhibited within the different expressions of God's active presence, we can identify a fundamental pattern of divine-human relationship, a covenant relationship that is best described as love.

God's Active Presence

The God of the Scriptures is most fundamentally the God with whom we are confronted. The Bible is a record of God's dealings with humankind, and a primary element of this record is *God's dealings*. God is "the one who"—"the one who appeared to Abraham," "the one who brought you out of Egypt," "the one who sent you prophets," "the one who brought you out of exile," "the one who sent his only Son," "the one who sends his Spirit," and so on. The psalms alone speak of God answering, delivering, forsaking, protecting, leading, rewarding, hiding, ruling, relenting, creating, forgetting, destroying, counseling, forgiving, healing, planning, and much more. We also find God *waiting*: God waits to rescue his people out of Egypt, to send deliverers in the time of the Judges, to heal Lazarus. (Are these waiting times moments of God's *inaction*, or should they be seen as other forms of God's active presence?)[35]

This understanding of God as active personal presence must be joined with our understanding of God's revelation. God's revelation is not simply manifestation. Rather, virtually all divine revelation is also interpersonal invitation. The invitational self-communication of God is not devoid of the communication of actual propositional truths about God. Rather, the propositional aspects of God's communication clarifies the invitation and specifies the appropriate responses. As we shall see below, this character of God's active presence that communicates both self and proposition is fundamental to understanding God's covenant relationship with human beings.

Signs of God's Active Presence: The Way of Causation

We often come to know God by paying attention to those places where God is actively present, recognizing the signs of God's presence. This is the way of causation. It is an act of seeing God as the cause behind things: seeing the designer behind the design present in the world, seeing the Good behind the "goods" of the world, seeing Being behind the beings of the world, and so on. In philosophy this kind of paying attention is often discussed under the heading of "arguments for the existence of God." Yet, while the way of causation has some value in guiding people unfamiliar to belief in God toward that belief, it is best understood as a natural movement of believing devotion.[36]

The way of causation leads us to see God as the source, the pattern, and the end of all things. One may examine the world, considering how it came to be, and conclude that whether over a long time or within a very short time, the world itself is left unexplainable without appreciating the Source from which what is arises (the cosmological argument). Another may think about ideas of goodness and discover that human conscience points to the active presence of God (the moral argument). Some may think about the things that are around, the beings of the world, and wonder whether there must not be a perfect Being as the standard from which all beings have their being (the ontological argument). Others may look at the design or purpose inherent in the universe and see behind them the hand of a designer, one toward which all purpose points (the teleological argument). Finally, one might consider the variety of religious experiences people have and wonder whether they do not point to the active presence of God (the religious experience argument). When we begin to ask the question, What would be necessary such that this world, these people, would be as they are? we begin to see signs of God's active presence all around us. Attending to these signs is a means of being introduced to the Christian God: Perfect Being, Designer, Good, the Purpose of all that is, that to which experience ultimately points. This is the way of causation.

A Few Spiritualities

As we have noticed, attention to God's active presence can take many different forms. As one or another of these forms of attending becomes central to one's experience of God, a particular type of spirituality develops. (This is spirituality at the second level, the level of formulation about the dynamics of relationship with God.) A few examples might help.

One influential approach to spirituality follows the lead of theologian Karl Rahner (1904–84). Rahner takes as his starting point human self-awareness. Behind this self-awareness, this human ability to transcend the objects of consciousness and become aware of one's own thoughts and actions, one can identify a mysterious core: what must be present in order for thinking to occur in the first place. As Rahner puts

---

It is only in Jesus Christ that the hidden God is truly revealed.

—Jean Daniélou[37]

---

it, "In the ultimate depths of his being man knows nothing more surely than that his knowledge, . . . is only a small island in a vast sea that has not been traveled."[38] Humans are radically confronted with their own reception of their being and with the mysterious openness toward which their being points. The giver of that being, and the holy mystery toward which being points, is God. God is thus actively present at the core of human thought and experience. By attending to our thought in depth, we can learn to identify God's active presence—not so much as particular impulses within consciousness, but rather as the source and aim of all truly authentic thinking. Relationship with God is then pursued through attention to and cooperation with human consciousness in depth.[39]

A second form of attention to the active presence of God centers itself around God's address to humankind in the giving of the Word, represented by the works of Karl Barth (1886–1968). For Rahner, the central act of God is in God's self-communication to human consciousness. For Barth, the central act of God is in the historical event of Christ. "The possibility of revelation," asserts Barth, is found "in the condescension whereby God in Jesus Christ becomes identical with a reality different from Himself."[40] To attend to the active presence of God in the historical work of God through Christ is, fundamentally, to come to terms with our mystical union with God accomplished on the cross prior to any efforts of our own. It is to root our growth in holiness (our sanctification) in our prior acceptance by God through Christ (our justification). It is to respond to the work of God with the commitment of faith.[41]

A third form of spirituality emphasizes God's active presence through the Holy Spirit. This emphasis can be seen in the thought of contemporary theologian Donald L. Gelpi. Gelpi—like Barth and unlike Rahner—sees the active presence of God not in the structure of human subjectivity but in events that reveal the self-communicating God. Gelpi, however, identifies these events "in a special way in the shared faith consciousness which results from sharing the charisms of the Spirit in community."[42] Elsewhere he speaks of responding to "every impulse of divine grace" or to "the divine touch."[43] The active presence of God meets us through the Holy Spirit as a force within our experience, a force through which we are addressed in the moment and to which we are invited to respond. Authentic spirituality involves the sensitivity and docile response to this active presence of God.[44]

The Covenant God: Active Presence and Divine-Human Relationship

We have learned not only that God transcends time and space, but also that he is actively present in time and space. This active presence of God within human experience is not merely a self-manifestation; it also normally arises as a personal invitation, an address that asks for response. As such, God's action is God actively present to humans *in relationship*. This is the foundation for understanding the biblical notion of **covenant**. The covenant God of Christianity is a God who is *relationally* present, initiating and offering relationship in and through his acts. As covenant partners, we respond to God's invitation to relationship. God in turn responds to our response. This self-existent, covenant-relational, active presence of God identifies God as one who is sovereignly responsive. Covenant responsiveness is a fundamental element of the divine character. Much of Christian spirituality is built on this dynamic. Frequently we speak of this aspect of God's character as *love*.

God's Active Presence as Love

In the *Book of Common Prayer* one of the psalms offered in the Noonday recitation (also known as the Noonday Office) is Psalm 121. Listen to this psalm, think of what you are feeling like by noon, and see if it wasn't the perfect choice for a noonday reminder:

> I lift my eyes to the hills—
>   from where will my help come?
> My help comes from the LORD
>   who made heaven and earth.
> He will not let your foot be moved;
>   he who keeps you will not
>   slumber.
> He who keeps Israel
>   will neither slumber nor sleep.
> The LORD is your keeper;
>   the Lord is your shade at your
>   right hand.
> The sun shall not strike you by day,
>   nor the moon by night.
> The LORD will keep you from all
>   evil;
>   he will keep your life.
> The LORD will keep your going out
>   and your coming in
>   from this time on and
>   forevermore.

The theme of "keeping" is central to the psalm. It describes the mode of God's active presence with us. God's active presence is *for* us. God is sincerely interested in the welfare of his people and is actively engaged for their sake. God's sovereign responsiveness is not capricious. Rather God's sovereign responsiveness is responsiveness *with regard*.

God's love is rooted in God's Trinitarian nature. God is by nature self-giving: Father to Son and Spirit, Spirit to Father and Son,

> Just as the cosmic idea of God is known through the creation, so the biblical God is known through the covenant.
>
> —Jean Daniélou[45]

Son to Father and Spirit. Our experience of the love of God is the experience of what is expressed within God entirely apart from human existence. God freely chooses to extend the love that God *is* beyond the boundaries of the creative Trinity to the creation itself. It is extended especially to those who need it the most: the mistreated women (for example, Genesis 16:7; 21:17–20; 29:31; 30:22), the alien (Leviticus 19:34; Deuteronomy 10:18), the poor (Proverbs 14:31; Jeremiah 22:16), and others in similar straits.

God's love toward us is sacrificial: it is self-giving, reaching out to us even when it is rejected. God's love toward us is also a delight in God's beloved. God recognizes our value, calling us "very good" (Genesis 1:31). God delivers "me" because "he delighted in me" (Psalm 18:19). God desires relationship as a husband to a wayward spouse (Hosea 1–3; Ezekiel 16) or as a mother to a child (Psalm 131). This is the motif that the "everlasting Father" who spoke to lay Dominican Catherine of Siena (1347–80) in her *Dialogue* returns to again and again: "The reason I provide for you what I provide, whether painful or wonderful, is for your good, because I love you and see you as lovable."[46] If the character of God's active presence toward us helps us to see who God *is*, then we can begin to understand the meaning of the passage "God is love." "God *is* love," writes Oden, "in these two senses—enjoyment of the beloved, and self-giving for the beloved's perfect good—in perfect fullness, balance, harmony, and completeness. God *feels the worth of creatures* and *longs to do them good*."[47] The God to whom Christians relate is a God who loves.

The Operations of God: The Ways of Analogy and Eminence

Our summary of God's character above stated that God is one *who is experienced in terms of operations bearing similarity to those of humans*. God's actions are not random, unintelligible actions. Rather, we experience God within time and space as one who acts evaluatively—who perceives, thinks, feels, decides, and acts—in a manner that bears some resemblance to our own evaluative experience. Following the Eastern Church, which speaks of God's energies, qualities, or operations (the West speaks more of God's relational attributes), we will speak of these evaluative patterns of action

(God's knowing, feeling, willing) as God's *operations*.[48]

We say that we experience God in terms of operations "bearing similarity to those of humans." When we learn something of the character of God by means of observing similarities with humans, we move from the ways of affirmation and causation—from asserting about and pointing to God—to the ways of analogy and eminence.

The way of *analogy* draws on a similarity between something within our experience and God to point to an aspect of God's character, even while acknowledging that there are clear ways in which God is *not* like that something. "The Lord is my rock," the Psalms declare, and we think of God's stability. Yet we know that the Lord is not localized like a rock, that the Lord is personal unlike a rock, and so on. While analogies are not as well defined as simple affirmations, they communicate something of the richness of God's character. We speak of God as knowing, feeling, and willing. God does not have a brain. God does not have adrenal glands. God's heart rate does not change. And yet we experience God's active presence in some way similar to our own evaluative experience.

The way of *eminence* points to the *kind* of difference between items compared, pointing to God as the supreme example of the item considered. We can think of God as father, and images of source, provision, and care may come to mind. In the way of eminence, however, it is not just that God is *like* a father to us, but that God is actually the *supreme* Father. Our understanding of fatherhood ultimately is derived from reflection on God. Thus, when we speak of God's operations by way of eminence, we are not simply saying that God's knowledge (feeling, willing) is *like* ours, but that God's knowing (and so on) is *supreme*.[49] The ways of analogy and eminence help to give us an imaginative sense of God. Through these metaphorical ways of speaking about God we are drawn into encounter with God and we make some sense of the God we encoun-

ter. Yet we must be careful: these methods both reveal and conceal God.

God's Knowing

Relationship to God as "one who knows" has been part of Judeo-Christian spirituality from the start. God was the one who appeared, bringing information about the future. God was the one to whom the Israelites turned for advice, the one of whom they inquired: by Urim and Thumim, by the prophets, by dreams. God is the one who remembered his people and his covenant with them. God's wisdom is greater than the wisdom of people, so God prods Job:

> Where were you when I laid the
>   foundation of the earth?
>   Tell me, if you have
>   understanding.
> Who determined its measure-
>   ments—surely you know! . . .
> Have you comprehended the ex-
>   panse of the earth?
>   Declare, if you know all this.
> (Job 38:4–5, 18)

And the Lord declares in Isaiah 55:

> For my thoughts are not your
>   thoughts,
>   nor are your ways my ways, says
>   the LORD.
> For as the heavens are higher than
>   the earth,
>   so are my ways higher than your
>   ways
>   and my thoughts than your
>   thoughts. (Isaiah 55:8–9)

As we have mentioned above, God is present to his people in *acts,* such as the Exodus or the Incarnation. Yet even as God addresses us through redemptive events, God also provides normative *meanings* of the same events through interpreters of the events such as Moses, the gospel writers, and the apostle Paul. God is not simply the one who acts. God is also the one who, in acting, knows why he acts and communicates his knowledge to others.

Here, then, are the ways of analogy and eminence. God reveals himself as one who knows, who possesses something akin to perceptions, judgments, perspectives. But at the same time, God's knowing supersedes human knowing in every possible way. Thus the psalmist declares to God, "You know when I sit down and when I rise up; you discern my thoughts from far away" (Psalm 139:2), and Jesus tells his followers that "even the hairs of your head are all counted" (Matthew 10:30; see also Proverbs 24:12). Thus we say that humans are scient (have the possibility of knowing) but that God is *omni*-scient.

While God's supreme knowing is a comfort to many, it has also been a problem to others from the time of Origen until now.[50] How are we to reconcile biblical passages that speak of God's knowing my words before I speak them with other passages that speak of God's "coming to knowledge" of freely chosen human action as if God did not earlier possess this knowledge (for example, Genesis 22:12)? How are we to reconcile philosophical understandings of God as all-knowing with our understanding of the presence of evil? These issues, moreover, are not irrelevant to Christian

... It's as if God were a large prepared ham and I were but a measly clove.

Pastor Brackerman secretly wishes that certain folks would leave analogy-making to the professionals.

spirituality. One views prayer on behalf of another, for example, quite differently depending on whether or not one believes that God knows all future events, including the free choices of humans. Our approach to divine guidance, our demeanor in times of suffering, our zeal for evangelistic or social issues—these may all be affected by our sense of God's knowing.

In spite of disagreement over particulars, the following points are affirmed by nearly all:

- God's knowledge is perfect. God knows all that can possibly be known.
- God knows reality as it is. For example, while the true character of freedom is debated, all agree that whatever it is, God knows it, and relates to it, as such.
- God's means of carrying out his plans in time are affected by the choices of people—especially by fervent prayer, sincere repentance, or persistent sin.
- God is acquainted with and involved in the most intimate details of our lives.
- God knows *some* choices or future events as certain, especially key events such as the coming of Christ or the eschaton.

Lying underneath this agreement is an intuitive apprehension of God's sovereign responsiveness, God's covenant relationality. The narrative structure of the entire biblical message—God's preservation of a people in the midst of the choices of the patriarchs, God's sovereign hand over the nation of Israel through times of redemption and rebellion, God's provision of his Son and the offer of salvation through Christ and the Spirit—reveals a God who both is sovereign over time and space and is experienced within (and who experiences) real relationships *in* time and space. The God with whom we relate is a God who knows, and who knows as only God can know.

God's Feeling

Just as the assumption of God's knowing is fundamental to Judeo-Christian spirituality, so also is the assumption of God's feeling or affectivity. Just as the Father delights in the glorification of the Son, and the Spirit delights to honor the Father and the Son, and the Son desires to share his joy with those whom the Father gave, so the God with whom we relate feels deeply for those who are his creation. When the scriptures speak of God, they speak of a God who feels. The Lord is pleased, angry, merciful, furious, jealous, calm; the Lord loves, delights, hates, laughs, cries, abhors, detests, grieves, finds favor; the Lord feels compassion, sorrow, fulfillment, satisfaction, peace, wrath; the Lord is deeply moved, intercedes with sighs too deep for words, hardens, welcomes, and wipes the tears from our faces. Hear what Yahweh says to the Israelites as they are ready to cross into the promised land: "Although heaven and the heaven of heavens belong to the LORD your God, the earth with all that is in it, yet the LORD set his heart in love on your ancestors alone and chose you" (Deuteronomy 10:14–15). Hear how the Lord empathetically communicates in Isaiah 49:15: "Can a woman forget her nursing child, or show no compassion for the child of her womb? Even these may forget, yet I will not forget you."[51]

In spite of this overwhelming biblical evidence, however, many of those who were instrumental in formulating the image of God in Christianity's first centuries minimized this passionate aspect of God's character. After all, while human emotions are often tied to physiological responses, God is not embodied as humans are. How are God's feelings to be imagined? Eager to avoid a portrait of the Christian God that would look like the (all too human) pagan gods, and attracted by the philosophical frameworks of Plato and Aristotle, many Christians described God as impassive or impassible: as impervious to such changes of nature as passions or suffering. Some felt that to attribute such feelings in God would imply ambiguity in God's will or knowledge. (We see the complications of trying to apply the way of analogy, which is necessarily vague.) This minimizing of God's affectivity, however, was not universal. Tertullian, a second-century theologian, speaks of God's feelings by way of analogy in this manner: "And this, therefore, is to be deemed the likeness of God in man, that the human soul have the same emotions and sensations as God, although they are not of the same kind; differing as they do both in their conditions and their issues according to their nature."[52]

Spiritual writers struggled with this aspect of God's character throughout history. On the one hand, they were trained to think of God as not subject to suffering. Yet their experience was of a God who was deeply passionate.[53] Recent theological reflection in the West concerning God has tended to reinterpret the notion of impassibility or impassivity to affirm that God's being is not simply subject to that of humans, but that, at the same time, God allows himself to be moved, affected, and influenced by his creation.[54]

It might be helpful to think of God not as *im*-passive or *im*-passible, but rather as *omni*-passible, or ***omni*-passionate**. God as experienced in time appears to display something like human knowing, yet God is beyond this in every aspect; so too (we might do well to think) God possesses something like human feelings, emotions, and affectivity, only God is beyond these in every aspect. God's feelings are rooted in fundamental concerns and accurate appraisals. God's emotions are not limited by mere physiology or cultural norms for expression. God's affectivity runs deeper than we could ever imagine.

God's Willing

Finally, we gain some grasp of God's character when we assume for God something of our own ability to choose, will, purpose, make decisions, and influence what is around us. We experience God as one who is not merely actively present in time

and space, but also *purposefully* involved in time and space. God chooses Israel and destines Israel to become a great nation. God plans for the coming of the messiah, the Son of God. The scriptures portray God as fully influential, as omnipotent. Storms are calmed, trees wither, people are healed (or struck blind), nations rise and fall, and hearts are hardened or softened, all at the hand of God. The God of the scriptures is a God who plans and acts.

And yet at times the scriptures also appear to portray God as vulnerable, as one whose plans are "at risk," as one who is not able to act. The Lord "grieves" at the creation of humans, telling Noah, "I will blot out from the earth the human beings I have created—people together with animals and creeping things and birds of the air, for I am sorry that I have made them" (Genesis 6:7). Moses pleads with God until God "changes his mind" (Numbers 14:1–25). Indeed this aspect of God's personality— that God relents—is an aspect that is actually praised. Hear what the Lord says through the prophet Jeremiah:

> "Can I not do with you, O house of Israel, just as this potter has done?" says the Lord. "Just like the clay in the potter's hand, so are you in my hand, O house of Israel. At one moment I may declare concerning a nation or a kingdom, that I will pluck up and break down and destroy it, but if that nation, concerning which I have spoken, turns from its evil, I will change my mind about the disaster that I intended to bring on it. And at another moment I may declare concerning a nation or a kingdom that I will build and plant it, but if it does evil in my sight, not listening to my voice, then I will change my mind about the good that I had intended to do to it." (Jeremiah 18:6–10; see also Joel 2:12–14)

Yet there are also times when God declares that he has made up his mind and will not relent or that God is not a man and so will not relent (for example, Numbers 23:19; 1 Samuel 15:29; Psalm 110:4; Ezekiel 24:14).

131

God's Operations

God's Knowing (omni-scient)

- God acts toward us in ways that resemble perceptions, judgments, apprehensions
- Yet God's knowing supercedes human knowing in every possible way
- and is ultimately beyond our understanding

God's Feeling (omni-passionate)

- God acts toward us in ways that resemble emotions, moods, feelings
- Yet God's feeling supercedes human feeling in every possible way
- and is ultimately beyond our understanding

God's Willing (omni-potent)

- God acts toward us in ways that resemble purposes, determinations, choices
- Yet God's willing supercedes human willing in every possible way
- and is ultimately beyond our understanding

It is not easy to construct a neat picture of this aspect of God's operations. It is clear that Jesus has the power to heal, yet in his own hometown he "did not do many deeds of power there, because of their unbelief" (Matthew 13:58). It is clear that the Lord answers prayer, and yet a variety of conditions are given in scripture for both answered and unanswered prayer. God clearly does not desire for evil to reign, and yet it does—sometimes with horrific consequences. And then there is the age old question of predestination and free will. On the one hand, we want to see God as sovereign, as intimately involved with the details of our lives. (Have you ever prayed for a parking place?) Yet if God appears *too* sovereign, then we appear as puppets. We want to understand God as responsive, as actively present in real relationship with us. Yet if God appears *too* responsive, then it is we who are directing God.

Theologians and spiritual writers throughout history have drawn attention to each side of this tension, emphasizing either God's sovereignty or God's responsiveness to human freedom. Once again we face the problems of the ways of analogy and eminence. God does operate with relation to us by means of plans, will, influence. Yet the vastness of God's knowledge and power, and the fact of God's existence both within and without time, point to a God who can sovereignly support the nuances of human freedom.[55]

The Christian God appears to have some similarities to people. God is revealed to us as actively present, evaluating as we evaluate: God is aware, perceiving, understanding, feeling, deciding, acting. Yet while God's use of these operations bear some similarity to our own use of these operations, God's thoughts are not our thoughts, God's feelings are not our feelings, God's plans are not like our plans. God is omniscient, knowing with infinite keenness, infinite breadth. God is omnipassionate, feeling with a sensitivity and depth unfathomable to human experience. God is omnipotent, carrying out his plans with infinite subtlety, infinite capability. By exploring the operations of God, we have begun to sense what relationship with God might look like as *person to person*, heart to heart, our will following God's will, our mind in tune with God's mind. By exploring the operations of God we have also learned something about knowing God by the ways of analogy and eminence. The ways of analogy and eminence enable us to grasp God with a greater personal relevance. It is one thing to think of God as self-existent Trinity, existing within and without time. It is another to ponder the fact that God knows us, feels our hurts, and acts on our behalf. But with the greater personal relevance that analogical knowing brings, there are the complications of correctly holding metaphorical portraits. We must be careful not to make more of our metaphors than is appropriate.

Names and Images of God

In scripture—and for most of us—God is grasped first in names and images. The sacred texts of the Christian faith speak of God in names and images: "the Living One," "the Mighty One," "I AM," "the Provider," "the Healer," "the Lord Most High," "the Eternal One," "the Lord of Hosts," "the Holy One of Israel," "Father," "beloved," "light," "mother," "fortress," "shepherd," "food," "fire," "hiding place"—on and on goes the list. Informal conversations generally reveal that people think of God most often in the form of names, images, and "the one who . . ." statements. As elements of God's active presence coalesce into recognizable patterns, we point to the One whom we experience and say, "*This* is God." The names or images identify particular configurations of operations as experienced: they represent the person of God as we have come to know God. And generally as a group or person grows to know God more, other names and images are introduced and integrated into one's God-image.

Images of God in the Philokalia

In order to explore this use of names and images more closely, especially with relationship to Christian spirituality, let us look at the stages of growth in relationship with God as outlined in the Eastern Orthodox classic, the *Philokalia*. The *Philokalia* is a collection of spiritual writings from the giants of Eastern Christianity (and especially the monastic tradition) from the fourth to the fifteenth centuries—what we might call today a "best of" sampler. The writers generally summarize the intentional Christian life into either two or three stages: either ascetical and then contemplative, or the practice of the virtues, the insight through meditation on created things, and then pure contemplation. Let us see who God is for the participant in each of the three stages of the latter list.

For the beginner in the spiritual life in the tradition of *Philokalia*, one practicing the virtues (or beginning to experience the fruit of the practice of the virtues), God is the one present in the struggle to gain victory over one's passions and to acquire the virtues. God is the dispassionate one, the

one beyond goodness, who both models and gives the virtues to those who seek.[56] God is also a source of fear, indeed a consuming fire, motivating those who take up the yoke of the priesthood to holy living and careful preaching.[57] God is the focus of, and the help in, our watchfulness;[58] the producer of an inner change that transcends mere ascetic performance;[59] the doctor of our souls, who learns from our responses to temptations and fashions the cures perfectly for our personalities;[60] and the one who condescends to our personal capacity.[61]

The second stage of growth involves an illumination of the intellect and a gradual coming to awareness of the truth of created reality. The fruit of this stage is often described as a process of becoming aware of the "inner nature of things" or of the "essence of created things." At this stage there is heavier application of the way of causation, and God is seen as the source and pattern behind all that is.[62] Theologian and spiritual writer Maximos the Confessor (580–662) encourages his readers, writing, "If, instead of stopping short at the outward appearance which visible things present to the senses, you seek with your intellect to contemplate their inner essences, seeing them as images of spiritual realities or as the

Draw your own picture/image of God here

New Images of God for a New Generation?

There is a wisdom, we have learned, in cultivating different images of God at different times for different people. A young boy may begin the spiritual life of faith by imaging God as Savior. But this same boy could, over time, end up with a distorted image of God by clinging solely to this very image of Savior. Could the same be the case for groups of people, or even for an entire generation? for our present generation? Sallie McFague, in her *Models of God: Theology for an Ecological, Nuclear Age*, argues that it is. She claims that "there is no way to do theology for our time with outmoded or oppressive metaphors and models. . . . In this situation, one thing that is needed . . . is a *remythologizing* of the relationship between God and the world."[63] She suggests that a new set of images—God as mother, lover, friend of the world—might be better able to facilitate relationship with God. Others have joined her, suggesting similar reimagining projects.[64] How do we face this question of corporate images of God? If some images have served to do great harm to the church or to others outside the church, perhaps it is about time we consider other images that might be more appropriate to a congregation or this generation. Let us explore this question as if we were giving wise spiritual direction—that ministry whereby one offers support and guidance to another regarding his or her relationship with God—to this generation.[65] How would we go about giving good counsel to this generation's relationship with God?

First, the wise spiritual director *knows the genuine need* of her directee (someone who comes for spiritual guidance). There is a difference between assisting someone one knows is stuck in an unhealthy God-image and imposing one's own God-images on others. Late-medieval anchoress and visionary Julian of Norwich (ca. 1342–1416), for example, felt perfectly comfortable speaking of Jesus as mother and, at the same time, using the monarchical image of God as Lord. She saw not patriarchy or dominance in the term, but the courteous, familiar care of lord for his people.[66] There is an equally unpredictable range of response to traditional God-language today.[67] We must be careful, in our guidance of congregations or generations, to diagnose carefully, lest our treatment be misplaced.

Second, the wise spiritual director *is prepared to introduce new images* to directees. She knows how to suggest neglected biblical material, to encourage new prayers, to recommend associations that might encourage new ways of thinking about God. She knows how to administer the medicine in the right doses in order to achieve the right ends. What would this look like in facilitating new God-images for a congregation, or a generation? Ultimately, it would mean fostering liturgical reform, altering formation, changing our styles of writing. Are we prepared to introduce these changes? in the right doses? in order to achieve the right ends?

Third, the wise spiritual director *is aware of the implications* of introducing new ideas to directees. Good directors know when an unhealthy God-image is damaging the spiritual growth of a directee. She also perceives the dynamics involved in reimagining God. How much avoiding of God might be involved in the exciting pursuit of a new image? How much will the introduction of a new God-image threaten to bankrupt the person of meaningful handles for

God? Should change take place slowly or by a severe break? These are not superficial matters. One's deepest concerns are wrapped up in an image of God, likewise with a congregation or a generation. Glib rejections of traditional images of God and substitutions with alternative models may be trendy and even appropriate at times, but these rejections and alternatives can leave many confused and without a God with whom to relate. Wise spiritual direction treads lightly on the sacred ground of another's relationship with God.

Finally, wise *Christian* spiritual direction *is grounded on the basic foundations of authentic Christian spirituality.* A wise Christian spiritual director reaches into the texts and traditions of historic Christianity to provide resources for those who are in need. She presumes the

richness of the Christian God, fully aware of the strengths and weaknesses of the ways of analogy and eminence. She is attentive to aspects of human experience that may be over- or underemphasized. She facilitates an authentic relationship of love between God and directee. The same will be true of our wise direction of congregations and generations.

It is easy to diagnose the problems of our society and to prescribe changes that will fix it. It is also easy to ignore the grievous harm that the church has caused in the name of certain images of God. We must become wise spiritual directors for our generation. We must not approach these questions casually, for our image of God, however conscious, is the North Star of our spiritual navigation.

inward principles of sensible objects, you will be taught that nothing belonging to the visible world is unclean."[68] Thus God the Creator and Logos are primary images (or ways that God's energies are experienced) for one in the second stage.

The third and final stage of growth involves the perception of God as beyond qualities, as pure intellect, as incomprehensible. Here God is pure light: "He is Light and the source of blessed light. He is Wisdom, Intelligence and spiritual Knowledge and the giver of wisdom, intelligence and spiritual knowledge."[69] At the peak of Christian perfection, the use of names and images of God begin to be unnecessary. Thus Maximos writes of the one who wishes to pursue spiritual knowledge, "Circumcision of the heart in the spirit signifies the utter stripping away of the senses and the intellect of their natural activities connected with sensible and intelligible things. This stripping away is accomplished by the Spirit's immediate presence, which completely transfigures body and soul and makes them more divine."[70]

The writings of the *Philokalia* give a helpful overview of some of the images and names of God that may be associated with different people at different stages of spiritual development within that tradition. But take note! This creative imaging of God is not simply a human fashioning according to our preferences. Rather God is actively involved in revealing himself in ways appropriate to our development, even to the point of stripping us from images when we no longer need them. We are in relationship with God even in the act of developing our images of God.

Kataphatic Spirituality

We have been following a five-fold schema of knowing God (affirmation, causation, analogy, eminence, negation). The ways of coming to know God have also been divided, in the history of the church, into a two-fold schema: the affirmative way (**kataphatic**—according to image) and the negative way (**apophatic**—apart from image). Thus, Maximos the Confessor writes, "If you theologize in an affirmative or cataphatic manner, starting from positive statements about God, you make the Logos flesh, for you have no other means of knowing God as cause except what is visible and tangible. If you theologize in a negative or apophatic manner, through the stripping away of positive attributes, you make the Logos spirit or God as He was in His principal state with God: starting from absolutely none of the things that can be known, you come in an admirable way to know Him who transcends knowing."[71]

Maximos, drawing from the work of Pseudo-Dionysius, draws attention to two different ways of "doing theology." The affirmative or kataphatic way explores the nature and character of God by starting with that which can be affirmed of God from scripture and nature. Nearly all that we have covered in this chapter so far would come under the general heading of kataphatic theology. The negative or apophatic way begins by discussing what God is *not*.

For early theologians, theology and spirituality were intimately connected. A theologian was not simply one who possessed academic training in the things of God, but rather one who *knew* God by intimate personal experience. Thus devotional practices and theological methods were inextricably linked. This means devotional exercises that made heavy use of the visible and of affirmation (meditation on passages of scripture; imagination of Gospel stories; reflection on nature, creeds, and so on) were more appropriate for doing affirmative theology. One's meditation, like one's study, would focus on the things that could be affirmed of God. When, however, one wished to pursue God by the way of negation, it was necessary to apply different devotional practices as well as different theological methods—practices that emphasized the removal of imagery and content from the mind in contemplation.

As theology and spirituality became increasingly separated and as theology developed new terms of specialization, the terms *apophatic* and *kataphatic* were retained as descriptions of two types of spirituality, though types less connected with theological pursuits. Kataphatic spirituality in this sense describes the awareness of God gained especially by means of meditation on scripture and creation, including the meditation on our own selves. Jesuit theologian Harvey Egan writes of katphatic (affirmative) spirituality, "As a mode of contemplative ascent to God, the affirmative way contends that God can be found in all things because all creatures are the overflow and expression of divine fecundity. It sees them as the shadows, echoes, pictures, vestiges, representations, and footprints of the triune God."[72] Good examples of kataphatic spirituality can be found in the first six of Franciscan theolgian Bonaventure's (1217–74) various means of contemplating God in *The Soul's Journey into God*, in Italian mystic Angela of Foligno's (ca. 1248–1309) Eucharistic devotions, in the meditations on Christ found in the literature of the *Devotio Moderna* (fourteenth-century Netherlands), in the use of icons in the Eastern Church, in the meditations and contemplations of Ignatius of Loyola's *Spiritual Exercises*, and in the wide range of exercises used in Puritan devotional life.

The One with Whom We Struggle

The God of the Struggle

The God with whom Christians relate is self-existent Trinity, existing inside and outside time, is actively present, and is referred to by a variety of names and images. But God is also vague, hidden, and at times confusing. The God with whom we relate is also the God with whom we struggle—and who struggles with us: hunting us, enduring us, and more.

The God with whom we relate is not only *Deus revelatus* (the God who is revealed) but also *Deus absconditus* (the God who is hidden). Both because of the infinitude of God and because of the nature of the human condition, God does not reveal himself in fullness. Some have thought of this *Deus absconditus* as the invisible God "behind" the revealed Son of God. Others think in terms of hidden and revealed aspects of God's communication. Thus there is something hidden in the midst of every revelation. Our perception of God is true perception, but it is not exhaustive.[73] Author Philip Yancey writes, "We live dangling between the secret things, withheld perhaps for our own protection, and the revealed things. The God who satisfies our thirst is also the great Unknown, the one who no one can look upon and live. Perhaps it takes God's absence and presence both for us to remain ourselves, or even to survive."[74] While theology has tended to emphasize God's omnipotence, omniscience, and omnipresence, Yancey recommends that we extend this list of attributes to include that God is shy, God hides, God is gentle, and God's presence varies.[75]

The Struggle with God

God comes to us, but God comes partially obscured. Take, for example, God's self-communication through creation. It is clear enough that God is noticeable therein (see Acts 14:15; Acts 17:22–31) and that we are culpable for our lack of response (Romans 1:18–23), yet it is vague enough that attention to God requires choice. Take, for example, God's manifestation in the Old Testament. It is clear enough that God's work can be documented, remembered: the time God parted the sea, the time that God swallowed up people in the earth, the time that David defeated Goliath. Yet his work is infrequent enough that God is more often forgotten. Take, for example, the Incarnation: God become man—his healings, his teachings, his character. It was clear enough that those who had ears could hear, but vague enough that those who didn't, couldn't.

And then there are the seemingly conflicting portraits of God presented in the scriptures. Is the God who "is not like a man that he would change his mind" the same God who changes his mind about the destruction of the wandering Israelites or about the destruction of Ninevah? Is the God who "will not leave us or forsake us" the same God to whom the psalmist cries, "My God, why have you forsaken me?"

And then there are the conflicts between the God presented in the scriptures or a given tradition and the issues of our day and age. Is the God who commands us to love our enemies the same God who obliterated his enemies in the Old Testament? Is the God who so visibly affirmed women through the ministry of Jesus the same God who directed Paul to instruct that women should not teach or have authority? How can we believe in a God who loves when this God appears to have allowed (if not *caused*) so much evil?

And then there are our own personal conflicts. Unanswered prayers, sufferings, questions, particular experiences (or the lack of experience) all contribute to the ambiguity of our knowledge of the God to whom we relate. Some people seem to fit into Christianity like a glove. For others it feels like a straitjacket. Perhaps we begin to feel like Jayber Crow, the chief character in Wendell Berry's novel of the same name who, when studying for the ministry, discovered not answers but questions. Jayber remembers that "by then I wasn't just asking questions; I was being changed by them . . . wasn't just a student or a going-to-be preacher anymore. I was a lost traveler wandering in the woods, needing to be on my way somewhere but not knowing how."[76]

Suggestions for the Struggle

Needless to say, we will not attempt here to solve all of the conflicts listed above. *Indeed, that is the point.* God is not grasped as one or another solution to a metaphysical conundrum. Each image of God points to God—truly perhaps, but certainly not completely. The God whom we know is both the God whom we cannot *but* know and the God we *cannot* know. God is known both by the affirmations that come through names and images and within the midst of the struggle with the same images and names. But, while we may not solve all the issues, it is still helpful to keep a few things in mind along the way.

First, we must be as careful with our biblical interpretation as possible. Sometimes God gets accused of something regarding which scripture gives no clear evidence. (God is a capitalist?) At times the history of theology has tended to emphasize one aspect of God (like God's impassibility) when contemporary questioning compels us to acknowledge the biblical evidence to the contrary. At other times, however, our attention to scripture only serves to show that a traditional portrait of God is clear and that contemporary trends must be rejected. If we are going to struggle with God, it might as well be the God of the scriptures.

Similarly, we must acknowledge the progressive nature of the revelation of God's character (and this even within the pages of scripture). The God who is present through spontaneous appearances in the patriarchal narratives is the God who is present through law, monarchy, temple, and prophet and is the God who is incarnate in Jesus and poured out through the Holy Spirit. Fresh aspects of God's character are encountered with each new season,

---

The knowledge of God is a work of reason and a challenge to reason.

—Jean Daniélou[77]

---

bringing both continuity and tension with the old. Themes barely introduced at one point of history are developed later. We are wise to clarify our struggles with God by attending to the big picture of God revealed over time.

Often our struggles with God are introduced as we come into contact with unfamiliar traditions. Perhaps, out of a tinge of dissatisfaction with a liturgical tradition, one visits a Pentecostal revival meeting and walks away asking, "God, are you really like that?" Or a postmodern agnostic attends Orthodox services during Great Lent and is taken aback with awe. Contacts with other communities can, in both healthy and unhealthy ways, stimulate struggles with God. They may stimulate reshaping a new God-image. They may require a life-and-death battle with the God we have always known and avoided.

We also must be careful in our use of the ways of analogy and eminence. When it comes to thinking about God through these ways, strict either-or thinking may not be the most helpful approach. It is difficult to harmonize disparate portraits of God (for example, God as judge and friend; God as Lord and lover) while respecting the contributions of each metaphor (judge, friend, Lord, lover). We must avoid both a superficial compatibilism as well as a resolution that reads one side in light of the other such that faithfulness to the sources are compromised. At times we must simply hold diverse experiences of God in painful tension. We are not after solutions. We are after *God*. Julian of Norwich's *Showings* and Anglican bishop and writer Jeremy Taylor's (1613–67) *The Rule and Exercises of Holy Living* and *The Rule and Exercises of Holy Dying*, both classics of spiritual writing, were written in the midst of great struggles, in times of terrible suffering, and in the context of an all-too-imperfect church. In patient struggle we may discover a synthesis of disparate elements of God's character unimagined before.

Finally, struggle can foster a move into the way of negation. Each way of knowing God has strengths and weaknesses. The collapse of kataphatic spirituality might just provide the doorway into apophatic spirituality. Our attempts at conceptualization run aground, and yet we still believe—rather, we *know* God. We run out of words to speak of God and find ourselves in a frustrated silence. And when we rest in this, perhaps it becomes a holy silence.

The One Who Transcends: The Way of Negation and Apophatic Spirituality

Yes, perhaps there comes a time, whether in struggle or in worship, whether early or late in growth, through an experience of utter darkness or of divine light, when we find that we comprehend God best not by statements or names or images but rather by silent recognition that God is beyond. We find that God is not just the one who, but also the one who is not. And in so doing we move toward the way of negation or apophatic spirituality.

The Bible is the first source to apply the way of negation. Elihu probes Job with the question, "Can you find out the deep things of God? Can you find out the limit of the Almighty?" (Job 11:7; cf. 37:15–24). The preacher of the book of Ecclesiastes declares that God "has put a sense of past and future into their minds, yet they cannot find out what God has done from the beginning to the end" (Ecclesiastes 3:11). Isaiah declares, "The LORD is the everlasting God, the Creator of the ends of the earth. He does not faint or grow weary; his understanding is unsearchable" (Isaiah 40:28). Likewise the apostle Paul writes, at the conclusion of his difficult discussion of the election and future of Israel, "O the depth of the riches and wisdom and knowledge of God! How unsearchable are his judgments and how inscrutable his ways!" (Romans 11:33); and again "For who has known the mind of the Lord so as to instruct him" (1 Corinthians 2:16; cf. Isaiah 40:13). The One whom we know is ultimately unknowable. The way of negation is learning to rest in this unknowing.

Many classic writings in the history of the Christian church echo this biblical theme. Thus Gregory of Nyssa writes, "For leaving behind everything that is observed, not only what sense comprehends but also what the intelligence thinks it sees, it keeps on penetrating deeper until by the intelligence's yearning for understanding it gains access to the invisible and the incomprehensible, and

there it sees God. This is the true knowledge of what is sought; this is the seeing that consists in not seeing, because that which is sought transcends all knowledge, being separated on all sides by incomprehensibility as by a kind of darkness."[78]

Perhaps the most influential document in the West developing negative or apophatic theology was *The Mystical Theology*, composed under the pseudonym of Dionysius (fifth or sixth century). *The Mystical Theology* is the last of a set of documents by the author presenting accounts of God according to various ways of knowing. It begins from the assumption that "the more we take flight upward, the more our words are confined to the ideas we are capable of forming; so that now as we plunge into that darkness which is beyond intellect, we shall find ourselves not simply running short of words but actually speechless and unknowing."[79] The author then proceeds step by step to deny of God those things we must deny of God: that God is not a material body, that God experiences no decay, that God is not soul or mind, that God is not sonship or fatherhood as we know it (carefully isolating the dissimilarities out from the way of analogy), and God falls within the predicate neither of being nor of non-being. The document closes by saying, "We make assertions and denials of what is next to it, but never of it, for it is both beyond every assertion, being the perfect and unique cause of all things, and, by virtue of its preeminently simple and absolute nature, free of every limitation, beyond every limitation; it is also beyond every denial."[80]

Examples of the way of negation can be drawn from every corner of the Christian church: from the fourteenth-century English classic the *Cloud of Unknowing*, to the work of Spanish mystic John of the Cross, to the writings of Lutheran shoemaker Jacob Boehme (1574–1624), to the more recent Thomas Merton's (1915–68) *Contemplative Prayer* and *The Inner Experience*, and many more. Contemporary author Mark McIntosh, following the lead of Augus-

Thus it is, as we have said, through the growth of the soul in the life of charity, that the Three Persons are known by the soul with that obscure and loving knowledge in which knowledge is in proportion to love. This is mystical theology, the royal dawn of the eternal vision.

—Jean Daniélou[81]

tine (354–430), suggests that the silence of mysticism is due not to the absence of God but rather to the supreme *fullness* of God, a muchness that cannot be grasped in speech.[82] This is similar to the point made by Gregory of Palamas that the Christian's experience of the Light of Christ is an encounter with the inexpressible richness of God—not at all a merely "negative" negative spirituality! For Palamas, "the negations of apophatic theology signify only the inability of reaching God without such a transfiguration by the Spirit."[83] Studies of the apophatic mystics tend to focus attention on the psychological aspects of the way of negation in the experience of prayer. More central, however, to the works of the negative way—and the point we must remember here—is the theological point: that God is not contained within the affirmations or analogies we can make of God. The essence of God, God in ultimacy, transcends any concept, feeling, or word we may wish to attach to God. God is simply *not*.

One final note on the way of negation. The way of negation both flows from and draws us into the elements of paradox inherent in our thought and experience of God. This has been a theme of increasing interest in current theological discussion. Scholars and spiritual writers are turning to the language of negation to bring people to God. A warning in this regard: an authentic practice of the way of negation must not serve as a convenient escape for deep and careful reflection on and struggle with God but rather must arise as the real, existentially experienced, resolution of that very reflection and struggle. Kataphatic and apophatic spiritualities, ways of affirmation and negation, must be seen and practiced in tension as complementing approaches. We cannot simply retreat within the God who is not. Rather God's self-communication demands that we know God as both the Known and the Unknowable.

CHAPTER SUMMARY

Christian Spirituality is the pursuit of a relationship between God and people. In order to better understand Christian spirituality, we must understand something about the God with whom Christians relate. In this chapter you have been introduced to that God, drawing from scripture, history, theology, and a variety of other sources. You have learned the following principles:

1. One goes about knowing or speaking about God through a process of internalizing images and experiences from those around us and from our own experiences. God-images are developed and changed in the contexts of both God's self-communication and our situation.

2. There are a number of ways of speaking of God. The way of affirmation speaks of what can be affirmed clearly from scripture and tradition. The way of causation points to aspects of God by looking at God's creation to see how it points to God as ultimate Cause. The way of analogy speaks of similarities between our world and God's character, while the way of eminence speaks of God as the supreme example of a given comparison. The way of negation focuses attention on what God is *not*.

3. The Christian God is revealed as a self-existent Trinity. God has no source other than himself and is the source of all that is. The Christian tradition affirms God as a Tri-unity, a three-personed God. The Trinity can be viewed through psychological or social perspectives, each suggesting different approaches to relationship with God.

4. God both transcends and is immanent to us in time and space. Because God is not limited to our time and space, all of time and space are available to God. Furthermore, scripture represents God as relating to humans within time and space. Based on these truths, we can begin to talk about the many ways of thinking about God's presence.

5. God's presence with us is an *active* presence; he interacts concretely with creation. God appears as a presence of mysterious Creator, redeeming Son, enlivening Spirit. The Christian God is a covenant God actively initiating relationship with humans, a relationship of love.

6. Scripture and tradition speak of God in terms of operations or attributes. These operations bear some similarity to our own experience, while transcending them. Thus God knows, but God's knowledge encompasses all that can be known. God is omnipassionate, feeling the depths of creation and his own heart with perfect affection. God wills, but with complete power. It is by getting in touch with God's operations that we relate to God person to person.

7. God is grasped by humans intuitively through a variety of names and images. We comprehend God imaginatively as light, as cloud, as shepherd, as lover, as friend, as savior, and much more. The use of varieties of images highlight particular configurations of God's use of operations in relationship but hides others.

8. God is also someone with whom we struggle. God is both revealed and hidden. There are aspects with regards both to God's revelation and to our experience of God that remain ambiguous. Therefore there is a necessary element of tension and struggle in our relationship with God. At times this may lead us into the way of negation, wherein we know God through unknowing—through realizing what God is not more than what God is.

Practicing Christian Spirituality

Enriching Our God-Image through Theological Meditation

The aspects of the character of God described above must become for us not merely theological propositions but elements of a real relationship with God. We must come to *know* God as Trinity, as in time, as fire, as More. One way of cultivating this knowing of God is called *theological meditation*. Theological meditation is when we structure a time of devotion around themes and passages related to the great truths of the Christian faith. This method is common to the saints of old and to believers today.[84] The method proceeds by a few simple steps.

Choosing the Topic and Passages

Theological meditation begins when you pick a great theme or doctrine and find passages that discuss it. You can find scriptures appropriate to a theme by using Bible appendices, a concordance, a Bible dictionary, or a theology textbook. If you choose the character of God as your theme, for example, you can look up words like *God* or *Trinity* (not in scripture, but in theology textbooks) or perhaps an image you may wish to focus on (for example, God as *fortress*). You might pick a few of these passages for use in your time of meditation. In our case we will use the working summary of God presented in this chapter as our guide, rewritten as the start of a prayer:

> *O my God,*
> *Self-existent Trinity,*
> *Who, though transcending time and*
> *space, accommodates yourself to time*
> *and space;*
> > *immanently present herein,*
> *the One who is actively present,*
> > *sovereignly responsive in love;*

> *the One who knows, feels, wills, acts;*
> *You who are known through a variety*
> *of names and images;*
> *the One with whom we struggle,*
> *and who ultimately transcends all*
> *attempts to fully comprehend You*
> *in concept,*
> > *language, act, or feeling—*
> *Hear our prayer.*

Choose one or more passages of scripture for one or more elements of this summary, either from this chapter or from your own study. Or perhaps you want to leave the topics open, waiting to choose scripture passages when they come to mind in your meditation on the summary of God. (Needless to say, to cover each phrase may take more than one sitting.)

Opening in Prayer and Reading

Begin meditating with a brief prayer asking God to reveal himself more deeply. In this example you might ask God to enlighten your heart and mind to know the person and character of God. Ask that God might grant you to know more of his knowledge of you, for example, or more of his holiness, his Trinitarian communion, or the like. Then read the summary of God's character and begin to read any passages you have chosen. Read them slowly, allowing your mind to move from text (what the summary and the passages say), to context (what was meant by the initial writing), to life (what it means to your personal situation).

Feeling and Reflecting on the Truths of Scripture

Just sit with each passage for a while. Allow the depths of its truths to work into your soul. You may have heard these truths many times before, but maybe you have never allowed them to sink into the deeper parts of your being. Theological meditation accomplishes this. It provides the means by which plain words become living truth. Allow your heart to be stirred, moved, and touched by the truth of God.

Move from passage to passage as you find nourishment for your soul. Some may not feed you in a given session. For example, you might begin with a passage on God's self-existence, perhaps Psalm 90:1–2: "You have been our dwelling place in all generations," the psalmist declares. "Before the mountains were brought forth, or ever you had formed the earth and the world, from everlasting to everlasting you are God." You may get a sense of God's priorness to human existence, but the passage may not "send you"—no great revelation comes. If so, you may wish to move on to another passage or perhaps to a passage about God's holiness, or to the Trinitarian blessing in 2 Corinthians 13:14.

On the other hand, other passages may provide rich nourishment. Perhaps, as you are reflecting on the blessing of the Father, Son, and Spirit in 2 Corinthians 13:14, you are struck concerning how the persons of the Trinity work together to bring you blessing. You stay with this awhile. What role does the love of the Father play in your life? How does the grace of the Lord Jesus Christ serve to bring you blessing? How have you known the communion of the Holy Spirit? Perhaps you are drawn from this to other passages about the work of the Holy Spirit. You remember time after time where you have known the communion of the Holy Spirit. You remember times when you have known the love of the Father, the grace of the Son.

In this manner you move from thought to thought, passage to passage. One insight begins to feed another, and you may find yourself delighting in the Trinity. The significance of the Trinity is made real to you as you slowly turn the passages over and over in your mind. As you spend time reading, feeling, and reflecting on these phrases and passages of scripture one by one, each may bring up new material for meditation, and your understanding of the theme will expand in prayer. This is the practice of theological meditation.

Questions

1. How does our understanding of God affect our habits of relating to God? Give examples.

2. People have often thought of concepts like Trinity or "self-existent" as being esoteric and having little to do with Christian living. Show the significance of one of these terms for Christian spirituality.

3. Is it fair to talk about God as being like a human—speaking of God's having thoughts, feelings, and such? Is this anthropomorphism? Why or why not?

4. Give an example of both a healthy and an unhealthy use of the same image of God. What would make these uses healthy or unhealthy? Demonstrate, in your answer, how God-image and spirituality are connected.

5. Review the start of a prayer similar to the one presented in the practical exercise. Use it to begin your times of intercession for a month. How do your intercessory prayers change in light of a focus on the character of God?

6. Prepare a class outline or sermon series on the topic of "God." How would you introduce your own circle of relationships to God in such a way that the core features of the Christian God would be available for fostering quality spiritual life?

LOOKING FURTHER

Practice

Alister McGrath's *Beyond the Quiet Time: Practical Evangelical Spirituality* (Grand Rapids: Baker, 1995) presents an interesting introduction to theological meditation, covering many of the great themes of the Christian faith. While the chapters do not focus on God, the book helps to bring us to God. *Knowing God*, by J. I. Packer (20th anniversary ed., [Downers Grove, IL: InterVarsity Press, 1993]) is a passionate call for us to get to know God personally and truly. See also A. W. Tozer's *The Pursuit of God* (Harrisburg, PA: Christian Publications, 1948).

Dynamics and Historical Models

The following books explore the theme of God in the history of Christian spirituality. Catherine Mowry LaCugna's *God for Us: The Trinity and Christian Life* (New York: HarperCollins, 1991) presents LaCugna's notion of the practical trinity. It is challenging in points, but helpful nonetheless. For a fine survey of God and spirituality via images of God as seen in the scriptures and texts of historical spirituality, see Kenneth Leech, *Experiencing God: Theology as Spirituality* (New York: Harper and Row, 1985). *Spirituality and Theology: Christian Living and the Doctrine of God* (Maryknoll, NY: Orbis, 1998), by Philip Sheldrake, is not only an excellent discussion of the relationship between spirituality and theology, but also a wonderful exploration of God in the history of spirituality.

Study

These works are more directly related to the theology of God from different perspectives. Walter Brueggemann's *Theology of the Old Testament: Testimony, Dispute, Advocacy* (Minneapolis: Fortress, 1997) deals specifically with the Old Testament, but it presents the theology of the Old Testament in terms of a dialogue about the character of God. John S. Feinberg's *No One Like Him: The Doctrine of God* (Wheaton: Crossway, 2001) is a comprehensive treatment of the doctrine of God from the perspective of moderate Evangelical Protestantism. A progressive Roman Catholic's creative synthesis of philosophical and theological approaches to the Trinity, Donald L. Gelpi's *The Divine Mother: A Trinitarian Theology of the Holy Spirit* (Lanham, MD: University Press of America, 1984) pays special attention to the theology of the Holy Spirit. *The Living God* (Peabody, MA: Prince, 1998), by Thomas C. Oden, is an attempt to summarize the consensus of the church in a systematic theological format. This volume covers theological method and the doctrine of God. *The Experience of God* vol. 1, *Revelation and the Knowledge of the Triune God,* trans. and ed. Ioan Ionita and Robert Barringer (Brookline, MA: Holy Cross Orthodox Press, 1994), by Dumitru Staniloae, the first volume of a well-respected Orthodox systematic theology, covers theological method and the doctrine of God.

Christian Experience

OBJECTIVES

In this chapter you will explore the meaning of human experience from the perspectives of Christian theological disciplines. Although this is not a chapter on theology, this chapter—like the previous one—covers many theological themes in order to provide a coherent way of looking at the foundations of relationship with God. You will glimpse something of the specialness of humanity in the plan of God. You will examine how human experience has been marred through a variety of factors. You will catch something of the hope of the restoration of humanity (and something of the character of God) through the work of Jesus Christ and the Holy Spirit. You will explore this threefold pattern in classic writings of Christian spirituality. You will ponder original blessing and original sin and consider their significance for Christian spirituality. You will discover how themes of creation, distortion, and restoration fit with the more philosophical and psychological presentation of human experience given in chapter 3. Finally, you will explore these themes in your own life as you experiment with the meditative practice of self-examen.

After reading this chapter, you should be able to

- summarize the meaning of human experience from the Christian perspective;
- retell the biblical story of God's covenant with humankind: partnership with God, covenant unfaithfulness, the special role of Israel, the work of Christ and the Spirit, and the fulfillment of the covenant in the church and in the eschaton;
- identify key theological terms related to the Christian presentation of the meaning of human experience (creation, image, sin, corporate evil, demonic, covenant, restoration, reconciliation, and the like);
- describe the significance, for the practice of spirituality, of different emphases with regard to the three major aspects of the Christian understanding of human experience (greatness, tragedy, restoration);
- describe the significance, for the practice of spirituality, of different emphases with regard to the meaning of Christ's restorative work;
- suggest ways in which insights from philosophy and the human sciences and insights from the theological disciplines mutually enrich an understanding of Christian experience;
- show how an understanding of human experience in terms of operations, stages, relationships, and such augments our understanding of Christian experience as great, tragic, and restored.

Christian spirituality is about relationship with God. We have introduced God in the previous chapter. And in chapter 3 we introduced human experience using the insights of philosophy and the human sciences. If, however, we intend on using our enhanced understanding of humanity as part of an account of *Christian* spirituality, then we must coordinate our philosophical and empirical model of human experience with insights drawn from disciplines directly within the Christian tradition. We must give a fuller account of God in terms of the story of God presented in the Christian gospel. And we must begin to bring God and human together. Thus, in this chapter we will consider the reflections of Christian theology and history, the themes that Christians have used to summarize an understanding of human experience. And we will sample writings of Christian spirituality, noticing how these themes have been expressed in the classics of the faith.

In drawing from the resources of the Christian tradition, we shift attention somewhat from our treatment of human experience in chapter 3. Whereas previously we considered human experience from a *phenomenological* point of view—simply asking what is there when we look at human experience (operations, stages, relationships, and so on)—in this chapter we will consider human experience from more of a *teleological* point of view, inquiring whence we came and whither we are going. We turn from asking about the *character* of human experience to asking about the *meaning* of human experience. And whenever we ask about the meaning of a thing, we find ourselves trying to understand that thing within the context of larger realities within which it can be comprehended. Thus (and here is our problem) we must know the whole in order to understand the part. It is impossible to give an account of the meaning of God or human experience apart from an account of our relationship with God. And thus, while there is some legitimacy in separately introducing each player in the divine-human relationship,

there is also a case to be made for looking at the meaning of relationship with God in order to comprehend, for example, what it means to be human.[1] And so in this chapter we will focus attention on a part (human experience) from the perspective of the whole (the Christian faith). In the process we will also learn more about God. By coordinating the insights of the philosophical and human science insights with those from the Christian tradition and bringing them together into a single perspective of human-experience-before-God, we will then be prepared to look at the dynamics of the divine-human relationship itself.

The Christian tradition tends to summarize the meaning of human experience in a basic structure. Adolphe Tanquerey's *The Spiritual Life*, a highly regarded manual of early twentieth-century Roman Catholic spirituality, for example, consecutively discusses "the natural life of man," "the elevation of man to the supernatural state," "the fall and its consequences," and "the redemption and its effects."[2] A similar structure is cautiously offered by Old Testament theologian Walter Brueggemann, who presents a threefold pattern: "creation for glad obedience," "a failed relationship," and "rehabilitation for a new beginning."[3] Others speak of creation, fall, and redemption.[4] Human experience cannot be understood *Christianly* apart from some reference to this structure. Thus we shall explore the Christian account of human experience by addressing the *greatness* of human experience, the *tragedy* of human experience, and the *restoration* of human experience. Like the previous chapters, this chapter is organized as a commentary on a working thesis regarding human experience from a Christian point of view:

> Humans are created in God's image and as God's covenant partners. Human experience has, however, become twisted through covenant unfaithfulness and sin. Furthermore, human experience is plagued by threatening social forces and is subject to evil powers. Nevertheless, God has

"Easter Wings"
by Anglican pastor and poet George Herbert (1593–1633)

Lord, who createdst man in wealth and store,	My tender age in sorrow did begin
Though foolishly he lost the same,	And still with sickness and shame
Decaying more and more,	Thou didst so punish sin,
Till he became	That I became
Most poor	Most thin
With thee	With thee
Oh let me rise	Let me combine,
As larks, harmoniously,	And feel this day thy victory:
And sing this day thy victories:	For, if I imp my wing on thine,
Then shall the fall further the flight in me.	Affliction shall advance the flight in me.[5]

acted, especially through Jesus Christ and the Holy Spirit, to bring to human experience both the hope and the reality of a full restoration of life.

The Greatness of Human Experience

> What are human beings that you are
>   mindful of them,
> mortals that you care for them?
> Yet you have made them a little
>   lower than God,
> and crowned them with glory and
>   honor. (Psalm 8:4–5)

One of the most obvious features about humankind, both individual and corporate, is our **greatness**. The human race has accomplished what no other species has even considered. We have altered the face of the earth. Even in our abuses our greatness is revealed. No other creature can cause the damage we can. The scale, the genius, and the creativity involved in human activity is unmatched. The Christian tradition often speaks of human greatness in terms of "whence we came" and "whither we are headed." But in so speaking, it uses a variety of different ways of treating the relevant themes. The sacred scriptures reveal their insights concerning human greatness progressively, as themes like covenant and kingdom are developed from one era to the next. Systematic theology has tended to reflect on human greatness through discussion of

the nature of human beings in the image of God. We will explore human greatness by examining three concepts: being created, image, and covenant partnership.

Being Created

Of all subjects of religious debate, the one that has perhaps received the most media attention in the twentieth century is the subject of **creation**. At times both the creationists and the evolutionists have come out looking like monkeys. Yet, while the *means* of God's creation may be debated, the *fact* of God's hand in the origins of humanity is universally affirmed by the Christian Church.[6] The most basic fact about humanity from the Christian point of view is that we are *created*. "In the beginning, God created"—these are the first words of the Hebrew and Christian Bibles. Our creation is narrated in the first few chapters of Genesis; it is implied rhetorically by God himself as God questions Job (Job 38–41); it is lifted up by the psalmists in praise to God (Psalm 139); it is proclaimed by Paul to those who have never heard of the Christian (or Jewish) God (Acts 14:15–17; 17:25).

Three features of human experience may be highlighted with regard to our createdness:

Distinct. First, human experience is *distinct* from the divine. We are not God. The early theologians of the Christian church were careful to distinguish creation as the free expression of God's *will* from a less adequate conception of creation as a necessary expression of God's *essence*. Thus, contemporary theologian John Meyendorff states in his *Byzantine Theology*, God "remains transcendent to the world after creating it," and the creator's actions in the world "presuppose difference and distinction between Him and His creation."[7] Some have found ways of blurring this distinction, pointing, for example, to the divine found at the true center of each human heart or identifying the Creator with the process of evolutionary change itself. Nonetheless, while acknowledging that God is available to all times and places, Christians have been careful to distinguish God's essential being from those times and places. This is what makes God *God*. God is one reality. Everything else is distinct.

Dependent. Second, human experience is *dependent* on God. God is self-existent. God's being and experience comes simply from God, nowhere else. We humans, however, cannot bring ourselves to life, and we are aware—especially at the edges of life—that the continuity of our embodied soul depends on the providential care of God. The psalmist declares,

> The young lions roar for their prey,
> seeking their food from God. . . .
> People go out to their work
> and to their labor until the evening. . . .
> These all look to you
> to give them their food in due
> season. (Psalm 104:21, 23, 27)

Our dependency on God is not always at the forefront of human consciousness. Often we act out our life as free subjects, trying to make a life for ourselves. And just as often, our efforts at making a living provide ways of avoiding what perhaps we know most deeply, that "in spite of his free subjectivity, man experiences himself as being at the disposal of other things, a disposal over which he has no control," and that "He comes to the real truth about himself precisely by the fact that he patiently endures and accepts this knowledge that his own reality is not in his own hands."[8]

Participants. Finally, we are *participants* in creation. As distinct from God and as embodied souls, we have much in common with rocks, plants, and with other animals and humans. Indeed, God placed us on earth, in the garden, "to till it and keep [literally, 'conserve'] it." Our life is lived in intimate relationship with the ecosystem, whether we are aware of this or not. Human experience is about "getting along with nature."[9] How and where we build our dwellings, the kind of work we pursue, the technologies we use, the food we eat—these decisions are enmeshed in our participation with creation. Furthermore, as participants in creation, we participate in the goodness of God's creation. Human life is to be lived in joyful identification with the limits of the fellow participants of creation. Through creation we are set free to celebrate the fullness of ordinary embodied life.

In the Image of God

While we are participants in creation, we are participants of a special kind. This is indicated in the creation narratives by human creation's being listed at the conclusion of the account, by God's use of the phrase *very good* to describe human creation, and by the account in Genesis 2 of God's breathing into Adam the breath of life. But the feature of the creation narrative that has received the greatest attention over the centuries is the claim that humankind is created in the **image** and likeness of God (Genesis 1:26–27). Early Christian commentary on this passage often made a distinction between the Hebrew terms for *image* (*selem*) and *likeness* (*demut*), pointing, on the one hand, to our natural capacities, which bear similarity to God's, and, on the other, to what we might become. Medieval theologian Peter Lombard's (1100–60) *Sentences*, the standard Western medieval manual of theology, summarized this distinction by

"The Loves of Taliesin" A Welsh Poem (fourteenth century)

The beauty of the virtue in doing
    penance for excess,
Beautiful too that God shall save me.
The beauty of a companion who
    does not deny me his company,
Beautiful too the drinking horn's
    society.
The beauty of a master like Nudd,
    the wolf of God,
Beautiful too a man who is noble,
    kind, and generous.
The beauty of berries at harvest
    time,
Beautiful too the grain on the stalk.
    . . .
The beauty of a hero who does not
    shun injury,
Beautiful too is elegant Welsh.
The beauty of the heather when it
    turns purple,
Beautiful too pasture land for cattle.
    . . .
The beauty of the word which the
    Trinity speaks
Beautiful too doing penance for sin
But the loveliest of all is covenant
With God on the Day of Judgment.[10]

identifying *image* with the operations of human experience—memory, intelligence, love, cognition of truth—and identifying *likeness* with innocence and righteousness, "which qualities are not naturally in the rational mind."[11] Martin Luther, dissatisfied with such a distinction, identified both image and likeness with human moral uprightness or righteous obedience to God. Many theologians associate image with the higher faculties (intellect, will, memory), feeling that these distinguish human experience from that of mere brutes. Others suggest that image (and likeness) may refer not to a capability or condition but rather

to our calling: that just as God has rule over all things, so we are called to have dominion over the earth. Still others emphasize the corporate dimension of human experience, conceiving our likeness to God in terms of relationality: as God exists in Trinitarian relationship, so we are corporately in the image of God, fundamentally relational toward God and toward others.[12]

In terms of biblical scholarship, the facts are simply that the Hebrew terms used for *image* and *likeness* are synonyms (see Genesis 5:3). The terms are perhaps best understood in the context of a Hebrew polemic with the mythologies of the surrounding ancient Near Eastern cultures. Whereas other cultures emphasized the *king* as being in the image of God, the Genesis passage affirms that *all people* (male and female) bear the divine image. Yet just what that image entails is not specified in Genesis 1. As theologian Stanley Grenz summarizes, "Although the use of the two nouns suggests that as the divine image humans are to resemble their Creator, Genesis 1:26–28 only hints at the nature of this resemblance."[13]

Two other Old Testament passages (Genesis 5:1–2; 9:1–6) link humankind directly with the image of God, and in doing so highlight their special status or role on earth. Human beings are unique among the inhabitants of the earth. A third passage (Psalm 8), while not using the terms *image* or *likeness*, is clearly a meditation on this theme as well, drawing attention both to the special status of human persons (NRSV gives "a little lower than God"; NIV gives "a little lower than the heavenly beings"; KJV gives "a little lower than the angels") and the role of people as rulers on earth ("given them dominion over the works of your hands"). If there is any aspect of likeness to God that is shared between the creation narrative and other Old Testament reflection, it is that humans are created with a special role and status (and perhaps, by implication, a certain dignity of capabilities as well). As God is infinitely capable and supremely glorious in character, and as God rules over all that is seen and unseen, so also humans possess

significant capabilities, are also glorious in character, and are assigned with the role of vice-regent of God's creation on earth.

Covenant Partners

While the theme of humans as the image of God is seldom mentioned in the scriptures, the theme of covenant is central. And what is most central in the Old Testament about the theme of covenant is the idea of Israel as God's **covenant partner**. Furthermore, as Old Testament theologian Walter Brueggemann states, "In the Old Testament human persons are understood as situated in the same transactional processes with the holiness of Yahweh as is Israel, so that in a very general way the character and destiny of human persons replicates and reiterates the character of Israel."[15] Just as Adam was created to be the representative of God on earth, so Abraham and his offspring find themselves to be a chosen influence for God's purposes on earth: to contribute to the restoration of the earth into harmony with God's design. Likewise God's intention in delivering Israel through the hand of Moses is that, as a covenant partner, the nation of Israel would fulfill something of the role that was designed for Adam, for Noah, for Abraham's family, and indeed for humankind as a whole: to cultivate a world ordered in harmony with God's character, to be the image, the reflection, of God on earth. The Mosaic law specified what must be done to cultivate and maintain such a world in the setting of the ancient Near East (in terms of relationship to others, to God, to oneself, and to the land). A similar invitation was made to king David (see 2 Samuel 7:1–29).

After David, God's chosen people were divided into two kingdoms: Israel and Judah. Both failed to keep the law. Despite repeated prophetic warnings, God's people continued on their own independent way. Rather than living into their covenant partnership with God, they failed it. Rather than realizing their role as representative and image of God, they lost it. But even as the Israelites were being dragged away into exile, the prophets spoke a word of covenant renewal, of God's establishing of a new covenant with his people. This new covenant not only would address their partnership with God as individuals and as a nation, but also would provide a new means of maintaining that partnership. As the Lord announces through Jeremiah, "But this is the covenant that I will make with the house of Israel after those days, says the LORD: I will put my law within them, and

I will write it on their hearts; and I will be their God, and they shall be my people. No longer shall they teach one other, or say to each other, 'Know the LORD,' for they shall all know me, from the least of them to the greatest, says the LORD; for I will forgive their iniquity, and remember their sin no more" (Jeremiah 31:33–34).

This promise shaped the hope of the people of Israel and their sense of identity (destiny and identity are connected), during their time of exile and on their return.

And as mentioned above, *humanity in general* shares something of this role of covenant partnership with Israel. The idea is not developed fully but is present and assumed in passages throughout the Old Testament. Brueggemann summarizes the characteristics of this "covenantal humanness" in the following outline:

- Yahweh is sovereign . . . the human person is summoned to obedience and deference
- Yahweh is faithful . . . the human person is invited to freedom and initiative
- Yahweh is covenantal in the enactment of sovereignty that claims and fidelity that authorizes . . . human persons are understood as Yahweh's transactional partners who are endlessly engaged in obedience and freedom, in glad yielding to Yahweh's sovereignty and in venturesome freedom from Yahweh's fidelity[16]

Even though the people of Israel received a special call to be instruments of God's deliverance (and to receive that deliverance themselves), and even though the primary attention of the Old Testament message is on this calling of *Israel*, humankind in general is never seen in any other way except within this same call to be God's partners, God's representatives on earth. No matter into what depths of degradation the nations may fall, humans are still to be seen in light of this greatness. The biblical portrait of humanity as God's covenant partners is that *all human*

experience—both individual and corporate, especially Israel—must be comprehended within the context of partnership with God and God's purposes on the earth. As Grenz puts it, "God has endowed humankind as a whole with the vocation to act as God's covenant partner and hence as God's representative within creation. Humankind is to be the representation of God—that is, to be that image through which God's presence and self-manifestation may be found."[17]

Partner and Image

In the period between the Old and New Testaments the connection between Adam and Israel was more explicitly developed.[18] By the beginning of the New Testament era, what it meant to be human was often described in terms of the person and role of Adam, and the hopes of the nation of Israel. Jewish expectations of a messiah, when present, would have carried with them something of this sense of the hope and destiny of Adam and Israel.

Which brings us to the New Testament. Only two verses in the New Testament mention humans in the image of God or likeness of God, neither of which offers any new insights other than to confirm a general sense of our special status and role (1 Corinthians 11:7; James 3:9). The Greek term (*eikon*) used to translate the Hebrew word for image (*selem*) is a strong term, often referring to the exact replica of an original. For this reason, some scholars think that the New Testament writers may have been reticent to use such a strong term to refer to the relationship of humans to God. It is perhaps for this reason that there are not more New Testament references to humans as the image of God.

Yet it was only natural for them to speak in this way of *Christ*. Grenz states that "the resultant heightening of the meaning of the *imago dei* [image of God] that occurred when it took on the characteristics associated with the Greek word *eikon* facilitated, perhaps even necessitated, the shift toward a Christocentric focus that epitomizes the New Testament use of the term."[19] Christ is "the image of the invisible God, the firstborn of all creation" (Colossians 1:15), the "reflection of God's glory and the exact imprint of God's very being" (Hebrews 1:3; see also 2 Corinthians 4:4). In the same way Christ is naturally called the "second Adam" (Romans 5:15–21; 1 Corinthians 15:22). Where Adam failed, Jesus lived out his life on earth in obedient relationship with God. He passed the test (to the death) and ascended to rule where Adam might have ruled. Covenant partnership and image are thus both fulfilled in the person of Jesus. New Testament scholar N. T. Wright summarizes Paul's grasp of these insights: "The resurrection forced Paul to regard that death [Jesus's] as an act of grace, and hence not as a denial of Israel's role in God's purposes but as the fulfillment of that role and those purposes; which meant that God's plan, and Israel's role, had to be re-evaluated. Jesus, as last Adam, had revealed what God's saving plan for the world had really been—what Israel's vocation had really been—by enacting it, becoming obedient to death, even the death of the cross."[20]

But the themes of image and covenant partnership do not end with Christ. The nature of human experience is comprehended not simply in the light of who Jesus was (or who Christ is), but also in the light of who we are called to become *in Christ*. The New Testament assures us that "those whom he foreknew he also predestined to be conformed to the image of his Son" (Romans 8:29), that "just as we have borne the image of the man of dust, we will also bear the image of the man of heaven" (1 Corinthians 15:49). Here we find not the image of God, but rather the image of the image of God: the image of Christ. We are chosen (notice the parallel) and provided with the means (of the Spirit—see earlier in Romans 8) to share with Christ in his life and rule as a new community in intimate relationship with God.[21] The fulfillment of the covenant promises belong to those

communities and individuals who become *in Christ* covenant partners and the image of God. New Testament scholar Ralph Martin speaks of an eschatological dimension to the *imago dei*, when "believers in Christ live in a new age where 'glory' is seen in the Father's Son and shared among those who participate in that eon. It is the Spirit's work to effect this change, transforming believers into the likeness of him who is the groundplan of the new humanity, the new Adam, until they attain their promised destiny as 'made like to his Son' (Romans 8:29) and enjoy the full freedom that is their birthright under the terms of the new covenant."[22]

Thus, an understanding of what it means for human persons to be created in the image of God, or for the human community to be covenant partners with God, is not solved simply by philosophical speculation on the Genesis narrative. Rather we must look to ourselves as part of a story, as fitting in to the designs of God expressed through history, especially in Christ. When seen from the perspective of the big picture, we find that image and call, ontology and eschatology, are tightly connected.

Consequences and Conclusions

What then are we to make of the nature of human nature—created, made in God's image, and intended as God's covenant partners? What are the consequences of these insights for our understanding of human experience in general? And how are we to coordinate the insights from scripture and theology with those of philosophy and psychology? A few conclusions may be offered.

First, there is good reason to believe that humanity possesses some fundamental similarity to God. Orthodox theologian Vladimir Lossky states that in spite of disagreement on details, "All the Fathers of the Church, both of East and of West, are agreed in seeing a certain co-ordination, a primordial correspondence between the being of man and the being of God in the

Through the wonder of a pyramid, the co-participation of creature and creation in farming, or the genius of brain surgery, we catch glimpses of the greatness of human experience.

fact of the creation of man in the image and likeness of God."[23]

Second, because there is no clear designation of any part of human experience that is assigned the image of God, it is reasonable to conclude that our being created in God's image does not relate specifically to any specific part; rather, it must involve the whole of human experience. This holism involves the fullness of human operations, stages, and relationships. Thus, Brueggemann writes of our partnership with God, "It is clear that obedience and responsibility touch every sphere and zone of human existence: sexuality, economics, religion, and personal integrity."[24]

Third, the nature of our character as the image, likeness, and partner of God is intimately tied up with our calling on the earth as God's representatives or vice-regents over creation. However we have abused the phrase over history, human beings possess a certain dominion over this planet. Again, Brueggemann's words are relevant: "Human persons are authorized to 'have dominion' over all creation, but that dominion, given the verbs of Genesis 2:15, is to 'till' (*'bd*) and 'keep' (*šmr*) the earth. The verbs suggest not exploitive, self-aggrandizing use of the earth, but gentle care for and enhancement of the earth and all its creatures. In this regard the mandate of obedience issues in stewardship, the wise care for the world and its creatures, who are entrusted to human administration."[25]

Fourth, we must recognize that within the Christian perspective, the nature of human experience is to be understood (and we shall see this as well in the sections to follow) contextually. Who we are simply depends on where history is going and how we are related to this teleology. Our "being" is understood in terms of a more fundamental "being-with" which gives shape to the experience that we are in space and time.

Fifth, while it is not developed explicitly in the scriptures, it seems reasonable to concur with spirituality scholar Steven Harper that "because we have been made 'like God' we are equipped for relationship with God. In the act of creation, God demonstrated a desire for relationship beyond and outside of the Godhead. By creating human beings with the *imago dei*, God made possible both the desire and ability for every person to relate beyond himself/herself—to others, to every other part of creation, and ultimately to God."[26] Some Christians throughout history claim even more, finding, in the structure of the human person, not only the possibility of divine-human relationship, but also some form of the active presence of God.[27] There is a sense in which God has set "eternity in our hearts" (cf. Ecclesiastes 3:11), in which God has designed our existence such that we "would search for God" (Acts 17:27), in which "in him we live and move and have our being" (Acts 17:28). While this vague connection with God should not be overemphasized, it is fair to see an important foundation of Christian spirituality in our special position as the image of God.

Finally, we must allow for the mystery of the human just as we have allowed for the mystery of the divine. Some Christian theologians make specific mention of the apophatic dimension not only of our approach to God (apophatic theology), but also of our approach to human experience (apophatic anthropology). Historian Bernard McGinn writes, summarizing the thought of British mystical theologian John Scotus Eriugena (ca. 810–977), "We are most truly image of God in our inability to grasp or define our true nature, which precisely as *imago Dei* remains forever mysterious."[28] Perhaps the terms for image and likeness are vague for a divine reason. They leave us in silence when we need to be silent.

The Tragedy of Human Experience

The greatness of human experience, however, reveals itself alongside another dimension of human experience, equally as evident. This is the **tragedy** of human experience. Just as humans are created in the image of God and as God's covenant partners, so also human experience is *twisted through covenant unfaithfulness and sin, plagued by threatening social forces, and subject to evil spiritual powers*. While some of the factors contributing to human tragedy (such as the subject of sin) are addressed at great length in the Christian scriptures, others (such as angelic and demonic influence) are not treated with any degree of systematic comprehensiveness. Systematic theologians, in their attempts to render the many terms, contexts, and metaphors of human tragedy into a single coherent outline, have tended to speak in terms of fall, original sin, concupiscence, or depravity. For some recent theologians however,

the situation is marked, claims theologian Robert Williams, "by the eclipse of the classical doctrine of sin and by the interest in and concern for the problem of evil,"[29] and consequently by a different set of terms and questions. Whether depravity or theodicy, the tragic side of human experience often leaves us with more questions than answers. Once again, there is wisdom in resting in a blend of knowing and unknowing.

We will explore human experience in its tragic dimension in terms of three characteristics. First, the character of human experience is twisted through sin and covenant unfaithfulness (an exploration of the flesh). Second, human sin involves not merely an individual but also a corporate dimension. Consequently humanity is under pressure from social forces that threaten our experience (an exploration of the world). Finally, the tragic side of human experience also derives its distinct character from its arising, its *being*, within the context of a conflict of spiritual forces, a cosmic conflict that bears on human experience without being limited to that experience (an exploration of the devil).

Twisted through Covenant Unfaithfulness and Sin

The notion of sin in Christian theology (and in common conversation) encompasses a wide variety of words and ideas—biblical, theological, historical, and practical. When we recite the Lord's Prayer, we ask Our Father to forgive our *debts* or *trespasses* (following the Matthean version) or our *sins* (following the Lukan version). Even here in this most central of Christian prayers, the language for sin is varied and general. In the vocabulary of Christian theology, *sin* functions as shorthand for a whole complex of ideas and metaphors speaking about our relationship with God. In terms of the *story* of scripture, however, the phrase ***covenant unfaithfulness*** is a helpful way of describing the development of the failed partnership between humankind (especially Israel) and God.

Covenant unfaithfulness points to the essentially relational dimension of human failure in the story of the scriptures.

Covenant unfaithfulness. The story of human failure begins with the creation narrative in Genesis. The narrative follows a basic structure:

1. First, God acts—creating, breathing life, speaking, inviting humankind into a relationship of cooperative leadership over the earth. Yet this invitation comes with stipulations in order to maintain life within the context of the relationship.
2. Then, Eve and Adam fail to keep the stipulations and, as a consequence, lose life.

We see the same structure in the account of Noah and his descendants (Genesis 9:1–19). After God destroys the earth, he establishes a covenant with Noah and his children. The passage immediately following this covenant describes a violation of Noah's dignity and the curse that follows (Genesis 9:20–27). In a similar manner, Abraham is invited into covenant relationship with God. God's most general covenantal condition to Abraham is found in the phrase "walk before me, and be blameless" (Genesis 17:1). Abraham vacillates in obedience, with significant consequences for history. The rest of Genesis presents an account of God's preservation of Abraham's descendants in spite of their failure to walk before God and be blameless.

And so the story goes, throughout the entire history of God's people. From the Exodus through the Exile and return, the people of God, as individuals and as a nation, are invited by God to follow leader and law and receive life. But they seek their own gain and leave covenant with God behind. The rich oppress the poor, the judicial system sidesteps justice, the people live an adulterous lifestyle, and the worship of Yahweh is compromised by the adoption of foreign gods and by corruption among the priests.

Rather than being a light to the nations, Israel was consumed by them. Instead of life, Israel received judgment. Furthermore, just as the foreign nations share in covenant partnership with Israel, so they share in the irresponsible neglect of God's way of life. The prophets who proclaim judgment on Israel issue the same condemnations on the surrounding nations.

Jesus, as many prophets before him, points to the roots of this covenant unfaithfulness. Covenant unfaithfulness was a matter not of failed observance but of a failed heart. Jesus's own life was an invitation of God. Stephen's final speech is presented in Acts as a rehearsal of Israel's covenant unfaithfulness, ending with the offer made through Christ (Acts 7:2–53). One more invitation rejected.

All people are called as covenant partners with God and therefore bear responsibility for relationship with God insofar as God has made that available. Yet all people, Jew and Gentile alike, have failed to respond to God's covenant invitations. Paul states it thus:

> For the wrath of God is revealed from heaven against all ungodliness and wickedness of those who by their wickedness suppress the truth. For what can be known about God is plain to them, because God has shown it to them. Ever since the creation of the world his eternal power and divine nature, invisible though they are, have been understood and seen through the things he has made. So they are without excuse; for though they knew God, they did not honor him as God or give thanks to him, but they became futile in their thinking, and their senseless minds were darkened. (Romans 1:18–21)

Thus, not only Israel, but all of humanity, as covenant partners with God, are found to be guilty of persistent covenant unfaithfulness, an unfaithfulness that lies at the core of human experience.

The twisting of sin. According to the *Anchor Bible Dictionary*, "one may count over fifty words for 'sin' in biblical Hebrew, if spe-

Historical Portrait: A Vision of Hildegard von Bingen

Hildegard of Bingen (1098–1179), a German nun, mystic, moralist, and composer, received a vision that encompasses the whole of the Christian story of human experience. Here are presented the entire vision and, following that, her comments on Adam's rejection.

And I, a person not glowing with the strength of strong lions or taught by their inspiration, but a tender and fragile rib imbued with a mystical breath, saw a blazing fire, incomprehensible, inextinguishable, wholly living and wholly life, with a flame in it the color of the sky, which burned ardently with a gentle breath, and which was as inseparably within the blazing fire as the viscera are within a human being. And I saw that the flame sparked and blazed up. And behold! The atmosphere suddenly rose up in a dark sphere of great magnitude, and that flame hovered over it and gave it one blow after another, which struck sparks from it, until that atmosphere was perfected and so Heaven and earth stood fully formed and resplendent. Then the same flame was in that fire, and that burning extended to itself to a little clod of mud which lay at the bottom of the atmosphere, and warmed it so that it was made flesh and blood, and blew upon it until it rose up a living human. When this was done, the blazing fire, by means of that flame which burned ardently with a gentle breath, offered to the human a white flower, which hung in that flame as dew hangs on the grass. Its scent came to the human's nostrils, but he did not taste it with his mouth or touch it with his hands, and thus he turned away and fell into the thickest darkness, out of which he could not pull himself. And that darkness grew and expanded more and more in the atmosphere. But then three great stars, crowding together in their brilliance,

appeared in the darkness, and then many others, both small and large, shining with great splendor, and then a gigantic star, radiant with wonderful brightness, which shot out its rays toward the flame. And in the earth too appeared a radiance like the dawn, into which the flame was miraculously absorbed without being separated from the blazing fire. And thus in the radiance of that dawn the Supreme Will was enkindled. . . .

And I saw a serene Man coming forth from this radiant dawn, Who poured out His brightness into the darkness, and it drove Him back with great force, so that he poured out the redness of blood and the whiteness of pallor into it, and struck the darkness such a strong blow that the person who was lying in it was touched by Him, took on a shining appearance and walked out of it upright. And so the serene Man Who had come out of that dawn shone more brightly than human tongue can tell, and made His way into the greatest height of inestimable glory, where He radiated in the plenitude of wonderful fruitfulness and fragrance.

Adam accepted obedience, but by the Devil's counsel did not obey

When this is done, the blazing fire, by means of that flame which burns ardently with a gentle breath, offers to the human a white flower, which hangs in that flame as dew hangs on the grass. For, after Adam was created, the Father in His lucid serenity gave to Adam through His Word in the Holy Spirit the sweet precept of obedience, which in fresh fruitfulness hung upon the Word; for the sweet odor of sanctity trickled from the Father in the Holy

Spirit through the Word and brought forth fruit in greatest abundance, as the dew falling on the grass makes it grow. *Its scent comes to the human's nostrils, but he does not taste it with his mouth or touch it with his hands*; for he tried to know the wisdom of the Law with his intelligence, as if with his nose, but did not perfectly digest it by putting it in his mouth, or fulfill it in full blessedness by the work of his hands. *And thus he turns away and falls into the thickest darkness, out of which he cannot pull himself.* For, by the Devil's counsel, he turned his back on the divine command

and sank into the gaping mouth of death, so that he did not seek God either by faith or by works; and therefore, weighed down by sin, he could not rise to true knowledge of God, until He came Who obeyed His Father sinlessly and fully.

And that darkness grows and expands more and more in the atmosphere; for the power of death in the world was constantly increased by the spread of wickedness, and human knowledge entangled itself in many vices in the horror of bursting and stinking sin.[30]

cific as well as generic terms are isolated."[31] At least seven words carry the concept of **sin** in the Greek of the New Testament. Ideas conveyed by these terms include missing a mark, willful violation of a standard, error, rejection of God, transgression of a statute, disobedience, unrighteousness, and more. Some highlight the human condition (wickedness), while others point to the divine standard (missing a mark, unrighteousness), and still others address the one being offended (rejection, disobedience). What we discover about human experience from this is a basic tendency (opposition or nonconsent to God) expressed in a wide variety of acts and attitudes and explorable from a number of different perspectives. Sin is complicated, both in its acts and in its comprehension.

Needless to say, a number of approaches to sin have been offered by the church throughout the centuries. The Fathers of the East linked human revolt "more to the composite nature of human beings [spirit and flesh] and the temptations that emerge from the senses."[32] In the patristic West, the issue of the human condition was a central battleground during the controversy between Augustine and the "Pelagians" (around 410), with Augustine teaching that human sinfulness was both universal and "original," and the Pelagians arguing that

God had granted all that humans needed to respond in obedience to God. Similarly, to Catholic humanist Erasmus's *Freedom of the Will* (1524), Protestant reformer Martin Luther responded with *The Bondage of the Will* (1525), while the Anabaptists argued for the freedom of the will in the midst of their own "protest" against the Catholic Church. Future centuries would see Socinians, Arminians, Methodists, Puritans, Jansenists, and others all contribute to the Western debates over the nature of the human experience of sinfulness. Three characteristics addressed in these discussions illustrate the character of sin as a fundamental twisting of human experience.

First, sin is *universal*. At the start of the creation, Adam and Eve are portrayed both as individuals and as representatives of humanity as such.[33] They are placed in God's garden and reminded that the trees are given to them as food—that is, with the exception of a single tree. Author Gil Bailie writes of the biblical passage,

The "test" that the tree represents is whether or not humans can tolerate even the most innocuous form of self-restraint and even the most beneficent form of transcendence without becoming resentful and rivalrous. . . . Even in a situation that is as unconducive to envy, covetousness, and resentment as the Garden of Eden, the serpent's gaudy desire is all that it takes to unhinge the human race and shove it on its grasping and violent "career."[34]

In the context of this grace-filled test, Eve and Adam choose to reject God's command. From that point on in the narrative, the atmosphere in the garden changes. In Genesis 4, we hear the story of Cain and Abel and of the beginnings of murder and hatred. By the time we reach the Noah story (Genesis 6–9), God is ready to destroy the entire human race. It might be instructive, in terms of the narrative of Genesis, to think of the Fall not simply as a single event, but in terms of a downward slide, a *process* that began with the eating of the forbidden fruit and that reaches a clear universality by Genesis 9.

The universality of sinfulness is acknowledged by theologians from all perspectives. "Even those who oppose the church dogma of original sin concur in this basic assessment of our reality," writes theologian Henri Blocher.[35] The biblical evidence is clear: "The LORD looks down from heaven on humankind to see if there are any who are wise, who seek after God. They have all gone astray, they are all alike perverse; there is no one who does good, no, not one," writes the psalmist (Psalm 14:2–3). "All have sinned and fall short of the glory of God," writes Paul in Romans 3:23. While we can acknowledge the existence of "good people," those who seem naturally to lead a fairly righteous life, the weight of theological reflection and historical experience is in favor of a belief in the universality of the tendency to sin. As founder of the Methodists, John Wesley (1703–91) wrote, "Still, then, sin is the baleful source of affliction; and consequently, the flood of miseries which covers the face of the earth,—which overwhelms not only single persons, but whole families, towns, cities, kingdoms,—is a demonstrative proof of the overflowing of ungodliness in every nation under heaven."[36]

Second, sin touches our very *depths*. The Old Testament speaks of this in terms of the failure of the human *heart*, the center or core of the human person. This heart is hard (Isaiah 63:17), deceitful (Jeremiah 17:9), false (Hosea 10:2), and far from God (Isaiah 29:13; Matthew 15:8). In Psalm 51:5, David declares, "Indeed, I was born guilty, a sinner when my mother conceived me." Paul's special use of the term *flesh* similarly points to the fundamental character of the human orientation away from God.

Human sinfulness is not simply an unfortunate event, a mere glitch in the works. Human orientation away from God is established in the deepest parts of human experience. In terms of our model of human experience, we can think of this in terms of the "depth dimension" discussed in chapter three. Sin is not simply a matter of thoughts, feelings, or behaviors that happen to be wrong. Nor is sin simply a matter of bad habits, of general concerns, of beliefs. No, the roots of sin go deeper still. There is an orientation, a tendency away from God that is embedded in the very lifestyles, the fundamental concerns, and the worldviews that hold communities and individuals together. Indeed, at our very deepest core, we are *self*-centered rather than *God*-centered. It is perhaps in such language that we can speak of a sinful nature.

Third, the tendency to avoid or reject God's invitation to life is somehow *transmitted* from generation to generation. Adam is not mentioned a great deal in the Old Testament outside of Genesis. But when he is, Adam is mentioned not as the image of God but as the prototype of human transgression (see Job 31:33; Hosea 6:7). The identification of Adam as the father of human sinfulness is developed even further in the intertestamental period. Fourth Ezra (which is probably a first-century Jewish document) asks, "O Adam, what have you done? For though it was you who sinned, the fall was not yours alone but ours also who are your descendants" (4 Ezra 7:118; see also Ecclesiasticus 25:24). The key passages in the New Testament are Romans 5:12–21 and 1 Corinthians 15:21–28. Romans 5:12 states that "sin came into the world through one man," yet it affirms our responsibility in the next phrase: "death spread to all because all have sinned." In 1 Corinthians 15:22, we read that "all die in Adam."[37] To draw on one metaphor, it appears that these passages communicate the idea of Adam as the parent of humanity and human sinfulness. Sin begins with Adam and is passed from the father to the children. The unfortunate consequences are passed as well. Nevertheless, just as children inherit predispositions from their parents yet have the possibility (and the responsibility) to address these predispositions as unique individuals, so too humans bear their own responsibility for what has been inherited from the first parents. Furthermore, in each of these passages, Adam is mentioned insofar as he is related to Christ. As we mentioned earlier, where Adam failed as God's image and covenant partner, Jesus succeeded. Where Adam introduces death, Christ introduces life. Our understanding of the role of Adam is fully understood only as we grasp the meaning of the work of Christ.

Let us consider the notion of sin in terms of the approach to human experience presented in chapter three. There we learned that our individual and corporate selves are experiences containing all that forms them into what they are at any moment. Each self, each experience, is *real* in that it is an identifiable set of physical and mental tendencies. Some of these tendencies, these patterns of activity, are developed over the entirety of human history. The longer and deeper a pattern is established, the more it becomes part of our nature. In this way our alienation from God—our inclination to disobey God and to distance ourselves from God's loving invitations—stems from the earliest moments of human history and the deepest parts of human experience. In this way we can, perhaps, begin to speak of "original" sin.[38]

THE TORTURES OF THE FLESH

We have seen something of the "whence" of sin. But we must move from the "whence" to the "what" of sin. What does this twisted greatness, which humans have inherited

through creation and fall, look like in the concrete? What does human experience look like in light of our characteristic tendency to sin?

Although Christian theologians throughout history have described in various ways the consequences of the fall and the character of human experience in sin, there is general agreement that in some form sin affects human experience as a whole, touching every part. The Calvinist understanding of total depravity emphasizes that every dimension of human experience is tainted. Similarly, Orthodox theologian Kallistos Ware writes of humans after the fall: "Instead of acting as mediator and unifying center, he ["man"] produced division: division within himself, division between himself and other men, division between himself and the world of nature."[39] Let us consider this by exploring the effects of sin on each of the dimensions of human experience presented in chapter three.

When we reflect on sin's effect on the experience of humans as *embodied souls*,

"As you can see on your handouts, today's topic is original sin."

we begin to explore the roots of the **flesh**, **concupiscence**, and the passions. While Paul's notion of the flesh is not a condemnation of the human body itself as sinful, it points to the effect of sin on our embodied existence. The Orthodox tradition is especially attentive to this. Thus, theologian Dumitru Staniloae speaks of "the state of disobedience as estrangement with God" being "reciprocally involved with the passionate impulse that takes its birth from the weaving together of sensuality and the sensible aspect of the world."[40] The Pauline notion of the flesh draws attention to the patterns and habits of our embodied existence insofar as these are oriented away from God. In this sense, *flesh* refers to sin's effect on every aspect of human experience. The Roman Catholic Church refers to the connection between sin and embodiment by speaking of "concupiscence." The 1994 *Catechism of the Catholic Church* identifies *concupiscence* as "the movement of the sensitive appetite contrary to human reason." It says further that concupiscence "stems from the disobedience of the first sin. It unsettles man's moral faculties and, without being in itself an offense, inclines man to commit sins."[41] To give an example in the language of the human sciences, the tight connection between physiology and emotion can give rise to the existence of disordered "passions." When the concerns that govern our drives, moods, and emotions are *self*-centered (owing to the patterning of our drives and affective tendencies since the earliest choices of humankind), we naturally find impulses inclining us into sin and away from God, impulses that are perceived in terms of our physiology (specifically what stimuli increase our heart rate, alter our breathing, affect our digestion, and so on).

Similarly, each of our *operational systems* exhibit not only the greatness of human experience, but also distortion due to sin. Our cognitive operations—our inquiries, insights, ideas, and the like—tend to be formed by bias, prejudice, and personal ambition. Thus Gregory of Sinai, a fourteenth-century monk, writes, "Mere skill in reasoning does not make a person's intelligence pure, for since the fall our intelligence has been corrupted by evil thoughts. The materialistic and worldly spirit of the wisdom of this world may lead us to speak about ever wider spheres of knowledge, but it renders our thoughts increasingly crude and uncouth. This combination of well-informed talk and crude thought falls far short of real wisdom and contemplation, as well as of undivided and unified knowledge."[42]

Our sinful inability to embrace one another in honest listening fosters the encrustation of selfish "regimes" of knowledge and prevents the advancement of learning together.[43] The foundations on which we build our thought, the methods by which we conduct thinking, and the results for which thinking is conducted are often narrowly directed by self-concerns—to the harm of the thinking itself. Likewise our affective operations—our moods, attractions, emotions, drives, and such—tend to be rooted in self-centered concerns. Our appraisals, our criteria of emotive regulation, and the action tendencies that express emotion are developed and navigated with reference to self, rather than to God. Frequently we are left unable to really experience the vibrancy of life as our emotional framework has been shrunk into the shallow categories provided by a damaged person or culture.[44] Finally, reflecting on the effects of sin on our volitional operations, one can begin to see how one's will can be free yet constrained by sin. The trajectory of the human self is simply away from God. The choices that move human experience from one moment to the next tend to move us away from God. This is a pattern established from the dawn of humankind.

Just as sin affects the operational systems, so it affects the way these operations are employed at the various *stages* of human experience (outlined in chapter three). At the stage of Being Aware, sin keeps us from desiring deeper or wider levels of awareness, thus preventing us from important insights about God. At the stage of Experiencing, sin makes us comfortable with our own shallow range of experience, or we question legitimate perception due to faulty worldviews. At the stage of Understanding, sin keeps us from honest inquiry, from well-considered insights, or from constructive hypotheses. We bury our heads in the sand, afraid to allow our own views to be placed under scrutiny. We inquire from the wrong motives and for the sake of the wrong results. We settle for much too little. At the stage of Judging, our logic is flawed because our minds are made up or because we are afraid to admit we might be wrong. Our judgments are made with inadequate grounding. We make no reference to standard criteria for authentic judgment. At the stage of Deciding and Acting our self-entrustments are made unwisely, without discernment, for selfish reasons. We tend toward unethical decisions. Finally, at the stage of Integration, we tend to leave God on the outside of our lives. We avoid even thinking about integration, especially a conscious integration oriented toward Christ.

Old Testament theologian Elmer Martens outlines Genesis in terms of four sins committed: Adam and Eve's sin against God; Cain's sin against man; the sins at the time of the Flood against the natural order; and the sin at the Tower of Babel against culture.[45] His schema points to something that is pervasive in scripture: sin has affected every dimension of human *relatedness*. Relationship with God becomes a matter of avoidance and rejection rather than response. This appears already in Genesis 3. Humans have chosen to go their own independent way, and fellowship with God is broken. Alienation from God is at the center of all the other consequences of sin. Likewise, we become alienated from ourselves. We are alone with ourselves, not understanding, not having direction— dis-oriented. Psychological neuroses and psychoses plague us. Sin keeps us from a knowledge and acceptance of ourselves as we really are. We are also alienated from nature. Compassionate dominion becomes careless domination. As we shall see, there is a further alienation with the realm of spiritual forces, an alienation that brings "**spiritual warfare**." Dis-integration of humans and nature brings disease and disaster. Rather than joyful participating in creation, we exhibit selfish abuse of creation. Finally, we are alienated from one another. Economic divisions, unjust patriarchal dominance, wars, and family divisions proliferate; relationships are characterized by strife rather than love. We exclude rather than embrace. Our personal imitations and corporate identities are reinforced by competition and self-interest, rather than by aesthetic fascination.

The patterning of sin is present with us at every developmental stage. Because sin involves tendencies and orientations that are deeply rooted and that trace back to the first human parents, it is not simply a matter of reaching some age of accountability. Just as a child grows into the personality she inherits from her parents, so too that child will also grow into the sinful tendencies that she inherits from her first parents. And just as personality traits may not show themselves for a time but develop as the child develops and responds to the traits themselves, so too we may or may not reveal our unique sinful tendencies right away. Rather, they develop in us as we grow and interact with them. As we grow older our sinful tendencies become more established. They are reinforced as we allow them to grow through various stages of our life. Finally, sin has its influence at every level of the depth of human experience: from bad thoughts to godless worldviews, from hurtful feelings to a deep core of selfishness, from wrong choices to a lifestyle lived apart from God.

It can be seen from this brief review that just as every aspect of human experience is involved in our bearing the image of God so too the whole of experience is influenced by sin. This does not, of course, mean that we all are haunted by sin in every dimension of our lives at all times. This outline simply presents how sin affects the character of human experience *in general*. Just as each of us have aspects of human experience toward which, for various reasons, we are more or less oriented (some are thinkers, others are feelers), so too sin will affect each person differently. One may be plagued with worry, another with unbelief. One may experience alienation from others, another from oneself. Some women, for example, tend to experience sinfulness differently than men.[46] Ultimately, we must grasp human sinfulness (and human greatness) not simply by academic analysis, but also by prayerful meditation.[47] The tragic side of human experience is illustrated in figure 5.1. Reflect on this chart in light of your understanding of covenant unfaithfulness and sin as individuals and communities. See how each element of human experience is affected. How does sin affect your thinking, your feeling, and your choosing? How have you seen sinfulness limit people's awareness, hinder their judgments, or shape their decisions and actions? How has covenant unfaithfulness toward God caused strained relationships with others that you have known? In what ways does a breach of covenant with God influence our relationship with nature?

Plagued by Threatening Social Forces

Unfortunately, the tragic side of human experience does not end with individual sinfulness. There is a **corporate evil** as well. Thus John Wesley, as mentioned above, referred to a sinfulness "which overwhelms not only single persons, but whole families, towns, cities, kingdoms." The story of covenant unfaithfulness is not simply the story of individual failures; it is the story of *community* unfaithfulness. The Apocalypse castigates not individuals but *city churches* for their sins (see Revelation 2–3). When we reflect on the tragedy of human experience, sooner or later we find ourselves crying out with Isaiah, "Woe is me! I am lost, for I am a man of unclean lips, and I live among a *people* of unclean lips" (Isaiah 6:5, emphasis added).

Our one-in-many-ness, embodied in social groupings, reflects the very character of the Christian God as Trinity, as One-in-Three. And indeed, it is perhaps not through individual accomplishment but rather through cooperative effort that the greatness of humanity shines brightest. The uniting of a community in compassion for some who have suffered or the joining of human genius for the sake of scientific research both illustrate this greatness of the solidarity of the social self. Unfortunately, however, just as sin touches every area of individual experience, it spreads throughout the various dimensions of social experience, as well. Thus we must speak not only of sin with reference to individuals; we must acknowledge the realities of social sin as well. Theologian Bernard Lonergan speaks of this phenomena in terms of "group bias": "Just as the individual egoist puts further questions up to a point, but desists before reaching conclusions incompatible with his egoism, so also the group is prone to have a blind spot for the insights that reveal its well-being to be excessive or its usefulness at an end."[48] Community life is a life of shared meaning. When we explore the tragic side of our shared meanings, we discover oppressive ideologies, self-serving regimes of knowledge, and hateful prejudice. René Girard discusses the sinfulness of social groups in terms of a developing identity through "mimetic desire," or socially influenced imitation. Acquisitive and accusatory gestures foster both solidarity and division within groups of people. Scapegoats are sacrificed to maintain group identity. Violence and social chaos are the end results.[49] As mentioned in chapter 3, comparison, imitation, and identity are important aspects of corporate experience. When these aspects of corporate life are twisted, we find not harmony and mutual enrichment, but rather factions, envy, rivalry, and violation. Whereas Lonergan's analysis tends to emphasize the failures of group cognition, Girard's analysis tends to emphasize the

FIGURE 5.1
The Tragedy of Human Experience

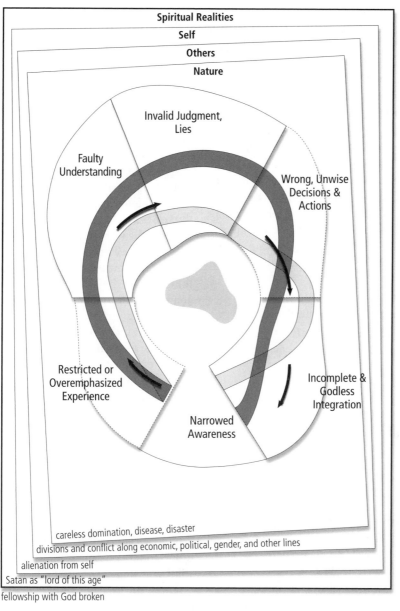

Spiritual Realities

Self

Others

Nature

Invalid Judgment, Lies

Faulty Understanding

Wrong, Unwise Decisions & Actions

Restricted or Overemphasized Experience

Incomplete & Godless Integration

Narrowed Awareness

careless domination, disease, disaster

divisions and conflict along economic, political, gender, and other lines

alienation from self

Satan as "lord of this age"

fellowship with God broken

Self-centered, dysfunctional affections often disconnected from thinking

Biased, self-serving cognitive system

Volitional system predisposed away from God, temptation, unfree freedom

Brokenness embodied at every level of development, every level of depth failures of group affectivity. Similarly, following our account of corporate experience in chapter 3, we could develop accounts of the failures of communication, of dysfunctional roles, of the self-serving nature of the institutions of culture, and so on. As with individual experience, all aspects of corporate experience communicate a twistedness that exhibits an orientation toward self (whether individual or group self is meant) and away from God.

Take a look once again at figure 5.1. This time meditate on the chart, seeing it not as a summary of the effect of individual sin, but as a reflection of specifically corporate sin, of the tragedy of the world. Where is Experience restricted or overemphasized in communities you know? Where have in-

---

The air was filled with phantoms, wandering hither and thither in restless haste, and moaning as they went. Every one of them wore chains like Marley's Ghost; some few (they might be guilty governments) were linked together; none were free.

—Charles Dickens,
A Christmas Carol[50]

---

stitutions prevented adequate Understanding for reasons of self-protection? Where have you seen a disconnect between family mind and family feeling? How have you seen economic institutions facilitate alienation between self and others, between self and nature, between humanity and God? And so on.

Social sinfulness—like individual experience—is expressed uniquely for each group, due to differences in history, geography, interests, and so on. One group may be quite generous with material resources, only to be viciously protective about ideological changes. Another group may be open about allowing a diversity of ideas into the group

and defensive about threats to leadership. Each have their own kinds of twistedness. The fact of twisted social forces is a defining feature of human experience. We know this all too well every time we hear a news report. Oppression, war, violence, selfishness, hatred, exclusion, intrigue, dishonesty, and such surround us on every side. In one way or another we are all both victims of and participants in evil social structures.

THE THREATS OF THE WORLD

Scripture, especially the Johannine literature, expresses the corporate dimension of sinful human experience by speaking of the "**world**." "Do not love the world or the things in the world. The love of the Father is not in those who love the world" (1 John 2:15). According to New Testament scholar John Painter, the Johannine use of *world* emphasizes "the world of humanity dominated by the darkness of false loves, false values, false knowledge."[51] The world is the corporate life of humanity—the cultural worldviews, the corporate institutions, and such—insofar as these are turned away from God. Human experience, both individual and corporate, is confronted with the world as a force that plagues human experience and threatens the advancement of God's desires on earth. This tends to happen in three ways: the world acts contrary to God's will, the world attacks God's people and concerns, and the world attracts God's people away from God's heart.

First, social groups, like individuals, tend to *act* contrary to (or independent of) God's will. Cain's violence against his brother Abel (Genesis 4:8) was an individual sin (but perhaps also a family sin and, as such, a sin of a dysfunctional system or world). The violence of the Ammonites against the pregnant women of Gilead (Amos 1:13; see Amos 1:1–12) was social sin. The nation was guilty and judged as a whole. The greed of Achan (Joshua 7:20–21) was an individual sin. The greed of those who were "at ease in Zion" (Amos 6:1–7; see also Amos 5:1–15) was a social sin. The leisure class was the "first to go into exile" (Amos 6:7).

While the omniscient God knows who acts contrary to his will, it is hard at times for us, who see from our limited perspectives, to point the finger of blame for social sin. The character of *persecution*, for example, can be easily recognized: a party is identified as excluded and actions are taken to express this. *Oppression*, however, is not so easy to nail down. In this case, exclusion is less clearly identified and the means of exclusion are enmeshed in complex economic and social dynamics. Yet, whether vague or clear, parties are being persecuted or oppressed just the same, and the sins offend God just the same.[52]

Furthermore, the crimes of social evil are often worse than those of personal evil. You know what it is like when that "good" ten-year-old boy gets together with those other "good" ten-year-old boys. They are fine alone, but just put them together and all hell breaks loose. Thus theologian Reinhold Niebuhr speaks of "moral man" but "immoral society." Similarly, psychiatrist M. Scott Peck suggests that perhaps groups are "less than the sum of their parts." In his "Mylai: An Examination of Group Evil," Peck gives a penetrating analysis of the Mylai massacre, a situation during the Vietnam War in which American soldiers brutally slaughtered five to six hundred local villagers, a situation that went unreported for over a year. He explores these questions of ambiguous blame and of "group immaturity." Peck suggests that in social evil, specialization enables the group to bypass the sense of personal responsibility. The ambiguity of blame and the devastation possible through group immaturity combine to make social evil an exceptionally painful factor in human experience.[53]

Insofar as the world acts contrary to God, God's people respond with righteousness—action in right relation with God. Indeed, righteousness ultimately involves a full-orbed right relatedness to self, to others, to nature, to the spiritual world, and to God. Righteousness, as a response to the world's contrary life, is the action of a counterculture (or perhaps we should call

it an "authentic culture"). In the face of the world's oppression, God's people live out compassion. In the face of the world's rivalries, God's people live out hospitality. In the face of group corruption, God's people live out edification.

The world is a plague to human experience because it acts against God, and ultimately contrary to the well-being of human experience. Because of this, it is often in direct conflict with God's interests and God's people. Second, social forces also *attack* God's people and concerns. In the language of the Bible, social forces are often enemies of God. In the Old Testament, these social forces are frequently identified with nations. God's purposes in the Old Testament had to do with raising up a nation in a land. Thus, the social forces that threatened Israel's perpetuity in the land (often neighboring nations) were threats to God's purposes. God delivers Israel out of *Egypt*, where the Hebrews were enslaved. God enables Israel to conquer enemy nations in order to inhabit the promised land. Jesus is crucified by social forces: the Jewish Sanhedrin and the Roman government. The Roman government is also represented in a veiled fashion as God's enemy in Revelation. For the most part, however, the New Testament does not emphasize the role of nations as threats to God's purposes. Caesar's rule is seen relative to the lordship of the risen Christ. After Christ's resurrection, God's purposes do not entail establishing a nation in a particular land so much as spreading a gospel by means of a transformed people throughout all lands. Thus, the primary enemies of God in the Christian era are the socially maintained lifestyles, worldviews, and central concerns that keep people from responding to the fullness of God's love.

The history of Christian spirituality has praised those who boldly stand up to the attack from evil social forces for the sake of Christ. Indeed, the memory of those who died in the face of evil social forces has shaped the character of Christian spirituality since its earliest period. Boniface Ramsey, in his article on martyrdom in the *New Dictionary of Catholic Spirituality*, asserts that "it is quite unquestionable that the spirituality of the Church's first three centuries, and of some centuries after, was strongly marked by the mystique of martyrdom— perhaps as strongly as it was by the mystery of baptism, with all its implications."[54] Our heroes of the Christian faith are often those who persevere in faith, love, and hope (who live out authentic culture) in the midst of the worst society can offer.

Finally, social evil manifests itself in human experience as a kind of *attraction*, pulling people away from the habits of thought, feeling, and action that are dear to God's heart. While this threat to God's purposes is no longer direct, it is still present; perhaps it is even more dangerous because of its being indirect. The Gentile nations were a threat to God's purposes in Israel, not simply because they sought to take over the land, but also (and perhaps even more so) because their patterns of life and worship drew the people of Israel into a way of being that ignored Yahweh's place in their midst. "Why be concerned with fair weights and measures? The merchants from the neighboring country cheat their poor at the scales, and they are doing just fine." "Why fuss over this 'just one God' thing? The priests from the neighboring countries appeal to a number of gods to help their crops, and last year they had a better harvest than Israel." And so the prophets declare judgment on the leaders of Israel for looking to the gods and the practices of the surrounding nations instead of honoring Yahweh. The ideologies, the entertainments, and the social intrigues of the world confront human experience as forces asking for attention, demanding response. Every aspect of human experience is indirectly under attack by the influence of the world.

Being especially conscious of this aspect of evil social forces, the monastic traditions of Christian spirituality have taken the Johannine warnings concerning the world very seriously. Property, family, prestige, luxuries, money, sex, power—all that the world has to offer—is left behind as the attractions of the world are confronted radically through monastic renunciation. A story is told of a monk who failed such a renunciation:

> A brother renounced the world and gave his goods to the poor, but he kept back a little for his personal expenses. He went to see Abba Anthony. When he told him this, the old man said to him, "If you want to be a monk, go into the village, buy some meat, cover your naked body with it and come here like that." The brother did so, and the dogs and birds tore at his flesh. When he come back the old man asked him whether he had followed his advice. He showed him his wounded body, and Saint Anthony said, "Those who renounce the world but want to keep something for themselves are torn in this way by the demons who make war on them."[55]

By acting against God, attacking God's people or concerns, and attracting God's people away from God's concerns, social evil threatens the advancement of God's purposes. The world *inhibits* and *weakens* the greatness of human experience. Directly, by attack, the thoughts, feelings, actions, decisions, relationships, and such that flow from and lead to God are minimized, persecuted, or prevented from expression. At times the people of God are prevented from life itself. Indirectly, by attraction, people are drawn further and further from expressing the heart of God, from living out their co-dominionship of reconciliation on the earth. Instead, the people of God are lured by distractions and luxuries into a comfortable and safe partnership with the world at its worst. Corporate embodiment of sinful tendencies can prevent individuals and groups from Being Aware, from really Experiencing, from asking the questions that might lead them to Understanding, and so on. Social evil shrinks one's relationship with self into those categories that the society allows. (What do most people think when they look into the mirror?) Social evil

FIGURE 5.2
The Threats of the "World"

1. The "world"—the corporate manifestations of sinful human experience:

Acts Contrary to God's Will	Attacks God's People & Purpose	Attracts God's People Away from God
(immoral society or "group evil") - excluding others through persecution - taking advantage of others through oppression - systematized disobedience	(institutionalized enemies of God) - socially maintained worldviews - socially maintained concerns - socially maintained lifestyles	(indirect force keeping God's interests out of focus) - self-serving ideologies - distracting entertainments - absorbing intrigues

2. The actions of the world threaten to:
- inhibit or weaken the full greatness of human experience
- exacerbate the sinful tendencies of individuals

3. God's people respond to these threats with:

Righteousness	Martyrdom	Renunciation
(authentic cultural living) acting in harmony with God	(voluntary suffering of attacks without compromise)	(joyful rejection of attractions)

restricts relationships with others or with nature insofar as people or creatures are deemed less or more important.

Social evil also threatens God's concerns insofar as it *exacerbates* the sinful tendencies already present in individuals. In this sense, the group is indeed less than the sum of its parts. Limited opinions become social biases, personal concerns become group agendas, individual anger becomes group violence, and what was unfortunate when expressed by the individual becomes horrific when expressed by the group. The social dimension of evil selves, both in numbers and intensity, multiplies the effect of evil on human experience.

The tragedy of human experience is not only found in the twistedness of personal sin. Rather, human experience is carried out within a tangled mess of selfish concerns and social agendas, a complex of personal and corporate bias, a world of private woundedness and public violations. Figure 5.2 summarizes the threats that the world presents to human experience.

Subject to Evil Spiritual Powers

The tragic side of human experience does not end with personal and social sin. Or perhaps we should say, it does not *begin*

there. Adam and Eve were not alone in the garden on that fateful day. And there is a long tradition identifying that serpent with the chief of an army of spiritual beings (**demons**) that was (and is) at war with God. As we have mentioned, human experience is a *related* experience. And part of that relatedness (and, in the fall, the alienation) consists in our relatedness (and alienation) with spiritual realities. Furthermore, there is indication that the war between these powers and God, on the one hand, and the war between these powers and the character of human experience, on the other, are somehow intertwined.

So why place discussion of this aspect of the tragedy of human experience at the end rather than at the beginning? Actually, in many theological discussions, angelology and demonology (the discussion of the creation and character of angels and demons) are placed earlier in the systematic order, during the discussions of creation or providence and prior to the discussion of sin and evil.[56] For others, however, especially in the West, perhaps due to a respect for the scant biblical material detailing angelology and demonology (or perhaps due to an abandonment of the warfare mentality implicit in the biblical material[57]), treatment of Satan, angels, demons, and such usually receives brief mention, commonly during discussion of the fall.[58] Here we will simply reflect briefly on a few matters that bear on the effect the demonic has on the character of human experience, especially as this relates to Christian spirituality.[59]

Spiritual conflict. First, although neither Satan nor the demonic is a primary focus of the Old Testament canon, nevertheless, the writers of the Bible assume (and develop within the canon itself) a narrative theology of the drama of human experience as played out within the context of cosmological conflict.

The word *Satan* is used in four Old Testament passages: 1 Chronicles 21:1; Job 1:6–2:7; Psalm 109:6 (also translated "accuser"); Zechariah 3:1–2. The word *devil* is not used at all. References to demons or evil

Original Blessing or Original Sin?

In 1983 Matthew Fox, a Dominican scholar and popular speaker, published a book entitled *Original Blessing*. He opens the book with two questions: "In our quest for wisdom and survival, does the human race require a new religious paradigm?" and "Does the creation-centered spiritual tradition offer such a paradigm?" He continues by stating that "my answer to both questions is: *yes.*"[60]

Fox divides Western spiritualities into two basic models. First, he identifies creation-centered spirituality, which begins its reflection on the human condition with *original blessing*. It affirms the things of creation: eros, play, and pleasure. It affirms the arts and sciences, compassion for the poor. Second, he addresses the "Fall/Redemption" model of spirituality, which begins with *original sin*. It fails to teach us to care for the cosmos and communicates pessimism and cynicism. The rest of Fox's book—along with his ministry at the Institute in Culture and Creation Spirituality—develops the case for a shift toward creation-centered spirituality.[61] Fox puts his finger on the significance of our theological views of human experience for our lived spirituality. The way we live our lives—our participation in or avoidance of many aspects of life—is evaluated in the context of a relationship with God that often views human experience either in light of creation or in light of the fall.[62] What are we to make of Fox's challenge today? Does the current global crisis beg for a return to some kind of creation-centered spirituality? How do we reconcile our spirituality with the stories of creation, fall, and redemption?

Human experience is characterized by greatness. Human beings are created by God, and he declares they are "very good." Human creativity, human relationality, human sexuality—every dimension of human experience received God's stamp of blessing.[63] Furthermore, humanity is created in the image of God, as God's covenant partners. We have been called together to think like God, to share God's heart, to cooperatively share God's compassionate rule over the richness of creation. What does this mean for Christian spirituality? A lot. Some Christian communities have followed the lead of the Puritan divine Lewis Bayly, who states (in his classic *The Practice of Piety*) that the practice of piety consists, with relation to knowing ourselves, in knowledge of "thy own self with respect to *corruption* and *renovation*."[64] Oh, if only his readers could have begun by meditating on the glory with which they were clothed from creation, the glory in which they were called to participate. And if our theology and our meditation is lacking, our lives will communicate that lack as well. Christians have often neglected to appreciate creation (which has, in turn, resulted in a neglect *of* creation). Christians have at times been hesitant to foster human creativity in the arts. For many Christians today, the general point of Fox's agenda is well taken: perhaps it is time for the pendulum to swing in the direction of affirming the "original blessing" of God's creation and affirming humanity as participants in that *very good* creation.

Yet *at the same time* we must recognize that each and every aspect of our participation in creation arises not in a pure reflection of divinity, but with a kind of twistedness. This twistedness touches every aspect of life, every relationship. Human experience is mixed: that which reflects the character of God through greatness can, simultaneously, reflect a disorientation away from God. Art can become exploitation or morbid self-obsession. Science can serve the senseless destruction of the earth rather than the sensitive care for the earth. And so on. Often both greatness and twistedness are expressed together. While a doctrine of original blessing recognizes the value of the poor, the weak, and the oppressed as special creations of God, a doctrine of original sin recognizes that the conditions perpetuating oppression are not mere accidents of nature, that the roots of exclusion go back to the garden of Eden. Rejection of the other is traced to the primordial rejection of the Other.

Thus it is not simply a matter of one paradigm *versus* another, but rather of the wise application of *both* to our relationship with God, both individually and corporately as a culture. By acknowledging both creation and fall, the resources of the history of spirituality are not set at odds with each other;[65] rather, they are respected in light of the contexts from which they arise and are employed in light of the contexts within which they are needed. The poems of Celtic Christianity feed those who need attachment with nature, with the ordinary, while the works of the more "spiritual" French writers of the seventeenth and eighteenth centuries feed

those who need to be directed from earth to heaven. The maxims of Thomas á Kempis's (ca. 1380–1471) devotional classic, *The Imitation of Christ*, foster a healthy detachment from our own selfish ambitions, while Dorothy Day's (1897–1980) autobiography, *The Long Lonliness*, fosters a healthy attachment with our own ambitions for good.

Fox claims that the human race is in need of a new religious paradigm and that creation-centered spirituality offers just such a paradigm. I disagree. What is needed today is not a shift from one paradigm to another. What is needed is the development of a culture of Christian wisdom that knows how to apply the fullness of the gospel—the knowledge of both the greatness and the sinfulness of human experience—in each situation, to each culture, to each individual. This kind of wisdom begins to realize not only the rich complexity of human experience, but also the glorious mystery of redemption.

---

spirits are notoriously vague. Nonetheless, there is evidence that the writers of the Old Testament viewed the world as connected to a conflict of cosmic proportions. God the divine warrior subdues the forces of the sea. Historical events like the crossing of the Red Sea are described with imagery describing cosmological conflict (see, for example, Psalm 77:16–20 and Daniel 10). And then there are the vague references to the origin of Lucifer (see Isaiah 14 and Ezekiel 28). These themes point to the Israelite assumption that events on earth are part of a conflict of a different order. And while the references are not always explicit, there is sufficient evidence to conclude with Gregory Boyd that, as Israel understood,

"there is a 'world in between' [distinct from the world of humans and the world of God]; it is largely characterized by warfare; and, for better or worse, it significantly affects the world as a whole, and therefore each of our lives."[66]

The Judaism of the intertestamental period developed the themes related to cosmic warfare significantly. Writers elaborated on the nature of spiritual powers and their cosmic battles with the forces of God. Increasingly they spoke of a single leader of this evil army. Cosmic warfare was seen as having increasing significance for their own lives as unfulfilled covenant-bearers. This kind of reflection led to the development of the Jewish "apocalyptic" worldview.[67]

The following is an excerpt from Athanasius's *Life of Antony*, written around 360. Antony of Egypt, considered the father of monasticism, lived from ca. 251 to 356:

> And someone else, a person of nobility, came to him [Antony] afflicted by a demon. That demon was so hideous that the man affected by him did not know that he was going to Antony; his state was such that he used to devour his bodily excrement. The ones who brought him begged Antony to pray for him. And Antony, having compassion for the young man, offered prayers and stayed up with him the whole night. Then as dawn approached, the young man, suddenly jumping on Antony, shoved him. Though the ones who had accompanied him were furious at him, Antony said: "Do not be angry with the young man, for he is not responsible, but the demon in him. And because of his censure and his banishment to arid places, he raged and he did this. So glorify the Lord, for in this way his assault on me has become a sign of the demon's departure." When Antony had said this, immediately the young man was well. And finally coming to his senses, he realized where he was and embraced the old man, all the while giving thanks to God.[68]

Jesus entered history in the context of this apocalyptic interest in cosmic warfare. And instead of rejecting the apocalyptic worldview, Jesus, along with those of his followers who wrote the New Testament, appear to have retained the central elements of the warfare mentality of apocalyptic, reinterpreting it in light of the place of Christ and the Holy Spirit. Jesus is presented in Mark as the warrior of God: heralded, anointed, tested, placed in battle with the cosmic enemy, and ultimately victorious.

Jesus casts out evil spirits with a word. Jesus calms the raging sea. Jesus rebukes sickness and makes people well. He interprets his own actions in terms reminiscent of holy war—the presence of God doing battle for his people. The apostles likewise describe the significance of Jesus's life, death, and resurrection in terms of cosmic warfare. Christ, through his death and resurrection, conquered the principalities and powers of darkness. While ultimate restoration is delayed until the final day of the Lord, through the empowerment of the Holy Spirit followers of Christ could be raised above the powers of the evil one to new life in the present. And indeed, early followers of Jesus traveled from place to place, demonstrating Jesus's victory by their healings and exorcisms, proclaiming that victory through the preaching of the gospel, and living that victory through a changed life. Thus, from the garden in Genesis to the destruction of Satan in Revelation 20, a story of cosmic conflict is assumed in the sacred scriptures of the Christian faith.[69]

Existence of the demonic. Second, although the details of Satanic and demonic origin and character are not described in scripture, the existence of evil spiritual powers that have some degree of autonomy and who influence human experience for the worse has been assumed throughout the history of the church. Indeed, the demythologization of the demonic, current in some circles, has only been a recent phenomena of Western modernism.

Bishop Irenaeus (ca.130–200) writes that "those who are in truth His disciples, receiving grace from Him, do in His name perform [miracles], so as to promote the welfare of other men, according to the gift which each one has received from Him. For some do certainly and truly drive out devils, so that those who have thus been cleansed from evil spirits frequently both believe [in Christ], and join themselves to the Church."[70] The Celtic tradition is also replete with prayers of cosmic protection and victory, reflecting warfare themes.[71] Medieval theologian Thomas Aquinas (ca.1225–74) states that "demons are in this dark atmosphere for our trial."[72] Central to Ignatius of Loyola's *Spiritual Exercises* is a set of "rules for the discernment of spirits," in which Ignatius speaks of interior motions stimulated by good or evil spirits.[73] Protestant Reformer John Calvin (1509–64) argues forcefully against the view that "devils are nothing but bad affections or perturbations suggested by our carnal nature." He argues instead that demons are "minds or spirits endued with sense and intellect."[74] Lorenzo Scupoli's *The Spiritual Combat* (1589) became a classic manual of spiritual warfare for Roman Catholic and Orthodox communities, just as William Gurnall's *The Christian in Complete Armour* (1655) became for Puritan readers.[75] More recently, writers in spirituality and spiritual direction such as Kenneth Leech, Gerald May, and Richard Lovelace have affirmed the reality of the demonic and the need to face this reality with spiritual maturity.[76] Guides for spiritual warfare have become especially popular among Evangelical Protestants in recent years.[77] Simply put, the Christian tradition has nearly universally affirmed some kind of belief in malevolent spiritual powers.

While biblical scholars and theologians wrestle with the existence of the demonic on one level, the fields of psychiatry, clinical psychology, anthropology, and pastoral counseling deal with the *perception* of demonic experience day after day. And while some therapists doggedly continue to deny the existence of the demonic, some are beginning to admit that, along with the recognition of human factors involved in demonic experience, there may be external independent environmental constraints shaping the character of a given client's experience.[78] (In other words, they might believe that demons exist.)

A philosophical step toward understanding the demonic may be taken by examining the issue in light of our broad view of experience. First, remember that in the broad view of experience, reality is not primarily about thingness, a kind of *form* present in a kind of *matter*. Rather, reality is about Tendencies of Quality and Force that become manifest. Thus, for example, we can speak of the *reality* of an "atmosphere" of conflict or hatred in a gathering of people. You know when that atmosphere is in the room. One might even speak of this atmosphere "controlling" the gathering. The patterns are simply *there*, a perceivable tendency with force and quality, present and influential within the experience of the group.

If, then, there are such things as *spiritual* beings that do not manifest in a bodily form (or at least do not do this often), these beings could, nonetheless, be perceived by virtue of the patterns of thoughts and feelings arising within our experience (conscious or unconscious), apart from any prior activity of our exterior sensations. Thus just as an atmosphere (atmosphere, wind, breath, spirit?) of hatred might be perceived as dominating a gathering, so also we might speak of a *demonic* "spirit" of hatred having influence in the meeting. Just as we can think of the Holy Spirit as a force doing work in the midst of human experience, so too good or evil spirits might be comprehended as forces, entities that operate habitually in recognizable ways in the experience of individuals, groups, or in society as a whole.[79]

Yet we must, in keeping with the biblical and historical evidence, acknowledge that these beings or experiences—these recognizable patterns of activity and sources of recognizable effect within human experience—have a certain degree of *autonomy*. The spirit of hatred has (or takes on) a "life of its own."[80] The world of the demonic appears to be something we know little about, yet it confronts us repeatedly. There is danger in seeing a demon behind every bush. There is another danger in beating around the bush when the demon is there.

The subjection of the Devil(s). While we must be cautious in developing a comprehensive characterization of the angelic and demonic, we may suspect that the range of demonic influence in terms of the breadth of human experience is actually quite wide.[81] With regard to our *embodied existence*, it appears that the demonic has the freedom to influence the presence of disease in some people. Thus Jesus heals a "woman with a spirit that had crippled her for eighteen years" (Luke 13:11) and a man who "could not talk because he had a demon in him" (Matthew 9:32 NCV). The relationship between disease and demonic influence is mentioned frequently in the New Testament.[82] An interesting case of spiritual evil and embodiment is found in 1 Corinthians 7, where Paul gives advice to the church of Corinth concerning sexual relations. He encourages couples, saying, "Do not deprive one another except perhaps by agreement for a set time, to devote yourselves to prayer, and then come together again, so that Satan may not tempt you because of your lack of self-control" (1 Corinthians 7:5). Paul, in his wisdom, is aware that couples can unwittingly find themselves on dangerous ground while pursuing a spiritual life. He probably encountered devout couples who wanted to serve the Lord and decided to separate themselves from sexual activity in order to give themselves entirely to spiritual pursuits. In the process of following their spiritual pursuits, however, Paul watched people become distracted or even shipwrecked in their faith due to the influence of sexual temptations. Indeed, Paul saw that normal physiological and emotional sexual urges, left unattended, could easily be exploited by Satan to lead believers into trouble.

With regard to the *operational systems* of human experience, we find the work of the enemy on all fronts. With regard to the cognitive system, Satan is described as "the deceiver" and the "father of lies" (Revelation 12:9; John 8:44). The demonic fosters false teachings (1 John 1–3; 2 John 7) and blinds unbelievers from recognizing the truth (2 Corinthians 4:4).[83] With regard to the affective system, Ephesians 4:26–27 speaks of putting anger to bed readily lest one "make room for the devil." If anger is allowed to sit and fester, the enemy will often suggest thoughts, images, and feelings that incline us away from the heart of God. Church leaders are to be chosen wisely and not from among the newly converted, or else a leader "may be puffed up with conceit and fall into the condemnation of the devil" (1 Timothy 3:6).[84] With regard to our volitions, Satan is called the "tempter." The devil tempts Jesus to make choices against God (Matthew 4:1–11) and the devil tempts us (1 Thessalonians 3:5), leading us from pure devotion to Christ (2 Corinthians 11:3).

Satan is active also in the full range of human relationships. With regard to our relationship to the self, Satan is called "the accuser" and he who "accuses them day and night before our God" (Revelation 12:10). It is the demonic that brings a person to such a state of disintegration that he would live among the tombs habitually performing acts of self-mutilation (Mark 5:1–13; see also Matthew 17:14–18). With regard to relationships with others, Satan is the one who incites divisions in the body of believers (Romans 16:17–20). In 2 Corinthians 2, Paul expresses his forgiveness for a man who had grieved the church at Corinth and was subsequently punished. Paul encourages the church to reaffirm their love for this man as well: "What I have forgiven, if I have forgiven anything, has been for your sake in the presence of Christ. And we do this so that we may not be outwitted by Satan; for we are not ignorant of his designs" (2 Corinthians 2:10–11). Paul was aware that when reconciliation between brothers and sisters in the body is left incomplete, it leaves open a door for gossip, slander, or bad feelings to spread among the body, leading to the decay of the gospel witness. He saw this as a scheme of the enemy. In Revelation 2:10 the church of Smyrna is warned that "the devil is about to throw some of you into prison." Here we see the larger social dimension of the work of Satan, which apparently has some influence over larger social forces such as the Roman officials. Similarly we can think in terms of evil spiritual powers influencing not only individual experience, but also corporate entities. It is in this manner of the social dimension of human experience that we often speak of "principalities and powers" or of "territorial spirits." Theologian Walter Wink writes,

> We in the West are so individualistic that we have ceased to regard corporate entities as anything more than the mere aggregates of their parts. But an institution is more than the sum of its visible parts. It has a momentum and trajectory through time and an entire set of unspoken values and goals. It replicates itself by selecting people compatible with its qualities. An institution can even impose on people behaviors that they would not freely choose. It is not a mere personification. It is an actual palpable force. Our incapacity to recognize the spirituality of institutions has left us tinkering with their parts while ignoring their essence.[85]

Interestingly, in a section of Mark's Gospel devoted to showing the breadth of Jesus's authority, we find Jesus *rebuking* the sea (Mark 4:35–41). This is the same action Jesus takes with the demons, and the language of the passage ushers the reader back to the battles of God with the sea in the Old Testament. In the description of the new heaven and the new earth, immediately following the destruction of death and Hades in Revelation 21:1, we simply find that "the sea was no more." Perhaps we find here hints of the demonic influence over nature. Finally, with regard to our relationship with God, the demonic is simply referred to as a spirit of Antichrist (1 John 4:3; 2 John 7). Through deception, false doctrine, temptation, accusation, oppression, and physical destruction, the enemy draws humanity further and further from identification with the person and life of the Creator, the Redeemer, and the renewing Holy Spirit.

Now take a *third* look at figure 5.1. This time look at it as a summary of the personal and corporate targets and vehicles of evil spiritual powers. How does Satan introduce

false thinking into the church? How have you seen patterns of feeling (fear, anger, envy . . .) perpetuated by a force that appears beyond the circumstances themselves? Where have you seen the demonic behind tragic patterns of un-Awareness, mis-Understanding, in-Action, or dis-Integration? How do spiritual enemies work to promote division and alienation between self and self, self and others, self and nature, self and the spiritual world, self and God? Think of this at the more shallow levels of human experience. Then think of this at the deeper levels of experience.

While we are wise not to place undue attention on the demonic, nevertheless, it would appear that acknowledging the influences of the demonic is essential for an adequate understanding of the tragedy (and the restoration) of human experience. As Dumitru Staniloae writes, "Evil manifests proportions and powers that cannot be explained by human freedom alone."[86] The serpent was present in the garden of Eden. Cosmic battle was present in the events experienced by the writers of the Old Testament. Jesus fought with the demonic spirits and won. And in Revelation 20:2 we hear that an angel "seized the dragon, that ancient serpent, who is the Devil and Satan, and bound him." From start to finish, human experience is somehow enmeshed not only with personal and social sin, but in a battle of cosmic proportions.

Conclusions

We have seen not only the greatness of human experience, but also how that greatness has been marred by tragedy. We have seen both the grandeur and the misery of human experience. Some of the tragedy is due to our own sinful choices. We choose to live separately from God and we experience alienation from God, ourselves, others, and the earth. Some of the tragedy is "original," passed on from parent to child through whatever complex of bio-psychosocial factors that communicate tendencies from one generation to the next. Some of

Through the dis-membering caused by the wars of the *world*, the dis-eases cased by the *flesh*, or the dys-function of unresolved anger (room made for the *devil*, see Ephesians 4), we catch glimpses of the tragedy of human experience.

our tragedy is inflicted on us and formed within us by means of the social structures that surround us. We are the victims of, and the participants in, corporate selves that, to a greater or lesser degree, express the same greatness and distortions as do individuals. Some of the tragedy of human experience is due to the influence of other malevolent powers or beings bent on doing harm to God and his creation.[87] We are alienated from God, enemies of ourselves, excluded by others, and attacked by demons. Even

> We are alienated from God, enemies of ourselves, excluded by others and attacked by demons.

nature itself is against us at times. Humankind is still great. Don't forget this. Even in the worst of situations, the image of God in humans still can be seen. Nevertheless, all these factors put together make human experience tragic indeed.

The Restoration of Human Experience

We have seen that human experience exhibits both a great side and a tragic side. But is there more? Specifically, is any change wrought in the very character of human experience as a consequence of the life, death,

and resurrection of Jesus? Or from the outpouring of the Holy Spirit on God's people? On the one hand, it would seem that humans "as such" are still humans before and after Christ's appearance. Humans, as humans, express both the greatness and the tragedy that characterizes human experience now, just as before the Incarnation. The coming of Christ did not automatically introduce some new dimension to human experience, such that people now naturally love others or the like. Yet there is *something* different, some new element brought to human experience through the events of the Christian faith. The coming of Christ introduced a new *possibility* to human experience, which for some becomes a new *reality*. In sum,

> *God has acted, especially through Jesus Christ and the Holy Spirit, to bring to human experience both the hope and the reality of a full restoration of life.*

Religious hope is characteristic of human experience. Human experience, *as human*, involves a radical confrontation with hope, a hope perceived incipiently within human experience, grounded in the history of God's acts in this world (and especially in Christ), and touched by the Holy Spirit who draws us to God. Some perceive this hope only as the vague possibility of improvement, of a change for the better.

For Christians, however, transformation is not merely a possibility but an experienced reality, a full **restoration** of every aspect of human experience. We will examine the content of that hope in the remainder of this chapter. We shall see how this hope becomes a part of the experience of the Christian more fully in the remainder of the book.

Human Experience and the Experience of Hope

In order to understand the effect of the gospel on human experience, we must begin by considering the nature of **hope**. Hope exists within a context of possibilities. Human beings live in a world of *possibilities*.[88] News is newsworthy because it is viewed in the context of what else may have happened (the ordinary). Human judgments are made in the context of reviewing alternative scenarios. Similarly, we feel anger in the context of a host of other feelings that we might experience in a given situation. The nature and range of one's perceived possibilities shape the character of human experience for a given individual. The child growing up in an inner-city ghetto or in an adobe-and-tin barrio perceives a very different range of life possibilities than the child of upwardly mobile suburban culture.

Hope arises when one possibility offers the potential of greater *satisfaction*.[89] A satisfaction brings together various elements into integration. A mocha integrates my interests in sweet, hot, bitter, rich smells, and so forth. For this reason, mocha is more satisfying to me than other beverages. We can speak of concepts that are intellectually satisfying (integrating a number of ideas together into a coherent whole) or events that are emotionally satisfying (containing all the nuances of affective experience desired in a given encounter). We can speak of trivial satisfactions (my love for mochas) and deep satisfactions (my love for my spouse). Deep satisfactions integrate worldviews, core emotional concerns, and basic lifestyles. *Religious* satisfaction is when the integra-

tion addresses the level of relationship with Almighty God.

Satisfactions are inherently partial. The fact of the matter is that we are all dissatisfied to one extent or another. Our drinks are too expensive, our theories don't explain it all, our spouses get up on the wrong side of the bed, our God-image doesn't match our deepest experience, and so on. And here is where *hope* is born. Ordinary hopes, like my hope for a better hot drink, anticipate greater levels of integrative satisfaction regarding the ordinary matters of life. *Religious* hopes, as elements of human experience, anticipate, in the context of the possibilities of life, the meaningful synthesis of all of human experience, a comprehension of the ultimate meaning and purpose of life (yet a synthesis that is, at the same time, not *too* integrated so that the ambiguity of experience is distorted).

Christians often write about a religious hope born of our fundamental dissatisfaction outside of living relationship with God. Augustine proclaims that "our heart is restless until it rests in you."[90] Philosopher and scientist Blaise Pascal (1623–62) speaks of humans as having a God-shaped vacuum in our hearts that can only be filled by God.[91] Bernard Lonergan writes of a "pure desire to know" that anticipates its fulfillment in the knowledge of God. Theologian Paul Tillich (1886–1965) speaks of God as the fulfillment of our "Ultimate Concern." Through our encounter with beauty, with world design, with time itself, there is something of an implicit sense of hope for something more, a Greatest Satisfaction, an Ultimate Concern, a Supreme Truth. Thus the apostle Paul's speech on Mars Hill declares that God made humans so that "they would search for God and perhaps grope for him and find him" (Acts 17:27). However vaguely experienced, humans appear to have an incipient hope for religious satisfaction—even if this hope arises in the context of our profound dissatisfaction with life. It is within the context of incipient hope that Christ appears, and thus human implicit hope interacts with the historical confrontation of hope presented in the Christian gospel.

The Christian Story: A Story of the World's Radical Confrontation with the Hope of Restoration

The acts of God in history, and especially in Christ, come to us, whether through the events themselves or through their proclamation in the Christian gospel, as a radical confrontation with hope. God, through these acts and their proclamation, offers the possibility of the complete restoration of human experience. When the creator of the universe comes to earth and walks among us—teaching us a new restored kind of life, dying for us, rising from the dead, and pouring out the Spirit of God on us—we are forced to respond, one way or the other. The coming of Christ is the turning point in human history.

One way of looking at the story of the Christian scriptures as a whole is to see it as the story of the world's radical confrontation with the hope of restoration. Greatness, tragedy, and hope weave their way through the scriptures like an intricate tapestry. We began with the story of Adam and Eve to account for human greatness and tragedy; we find in the same story our first reference to restoration, a vague promise regarding Eve's offspring (spoken to the serpent) that "he will strike your head, and you will strike his heel" (Genesis 3:15). Likewise in Genesis 9, we find God providing hope through the symbol of the rainbow, a sign of God's enduring commitment to humankind. Similar promises are given to Abraham and his offspring throughout the rest of the book of Genesis. The hope of restoration, then, winds its way through the Old Testament in a series of deliverances, callings, failings, and further promises. The acts of God and the promises of God mutually interpret one another throughout history. The act of the parting of the waters is interpreted repeatedly as a sign of God's promise of restoration. God's act of bringing a remnant of Israel back from exile is seen as a state-ment of God's intention to restore humanity and to use Israel (a light to the nations) to accomplish this. Walter Brueggemann summarizes this aspect of Old Testament theology as follows:

> At the culmination of Israel's portrayal of reality is a certitude and a vision of newness, a full restoration to well-being that runs beyond any old well-being. This culmination in well-being, assured by the resolve of Yahweh, is articulated in the conclusion of most psalms of complaint and in prophetic promises that eventuate in messianic and apocalyptic expectations. Israel's speech witnesses to *profound hope*, based in the promise-maker and promise-keeper for whom all things are possible.
>
> Israel refuses to accept that any context of nullity—exile, death, chaos—is a permanent conclusion to reality. Israel, in such circumstances, articulated hope rooted, not in any discernible signs in the circumstance, but in the character of Yahweh (based on old experience), who was not a prisoner of circumstance but was able to override circumstance in order to implement promises. This hope is not incidental in Israel's life; it is a bedrock, identity-giving conviction, nurtured in nullity, that Yahweh's good intentions have not and will not be defeated. As a consequence, complainers anticipate well-being and praise. Israel awaits homecoming, the dead look to new life, creation expects reordering.[92]

As Brueggemann mentioned, Israel's hope in Yahweh eventuated "in messianic and apocalyptic expectations." While a remnant of Israel had returned to their homeland from exile in 538 BC, their hopes were not fulfilled. They were a much-reduced people, ruled by governments not their own. The Hasmonean revolt and the ensuing struggles with Roman oversight of Israel became the sociopolitical soil within which apocalyptic and messianic expectations flowered. According to Jewish hope, God's covenant partnership was to be expressed through God's people leading the world into a government of righteousness. The tragedy of brokenness with God would be wiped away and God's people would serve God at the temple and would become the light to the nations that God promised. This was both a religious and a political hope. Apocalyptic hope was not always articulate, pointing vaguely to portents and powers acknowledged to be signs of the promised fulfillment. All were agreed that the satisfaction or fulfillment of Israel's hope would be brought about by the sovereign act of God. Some, however, thought God might use Jewish rebellion in this restoration. At times all these hopes were placed on the shoulders of one or another military leader. Thus the experience of Judaism at the time of Christ was deeply shaped by hopes of some sort. This must be understood clearly, for Jesus "can be understood only within a climate of intense eschatological expectation."[93]

Into this context of eschatological expectation Jesus entered, healing the sick, casting out demons, forgiving sins, and preaching about a new kingdom. The Christian faith proclaims that the one who lived in Galilee, who was "crucified under Pontius Pilate,"[94] has risen and now sits at the right hand of the Father. While scholars have at times driven a wedge between the "Jesus of history," the person who lived in Palestine around AD 30, and the "Christ of faith," the person believed in (or created?) by the apostles and their followers, historical evidence suggests that the division is not so wide as we might have thought.[95] Jesus's life and teachings indicated that he was the living fulfillment of Israel's hope for restoration. Every area of human tragedy was addressed in this man. Jesus lived a life without personal sin, rising above temptation and self-interest again and again to give himself for others. He taught a message that identified sin from within rather than from superficial externals. He recognized social as well as personal sin, for example, by confronting the power brokers of his day with their corporate responsibility for evil or by stretching the boundaries of cultural acceptability in order to honor women. He confronted evil spiritual powers as well, casting out demons and healing disease.

An exploration of the word *save* or *heal* (*sodzo, soteria*) in the Lukan writings reveals the breadth of Jesus's work. Restoring the balance between rich and poor, forgiving sins, healing bodies, delivering people from the oppression of evil spiritual powers or oppressive social expectations, bringing people into reconciliation with God—all of these were part of Jesus's saving ministry on earth, of the kingdom that Jesus was introducing into the world. Jesus's presence on earth was the bringing of hope to the world (and confronting people with that hope: "the kingdom of God is at hand") not only in his radical authority over the areas of human tragedy, but also in the sheer positive aesthetic vision he provided to those who met him.[96]

If the experience of the historical Jesus was a confrontation with the hope of restoration, the experience of the risen Lord and of the outpouring of the Holy Spirit was an experience of the reality of that restoration. The Gospels reveal the shattered hopes of the disciples after the death of Jesus. The news of the resurrection came as a shock to many, unbelievable to some. The account of Jesus's ascension in Acts indicates that Jesus's followers were still expecting Jesus to establish an earthly rule up until Jesus's ascension. It was not until they experienced the filling of the Holy Spirit in the Upper Room (Acts 2) that they comprehended the events of the past three years (and especially the past few weeks) as the turning point in history, as the making available the restoration of all that humankind was meant to be. Just as Moses ascended to Sinai and brought the law, so Jesus had ascended and brought the Spirit.

Those who witnessed something of the Pentecostal outpouring and heard Peter's first speech about the fulfillment of hope through the outpouring of the Spirit immediately recognized it as a confrontation with hope, an invitation to an entirely new kind of existence. "What shall we do?" they asked. The disciples' response to the ques-

Practicing Christian Spirituality

An Ignatian Contemplation

The best way to appreciate the beauty of Jesus and the full import of the Christian story is through a combination of academic study and prayerful reflection. Here is a sample of prayerful reflection, taken from a survey of spiritual exercises by author Anthony de Mello:[97] a passage from the Gospels (John 5:1–9) is followed by some directions to lead you in meditation. Read it through once and then go back and follow as you are led through the story.

> After this, there was a Jewish religious feast, and Jesus went to Jerusalem. There is in Jerusalem, by the Sheep Gate, a pool with five porches. In the Hebrew language it is called Bethesda. A large crowd of sick people were lying on the porches— the blind, the lame, the paralyzed. . . .
>
> (They were waiting for the water to move; for every now and then an angel of the Lord went down into the pool and stirred up the water. The first sick person to go down into the pool after the water was stirred up was made well from whatever disease he had).
>
> A man was there who had been sick for thirty-eight years. Jesus saw him lying there, and he knew that the man had been sick for such a long time; so he said to him, "Do you want to get well?" The sick man answered, "Sir, I don't have anybody here to put me in the pool when the water is stirred up; while I am trying to get in, somebody else gets there first."
>
> Jesus said to him, "Get up, pick up your mat, and walk." Immediately the man got well; he picked up his mat, and walked.

Now imagine the pool called Bethesda . . . the five porches . . . the pool . . . the surroundings . . . Take time out to imagine the whole setting as vividly as possible, to *compose yourself, seeing the place,* . . . . What kind of place is it? Clean or dirty? Large or small? . . . Notice the architecture . . . Notice the weather . . .

Having prepared the stage, let the whole scene come to life now: see the people near the pool. . . . How many people are there? What sort of people? . . . How are they dressed? . . . What are they doing? . . . What kind of illnesses are they suffering from? . . . What are they saying? . . . What are they doing? . . .

It is not enough for you to observe the whole scene from the outside, as if it were a movie on the screen. You must participate in it . . . What are you doing there? . . . Why have you come to this place? . . . What are your feelings as you survey the scene and watch these people? . . . What are you doing? . . . Do you speak to anyone? . . . To whom? . . .

Now notice the sick man that the gospel passage speaks about . . . Where in the crowd is he? . . . How is he dressed? . . . Is there anyone with him? . . . Walk up to him and speak with him . . . What do you say to him or what do you ask him? . . . What does he say in reply? . . . Spend some time getting as many details of his life and his person as possible . . . What sort of an impression does he make on you? . . . What are your feelings while you converse with him? . . .

As you are speaking with him you notice, out of the corner of your eye, that Jesus has entered this place . . . Watch all his actions and movements . . . Where does he go? How does he act? . . . What do you think he is feeling? . . .

He is now coming toward you and the sick man . . . What are you feeling now? . . . You step aside when you realize that he wants to talk to the sick man . . . What is Jesus saying to the man? . . . What does the man answer? . . . Listen to the

> whole dialogue—fill in the sketchy account of the gospel . . .
>
> Dwell especially on Jesus's question, Do you want to get well? . . . Now listen to Jesus's command as he tells the man to get up and walk . . . the first reaction of the man . . . his attempt to get up . . . the miracle! Notice the reactions of the man . . . notice Jesus's reactions . . . and your own . . .
>
> Jesus now turns to you . . . He engages you in conversation . . . Talk to him about the miracle that has just taken place . . .
>
> Is there any sickness that you are suffering from? . . . Physical, emotional, spiritual? Speak to Jesus about it . . . What does Jesus have to say? . . .
>
> Spend a while now in quiet prayer in the company of Jesus . . .

tion assumed that the gift of the Holy Spirit, the indwelling fulfillment of Israel's restoration, was available to all. And as with the coming of Jesus, we hear of the restoration of personal and social life and power over evil forces, which ensues from the coming of the Spirit (Acts 2:41–47). Through encounter with Jesus, the disciples were confronted with the hope of a new kind of existence. Through encounter with the Holy Spirit, they were confronted with the reality of that existence.[98]

From this point on, the apostles saw the people of God—those who have the Spirit of God—as the new living embodiment of Jesus (the body of Christ), acting toward the world as a living example of the hoped-for restoration, a symbol or icon of what might be. However partially this was realized, the church was to be the restoration of Israel's calling, the new Israel, the new Jerusalem, the bride of Christ. Just as Israel was to be a light to the nations, so now the Spirit-empowered Christian community was to be the light of the world, an aroma of Christ, the salt of the earth, the leaven of God into the world. And the proclamation of the gospel was the vehicle for bringing the news about this turning point in history and the confrontation of hope that follows from that news. Thus the church as the living Word of the Spirit and the gospel as the proclaimed Word of the Spirit become the means by which the confrontation with hope initiated in Jesus is communicated throughout space and time.

The early leaders of the Christian communities were forced to come to grips with the meaning of the man many of them had known in person but now knew as a risen Lord and empowering Spirit. Likewise, they re-visioned the meaning of human experience in light of this Christ-man. As Walter Lowe expresses, "Beginning with what they had witnessed, the community reached back into their thought world, which was informed by both Judaism and Hellenism, in search of ways of understanding."[99] The results of their Spirit-inspired reflections are the New Testament and the earliest traditions of the Christian church. Drawing on Old Testament stories, Jewish tradition, Greco-Roman philosophical categories, and such, the writers of the New Testament compose a symphony of the meaning of the fundamental events of the Christian faith that weaves together a variety of motifs and melodies. New Testament scholar Joseph Fitzmyer summarizes the thought of the apostle Paul as if Paul gazes at the meaning of Christ from different angles, making use of a number of different images: justification, salvation, reconciliation, expiation, redemption, freedom, sanctification, transformation, new creation, and glorification.[100] Matthew sees Christ as the new Moses. The author of the book of Hebrews sees Christ in light of sacrificial practice. What differs are the metaphors and images used to re-present the meaning of Christ to others. What is constant is the conviction that in Christ and in the Spirit humankind is faced with the fulfillment

The Resurrected Christ, our confrontation with hope.

of the hopes of all history, the supreme satisfaction—the Almighty God.

The Character of the Restoration Hoped-For and Experienced

We have looked at human experience as an experience that involves hope. And we have seen that the Christian message comes to human experience as a radical confrontation with hope, the hope of restoration. Now we must take a closer look at the restoration itself, whether simply present in human experience as the hope of a better life or a living reality among those who experience the restoration through Christ and the Spirit. How is this restoration described by the Christian tradition? How has the history of theology and spirituality understood the meaning of the Christ-event for human experience?[101]

In *Against Heresies*, early-church father Irenaeus spoke of Jesus as **recapitulating** Adam's task in himself. Where Adam failed in the flesh, Jesus succeeds. Adam disobeyed at the branches of a tree, Jesus succeeds hanging on a tree. Adam's disobedience is canceled by Christ's obedience. As the human race fell into bondage through the hands of a virgin (Eve), so it was rescued

by a virgin (Mary). "He has therefore, in his work of recapitulation, summed up all things, both waging war against our enemy, and crushing him who had at the beginning led us away captives in Adam, and trampled upon his head. . . . And therefore does the Lord profess himself to be the Son of man, comprising in himself that original man out of whom the woman was fashioned, in order that, as our species went down to death through a vanquished man, so we may ascend to life again through a victorious one."[102]

Athanasius, bishop of Alexandria (300–373), argued for the victorious significance of Christ's becoming flesh in his *On the Incarnation*. The Incarnation, for Athanasius, not only grounds the believer's understanding of relationship with God, but also enables the believer to experience that relationship. Only the life and death of the God-man Jesus Christ was able to break the power of death, sin, and the devil and thus make life available to any who would follow after him in faith. Through his death and resurrection Christ has conquered the enemies of the human race: death, the devil, and sin. If new life is manifesting itself in the works of believers, it is a sign that Christ is no mere creature, but is the true deity, as the Holy Spirit is also deity.

Augustine speaks of the work of Christ in terms of a variety of roles. Through his earthly activity Christ is our *revealer and example*. In his inward devotion and total obedience he is our *reconciler*, making a sacrifice for sin as a priestly representative. Christ is our *redeemer*, who by undergoing an undeserved punishment discredits the forces of evil and ransoms humans from their solidarity in guilt. Christ plays an ecclesiastical and eschatological function as *pioneer* and *head* of a redeemed humanity.[103] Finally, Christ is the *source of love*. Augustine's works are replete with mention of love. We share as humans in the divine love that is characteristic of the Godhead itself.

Maximos the Confessor highlighted the cosmic dimensions of the Christ-event. He saw the universe in terms of a series of divisions: uncreated and created, intelligible and sensible, heaven and earth, paradise and inhabited world, and male and female. Human beings participate and are created to mediate between each of these divisions.[104] Sin, however, introduced a fundamental disorder into things, and thus human beings are not moved naturally toward unification but rather are inclined by passions toward things below, resulting in increasing fragmentation and division. Through Christ's life, death, resurrection, and ascension, each of the fundamental divisions of the universe are united (for example, Christ united heaven and earth by appearing to the disciples after his resurrection), and Christ makes possible the unification of the cosmos through the mediation of humankind.

Anselm of Canterbury, one of the originators of medieval scholastic philosophy (1033–1109) probes the logic of Christ's incarnation and death in his *Why God Became Man*. Anselm emphasizes sin as an offense to God's honor, an offense that God must address in order to be consistent in his character. The satisfaction for this offense must be proportionate to the guilt incurred; and since an offense to God is an infinite offense, a human being is incapable of adequately making reparation. Yet payment for such a penalty must come from a human in order to satisfy the offense. Thus it is necessary for payment to be made by the God-man. Jesus is this God-man, who in perfect obedience to God need not die himself, but rather lays down his life of his own will as a gift that is presented to the honor of God on our behalf.

Philosopher and theologian Peter Abelard (1079–1142), our final example from early Christian theological history, highlighted the exemplary function of Jesus's death on the cross. Jesus's death was the supreme example of the statement "No one has greater love than this, to lay down one's life for one's friends" (John 15:13). Contemporary theologian Bruce Demarest summarizes this aspect of Abelard's thought

as follows: "Abelard depicted Christ's death as providing compelling demonstration of God suffering with his creatures. The spectacle of Christ impaled on the cross frees people from fear of wrath, melts their stony hearts, and moves them to amend their lives. The sufferings of the innocent Christ stir sinners to love the One who demonstrated such love for them. In sum, people are saved by the power of divine love that compellingly elicits human love."[105]

Over the next millennium, the themes introduced by these and others would wind their way in and out of the Christian tradition's appropriation of the meaning of the Christ-event. The scriptures themselves present a tapestry of metaphors illumining the meaning of the mystery of the Christian faith, and the history of theology presents a similar tapestry in which the whole presents a clearer re-presentation of the meaning of Christ than any of its individual parts. Furthermore, as we learned with regard to our understandings of God, emphasizing one or another metaphor (in this case, metaphors of restoration) encourages the fostering of distinct forms of spirituality. Let us examine five aspects of the restoring work of Christ and see the spiritualities that are fostered.

DEMONSTRATED AND EMPOWERED A NEW KIND OF LIFE

Let each of you look not to your own interests, but to the interests of others. Let the same mind be in you that was in Christ Jesus, who, though he was in the form of God, did not regard equality with God as something to be exploited, but emptied himself, taking the form of a slave, being born in human likeness. And being found in human form, he humbled himself and became obedient to the point of death—even death on a cross. (Philippians 2:4–8)

By Jesus's self-emptying birth, life, death, resurrection, and ascension, and by the sending of the Spirit of Christ, humans have before them the model and the means of a new life. Jesus's humble birth provides

Franciscan Spiritual Mother Angela of Foligno's *Instructions*

There are three kinds of poverty that we should make our own.

The first poverty is the lack of temporal goods, which Christ practiced perfectly. Each of us ought to imitate him in this poverty, and perfectly, if we can. Those who cannot do so perfectly, either because they belong to the nobility or have a family, should at least have a sincere love for poverty and renounce affection for worldly belongings.

The second poverty is that of friends, which Christ experienced to such an extent that none of his friends, nor any of the people he was related to through his mother, could shield him from a single blow. Thus we too must be poor in terms of friends and any creatures which interfere with imitating Christ.

The third poverty of Christ was that he was poor in terms of his own self. Even though he was omnipotent, he willed to become weak so that we might imitate him—not by hiding power as he did, which we cannot do because we do not have his power, but by attentively considering and weeping over our defects, vileness, and misery.

Therefore, the soul seeking to do the will of the Beloved, which he showed us by the example of his poverty, should strive to be transformed into his poverty as perfectly as it can.[106]

an example of unassuming presence. His life was one of unconditional welcome to the least. Abelard was right: the vision of Jesus impaled on the cross is a compel-ling aesthetic vision of love, inspiring us to self-giving love. His resurrection gives both a hope and a metaphor of a new kind of life.

The spirituality that flows from Christ's example is a spirituality of **imitation**. From the encouragements in Ephrem the Syrian's (306–73) *Hymns on the Nativity*, Thomas á Kempis's famous *Imitation of Christ* (1441), and Adolph Harnack's *What Is Christianity?* (1900) to the recent interest in "what would Jesus do" (WWJD), relationship with God has been lived out with special attention to aesthetic mimesis: copying the thoughts, the lifestyle, the actions, the heart of Christ.

The Christ-event was not, however, simply an exhibit of an example of moral living. Especially through the resurrection and outpouring of the Spirit, a new kind of life is both inspired and empowered. Thus Paul proclaims that "the law might be fulfilled in us, who walk not according to the flesh but according to the Spirit" (Romans 8:4). Attending to the work of the resurrection and the Spirit fosters a spirituality that moves beyond *imitation of* the life of Christ to *sharing in* the life of Christ. "Such a life," asserts Vladimir Lossky, "in the unity of the body of Christ provides human beings with all the conditions necessary for the acquisition of the grace of the Holy Spirit, and thus for participation in the very life of the Holy Trinity, in that supreme perfection which is love."[107] The life of Christ is an influential moral example, and much, much more.

BATTLED VICTORIOUSLY OVER ALL ENEMY POWERS

And having disarmed the powers and authorities, he made a public spectacle of them, triumphing over them by the cross. (Colossians 2:15 NIV)

Christ not only modeled and empowered a new life for those who would follow him; he also defeated those powers that threatened the fulfillment of God's purposes on earth. This victory is present even in Jesus's earthly life (Matthew 12:22–30). It was shared by his followers during his lifetime (Luke 10:17–20) and after his resurrection (Acts 19:11–20). Acquired yet unfinished (see 1 Corinthians 15:20–26), this victory must be realized as Christians fight "in the strength of his power" against the forces of evil (Ephesians 6:10–17). Thus Christ's work is rightly to be understood as a conquering of sin, death, and the devil.[108]

The spirituality that flows from this approach to Christ's work is one of courageous *spiritual warfare*. Antony, in a speech to his fellow desert monks, proclaims, "We need, therefore, to fear God alone, holding them [demons] in contempt and fearing them not at all. Indeed, the more they do these things, let us all the more exert ourselves in the discipline that opposes them, for a great weapon against them is a just life and trust in God. . . . For they know the grace that has been given to the faithful for combat against them by the Savior, in his saying, *Behold, I have given you authority to tread upon serpents and scorpions, and over all the power of the enemy.*"[109]

A life of courageous spiritual warfare recognizes that at least some of the evils of this world (indeed, perhaps most of the evils) are not conditions to which Christians are obliged to be resigned. Rather, in the strength of the Lord's power, we stand up and fight. Whether these powers be demons of infirmity, strongholds of sin and shame, or worldviews and patterns upholding evil social structures, our job as inheritors of the victory of Christ is to take ground against the powers of darkness, rejoicing in the victory won by Christ through his death and resurrection.[110]

Paid the Penalty and Broke the Power of Sin

And every priest stands day after day at his service, offering again and again the same sacrifices that can never take away sins. But when Christ had offered for all time a single sacrifice for sins, "he sat down at the right hand of God," and since then has been waiting "until his enemies would be made a footstool for his feet." For by a single offering he has perfected for all time those who are sanctified. (Hebrews 10:11–14)

The motif of satisfaction and sacrifice is strong in scripture. God warns Adam in Genesis 2 that the consequence of disobedience would be death. And in Genesis 3, after Adam and Eve's disobedience, God finishes the "curse" by declaring that "by the sweat of your face you shall eat bread until you return to the ground, for out of it you were taken; you are dust, and to dust you shall return" (Genesis 3:19). In the very next chapter we find Cain and Abel making offerings. Later, an elaborate sacrificial system was developed to make atonement for people's sins so they would be forgiven (Leviticus 4). Jesus's death is interpreted in light of this sacrificial background. Thus Paul, perhaps drawing on a primitive Christian confession, speaks of Jesus, "whom God put forward as a sacrifice of atonement by his blood" (Romans 3:25). Jesus died on our behalf and in our place.[111] The penalty for sin has been paid.

The spirituality flowing from Christ's sacrificial work on the cross is a spirituality of trusting rest. Through the work of Christ, the Christian individual or community need not fear divine rejection. Relationship with God is lived not with a view to meriting God's favor, but rather *in light* of that favor expressed and accomplished through Christ. Thus Martin Luther, commenting on Galatians 2:20 ("And the life I now live in the flesh I live by faith in the Son of God, who loved me and gave himself for me"), rejoices: "Christ therefore in very deed is a lover of those who are in trouble or anguish, in sin and death, and such as lover as gave himself for us. . . . Read therefore with great vehemency these words, 'ME' and 'FOR ME,' and so inwardly practice with thyself that thou with a sure faith mayest conceive and print this 'ME' in thy heart, and apply it unto thyself, not doubting but that thou art of the number of those to whom this 'ME' belongeth."[112]

"The Cleansing Wave," a Hymn of Phoebe Palmer

I rise to walk in heav'ns own light
Above the world and sin
With heart made pure and garment
white
And Christ enthroned within.
The cleansing stream I see, I see!
I plunge and O it cleanseth me;
O praise the Lord it cleanseth me.
It cleanseth me, yes cleanseth
me.[113]

The Christian tradition speaks, however, not only of our rescue from the penalty of sin. It also speaks of our freedom over the power of sin. Paul writes, "We know that our old self was crucified with him so that the body of sin might be destroyed, and we might no longer be enslaved to sin" (Romans 6:6). The work of Christ loosened the hold of those habitual Tendencies to avoid or refuse the invitations of God, thereby initiating the possibility of living apart from the domination of sin. John Meyendorff writes of Jesus's resurrection, "For the Resurrection of Christ means indeed that death has ceased to be the controlling element of man's existence and that, therefore, man is also free from the slavery to sin."[114] Thanks to Jesus, we are given a means of obtaining not only a new relationship *with* God, but, through that relationship, a new life *in* God.

RECONCILED US TO GOD AND OTHERS

So if anyone is in Christ, there is a new creation: everything old has passed away; see, everything has become new! All this is from God, who reconciled us to himself through Christ, and has given us the ministry of reconciliation; that is, in Christ God was reconciling the world to himself, not counting their trespasses against them, and entrusting the message of reconciliation to us. So we are ambassadors for Christ, since God is making his appeal through us; we entreat you on behalf of Christ, be reconciled to God. For our sake he made him to be sin who knew no sin, so that in him we might become the righteousness of God. (2 Corinthians 5:17–21)

Another motif describing the effects of the work of Christ is that of **reconciliation**. In contrast to many world religions that pay special attention to precise gifts and rituals in attempts to conciliate the gods, the Christian religion proclaims a God who comes to earth and dies in order to reconcile himself with us. Thomas Oden writes, "Individuals do not become reconciled to God on their own initiative—rather they are being reconciled by God's own initiative to which they are being called to respond."[115] Karl Barth divides his entire theological enterprise into four categories: the doctrine of the Word of God, the doctrine of God, the doctrine of creation, and the doctrine of reconciliation. Reconciliation, for Barth, expresses the essence of the Christian gospel. The presupposition of this reconciliation is our covenant partnership with God. Reconciliation is the fulfillment of the broken covenant. Barth writes, "But this fulfillment of the covenant has the character of atonement. The concept speaks of the confirmation or restoration of a fellowship which did exist but had been threatened with disruption and dissolution."[116] And as with the other motifs presented above, the theme of reconciliation has ramifications for the life of the believer. Paul writes, "For if while we were enemies, we were reconciled to God through the death of his Son, much more surely, having been reconciled, will we be saved by his life" (Romans 5:10).

The theme of reconciliation—a very interpersonal metaphor—is of special interest for spirituality, as spirituality addresses the lived relationship between God and humans. Union with Christ is at the center of Christian mystical reflection. A spirituality of mystical union is rooted in an understanding of Christian restoration as reconciliation. The theme is prominent throughout the history of Christian spirituality not only in literature, but also in architecture, liturgy, and many other texts of Christian history. For example, Maximos the Confessor, in his *Mystagogia*, interprets the structure of the nave and sanctuary in the Orthodox Church—and the congregation's processions therein—in terms of the movement of the individual soul toward God.

Formed a New Cosmic and Social Order

God put this power to work in Christ when he raised him from the dead and seated him at his right hand in the heavenly places, far above all rule and authority and power and dominion, and above every name that is named, not only in this age but also in the age to come. And he has put all things under his feet and has made him the head over all things for the church, which is his body, the fullness of him who fills all in all. … So then you are no longer strangers and aliens, but you are citizens with the saints and also members of the household of God, built upon the foundation of the apostles and prophets, with Christ Jesus himself as the cornerstone. In him the whole structure is joined together and grows into a holy temple in the Lord; in whom you also are built together spiritually into a dwelling place for God. (Ephesians 1:20–23; 2:19–22)

Finally, the work of Christ stretches beyond individual human experience, establishing a completed expression of humanity through the church of Christ and ultimately through a reestablishing of the new heavens and the new earth. The Trinitarian, interpersonal God creates, by the outpouring of the Spirit, not only a new human, but a new humanity. Theologian Hans Küng writes of the earliest church, "This community realized more and more clearly that through faith in Jesus as the Messiah it was the *true* Israel, the *true* people of God. And as a consequence of the rejection of their message by the Gentiles, the disciples of Jesus realized more and more clearly that they were at the same time the *new* Israel, the *new* people of God: the new eschatological people of God."[117] Paul speaks of this community in terms of a baptism by the Spirit into the body of Christ (1 Corinthians 12:13). This charismatic and persecuted community established by the Spirit is described in the Apocalypse as a "holy city," the "new Jerusalem," a "bride adorned for her husband" (Revelation 21:2), a corporate unity fulfilling the purposes of the children of Abraham; not only worshiping God, but also *reigning* with him; fulfilling the call to dominion given to the first humans (Revelation 22:5). And furthermore, God's eschatological reordering initiated by Christ not only includes the human and social, but ultimately leads to a new order between heaven and earth, between the natural and the supernatural. The work of Christ is not just a work accomplished *for us*. It is also a work which *remakes the cosmos* into the fulfillment of God's original purposes.

The spirituality that flows from Christ and the Spirit's work of creating a new cosmic and social order is itself a reordered spirituality: a charismatic, communal, and sacramental spirituality. Kallistos Ware asserts that "salvation is *social* and *communal*, not isolated and individualistic."[118] This spirituality is charismatic, ordered by the leadership of the Spirit. It is communal, the embodiment of the diversity in unity characteristic of God. And it is sacramental, integrating the fullness of the faith using the materials of earth through the identity-signifying practices of church life. Christ and the Spirit have initiated a new community designed to fulfill the purposes of God here on earth and into eternity. A

John Ruusbroec's (1293–1381) *Spiritual Espousals*

"See, the bridegroom is coming. Go out to meet him" (Matthew 25:6). These words, written for us by St. Matthew the Evangelist, were spoken by Christ to his disciples and to all persons in the parable of the virgins. The Bridegroom is Christ and human nature is the bride, whom God created according to his own image and likeness. In the beginning he placed his bride in the noblest and most beautiful, the richest and most luxuriant place on earth, that is, in Paradise. He subordinated all other creatures to her, adorned her with grace, and gave her a commandment so that through obedience to it she might deserve to be made firm and steadfast with her Bridegroom in eternal faithfulness and so never fall into any adversity or any sin. But then came an evildoer, the enemy from hell, who in his jealousy assumed the form of a cunning serpent and deceived the woman. They both then deceived the man, in whom nature existed in its entirety. Thus did the enemy seduce human nature, God's bride, through deceitful counsel. Poor and wretched, she was banished to a strange land and was there captured and oppressed and beset by her enemies in such a way that it seemed that she would never be able to return to her homeland or attain reconciliation.

But when it seemed to God that the right time had come and he took pity on his beloved in her suffering, he sent his only-begotten Son to earth into a magnificent palace and a glorious temple, that is, into the body of the glorious Virgin Mary. There the Son wedded this bride, our nature, and united her with his own person through the purest blood of the noble Virgin. . . . Thus did Christ, our faithful Bridegroom, unite our nature with himself. He came to us in a strange land and taught us through a heavenly way of life and with perfect fidelity. He worked and struggled as our champion against our enemies, broke open the bars of our prison, won the struggle, vanquished our death through his own, redeemed us through his blood, freed us through his water in baptism, and made us rich through his sacraments and gifts, so that, as he says, we might "go out" with all virtues, "meet him" in the palace of glory, and enjoy him forever in eternity.[119]

charismatic, communal, and sacramental church prepares for this corporate design by "living into it" in the details of life here and now.

The restoration initiated by Christ has many facets. Jesus is our Reconciler, our Savior, our Sanctifier, our Healer, our Teacher, and much more. The restoration that Christ brings ushers us into a new kind of life—victory over sin and death, reconciliation with God and others, and an eternity of reigning with God. Figure 5.3 summarizes these images of restoration found in Christ and the spiritualities associated with them.

The Consequences of the Restoration

We have seen that the greatness of human experience—what it means to be in God's image and created as God's covenant partners—involves more than just humans being thinking creatures or being relational. The greatness of human experience is the whole of human experience itself brought into being by God in order that we may share that experience as enfleshed co-rulers and co-creators with God in the likeness of Christ, the supreme image of God. Our greatness is reflected in every

Figure 5.3
Images and Spiritualities of Restoration

The work of Christ	This leads to
1. Modeled a new kind of life	A spirituality of aesthetic imitation
Jesus demonstrated and modeled a life rightly ordered in every respect. The Spirit of Christ enables the believer to live this kind of life (Philippians 2:4–8).	
2. Achieved victory over enemy powers	A spirituality of courageous spiritual warfare
Christ defeated those powers that threatened fulfillment of God's purposes on earth (Colossians 2:15).	
3. Dealt with sin	A spirituality of trusting rest
Jesus's death paid the penalty for sin and, together with the work of the resurrection and the Spirit, broke the power of sin.	
4. Reconciled us to God and others	A spirituality of mystical union
Jesus's life, death, and resurrection brought together God and humanity.	
5. Formed a new cosmic/social order	A re-ordered spirituality: charismatic, communal, sacramental
Christ establishes a new social order (the church) and begins to set in place the proper relationships between natural and supernatural, earth and heaven—a new cosmic order.	

aspect of human experience: thoughts, feelings, relationships, embodiment, development, and the like. We have also seen that tragedy affects every area of human experience. Our habits of selfishness and our rejection of God become expressed in bias, prejudice, exclusion, self-hatred, violence, oppression, exploitation, and so on. Our relationships are dysfunctional; our thoughts are erroneous; our feelings are based on inappropriate concerns. What, then can we say about the restoration Christ brings? What does salvation mean? What can we hope for through Christ in terms of our model of human experience?

We have much to hope for indeed! Christ brings the hope, and the reality, of the restoration of every area of human experience. As Ware writes, "Salvation is nothing less than an all-embracing transformation of our humanness. To be saved is to share with all the fullness of human nature in the power, joy, and glory of the Lord."[120]

In terms of human *embodiment*, Christ the Healer, Christ the God-become-flesh brings the body back to its proper functioning. Dumitru Staniloae presents an Orthodox perspective of this reality: "If

it is true that Satan compromised the body and its human sensibility and the surface of the world that is perceptible to the senses, it is also true that Christ has reestablished the worth of the body and of the sensible world. In Christ the body and the senses have become what they ought to have been—means for apprehending the world in purity—while the world itself has become a place transparent of the presence of God."[121]

Likewise, each of the *operational systems* of human experience are objects of restoration. The Spirit of Truth reveals truth, convicts us of false bias and prejudice, and enlightens the perspective by which we understand what confronts us. The regenerating Spirit who enlightens the mind also enlivens the heart. Christian restoration thus involves not only the cognitive but the affective operations as well. The core concerns of communities and individuals are reoriented from self to God, and we have the possibility of deep compassion and full appreciation of life as it really is. Similarly, human volition is transformed from a stubborn self-will to a yielded will.

God invites each of the stages of human experience into the fullness of life. Rather than living in shallow frames of awareness due to fear or pride, the Spirit of God opens us to new habits of Being Aware, making possible new realms of Experiencing. As we are restored in Christ our Understanding and Judging are informed by the insight, the humility, and the logic of faith, as we are "transformed by the renewing of [our] minds" (Romans 12:2). Our Deciding and Acting are increasingly conducted according to the prudence, wisdom, and standards of the One who transcends all created things. We choose rightly, living the kind of life Christ would live in our bodies. Finally, as we "put on Christ," we begin to approach life itself increasingly from a God-oriented perspective. Our means and framework of Integrating reality take on a different character.

Each of our relationships are also affected (either in hope or reality) through

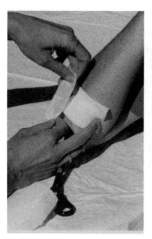

Healng the body; restoring creation(s); reconciling relationships;
we catch glimpses of the restoration of human experience.

the work of Christ. Salvation is a reconciliation with God, an at-one-ment brought about between God and human beings. Where there once was a distance between humans and God, now there is closeness at the root. Salvation also involves the renewal of our selves. Following the lead of spiritual writers like Bernard of Clairvaux or Johannes Tauler (d. 1361), we might speak of a shift from self-consciousness or self-referential experience to God-conscious or God-referential experience. When human experience returns from inappropriate to proper functioning and from substitute satisfactions to the fullness of Christ, our self-image and self-relationship are transformed in Christ. Salvation also brings wholeness (*shalom*) into relationships with others. This has implications for families, friendships, economics, and politics. Thus, for example, efforts for peace and justice in the world are not mere good works peripherally related to the Christian gospel. From the most incidental relationships to the largest social structures, Christ invites us to a new way of ordering our lives with others. Salvation is also a victory over enemy spiritual forces, a reordering of our relationship with the spiritual world. Finally, salvation involves an invitation to a reconnection with nature. "The creation waits with eager longing for the revealing of the children of God," Paul writes, "for the creation was

subjected to futility, not of its own will but by the will of the one who subjected it, in hope that the creation itself will be set free from its bondage to decay and will obtain the freedom of the glory of the children of God" (Romans 8:19–21). Paul affirms what we all know intuitively—"that the whole creation has been groaning in labor pains until now" (Romans 8:22)—but because of the work of the Life-giver, we now see the possibility of a new birth of the world, a new city and a new garden in which all are harmoniously related (and where righteousness reigns).

Turn now to figure 5.4. Here we see human experience in terms of the restoration possible through Christ. Use this chart as a guide for meditation. Reconsider each operational system, each stage of experience, each relationship, every developmental stage, every level of depth. Remember what you thought about as you reflected on the chart illustrating the tragedy of human experience. Recall specific examples. Now see these examples, one by one, as restored through Christ and the Spirit of God. What might it mean to have our self restored, to be re-Integrated with ourselves? What might it mean to see churches and cities feeling for others as Christ does, acting for others as Christ does, and so on?

All aspects of the fullness of human experience—from the shallowest thought to the deepest core concern, from the habits of a child to the fears of the elderly, from the secret sins of an individual to the shared visions of a nation—constitute the hope and reality of human experience in light of the restorative work of the gospel. How this restoration works will be explored in the chapters ahead.

FIGURE 5.4
The Restoration of Human Experience

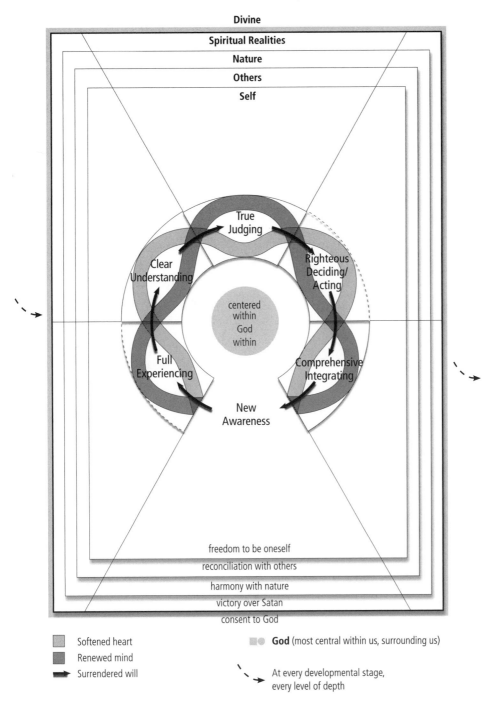

Divine
Spiritual Realities
Nature
Others
Self

True
Judging

Clear
Understanding

Righteous
Deciding/
Acting

centered
within
God
within

Full
Experiencing

Comprehensive
Integrating

New
Awareness

freedom to be oneself
reconciliation with others
harmony with nature
victory over Satan
consent to God

Softened heart
Renewed mind
Surrendered will

God (most central within us, surrounding us)

At every developmental stage,
every level of depth

Practicing Christian Spirituality

An Exercise in Self-Examination

One of the most valuable means of becoming aware of our own experience—its greatness, tragedies, and restoration—is a practice called *self-examination*: the act of prayerfully thinking over the events of one's day at the close of the day, often paying special attention to areas of life in need of improvement. Anglican divine William Law (1686–1761) writes of this practice, "This examination, therefore of ourselves every evening is . . . as necessary as a daily confession and repentance of our sins, because this daily repentance is of very little significancy and loses all its chief benefit unless it be a particular confession and repentance of the sins of that day." [122] Furthermore, daily self-examination can become a vehicle of recognizing not only our sins, but the fullness of our experience in God.

Take some time to be alone and think of your day. Think of yourself in the day. Just let the film of your day roll by. Look at your thoughts, your feelings, your relationships, your surface things, and your deep things. Just remember your day. Then ask yourself the following questions:

1. Where did I experience the greatness of human experience? In myself? In others? Where did I see evidence of that wonderful createdness, the expressions of God's image, the covenant partnership we have with God simply as human beings? How did I notice this? What was it like? (Relish your appreciation of that greatness in yourself or in others.)

2. Where did I experience the tragedy of human experience? In myself? In others? Where did I see evidence of the twistedness of human experience? Where did I see bias, prejudice, misguided emotion, wrong choices, or dysfunctional relationships? How did I respond to the signs of social evil (political, economic, or ecological disintegration) that surrounded me today? How did I identify any evil spiritual powers at work in my day? How was I confronted by these powers?

3. Where did I experience the restoration of human experience? Where did I sense the hope of something new? Where did I experience the reality of something new? Do I see any holy reconciliation, any renewal, any rebuilding? Where do I see hope today in my life? In the experience of others?

Self-examination is especially helpful when used in conjunction with the discipline of keeping a journal, for the journal can be used for recording progress in areas. You can note factors influencing transformation, write personal prayers, or copy special scriptures, songs, prayers, or quotes from books that can stimulate your reflection.

Self-examination need not be a depressing habit of morbid introspection. Rather it can be an honest and thankful review of the day, thanking God for victory and pressing on toward further growth in awareness of the richness of human experience. Remember, "He who began a good work in you will carry it on to completion until the day of Christ Jesus" (Philippians 1:6 NIV).

CHAPTER SUMMARY

1. While the *character* of human experience is illuminated through dialogue with philosophy and the human sciences, the *meaning* of human experience is expressed through dialogue with the resources of the Christian tradition. These resources present the meaning of human experience in terms of a threefold pattern: the greatness, the tragedy, and the restoration of human experience.

2. The greatness of human experience is found in our being created—we are distinct from God, dependent on God, and participants with the rest of the created order. It is also found in the fact that we are created in God's image; we share a mysterious likeness with God in operation and function, an image that sets us above other creatures and gives us a special share in relationship with God. The greatness of human experience is also found in our being ordained as covenant partners with God: we are chosen to share God's compassionate rule over all creation. As partner and image, humankind is called ultimately to share in the life and ministry of Christ, the supreme image of God. Every aspect of human experience is included in some way in this greatness.

3. The tragedy of human experience arises because of our covenant unfaithfulness and sin. Humans have universally chosen not to respond to God's initiatives of relationship, and this has altered the character of human experience itself. Once again, every dimension of human experience tends to a twistedness. The twistedness of human experience is not simply an individual matter either. Human experience is constantly plagued by evil social forces that act contrary to God, attack God's people and concerns, and attract people from the concerns of God. Furthermore, human experience is tragic because it is subject to evil spiritual powers. The drama of human existence is played out on a stage wherein demons dwell, subjecting human experience to tragedy.

4. The restoration of human experience brings to all human experience a hope. Some experience this hope implicitly simply as a vague hope for something better. For the Christian the hope of restoration is tangible because it is real. The restoration is communicated especially through the life and work of Jesus Christ and through the sending of the Spirit. This hoped-for and experienced restoration is understood by means of a number of metaphors, each of which fosters a distinct expression of spirituality. Just as every aspect of human experience is touched by greatness and tragedy, so too the restoration of human experience addresses every aspect of life, both corporate and individual.

LOOKING FURTHER

The first list presents a few classics of spirituality that explore Christian experience in terms similar to the categories presented in this chapter. Following this are lists of contemporary works. Most of the contemporary works listed below are more scholarly, presenting accounts of Christian experience that can help ground our understanding and practice of Christian spirituality.

Classics

Augustine's *Confessions* (originally published around 399) are a classic personal reflection on sin and salvation. I recommend the contemporary translation by Henry Chadwick (Oxford: Oxford University Press, 1991). Maximus the Confessor's (580–662) influence in the Eastern Church may be compared with that of Augustine in the West. Unfortunately, it is difficult to gain entry into his thought. A helpful collection of writings and introduction to Maximus, with sensitivity to issues of spirituality, can be found in *Maximus the Confessor*, trans. Andrew Louth, The Early Church Fathers (London: Routledge, 1996). See also *The Complete Works* by Hadewijch trans. Mother Columba Hart, Classics of Western Spirituality (Mahwah, NJ: Paulist Press, 1980)—the visions of this fourteenth-century beguine (lay religious) present many of the central themes of Christian experience in an imaginative genre—and Catherine of Siena's *The Dialogue*, trans. Suzanne Noffke (New York: Paulist Press, 1980). Book two of Walter Hilton's *The Scale of Perfection* trans. John P. H. Clark and Rosemary Dorward, Classics of Western Spirituality (New York: Paulist Press, 1991), a classic fourteenth-century treatise, explicitly treats human experience in terms of image, fall, and redemption. A version of the first "book" of *True Christianity: A Treatise On Sincere Repentance, True Faith, The Holy Walk of the True Christian* by Johann Arndt trans. Peter Erb, Classics of Western Spirituality (New York: Paulist Press, 1979); originally published in 1610), a Lutheran, Pietist treatise, is included in the Classics of Western Spirituality series; but in order to see Arndt's full treatment of the topic, it is helpful to read the later books. See the more inclusive volume published by General Council Publication House in 1910.

General

New Testament theologian N. T. Wright's works—including *The Climax of the Covenant*; *The New Testament and the People of God*; *Jesus and the Victory of God*; and *The Resurrection of the Son of God* (Philadelphia: Fortress, 1991, 1992, 1996, and 2003, respectively)—are building into a comprehensive retelling of the New Testament Christian message. Themes of image, covenant, tragedy, evil, and restoration wind their way throughout Wright's works. *Dynamics of Spiritual Life: An Evangelical Theology of Renewal* (Downers Grove, IL: InterVarsity Press, 1979) by Richard Lovelace is a classic Evangelical presentation of the foundations of Christian spirituality. It addresses both our view of God and our view of sin and redemption; it then explores the significance of these for our experience and practice of the spiritual life. Jesuit theologian Karl Rahner's understanding of the nature of Christian experience has been helpful to many students of Christian spirituality; see his *The Practice of Faith: A Handbook of Contemporary Spirituality*, ed. Karl Lehmann and Albert Raffelt (New York: Crossroad, 1992). *The Orthodox Way* (Crestwood, NY: St.

Vladimir's Seminary Press, 1995), a well-respected little book by Bishop Kallistos Ware, presents a concise summary of the Orthodox perspective on Christian experience.

On the Theme of Greatness

Stanley J. Grenz's book *The Social God and the Relational Self: A Trinitarian Theology of the Imago Dei* (Louisville: Westminster John Knox, 2001) incorporates biblical and historical theology with an exploration of postmodern philosophical categories in an effort to reconsider the theology of the image of God for today. *In the Image and Likeness of God* (Crestwood, NY: St. Vladimir's Seminary Press, 1974), a collection of essays by Vladimir Lossky, one of the most respected Orthodox scholars of the post–WW II generation, addresses the meaning of human experience.

On the Theme of Tragedy

In *Original Sin: Illuminating the Riddle*, New Studies in Biblical Theology (Grand Rapids: Eerdmans, 1997), Henri Blocher explores the neglected doctrine of original sin with a sensitivity to modern questions and ancient texts. Ronald J. Sider's chapter on structural sin in *Rich Christians in an Age of Hunger: Moving from Affluence to Generosity* 20th anniv. ed. (Nashville: Word, 1997) is a helpful introduction to the concept. Psychiatrist and best-selling author M. Scott Peck's *People of the Lie: The Hope for Healing Human Evil* (New York: Simon and Schuster, 1983) explores the problems of evil compatible with, but different than, traditional theological presentations. *Naming the Powers: The Language of Power in the New Testament*, by Walter Wink (Philadelphia: Fortress, 1984), and *God at War: The Bible and Spiritual Conflict* (Downers Grove, IL: InterVarsity Press, 1997), by Gregory A. Boyd, provide samples of different approaches to evil spiritual forces.

On the Theme of Restoration

Salvation in Christ: A Lutheran-Orthodox Dialogue, ed. John Meyendorff and Robert Tobias (Minneapolis: Augsburg, 1992) is just what it says it is—a dialogue between Orthodox and Lutherans around the idea of salvation. Bruce Demarest's *The Cross and Salvation: The Doctrine of Salvation* (Wheaton: Crossway, 1997), a summary of the doctrine of salvation, is written from the perspective of an Evangelical Protestant. The first chapters of Adolphe Tanquery's *The Spiritual Life: A Treatise on Ascetical and Mystical Theology* trans. Herman Branderis, 2nd and rev. ed. (Tournai, Belgium: Desclée, 1930) and Jordan Aumann's *Spiritual Theology* (London: Sheed and Ward, 1980), two manuals of traditional Catholic spirituality, present a clear outline of the theological framework within which Christian spirituality is understood.

Questions

1. Having read the chapter, how would you summarize the meaning of human experience from a Christian perspective?

2. We have looked at human experience through the lenses of philosophy and the human sciences and in dialogue with theology and the history of the church. What other disciplines might be used to illumine the nature of human experience? What might we see in doing so?

3. What do you think of Matthew Fox's challenge? Do you think the focus of today's culture needs to be redirected toward creation spirituality? How would you balance the emphases between original blessing and original sin today?

4. Review the condition of your community of faith in light of our model of human experience. At what points do you see the greatness shine brightest (in what operational systems, stages, relationships, and so on)? What aspects of community life seem to have the greatest predisposition toward the tragic? Where do you see God's hand of restoration the most?

5. To which of the five aspects of the restoration of Christ were you drawn the most? How would you describe your own personal spirituality with regard to your approach to the work of Christ?

6. How does your reading of this chapter affect the way in which you look at the future of the human race, both here on earth and in the eschaton? How does this, in turn, affect your lived spirituality?

The Divine-Human Relationship

6

OBJECTIVES

In this chapter you will begin to explore the core of Christian spirituality—how God and human beings relate to each other. First, you will learn something about what a relationship is; then you will learn what relationship with God might look like. You will learn some of the most basic features of divine-human relationship: the wide range of differences that characterize our relationship with God and the fundamental patterns common to all of us. Finally, you will get a chance to recount the history of your own relationship with God.

After reading this chapter you should be able to

- describe something of the character of relationships in general and explain how these characteristics apply to our understanding of relationship with God;
- distinguish how differences in human experience might naturally affect the character of an individual or community's relationship with God and give examples of how these differences affect individuals and communities in your own experience;
- recognize patterns of God's initiation, human response, and divine response in scripture, history, and life;
- summarize the character of God's initiative through revelation, grace, the gospel, and the Spirit, identifying examples of each;
- describe the nuances of perception of God, showing how these nuances are lived out in concrete experience;
- identify patterns of resistance and welcome, longing and contentment in the lives of individuals and communities;
- name key tendencies of divine response.

Christian spirituality explores the relationship between God and human beings. We now know something about each of the participants in this relationship. In chapters 3 and 5 we examined the nature of human experience: its operations, stages, and relationships, and its themes of greatness, tragedy, and hope of restoration. In chapter 4, and to some extent in chapter 5, we were introduced to the Christian God: the self-existent Trinity, the One described by so many metaphors, the One with whom we struggle, the Redeemer and Restorer. Now we can look at the divine-human relationship itself—not that we have been able to avoid exploring that relationship even as we spoke of each of the participants in Christian spirituality. For in speaking of God and humankind, we could not but speak of each as related and interrelated. We are unable to comprehend the Christian God apart from *Trinity* and apart from God as communicated *to us*. Likewise, we are unable to grasp human experience apart from human relatedness and apart from our situatedness in the history of God's salvation. So, in reality, we have learned a bit about divine-human relationships in order to understand both God and humans, and we will learn something of God and humans in the process of understanding the divine-human relationship. Our aim in this chapter is to use the insights gained about God and human beings in order to introduce Christian spirituality specifically *as relationship*. Here we will only cover the most basic dynamics of the divine-human relationship. More will come in the chapters to follow.

What Is a Relationship?

In order to understand relationship with God, we must first take a peek at the general notion of relationship in the context of our broad understanding of experience. What is a relationship, any relationship, an interpersonal relationship, relationship with God?

Any Relationship

In mathematics we say that −3 bears a particular relationship to 3. Because they share properties (they are both integers), they can be *coordinated* in terms of our understanding of integers. Thus we can say that −3 and 3 bear a similar relationship to 0. We cannot say such things about the relationship between −3 and a black dog. The simplest form of relationship is thus a capacity of terms or entities for coordination. But even this basic form of relationship is by no means unimportant. Some of the greatest scientific insights of the twentieth century were Albert Einstein's theories of relativity, wherein such terms as *where* and *when* are determined only by establishing the relationships of systems of coordination.

As we throw a pinch of baking soda in with vinegar, the atoms of sodium and ascetic acid are related not simply as coordinates on a common scale (though we can speak of one atom being larger than another). These atoms are also related by *interaction* with each other. Indeed chemists speak of different kinds of *bonds* as atoms interact and adapt to the presence of other atoms: ionic bonds, which involve the transfer of electrons from one atom to another, and covalent bonds, which involve the actual *sharing* of electrons between atoms.

As we move from atoms to molecules to compounds and so on, we are confronted with ever more complex and profound levels of coordination, interaction, and sharing. Some kinds of relationships are possible only within certain conditions. Thus, biologists speak of various forms of symbiotic relationships, wherein the life of one organism is dependent on another. Some species of lichen, for example, cannot even be identified apart from an explanation of the *mutuality* of the algae and fungus that form the context of the life of the lichen. Often, *symbols* are employed to facilitate shared experience, as with the dancing communication used by some species of bees. Coordination, interaction, adaptation, mutuality, sharing of experience, identity gained from context, symbolic communication—all of these are important aspects of relationship.[1]

Interpersonal Relationships

Interpersonal relationships exhibit the same characteristics described above, but they do so with even greater complexity, depth, and significance. Remember, a person is not simply a physical thing, but rather a complex of tendencies—embodiment, operations, stages, relationships, and more. An interpersonal relationship is the sharing of all of these.

To explore this we must add one piece of information to the model of human experience presented in chapter 3: *the process of human experience is also a process of knowing.* The development of human experience—from Being Aware, to Experiencing, to Understanding, to Judging, and so on—is a process of adapting our thoughts and life to that which confronts us. In common parlance we say we "know" something when our thoughts (and life) correspond or cohere in some fashion with that something. Furthermore, we often distinguish between *knowing about* something and *knowing* something. Thus I may speak of knowing about a famous personality—having read articles in magazines or having seen interviews on television. Yet it is quite a different matter to say that an individual or community knows that same person. Much more of human experience is involved in the latter.[2] It is within the context of knowing another that we live in interpersonal relationship. An *interpersonal relationship*, then, *is the mutual experience of another along with the shared knowledge of that experience.* I Experience something of your feelings. You Understand something of my Decision. I allow my habits to be shaped by the worldview of my community. We share something of life together, and in doing so, we know each other and have relationship.

We have explored this somewhat already in chapter 3, as the foundations

---

Relationship with God

Think about each of these, one by one.
- *relationship*—involving coordination, interaction, bonds, sharing, mutuality, symbols
- *corporate*—involving self-disclosure, symbolic expression, communication, comparison and imitation, common and shared experience, identity and roles
- *interpersonal*—involving interest and consent (quality), various shared spheres (type), stages of maturing, skills of "relationshipping," depth of sharedness (intimacy)

---

for corporate experience were presented (though it might be helpful to reread that section). We learned that human experience as *corporate*—as interrelated unity—involves self-disclosure, symbolic expression, communication, comparison and imitation, common and shared experience, and the development of identity and roles in the context of others. Interpersonal relationship—whether of individuals or of communities—involves all of these. But it is further developed by examining a few more features.

One significant aspect of interpersonal relationship, especially at the onset of the relationship, is *interest* or *consent.* Our interest in another draws us into relationship. Our consent to who they are deepens the relationship. Social psychologists speak of this in terms of the dynamics of "attraction" in interpersonal relationships. Object relations theorists speak of the strength of "projected" or "cathected" objects in relationship.[3] Jonathan Edwards speaks of relational movement in terms of "consent" or "dissent" in which the character of relationship is determined by the nature of the consent of one to the other.[4] Likewise, theologian Catherine Mowry LaCugna speaks of the divine persons as "irresistibly drawn to the other" or as "other oriented."[5] This factor of interest (a factor that functions at the junction between Integrating and Being Aware), in its varying degrees, combines with the types of responses enacted within encounters to produce the *quality* of a relationship. Thus the difference between a relationship of love or of hate is to be determined by examining this aspect of the relationship. Indeed, even distinctions between types of love are to be discerned through a careful exploration of interest and consent.

Just as interest or consent indicates the quality of interpersonal relationship, the spheres included in shared experience determine the *type* of relationship. This factor enables us to recognize the difference between a colleague, a drinking buddy, a sister in Christ, and a spouse. Furthermore, relationships shift in type as other dimensions of experience become mutually experienced. Thus a colleague at work (sharing only experiences related to the job) may gradually become an intimate friend, leading to marriage. The transition from one type of relationship to another often comes with a certain degree of awkwardness, owing to the expectations of the parties involved.

As with human experience in general, interpersonal relationships often develop in identifiable *stages*. Social psychologist Steve Duck divides friendship into a sequence that can be summarized as finding, encountering, growing, and changing. Philosopher John Macmurray speaks of a rhythm of "withdrawal and return" in interpersonal relationships.[6] We have already spoken of a pattern of God's initiation, our response, and God's response to us that is characteristic of relationship with God. All of these patterns and more can be identified in interpersonal relationships.

Furthermore, interpersonal relationships are navigated by the use of particular *skills*. Duck lists a few of these regarding human friendships: "assessing the other person's needs accurately; adopting appropriate styles of communication; indicating liking and interest by means of minute bodily activities, like eye movements and postural shifts; finding out how to satisfy personality needs; adjusting our behavior to the relationship 'tango' with the other person; selecting and revealing the right sorts of information or opinion in an inviting, encouraging way in the appropriate style and circumstances; building up trust; making suitable demands; and building up commitment."[7] While we might not think of the Trinitarian "processions" as the use of skills within the Trinity, we still find that there are particular patterns and habits of "relationshipping," as Duck calls it, whether we are talking of relationship between human beings or relationship with God.

Finally, the number, duration, intensity, and character of encounters produce the *depth* of a relationship. Here we distinguish between an acquaintance, a friend, and a close friend. *Intimacy* is perceived as a function of these kinds of factors. How often do we meet? for how long? How long have we known each other? What is shared together? How many different elements of experience do we share? At what levels of depth are our mutual interactions? How significant or important does the one figure in the other's Integrating? The answers to these questions reveal the depth of relationship. Theologian Donald L. Gelpi refers to the depth of the Trinitarian relationship by speaking of the divine persons' "perfect mutual self-donation."[8] All that is of the Father is open to the Son, which is revealed through the Spirit to us (John 16:15). We experience relationships in a variety of levels of depth.

Interpersonal relationship, then, is the activity of maintaining and developing one's experience and shared awareness of another. Understanding relationship for both individuals and communities enables us to explore, for example (1) how one is Aware of the other, (2) how the relationship is fostered, (3) what happens in the encounters and how the relationship is Experienced, (4) what Understandings and Judgments of the other are perceived, (5) what Actions characterize the mutual responses within the relationship, and (6) how the relationship functions to Integrate each person anew.

Relationship with God

Here and in the previous chapters, we have established that God and humans are indeed persons and that they have the capacity for understanding, for self-disclosure, for encounter, and for communication (*commune*-ication). We have also maintained that God is the One who reveals, that God has condescended to human capacities of understanding such that authentic relationship between God and humans is possible. Furthermore, we have seen that our understanding of each (God and human) depends somewhat on our understanding of the relationship between them both. Human persons cannot be comprehended apart from our situatedness in relationship with the divine Person. God cannot be understood except as *our* Creator, Savior, Comforter. Furthermore relationship with God is not only possible, it is actual.[9]

What Do We See When We Look at the Divine-Human Relationship?

Thus when we explore Christian spirituality, we are not exploring the possibilities of what might be; we are examining the realities of what is. In Christian spirituality we explore the relationship—the mutual sharing, the interest and consent, the intimacy, and so on—that characterize human-divine encounter. But what do we see when we look at the lived relationship between humans and God? This is a central question of Christian spirituality. In chapter 1, we learned that Christian spirituality reveals a wide range of diversity built on the foundation of a fundamental unity. In this chapter we will flesh out the structure of this diversity and unity. We will outline the basic elements here. The rest of the book will be given over to working out the dynamics (and the skills involved in their practice) in greater detail.

A Wide Range of Diversity

The first thing we notice when we begin to look at people's relationships with God is a wide range of diversity. In this sense, it is somewhat presumptuous even to speak of Christian *spirituality*. Rather we encounter *spiritualities*. It is out of attention to this diversity that many introductions to Christian spirituality have chosen to cover the topic from a historical, rather than a thematic, approach. It is important to keep the differences of relationship with God in mind right from the start. If we do not, the temptation to look at others' relationships with God through the lens of some cookie-cutter model without realizing it as just that—a *model* of a very complex reality—may be too great.

We have looked at the diversity of Christian spirituality in our introduction to the *forms* of Christian spirituality in chapter 1. We learned that because people differ, we can expect to find a variety of approaches to the actual cultivation and experience of relationship with God, a number of different models formulating teachings about the dynamics of relationship with God, and identifiable schools of thought related to the methods and content of the academic field of Christian spirituality. In this section we will explore those factors that shape the variety of actual lived spiritual practice found in individuals and communities.

Historical or Cultural Setting

Perhaps the most obvious aspect of our diversity is that of *historical or cultural setting*. It is this aspect that identifies the primary divisions for many surveys of Christian spirituality. Historical or cultural setting identifies the shared activities, values, aesthetics, and such that coalesce around groups of people in place and time, that are assimilated by individuals and groups raised within that place and time, and that are often embodied in particular institutions. Celtic spirituality, for example, originates from early medieval British Isles, and even when it is reappropriated in the present, it carries something of that character: a sense of harmony with the land, an orientation to the monastery. Puritan devotion derives from a different time and place and carries something of its time and place: a concern for detail, a sense of home and parish. Likewise, we can speak of late-medieval mysticism, of Ignatian spirituality, or of the Hesychast movement, each with their own activities, values, and institutions. Since we currently live in a transition of historical or cultural eras—between modernism and what follows after modernism—we can expect that some people will live out their relationships with God differently than others depending on their orientation within this particular transition (hence, discussions of postmodern spirituality).[10]

In a similar way we might speak of how our historical or cultural setting provides certain economic and social orientations to life that color our relationship with God. The spirituality of the wealthy and educated is interested in different aspects of God's character and shares a depth of worldview and core concern different from the spirituality of those who have no education or wealth. (Consider, for instance, how each might relate to suffering.) Even the skills of relationship are navigated differently by rich and poor. Thus, each will

"Couldn't I talk to a burning bush or something?"

approach relationship with God from her or his own socioeconomically shaped orientations.

Experiences

People also *experience* relationship with God in different ways. Just think—how have you experienced God? Do you know someone who experiences God differently? The range of spiritual experiences mentioned in the narratives, letters, and treatises of Christians throughout history is vast. New Testament scholar Luke Timothy Johnson, for example, explores the diversity of first-century spiritual experience in order to provide the context of the earliest Christians' understanding especially of baptism, speaking in tongues, and common meals.[11] John of the Cross, in his well-known *Ascent of Mount Carmel*, speaks of different experiences of God in terms of "apprehensions" of the intellect and memory. He differentiates between intellectual apprehensions received through exterior bodily senses (natural and supernatural), apprehensions received through interior bodily senses (natural meditations and supernatural visions), spiritual apprehensions (including visions, revelations, locutions, and spiritual feelings), and apprehensions of the memory (natural, supernatural, imaginative, and spiritual).[12] From a more "scientific" perspective, psychologist William James recounted narratives of a wide range of mystical experiences, both within and without the Christian faith in his lectures (delivered 1901–02) on the varieties of religious experience.[13] Psychologists since James have explored this diversity of experience with increasing rigor and differentiation: one team of researchers identifies sixty-one separate elements listed in three thousand solicited reports of religious experience.[14] And just as with individuals, so with corporate experiences: sociologists and anthropologists speak of corporate experience in terms of a "spectrum of ritual action."[15] Some people, however (even believing Christians) say that they have had no experience of God whatever. They do not know what these words might mean. Our experiences of relationship with God vary as much as our experiences of any other relationship.

Personality and Temperament

Because people are different, factors that affect *personality* will also affect relationship with God. Consequently, when we look at relationship with God, we see a diversity resulting from differences of personality. Author James Houston, for example, explores the experience of prayer in terms of the four classical personality divisions of sanguine, phlegmatic, choleric, and melancholy:

> A sanguine person becomes restless if he or she spends more than ten minutes alone in prayer. This is because sanguine types are very active. They generate enthusiasm, act spontaneously and find discipline very trying. They therefore find prayer in the company of other people much more easy than long hours spent on their own. Phlegmatic people, by contrast, are much more dependable, stable, and conservative. They find security in routine, and so find it easy to develop a discipline of prayer. Phlegmatics are faithful, but they are not usually creative or spontaneous in their worship. The choleric person tends to be logical and rational, lacking in feelings and in the quality of relating well to others. One choleric who struggled with prayer said, "My prayer life is all exegesis, like preparing a series of sermons!" Cholerics need plenty of space for their times with God, but they do not experience the ecstasy of others who pray. The melancholic are creative, persuasive and imaginative people who think reflectively and deeply. But they can also be touchy, or set themselves impossible standards. Their prayers are often creative and spontaneous, but they happen more intermittently.[16]

While temperament schemas are not always the most empirically grounded descriptions of human experience, they do provide a somewhat heuristic typology of the styles with which we interact with our environment. Models of personality difference and temperament have proven to be popular means of illustrating differences in our approach to relationship with God.[17]

Developmental Differences

Likewise, our experience of relationship with God will vary with our *developmental level*. Not only can we recognize movement toward maturity *as a Christian* (which we will discuss in chapters 7 and 8), but we can also acknowledge differences of Christian experience simply due to our developmental level *as persons and communities*. Generally, there are differences between a child's experience of God and the experience of a youth, adult, or senior.[18] We cannot normally expect as adults to have the kind of experience of God we had in our youth. For example, Elizabeth Liebert argues that the more nuanced aspects of Ignatian discernment require a developed affectivity, which in turn informs a mature conscience. She writes, "With the appearance of mature adult conscience, then, the possibility of discernment in its rich, inner self-directing sense at last becomes possible for directees themselves. This new possibility creates a watershed in terms of spiritual direction."[19] Similarly, certain key events of life (such as adolescence or midlife crisis) can stimulate spiritual interests and facilitate significant changes in one's experience of relationship with God. Likewise, the more stable mind of a mature community will interpret a move of God's Spirit differently than the mind of a community in the early stages of formation will.

Embodiment

People also differ with regard to *embodiment*. Consequently, our embodied experience, our sexuality, and the encultured gender roles associated with certain embodiments result in differences in our

The Dynamics of Diversity:
A Suggestive Outline for Individuals and Communities

Ask the following questions of yourself. If you are applying this to a community, substitute *we* for *I* and adapt the questions as needed. (Ask, for example, Where were we first formed? and What about our relationship with God did we inherit from our culture of formation?)

Initial Questions	Deeper Questions
Where did I grow up?	What about my relationship with God did I inherit from my culture of formation?
When was I born?	How does my relationship with God look different from that of those born ten, fifty, or two hundred years before me?
What experiences (if any) of God have I had?	How have these experiences shaped my own expectations of relationship with God?
What kind of person am I?	What kind of relationships do I look for or need from others? from God?
How old am I?	How does my relationship with God reflect the ways of living characteristic of others my age?
What do I look like? feel like?	How does my body, gender, and ethnicity shape my relationship with God?
With whom have I lived in the past? With whom do I live now?	What about my relationship with God have I inherited from family or close community? How do they affect the way I live out my relationship with God now?
How have I worshiped in the past? How do I worship now?	What does my association with religious tradition bring to my relationship with God?

relationship with God. Bodily existence significantly shapes our ways of perceiving and relating to our world. (Consider, for example, how we are changed by puberty, childbearing, or menopause.) A blind person will be predisposed to relate to the world differently than will a sighted person. Differences of embodied experience, in turn, influence one's experienced relationship with God. An adolescent male will normally approach God differently than will a woman going through menopause. Different kinds of activity, different ways of perceiving, different patterns of relating may be stimulated simply by differences in hormonal activity.

This is true of our embodied sexuality as well. As Wendy Wright writes, "Do men and women know God differently because they are differently embodied?' 'Yes, although one way of knowing should not be considered superior to the other.' My own experience of being wife and mother had given me intimations of divine life that were distinct from my husband's. Furthermore, it was not simply my biological experience as a woman that taught me about God. It was my gendered identity, my being a woman in the culture and time, and the subtle roles assigned to me that shaped my ways of knowing God."[20]

Natural embodied differences are accompanied by culturally created gender roles, those expectations concerning how people experience life and those assumptions concerning how life is to be lived. On the one hand, the identities and roles we play predispose us to a healthy diversity of relationship with God, just as our embodied differences do. Yet, this matter of culturally shaped differences with regard to gender is complicated, because at times cultural norms (such as those concerning wealth and poverty, ethnicity, class, acceptable physical appearance, and other areas) operate from an unconscious (or worse, a conscious) ignorance. Thus, to use the language of developmentalist Carol Gilligan, it could be said of much of Christendom that "implicitly adopting the male life as the norm, they have tried to fashion women out of masculine cloth."[21] And as with gender, so with ethnicity. Embodiment and cultural norms combine, facilitating both healthy and unhealthy predispositions in relationship with God.[22]

Family and Close Community

Another source of diversity in spirituality comes from our own settings within *family and close community*. As we mentioned in our discussion of the knowledge of God, our basic image of God arises in the context of the world in which we grow up as children. Hence, part of growing in relationship with God is acquiring images of God through family and close community and refining them through interaction with God's own revelation. Authors Ann and Barry Ulanov give us a picture of this process in the context of a psychological treatment of prayer:

> In prayer we must begin where we are, with the images of the divine that we project or find ourselves projecting onto the unknown. . . . Only then, after we have examined and recognized our introjections and projections for what they are, can we really hear another voice than our own. . . . One of the first tasks in prayer is to face that process openly, to notice what images we have of God and to welcome them into our awareness. . . . We may be shocked to find entering our prayer a picture of God as a nasty shopkeeper tallying up our faults in indelible ink. . . . God does match our image-making with a parallel creation, presenting Himself in images—as a servant, for example, the all powerful one emptying himself to come to us in a way that will not offend us and make us flee. . . . In the meeting of these two sources of imagery, the human and the divine, we experience our purgation—that sorting, breaking, abandoning and transforming of images in which we are led to confront being itself and are made

pliable enough to receive that being into ourselves.[23]

Different people have different family histories, and these histories will naturally show themselves in our different God-images. Comprehending the nature of relationship with God requires that we be sensitive to the diversity of God-images expressed by others and by ourselves.

Tradition

As history, culture, theology, and community coalesce, we identify differences of spirituality due to religious *tradition* or denomination. It does not take too long for those of us in the Christian world to realize that we who meet together over here approach relationship with God differently from those Christians over there. Methodist, Greek, Benedictine, Pentecostal, Jesuit traditions—all have different habits of prayer, community, and action. Recognizing and appreciating the diversity of Christian traditional expression is an important aspect of understanding Christian spirituality. We will speak of this more in chapter 10.[24]

We attend to the diversity of the divine-human relationship because each individual's relationship with God is sacred. It is a sin (perhaps the unforgivable sin of Mark 3:22–30?) for me to attribute to the devil what is born of the Spirit of God. Recognizing these differences protects us from expecting others' relationship with God to look like ours (or from condemning ourselves because ours does not look like theirs). For this reason it behooves us to gain a sensitivity to the wide range of experiences, perceptions, and expressions surrounding Christian spirituality. History, personality, sexuality, community—all these and more shape the variety of forms we see when we look at Christian spirituality. What do we see when we look at relationship with God? A wide range of diversity.

Fundamental Patterns of Relationship with God

But underneath that wide range of diversity one can detect forms, patterns, and ways of being that make Christian spirituality a *relationship* and that make it specifically the kind of relationship it is. Luke Timothy Johnson affirms this as he concludes his study of religious experience in earliest Christianity: "Despite the diversity within earliest Christianity, a diversity so obvious that it scarcely needs underscoring, the evidence also suggests that from the beginning a certain unity of experience and conviction was sufficient to distinguish this collection of people from others in the Mediterranean world and to provide the basis for its life, movement, change, and growth."[25] Just as one can observe stages, levels of depth, and other basic dynamics in human-to-human relationships and Trinitarian relations, so too we can observe similar patterns in the divine-human relationship that is Christian spirituality.[26] We introduced one basic pattern in our discussion of the covenant God: The Christian God—actively present, sovereign-responsive—is not distant from humankind but rather is *relationally* present to his creation. God **initiates** and offers relationship, we respond to God's invitations, and God responds to our response (initiation, response, response, or I-R-R). Let us explore this pattern further.

In any relationship, this structure is present: a self-communication of one, which demands a response of the other, to which the first responds. We pass by one another on the street. You look at me and offer greetings (I). I give my greetings and take the conversation further, asking about your health, or I choose not to take the conversation further (R). You respond to either of my choices (R). And the relationship grows from here. The Father sends the Son (I). The Son does what the Father initiates (R), and the Father glorifies the Son (R). Initiation, response, response. The pattern is paradigmatic for understanding God's ways with humanity. The covenant relationship of God with his people is a relationship offered by God and accepted (or rejected) by his people. Furthermore, God allows himself to be moved by our response, adjusting his relationship with us accordingly.

First, God initiates, invites, acts. God is the one who calls Abraham out of his homeland, rescues Israel from slavery, plants his people into the land of Canaan, sends the prophets to warn, sends his only Son, and offers the Spirit. Jesus heals and says, "Come and follow." The Spirit is given to the church and Peter cries, "Repent and be baptized." These are not just random acts of God's presence. They are invitations to a relationship. The task of humanity is to respond to the reality of this God, this active presence, this "I AM." Appropriate responses to God's invitation vary with the context: Abraham's response to God's call to covenant circumcision, the Hebrew slaves' response to God's call for the redeemed to obey the law, the listeners' response to God's call through Hosea for the return of God's beloved, Mary's response of faith to the angel's message, the believers' response to being led by the Spirit. And then there are not-so-appropriate responses. John Cassian writes, "Our situation is that we respond eagerly or in a laggardly manner to these opportunities made available by God to us."[27] In turn, God responds to our response: "If you circumcise, I will make you numerous. If you obey, I will bless your land. If you disobey, I will curse your land." When we "return," God will restore. "Our task is," writes Cassian, "laxly or zealously, to play a role which corresponds to His grace and our reward or our punishment will depend on whether we strove or neglected to be at one, attentive and obedient, with the kindly dispensation of His providence toward us."[28] Similarly, theologian Donald Bloesch asserts that God "alters his ways with his people in conjunction with their response to his gracious initiative," and Thomas Oden writes that "it is precisely because God is so unchanging in the eternal purpose of self-giving love that God is so

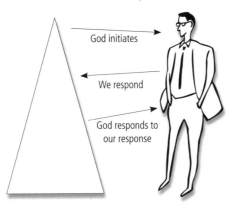

FIGURE **6.1**
A Basic Pattern of Divine-Human Relationship

God initiates

We respond

God responds to our response

attentively answerable, so free in responding to changing historical circumstances, and so versatile in personal response."[29] Initiation, response, response.

Patterns of Divine Initiation

God comes to us. God reveals himself to us. God invites us to relationship, initiates relationship. The Christian tradition also recognizes those times when we initiate relationship with God—such as Jesus's cry, "My God, why have you forsaken me?" (which we will explore later in our chapter on prayer). But more often the focus is on God, who draws us into communion. Let us explore a few of these aspects of God's initiation.

Revelation and self-disclosure. First, God's initiation involves revelation and self-disclosure. As we mentioned above, relationship is built on self-disclosure. And so it is in our relationship with God. The Triune God has made himself both knowable and known to us: God uncovers something of the divine nature such that we might be able to perceive God; God unveils not simply facts *about* God (although this is included), but something of the whole of the divine experience—a *self*-disclosure.

God appears as something that *presents itself* to human experience, functioning in some way as a force or object for human experience. God is present *as____*. God

is not a quality-less vacuum but rather reveals himself *as* something in this or that situation. God's presence is also a presence *to____*. Revelation is a mediation or disclosure of God that has the potential of affecting another who receives that revelation. Furthermore, God's presence is a presence *through____*. We become aware of God's presence by the means of the signs of God's presence, the means of grace. God manifests himself in a fashion that we can understand: presence *as*, *to*, and *through*.

Yet revelation is not simply divine self-display (although it includes this), but also interpersonal self-disclosure. God's revelation is given in the context of an active interest in relationship, a presence of love. John Ruusbroec writes in his *Spiritual Espousals* of a threefold "coming" (revelation) of God. Each coming invites a different response to the active, loving, presence of God:

> The first coming, namely, when God became a human being, lived humbly, and died out of love for us, is one which we should imitate exteriorly through the perfect practice of the virtues and interiorly through charity and genuine humility. The second coming, which is in the present and which takes place when Christ comes with his graces into every loving heart, is one which we should desire and pray for every day, so that we might persevere and progress in new virtues. The third coming, at the Judgment or at the hour of our death, is one which we should await with longing, confidence, and awe, so that we might be released from this present misery and enter the palace of glory.[30]

Revelation and self-disclosure speak of God's presence as a presence *through*. Just as you might learn something of my presence or character or activity through a footprint of mine, through my writings, through getting to know my children, or through a personal conversation, so we get to know God by the different signs of his presence. And the signs are many. The "word of the LORD" appeared to Abraham in a vision

focus

Biblical Portrait:
Hosea and the Divine-Human Relationship

"Therefore I am now going to allure her; I will lead her into the desert and speak tenderly to her. . . . There she will sing [or respond] as in the days of her youth, as in the day she came up out of Egypt." . . ."In that day I will respond," declares the LORD. . . ."I will plant her for myself in the land." (Hosea 2:14, 15, 21, 23 NIV)

The language is passionate. God will allure, he will speak tenderly, and he will woo his people, his bride, to himself. And God's beloved will respond to God's tender invitation as she did long ago. And God will respond in turn with blessing and restoration. This metaphor—the image of the passionate husband longing for his beloved—is the driving metaphor throughout the book of Hosea. The bulk of Hosea was probably written between 752 and 721 BC in Israel, the northern kingdom of the Hebrews. Israel was frequently tempted to establish her security by means of alliances with either of two superpowers, Egypt or Assyria. It was a time of religious corruption. The people of Israel worshiped Yahweh along with the other gods of the surrounding cultures. It was also a time of sexual promiscuity.

The book of Hosea, a collection of poetic prophecies, divides into two major parts: chapters 1–3 introduce Hosea and Gomer, Hosea's wayward spouse, along with the major themes of the book; chapters 4–14 present the prophetic message of warning and restoration. At the start of Hosea 1, Gomer, Hosea's "wife of whoredom," bears three children, and the name of each child symbolically speaks God's message of warning to the people who surrounded the couple (Hosea 1:1–9). In Hosea 3 we find God commanding Hosea a second

time to "love a woman who has a lover and is an adulteress" (v. 1). Hosea's family experience, then, forms the primary image through which his prophecies are presented. Hosea initiates relationship with Gomer, knowing that he faces the distinct possibility of an unfaithful response from his spouse.

Sandwiched between these stories of Hosea's family is a composite prophecy of judgment and restoration (Hosea 1:10–2:23). Hosea 2 begins with God's plea that his wife "put away her whoring" (v. 2). Otherwise, God will act toward his bride (Israel) with judgment. "I will have no pity," God declares (v. 4). Why? Because Israel has "played the whore. . . . For she said, 'I will go after my lovers'" (v. 5). God has initiated relationship with his beloved. Her response? Unfaithfulness. God's response to her response? Judgment—unless she puts away her adulterous ways. The same themes are repeated in verses 9–13. Then the theme shifts from judgment to hope. God will *allure* his beloved, will "bring her into the wilderness, and speak tenderly to her" (v. 14). Once again God will initiate relationship. This time, however, the response of the beloved is a response of consent, recalling her previous experience of love ("She shall respond as in the days of her youth," v. 15). And in response to her response of consent, God gives blessing (vv. 17–23).

This theme of passionate reciprocity reappears throughout the book of Hosea, much as the primary themes of a symphony reappear with slight variations. In Hosea 9:10–13, we see God as one who "found," who "saw" Israel, or Ephraim (these terms are used as symbols of

God's loving attention). But they "consecrated themselves to a thing of shame" (v. 10), "they have not listened" (v. 17). And in response God will "depart from them" (v. 12), will "drive them out of my house" (v. 15), and will "reject them" (v. 17).

Again, in Hosea 11 we read, "When Israel was a child, I loved him, and out of Egypt I called my son [here a parent-child image of relationship]. The more I called them, the more they went from me" (vv. 1–2). The presentation of God's care is especially tender in verses 3–4. But "they have refused to return to me" (v. 5). Here God's response is not dictated simply by Israel's rebellion. The heart of God "recoils within" (v. 8)

at the thought of giving up his beloved to utter destruction. God's own compassionate character gains the upper hand, and God's response is that of mercy (vv. 9–11). God's initial initiation to relationship is grounded in both our need and God's self-communication. God's response to us is a response both to our response and to the demands of his own character (see also Hosea 13:4–6). The book of Hosea graphically portrays relationship with God in terms of a mutual reciprocity. God initiates, we respond, and God responds to our response. This pattern is characteristic of the God who is sovereign yet personally involved in the well-being of his people.

(Genesis 15:1). The Lord descended on Mt. Sinai with lightning, fire, and thunder as he made contact with Moses and the Israelites (Exodus 19:18–19). The very firmament of the heavens points to the presence and activity of God; it "proclaims his handiwork" (Psalm 19:1). We look around us and we see evidence of God's presence on every side, such that "what can be known about God" by human persons as human "is plain to them" (Romans 1:19).

God dwelt with his people in the temple. God acted on behalf of his people through the monarchy. God spoke to his people through the prophets. And the prophets and poets and historians recorded God's acts and words in scripture—not simply as a record of God's revelation, but as part of the revelation itself. Jesus is the living Word of God. God's character is present through the life of Christ; God's purposes are present through the death of Christ; God's power is present through the resurrection of Christ. In every step, God discloses himself through Jesus to the world, inviting us into relationship.

God is disclosed not only as we look without, but also as we look within. God has set "eternity in the hearts of men"

(Ecclesiastes 3:11 NIV). "What the law requires is written on their hearts" (Romans 2:15). Our very searching and groping for God reflects the hand of the One who is the End of that very quest (Acts 17:26–27). As mentioned in our previous chapter, our very constitution in the image of God, with the capacity of communication (*commune*-ication) with God, is itself at least a hint of God's own invitation to relationship. Finally, God is present to us through his Spirit. "He abides with you," Jesus tells his disciples, "and he will be in you" (John 14:17).

Initiation and grace. God's presence to us is also his initiation of relationship with us. Thus God's *goodness* (referring to an attribute of God's character in himself) is inseparable from God's **grace** (referring to the character of God's relationship with human beings). Using the language of interpersonal psychology, we might speak of God's style of "relationshipping" as being characterized by grace. Thus, when we speak of God's presence *as*, in terms of the quality of God's initiation of relationship with humankind, we must begin by speaking of God's grace.[31]

God's initiation of relationship with us, as gracious, is not compelled. God's grace is his freely offered self-communication and invitation. Grace is ultimately rooted not in human capacity or incapacity but rather in the freely expressed love of God.[32] God's offer of relationship is also *unearned*. Paul writes that those who believe in Jesus Christ "are now justified by his [God's] grace as a gift" (Romans 3:24), and that "for the wages of sin is death, but the free gift of God is eternal life in Christ Jesus our Lord" (Romans 6:23). God's welcome is not determined by our religious performance. Rather it comes to us as an expression of God's unconditional love.

God's initiation of relationship is also an offer of God's *favor*. Unmerited favor—this is a common summary definition of grace. We speak about a judge who looks with favor on our case and we express gratitude for the judge's approving consideration offered on our behalf. We ask another, "Could you do me a favor?" and we solicit action from another on our behalf. Grace is God's attitude and action released on our behalf. Theologians speak of common grace (God's favorable preservation of humankind in general), of prevenient grace (God's enabling persons to respond to other expressions of God's offer of relationship), of saving grace (whereby God receives undeserving sinners into fellowship), and of operative and cooperative grace (God's favor expressed in our transformation both apart from and in harmony with our own exercise of freedom). Whatever the terminology, the point is that God is disposed with favor toward humans: God is actively present on their behalf to do for them what they are unable to do for themselves.

As favorable action toward another, God's grace is also *power*. It accomplishes something. It produces real and tangible effects. Grace involves God's receptive attitude toward sinners, but it also includes more. Grace attested the success of the apostles' mission (see Acts 6:8; 11:23; 14:3, 26; 18:27; 20:32). Grace empowers the transforming work of God, given

generously and making us new creatures (and a new society) in Christ (see Romans 12:6; 1 Corinthians 15:10; 2 Corinthians 4:15; 6:1; 8:1; 12:9).[33] The dual aspects of both pardon and power in the spirituality of grace are reflected in the lyrics to the famous hymn "Amazing Grace":

> Amazing grace! How sweet the
> sound
> That saved a wretch like me!
> I once was lost, but now am found;
> Was blind but now I see. . . .
> Through many dangers, toils, and
> snares,
> I have already come;
> 'Tis grace hath brought me safe thus
> far,
> And grace will lead me home.

Let us consider grace in terms of our working model of human experience. God initiates relationship by entering into my experience in some fashion (the stage of Experiencing). God's presence *to me* at a given point in time (Force) introduces a new dimension and perhaps new patterns or tendencies into my experience. By becoming present *to me*, God introduces a new way of orienting my experience, a new way of Integrating my experience. Every dimension of human experience, both individual and social, is thus potentially subject to God's welcoming and transforming grace, especially as new life spreads from one area of experience to another and from one person to another and back to God. This introduction is known as grace insofar as God enters my experience *as* freely self-giving and uncompelled, receiving me undeserved, accomplishing in or for me that which I cannot do for myself. It is *divine* grace when it is the expression of God's omnipotent goodness: favor and power from on high (Quality).[34]

The gospel. God's initiation of relationship is expressed by virtue of God's presence—*as* a free, actively involved, self-communicating, welcoming, transforming God. Our relationship with God is rooted in

God's grace. God's initiation of relationship as presence *to*_____ must be understood not only in light of a general account of human experience, but also in terms of the role of humanity as covenant partner with God, as participant in the restoration of the cosmos. As was made clear in the previous chapter, our place in history, indeed our very being, is not something we possess in a rigidly static way. Rather we are invited into ourselves; our being is defined by who we become. On the one hand we are creations of God, made in the image of God, with the mandate of covenant partnership hard-wired into our souls. Yet the living out of this covenant partnership is offered, not imposed.

Grace is free, unearned. But this does not make grace inexpensive. Rather it is costly indeed. German theologian Dietrich Bonhoeffer (1906–45), speaking of Jesus's invitation to Peter to follow him, writes,

> This grace was certainly not self-bestowed. It was the grace of Christ himself, now prevailing upon the disciple to leave all and follow him, now working in him that confession which to the world must sound like the ultimate blasphemy, now inviting Peter to the supreme fellowship of martyrdom for the Lord he had denied, and thereby forgiving him all his sins. In the life of Peter grace and discipleship are inseparable. He had received the grace that costs.[35]

God's initiation of relationship is not bare manifestation, not empty revelation, but manifest invitation, expensive confrontation. And this confrontation with the inviting presence of God is especially made clear to humankind through the person and work of Jesus Christ. In this sense, God's initiation of relationship with humankind is to be understood as **gospel**. The Jews believed that the One God, who had called Israel to be his people, had also chosen them to be special agents of God's purposes in the world through their obedience and their suffering. Jesus came as the fulfillment of these very purposes. Thus

N. T. Wright states, speaking of Acts 17:28, "The resurrection, as an event within recent history, means that the judgment of the world, long awaited within Judaism, is now announced to all."[36] Through Christ, both Jews and Gentiles are confronted with their Messiah and Lord, a confrontation that demands response.

In the previous chapter we spoke of humanity as radically confronted with hope, speaking from the perspective of the *objective* side of salvation—what the work of Christ has accomplished for us. At the transition point from the objective to the subjective side of salvation, we speak of the gospel offer. From the perspective of relationship, our confrontation with hope is not simply part of the character of human experience; it is the relational offer of a new experience with God. And new Understanding must ultimately have its effect on Acting and Integrating. The gospel of Christ comes as a challenge to all of human experience. In Jesus, God entered human experience. Jesus is God's initiation of relationship with humankind "in the flesh," inviting us to a transformed heart, mind, and life. The gospel message of the apostles was that Jesus Christ is Lord. Yet this proclamation carries implicitly with it the invitation to act as if the proclamation is indeed the case: to believe, to repent, to "turn from these worthless things to the living God" (Acts 14:15). Thus gospel invitation confronts us at every level of human experience, offering us acceptance by God, freedom from bondage to sin, fellowship with God through the Holy Spirit, and victory over the power of the enemy.[37]

The Spirit. Lars Thunberg, summarizing the theology of Maximos the Confessor, writes, "It is certainly only through revelation that one can understand the essential secret of the act of salvation, but revelation, in its content, is made a reality at the same time on both the 'historical' and on the mystical levels."[38] We have discussed something of the historical level in our look at the gospel of Jesus Christ. With the mention of the mystical level, we are brought

Is the Spirit Active in the Life of Unbelievers?

One of the cardinal assumptions of the work of spiritual direction, that ministry whereby one offers support and guidance to another regarding her or his relationship with God, is that the Holy Spirit is actively involved in the life of the person coming for direction. Is this a legitimate assumption? Can it be assumed for believer and unbeliever alike? What can we conclude from scripture?

References to the Spirit in Genesis point to a Spirit of God who not only brings life to the formless earth, but also in some sense brings life and breath to humankind.[39] The Wisdom of Solomon explicitly refers to the Spirit's correcting, revealing, convicting influence among "the nations."[40] While Psalm 139:7 affirms the omnipresence of the Spirit ("Where can I go from your spirit? Or where can I flee from your presence?"), the context of the statements suggest that we may be reaching beyond the evidence to argue that this text demonstrates God's active influence on all peoples everywhere. In Joel 2:28–29, the Lord speaks, looking forward to a time when

> I will pour out my spirit on all flesh;
> your sons and your daughters shall prophesy,
> your old men shall dream dreams,
> and your young men shall see visions.
> Even on the male and female slaves,
> in those days, I will pour out my spirit.

The messianic expectations of an outpouring of the Holy Spirit is fulfilled in Jesus. Peter points to this prophecy, claiming that the Spirit promised in Joel is now made available and that "everyone who calls on the name of the Lord shall be saved . . . For the promise is for . . . everyone whom the Lord our God calls to him"

(Acts 2:21, 39). While we have here a reference to the universal *availability* of the Holy Spirit, we may, once again, be overstating our case to claim that the passage here implies the universal, equal ministry of the Holy Spirit with regard to every single human being. John 14–16 presents Jesus's most developed speech on the ministries of the Spirit. John 16:8–11 confirms the sentiments recorded in the Wisdom of Solomon: "And when he [the Spirit] comes, he will prove the world wrong about [or convict the world of] sin and righteousness and judgment" (John 16:8). It is the world that is judged, the system of humankind organized apart from consideration of the light of truth in Christ. This passage interprets the Spirit's convicting influences in light of the gospel of Christ. Could this convicting work of the Spirit be connected with the Father's work of drawing others to himself (John 6:44)? Finally, the Spirit is involved in the lives of those who are not of the family of God by arranging for at least some to hear the gospel (see Acts 8:29–35) and by giving new life to those who do believe in God (John 3:1–8).

What are we to say? Are we justified, from the passages above, in assuming that the Spirit is actively present or working in some fashion with every person we meet? The Spirit of God gives life to the earth, animating lifeless material into God-inspired (filled with God's breath) order. The Spirit of God fills the earth, much as wisdom fills the earth—correcting, judging, convicting. The Spirit of God is universally available. The Spirit of God orchestrates the conditions for the conversion of some and gives life to those who believe in Christ. While these passages are not clear about the *nature* of the Holy Spirit's active presence to all humanity, it is reasonable to conclude (cautiously) that the Holy Spirit *is* indeed actively present in some fashion to all of humanity, inviting us into relationship with God.

We must not, however, allow this assumption to blur the *very clear distinction* in the New Testament between those who have and have not received the Spirit. True, Peter's first sermon as recorded in Acts points to the fulfillment of the messianic expectations of the universal availability of the Spirit, but the same passage makes the appropriation of that universally available Spirit dependent on the *reception* of that Spirit in conjunction with repentance and baptism (Acts 2:37–39). Jesus, at the onset of his discussion of the Spirit in John 14–16, speaks of "the Spirit of truth, whom the world cannot receive, because it neither sees him nor knows him" (John 14:17). While the Spirit is active among all peoples, drawing them to God, not all will welcome that drawing impulse. Similarly, Paul distinguishes clearly between those who do and do not have the Spirit of God (for example, Romans 8:9–11).

To state that the Spirit of God is actively present to humanity, or to state that humankind is constituted such that we are implicitly hearers of the Word, or even to state that the Spirit is especially evident when we search the deepest places in our being (speaking perhaps, as some have throughout the history of Christian spirituality, of a Ground or Spark of the soul, or of an Inner Word), is not necessarily to state that all humans are equally attuned or oriented toward this Spirit. Our attunement or orientation is a matter of our relationship to that which confronts or invites us. The Spirit can be opposed (Acts 7:51), lied to (Acts 5:3), grieved (Ephesians 4:30), quenched (1 Thessalonians 5:19), outraged (Hebrews 10:29), and put to the test (Acts 5:9).

Is the Spirit actively involved in the lives of all those who come to me for spiritual direction? I say, cautiously, yes. Nonetheless, my assumption of the *fact* of the Spirit's influence must not overshadow my attention to the *character* of that influence and the other's response.

to a discussion of the Holy Spirit and the initiating work of God. We do call it *spirituality*, after all. In some sense for all people, but especially when we consider the life of the Christian, divine-human relationship is initiated by the Holy Spirit.[41]

The Spirit initiates relationship with God from the very start, drawing our spirits to the heart of God, presenting us with tangible experiences of God, enlightening our eyes to see the truth of God. The Spirit also initiates throughout our ongoing relationship with God. Puritan divine John Owen (1616–83) says this of the Holy Spirit's influence on Christians attempting to pray according to the promises of God:

But this is that which he [the Spirit] doth herein:—he openeth their eyes, he giveth an understanding, he enlighteneth their minds, so that they shall perceive the things that are of God prepared for them, and that are contained in the promises of the gospel; and represents them therein in their beauty, glory, suitableness, and desireableness unto their souls: he maketh them to see Christ in them, and all the fruits of his mediation in them, all the effect of the grace and love of God in them; the excellency of mercy and pardon, of grace and holiness, of a new heart, with principles, dispositions, inclinations, and actings, all as they are proposed in the truth and faithfulness of God.[42]

The Holy Spirit communicates the experience of God into our own experience. Thoughts arise, the heart is softened, an inclination is perceived. Just as my experience is affected when another human communicates, I am also affected when

---

God initiates relationship

- through self-disclosing *revelation*,
- as an expression of God's *grace*,
- by means of the presentation of the *gospel* of Christ,
- through the existential invitations of the *Spirit*.

---

the Spirit speaks. The God who reveals himself graciously through the gospel of Jesus Christ brings that gospel to bear concretely in our lives through the ministry of the Holy Spirit.

God the Spirit enters into our experience, encountering us, sharing God with us, inviting and initiating relationship with God. There is always a certain ambiguity with God the Spirit. Even the metaphors used in scripture attest to that ambiguity: wind, fire, dove, force. Through the Spirit of God, we can be sure of the work of God *in* human experience. We are in no position, however, to make a simplistic identification of God *with* our experience. Both human experience and the work of the Spirit are too subtle to allow for such assumptions. For now it is enough to affirm the fact of God's gracious initiation through his Spirit. We will explore the mysterious and transforming work of the Spirit in the chapters to follow.

We have learned that God initiates relationship with humanity. Indeed God does this *characteristically*. We can expect it. God's initiation is rooted in revelation, in God's self-communicating activity. God is present *as*, is present *to*, and is present *through*. God's self-communicating revelation is characterized by *grace*. God's initiation of relationship is freely given, uncompelled, unearned. God invites, welcomes, and receives us on the basis not of our righteousness, but of his love. Because God's initiation is based on his love it is tailored to each individual, each community. To some, relationship with others is primary and we are brought

to God through a call to love others; to others a relationship with nature or an experience of spiritual forces (perhaps an angel) is primary. God's way of initiating relationship is tailored to the trajectory of a person's spirituality. Those who are moving from good to better are drawn with consolations, feelings of tranquility, courage. Those moving from bad to worse are drawn by stings to the conscience.[43] This grace is communicated to us historically through the *gospel* of Jesus Christ. Through Jesus we are confronted with the grace of God in the flesh. The gospel comes to us as both proclamation and invitation. We must respond. Finally, God's invitation of relationship is made through the work of the *Spirit* of Christ. Through the Spirit we receive the communication of God into our own personal experience. Heart, mind, conduct, and relationships are all subject to the touch of God's Spirit. We can expect that God will initiate relationship. We cannot expect just how that initiation will be expressed to us.

Patterns of Perception

Between God's invitations and our responses lie our *perceptions* of God's invitations. It is one thing to say that God reaches out to us in patterns of self-disclosure, grace, gospel, Spirit. It is another thing to *recognize* these invitations. Yet just as there are recognizable patterns of God's initiation of relationship, so also are there tendencies in our perception of God's initiation that can be identified and explored as particular dynamics of the divine-human relationship.

Clear and vague. First, we perceive God's self-communication on a continuum running from clear to vague. We are all aware of the ambiguities of interpersonal communication. Is that a look of confidence or condescension? Is that person knitting in the corner of the meeting room communicating boredom, or does that activity simply facilitate her concentration on the meeting?[44] Within human-to-human communication, ambiguity often arises as we interpret an action within shared frameworks of meaning. Both the person communicating and the person receiving communication know that certain looks convey confidence or condescension; and furthermore, they generally know how those looks might appear. The question for the one receiving communication from one unconsciously communicating is, "Am I correctly interpreting the cues for confidence or condescension?" We all assume that animation generally indicates interest. What we do not know is whether *this* animation is caused by interest or coffee.

We struggle with similar problems in our relationship with God. While there are moments where we are knocked off our horse, more often we perceive God's active presence through ambiguous leadings, where we find ourselves struggling to assess the indications of God's presence or action.[45] We ask, Is the thought that just arose in my mind the voice of God or not? Is that slight shift of the circumstances a sign of the Lord's guidance or not? Sometimes it is hard to tell.

Part of this mixture of clear and vague in our perception of God's initiations lies in *God's character* as both known and unknowable. God is the One whom we cannot avoid. And at times we are riveted to an aspect of God's revelation and all is known clearly. At other times, however, we are drawn into hitherto unexplored aspects of God, and we find ourselves thrust into a "cloud of unknowing."[46] Moses was confronted with the living God at the burning bush and asked, "Who are you?" Jesus's disciples were confused when asked to identify Jesus. People thought those filled with the Holy Spirit were drunk. In God, we are confronted with irresolvable ambiguity. Yet part of our sense of ambiguity may also lie in *God's choice* to remain somewhat hidden so as to allow us to grow in wisdom and love. Paul Hinnebusch, reflecting on the experience of the Catholic renewal movement, writes,

In the human body, the muscular system is the instrument of power, while the nervous system is the instrument of control. Power without control can work havoc; strong muscles without coordination can dissipate all their energy. In a similar way, it is not enough for us to have the power of the Holy Spirit released in our lives. We also need discernment in using that power, and in letting it use us. We can come to disaster through an undiscerning implementation of the Spirit's inspirations. And so, in order to bring us into mature discernment, God allows his self-disclosure to be veiled.[47]

Furthermore, part of the ambiguity of our perception of God lies in *our differences*. Some of us are more attentive to powerful experiences of short duration. Others of us are more attentive to the simple rhythms of everyday life as experienced over a very long duration. Some are more attentive to ideas, others to feelings or action. And we find ourselves changing in these areas over time. We need discernment. Spiritual theologian William Barry writes, "Discernment is necessary not only because of the possible influence of the evil spirit, but also because of the multidimensionality of human experience."[48] There is much more to say about the ambiguity of our perception of God's active presence. We shall explore this in our chapter on discernment.

Nearness and absence. We perceive God's initiation not only with a mix of clearness and ambiguity, but also with a sense of both God's nearness and his absence. We might think these two are positively linked together: clearness to God's nearness, vagueness to God's absence. But it's not always like that. Many saints in the history of Christianity will attest to a clear sense of God's absence or a vague sense of God's nearness. Nonetheless, we perceive God's active presence with a combined sense of nearness and absence.

Once again, this is due in part to the *character of God*. God is both transcendent and immanent—absolutely beyond our reach, yet closer than our dearest friend. James Houston writes that "in prayer, we experience both poles: God's majesty and his humility, his otherness and his nearness. True prayer is to recognize that he is both above us, calling for our worship, and walking along side us, understanding us completely."[49] Likewise, the *sovereign work of the Spirit* of God himself may contribute to our sense of God's nearness or absence. At times God will flood us with light; other times he will withdraw that light and we will perceive ourselves to be in the dark. Symeon the New Theologian recounts an experience of the flooding and withdrawing of the Light of God:

> So I entered the place where I usually prayed and, mindful of the words of the holy man I began to say, "Holy God." At once I was so greatly moved to tears and loving desire for God that I would be unable to describe in words the joy and delight I then felt. I fell prostrate on the ground, and at once I saw, and behold, a great light was immaterially shining on me and seized hold of my whole mind and soul, so that I was struck with amazement at the unexpected marvel and I was, as it were, in ecstasy.... "Whether I was in the body, or outside the body" (2 Corinthians 12:2–3), I conversed with this Light. The Light itself knows it; it scattered whatever mist there was in my soul and cast out every earthly care.... Thus all the perceptions of my mind and soul were wholly concentrated on the ineffable joy of that Light.
>
> But when that infinite Light which had appeared to me ... in some way had gently and gradually faded and, as it were, had withdrawn itself, I regained possession of myself and realized what its power had suddenly done to me. I reflected on its departure and considered how it had left me again to be alone in this life. So severe was the grief and pain that overcame me that I am at a loss properly to describe how great it was.[50]

God has reasons for sending us—or for withdrawing from us—experiences of his presence.

Our sense of the nearness or absence of God can also be due to *our spiritual condition*. Persistent sin, resistance to God's callings, or unwillingness to consider God's involvement in our lives may have their effects over time, and our perception of God's active presence may become dulled. "Your iniquities have been barriers between you and your God" (Isaiah 59:2). Consequently God may appear absent. And finally, our perception of God's nearness and absence can be affected by *the changes in life*. We have learned that our relationship with God differs with regard to personal development and community involvement. It is quite common, during a time of personal or community transition, to feel like God isn't there anymore. The ways that we perceived God do not have the meaning they did before. Yet we are not used to God's patterns of invitation in our new stage or community. In time, however, we begin to attune ourselves to God's active presence in our new setting and our sense of God's nearness returns, albeit with new qualities. Just as interpersonal relationships peak and plateau, so too our relationship with God may experience natural highs and lows, wherein the sense of closeness ebbs and flows.[51]

We perceive God in a mix of both nearness and absence, and we shall return to these themes in the chapters on spiritual formation and prayer.

True and false guilt. Finally, our perception of God's self-communication is tied up with our own preconceptions of our relationship with God. One of the clearest examples of this is the phenomena of false guilt or, as it is often labeled, **scruples**. The *Catholic Encyclopedia* defines *scruple* as "an unfounded apprehension and consequently unwarranted fear that something is a sin which, as a matter of fact, is not. It is not considered here not so much as an isolated fact, but rather as an habitual state of mind known to directors of souls as a 'scrupulous conscience.'"[52] Having scruples is a slightly different dynamic than those addressed above in that it deals not simply with our perception of God's invitations, but more generally with our perception of our relationship with God. Nonetheless, our perception of God's invitations is *always* conducted within the context of our assessment of our relationship with God in general. Just as with any interpersonal relationship, when we assume things are on the rocks, we will interpret statements or other signs of communication as expressions related to our problematic situation. So it is with our relationship with God.[53] We perceive God's active presence, or God's present activity, in terms of our own perceived understanding of God and of our relationship with God. Overconfidence can lead to a misguided **antinomianism**. Underconfidence can lead to scruples. Satan is called "the accuser" in Revelation 12, and we see that strategy present among those who constantly feel under God's judgment.

We have, for the most part, been giving examples of perception from the spirituality of individuals. The same dynamics, of course, apply to corporate entities. The gospel may be offered to a family or a people group just as to an individual. The Spirit may be described as falling on a gathering of people, considered as a whole, just as on an individual. A particular denomination may have a predisposition to perceive God's presence to the neglect of his absence. One might find an entire congregation suffering from scruples.

Patterns of Human Response

As God initiates relationship with us—sharing the divine experience with us—and as we perceive that initiation, we respond. In response, we communicate ourselves toward God, sharing our own experience with God. Though God's initiation of relationship can arise within any aspect of human experience (thus, God can introduce an idea, a feeling, a new pattern of Experiencing, a new way of Integrating, a new relationship, and so on), our response to God's initiation is ultimately expressed at the level of Deciding and Acting. There is an intention, a commitment of ourselves, to a particular kind of response at this particular

moment. We are defining ourselves through the response and entrusting ourselves to it. The dynamics of our response to God involve many factors: God's influence on us, our own attitude toward God, our perception of God, our social structures, and so on. Here we will explore only two dynamics: we respond to God's initiations of relationship with resistance and welcome, and we respond to God with longing and contentment.

Resistance and welcome. In every relationship, in nearly every moment of relationship, there is present a degree of attraction or aversion. Interest is triggered in the other or through the other, and we adapt our response in view of that interest. We are captivated by the conversation of a friend, drawn to the ideas of a colleague, bored by the irrelevance of an acquaintance. As mentioned in our discussion of relationship in general, it is this dimension of interest that forms the *quality* of a relationship. We are constantly responding in relationships with a kind of positive or negative evaluation. These evaluations are often made in the context of assessments of power (who has power over whom, what is desired by whom, and so on). This positive or negative evaluation of the relationship is embodied both in fundamental moments of commitment (like saying "I do" at a wedding ceremony) and in the gestures, expressions, and actions of everyday life with another. Relationship is constantly navigated in the context of resistance and welcome to the initiations of that relationship.

It is no different in our relationship with God. The most fundamental dynamic of our response to God's initiation of relationship is this matter of negative or positive evaluation. The scriptures use a variety of pairs of terms to describe this dynamic: disobedience or obedience, unbelief or belief, ignoring or heeding, following or leaving. Some have spoken of dissent or consent with the Spirit of God, or of our avoidance of or openness to God. Each term has its own special nuance.

We **resist**. Sometimes God initiates relationship with us, and we are just not interested. For example, after rehearsing the laws that will bring life to the Israelites, Deuteronomy 28 lists a variety of curses that shall fall on the them "if you will not obey the Lord" (v. 15). God cries out in Hosea 11:2, "The more I called them, the more they went from me." Jesus looks to his twelve key disciples after a particularly frank discussion about himself and asks them, "Do you also wish to go away?" (John 6:67). Paul asks of our response to God's grace, "Should we continue in sin in order that grace may abound?" (Romans 6:1). In a variety of situations, in a variety of ways, we resist God's initiation of relationship.

In theological discussion a distinction is often made between *original sin* and *personal sin*.[54] *Original sin* describes our predisposition as human beings to resist God. We have discussed this in our overview of the tragedy of human experience. *Personal sin* refers to our choices—day by day, one by one—that are contrary to God's will or invitation. The variety of language used for original sin is used for personal sin as well (transgression, missing the mark, iniquity, and so on). Needless to say, there is a deep connection between original and personal sin. Forms of resistance that have become habituated in a given family, culture, or era are more likely to be practiced by individuals concretely.[55] Thus cultural bias may blind us to the riches of God's will, as when racial prejudice prevents us from appreciating the possibilities created when different ethnicities work together. Similarly we may have grown up to expect rejection—to expect that promises won't be kept—and so responding positively to God's invitation feels just like setting ourselves up for disappointment. The invitation of God's unconditional love is too much to handle. And so we keep ourselves at arms length from God: just close enough to feel comfortable, just far enough to feel safe.[56]

And then there is the whole issue of spiritual warfare. As mentioned in the previous chapter, we are not alone in this world. We are, to some extent, still subject to evil spiritual forces, forces that seek to keep us from intimate relationship with God. The spiritual classic *Unseen Warfare* summarizes some of these strategies of the enemy with regards to human diversity:

> Know, my beloved, that the devil cares only for compassing the ruin of everyone of us, but that he does not use one and the same method of warfare against us all. To help you to see and understand this more clearly, I shall describe to you five inner states of people and the corresponding wiles, and circuitous approaches and enticements of the enemy. These states are the following: some people remain in the slavery of sin, with no thought of liberation; others, although thinking of this liberation and desiring it, do nothing to achieve it; there are also people who, having been freed from the shackles of sin and having acquired virtues, again fall into sin with still greater moral corruption. In their self-delusion some of these latter think that, in spite of it all, they are still advancing towards perfection; others heedlessly abandon the path of virtue; yet others turn the very virtue they possess into a cause and occasion of harm for themselves. The enemy influences each of them in accordance with their state and disposition.[57]

At times our resistance is connected with family of origin issues. We have grown up in a family that was untrustworthy (perhaps even violent), and the idea of unconditional surrender to a Supreme Power is hard to swallow. We have inherited fears, patterns of intentional ignorance, or the like that make it hard to receive God's invitation of grace. At times a touch of healing and unconditional acceptance is needed to open the way to our consent to divine invitation.

Other times, however, our resistance appears less connected to our spiritual or social context. We resist because we simply do not want to grow. We sense that we are being invited to change, and we are too comfortable, too secure, to change. We rest in the memory of relationship with God that we had years ago and in the rituals and structures of Christianity to which we have become accustomed—confident that we are saved based on what happened back then, but unwilling to take the risks that radical response to God might require of us here and now. Then there are those moments when we resist God's initiation of relationship out of simple independent self-will. "I want to do what I want to do, and ain't nobody gonna tell me otherwise." There is a battle for the self in response to God's initiation of relationship (as in any relationship). One's situatedness with regard to another is also a defining of one's self. How will we see ourselves in relationship to *this* invitation, *this* situation, *this* person? Relational response and self-image are inextricably connected. At times, we just refuse to go there.

In sum, resistance arises in the context of a variety of factors. The first few books of Augustine's *Confessions* recount his own resistance, giving mention of a number of the factors listed here. We will do well to reflect deeply on the character of resistance in our own lives and in the lives of those persons and social structures with which we are involved. We cannot understand resistance, however, apart from a grasp of the welcoming responses with which resistance is contrasted. Indeed, perhaps resisting is best understood as "not welcoming."

We resist, but we also **welcome**. The True Light, the Living Word (Logos) of God, was in the world, so states the beginning of the Gospel of John: "He was in the world, and the world came into being through him; yet the world did not know him. He came to what was his own, and his own people did not accept him" (John 1:10–11). The invitation was made and resisted. Yet it is not always resisted: "But to all who received him, who believed in his name, he gave power to become children of God" (John 1:12). Commentator George Beasley-Murray writes of this passage that "the positive aspect of the ministry of the Logos is here described: there were those who 'received' the Logos, i.e., welcomed the

Word in faith."[58] Sometimes God initiates relationship, and we say yes. We welcome relationship with God. We choose to obey the commandments. We heed the warnings of the prophets. We enter into God's presence in the temple. We choose to follow Jesus's call to discipleship. We receive the Spirit of life. The variety of biblical terms for welcome are just as diverse as those used for resistance. Each in its own way communicates something of the positive response of the person or community to God's initiation of relationship. "There she shall respond . . . and I will take you for my wife forever" (Hosea 2:15, 19). We respond, and God responds to our response.

A few terms for our positive response to God's initiation of relationship have gained special attention through the history of the church. Perhaps the most significant is the term *belief* or ***faith*** (the word *pisteuo* in Greek is translated by both words). The New Testament uses these words frequently to describe our positive response to God's invitation. The Gospel of John was written "so that you may come to believe that Jesus is the Messiah, the Son of God, and that through believing you may have life in his name" (John 20:31). Paul writes that "the life I now live in the flesh I live by faith in the Son of God, who loved me and gave himself for me" (Galatians 2:20). Faith is both an initial response to God's call and an ongoing mode of life-response to God's active presence. Martin Luther made the concept of faith a matter of special concern. He described faith in terms of both assent to fundamental Christian truths and trust in the person and provision of Christ. Faith is not just assent to the answers; it is an investment in the Mystery. Faith, as a response to divine initiations, involves an entrustment of ourselves into relationship with the Living God: an entrustment of mind, heart, and life. This entrustment of ourselves to God occurs both in times of special commitment and in a lifestyle of ongoing relationship.

A second term for our positive response to God's initiation of relationship that is common in the scriptures and in the history of spirituality is **obey**. The book of Hebrews writes of Jesus that "although he was a Son, he learned obedience through what he suffered; and having been made perfect, he became the source of eternal salvation for all who obey him" (Hebrews 5:8–9). Peter calls his readers those "who have been chosen and destined by God the Father and sanctified by the Spirit to be obedient to Jesus Christ" (1 Pet 1:2). Likewise, Paul considers his mission "to win obedience from the Gentiles" (Romans 15:18; see also 1:5). Christians have highlighted obedience throughout the history of the church. For example, Gregory of Sinai suggests,

> If you are feeble in practising the commandments yet want to expel your inner murkiness, the best and most efficient physic is trustful unhesitating obedience in all things. This remedy, distilled from many writers, restores vitality and acts as a knife which at a single stroke cuts away festering sores. If, then, in total trust and simplicity you choose this remedy out of all alternatives you excise every passion at once. Not only will you reach the state of stillness but also through your obedience you will fully enter into it, having found Christ and become His imitator and servitor in name and act.[59]

Likewise John Calvin writes of the Holy Spirit that "he is given to us for sanctification, that he may purge us from all iniquity and defilement, and bring us to the obedience of divine righteousness."[60] While some Christians have been reticent to think of relationship with God in terms of obedience, response to God through obedience makes a necessary complement to the response of faith. Faith expresses our response to the supreme provision of God as God. Obedience expresses our response to the supreme demand of God as God. "Trust and obey / for there's no other way / to be happy in Jesus / but to trust and obey."

A third term of response less common today is the term **yieldedness**. The term *yieldedness* actually translates a word used in German spiritual writings, especially those from the fourteenth through the seventeenth centuries: *Gelassenheit. Lassen* often carries the sense of "to leave" or "to let go." Thus one might translate *Gelassenheit* as "letting-go-ness." While faith and obedience communicate our response to the gospel, yieldedness is especially appropriate for describing the nuances of human response to the invitations of the Holy Spirit. Protestant Reformer Andreas Bodenstein von Karlstadt (1477–1541) wrote three separate essays on *Gelassenheit*, the final one written shortly before his death. The theme of yieldedness, important to him his entire life, expressed both a renunciation of everything "in which I may cling" and a state of mind given over to the leadership of the Spirit. Similarly, early Anabaptist leader Peter Walpot (1520–78) spoke of the value of yieldedness fostered by the sharing of possessions practiced by the Anabaptist communities. Walpot calls community life "an oven of yieldedness in which the person is tried like gold in the fire."[61]

Another term that offers interesting insights concerning our positive response to God's initiation of relationship is the term **open**. Think of being open to another, as opposed to being closed to that person. What is involved in this? Steve Duck writes, in his survey of interpersonal psychology, that "the development of relationships is not automatic but rather occurs through the skills of partners in revealing or disclosing first their attitudes and later their personalities, inner character and true selves."[62] How is this process navigated? Through a sense of the openness of one to the other. How does she respond when I show her this side of myself? How does he respond to my angry moments, to my way of expressing intimacy, to my seasons of depression? While not being a classic theological term, I suggest that *openness* may illumine the interpersonal dimension of our positive response to God's initiation of relationship. What does it mean for us to be open to the winds of the Spirit?

All these terms of positive response to God (such as *faith, obedience, yieldedness, openness*) stand in contrast not only to negative responses to God, but also to false positive responses to God—those responses that appear positive at first blush, but on closer inspection are seen to be mere shadows of authentic response, or worse yet, are seen to be means of avoiding authentic response to God posing as religious success. An example of this kind of false response is called the sin of **religiosity** or **spiritual pride**. Religiosity describes a way in which religious people behave *as religious people* that enables them to have a high social standing in their religious community and avoid real authentic relationship with God at the same time. It is a sin that is created and perpetuated by the complex dynamics of religious social systems. It is condemned in numerous classical spiritual writings as preventing real love of God and neighbor. Listen to the anonymous author of *The Cloud of Unknowing* speak of these hypocrites:

> There are, however, others who study with all their might, inward and outward, how they can inflate themselves in their speech, and prop themselves up on every side with many humble-sounding words and gestures of devotion. Their aim rather is to seem holy in the sight of men, than to be holy in the sight of God and his angels. Such people care more and sorrow more for a disordered gesture, or an unseemly and unfitting word spoken before men, than they do for a thousand idle thoughts and foul stirrings of sin deliberately accepted or carelessly committed in the sight of God and of the saints and angels of heaven.[63]

Religiosity is especially dangerous, as it gives the impression of relationship with God without the risks of the reality of that relationship.

One final note—while we have described our response to God as neatly divided between resistance and welcome, the reality of our response is actually more complicated. You know how it is with relationships. We respond ever so tentatively with a bit of openness, all the while holding our guard up toward the other, protecting ourselves from hurt. We allow another to offer opinions, yet all the while we wait for their opinions about life in general to turn into judgment of us. We can be both welcoming and resistant at the same time. We are not sure what we want from the other. And again, it is the same with God. We open ourselves up to the possibility of a new experience with God, a new image of God, a new pattern of action toward God, but at the same time we hesitate. We avoid those disciplines that we know would bring desired change. We go a certain distance in prayer but are shy to go further, afraid of what might be experienced or expected in the context of God's unconditional love. We keep up enough of a facade of religiosity both to satisfy our sense of self to ourselves and others without taking too many risks and to give us a chance to stick our toes deeper in the water when we feel brave enough. Even apathy or "unresponsiveness" reflects the character of God's presence (in clarity and ambiguity), and our mixture of resistance and welcome. Relationship with God is conducted in this interesting blend of welcome and resistance.

Contentment and longing. One of the best indicators of spiritual health is the appropriate balance (for a given individual or community at a given time) of **contentment** and **longing**. Too much contentment can become complacency or quietism; too much longing can become anxious legal-

We respond with both welcome and resistance.

ism. The right blend shows an authentic welcome response to God's initiation of relationship. Longing and contentment are fundamental ways of responding to God's initiation of relationship. These themes are developed in scripture and in the classics of the history of spirituality. Consider the expression of contentment found in Psalm 131:

> O Lord, my heart is not lifted up,
>   my eyes are not raised too high;
> I do not occupy myself with things
>   too great and too marvelous for
>   me.
> But I have calmed and quieted my
>   soul,
>   like a weaned child with its
>   mother;
>   my soul is like the weaned child
>   that is with me.
> O Israel, hope in the Lord
>   from this time on and
>   forevermore.

Consider also the expression of longing found in Psalm 42:

> As a deer longs for flowing streams,
>   so my soul longs for you, O God.
> My soul thirsts for God,
>   for the living God.
> When shall I come and behold
>   the face of God?
> My tears have been my food
>   day and night,
> while people say to me continually,
>   "Where is your God?" (vv. 1–3)[64]

Authentic response to Jesus in the Gospels is sometimes expressed by contentment: by not worrying about tomorrow, by not fussing about the storm, by resting one's head on Jesus's chest. But it also is expressed at times by pouring out one's tears on Jesus's feet, by desiring the pearl so much that one sells all, by leaving home and family to follow Jesus. The book of Hebrews speaks of "entering his rest," the fulfillment of the Old Testament promise of inheritance and contentment; but at the same time it speaks

of the diligence needed to enter that rest. Longing and contentment—response to God is expressed in a combination of longing and contentment.

This, like the other fundamental dynamics discussed above, is characteristic of interpersonal relationships in general. Interest in the other is expressed through attraction and longing. We desire to spend time with the other, to learn more about the other, to experience the other in new ways. At the same time, the unity of the relationship is expressed in a kind of contentment with each other. We get along. There is a minimum of conflict. Longing leads the relationship into uncharted territory, or into tension and anxiety. Contentment leads the relationship into peace, or into complacency and boredom. We are constantly navigating our responses to another within this continuum of longing and contentment. So it is with God.

The dynamics of longing and contentment can become characteristic of forms of spirituality for individuals or groups. (We all have our own predispositions to one or the other.) A spirituality of contentment is expressed, for example, in this sample from Thomas à Kempis's *Imitation of Christ*:

> You, O Lord my God, are supreme above all things. You alone are most high, you alone are most powerful, you alone are self-sufficient and complete, you alone are most sweet and delightful, you alone are most beautiful and loving, you alone are most noble and glorious above all things. In you all good exists perfectly and at once; it always was and it always will be. Therefore, whatever you give me other than yourself, or whatever you reveal or promise to me is far too little, is not enough, as long as I do not see you or fully embrace you. My heart cannot truly rest nor be fully content, if it does not rise above all gifts and all created things and rest in you.[65]

It is also expressed by Hannah Whitall Smith (1832–1911) in *The Christian's Secret of a Holy Life*:

You ask whether you ought to express desires for any thing God does not give. I always feel a "check" myself from expressing such things, because they really are not true, for if God does not give it I do not want it. I would be afraid to have anything He thought best for me not to have. And therefore I would advise you not to say such things. They all help the soul to be discontented with what it has, and God's lesson to us is always one of contentment. I am sure our words and our expressions do affect our inner life. We overcome by the blood of the Lamb and the word of our testimony. Let us always say then the thing our wills are choosing as best.[66]

Augustine, however, proclaimed, "The whole life of the good Christian is a holy longing."[67] Just as there are spiritualities of contentment, so there are spiritualities of longing as well. Pastor and leader of a movement of intercessory prayer, author Mike Bickle writes in his book *Passion for Jesus*, "God designed the human soul to be passionate, abandoned and committed. That is the way the soul functions best. It sinks into restlessness, boredom, passivity and frustration if it has nothing worthy of giving itself to or sacrificing itself for. In other words, if we have nothing to die for, then we really have nothing to live for."[68]

William Stringfellow's (1928–85) response to God was expressed through a longing for God's kingdom of justice on earth. Stringfellow was a lawyer who was concerned with the outcasts of society. He moved into Harlem, a rough neighborhood in New York City, to share his life and his work with the outcasts who surrounded him daily. He writes, "To be concerned with the outcast is an echo, of course, of the Gospel itself. Characteristically, the Christian is to be found in his work and witness in the world among those for whom no one else cares—the poor, the sick, the imprisoned, the misfits, the homeless, the orphans and beggars. The presence of the Christian among the outcasts is the way in which the Christian represents, concretely, the ubiquity and

universality of the intercession of Christ for all men."[69]

A life of intercession, whether expressed in charismatic prayer or in defense of the outcast, is a life of holy longing.

The dimensions of longing and contentment differ from person to person. On the one hand, Bickle argues that "passion for Jesus is not a personality trait. You can have the gentlest human makeup possible and still be consumed with the fire of God. You may not express your passion in the same way a '220 volt' type personality does, but that fiery devotion will be there, and it will be just as real."[70] Yet some are more predisposed by personality, history, or culture to either a more contentment-oriented or a more longing-oriented spirituality. Theologian Ron Sider illustrates this well while comparing Reformers Martin Luther and Andreas Bodenstein von Karlstadt. Commenting on a historian's observations, Sider states, "Gordon Rupp has noted that Luther 'knew as Karlstadt did not, what it meant to begin with the bruised conscience which needs peace with God.' It would be equally true and more illuminating to say that Karlstadt knew, as Luther did not, what it means to begin with a petty, intensely egocentric personality which badly needs God's regenerating grace."[71] Luther needed the rest in Christ provided by the contented assurance of God's forgiveness. Karlstadt needed to move beyond petty religion into passionate longing for Christ. And God initiated relationship with each such that each received what was needed. The blessing comes in receiving what we need. The danger comes in viewing God's way of initiation to meet *our* needs as normative for meeting *everyone's* needs.

As our self is remade through initial conversion to Christ, and as we increasingly comprehend ourselves in terms of relationship with God (Integrating ourselves in Christ), our sense of contentment in God and longing for God both increase. We no longer avoid the presence of God in our life; rather, we attend to it with rejoicing. Longing—desire for something more,

We respond with both contentment and longing.

hunger for God—is not eliminated but is in fact intensified as we perceive and respond to the One to which our being points and from which our being comes. Alongside our contentment there is our longing, a desire for more of what we already have.

Patterns of Divine Response

God initiates, we respond, and God responds to our responses. We obey and God blesses. We disobey and God has mercy. We continue to disobey and God judges. We believe and then receive. We walk in the Spirit and then experience the fruit of the Spirit. God's initiation to relationship comes as invitation. God's response to our response comes both as new initiation and as an opportunity for our transformation. Every moment of openness, of hesitation, of welcome, of fear shapes the character of relationship with God. God continues to share his experience with us: his concerns, his pain, his joys. But he does so insofar as we are willing and able to receive.

We obey and God **blesses**. We believe and we receive from God. *Generosity* is characteristic of God's interactive response. But we must understand that God's generous blessing is not simply a mechanical reward for our responses. The blessing of God contributes to a developing relationship. Old Testament scholar Kent Harold Richards writes, "The primary factor of blessing is the statement of relationship between parties. God blesses with a benefit on the basis of the relationship. The blessing makes

known the positive relationship between the parties, whether a single individual (Genesis 12:1–3) or a group (Deuteronomy 7:12–15)."[72] Consider a relationship between a parent and a child. Your child exhibits obedience to your wishes, shows interest in the kinds of things that interest you, asks you to guide her into maturity in the kinds of values that are important to you. How will you respond to this child? You will be generous, blessing her with time, energy, and support. And it is not simply a matter of rewarding her for good behavior. Rather, your blessing is an expression of positive relationship, your showing approval and using expressions of that approval to develop her further. Furthermore, God's blessing is tailored to our specific situations. "When the righteous cry for help, the LORD hears, and rescues them from all their troubles. The LORD is near to the brokenhearted, and saves the crushed in spirit" (Psalm 34:17–18; see also Psalm 146:7–9). As we open ourselves to God, yielding ourselves to his care, God is free to open himself to us, showering on us his rich generosity.

When we resist or avoid God's invitations, God generally perseveres with us. God responds with **mercy**. "But you, O Lord, are a God merciful and gracious, slow to anger and abounding in steadfast love and faithfulness" (Psalm 86:15). God sends prophets to Israel to warn them—again and again—before he sends armies. God desires the best for us. But God is also faithful to his concerns. The tension between these is expressed in the parallel phrases of 2 Timothy 2:11–13:

> If we have died with him,
>   we will also live with him;
> if we endure,
>   we will also reign with him;
> if we deny him,
>   he will also deny us;
> if we are faithless,
>   he remains faithful—
>   for he cannot deny himself.

Even in the midst of our resistance, God continues to draw, to call, to invite. Even through our own distractions and dissatisfactions, God woos us to himself in a way that is appropriate to who we are at that moment. We cop an attitude of discontent with the system, only to wonder how much our own discontent is a function of our own little system. And we are drawn to something deeper underneath. Or we consider God a distraction to our ladder climbing, only to find that our ladder is precariously balanced on an uncertain foundation. Or in our boastful maintenance of spiritual practice (religiosity) we find ourselves "accidentally" confronted with the Living God. And so God continues to draw, to call, in and through and around our own resistances.[73] Thus French spiritual writer Francis de Sales (1567–1622) expresses, "See the divine lover at the gate. He does not simply knock once. He continues to knock. He calls the soul: come, arise my beloved, hurry! And he puts his hand on the lock to see whether he can open it. . . . In short, this divine Savior forgets nothing to show that his mercies are above all his works, his mercy is greater than his judgment, that his redemption is copious, his love is infinite and, as the Apostle says, he is rich in mercy and so desires that all should be saved and none perish."[74]

But there are, finally, those times when God chooses to chastise, to punish, to judge. "If you are willing and obedient, you shall eat the good of the land," Isaiah cries, "but if you refuse and rebel, you shall be devoured by the sword" (Isaiah 1:19–20), a wrath perhaps we ourselves have stored up (see Romans 2:5). Yes, God judges. Indeed, it is the very "serious nature of God's wrath" that gives meaning to God's turning away of wrath in mercy.[75] For this reason, meditation on the judgment of God has provided a stimulus for Christian devotion throughout the Christian church.[76] But even judgment exhibits God's sensitivity to his people. "Do not despise the LORD's discipline or be weary of his reproof, for the LORD reproves the one he loves, as a father the son in whom he delights" (Proverbs 3:11–12; see also Hebrews 12:6).

Relationship grows as those in relationship share experience. As we reveal our thoughts, feelings, Decisions, Integrations, relationships, and so on (at various levels of depth) to God—and as God reveals the same to us—we are incorporated in Christ, into the sphere of God's experience. And the Spirit of God indwells us, influencing us at every level of experience. We are transformed through relationship with God. As interest, depth, skills, and familiarity develop further, relationship with God becomes a rich experience of love. We shall explore this further in the chapters to follow. In the next chapter, we will take a look at the development of relationship with God through Christian transformation. In chapter 8 we will explore the stages and skills of relationship with God as we explore Christian spiritual formation. In chapter 9 we will venture into the depths of relationship with God as we discuss prayer. In chapter 10 we will explore how relationship with God informs our relationships with others. And in chapter 11 we will discuss the issue of the clarification of relationship through discernment.

Practicing Christian Spirituality

A History of My (or Our) Relationship with God

These two short exercises are provided to help you get an overview of your relationship with God as it has developed, especially in its most recent season. They may also give you new perspective on the directions in which you see your relationship with God to be moving in the near future. Take your time with each question. It may be helpful, after completing the worksheet, to process the experience of reviewing your relationship with God with a trusted friend or spiritual director. Perhaps the completing of this worksheet itself will be an enlightening encounter with God.

Exercise 1: History of My Relationship with God

On a blank sheet of paper draw a graph describing the history of your relationship with God from its beginning to the present. Show the highs and lows of this relationship from its beginning to the present. Identify (and date if appropriate) key peaks, valleys, plateaus, transitions, and developments. Where were those key moments of God's invitation, your response, and God's response to you? Now sit back and prayerfully look at this chart. What has characterized your most recent season with the Lord? How does this season differ from previous seasons? Where does your relationship with the Lord appear to be moving now?

Exercise 2: Pictorial Summary of My Relationship with God

On another blank sheet of unlined paper, draw a picture representing your relationship with God. This picture can be abstract or realistic, black-and-white or color, an imitation of Rembrandt or a collection of stick-figures. The sincerity of expression is important; the quality of product is not. Allow yourself to deeply feel the movement of your relationship with God as it has been taking shape in the present period. Allow that sense, that feeling, to be expressed naturally on paper. (If you want to use another visual expressive medium—sculpture, dance, or the like—go for it.) If you want to, feel free to title your art work or to adorn it with a verse from scripture that has been meaningful to you recently.

Now you may wish to comment on or to analyze the relationship you have just described. How did this period of your life develop? What are the distinctives of your particular relationship with God in this season? What are the distinctives of your relationship with God just because you are you? How has God invited you into relationship this season? Where do you see signs of God's self-disclosure, grace, gospel, Spirit? How have you perceived God's initiations? What do the mixtures of clearness and vagueness, nearness and distance, look like for you? How have your assumptions about your relationship with God in general affected your perceptions of God's touch? How have you responded to God lately? Describe the various resistances and welcomes, contentments and longings that have characterized your relationship with God recently. Finally, reflect on God's responses to you: his blessings, mercies, judgments. What do these indicate about the direction of your relationship with God in the next season? Try not to be too self-critical in this evaluation. Just be honest.

CHAPTER SUMMARY

1. Relationship is a part of every aspect of human (and *all*) experience. Interpersonal relationships involve (in addition to self-disclosure, communication, and the other features mentioned in chapter 3): interest and consent—leading to the quality of the relationship; the sharing of various spheres of life—leading to the type of relationship; the exercise of various skills; and the mutual experience of various levels of depth—leading to the degree of intimacy of the relationship. Relationship with God, like human relationships, exhibits all of these dimensions.

2. When we look at people's relationships with God (both individuals and communities), we see a great deal of diversity. Different peoples have different relationships with God. This diversity is due in part to the diversity of human experience itself. We differ from one another in historical-cultural setting, kinds of spiritual experiences, personality and temperament, development, embodiment, family and close community, and tradition. Our uniqueness in each of these areas leads to a lived experience of relationship with God that is distinct to a given group or individual. Recognition of these differences protects us from expecting others' relationship with God to look like ours (or from condemning ourselves that ours does not look like theirs).

3. While our relationships with God demonstrate a great deal of diversity, we can still recognize common patterns of divine-human "relationshipping." One of those patterns common throughout scripture and the history of the church is the pattern of divine invitation, human response, and divine response to human response.

4. God's initiation to us is his own self-giving in relationship. God initiates relationship through the self-disclosure of revelation. This revelation is a revelation of grace: uncompelled, undeserved, powerful, active, favor. It confronts us most directly through the gospel of Jesus Christ. It is made real to us personally through the ministry of the Holy Spirit.

5. Between God's initiation of relationship and our response, we recognize the dimension of our perception of God's self-giving initiation. Just as there are patterns of God's initiation, so there are identifiable tendencies of our perception of God's active presence. For reasons which involve both God's character and our situation, we perceive God's invitations with a mix of clarity and vagueness, nearness and distance. Furthermore, our sense of the condition of relationship with God in general affects our perception of God's work in our lives, for example, in the case of "scruples."

6. As with any other relationship, we respond to God's initiations. At times we avoid or resist God. The dispositions of original sin are embodied in the choices of personal sin. Cultural bias, spiritual warfare, family of origin issues, our own self-protectiveness, and more, all color the kinds of avoidance and resistance we might exhibit toward God's loving invitations. At other times (or combined with our resistance—we often express elements of these together), we welcome God's invitation. We receive God in faith, obey God in life, yield heart and will to God, and open ourselves to God's own experience given to us.

7. Finally, God responds to our responses to him. We experience God's responses as a blessing that communicates his favor and support, a mercy that is patient with us even when we resist, and a judgment that expresses both God's righteous wrath and his loving chastisement for those he loves.

LOOKING FURTHER

General

The dynamics of interpersonal relationships in general are explored within an entire sub-component of social psychology. See, for example, *Understanding Relationships: Selected Readings in Interpersonal Communication*, ed. Benjamin J. Broome (Dubuque: Kendall/Hunt, 1986) and Steve Duck's *Understanding Relationships* (New York: Guilford, 1991). For relationally centered approaches to philosophy see, for example, Josiah Royce, *The Problem of Christianity* (Washington, DC: Catholic University Press of America, 2001); John Macmurray, *Persons in Relation* (Atlantic Highlands, NJ: Humanities Press, 1961); and Emmanuel Levinas, *Entre Nous: On Thinking-of-the-Other*, trans. Michael B. Smith and Barbara Harshav (New York: Columbia University Press, 1998).

Diversity

A number of works have explored our varied experience of relationship with God. See the notes in the text for more details. A few examples might include the following: *The Psychology of Religion: An Empirical Approach*, 2nd ed. (New York: Guilford, 1996), edited by Ralph W. Hood, Bernard Spilka, Bruce Hunsberger, and Richard Gorsuch; Chester P. Michael and Marie C. Norrisey, *Prayer and Temperament: Different Prayer Forms for Different Personality Types* (Charlottesville, VA: The Open Door, 1984); Francis Kelly Nemek and Marie Theresa Coombs, *The Spiritual Journey: Critical Thresholds and Stages of Adult Spiritual Genesis* (Wilmington, DE: Michael Glazier, 1987); *Women's Spirituality: Resources for Christian Development*, 2nd ed. (New York: Paulist Press, 1996), edited by Joann Wolski Conn; Richard Rohr and Joseph Martos, *The Wild Man's Journey: Reflections on Male Spirituality* (Cincinnati: St. Anthony's Messenger Press, 1996); Flora Wilson Bridges, *Resurrection Song: African-American Spirituality* (Maryknoll, NY: Orbis, 2001); and *Exploring Christian Spirituality: An Ecumenical Reader* (Grand Rapids: Baker, 2000), edited by Ken Collins.

Fundamental Patterns

Descriptive studies of the fundamental patterns of relationship with God are harder to find. These dynamics are discovered only through synthesizing a review of works in biblical and systematic theology, history of spirituality, and spiritual direction. For biblical and theological reflections see, for example, Walter Brueggemann, *Theology of the Old Testament: Testimony, Dispute, Advocacy* (Minneapolis: Augsburg, 1984); Donald L. Gelpi, *The Gracing of Human Experience: Rethinking the Relationship Between Nature and Grace* (Collegeville, MN: Liturgical Press, 2001); Richard Lovelace, *Dynamics of Spiritual Life: An Evangelical Theology of Renewal* (Downers Grove, IL: InterVarsity Press, 1979); and Vladimir Lossky, *The Mystical Theology of the Eastern Church* (Crestwood, NY: St. Vladimir's Seminary Press, 1998).

Classics of the history of spirituality that are especially oriented around the theme of interpersonal relationship might include John Ruusbroec, *The Spiritual Espousals and Other Works*, trans. James A. Wiseman, Classics of Western Spirituality (New York: Paulist Press, 1985); Bernard of Clairvaux, *Selected Works*, trans. G. R. Evans, Classics of Western Spirituality (New York: Paulist Press, 1987); and Mechthild of Magdeburg's *The

Flowing Light of the Godhead, trans. Frank Tobin, Classics of Western Spirituality (New York: Paulist Press, 1998).

Mike Bickle's *Passion for Jesus: Perfecting Extravagant Love for God* (Orlando, FL: Creation House, 1993) is a contemporary Protestant/Charismatic example of relational spirituality.

William A. Barry and William J. Connolly's *The Practice of Spiritual Direction* (New York: Seabury, 1982) and Gerald May's *Care of Mind, Care of Spirit: Psychiatric Dimensions of Spiritual Direction* (San Francisco: Harper and Row, 1983) are especially helpful with regard to relational dynamics.

Questions

1. This chapter spends a lot of time comparing relationship with God to ordinary human relationships. Given what was said about the dangers of the way of analogy in chapter 4, is this a legitimate approach? To what degree is the divine-human relationship like any human relationship? When do we cross the line and venture into unhealthy anthropomorphisms? Have you seen errors of this sort expressed in the history of Christian spirituality? How can we avoid them?

2. What other aspects of diversity could be added to the list given in this chapter? Evaluate your own history of church attendance. How might you characterize the different spiritualities of the churches in which you have participated?

3. This chapter focused on the "divine initiation, human response, divine response" pattern of relationship. Is this the only pattern there is? What about those times where *we* initiate first? Can you develop your own theory about other fundamental patterns of relationship?

4. We explored God's initiation in terms of revelation, grace, gospel, and Spirit. But there are other dimensions to be explored. How might you develop a spirituality sensitive to a theology of calling or election or the like?

5. Consider someone to whom you are ministering currently. Evaluate their perception of God's initiations based on the categories given in the chapter. Or perhaps add a few other categories of your own. What do you learn about their relationship with God by this kind of reflection?

6. Look at your own life. What are the ways that you habitually avoid or resist God? What are the ways in which you habitually welcome God? How do you see elements of each simultaneously active at moments in your experience?

7. What might happen if you lead your small group through an experience of meditation on God's judgment?

227

Christian Transformation

7

OBJECTIVES

In this chapter you will see how relationship with God is a transforming relationship. You will learn about the character of Christian transformation: how transformation flows out of interpersonal relationship with God, the ways that God's action and human volition contribute to this transformation, and how transformation is at the very center of the Christian's hope and life. You will get a personal feel for Christian transformation by reading from the stories of a few well-known Christians. You will discover how Christian salvation begins with the work of Jesus, is received initially as we are converted to Christ, grows through ongoing transformation, and is completed in the eschaton. You will explore the impact of transformation upon the whole of human experience. Finally you will get a chance to foster transformation through composing your own spiritual autobiography.

After reading this chapter, you should be able to

- explain how Christian transformation is (and is *not*) like the transformation of other inter-personal relationships;
- identify key moments of Christian salvation, showing how the transformation of humanity encompasses human history and our personal histories;
- distinguish between transformation "from the inside" and "from the outside"; distinguish between "once-born" and "twice-born" transformations;
- summarize the basic stages of initial salvation for "twice-born" individuals or communities, describing the value of a sensitivity to these stages for ministry to others;
- describe and discuss various stage-theories of development for ongoing salvation;
- recognize the work of transformation in a variety of areas of your life: thoughts, feelings, actions, relationships, shallows and depths, and so on.

Introducing Christian Transformation

> So if anyone is in Christ, there is a new creation: everything old has passed away; see, everything has become new! (2 Corinthians 5:17)

Perhaps my favorite image of **transformation** is a simple chemistry demonstration I saw when I was a young boy. Just for fun, I reconstructed this demonstration just before writing this paragraph. First I took a test tube (we had an old glass milk bottle in the recycling bin), cleaned it and dried it, and then added two spoonfuls of white sugar. I turned on the Bunsen burner (in this case the unit on our gas stove). Then I held the "test tube" over the "Bunsen burner" to heat it up and watch what happened. And sure enough, in a couple of minutes, the glass bottle broke and I had sugar and broken glass all over the stove. Once I cleaned up the mess I tried again, this time with the sugar in a metal measuring cup for a "test tube." I also turned the stove down a little, so the heating would be slower.

As the sugar began to heat, I saw the crystals on the edges start to melt little by little. First the liquid was clear, then yellow, then brown, getting darker all the time. The liquid area started to bubble, first just a little and then more. I watched as the amount of bubbling liquid grew and the amount of crystallized sugar shrunk. A stinky smelling gas rose from the mixture. (I ran to open the door and turn a fan on to clear the kitchen of smoke.) The bubbling mixture got darker and thicker; there was a time where you couldn't tell just what it was or what it might become. It bubbled up and formed a kind of balloon inside the measuring cup. (I thought it was going to drip out over the stove for a moment.) Then the bubbling subsided and the mixture got drier. Soon the stuff seemed to stabilize: a black, hard, dry, airy substance that looked kind of like the surface of the moon. Cool! One moment I had pure white sugar and now I had this black ball inside my measuring cup. Transformation!

In the previous chapter we explored the divine-human relationship. We discovered that Christian spirituality involves the human person or community in an interactive relationship with God. Our relationship with God, however, is not just an interactive relationship but also a *transforming* relationship—a powerfully transforming relationship.

Another image of transformation is that of a pilgrimage—a journey from a starting place to a holy destination, where the person who finishes the journey is a different person than the one who began. During a pilgrimage one encounters forces (like the heat in my sugar experiment) that stimulate changes. Just as in chemical transformations, there may be times in a pilgrimage where one is not quite sure what one is or is becoming. Small changes at one point could end up fostering great changes further on down the road. But good pilgrimages, like good chemistry demonstrations, move the pilgrim (or the sugar) ultimately from uncertain identity to new identity.[1]

The idea of Christian transformation brings up thoughts of a number of other related terms: salvation, justification, conversion, sanctification, deification, spiritual formation. To focus on transformation, rather than justification, for example, is to approach transformation from the point of view of spirituality rather than theology. To explore the dynamics of transformation as *spirituality* is to explore patterns of change present in the actual, lived relationships with God of individuals and communities. To focus on transformation rather than sanctification, then, is to approach transformation with a broader sense of time in view. Christian transformation includes the changes involved in initial conversion, sanctifying growth, and on to glorification. Finally, to explore transformation rather than spiritual formation is to attend to the *dynamics* of change instead of the *means* of that change (which shall be addressed in the following chapter). In this chapter, then, our aim is to explore the changes in human experience insofar as they embody movement toward Christ or into conformity with Christ. In chapter 5 we learned that human experience is confronted, through Christ and the Spirit, with a radical hope: the hope of a full restoration of human experience itself, both personal and corporate. This full restoration is the aim of God with humanity. Transformation is the realization of that restoration in concrete life. In this chapter we learn just how this restoration is realized in the context of relationship with God.

As in previous chapters, our exploration of Christian transformation will involve the integration of the perspectives of a number of disciplines. We will take a look at models of transformation in scripture and in Christian theology. We will tell stories of changes in communities and individuals. And we will consider insights that the human sciences have to offer concerning factors that affect our transformation.

The Character of Christian Transformation

> You were taught to put away your former way of life, your old self, corrupt and deluded by its lusts, and to be renewed in the spirit of your minds, and to clothe yourselves with the new self, created according to the likeness of God in true righteousness and holiness. (Ephesians 4:22–24)

Just as chemical transformations have their own unique characteristics, so also Christian transformation has its own unique features, characteristic of the divine-human relationship. Let us examine four of these: Christian transformation involves a change in relationship, it is characterized by a Godward reorientation of life, it is the work of both God and humans, and it is the goal of the Christian faith.

A Change in Relationship

Transformation is change. One form passes over (*trans*) to some other form. The white sugar becomes black; the pilgrim becomes a different person. Yet while Christian transformation involves changes in persons, it is larger than this. Christian transformation involves not only changes in individuals and communities, but also changes in *relationship*, in the ways that individuals and communities interact with God and one another. Furthermore, Christian transformation is structured within the context of the unique, interpersonal dynamics of the *divine-human* relationship. It is the shared experience of a sovereign-responsive God and an embodied-spirit human that is the object of change in Christian transformation. We have learned that relationship is characterized by mutuality and by the shared awareness of that mutual sharing. It involves interest, skills, shared elements of life, and so on. A *transformation of relationship with God* means that we grow interested in God, that we sense God's interest in us. It means that we learn the skills of perceiving and responding to God's invitations. It means that God shares with us and we with God. Greater depth leads to greater intimacy, and we are not the same people we once were. In chapter 5 we spoke about reconciliation with God. These kinds of change *are* that reconciliation in lived experience.

Christian transformation can arise in a moment of insight, when one partner realizes something about the other and something entirely new is shared, a sharing that changes everything. Emilie Griffin gives an example of this from the movie *Lili*, describing an aspect of transforming insight she calls the moment of relational "Surrender":

> In a film called *Lili*, there is a scene which is for me a metaphor of this kind of recognition of the Lord. The film concerns a young woman who loved a puppeteer, but was never able to perceive his love for her. At the last, when she is preparing to leave the traveling circus, he speaks to her through his puppets; they tell her of their love. She returns and speaks to the puppets

as though they were alive. It is only after a few moments that she knows it is not the puppets who are speaking, but the puppeteer behind the curtain, who is giving them life. I think the Surrender is this same kind of mutual recognition. The Lord has expressed his love to us through human beings and through events; but we have not been fully able to perceive his love until this final moment, when we can say, "My Lord and My God."[2]

Singer-songwriter Billy Crockett uses the image of a spreading infection to describe the unique relational changes in Christian transformation:

> You're into everybody's scene,
> You never heard of quarantine,
> You love without a compromise,
> Exposing those who immunize,
> Attacking every barrier,
> You living breathing Carrier of love.[3]

Whether through a sudden discovery or a slow "infection," Christian transformation involves the introduction of new elements into our relationship with God and others.

A Godward Re-orientation of Life

The changes of relationship in Christian transformation involve a **reorientation** of one's life toward God and others. Transformation is the lived experience of restoration. The changes in relationship introduce new ways of being aware of God, of perceiving God, of responding to God. While Christian transformation affects every area of human experience (we shall see this below), by discussing transformation we draw special attention to the ways in which this relationship affects our Integration of life. Philosophers speak of paradigm shifts, or of adopting new research programs or new standpoints to describe these kinds of shifts. Transformation is not simply the adding of new information to our current perspective; it is also the remaking of the perspective itself. This is what we mean by

re-*orientation*. When we are transformed in Christ, we do not just see new things; we see all things in a new way.[4] Becoming a Christian in the first centuries of the faith was distinct from Greco-Roman religious belief formation in that while the average pagan felt free simply to add new gods to an already existing pantheon, Christian conversion required the renunciation of other gods and the reorganization of one's entire belief system *in terms of* the supremacy of Christ.[5]

The Christian tradition speaks of this reorientation by means of a variety of stories and images. The Gospel of John speaks of belief in Jesus, of being "born again" (or "born from above"), of walking in light rather than in darkness. The Pauline epistles speak of identification with Christ, of repentance, of faith, of receiving the Spirit, of incorporation into the family of God, of growing in holiness. Mark presents an unfolding encounter of those who were learning to follow Jesus, a developing encounter wherein they grew to know Jesus the teacher, the prophet, the Messiah, the Son of Man, the son of David, and finally the Son of God. Late-medieval theologian and mystic Meister Eckhart (1260–1327) speaks of the need to transcend mere religious duty by means of a "breakthrough" into the knowledge of God. Similarly, Eckhart's student Johannes Tauler speaks in his sermons of a number of "births" of Jesus: his eternal birth in the Trinity, his birth in Mary, and his birth in the soul of the believer "every day and every hour." We have already mentioned the image of pilgrimage used by many. Different aspects of this reorientation toward God are expressed with different images.[6]

The Work of God and Humans

This reorientation of relationship known as Christian transformation is both a *work of God* and a *work of humans*. This is easy enough to state—with confidence—but very difficult to explain. If the ways of a

focus

Historical Portrait: Dorothy Day (1899–1980), founder of the Catholic Worker Movement

In this first portrait, Dorothy Day, a woman who in her younger years was immersed in Communist and anarchist thought, begins to learn about prayer.

I was surprised that I found myself beginning to pray daily. I could not get down on my knees, but I could pray while I was walking. If I got down on my knees I thought, "Do I really believe? Whom am I praying to?" A terrible doubt came over me, and a sense of shame, and I wondered if I was praying because I was lonely, because I was unhappy.

But when I walked to the village for the mail, I found myself praying again, holding in my pocket the rosary that Mary Gordon gave me in New Orleans some years before. Maybe I did not say it correctly but I kept on saying it because it made me happy.

Then I thought suddenly, scornfully, "Here you are in a stupor of content. You are biological. Like a cow. Prayer with you is like the opiate of the people."

And over and over again in my mind that phrase was repeated jeeringly, "Religion is the opiate of the people."

"But," I reasoned with myself, "I am praying because I am happy, not because I am unhappy. I did not turn to God in unhappiness, in grief, in despair—to get consolation, to get something from Him."

And encouraged that I was praying because I wanted to thank Him, I went on praying. No matter how dull the day, how long the walk seemed, if I felt sluggish at the beginning of the walk, the words I had been saying insinuated themselves into my heart before I had finished, so that the trip back I neither prayed nor thought but was filled with exultation.[7]

"man with a girl" are difficult to understand (see Proverbs 30:19), the ways of the God-human relationship are even more mysterious, for the transformations of Christian spirituality involve both changes *in* relationship and changes *through* relationship, a relationship with the infinite Spirit. In terms of theology this means that to explore the dynamics of Christian transformation is to enter into the minefield of theological debates concerning the relationship between the roles of God and human: monergism or synergism, divine sovereignty or human freedom, certainty of God's perseverance with the saints or uncertainty of God's perseverance, and so on. Nonetheless, there is virtually no Christian community that emphasizes the work of God to the complete denial of human activity in the sanctifying life of the believer. And, conversely, there is no Christian community that emphasizes the work of the human to the denial of God's gracious initiation in some form. Given that one's understanding of the theology of Christian transformation falls somewhere between these extremes, we can—as students of spirituality—appreciate the various emphases of different Christian traditions regarding the diverse dynamics of Christian transformation.

First, Christian transformation is a work of God. Drawing on insights from chapters 4 and 5, we can expect the divine loving Presence to be actively involved in the changes that take place as a community or individual grows into relationship with God. We can expect God's personal self-communication toward us as persons and communities: a communication of knowledge, of feeling,

focus

Historical Portrait: Ignatius of Loyola (1491–1556)

Here is a story of the beginnings of Ignatius of Loyola's change from a proud Spanish knight to a soldier for Jesus and the founder of the Order of the Jesuits. In this portion of the story Ignatius recounts (in the third person) how he recovered after being struck by a cannonball in battle.

As he was much given to reading worldly books of fiction, commonly labeled chivalry, when he felt better he asked to be given some of them to pass the time. But in that house none of those that he usually read could be found, so they gave him a life of Christ and a book of the lives of the saints in Castilian.

As he read them over many times, he became rather fond of what he found written there. But, interrupting his reading, he sometimes stopped to think about the things he had read and at other times about the things of the world that he used to think of before. Of the many foolish ideas that occurred to him, one had taken such a hold on his heart that he was absorbed in thinking about it for two and three and four hours without realizing it. He imagined what he would do in the service of a certain lady; the means he would take so he could go to the place where she lived; the quips—the words he would address to her; the feats of arms he would perform in her service. He became so infatuated with this that he did not consider how impossible of attainment it would be, because the lady was not of ordinary nobility; not a countess nor a duchess; but her station was higher than any of these.

Nevertheless Our Lord assisted him, by causing these thoughts to be followed by others which arose from the things he read. For in reading the life of Our Lord and of the saints, he stopped to think, reasoning within himself, "What if I did what St. Francis did, and what St. Dominic did?" Thus he pondered over many things that he found good, always proposing to himself what was difficult and burdensome; and as he so proposed, it seemed easy for him to accomplish it. But he did no more than argue with himself, saying, "St. Dominic did this, therefore I have to do it; St. Francis did this, therefore I have to do it." These thoughts also lasted a good while; then, other things coming in between, the worldly ones mentioned above returned, and he also stayed long with them. This succession of such diverse thoughts lasted for quite some time, and he always dwelt at length on the thought that turned up, either of the worldly exploits he wished to perform or of these others of God that came into his imagination, until he tired of it and put it aside and turned to other matters.

Yet there was this difference. When he was thinking of those things of the world he took much delight in them, but afterwards, when he was tired and put them aside, he found himself dry and dissatisfied. But when he thought of going to Jerusalem barefoot, and of eating nothing but plain vegetables and of practicing all the other rigors that he saw in the saints, not only was he consoled when he had these thoughts, but even after putting them aside he remained satisfied and joyful.

He did not notice this, however; nor did he stop to ponder the distinction until the time when his eyes were opened a little, and he began to marvel at the difference and to reflect upon it, realizing from experience that some thoughts left him sad and others joyful. Little by little he came to recognize the difference between the spirits that were stirring, one from the devil, the other from God.[8]

Historical Portrait: Jackie Pullinger-To (b. 1944)

Here a story of transformation in the life of a woman who, in 1966, at age 22, left England alone on an around-the-world trip and ended up in Hong Kong's infamous Walled City, where prostitution, crime, and addiction were rampant. Since that time she has led hundreds out of bondage and into new life in Christ. At this point in her story, Jackie is a young girl preparing for confirmation in the Anglican Church.

Confirmation came round and it was our form's turn to be done. I was rather serious about all this, feeling that I was one of the few who really believed in God. The others were only doing it for the dresses and the Confirmation Tea to which we could invite relatives and godparents. Yet my real fear was that the vicar would ask us individually what we believed, before we could get through; but I need not have worried—he never did. So that was all right. But I had to ask him a question first.

"What should I think about when the Bishop puts his hands upon my head?"

The vicar thought for a moment, "Ah—I should er . . . er—pray!" he concluded triumphantly. Gilly and I walked forward in our school-issue white dresses and knelt down. The Bishop laid hands on us—I can only remember walking back to my seat filled with joy. Actually I felt like laughing—like splitting my sides. How improper—this was a confirmation service, and this was the solemn bit. Laughing was for the tea after. I found my service sheet and covered up my face so that no one should see me smiling in the pew, and then quickly put my head down in an attitude of prayer. I had hoped to carry off the ceremony looking both reverent and graceful and there did not seem to be any connection between the service and this unseemly gladness. I was giving my life to God; I had expected nothing back.[9]

of will. This self-communication comes as expression and as invitation, an invitation of grace, gospel, and Spirit. And it affects or transforms us just as communication between one person affects change in another. (Think—how *does* communication change you?) Yet we can also expect that the divine-human communication—this communication of Person to person, of Trinity to community—will transcend mere human expressions. We can expect to be confronted with surprise, with wonder, with mystery. To become acquainted with Christian transformation as a work of God demands theological reflection, prayerful devotion, and authentic action.

Second, Christian transformation is also the work of humans. As the transformation of a divine-*human* relationship, Christian transformation is subject to all the nuances of ordinary human experience. Christian transformation will reveal the greatness, the tragedy, and the restoration of human experience in all their ordinary humanness. Psychological and social factors shape the way that we experience our religious transformation.[10] Similarly, human patterns of decision making structure our transforming religious decisions: for example, we may be inclined to evaluate Christianity in terms of a few salient examples.[11] Furthermore, Christian transformation, as transformation of a *human* relationship, is subject to the dynamics of other interpersonal relationships: for example, learning to attend to the partner, developing intimacy through appropriate self-revelation, and communicating about the relationship through

235

The Length of Christian Transformation

Historical Salvation	You *have been* saved	at the cross
Initial Salvation	You *were* saved	at baptism or at decision
Ongoing Salvation	You *are being* saved	in Christian life
Final (or Eschatological) Salvation	You *will* be saved	in the end of things

signals to others.[12] Finally, as the work of humans, Christian transformation will be experienced within the context of the ordinary stages of human experience.

The Goal of the Christian Faith

One other characteristic of Christian transformation needs to be mentioned: transformation is the *goal of the Christian faith*. As we looked at the meaning of Christian experience in chapter 5, we discovered that restoration—personal, corporate, cosmic—is our destiny as humans. And restoration necessitates transformation. We are meant to share covenant partnership with God: to share God's heart, God's mind, God's reign. Again, Christian transformation is not simply a matter of becoming better persons. Rather, our transformation as persons is only part of a much larger cosmic transformation that will be the fulfillment of all of history and creation. Gordon Smith, speaking of initial conversion to Christ, writes, "Transformation is ultimately eschatological—it will come and will be complete in the kingdom that is yet to come. The experience of conversion enables us to know the transforming grace of God in this life, but it is given to us only as a 'down payment' of the ultimate experience of God's grace, which will be at the consummation of the kingdom."[13] If we are to understand Christian transformation, we must understand the goal to which this transformation is directed.

The Length of Christian Transformation

At times, among some segments of Christendom, transformation was identified almost completely with the moment of becoming a Christian. Yet at other times this has not been so. Early Protestant theologians, for example, elaborated what was called the *ordo salutis*, or order of salvation, identifying Christ's transforming work through stages of election, calling, illumination, conversion, regeneration, justification, mystical union, renovation, preservation, and glorification. "All agree," states the foreword of a survey of views of Christian sanctification, "that the Bible teaches a sanctification that is past, present, and future. It is past because it begins in a position of separation already gained in Christ's completed work. It is present in that it describes a process of cultivating a holy life. And sanctification has a future culmination at the return of Christ, when the effects of sin will be fully removed."[14] Here we will view the span of Christian transformation in terms of four "moments of salvation"—**historical salvation, initial salvation, ongoing salvation**, and **final salvation**[15]—paying special attention to the moments of initial and ongoing salvation, for these are the two moments of particular concern to Christian spirituality.

Historical Salvation

You *have been saved* through Christ. Second Timothy 1:9 speaks of God "who saved us and called us with a holy calling, not according to our works but according to his own purpose and grace. This grace was given to us in Christ Jesus before the ages began." Likewise, Colossians 1:20 says of Christ that "through him God was pleased to reconcile to himself all things, whether on earth or in heaven, by making peace through the blood of his cross." Just as one might consider a house "as good as built" when a trustworthy contractor has signed the contract to build, so too there is a sense in which our transformation has already been assured through Jesus Christ, who signed the covenant between God and humanity with his blood. The finished work of Christ on the cross, the historical moment of our transformation, is a special emphasis of Reformed theology and spirituality. "Redemption accomplished and applied," proclaims Reformed theologian John Murray.[16] In a similar manner, Karl Barth writes, "For when we name the name of Jesus Christ and remember the new creation of man that has taken place in Him, we have really spoken the last Word—not our last word, but God's (and therefore ours as well)."[17]

God has expressed his orientation to us and made possible our reorientation toward God, through the work of Christ. The hope of restoration is real because of the *availability* of restoration. Thus, Christian transformation is not simply a hoped-for possibility. In a very significant sense our transformation has been already accomplished—a historical salvation.

Initial Salvation

You *were saved* when you believed. First Corinthians 1:21 states, "For since, in the wisdom of God, the world did not know God through wisdom, God decided, through the foolishness of our proclamation, to save those who believe." (See also Ephesians 1:13.) And again we read in Titus 3:5, that "he saved us, not because of any works of righteousness that we had done, but according to his mercy, through the water of rebirth and renewal by the Holy Spirit." This moment of salvation is generally what most people call conversion (though some use the term *conversion* to speak of ongoing salvation as well). A fundamental transformation took place as we made the choice for relationship with God, as we received the rebirth of the Spirit. Some would refer to this moment simply as "when I became a Christian."

Initial salvation is a mystery. Psychologist of religion Lewis Rambo sums up the mystery of initial salvation nicely in the conclusion of his book on the topic (using the term *conversion*):

> Conversion is paradoxical. It is elusive. It is inclusive. It destroys and it saves. Conversion is sudden and it is gradual. It is created totally by the action of God, and it is created totally by the action of humans. Conversion is personal and communal, private and public. It is both passive and active. It is a retreat from the world. It is a resolution of conflict and an empowerment to go into the world and to confront, if not create conflict. Conversion is an event and a process. It is an ending and a beginning. It is final and open-ended. Conversion leaves us devastated—and transformed.[18]

The Dynamics of Initial Salvation. The transformation of initial salvation is a work of God, a work of the convert, and a work of the body of Christ. From the side of God, this transformation is a work of *divine grace*. It is the expression of the loving action of God on our behalf apart from any merit of our own. It is the action of God communicating himself to us, stimulating and enabling our response to him, effecting our reorientation.[19] Theophan the Recluse, in his classic *The Path to Salvation*, identifies a number of "special actions of divine grace in arousing sinners from the slumber of sin." He specifically mentions the giving of miracles and sensible manifestations, the direct impression of thoughts and feelings on the mind, and the indirect loosening of ties one might have to the world, flesh, or devil. These actions of grace arouse in one an awareness of something more, a hunger for something more, the stimulation of intent toward God.[20]

The transformation of initial salvation is also the work of *God's Spirit*. Gordon Smith writes, "The Holy Spirit effects Christian conversion. It is the Holy Spirit who illuminates the mind, convicts the heart of sin and enables the will to act in response to truth."[21] The Spirit initiates and effects the "junction" of divine-human relationship itself. Scripture speaks of the Spirit in action (just as we learned of the active presence of the Christian God generally). The verbs used to describe the work of the Spirit give us a fair picture of the active presence of the divine Spirit, entering into human experience and facilitating new "relationshipping" with God. For example, the Spirit of Christ *baptizes* us, placing us within the sphere of Christ, of the Body of Christ, and of the Spirit itself (Mark 1:8; John 1:33; Acts 1:5; 11:16; 1 Corinthians 12:13). The Holy Spirit is *poured out* on God's people, initiating a new and powerful dimension to human experience, a dimension readily identifiable as being "from God." (For *poured out* and similar terms, see John 7:38–39; Acts 1:8; 2:17–18, 33; 10:45; 19:6; Romans 5:5; Titus 3:5–6.) The Holy Spirit *fills* believers, bringing an intense sense of the presence of God or an unusually strong expression of the activity of God to others, facilitating the expansion of God's kingdom on earth (see Luke 1:15, 67; 4:1; Acts 2:4; 4:8, 31; 7:55; 9:17; 13:9, 52; Ephesians 5:18; for references to those who become "full" of the Spirit, whose lives are particularly marked by the work of the Spirit, see Acts 6:3, 5; 11:24). The Spirit is *given* or supplied to believers (John 1:32; Romans 5:5; Galatians 4:6; Philippians 1:19; 1 Thessalonians 4:8). The Spirit *regenerates* persons, giving them a new "birth" (John 3:8).[22] What we discover from these terms and passages is that God the Spirit both invites us into relationship and to a certain extent "jumpstarts" that transformed divine-human relationship by entering into our experience concretely, bringing to us a new sense of the divine.

From the side of the human, the transformations of initial salvation are experienced in the context of the web of human relationships and through the systems and stages of human experience. We experience God, and act toward God, as humans. Theologically, the human side of conversion is an act of repentance and faith, our welcoming response to God's invitation of relationship. "Repent, and believe in the good news," is the invitation of Jesus (Mark 1:15). Repentance and faith involve mind, heart, and will. One understands the distance between human and divine. One feels sorrow for sin. One intends to change and make the choice for God. Christian faith assumes some intellectual knowledge of "the faith," emotional assent to its truth "for me," and willingness to trust in Christ.[23]

This repentance and faith will be experienced psychologically and socially, however, with all the diversity of human experience. Ignatius of Loyola's transformation knew the tensions between the life of chivalry and the life of renunciation presented in the stories of the saints. Dorothy Day experienced the tensions of Marxist theories and personal delight in prayer. Christian transformation is the transformation of *human* experience. As *human* experience, initial transformation can be (and has been) explored through empirical investigation. Religious conversion (along with similar religious behaviors, such as apostasy, intensification or revival, or switching religions) has been studied by social scientists since the beginning of the twentieth century. Early psychologists took inspiration from the account of Paul's conversion and explored conversion as a radical transformation of the self. They identified adolescence as the prime age of conversion. They emphasized the emotional factors present, the suddenness of change, the passiveness of the convert, and the permanence of transformation. Later research in conversion tended to draw greater attention to rational processes, to the convert's active role, and to the impermanence of conversion. Recently conversion has been explored more as a transfer of social alliance than as an internal psychological change. While not invalidating the role of the divine in Christian conversion, we attempt—by examining things like context, precipitating events, supporting activities, and participation or commitment—to sort out the complexities of converting transformation, understanding patterns that are common to many or unique to given individuals as human persons.[24]

When psychological and theological insights are joined, the wisdom of the Spirit is fostered. This wisdom, recorded in the classics of Christian spirituality and reappropriated by informed spiritual guides today, speaks of the ways of converting transformation. The wisdom of the Spirit notices, for example, the tendency for one's sense of the divine call to weaken through repeated neglect. Wisdom recognizes the distinction between a powerful experience of divine invitation and the authentic expression of converting repentance and faith. Wisdom discerns the presence of God in the details of human experience. Wisdom notes the stratagems of the enemy: distracting one from conversion with activities, drawing another away with temptations of pleasure, holding another captive through guilt and shame. Wisdom sees through the debates about faith and reason into the sincere needs that must be met by an individual or group in order to take the next step toward God. Wisdom makes use of appropriate means for clarifying the mind, for softening the heart, for motivating the will to respond to the converting impulses of the Spirit.[25]

The transformation of initial salvation is also a work of the community. Contemporary research is correct to draw attention to the corporate dimensions of conversion. Our salvation is a process of leaving the world and becoming incorporated into the body of Christ. Earliest Christianity saw, in its approach to the rite of baptism, a break with pagan understandings of perfection. Through baptism, Christians are, to use the language of New Testament scholar Luke Timothy Johnson, "ritually imprinted"— without distinction between gender, race, or status—into a new community, a community that expresses its growth to perfection not merely through repeated rituals but through a transformed manner of living.[26] As mentioned in chapter 3, we are increasingly seeing the self in terms of the networks of relationships that define who

we are. From such a perspective, we see conversion in terms of the transformation of our sense of relatedness and "belonging-to-ness." Hence initial salvation is not simply a matter of an inner experience or an intellectual profession of belief, but also a reconfiguration of community. And in such a case, Christian community is viewed as both the midwife and the host of conversion.[27] The restoration of human experience is made available through the work of Christ. It is realized through a combination of the Spirit's influence, human response, and community welcome.

Considering conversion from the perspective of "social alliance," we can distinguish two (or maybe three) types of initial salvation encompassing conversion from the "inside" and from the "outside." Conversion from the inside is the natural maturing of faith of one raised within the context of Christian faith and community. Conversion from the outside refers to the birth of Christian faith for one not raised within the Christian community. Different dynamics can be identified, and distinct wisdom can be advised, for each of these two groups. In the previous chapter we noted that relationships develop in identifiable stages: finding, encountering, growing, and changing. Initial salvation covers the steps of finding and encountering. Finding and encountering relationship with God develops differently for "insiders" and "outsiders." Between these two is the ambiguous category of the "once born."

As any preacher's kid will tell you, it is a much different thing as an **insider**, growing up in the faith, than coming to Christian belief "from the outside." The perspectives from which questions of belief are asked, the sense of felt spiritual need, and the structures of belonging are all distinct for "cradle believers." Consequently, these believers must be treated distinctly by family and church community. For example, we do not need to expect those raised within the faith to experience a Pauline "crisis of faith." Theophan the Recluse devotes two chapters of *The Path to Salvation* to the guid-

239

ance of those who come to faith from the inside. He writes,

> In the natural course of the development of one's capabilities, everyone naturally comes to the awareness that he is a man. But if to his nature there is ingrafted the new principle of the grace of Christianity at the very moment when a person's powers and their movements are awakened (in Baptism), and if then in all the points of the development of these powers this new principle not only does not yield first place—but on the contrary always prevails and gives as it were the form to everything—then when a man comes to full awareness he will find himself at the same time acting according to Christian principles and will find himself to be a Christian.[28]

Fostering the maturing faith of insiders (some might speak of "preserving the grace of baptism" here) requires a unique sensitivity. One must carefully discern for each person the age of accountability. (Perhaps we should speak of levels of accountability?) One must know the degree of seriousness with which to take prayers of conversion or confirmation commitments at different ages and contexts. One must know how to foster the perception of the work of the Spirit in a young person without fostering expectations that the Spirit will act in the same way throughout his or her life. One must distinguish between loving encouragement and inappropriate coercion. One must accompany some through a season in

As we sing the 314th verse of "Just as I Am," isn't there ONE MORE who will come?

which they "outgrow" their faith in order to find it again.[29]

Lying between those who come to faith naturally within the Christian community and those who either leave the faith and return or come to faith from outside Christendom ("outsiders") is a kind of transitional group: the **once-born**. William James, in his classic study *The Varieties of Religious Experience*, distinguishes between the once-born and the twice-born. His description of the once-born does not necessitate being raised within a community of faith. By this designation, rather, James simply wants to acknowledge the existence of those who throughout life develop in a responsive relationship with God apart from a perceived conversion or who change from one thing to another. James borrows from an essay by Francis Newman to clarify his understanding of the once-born:

> They see God, not as a strict Judge, not as a Glorious Potentate; but as the animating Spirit of a beautiful harmonious world, Beneficent and Kind, Merciful as well as Pure. The same characters generally have no metaphysical tendencies: they do not look back into themselves. Hence they are not distressed by their own imperfections: yet it would be absurd to call them self-righteous; for they hardly think of themselves *at all*. This childlike quality of their nature makes the opening of religion very happy to them: for they no more shrink from God, than a child from an emperor, before whom the parent trembles; in fact, they have no vivid conception of *any* of the qualities in which the severer Majesty of God consists. He is to them the impersonation of Kindness and Beauty. They read his character, not in the disordered world of man, but in romantic and harmonious nature. Of human sin they know perhaps little in their own hearts and not very much in this world; and human suffering does but melt them to tenderness. Thus, when they approach God, no inward disturbance ensues; and without being as yet spiritual, they have a certain complacency and perhaps romantic sense of excitement in their simple worship.[30]

We must try to get beyond the portrait of nineteenth-century liberalism embedded within the description. The student of Christian *spirituality* must address the facts of people's real, actual experienced relationship with God. And in that regard, the point is simply this: there appear to be some who do not "come" to faith in any significant way. Rather, for them, faith, or relationship with God, is experienced as simply being always present. It is a faith that grows and changes, but it is never absent. And some of the once-born are people who have not had much contact with the Christian faith. If a Christian perspective is accurately introduced, the once-born might say, "This is the God I have always known," though the doctrinal framework of once-born individuals are often underdeveloped and sometimes eccentric. James devotes more of his attention to the twice-born in *Varieties of Religious Experience*, as we will here. Yet James is compelled to acknowledge that such people exist. Have you known any such people? What we make of their claims—how we integrate claims of once-born-ness with our theologies of exclusivism, inclusivism, or pluralism—is another question, one not to be answered here. For now it is simply enough to acknowledge those who *claim* such once-born faith and to wonder how one might facilitate ongoing maturity and authentic Christian transformation for the once-born.

And then there are those who "come" to faith, who join the Christian community, *from the **outside***. These are James's **twice-born**, who find faith out of a sense of sickness or of a divided self. James sees the process of conversion, whether gradual or sudden, as a shifting of one's center of personal energy and a lighting up of new crises of emotion. He draws attention to conscious processes of the will and of a subconscious maturation of motives that, when ripe, burst into flower. For James, the results of authentic conversion are a new sense of reality and sanctification.[31] Others draw attention to the dynamics of separation and association involved in joining a new community: building relationships, sharing worldviews, adapting language, and so on. The fact is, people claim to experience initial transformation into the Christian faith a variety of ways: from the inside, from the outside; once-born, twice-born. Each faces different needs and requires different care in order to secure faith and to mature in faith.

THE STAGES OF INITIAL SALVATION (FOR THE TWICE-BORN)

Building on the work of James, scholars have endeavored to organize the process of initial conversion by speaking in terms of a set of stages.[32] Recognizing that any categorization of experience is bound to suffer at points from simplification, we will follow the schema suggested by Lewis Rambo: context, crisis, quest, encounter, interaction, commitment, and consequences.[33]

First, conversion springs from within a ***context***. There is the larger context of the availability of the gospel in the convert's general culture. There is the more narrow context of a convert's local setting (family, friends, ethnic group, and such). There is the background awareness (intellectual, affective, more strictly "spiritual") that one may have of the things of religion. There are social, personal, or religious experiences that shape, in a potential convert, an accumulated sense of the divine and relationship with "god" that is addressed in the process of conversion. There are coercive pressures from within

FIGURE 7.1
A Sequential Stage Model

Stage 1	Stage 2	Stage 3	Stage 4	Stage 5	Stage 6	Stage 7
Context	Crisis	Quest	Encounter	Interaction	Commitment	Consequences

241

Contours of Crisis

Various qualities or characteristics of the stage of crisis shape the way the sense of need or the crisis is experienced. Each of these qualities may be plotted on a continuum.[34]

FIGURE 7.2

- Intensity   Mild ⟷ Severe
- Duration   Brief ⟷ Prolonged
- Scope   Limited ⟷ Extensive
- Source   Internal ⟷ External
- Old/New   Continuity ⟷ Discontinuity

and without Christiandom. These kinds of factors open paths of conversion to some that are unavailable to others. They shape the sense of congruence or incongruence that, in turn, affect the ease of conversion. And then there is the presence of God, always an active part of our context. Psychiatrist and spiritual writer Gerald May writes of this divine context, "the journey toward greater love is not something to be instilled in people; it is already there to be tended, nurtured, and affirmed."[35]

Second, conversion proceeds in response to a *crisis*. Perhaps *crisis* might be too strong a term for what occurs in some conversions, but at least we may fairly speak of a sense of need or desire. We learned in chapter 5 of the birth of religious hope from our fundamental dissatisfaction with life. Emilie Griffin speaks of this dissatisfaction and the crisis it brings: "So, out of our human longings, out of a nostalgia for childhood joys, out of a sense of alienation from things as they are, out of disenchantment, we come at last to an understanding—some sooner, some later—that there is a desire within us for something greater than ourselves, a hunger which we ourselves can never satisfy. To see this for the first time is to feel a sudden isolation, a sudden helplessness." She says further, "It is one thing to feel these longings; it is quite another to consent to them."[36] The catalysts for conversion (or at least the stimuli for our converting quest, for we are active agents in our own conversion) can be as spectacular as an experience of healing or as ordinary as raising the question, Is this all there is? For some, the quest for something more is triggered by an awareness of our own stuff.

Third, the sense of dissatisfaction stimulates our openness to something more, and thus *crisis* leads to **quest**. Our quest can manifest as an aggressive exploration of a particular religious community or as a quiet openness to wonder. For some it is a quest for community; for others it is a quest for truth. For some it is a quest for purpose; for others, a quest for peace. Some quests can last nearly a lifetime. Other quests may only last from the beginning of a sermon (when our need is made known) to the end (when we find satisfaction of that need in Christ). We may hold a kind of inner dialogue, posing and evaluating secular and religious hypotheses. Or we may find ourselves listening to new music, talking to different people, trying something new. Our sense of dissatisfaction, our glimpse at something else, challenges our stability. Motivations of one sort and another shape the character of our quest. Particular experiences may cause us to explore religious matters and motivate a quest. We may take different quests, depending on whether we are motivated by physical hunger, by the need for safety, or by a sense of belonging, achievement, or actualization. And our quests are shaped by our different styles of response to the options before us.

Fourth, our quest leads us "out," and our "outness" leads us to **encounter**. We encounter *ourselves* in our "outness." We encounter the discomfort of uncertainty—the temptation to settle for the dissatisfactions we have always known rather than to face the confusion of the unknown. We are plagued with arguments, with feelings that go here and there, with mixed intentions and strained commitments. We also, in Christian conversion, often encounter an *advocate*, someone who represents (or presents) Christianity for us. This advocate (or

Modes of Response

The presence of a new religious option may stimulate a stage of *questing*. But then again, it may not. There are many possible responses to a new religious option, depending on a variety of factors.[37]

FIGURE 7.3

Active	Receptive	Rejecting	Apathetic	Passive

Active questing	A person looking for new options because of dissatisfaction with the old ways and/or a desire for innovation and/or a search for fulfillment and growth
Receptive	A person is "ready" for new options for a variety of reasons
Rejecting	Someone consciously rejects the new option
Apathetic	Someone has no interest in a new religious option
Passive	Someone is so weak and fragile that he or she is easily manipulated by external influences

advocates) comes to us with his or her own sense of what Christianity is all about and what conversion would look like. Religious advocates come with their own persuasive strategies (just as do those who present to us opportunities for other, more mundane satisfactions—"Mocha anyone?") and style of how one should undertake and navigate a quest. Ultimately, we encounter the *divine invitation*. As discussed in the previous chapter, whether or not we are conscious of it, God is actively present, stimulating thoughts and feelings, drawing the seeker to himself.

Fifth, encounter becomes **interaction** as self, advocates, and God each have their own say in our quest. *Relationships* may strengthen bonds to a new community. *Rhetoric* may support the decision to make a paradigm shift. *Rituals* may provide modes of integrating a new way of life. *Roles* may suggest new meaning and purpose to the potential convert. Or they may not. The voices of the divine and the enemy conflict as things heat up. We reach that liminal moment (or season) where we are not quite sure who we are. We begin to become

Prescriptions and Proscriptions of the Advocate

Advocates of a new religious option bring that option in the context of their own approach, with their own expectations of the way that conversion should proceed or appear. In order to get a sense of how advocates see the conversion process, one might ask questions like the following:[38]

FIGURE 7.4

1. Are the requirements of the new option general or specific?
2. Are the changes mandatory or optional?
3. Are different levels of commitment allowed?
4. Are requirements explicit or implicit?
5. How much time is allowed to conform?
6. Is the convert allowed to negotiate changes?

243

aware that conversion will require change, repentance, leaving something behind. And interaction may lead to struggle. Griffin expresses the feelings of many in the later stages of this interaction, which she calls "the Struggle": "What characterizes the Struggle, then, is a growing realization of the truth of God's existence, and at the same time a last-ditch reluctance to accept him. It seems as though the nearer we come to the Lord, the more we sense his overwhelming power, the more we begin to believe that he is real, the more we resist him."[39]

Sixth, we then make a *commitment* to Christ. There is the decision to be baptized, to go forward in response to an "altar call," to pray that prayer—and a new relationship with God begins. American Evangelicalism has often comprehended the whole of Christian transformation within this "hour of decision," but it is now in the process of rethinking that perspective, seeing conversion from a broader perspective.[40] Conversely, those in Roman Catholic circles have tended to minimize this stage, but they are now rethinking their perspective, with a new emphasis on the Rite of Christian Initiation for Adults.[41] Conversion is expressed in an act of the will. "Desire, once claimed," writes Gerald May, "becomes intention. Intention, given the grace not to derail itself into superstitious control, becomes a willing,

honest turning toward the source of love." Elsewhere May says that "the yes to love, chosen with immediate awareness and full responsibility in the absence of certain knowledge, is the most free and authentic thing a human being can do. It is what the human will was created for."[42] Christian commitment is experienced as surrender. For some this surrender is an occasion for great joy. "But not every Surrender is accompanied with such euphoria," writes Griffin. "For others, the experience is just as real, but it is accompanied instead with an absence of feeling. It is without consolation. It is a humbling, a being brought low, and brings with it, not the tears and floating sensations of a near-mystical experience, but instead a kind of passage through a dark alley, without romanticism, without beauty, without joy. It is a crossing made in utter faith. It is a step into the darkness, an encounter with the unknown, for which the only resource is trust."[43]

Commitment is sealed with ritual. The rites of baptism, confirmation, and reconciliation have been the public expressions of adult conversion throughout its history. And new commitment ultimately leads to the development of a new sense of ourselves and a new story of ourselves.[44]

Seventh, and finally, in the end, conversion has *consequences*; conversion is transformation. We are changed through beginning relationship with God. Our feelings and thoughts may begin to change. We have new relationships and a new *kind* of relationship with others, with nature, with ourselves. There are other positive consequences of new life in Christ. We find the peace we were looking for. We are relieved of the oppression of the world, the flesh, the devil. We are welcomed into a new community. But conversion has its own downside, which spiritual guides are wise to anticipate. One can experience a sense of loss that comes with leaving something behind (even when what we leave may have been very destructive). There is also what Griffin calls the "wreckage" in our personal relationships caused by our

"Remember the good ol' days when we'd just give 'em a Gospel of John?"

focus

Historical Portrait: Effects of the Welsh Revival

POPULAR WELSH REVIVAL HYMNS.

Initial and ongoing salvation are not only matters of personal transformation. Families, small groups, and entire regions can, *as corporate entities*, experience transforming relationship with God. Here is J. Edwin Orr's summary of the effects of the transformation of Wales during a powerful revival of the Christian faith in 1904.

> By the New Year of 1905, the Welsh Revival had reached its greatest power and extent. All classes, all ages and every denomination shared in the general awakening. Totals of converts added to the churches were published in the local newspapers, 70,000 in two months, 85,000 in five, and more than a hundred thousand in half a year. Eighty thousand were still in the membership of the Welsh churches in 1914, in spite of leakage to mission halls and emigration overseas. . . . After the 1905 New Year, the Swansea County Police Court announced to the public that there had not been a single charge for drunkenness over the weekend, an all-time record. The great wave of sobriety which swept over the country caused severe financial losses to men in the liquor trade, and closed many of the taverns. A great improvement in public morals resulted in turn from the closures. Stocks of Welsh and English Bibles were sold out. Prayer meetings were held in coal mines, in trains and trams and places of business. The works managers bore testimony of the change of conduct of their employees. The magistrates were presented with white gloves in several places, signifying that there were utterly no cases to try.[45]

conversion.[46] Ultimately, a "good" initial conversion—a conversion that is likely to persevere, a conversion that empowers an ongoing life of transformation—will exhibit certain features: some degree of belief, repentance, trust and the assurance of forgiveness, commitment, sacramental expression, reception of the gift of the Holy Spirit, and concrete incorporation into the Christian community.[47]

Ongoing Salvation

You *are being saved* through the Spirit. Our historical salvation was accomplished on the cross. The transformation of initial salvation is expressed in a fundamental commitment to the Christian faith. Then there is the transformation of ongoing salvation. "There is 'first conversion,'" writes Griffin, "that upheaval in our minds and hearts which we resolve when we first acknowledge the Lord and give ourselves to him.

That is turning in the sense of a turnabout: a reversal, a change of course. Beyond that first conversion—as many converts learn to their surprise—there is another turning which is to last our whole life long. That is turning in another sense: transformation."[48] Bruce Demarest comments on this as well: "Scripture thus calls men and women not only to an initial conversion to Christ that enrolls them among the justified, but to a continual conversion that makes them more like Jesus Christ in word and deed. Progressive conversion validates the reality of initial conversion."[49] "Continuous conversion," writes Bernard McGinn, "is the essence of the Christian life."[50]

We *are* being saved. Paul writes, "For the message about the cross is foolishness to those who are perishing, but to us who are being saved it is the power of God" (1 Corinthians 1:18). While the transformation of initial salvation places us in the sphere of Christ and within the influence of his body and Spirit, the transformations of ongoing salvation happen continually as more and more areas of our lives are "saved." In terms of interpersonal dynamics, ongoing salvation represents the ways that (to use the language of romantic movies) "getting to know you" changes everything. In terms of theology, ongoing salvation often comes under the rubric of sanctification.

THE DYNAMICS OF ONGOING SALVATION

The character of ongoing salvation is similar to that of initial salvation: it is a work of God, a work of the believer, a work of community. Paul exhorts the Philippian church, saying, "Therefore, my beloved, just as you have always obeyed me, not only in my presence, but much more now in my absence, work out your own salvation with fear and trembling; for it is God who is at work in you, enabling you both to will and to work for his good pleasure" (Philippians 2:12–13). Ongoing salvation is something that we work *out* and that God works *in*.

God's initiation of relationship does not end with the giving of *the Spirit* in initial salvation. Indeed, this is only the beginning of the Spirit's transforming work. For the Christian, every area of life is subject to the Spirit's life-giving initiations. As with initial salvation, the scriptures speak of the Spirit's work in terms of a number of verbs. The Holy Spirit *reveals* the divine, communicating God's voice to individuals and groups through a variety of signs and symbols—through scripture (Mark 12:36; Acts 1:16; 4:25; Ephesians 3:5: Hebrews 3:7; 2 Peter 1:21), prophetic utterances (Acts 11:28; 13:2; 20:23; 21:4, 11; 1 Corinthians 12:4–11; 1 Thessalonians 5:18–20; Revelation 2:7; 19:10), "inner voices" (Acts 8:29; 9:31; 11:12; 15:28; Romans 8:6, 14; Galatians 5:16, 18, 25), dreams (Acts 10:19), and the gifted body of believers (1 Corinthians 12:7–11; 14:2, 15). The Spirit *dwells* in or with the believer, fostering a new orientation of life and lifestyle, a new sphere of Christian experience. (See John 14:16–23; 16:7; Romans 8:10–11, 26–27;

14:17; 1 Corinthians 3:16; 6:17–19; 14:2, 14; 2 Corinthians 6:6; Ephesians 2:18–22; 3:16; 6:18; 1 Thessalonians 1:6; 2 Timothy 1:14; Hebrews 6:4; Revelation 1:10; 4:2.) The Spirit initiates covenant-conforming character: *leading, sanctifying,* and *transforming* believers increasingly into Christlikeness in concrete living (Romans 8:4; 2 Corinthians 3:6; Galatians 5:5; 1 Peter 1:2). The Spirit *produces conviction* of belief (Romans 8:15–16; 9:1) and a *supernatural dimension* to worship, evangelism, and relationships with others (Acts 2:4; Romans 15:17–19; 1 Corinthians 2:4; 12:4–7, 11; Ephesians 5:18–20; 1 Thessalonians 1:5). The Spirit of God is God's transforming presence with us here and now.

Ongoing salvation is also a work of *the believer*. God invites and we respond. We change our habits of pride or self-hatred in response to our experience of God's love. Step by step our worldview is expanded to encompass an increasingly divine perspective. We welcome new divinely initiated feelings into our experience (for example, a compassion for those in foreign countries without adequate water supply), and our feelings are increasingly restored to truth. There really are dos and don'ts in scripture;[51] and while it is dangerous to reduce Christian spirituality to following commandments, it is also dangerous to ignore the place of obedience in the Christian life. The repentance and faith of initial salvation are deepened and broadened as we become increasingly aware of the character of God, of our own mixed condition as humans (great and fallen), and of the restoration toward which we are called. The Orthodox tradition speaks of *kataneixas*, or "compunction," and *penthos*, a "mourning for lost salvation."[52] As our view of the heights of salvation is raised, our grief for what is still lost is intensified. Furthermore, as a work of *humans*, our ongoing salvation, like our initial salvation, will be subject to all the psychological and social dynamics of human life. And just as theological and psychological insights together provide a wisdom of the Spirit regarding the dynamics, the means, and the nurturing of initial conversion, so also they guide the wisdom of the Spirit with regard to ongoing salvation.

Ongoing salvation is also a work of *the community* of Christ. As mentioned above, community is both means and ends of Christian transformation. We are nurtured by the body to become incorporated within the body. We come to understand God within the context of specific informal relationships and Christian traditions. We come to experience God not merely in private worship, but in and through the language of corporate worship. Our transformations are often corporately received and ritually celebrated through the sacraments of the church. Theologian John D. Zizioulas writes, "The application of Christ's existence to ours then amounts to nothing other than a realization of the community of the Church. This community is born as the Body of Christ and lives out of the same communion which we find in Christ's historical existence. . . . The eucharistic community is the Body of Christ *par excellence* simply because it incarnates and realizes our communion within the very life and communion of the Trinity, in a way that preserves the eschatological character of truth while making it an integral part of history."[53]

The field of Christian spirituality is especially concerned with aspects of ongoing salvation: its cultivation, contexts, content, character, and consequences. Ongoing salvation deals with the growing and changing stages of relationship. The remaining chapters of this book will deal with aspects of ongoing salvation (spiritual formation, prayer, community, discernment, and renewal).

The Stages of Ongoing Salvation

Just as scholars and spiritual writers have suggested stages of development in initial conversion, so they have also suggested stages of ongoing Christian life. Viewing the Christian life from the perspective of one model of Christian growth or another generally can be very helpful. Models of the stages of Christian growth give us a sense

of where we are in relationship with God: the kinds of struggles we may expect, the lessons we may need to learn, the experiences common to a given stage. Pastors and spiritual guides use models to help them discern the signs a person gives of her or his maturity and to help them target their ministry to the needs of that particular individual or group. (Groups go through stages of development, just like individuals.)

At times, however, viewing the Christian life from the perspective of a particular model of Christian growth can be very *unhelpful*. There are those times when we feel pressed into certain experiences just because they are considered necessary for the "expected" stage of growth. There are those times when we feel inadequate because we don't show the right signs of a stage of growth. There may also be times when we are exalted because we *do* exhibit the right signs when in fact we really are not all that mature (and that feels odd, too). There are the times when a spiritual friend misunderstands our struggles because he has incorrectly "labeled" us as being in a certain stage of growth.

Models of the stages of Christian growth are powerful tools in the hands of those

Pastor Newburg installed altar call ejection seats, believing, "If we do our part, God will do his."

247

Historical Portrait: More from Jackie Pullinger-To

Here is another look at transformation in the life of Jackie Pullinger-To. We saw a glimpse of her confirmation as a young girl in England. In this story, she is a young woman in Hong Kong. Notice the combination of Spirit, human, and community in her experience of ongoing transformation.

It was two years since I had left England—a year since I had supposedly received the "gift of the Spirit." I felt quite an authority on prayer meetings in the Colony. But my clarinet pupil's mother—Clare Harding—urged me to go [to another prayer meeting], saying it would be charismatic. This new term described a meeting where they expected the various gifts of the Spirit—charisma—to be manifested.

"Well, I'll just go for a few weeks until I've learned all about it—then I'll go back to the other meetings," I told Clare. And so I was introduced to Rick and Jean Stone Willans.

. . . To my horror they suggested we pray together in tongues. I was not sure if this was all right since the Bible said that people should not all speak aloud in tongues at the same time. They explained that St. Paul was referring to a public meeting where an outsider coming in would think everyone was crazy; we three would not be offending any one and would be praying to God in the languages He gave us.

I could not get out of it. We prayed and I felt silly saying words I did not understand. I felt hot. And then to my consternation they stopped praying while I felt impelled to continue. I knew already that this gift, although holy, is under our control; I could stop or start at will. I would have done anything not to be praying out loud in a strange language in front of strange Americans, but just as I thought I would die of self-consciousness God said to me, "Are you willing to be a fool for My sake?"

. . . After about six weeks I noticed something remarkable. Those I talked to about Christ believed. I could not understand it at first and wondered how my Chinese had so suddenly improved, or if I had stumbled on a splendid new evangelistic technique. But I was saying the same things as before. It was some time before I realized what had changed. This time I was talking about Jesus to people who wanted to hear. I had let God have a hand in my prayers and it produced a direct result. Instead of my deciding what I wanted to do for God and asking His blessing I was asking Him to do His will through me as I prayed in the language He gave me.

Now I found person after person wanted to receive Jesus. I could not be proud—I could only wonder that God let me be a small part of His work. And so the emotion came. It never came while I prayed, but when I saw the results of these prayers I was literally delighted. The Bishop should have told me what to expect at my confirmation when this could have started.[54]

who use them: they enable the wise surgeon to cut to the heart of a person's need, but they also permit the unwise to slash another and leave her to bleed. Models of Christian growth are tightly woven into our various traditions and communities. Most are connected in some form with scripture. Some reflect insights from the human sciences. Some are prescriptive; others are descriptive. Some focus on process; others focus on crisis. Some aim for perfection; others deny that possibility. Some assume that a few people have a special call to holiness; others assume that God has given a universal call to holiness. A *good* model will be constructed upon the foundations of authentic Christian spirituality established in chapter 1: (1) it will grow from the fundamental truths of the Christian faith, (2) it will acknowledge the reality of the spiritual world and the multidimensionality of human experience, (3) it will embrace the fullness of the gospel of divine-human relationship, and (4) it will express relationship with God in relationships of love. Here we will survey and evaluate some of the models of Christian growth. We will then explore yet another summary of Christian growth in an effort to synthesize the wisdom of the past and encourage more for the future.

History of Stage Models of Christian Growth. References to stages of Christian growth can be found as early as the Christian scriptures themselves. Paul writes in 1 Corinthians 3:1–2, "And so, brothers and sisters, I could not speak to you as spiritual people, but rather as people of the flesh, as infants in Christ. I fed you with milk, not solid food, for you were not ready for solid food. Even now you are still not ready." Ephesians 4:13–14 speaks of God's giving ministers to the church, "until all of us come to the unity of the faith and of the knowledge of the Son of God, to maturity, to the measure of the full stature of Christ. We must no longer be children, tossed to and fro and blown about by every wind of doctrine, by people's trickery, by their craftiness in deceitful scheming." Likewise, the author of Hebrews writes, "Therefore let us go on toward perfection, leaving behind the basic teaching about Christ, and not laying again the foundation: repentance from dead works and faith toward God, instruction about baptisms, laying on of hands, resurrection of the dead, and eternal judgment" (Hebrews 6:1–2). From children to adults, milk to solid food, immaturity to maturity, basic teaching to perfection—the stages may be simple, but the message is clear: people develop spiritually through recognizable stages. Those at one stage need different kinds of teaching and treatment than those at another. It is reasonable to assume that the spiritual life of others can be assessed in terms of a continuum between the beginning and end points of their metaphorical models. Christian growth is about moving as close to the mature side of the model as one can here on earth.

Subsequent to the writing of the scriptures, Origen of Alexandria's threefold schema offered a very early and very influential model of the stages of Christian growth. Drawing both from biblical and Neoplatonic influences, Origen suggested, in the prologue of his commentary on the Song of Solomon (Canticles), that the soul passes successively through three stages: learning virtue (*ethike*, associated with reflection on the book of Proverbs), reflecting on natural science (*physike*, associated with Ecclesiastes), and the contemplating of God (*enoptike*, associated with Song of Solomon). Origen's outline became the foundation for the development of two influential schemas in Christian history. Of the influence of Origen's outline in the West, Andrew Louth writes that "we clearly

> Models of the stages of Christian growth are powerful tools in the hands of those who use them: they enable the wise surgeon to cut to the heart of a person's need, but they also permit the unwise to slash another and leave her to bleed.

have here the beginning of the idea of the three ways of the mystical life, and very nearly the later familiar language of the way of purification (Origen's *ethike*), the way of illumination (*physike*) and the way of union (*enoptike*)."[55]

The Western church suggested a number of influential models during the Middle Ages. Bernard of Clairvaux wrote "On Loving God," his famous treatise in which he speaks of our motivation for spirituality in terms of four degrees of love: love of self for self's sake, love of God for self's sake, love of God for God's sake, and love of self for

249

God's sake. (See the excerpt from this essay in chapter 1.) Spiritual father Guigo II (d. ca. 1188) relates the development of the Christian life to the progression of *lectio divina* (see chapter 2): "Reading is an exercise of the outward senses; meditation is concerned with the inward understanding; prayer is concerned with desire; contemplation outstrips every faculty. The first degree is proper to beginners, the second to proficients, the third to devotees, the fourth to the blessed."[56] These models were developed largely within the context of monastic life, and they were especially directed to the believer's experience of prayer. While many Franciscans (and preeminently Bonaventure) promoted the threefold division of purgation, illumination, and union, the early Dominicans were cautious about precise models of prayer; perhaps for that reason, Dominican theologian Thomas Aquinas referred to stages of spiritual growth with the simple categories of beginners, proficient, and perfect.[57]

Protestant Reformers were often wary of models of spiritual growth. Martin Luther entered monastic life in obedience to a vow made in fear. His efforts at purgation brought him no illumination, no assurance of God's favor, and no union. Ultimately it was his surrender in faith to Christ's meritorious work on the cross that ushered Luther into union with God. This sense of acceptance, justification, and union with God then led Luther to illumination: illumination concerning his nature as simultaneously justified and sinful, and concerning the place of law and gospel in his life. He was now free from the burden of the works of purgation, undertaken to achieve God's favor, and free to express faith in love, as the Spirit leads through the Word. In a similar spirit, John Calvin stressed the priority of the Christian's mystical union with God as the basis for the illumination of justifying faith and the self-denial of Christian life. Anabaptists, "Spiritual" reformers, and such expressed varying approaches to models of spiritual growth.[58]

Protestant discussion of these matters settled into debates about the *ordo salutis* (order of salvation). Puritans discussed the issue of "preparationist" schemes of understanding conversion and the implications for Christian growth. In contrast to the Roman "triple way" of purgation, illumination, and union, "the main stream of Puritan thinking, in its treatment of sanctification," writes Richard Lovelace, "either abandoned the three stages or else reversed the order of them, beginning with the *unio Christi* as a basis for spiritual growth and proceeding through the illumination of faith to the mortification of sin."[59] A few Roman Catholics offered influential models of Christian growth in this period: the most notable of those models are Ignatius of Loyola's "weeks" in his *Spiritual Exercises*, Teresa of Avila's "seven mansions" in her *Interior Castle*, and John of the Cross's presentation of the various "dark nights" of the Christian life in his *Ascent of Mount Carmel* and the *Dark Night of the Soul*.[60]

Through the nineteenth and early twentieth centuries Protestants searching for the fullness of Christian growth struggled with questions of the role of particular postconversion experiences such as "entire sanctification" and the "baptism in the Holy Spirit." The spiritualities of the Holiness and Pentecostal movements are significantly shaped by models of spiritual growth. Roman Catholic manual spirituality summarized spiritual growth in terms of the threefold models of Thomas Aquinas or Bonaventure, illumined by the insights of Ignatian and Carmelite spirituality (especially as influenced by Teresa of Avila and John of the Cross).[61]

A significant contribution to the Christian understanding of the stages of growth came from research in developmental psychology in the late twentieth century. For example, drawing on developmental insights, James Fowler provided a model of the ways people tend to approach the things of religion at various age levels (Intuitive-Projective, Mythic-Literal, Synthetic-Conventional, Individuative-Reflective,

Conjunctive, and Universalizing Faith).[62] Others have drawn together insights from developmental psychology and specific religious traditions, suggesting a "wisdom of the Spirit" that is informed by both traditional and empirical sources.[63] Authors Janet Hagberg and Robert Guelich have promoted a model based on pastoral and scriptural reflection, identifying six separate stages and a time of struggle they call "the wall" (Recognition of God, Life of Discipleship, Productive Life, Journey Inward, the Wall, Journey Outward, Life of Love).[64] Still others explore the development of the Christian faith in terms of the different tasks or foci that characterize Christianity at different levels of maturity.[65]

The church today is the inheritor of an odd collection of models of spiritual growth. We are surrounded by many different—and at times conflicting—models of the stages of Christian growth. These models originate from a number of different settings, draw from a variety of different influences, and suggest different expressions of wisdom in practice.

Evaluating Stage Models of Christian Growth. Having surveyed models of the stages of spiritual growth found throughout the history of Christianity, we are now in a place to assess their value for us today. As mentioned above, a *good* model will be constructed upon the foundational principles of authentic Christian spirituality. Let us explore the possibilities and problems in employing such models of Christian development today in light of a few of these principles.

First, an authentic model or use of models of Christian development will arise from the fundamental truths of the Christian faith, grounded in the teachings of scripture as illumined through the history of the church's interpretation of the sacred text. While many will be able to appreciate the *descriptive* value of stage theories such as the traditional threefold way (in either the Eastern or Western expressions), we are in danger when we think of the threefold way as a biblical *normative* pattern for all

Christians. The pattern of purgation, illumination, and union, for example, is simply not taught in scripture. While the analogies between our spiritual development and the details of Moses's journey as developed by Gregory of Nyssa (or the analogies between our spiritual development and the books of Proverbs, Ecclesiastes, and Songs as developed by Origen) may be suggestive, they fail to account for the narrative, canonical, and poetic structure and language of the biblical texts concerned. Nor do we find a similar pattern reflected elsewhere. Certainly we find in scripture encouragement toward the purification of passions, toward the illumination of the heart and mind, and toward the union of believer and Christ. But these are so variously placed in scripture that no normative *succession* of elements can be determined. The narrative pattern of initiation-response-response can be determined with confidence, whereas purgation-illumination-union cannot.

Likewise, it can be dangerous to determine too closely the finer nuances of a Protestant *ordo salutis*. As we have already seen with the term *salvation*, terms like *repentance, called,* or *justified* may express ideas referring to a wide range of events or seasons. A precise schematization of an *ordo salutis* may require a systematization beyond the evidence of what is given in scripture. While such an order may be helpful for exploring the elements of our saving transformation and for considering the interaction among those elements, we must try to honor the ambiguities of the scripture itself. Likewise, while many Christians may experience a shift from an inward journey to an outward one, there is simply no normative support for this shift for all believers. While, as mentioned above, some passages indicate that there *are* stages of growth that require different teaching and pastoral treatment, we must be careful not to exaggerate the degree of *specificity* in the normative patterns we claim to find in scripture.[66]

We also must be careful of identifying "required" experiences from the scriptures. It seems clear from the New Testament *that* we are to experience the Holy Spirit. But just *what* experience is normative for all Christians in order to advance to another stage of growth seems beyond what we can confidently determine. Certainly we are all called to maturity. But whether that maturity is necessarily characterized by an experience of "infused contemplation," a "baptism of the Spirit," or a moment of "entire sanctification" is less clear. Rather, scripture and tradition affirm the diversity of giftedness and experience within a general framework of growth.

Second, an approach to the stages of Christian transformation will attempt to embrace the whole of the Christian gospel. Authentic spirituality aims at being Christ-centered, Spirit-led, and love expressive. An authentic model of spiritual growth (or an authentic use of models of spiritual growth) will seek to reconcile, for example, faith and works, or evangelism and social action. For this, we will need a sufficiently broad understanding of maturity, joining love for God to love for others. We can find precedent for this in the classics of spirituality themselves: for instance, in the final chapter of Teresa of Avila's *Interior Castle*, she concludes that the heights of prayer are given to equip us for the depths of service. Our approach to the stages of transformation must make room for growth both in the experience and in the expression of the Spirit. Likewise, an approach to the stages of growth that embraces the whole of the Christian gospel will embrace both individual and corporate dimensions of the gospel. We must move from thinking of Christian growth simply in terms of personal, interior maturity. The New Testament epistles were written to *communities*, and it is time that we reflect on what it might mean for our communities of faith to mature and that we ask what stages we might journey through on the way to corporate maturity. Consider, for example, pastor Rick Warren's well-known illustration of the baseball diamond, a model of congregational development in which the community passes through stages of commitment: from membership (first base), to maturity (second base), to ministry (third base), to missions (home plate).[67]

Third, we must respect the multidimensionality of human experience. We have discussed that multidimensionality itself in chapter 3 and have explored something of the diversity of relationship with God in chapter 6. We have learned that human experience is an integration of operational systems—cognition, emotion, volition— all working together all the time. In light of our account of human experience, we can see that an approach to the stages of spiritual maturity which assumes that one operational system is a higher faculty than the others (such as those of Origen or Guigo II) is simply inadequate to account for the complexities of personal (and corporate) spiritual development. While we can appreciate how the *purification* of every aspect of human experience might enable us to perceive the things of God more clearly, to receive God's *illumination*, and then to walk into *union* with God in ongoing relationship, we can also see how a fundamental sense of *union* with God (a re-Integration) might open up *illumining* transformations in our perception and make possible *purifications* unavailable prior to a given stage of encounter with God.[68] What has become clear throughout our exploration of human experience is that individuals and groups exhibit unique tendencies within operational systems, stages, relationships, and so on. We must give room for the stages of spiritual development to be experienced differently by people of different ages, cultures, genders, and personality types. From this perspective we can celebrate the multiplicity of models as expressions of wisdom arising within distinct contexts and times.

And yet at the same time, human beings are similar enough that *some* tendencies common to all can be identified. Thus we must find ways of appreciating different "micromodels" of growth within a larger

FIGURE **7.5**
Stages of Ongoing Christian Salvation

1. Crawling, Standing, Walking: The First Year of Life
   This stage (which will be different for those coming to Christ "from within" than for those coming "from without") usually involves the acquisition of the following:
   - basic Christian truths
   - a felt sense of identity with Christ
   - basic habits
   - a fundamental break with the past
   - a sense of one's community
   - a formal initiation into the Christian faith and community
2. Stepping, Playing, Working: Solid Growth as a Child of God
   This stage usually involves:
   - an increased depth of heart, mind, and life
   - a beginning perception of and participation in the basic cycles of Christian discipleship:
     (a) initiation, response, response
     (b) presence, lesson, action, integration
   - a navigation of the "Who's right?" question (theology, community, identity)
   - a basic understanding of four primary means of grace (Holy Spirit, ordinary events of life, planned disciplines, community)
   - a shift from walking to stepping out: the beginnings of Christian service
3. Climbing, Dancing, Journeying: Exploring the Christian Life, Thriving within Tension
   This stage usually involves a development of the following:
   - a broader or deeper understanding and experience of God
   - an acquaintance with different traditions of the church
   - an exploratory attitude toward the breadth of Christian transformation (see below)
   - a familiarity with a wider range of means of grace
   - a life of active service and giftedness in the body of Christ
   - a practice of Christian discernment and reintegration
4. Active Resting, Restful Acting: Living a Mature Christian Life
   After a season of exploration, this stage involves an integration of what was gained and lost:
   - settling into a lifestyle of exploration, discernment, and reintegration
   - settling into a sense of identity, call, rhythm
   - settling into community and theology
   - settling into possibilities and limitations
   - navigating crisis and resettling
   - settling into short- and long-term investments

"macromodel." This macromodel must be broad enough to encompass the growth of Christians in general to the best of our knowledge (scripture assumes anyone can mature) yet narrow enough to assert *real* categories (scripture assumes that there are recognizable stages). And yet to honor the diversity of people (and to honor our own fallibility), we must hold this macromodel loosely, as a working hypothesis. Not an easy task, indeed!

In sum, an approach to the stages of Christian maturity will follow scripture in recognizing the possibility of identifying basic stages of growth, yet it will shy from identifying normative stages or experiences too narrowly. Such an approach will recognize the maturity of the inner and the outer, the individual and the corporate. It will seek to find categories that can make room for a wide range of diversity of experience, yet it will lump together what needs to be lumped together in order to be a useful model. Figure 7.5 presents an outline of a working macromodel, drawing somewhat from the biblical metaphor of growth from infancy to adulthood. We will explore this model more—especially in terms of how it might be useful in the context of the practice of spiritual formation—in the following chapter.

Final or Eschatological Salvation

You *will be saved* in the end. In the final glory, "we will be like him" (1 John 3:2). Our salvation will be complete. His rule will be entire; it will extend, indeed, over all areas of life. "Much more surely then, now that we have been justified by his blood, will we be saved through him from the wrath of God" (Romans 5:9). "He will transform the body of our humiliation that it may be conformed to the body of his glory, by the power that also enables him to make all things subject to himself" (Philippians 3:21). New Testament scholar Ralph Martin, commenting on this passage, says, "Now Paul expresses the hope that complete conforming to his Lord (3:21) will come at the resurrection from among the dead."[69] As mentioned above, our transformation is ultimately eschatological.

This too is the work of the Spirit, who is the guarantee of the final fulfillment of the divine-human relationship. The Spirit who raised Jesus will *raise* us as well (Romans 8:11) and is presently *transforming* us into the image of Christ, to which we shall be conformed in the end (2 Corinthians 3:18). Our experience of the Spirit *points to our destiny* in Christ (Romans 8:23). The Spirit is itself the *down payment* of our future inheritance (2 Corinthians 1:22; 5:5; Ephesians 1:13; 4:30). It is also the work of human persons, individual and corporate: a *deification* of humanity wherein we share the life of Christ increasingly and ultimately completely. Second Peter 1:4 states, "Thus he has given us, through these things, his precious and very great promises, so that through them you may escape from the corruption that is in the world because of lust, and may become participants of the divine nature." Deification is the ultimate transformation of every aspect of human experience into conformity with that of Christ. Spiritual writings first acquaint us with a proximate deification embodied in the person (or community) who, on account of the work of the Spirit, "transmits and radiates the eternal and divine Light and burns with divine love."[70] It

"will be realized in its fullness only in the age to come, after the resurrection of the dead."[71] And, as with the other moments of salvation, final salvation is a work of the community, the bride of Christ prepared for the groom.

The Breadth of Christian Transformation

Christian transformation touches us from the beginning to the end of our lives. And Christian transformation touches every aspect of our being. We have seen in chapter 5 that God's restoration addresses the whole of human experience. But, as we have learned, transformation is not instantaneous. We discover different aspects of God at different points along the journey; so also we discover different aspects of ourselves. Changes in relationship (a new intimacy, for example) are stimulated here and mature there. The particular sin we struggled with a few years ago may not be the sin we struggle with today. Christian transformation spreads, like a wonderful disease: "Attacking *every* barrier / You living breathing Carrier of love."

That is the way of relationships. They begin with an area of common ground, a doorway, so to speak. I meet you at work, in a class, waiting in line. And we find something in common. We talk about our work, our studies, the line. The relationship begins. Perhaps the relationship stays at this one-thing-in-common level for some time. Then perhaps you invite the relationship a step further by revealing something else: you have a model train set. "Really," I respond. "I *love* model train sets!" And the relationship grows. Perhaps awhile later, while working on the train set with you, I bring up what it must have been like to live in the era portrayed in our train setup (say, mid-nineteenth-century pioneer America). We begin to discuss whether our society has really progressed that much at all over time. You say you have wondered about this. We have a friendly discussion, and both of us come out of the discussion having learned something. Now we are sharing ideas and values. We begin to discover one another's distinctives. I am meticulous about things being in order. You are inconsistent about showing up on time. Now the relationship begins to experience tension as confrontation and change are introduced. And so the relationship spreads, infecting many different areas of our life. The closer we get, the more areas of our lives are involved in the relationship.

That's the way it is with God. Even at the start of the relationship, at initial conversion, the points of common ground with God will vary from person to person. Different areas of human experience become the doorways of God's transforming work. Our sense of need, and therefore our quests, are related to different aspects of human experience. For Francis of Assisi, it was his experience of the divisions between rich and poor that first pushed him in a Godward direction. For Ignatius of Loyola, his felt sense of the difference in his fantasies of the future, and the meanings they provided for his life, led to his transformation. For young Jackie Pullinger, her transformation began with her personal devotion and experience of God. For one community, such as the Dani tribe of West Papua, matters of worldview were critical to their initial acceptance of Christ.[72] It might be different for another community. As we have discussed in chapter 3, some of us are more sensitive to the affective system, others to the cognitive system. Some live for Experience; some live to Act; others Integrate. Some are very aware of themselves; others are aware of their environment; yet others are attentive to spiritual realities. Hence, just as the initiation of God is unique to each, so too the "repentance and faith," and the commitment, of initial salvation will look different for different individuals or groups.[73]

Likewise, ongoing salvation will address different aspects of our lives at different times. As dysfunctional patterns of affective experience are exposed and transformed by the touch of God, we may be freed to experience the love of God and others in new (and more true) ways. As we are awakened to the plight of the unconverted and God's heart for the spread of the gospel, we may find both a new freedom and a new burden emerge in our experience. At times we may be awakened to these hitherto unnoticed dimensions of Christian living over a long period. At other times, we may be confronted with transformation in a moment of crisis. Thus, there is a sense in which we may experience many "conversions" in our lives: many times in which, while still retaining our fundamental Christian faith, we find ourselves in need of rethinking (or re-experiencing, or re-embodying) the whole once again in order to appropriate our growing relationship with God. Thomas Merton writes, "We are not converted only once in our lives, but many times; and this endless series of large and small conversions, inner revolutions, leads to our transformation in Christ."[74] Donald L. Gelpi speaks of a number of forms of conversion: moral, religious, affective, intellectual, and sociopolitical. Others have suggested other forms of conversion. Let us look at a few of these as a way of exploring the breadth of God's transforming work.[75]

Affective Conversion

"True religion, in great part, consists in the affections," writes Jonathan Edwards.[76] Religious reality, like aesthetic reality, is often *felt* more than *thought*. Sometimes, however, we view relationship with God simply as a set of beliefs to adopt, and we do not consider emotion (or we consider it as unimportant). Then God decides—in his perfect timing—to address our emotions, our dysfunctions, our stuff. Whether early or late, sooner or later many of us find ourselves in the midst of "**affective conversion**." For Gelpi, this came in midlife: "In my own case, affective conversion came last of all. One cannot make the Ignatian long retreat and experience regular spiritual direction without dealing at some level with one's affectivity. Only the mid-life crisis, however, forced me to face methodically my own emotional development. Over the years, affective conversion has produced a measure of emotional healing. It has also freed me to acknowledge unhealed areas in my heart and to name longstanding neuroses as old familiar friends."[77]

Perhaps affective transformation is triggered by reflection on scripture. We discover the repeated references to emotion: fear, hope, hatred of sin, desire, sorrow, zeal. We read of Jesus's compassionate identification with the feelings of others. We reflect on sin as a hardness of heart. We experience the passionate rhetoric of the epistles. And we realize that we must learn to feel for things as God feels for things. Or perhaps we are confronted with our own dysfunctional emotional system. We value the wrong things and so get unduly excited when we wish we were not. We find ourselves overreacting in anger in situations. We experience a depression hanging over us, weighing us down. We have this habit of stuffing emotions and consequently cannot seem to experience life to its fullest. We are simply confronted by God and are "undone" (Isaiah 6:5 KJV).

This sense of dissatisfaction, then, stimulates a process of conversion. And the process of affective conversion continues until there is some sense of commitment and resolution regarding the restoration of affective experience. The restoration may come through relationships with others, through nature, through music, or through a spontaneous experience of the Spirit (or through some combination of these). It may come suddenly or it may come over time. The conversion may involve a complete rethinking of lifestyle and worldview, or it may simply be the introduction of a new way of feeling about things. In the end we find ourselves aroused by compassion rather than lust, or we find ourselves reacting in patience rather than anger. Or, having really felt God's forgiveness, we can now forgive the ones who have hurt us. In the end we experience the grace of transformation, especially in the dimension of our emotions.[78]

Intellectual Conversion

Sometimes conversion is not a matter of the heart but the head. Consider the student who grew up in a church that greatly prized one's sense of the Spirit. He finds himself in college desperately needing to make sense of his faith: what he believes and why he believes. He needs to start again from scratch, for himself, until he is able to find a solid intellectual foundation for his faith. Until then, he feels that he cannot pursue his relationship with God. Indeed, his persistent questioning *is* his pursuit of relationship with God. Consider another for whom intellectual questions were simply not primary at initial conversion. But later she encounters the need to reconvert intellectually. Hers may be a joyful discovery of the riches of God's salvation. Or it may be a difficult period of questioning the foundations of her faith, of wondering whether she will remain a Christian. Transformation takes us on strange journeys at times, if we follow its lead.

Human beings feel. Human beings also think. We analyze, categorize, hypothesize, and synthesize what confronts us in life. Quite often the frameworks that give shape to our thinking and the procedures by which we do our thinking are perfectly adequate to facilitate and express our relationship with God. But sometimes they are not. Sometimes we find ourselves praying what we don't really believe. Sometimes we find that our beliefs have been rooted not in scripture and tradition, but in culture and perdition. Sometimes the biases of our society or our own interests cloud our thinking and prevent us from seeing things the way God sees them. We may be irrational, or we may hide beneath a phony rationalism. Or we may just be a little lost.

Intellectual conversion can be a doorway to initial salvation for some. Griffin's reflections on conversion are especially sensitive to this dimension, as her own conversion required some rigorous intellectual activity. She writes, regarding two people who influenced her own conversion, "What appealed to me most strongly was their growing realization that thought could be trusted as a way of discovering reality."[79] We face questions of the reasonableness of the existence of God, the problem of evil, the reliability of the scriptures, or the relationship between Christianity and other religions. And for some of us, one or the other of these questions simply *must* be answered to our satisfaction before we are able to entrust ourselves to the God of Christianity. But be warned: there is a fine line between aggressive questioning as authentic pursuit of God and aggressive questioning as a means of avoiding God.

Often intellectual conversion (whether part of initial or ongoing salvation) will require a rethinking of conventional beliefs. Gelpi writes that "one cannot lead a fully responsible intellectual life until one reflects critically on conventional beliefs. If conventional morality inculcates a mixture of virtue and vice, conventional wisdom inculcates a mixture of truth and error. The intellectual traditions of every human community hand on some truths, but they also hand on unverifiable prejudices, ideological obfuscations, and lies. Intellectual conversion, therefore, means recognizing that one cannot automatically accept everything one learns as true. The acquisition of truth involves more than memorizing set formulas and creeds. It engages the mind actively."[80]

The journeys of the mind, like those of the emotions, cannot be predicted. The questions posed by one person or community will not be the same questions posed by another. What *is* clear, however, is that in a way appropriate to each, God desires that we renew our minds, that we possess knowledge in increasing measure (2 Peter 1:5–6). This is intellectual conversion.

Moral Conversion

And then there is **moral conversion**, the transformation of habits of choice or

"What might conversion look like?"

action. Most of us are familiar with this. Cycles of compulsive behavior entrap us in lives we would rather not have. These behaviors could be as minor as talking too much in small-group settings or as serious as serial rape. Moral conversion is a significant aspect of initial salvation for many, as we turn to Christ for help in breaking these habits in our lives. But even as we mature in Christ, we discover habits we may not have noticed in our spiritual childhood. And at times we discover that these habits, while perhaps less obvious, are more harmful to others than those we dealt with in our early years of faith.

It is easy to distinguish affective, intellectual, and moral conversion on paper, but it is often tougher in reality, especially when the issues get deep. Immoral habits, false beliefs, and dysfunctional patterns of emotion get all tied up with each other as the lines between lifestyle, worldview, and core emotional concerns merge; and we find that transformation in one sphere may lead to (or even require) changes in other areas of our lives.

Religious Conversion

Affective, intellectual, and moral conversion address the transformation of human experience with regard to operational systems. But transformation also addresses us with regard to our web of relationships. We wake up to the reality of God and look at ourselves for the first time as "God-related": our way of being is now formed (or perhaps re-formed, in a season of renewal) by relationship with God. We see ourselves as creatures of God in a new way. At this point we might want to speak of a **"religious" conversion**, a new awakening with regards to relationship with God.

Psychological Conversion

Or we discover ourselves in a new way. We wake up to ourselves. God reveals who I am to who I am, and we find ourselves. This may be connected with a reworking of affectivity, worldview, or habit; or it may simply be a matter of reconciling ourselves to ourselves, of becoming comfortable with our values, preferences, purposes, and lifestyle. This transformation of our self-relatedness may happen suddenly, say, following a near fatal accident. Or it might happen over time as the development of a self-searching quest or encounter. We find at the end of this quest that God desires that we be properly related not only to God, but to ourselves as well. Religious transformation changes us in terms of our relatedness to God; **psychological conversion** changes us in terms of our relatedness to ourselves.

Social Conversion

Social conversion changes us in terms of our relatedness to others. It may be that we entered Christianity to be rescued from Hell. While this is not necessarily a wrong motive for responding to God's invitation to relationship (indeed it is a common motive in scripture and in the history of Christian spirituality), it may not place our relatedness to others front and center. The social implications of our faith—for example, questions of compassion, justice, and so on—may arise only after we have been Christians for a while. Or perhaps conversely, seeing the gospel in terms of

our relatedness to others is the *doorway into* initial salvation, as it was for Francis of Assisi or Dorothy Day. For some, social conversion is a significant experience. We find ourselves reading our Bibles with new eyes. We begin to mourn or to rejoice for others as we have never done. We see Christianity not only in terms of what God has done for *me*, not only in terms of what God wants of *me*, but now also in terms of God's heart for *us*, communities both small and large. We understand sin as structural as well as personal. And we perceive the kingdom of God not just in terms of an increase of the numbers of individual believers, but also in terms of the remaking of society.

Ecological Conversion

Finally, we might discover a new sense of identification with the creation: with our bodies; with the land; with plants, animals, and stars; with the sheer physicality of things. We find ourselves related (or re-related) to nature—hence, **ecological conversion**. (*Ecology* refers, by definition, to our interrelatedness with the earth.) As with other transformations, scripture and tradition may play a role. We may find that God is about building a new heaven and a new earth, that we have been placed on the earth to be keepers of the earth; or we may simply discover that we are creatures ourselves, physical bodies who happen to relate to God as such. Or a fascination with natural science may drive us into our relationship with nature. Or it may be a matter of making commitments: we embrace the combination of wildness and domesticity necessary for "getting along with nature."[81] We choose to treat our bodies as temples of God. And we are changed.

A transformation in any segment of the web of our relationships has a tendency to affect our experience of affective, intellectual, and moral action. When we see the world from the perspective of a social conversion, we feel the consequences of social sins more sharply. After conversion to the reality of God, one may never think about the nature of the universe the same again. Likewise, changes in social systems and spiritual life influence one another. Consider for example, a stereotypical beer-drinking, football-watching, couch potato husband. His wife wishes he would get a life, so she talks her brother into inviting the husband to a large men's religious conference at the stadium. Well, husband comes home an entirely different man. He goes into his room and reads the Bible; he goes to men's prayer meetings; he talks about God all the time. And the wife finds herself feeling somewhat abandoned. His spiritual transformation has changed the dynamics around the house. Conversely, changes in social systems can stimulate changes in spiritual interest (for example, in the case of a death or divorce).[82]

Furthermore, one conversion tends to influence the others. For example, affective conversion animates the other forms of conversion, providing enthusiasm to our transforming work elsewhere. Intellectual conversion informs the other forms of transformation, providing frameworks and methodological procedures that assist us when we address our habits or our relationships with others. Social or ecological conversion de-privatizes affective and moral conversion by raising normative feelings and actions from the realm of personal experience to their place in the context of a larger world. One transformation supports others, and so salvation spreads, like a wonderful infection.[83]

And, as we learned above, transformation is a cooperative venture. Individuals experience affective conversion; so do congregations. (Consider what happens after that special meeting when the whole congregation is touched.) Just as individuals may go through a period of discovering the social impact of their own personal relationship with God, so also communities can have a psychological conversion where the community realizes in a new way its corporate identity before God. Just as the faith of individuals is shaped by their association with the community surrounding them,

The Breadth of Transformation

Transformation touches every part of human experience.

our emotions and concerns	*affective conversion*
our beliefs and worldviews	*intellectual conversion*
our habits and lifestyles	*moral conversion*
our relationship with God	*religious conversion*
our relationship with ourselves	*psychological conversion*
our relationship with others	*social conversion*
our relationship with nature	*ecological conversion*

so also the faith of a community is shaped by the individuals who weave their way in and out of the community over time. The breadth of transformation is experienced on both corporate and personal dimensions simultaneously, making life incredibly complicated at times.

As we grow to know God, we begin to discover, and then to share, God's own thoughts, feelings, choices, relationships, and such. God's desire is that we put on his mind, that we increasingly feel like God feels for the world, that we experience what God experiences, that we understand what God understands, that we are increasingly aware of what God is aware of, that we do the kinds of things God does. God's desire is that we love him with *all* our heart, mind, soul, and strength. The breadth of Christian transformation covers every aspect of our being.

The Depth of Christian Transformation

Our restoration is experienced from the beginning to the end of our spiritual lives. It touches every area of our being. Likewise, God makes his presence known in the simplest, most ordinary aspects of life as well as in the deepest parts of our being. In chapter 3, we discovered the *depth dimension* to human experience. On one level, we deal with thoughts, feelings, choices, and actions. On a deeper level, we deal with beliefs, emotions, and habits. Still deeper, we deal with worldviews, nuclear concerns, and lifestyles. And this level itself is, perhaps, followed by one that goes still deeper. The deeper we go, the more the content of human experience begins to affect everything else. It is experienced as being more significant, as being at the center of our lives. In chapter 6, we returned to this dimension again, suggesting that part of *intimacy* in relationships involves the level of depth at which relationship is shared. Intimacy in any relationship is shaped by the levels at which the other's invitations are experienced; so intimacy in one's relationship with God is shaped by the levels at which God's invitations are experienced. Hence, it is only natural for us to consider transformation as possessing not only length and breadth but also *depth*. Our changes in Christ may address the minor matters of life. They can also encompass the deepest core of our being.

This aspect of transformation was especially significant to Protestantism in the late nineteenth and early twentieth centuries. In both America and the United Kingdom, "deeper life" conferences were attended by thousands seeking to find a way into greater intimacy with and surrender to God. The deeper life movement (also called the Keswick movement and the "higher" or "victorious" life movement) emphasized our need for full identity in Christ, contact with the Holy Spirit at the depths of the human spirit, the potential for significant transformation in this life, and the centrality of the cross as the focal point of transformation. Bible expositor J. Sidlow Baxter identifies the longings of this movement in a concise definition:

> It is that experience, originating at the crisis-point of utter self-yielding to God (not always emotionally vivid but always most definite) in which the Holy Spirit infills the heart, making fellowship with God and possession of Christ real as never before, and effecting within the fully consecrated believer a moral and spiritual renewal into

holiness deeper and fuller than could ever be known otherwise.[84]

Jesus complains about the Pharisees' lack of deep transformation present, crying, "But woe to you Pharisees! For you tithe mint and rue and herbs of all kinds, and neglect justice and the love of God; it is these you ought to have practiced, without neglecting the others" (Luke 11:42). Jesus's cry echoes the voices of the Hebrew prophets, who urged their hearers beyond a shallow understanding of their sacrifices, to consider the sacrifice of the depths of their heart. God's call to intimacy sounds, at times, like the call of a lover to the beloved:

> There's a lot of things that I would
>   know
> If you would let me climb into your
>   soul and see
> Your deeper side.[85]

Research indicates that there are two key aspects to developing intimacy in relationships: "the pacing of the deepening of intimacy, and the timing of revealing negative or positive information about yourself."[86] There is an art to knowing when and how much to reveal. Happily, this is not a problem in terms of our relationship with God—at least from God's side. God will not feel threatened if we reveal too much too quickly. God will not give up on the relationship if we pray shallow prayers for a long time. Furthermore, God knows just how much we can handle of his own self-revelation. God invites us into his depths at a pace that is just right for us. At times we may feel rather confronted by some aspect of God, but we can trust God's timing. The Triune God knows about relationship!

The transformation of the Spirit touches all levels of human experience. Here it might be the simple presence of joy as you watch a child. There it might be the presence of profound joy in an experience of deep spiritual healing. Here it might be a new insight while reading a text of scripture. There it might be an overthrow of one's entire framework of thinking about God. Here it might be the change of an insignificant habit, like changing one's diet. There it might be the adoption of a whole new way of living, like taking monastic (or marital) vows. God's Spirit is present in the large and the small, the shallow and the deep. Neither the trivial nor the profound is necessarily more holy than the other. Indeed, sometimes in relationships, depth is realized in discovering that we have shared in the small things for a very long time.

Nevertheless, relationship with God must be experienced at a certain minimal level of depth in order for it to get off the ground. Initial salvation requires a certain degree of commitment. One must be willing to make a go of it, so to speak. Needless to say, one flounders trying to prescribe precisely what level of depth may be required for any given individual, especially when we take into consideration the diversity of God's transforming work in terms of the stages of human experience discussed above. Nevertheless, nearly all of us would agree that conversion must touch to some extent not only our thoughts and actions, but also our worldview, our nuclear emotional concerns, or our way of life.[87]

Ongoing salvation will be experienced at varying levels of depth, just as any relationship is experienced at various levels of depth. Relationships get in ruts at times. One may start out with a great deal of self-revelation, only to shy away. What was once deep and significant becomes old hat and in need of renewal. Psychological research speaks about "intensification." Evangelicals cry out for revival. Spiritual directors talk about developing transparency in prayer.[88] Lived relationship with God is the navigation of these seasons of shallowness and depth.

Christian transformation, whether initial or ongoing, is, to a greater or lesser extent, a kind of "depth reception" of the gospel. In this depth reception of the gospel, awareness of God's holiness or love, comprehension of human dignity or sinfulness, understanding of the salvation brought to us through Christ, or other themes of the faith are internalized in depth to some degree. The common content of the Christian faith is made real for each person or group at appropriate depths. "O the depth of the riches and wisdom and knowledge of God! How unsearchable are his judgments and how inscrutable his ways!" (Romans 11:33).

Questions

1. How do different theologies present the roles of God and humans in Christian transformation? Take two sample theological perspectives. How might these perspectives work their way out into different approaches to perceiving the divine and human roles in transformation? How might this, in turn, lead to differently lived spiritualities?

2. How might a focus on one or the other moments of salvation lead to different emphases in the spiritual life? For example, how might an emphasis with regard to the finished work of Christ (historical salvation) affect one's interest in or practicing of spiritual disciplines and such (ongoing salvation)? Or how might an acute interest in sanctification lead to tension with others who are especially concerned with justification?

3. Review your own relationship with God (or that of your own congregation). Can you identify the stages of your initial salvation (or the congregation's initial rootedness in Christ)? Where is it similar (or different) from the presentation in the text? Why?

4. Make a list of people you know who might be labeled "from the inside," "once-born," "twice born." Think about advice you might give each one along the way. What lessons do you learn from such reflections for the education programs or the evangelistic efforts of your own Christian community?

5. With which aspects of the breadth of Christian transformation are you most familiar? Least familiar? Where are you deep with God? Where are you shallow? Why? What might you like to do about this?

6. This chapter addressed the breadth of transformation in a very cursory manner. Design a research project to explore one of these dimensions. What disciplines might you need to draw on in order to explore, for example, ecological conversion? What texts of scripture, what theological themes, what writings in the history of the church might inform your own developing wisdom about this one aspect of transforming relationship with God?

Practicing Christian Spirituality

My Spiritual Autobiography

There are stories from our lives through which God is trying to tell us things we need to know. We need to identify these stories, tell them, and try to sort them out. We need "to read our own history, to see the turning points, the moments of change, the unfolding of God's plan for us each step of the way."[89]

Biography has been a central part of Christian spirituality since the Gospels themselves. And autobiography has been an important genre of spiritual literature since Augustine's *Confessions*. We love to tell our stories. In fact, we *need* to tell our stories. The mere act of telling our story helps us to define and to understand who we are, what God has done. For some, giving our testimony was an oppressive ritual, especially if our story did not fit the model of conversion held dear to a particular tradition. But for others, the chance to recount our experience of God's transforming work in our lives is itself life-giving. Perhaps it is time we renew the art of spiritual autobiography or "giving testimony."[90]

To create your spiritual autobiography you must be sensitive to a few things. First, you must welcome God's timing in your life. To see the work of God over your whole life, you must see where and how God has taken his time with you. Recognize both the sudden and the gradual changes. Second, you must welcome your context. You must learn to appreciate God's use of all kinds of forces around you to shape your transformation. If you want, you can think in terms of three categories of context: *macrocontext* (the larger cultural milieu in which you were formed), *microcontext* (family, religious community, work, neighborhood), and *individual* context (your personal experience). But don't get lost trying to list all the macro- and microcontexts. While it can be helpful to recognize their influence in your life, it is *your* story you are telling.

Take some time and look back. Look back over your whole life. This is not just about the time you went forward at an altar call. This is not just about your baptism or confirmation. Try to see where God has been active in your whole life. Where have you experienced God's initiation or transformation at each stage of life? Identify key events or seasons of your spiritual life. Then formulate an *interpretation* of them. Part of the grace of composing spiritual autobiography is the opportunity to make sense of our past, to give it meaning. But beware of religious jargon. Don't just speak of "receiving Jesus in my heart" or of being "filled with the Spirit"; speak of the influences, the context, the real experience of the thing. Tell what actually happened. Give yourself permission to look at both the small and the big things, to see where transformation deepened and where it did not. Avoid the temptation to smooth over times of ambiguity and uncertainty. Your aim is not to compose a good autobiography but to honestly discover and interpret your own transforming relationship with God.

After you have reviewed each stage of the past, ask yourself, Where does this leave me in the present? One of the blessings of spiritual autobiography is that it helps us clarify our call. Here you prayerfully consider where you and God have been; and in doing so, you gain a sense of where you may be going. You see into the heart of your identity in Christ. Knowing the past may give wisdom for the future.

Now, having reflected on your story, you are ready to tell it. You may write it down and keep it in a private journal. But I also encourage you just to tell it. You gain some things from prayerfully reflecting on your life. You gain different things from sharing it with others.

CHAPTER SUMMARY

1. Christian transformation is about the changes that take place when we establish and grow in relationship with God through Christ. Transformation is not only about changes in us, but also about changes in the relationship itself, the ways that we interact with God and others. It is a Godward reorientation of life, wherein our relationship with God governs how we conduct our thinking, our feeling, our acting. It is a cooperative work, involving God's gracious work of invitation—the work of the Spirit of life—and the work of humans. As a *human* work it is subject to all the idiosyncrasies of human experience. Finally, transformation is the goal of Christian faith. To be transformed into the image of Christ is the destiny of the church.

2. Christian transformation is acted out from the cross to the eschaton. We can speak of the length of Christian transformation in terms of four moments of salvation: historical salvation, initial salvation, ongoing salvation, and final salvation. Christian spirituality deals with initial salvation and especially ongoing salvation.

3. With regard to the dynamics and stages of initial and ongoing salvation, there is a spiritual wisdom to be gained from attending the lessons to be learned from scripture, the writings of Christian spirituality, and careful observation of real people. By drawing together information from a number of sources we guard ourselves against mislabeling spiritual stages or misdiagnosing spiritual problems.

4. We come to faith—insofar as coming to faith involves associating ourselves with the Christian community—"from the inside" or "from the outside." Some have grown up within the Christian community and are familiar with the ideas and practices of the faith. Others have little contact or background in personal history to acquaint them with Christianity. Still others can be labeled "once-born": they have not necessarily been raised within the church, but they find themselves to have been in some kind of relationship with God all their lives. Those who leave the faith and return, or those who come to faith from the outside, can be labeled "twice-born."

5. Both initial and ongoing salvation develop in generally recognizable stages (though these should not be pressed too strictly). In initial salvation we often see a progression from a context, through some kind of crisis and quest, into significant encounters and interactions, and finally into a commitment that produces important consequences. In ongoing salvation we generally mature from a spiritual infancy of getting acquainted with the faith; through childhood, where that faith is established through solid growth in key areas; on through adolescence and young adulthood, where we explore new dimensions of relationship with God; and into a mature Christian life, where we settle into God, community, and ministry.

6. Christian transformation encompasses every aspect of human experience. As a new aspect of human experience is integrated into relationship with God, we might speak of a different "conversion." Thus, as different areas of our lives are transformed, we can identify affective, intellectual, moral, religious, psychological, social, and ecological conversions. Each transformation influences the others, fostering further union of individual and community with the fullness of the Trinitarian God.

7. Likewise, Christian transformation addresses every level of depth in human experience. Just as human-to-human relationships grow in depth through fits and starts, so also our relationship with God experiences the normal course of ups and downs as we allow our depths to be revealed to God or as God allows a new depth of his own heart to be revealed to us.

LOOKING FURTHER

In addition to the many stories of transformation in the classics of Christian spirituality (see notes for examples), consider these texts.

Characteristics

On the characteristics of transformation, see William James, *The Varieties of Religious Experience* (New York: Simon and Schuster, 1997); Richard Peace, *Conversion in the New Testament: Paul and the Twelve* (Grand Rapids: Eerdmans, 1999); and *The Psychology of Religion: An Empirical Approach*, ed. Ralph W. Hood, Bernard Spilka, Bruce Hunsberger, and Richard Gorsuch, 2nd ed. (New York: Guilford, 1996).

Length

See Gordon Smith, *Beginning Well: Christian Conversion and Authentic Transformation* (Downers Grove, IL: InterVarsity Press, 2001); Emilie Griffin, *Turning: Reflections on the Experience of Conversion* (Garden City, NY: Image, 1982); Lewis R. Rambo, *Understanding Religious Conversion* (New Haven: Yale University Press, 1993); James W. Fowler, *Stages of Faith: The Psychology of Human Development and the Quest for Meaning* (San Francisco: Harper and Row, 1981); and Janet Hagberg and Robert Guelich, *The Critical Journey: Stages in the Life of Faith*, rev. ed. (Salem, WI: Sheffield, 2005).

Breadth

See Bernard Lonergan's *Method in Theology* (Minneapolis: Seabury, 1972); Donald L. Gelpi's *Committed Worship: A Sacramental Theology for Converting Christians*, 2 vols. (Minneapolis: Liturgical Press, 1993); and *The Conversion Experience: A Reflective Process for RCIA Participants and Others* (Mahwah, NJ: Paulist Press, 1998).

Depth

A couple of good examples of "deeper life" spirituality can be found in J. Sidlow Baxter's *Going Deeper* and *His Deeper Work in Us: A Further Enquiry into New Testament Teaching on the Subject of Christian Holiness* (Grand Rapids: Zondervan, 1959 and 1967, respectively).

Christian
Spiritual Formation

OBJECTIVES

In this chapter you will learn about Christian spiritual formation—how we cooperate with the work of God to facilitate ongoing transformation in our relationship with God as individuals and communities. You will learn a few basic principles on which Christian spiritual formation is founded. You will see why the Methodists are called *Methodists*. You will consider the aims of spiritual formation, struggling with questions of holiness, perfection, deification, kingdom, and increase. You will examine the central tasks and means of Christian spiritual formation. You will consider questions of asceticism and hedonism. Finally, you will take steps toward your own spiritual formation by writing your own "spiritual agenda."

After reading this chapter you should be able to

- distinguish Christian spiritual formation from other sorts of Christian activities;
- identify both general and specific contexts within which an individual or community is formed, suggesting how the context might shape the formation process;
- recommend appropriate agents of spiritual formation for individuals or groups;
- clarify both ultimate and proximate aims for spiritual formation for an individual or group such that they might be able to see both how a given aim is connected with the gospel itself and how this aim makes sense to the concrete details of this individual's (or group's) life;
- describe the process of spiritual formation, identifying steps of that process and giving examples of how those steps are worked out through the breadth and length of human experience;
- identify wise means that might be used to facilitate Christian spiritual formation.

Introducing Christian Spiritual Formation

A potter forms a lump of clay into a pot or a mug, pushing the clay a little this way and pulling it a little that way. Parents and teachers talk about children being in their "formative years." The term *formation* brings to mind shaping and molding, influencing the development of a potential into a completed actual. *Christian spiritual formation* refers to a similar shaping process with reference to our relationship with God. We have learned that Christian spirituality is about relationship with God, an interactive give-and-take between God and humans. We have also learned that relationship with God involves *trans*-formation: changes *in* the relationship and changes that happen *on account of* the relationship. The restoration made available through Christ is realized through the transformation of corporate and personal life, a transformation that involves both God and human. Divine *trans-formation* is joined with human efforts of spiritual *formation*. Gordon Smith writes, "Conversion is never an end; it is a beginning and a means to an end. Thus it must be followed by a program of spiritual formation that should mirror the very nature and contours of Christian conversion."[2]

The use of the term *spiritual formation* is a fairly recent development in Christian (and especially Protestant) circles.[3] Its connection to the history of Christian spirituality is through the training of "religious" (monks, nuns, priests and such). For example, in the "complementary norms" of the Constitution of the Order of the Society of Jesus (the Jesuits), we find the encouragement regarding the training of young Jesuits that "there should be an organic unity in the entire formation, so that from the beginning of the novitiate and throughout the entire course of studies, spiritual formation, the work of study, and apostolic activity should be closely integrated. All who have charge of the training of our members, either in government or in teaching, should diligently and harmoniously work together for this integration."[4]

Interest in spiritual formation spread from Roman Catholic training to Protestant circles in the 1960s and 70s. Seminaries and "centers" developed programs to provide clergy training in spiritual development unavailable in traditional seminary education or to offer similar training to the laity. Thus whereas *transformation* may refer to the process of Godward change flowing from relationship with God (involving both God and human), *spiritual formation* tends to refer to the human side of the equation, to the initiatives and means by which we seek to foster and "work out" the transformation that God "works in." The following may serve as a working definition of Christian spiritual formation:

> Christian spiritual formation refers to the intentional and semi-intentional processes by which believers (individuals and communities) become more fully conformed and united to Christ, especially with regard to maturity of life and calling.[5]

Basic Principles of Christian Spiritual Formation

Colossians 2:16–3:17 directly addresses issues of spiritual formation. At the close of Colossians 2, Paul describes how *not* to approach ascetical practice, warning his readers about imposed regulations concerning new moons, sabbaths, angels, and what not to taste or touch. Then, in Colossians 3:1–17, he presents in general terms his position regarding how *to* approach spiritual formation, setting our eyes on the things above, stripping ourselves of the old, and clothing ourselves with the new. By looking at this passage in its two divisions we can discover a few basic principles of Christian spiritual formation.

What Christian Spiritual Formation Is Not (Colossians 2:16–23)

Our first principle of Christian spiritual formation is this: Christian spiritual formation does *not* focus on the appearance, the politics, or the particulars of spirituality. Paul calls those imposing regulations on others "puffed up" (Colossians 2:18) and says their actions have an "appearance of wisdom" (Colossians 2:23). Jesus uses similar language of the Pharisees, asserting that their deeds are done "to be seen" (Matthew 6:1, 5, 16; 23:5). Paul warns the Colossians not to get caught up in this kind of spiritual fashion show. In a similar manner he rebukes spiritual practice rooted in political positioning. It is the *imposition* of these practices—these "regulations" and "human commands," as Paul calls them—that is of concern to him (Colossians 2:20–22). Again, Paul is following Jesus in this, for Jesus complained that the Pharisees "tie up heavy burdens, hard to bear, and lay them on the shoulders of others" and "lock people out of the kingdom of heaven" (Matthew 23:4, 13). Finally, Paul warns the Colossian believers not to be overconcerned with the particulars of religious practice: observing festivals, new moons, sabbaths. "These are only a shadow of what is to come," Paul writes, "but the substance belongs to Christ" (Colossians 2:17). Do not mistake the means for the ends, Paul cautions. Likewise Jesus says of those who focus on the particulars, "they have received their reward" (Matthew 6:5, 16). Furthermore, by focusing on the particulars, believers find themselves majoring in the minors, "not holding fast to the head" (Colossians 2:19; see Matthew 23:23–28). Ultimately this kind of approach to spiritual practice is bound to end in failure (Colossians 2:23).

What Christian Spiritual Formation Is (Colossians 3:1–17)

The second principle of Christian spiritual formation is this: Christian spiritual formation, responding to the gracious work of God and requiring both perseverance and progress, is the intentional and God-ward reorientation and rehabituation of human experience. It aims at mature harmony with Christ and is expressed in the concrete realities of everyday life. Let's unpack this a bit.

Reorientation and rehabituation. First, the task of Christian spiritual formation is the *re-orientation* and *rehabituation* of human experience. Reorientation of life is a transformation, an Integrating, of the concerns that drive our emotions, of the worldview that drives our opinions and evaluations, and of the core lifestyle that drives our habits and actions. Paul speaks of this in terms of a fundamental shift from the "things that are on earth" to "the things that are above" (Colossians 3:1–2), from the "old self" to the "new self" (Colossians 3:9–10). Spiritual formation is also a **rehabituation**, a transformation of particular patterns of emotions, conducts, thoughts, and intentions of our experience. Paul speaks of this in terms of leaving "the *ways* you . . . once followed" (Colossians 3:7), giving a specific list of vices and virtues in Colossians 3:5–15. In Colossians 3 he specifically mentions our minds (vv. 2, 10), our hearts (v. 15), and our practice (vv. 9, 17)—saying, essentially, that we are to love the Lord our God with all our heart, mind, soul, and strength. Ultimately, the aim of this divine-human effort is *mature harmony with Christ*. Observances are shadows; *Christ* is the substance (Colossians 2:17).

Response to grace. Paul makes it clear, however, that spiritual growth in relationship with God, growth into the image of God, is not simply a matter of human effort. God initiates, and we respond. Christian spiritual formation is a *response to the gracious work of God*. We have died and been raised with Christ, Paul says. Our life is "hidden with Christ in God" (Colossians 3:1–3). Likewise, in Romans 8, Paul urges his readers to put to death, "by the Spirit," the deeds of the flesh (Romans 8:13). The wisdom of what to address in our lives, the guidance on how to address it, the empowerment to actually face it, and the results of the work are all from the Spirit.

Christian Spiritual Formation

Christian spiritual formation refers to the process by which believers become more fully conformed and united to Christ, especially with regard to maturity of life and calling.

- Christian spiritual formation does *not* focus on the appearance, the politics, or the particulars of spirituality.
- Christian spiritual formation responds to the gracious work of God and requires both perseverance and progress.
- Christian spiritual formation is the intentional and Godward reorientation and rehabituation of human experience.
- Christian spiritual formation aims at mature harmony with Christ.
- Christian spiritual formation is expressed in the concrete realities of everyday life.

Intentional. Nonetheless, Christian spiritual formation *is* a matter of human effort. Though guided and empowered by the Spirit, it demands an *intentional* and even, at times, *aggressive* effort on the part of the believer. Although Paul rebukes the Colossian imposition of regulations, he does not advise passivity. Listen to the images Paul uses: "put to death," "strip off," "get rid of," "clothe yourselves with" (Colossians 3:5–12). And these are not rare instances. Elsewhere we hear Paul urging believers with phrases such as "devote yourselves to," "persevere in," "do not neglect," "pursue," "turn away from," "rid yourselves of," "have nothing to do with," and so on. Furthermore, for Paul, remaining within the boundaries of gospel spirituality involves both *perseverance* and *progress* in the faith. The new self "is being renewed." "Let the word of Christ *dwell* in you," Paul writes.[6] Formation is intentional and ongoing.[7]

Expressed in life. Finally, Christian spiritual formation *is expressed in the concrete realities of everyday life.* Spiritual formation is not some ethereal change known only in the interior recesses of the prayer life of the advanced believer. Although it may involve a transformation of our prayer (how could setting our minds on the things above *not* have an effect on our prayers?), authentic Christian spiritual formation will produce tangible changes in the lives of individuals and communities. Paul speaks in terms of both specific vices that should be less evident and specific virtues that should be more evident in the life of the Colossian church (Colossians 3:5–17). Christian spiritual formation involves a reorientation and rehabituation of our lives. It aims at full harmony with Christ. It is divine insofar as it responds to divine grace; it is human insofar as it is intentional and ongoing. It is expressed in life.[8]

The Contexts and Agents of Christian Spiritual Formation

The first thing we must understand about the processes of Christian spiritual formation is that they do not happen in a vacuum. Formation is change of existing form, a form that is what it is because of a context. It is critical to understand this from the start. Lack of attention to the contexts of spiritual formation can result in a number of pitfalls in the spiritual life. We may apply means of grace to our lives (for example, fasting) out of a sense of duty or guilt (or, worse yet, it may be imposed on us by those in leadership in a given community) without any knowledge of our own diet and health. We may incur serious harm to our health (and to our spiritual growth) due to an inappropriate application of this means. We may, consequently, give up the idea of ascetical practice as ineffective or stupid. Thus, the *intention* of formation must be balanced with the *wisdom* of formation. Wisdom pays attention to the way things are.

The Formative Life

The general context of spiritual formation is life itself. As we have seen, we live in

focus

Historical Portrait:
The Wesleys and the Methodists

Ever wonder why the Methodists are called *Method*ists? The answer is found in the delightful story of the early history of John and Charles Wesley and their followers, a story that points to a defining characteristic of Methodism: their attention to spiritual formation.

John and Charles Wesley were brought up in a Christian home. John maintained, for the most part, a pattern of outward conformity to religious duties, although "I had not all this while so much as a notion of inward holiness," he writes in his journal. When he was about 23 years old (1726), while at Oxford University, he discovered Jeremy Taylor's *Rules and Exercises of Holy Living and Holy Dying*, a classic of Anglican spirituality (published 1651). He was deeply affected by the book, especially its discussion of "purity of intention." He was then led to other devotional classics that confirmed his quest for a deeper relationship with God.

John's brother Charles had gathered a group of fellow students interested in exploring the things of God. John ultimately found himself taking leadership of this group. They discussed works in theology and devotional classics. They made commitments to personal devotions and to frequent communion. They also visited the sick and prisoners to offer comfort. Their group was formally named the Holy Club, although other students made fun of them, calling them "sacramentarians," "enthusiasts," and "*method*-ists" (for their determined practices, or methods).

John and Charles left England in 1735 for the American colony of Georgia with the intent of ministering to the native tribes. There John discovered both his own shallow faith and a simultaneous attraction to the faith of a group of German Moravian believers. His own fear during the storms at sea contrasted greatly with their own confident faith. The lives of these Germans challenged John to see that while a spirituality of "right intent and right endeavor" could "instruct in the spiritual self-discipline through which a person could find God, it did little to foster an expectancy of the divine initiative."[9]

The Wesleys returned to England in 1738 and began visiting religious societies. A friendship with other Moravian believers further stimulated the Wesleys' pursuit, and soon both Charles and John had profound conversions of faith, experiencing firsthand the gracious transformation of the Spirit (including John's famous "Aldersgate experience").

John and Charles continued leading small groups. They drew up rules for their meetings similar to those for their earlier meetings of the Holy Club, but this time they emphasized one's internal sense of sin and forgiveness. Members of the society would ask one another such questions as, "What known sins have you committed since our last meeting?" "What temptations have you met with?" "Have you the forgiveness of your sins?" "Is the love of God shed abroad in your heart?" and so on.[10] In these meetings, personal devotion and interpersonal accountability were wedded in a program of intentional spiritual formation.

Partly at the encouragement of another friend, George Whitfield, John began preaching in marketplaces and other working-class gathering places. And people responded. Men and women accepted the gospel of faith in large numbers. The Wesleys gathered seekers and new believers into groups called "class societies" for the purpose of supporting their faith.

Their relationship with some of the German Moravians began to grow strained. The Germans so emphasized inward assurance that the use of traditional "means of grace" (attending communion, scripture reading, fasting, and such) was discouraged. John simply could not accept this. He welcomed the development of faith in the context of the traditional means of grace. In 1740 the Wesleys founded the first *Methodist* society, using the name of ridicule given to the earlier Holy Club. The use of the name Methodist symbolizes the value of intention and means in the context of a spirituality of grace. As

Methodist scholar David Lowes Watson states, John Wesley's "acceptance of the divine initiative as the *dynamic* of his spirituality did not negate the importance of spiritual disciplines as its *form*."[11] The Wesleys never wished to break formally with the Anglican church. The meetings of Methodist societies were normally held on evenings that did not conflict with Anglican services and it was not until the organization of the Methodist societies in America and later, after John's death in England, that the Methodist denomination was officially formalized. Yet throughout the Methodists' history, this balance of the divine and human initiatives has characterized the Methodist approach to spiritual formation, and it remains a legacy that we can see in Methodism today.

relationship with ourselves, nature, others, spiritual forces, God. All of these are part of the context of our formation. What we are at any given moment is the shape (the form) of that which has formed us, giving rise to our tendencies to form and be formed in certain ways. We are constantly being formed, and it is this interpenetration of forming tendencies that constitutes the context (or contexts) of our formation as individuals and communities—including the formation of our relationship with God.[12] As we shall see, attending to who we are, to the form of our lives at any given time—our embodiment, our story, our emotional needs, our experience of the Spirit of God, our relational networks, and so on—enables us to focus intention and means where they can best foster union with Christ.

Specific Contexts

Nonetheless, there are also specific contexts of distinctly Christian spiritual formation. These are the settings and life situations wherein the gracious invitations of God are discerned, the aims of our

growth in maturity are clarified, and the means of formation are specified.[13] "Our part" of the cooperative venture of Christian spiritual formation is pursued within the contexts of solitude, home, spiritual direction relationships, and congregation. Within these specific contexts care is applied from self to self, and something of one is shared for the benefit of the other. The context of solitude strips off all unnecessary responsibilities, occupations, and distractions and places one simply *there*, alone with the care of God and the battle with demons, to discover one's own formation. The context of home provides a setting of lifelong compassionate oversight, one for another. The way of spiritual guidance provides opportunities for persons to find support for spiritual formation within a one-on-one or small-group relationship. The context of intentional community or congregational life sees corporate life as a valuable crucible of spiritual formation. Thus, the Rule of the Order of St. Benedict speaks of the community as "a school for God's service."[14] Likewise, author Susanne Johnson speaks of the congregation as "an ecology of spiritual guidance and formation."[15]

Agents of Christian Spiritual Formation

More specific still, there are those who take initiative in the formation of an individual or community; we speak of these as the *agents* of Christian spiritual formation. The agents of Christian spiritual formation can be individuals (such as a spiritual director or pastor) or groups (such as the way a Presbyterian session may plan for spiritual formation as part of congregational life).

The primary agent of Christian spiritual formation is, of course, the Holy Spirit. As an agent of spiritual formation, the Holy Spirit takes initiative in our own spiritual maturity. The Spirit affects the forming of our lives. First, the Holy Spirit *initiates experience* that introduces or reinforces patterns of Godward transformation. The Spirit *leads* or prompts us into a new idea or pattern of action (Mark 1:12; John 16:13; Romans 8:2–5). Thoughts or feelings *appear* in our minds (Romans 8:15–16). We are increasingly *inclined* to certain actions (Galatians 5:22). We find ourselves experiencing the presence of God through the Spirit (Acts 2:4; Romans 8:26). Thus, for example, through an expression of prophecy in the gathered congregation, a community may be introduced to a deeper unity than hitherto experienced. Through the nudge of the Spirit, an individual may be led to explore evangelism within his workplace. Through the conviction of the Spirit in prayer, a couple may be reinforced in their previous commitment to fidelity.

The Holy Spirit also provides a unique *supernatural dimension* to existing patterns of human experience. One aspect of this is what Donald Gelpi calls "transvaluation."[16] The Holy Spirit transvalues our practice of self-control, for example, by enabling us to see our practice not simply as an independent effort at mastering our vices, but rather as part of a dynamic relationship of response to the initiation of the Living God. Issues of social justice are not seen simply in light of one political party or another but are transvalued in light of the heart of God revealed to us and through us by the Holy Spirit. Our feelings, thoughts, habits, ministry, and such begin to share and to express not only the human but the divine as well. Thus, as Vladimir Lossky writes, "Through the coming of the Holy Spirit the Trinity dwells within us and deifies us; confers upon us the uncreated energies, Its glory, and Its deity which is the eternal light of which we must partake."[17]

Yet while the Spirit is the primary agent of spiritual formation, other agents are still involved. We are all to some extent (consciously or unconsciously) self-directed, ordering this and that aspect of our lives in hopes that the Spirit will effect change through our efforts. And frequently we look to others, allowing the body of Christ to speak into our formation, lest our Christian life become isolated or haphazard.

The human agents of spiritual formation will vary with each individual or group, depending on the context. In professional

After the annual all-church potluck,
Wes Linn's heart felt stangely warmed.

273

or formal religious settings, the human agents of spiritual formation are district supervisors, directors of conscience, novice masters, bishops, spiritual directors, and such. These are often people who are assigned (though often now there is some mutuality of assignment and free choice), and the relationship is part of one's career. These agents of spiritual formation are easy to identify.

Others, however, may have difficulty naming the agents of their spiritual formation. Nonetheless, we often allow others to take initiative for the sake of our growth, whether we are aware of it or not. Who are our "spiritual friends," those we allow to guide or correct us? What aspects of church life form us most? Are we a part of a small group? In what ways do we give permission for a parent, a spouse, or a sibling to take steps to facilitate our formation in Christ? Have we a confessor, a mentor? Spiritual formation refers to the *intentional* and *semi-intentional* processes by which we are formed in Christ. Part of that intention is choosing to allow others leadership in our lives.[18] Attending to the *contexts* of our spiritual formation presents a passive side of spiritual formation—what shapes us. Attending to the *agents* of spiritual formation presents a more active side of spiritual formation—who is taking initiative to change our lives.

The Aims of Christian Spiritual Formation

Christian spiritual formation, in all its contexts and with all its agents, refers to processes through which we may be *conformed to and united with Christ.* The *intentionality* of spiritual formation is tied to the *aims* of spiritual formation. First there is the ultimate aim of Christian spiritual formation, summarized generally in terms of *mature harmony with Christ.* The epistle to the Ephesians states this aim in terms of God's purposes, namely "to gather up all things in him [Christ], things in heaven and things on earth" (Ephesians 1:10). We

might suggest, drawing on the comments of Andrew Lincoln regarding this passage, that God's aim for spiritual formation is that we would be "caught up in God's gracious purpose for a universe centered and reunited in Christ."[19] We are to share the heart of Christ and the mind of Christ. We are to participate in the suffering of Christ and in the reign of Christ. Mature harmony with Christ—*this* is our goal. This ultimate aim has been discussed with regard to a variety of terms: *deification, holiness, perfection, kingdom,* and others.[20] And then there are the more proximate aims of the increase of maturity appropriate to each individual or community. We will explore the ultimate aim of Christian spiritual formation by taking a look at a few of these terms. Then we will consider the proximate aims of Christian spirituality, the increase of the next step of growth.

Deification

In the Christian East, a term often used to identify the ultimate aim of spiritual formation is **deification** (*theosis*). Theologian John Meyendorff writes, "In deification man achieves the supreme goal for which he was created."[21] Likewise, Bishop Kallistos Ware discusses deification in answer to the question, "For what am I saved? What is my end-point or final aim?" stating that "to be saved is to share with all the fullness of human nature in the power, joy, and glory of God."[22] The roots of this idea can be found in the encouragement in 2 Peter 1:4 that through the promises of God we "may become participants of the divine nature." It is difficult to communicate this aim without expressing some theological error. Yet the ancient fathers of the church were confident to state that "God became man in order that man might become god."[23]

Some Greek fathers reflected on deification following the analogy of the union of the human with the divine in Christ. As Christ possesses both human and divine natures, each communicating with the other without mixture or confusion, so we through deification share in God ever more fully, yet without changing or violating our own human nature. Others emphasized our sharing of God's *energies* as opposed to his *essence*. However expressed, deification is not merely a conformity of imitation but rather a full sharing of the life—the energies—of Christ insofar as they can be incorporated by humans. Deification is "realized in its fullness only in the age to come after the resurrection of the dead," yet it is "fulfilled ever more and more even in this present life, through the transformation of our corruptible and depraved nature and by its adaptation to eternal life."[24]

Holiness

Another term frequently used to identify the ultimate aim of spiritual formation is **holiness**. Indeed, the word *sanctification* (*hagiasmos*) has its origins in holiness (*hagios, sanctus*). First Peter affirms the aim of holiness clearly: "Instead, as he who called you is holy, be holy yourselves in all your conduct; for it is written, 'You shall be holy, for I am holy'" (1 Peter 1:15–16). The idea of holiness carries nuances of cultic purity, of righteous living, of personal integrity, and of a quality of being touched with the power of God. The very first of Jonathan Edwards's famous "Miscellanies" is on holiness:

Holiness is a most beautiful and lovely thing. We drink in strange notions of holiness from our childhood, as if it were a melancholy, morose, sour and unpleasant thing; but there is nothing in it but what is sweet and ravishingly lovely. 'Tis the highest beauty and amiableness, vastly above all other beauties. . . . It makes the soul like a delightful field or garden planted by God, with all manner of pleasant flowers growing in the order in which nature has planted them, that is all pleasant and delightful, undisturbed, free from all the noise of man and beast, enjoying a sweet calm and the bright, calm, and

gently vivifying beams of the sun forever more: where the sun is Jesus Christ; the blessed beams and the calm breeze, the Holy Spirit; the sweet and delightful flowers, and the pleasant shrill music of the little birds, are the Christian graces. . . . How, if one were holy enough, would they of themselves and as it were naturally ascend from the earth in delight, to enjoy God as Enoch did![25]

At times in the history of the church, holiness became identified with a narrow range of behaviors such as sexual continence.[26] One consequence of emphasizing certain aspects of the tragedy (or the greatness) of human experience is that holiness becomes identified with a narrow range of activities and our understanding of spiritual formation is truncated. Some may *need* to hear that holiness has to do with the effects of the tangible power of the Holy Spirit of God (and not merely virtues of justice and tolerance), whereas others may *need* to hear that the outpouring of the Holy Spirit was given to facilitate righteous structures as well as powerful experiences. The aim of spiritual formation is holiness in all its fullness.

But is everyone called to holiness equally? This question was debated in the Roman Catholic manuals of ascetical and mystical theology in the past two centuries. Some, such as Adolphe Tanquerey, emphasized the distinction between ordinary Christian maturity and the more extraordinary gifts of mystical prayer. He felt that whereas all were called to progress in the moral (ascetical) life, only a few received the grace and calling to the mystical life (therefore there was not the same need to burden believers with the demands of this calling). Others, such as Réginald Garrigou-Lagrange, emphasized the continuity of Christian formation. He saw mystical prayer as a legitimate goal of all Christians.[27] The field of spiritual theology was developed in part to reconcile controversy over this issue. In any case, this debate reminds us of the need to pay careful attention to both the ultimate standard of holiness and the realistic standards we place before others.

For example, some people appear to be incapable of integrated thinking or feeling. Does the path to holiness necessarily travel *through* the healing of their neuroses and dysfunctions, or does the path to holiness *transcend* the healing of neuroses and dysfunctions, such that one may find real holiness *in the midst of* crippling psychological conditions?[28] There is a tension that must be maintained here. As we have stated throughout this text, all of human experience is subject to restoration. God's will is to redeem thought, feeling, intention, relationship, and so on. God can and does at times heal even physiological conditions. Yet we must also recognize an intimacy with Christ—indeed, a *holiness*—possessed and possessable in spite (or even because of) those aspects of our experience that may never be restored in this life.

Perfection

A third word used to identify the ultimate aim of spiritual formation is **perfection**. Paul prays for the Corinthians, "that you may become perfect" (2 Corinthians 13:9). He urges them to cleanse themselves, "making holiness perfect" (2 Corinthians 7:1). Paul declares to the Colossians the purpose of his ministry of proclamation, "that we may present everyone mature [perfect] in Christ" (Colossians 1:28, the Greek word *tebs* can be translated as either "mature" or "perfect").[29] Yet this same Paul elsewhere confesses, "Not that I have already obtained this or have already reached the goal" (Philippians 3:12; or "have already been made perfect," NIV). James encourages his readers to let endurance accomplish its work, "so that you may be mature [perfect] and complete, lacking in nothing" (James 1:4). Jesus affirms the same, commanding his followers to "be perfect, therefore, as your heavenly Father is perfect" (Matthew 5:48). Perfection

has been frequently used in the history of the church to identify the final stage of spiritual maturity: beginners, proficient, perfect.

But, as with deification and holiness, clarifying what is meant by "perfection" as the aim of spiritual formation is fraught with controversy. Early in the history of the church a distinction was made between the supreme perfection achieved through martyrdom, monasticism, and virginity and the perfection made possible through ordinary baptism and Christian growth.[30] The attitude of British monk Pelagius in the early part of the fifth century toward the possibilities of Christian perfection stimulated a historic debate regarding the nature of human freedom and the grace of God (the Augustinian-Pelagian controversy). In Protestant circles, the teaching of John Wesley regarding "entire sanctification" stimulated debate concerning perfection as a legitimate aim of spiritual formation. Indeed, the term *perfection* can be difficult to clarify. There is both the Pauline goal (to present Gentiles perfect) and the Pauline confession (that he has not arrived). There are the nuances of *telos* itself: maturity and perfection. And to be fair to the Christian faith, one cannot simply reduce perfection to character change, for Christianity is about a relationship of *love* between God and humans. Nonetheless, however difficult to define, perfection still remains as a biblical and historical reminder of the fullness of our ultimate aim of Christian spiritual formation.

Kingdom of God

Perfection, holiness, and deification are used to identify the ultimate aim of spiritual formation especially with reference to individuals. But, as we have seen, Christian spiritual formation is not simply the formation of individuals. The Spirit's initiation is not simply a call to individuals but an invitation to communities. Our eschatological communion is described not as the union of personal human to personal God but rather as a wedding of Trinitarian God and communal bride. God's restoration is not merely the rescuing of souls; it is the recreation of the heavens and the earth. We distort the biblical portrait of salvation (and of spiritual formation) when we reduce it to the individual dimension.[31]

And so we must speak of the aim of spiritual formation as the "**kingdom of God**." J. Heinrich Arnold, speaking to his flock of the Bruderhof, pleads, "I sometimes wonder whether our community has not completely forgotten the kingdom of God, and whether the distinction between personal salvation and the kingdom is clear enough to us. Both are of great importance. Eternal salvation is very important—it is wonderful to experience the nearness of Christ and to be redeemed by him. But the kingdom of God is still greater!"[32]

The theme of the kingdom of God is one of the primary metaphors used in the Gospels to describe God's purposes. The idea of a kingdom or realm of God suggests a sphere within which the influence and authority of the Living God is welcomed and recognized. God's kingdom may include the fullness of individual life (hence we can think of God having sway over every area of personal life). But a kingdom is primarily a corporate ideal. The Jewish apocalyptic expectation—and the Christian fulfillment of that expectation—pointed to the coming of a divine king who would not simply bring safety and a new presence of God into the lives of individuals, but rather reclaim a "people" for God and initiate a new corporate life of peace, justice, and righteousness. This has begun with the outpouring of the Holy Spirit of Christ on the followers of Jesus. The presence of the King becomes also the establishment of a visible king-oriented and king-ordered society.

As a metaphor for the ultimate aim of spiritual formation (formation in and by the Spirit), the ideal of the kingdom of God

urges the church into maturity. The church is the community of the king, the collective body of subjects ordered around and expressing the character of the king. Thus, "as the messianic community functioning as a charismatic body, it can and does reveal the true nature of the Kingdom."[33] Hence the passions to be removed en route to the ultimate aim of spiritual formation are not simply the private passions of individual sensuality (greed, lust, avarice, and the like), but also the public vices of "enmities, strife, jealousy, anger, quarrels, dissensions, factions, envy" (Galatians 5:20–21). Just as Ignatius of Loyola can speak of "disordered" affections inhibiting the individual's discernment and following of the will of God, so we may also think of "disordered" patterns of corporate life inhibiting the communal discernment and following of the will of God. The aim of the kingdom of God, then, is to see the deification, the holiness, and the perfection of corporate life, the reorientation and rehabituation—a realization—of the *community* of the King.[34]

Increase

Harmony with Christ, deification, holiness, perfection, the kingdom of God—these are the ways we express the ultimate aim of spiritual formation. More proxi-

mately, however, we can identify the aims of Christian spiritual formation simply as "increase." As we mentioned earlier, Christian spiritual formation is *intentional* and *ongoing*. Thus formation, for individuals or for communities, is about taking the next steps forward.

If we take the New Testament as our guide, increase is important to God. Both John the Baptist and Jesus "grew and became strong in spirit" (or "became strong, filled with wisdom" Luke 1:80; 2:40). When the Holy Spirit was acting on the church, "day by day the Lord added to their number," "living in the fear of the Lord and in the comfort of the Holy Spirit, it increased in numbers" (Acts 2:47; 9:31. See also Acts 4:4; 5:14; 6:1; 11:21, 24; 12:24; 16:5; 2 Corinthians 4:15). Paul encourages his readers' love to increase (1 Thessalonians 3:12; see also Philippians 1:9), "being transformed into the same image [Christ's] from one degree of glory to another" (2 Corinthians 3:18).

> Conformity to Christ is achieved in approximation through authentic increase as individuals begin to act and to feel like Christ, as communities participate more and more in the charismatic life of Christ, and as the world is subject to a growing influence of Christ through the community of the King.

The second epistle of Peter summarizes this theme nicely, exhorting believers to "make *every effort* to support your faith with goodness, and goodness with knowledge, and knowledge with self-control, and self-control with endurance, and endurance with godliness, and godliness with mutual affection, and mutual affection with love. For if these things are yours *and are increasing* among you, they keep you from being ineffective and unfruitful in the knowledge of our Lord Jesus Christ" (2 Peter 1:5–8, italics added).

We should employ "every effort" to find appropriate means and relationships to foster growth in relationship with God. Let us respect the tension here. On the one hand, God is personal Holy Mystery, transcending our every model or formula. Relationship with God is sacred ground, traversed in its own time and manner, subject to no personal or communal plan. Yet, on the other hand, there is this mandate for growth, for increase, and for our participation in each other's growth by the intentional use of particular means. So we step into each others' lives, carefully, attentively, speaking when we must to facilitate growth, but cautious lest we presume on the sovereign work of the Spirit.[35]

On Motive

Related to the idea of aim is the notion of *motive*. We are motivated to grow because of the aims we hope to achieve. But our motives may involve factors other than simply our understanding of the aim of spiritual formation. We pursue a given *aim* for a variety of different rational or psychological *motives*: reward, duty, gratitude, and so on. The motives of spiritual pursuit have been discussed throughout the history of the Christian community. Bernard of Clairvaux speaks of four degrees of loving God: when one loves himself for one's own sake, when one loves God for one's own good, when one loves God for God's sake, when one loves oneself for the sake of God.[36] The *Theologia Germanica* (1350) speaks of four ways of dealing with order and rule in life: some are compelled into order; others observe rules for the sake of reward, to "earn the kingdom of heaven"; some "fancy themselves as perfect" and "imagine that they are in no need of a rule"; and the final group (the "illumined ones") practice the ordered life out of love.[37] William James claims that the religious ascetic may be associated with such diverse psychological conditions as "organic hardihood, disgusted with too much ease"; temperance expressed out of the "love of purity," the "fruits of love," or sacrifices of gratitude; "pessimistic feelings about the self combined with theological beliefs concerning expiation"; irrational pathological fixation; or "perversions of the bodily sensibility."[38] Catholic writer Adolphe Tanquerey writes, in his influential manual on the spiritual life, that "ordinarily, our love of God is a *mixture of pure and interested love*; that is to say, we love God both for His own sake, because He is infinitely good, and also because He is the source of our happiness."[39] More recently, Evangelical Protestant author Ken Boa has explored the motivation of spiritual formation biblically, identifying seven distinct authentic motivators: no other options (when we have reached our limits); fear; love and gratitude; rewards; our identity in Christ (we act because of who we see ourselves to be); purpose and hope; and longing for God.[40] Spiritual formation is clarified by a broad understanding of aim. It is purified by a deep understanding of motive. We shall return to the question of motive in our focus on asceticism and hedonism, below.

In Christian spiritual formation (however motivated), individuals and communities "live into" our eschatological destiny as co-rulers with God, expressing the heart of God throughout creation. As missions writer Emilio Castro states, "A faithful evangelism that aims at the transformation and permeation of societies from within, looks to the kingdom that is coming as the recapitulation of all things in Jesus Christ. That recapitulation will include our lives and also our cultures."[41] Harmony with or conformity to Christ, as the aim of Christian spiritual formation—whether understood as deification, perfection, holiness, or as the kingdom of God—is achieved in approximation through authentic increase as individuals begin to act and to feel like Christ, as communities participate more and more in the charismatic life of Christ,

and as the world is subject to a growing influence of Christ through the community of the King.

The Task of Christian Spiritual Formation

Having gained some sense of the aims of formation, we are now ready to explore the task of formation itself. As we have defined it, Christian spiritual formation is a set of somewhat intentionally introduced *processes* aimed at fostering union with Christ. Christian spiritual formation introduces elements into human experience that facilitate the reorienting of our perspective and the rehabituating of our lives toward Christ. Two images illustrate this task, the first from scripture and the second from the social sciences.

"Putting On" and "Putting Off"

Following our passage in Colossians, we might summarize the task of Christian spiritual formation as a process of "putting off" and "putting on" (see Colossians 3:9–14). We have already reviewed the language used to describe our intentional role in spiritual maturation. The metaphor of putting off and putting on suggests a process of undressing and dressing, clothing ourselves with "attire" appropriate to our new life in Christ. This is not a shallow do's-and-don'ts spirituality. The task of formation is not merely the performance of particular behaviors but the fostering of a transformation of life: quality interpersonal relations, sincere and affective experience of God, control of addictive inclinations, decent public decorum, virtuous treatment of others, faithfulness to vocation, Godward mental attention, right doctrine, and trust in and devotion to God. Nonetheless, there *are* things to put off and put on. Paul is specific about this. Can you imagine Paul's response when a member of the Colossian church proclaims, "I'm not going to deal with my anger because I don't feel God's grace leading me to this right now"? Author Dallas Willard reflects

Historical Portrait: John of the Cross (1542–91) and the Dark Nights

The history of Christian spirituality affirms the centrality of the task of reorientation and rehabituation outlined in scripture, although it is pictured differently at different times. One of the most influential pictures of this process is that of John of the Cross's "dark night of the soul." Actually, John of the Cross, a Carmelite, spoke in terms of a series of *four* purifying detachments, or "nights," each initiated by different agents and aimed at different dimensions of human experience.[42] The *active night of the senses* addresses disordered affective operations (passions, appetites, and attachments dependent on the "lower faculties"). We confront these unhealthy passions by aggressive self-denial. The *active night of the spirit* addresses disordered patterns of our "higher faculties," patterns ingrained in the intellect, memory, and will. Whereas the objects of the active night of sense are our worldly vices, the objects of the night of spirit are our "spiritual possessions," those attachments we have to particular concepts or experiences of God. The active night of the spirit is lived out through intentionally weaning ourselves from these inadequate conceptual or experiential expectations involved in our relationship with God (for example, as we refrain from relying on God merely as an "indulgent grandfather").

The two active nights are described in contrast to two passive nights, which are effected by divine rather than by human action. The *passive night of the senses* purifies our affective system insofar as it concerns relationship with God. As we mature in the Christian faith, we can develop "spiritual vices": gluttony for spiritual experience, spiritual envy of another's faith, and so on. These spiritual vices are not easily noticed, yet they can be deeply ingrained and

can inhibit the maturation of authentic spiritual life. God addresses these by withdrawing satisfactions we may have had in spiritual things (hence an experience of darkness or "night"). Our role in these times is to remain faithful and unconcerned in the absence of these satisfactions. The *passive night of the spirit* addresses tendencies within human experience at its deepest center (beyond both lower and higher faculties) that prevent the fullest possible union with God. It is caused by an infusion of God into human experience transcending our comprehension. Through these four nights, John of the Cross teaches, every dimension of individual experience is reformed into a vessel capable of holding the fullness of the divine.

Now consider your own experience. What *active nights of the senses* have you experienced? How have you intentionally denied the senses the fulfillment they seek outside of Christ? What *active nights of the spirit* have you seen? Have you ever discovered that you are dependent on certain images of God or certain experiences of God that inhibited real growth in relationship with God? What did you do about this? What *passive nights of the senses* have you experienced? Do you know of times when God simply withdrew the sense of his presence? Have your familiar means of prayer ever simply dried up, and not because of unconfessed sin or some other personal reason? Have you ever entered into a *passive night of the spirit*, in which you feel separated from God at the core of your soul, in which God empties you of all previous foundations in order to rebuild a purer foundation of faith?

on this putting off and putting on when he speaks of "disciplines of abstinence" and "disciplines of engagement."[43]

What the scripture does *not* provide is a *normative phenomenology* of formation, a comprehensive description of the particular stages, means, and experiences necessarily included in a growing relationship with Christ. What it *does* provide is a *theology* of formation, a basic framework of understanding relationship with God and what righteous response to God means—putting off and putting on. So while we can learn from the New Testament that believers are to avoid anger and cultivate kindness, we do not learn *what* that will require or look like for every believer. The New Testament does not provide normative detail on church government, evangelistic methods, or political platforms; nor does scripture detail precise stages, experiences, or strategies of spiritual formation. There is room for the wisdom of each generation and each community to discover how theology should best be realized in practice. This is one of the functions of an ecclesial tradition. The task of spiritual formation as presented in the New Testament is simply one of putting off and putting on (reorientation and rehabituation), increasingly fostering tendencies within human experience that share and express those of the Triune God.

Practice

A second image of the task of spiritual formation, in addition to the biblical image of putting off and putting on, is that of putting the gospel "into practice." The task of spiritual formation is the practice of our faith. This is true of both our individual and our corporate formation in Christ. Sociologist Robert Wuthnow proposes, as an alternative to the "dwelling" and "seeking" spiritualities that have characterized the United States, what he calls "practice-oriented spirituality": "To say that spirituality is practiced means that people engage intentionally in activities that deepen their

relationship to the sacred. Often they do so over long periods of time and devote significant amounts of energy to these activities."[44] Similarly, Walter Brueggemann unites anthropological insight with biblical scholarship when he writes of the role of law, king, prophet, cult, and wisdom in ancient Israel: "These mediations are *concrete, communal practices* conducted by human agents. . . . Israel is practiced into Yahweh, and consequently into its life as Israel."[45] And if Christian spiritual formation is an increasing "putting into practice," it is also a process of education and socialization. We *learn* new habits of thought, feeling, and behavior in concrete living. And we are *socialized* into the body of Christ, complete with the practices that may accompany a given local expression (or network of expressions).

Furthermore, as an increasing practice of faith, spiritual formation will also include works of healing and deliverance or warfare. For example, where there are emotional wounds or scars that prevent the freedom to receive and give love, the ministry of healing facilitates reorientation. Where patterns of sin plague the individual or community, the stance of struggle is in order. (The Russians use the term *podvig* to describe this dynamic.) Where unforgiveness between parties fractures churches (or nations), the ministry of reconciliation facilitates kingdom practice. Where an individual is oppressed by a spirit of accusation (scripture calls the enemy "the accuser"), personal deliverance enables the practice of authentic Christian faith. Where a people group determines that it is oppressed with an evil spirit, preventing the group's putting of the gospel into practice, the work of spiritual warfare releases communities to the reign of Christ. Even the works of physical healing and spiritual formation may need to be integrated, as is suggested by the connection of healing, confession, and the ministry of the elders in James 5. In this work the gifts of the Spirit, the family of believers, and the ritual enaction through the sacraments of the church (reconciliation, deliverance

Spiritual formation is a "putting off,"   a "putting on,"   and a "putting into practice."

and healing, and so on) combine to *become* the practice of the faith in community. The task of spiritual formation is therefore the fostering of our embodiment of the gospel, our putting the gospel into practice.

Process

Having looked at the task of spiritual formation through a couple of images, we are now prepared to explore the process of spiritual formation itself. The task of spiritual formation as a *process* involves a series of acts and attitudes that together integrate the context, agents, aims, and means of formation. Both communities and individuals engage in the process of spiritual formation. This process (summarized as a formal intentional process) may include such steps as these:

- Gaining a *clear vision* of the aims of spiritual formation. This is accomplished in a general way by acquiring a knowledge of (and attraction to) the greater glory of God and the ultimate aim of spiritual formation, however defined. But the vision must move beyond the general to the particular. What would the ideal rule of God look like in *my* life (or *our* life), right here and now? What are some realistic proximate aims of spiritual formation?
- Cultivating a *strong determination* not to give up the process of growth—even if things don't seem to work.

- Nurturing *community support* to facilitate Godward re-orientation and re-habituation.
- *Identification*—where I/we may be suffering from *de*formation, *dis*orientation, wrong habituation. What must I put off, what must we put on—not just generally, but here and now?
- *Selecting* disciplines, practices, rules, circumstances, relationships, experiences, and the like, through which one hopes to introduce or reinforce a new and Godward orientation (or a new and Godward habit).
- Giving careful **attention** to the nuances of one's own context such that selection and revision are made in light of one's own real situation.
- *Implementing* an intentional program of activities (or leaving off certain activities).
- *Experimenting* with and revising the ongoing process.

Ultimately, people experience *re-habituation* whether spiritual formation is undertaken as a formal process or whether these steps are included here and there as a part of ongoing community life. This is where the means of grace accomplishes increasingly permanent work in our lives. Rehabituation is complete when a new pattern of life persists even in the face of negative reinforcement.

At times transformation occurs with little "effort" on our part. At other times (perhaps even frequently) the introduction of a means of grace results not in Godward transformation, but rather in "failure." Through repeated failures at persevering in spiritual disciplines, perhaps we become aware of deeply ingrained (perhaps even unconscious) self-destructive patterns hindering our transformation. And we are drawn into an unplanned-for process of healing. Or perhaps we find ourselves, through our apparent lack of change, broken and thrown into the hands of God—right where God wanted us to be in the first place. This is part of God's work. Through both unexpected success and failure, we come to see the gracious hand of God more clearly and we grow in surrendered relationship with God, which is what this is all about anyway. Theophan the Recluse, speaking of the "zealot," or one who is eager to pursue God, writes, "Thus the inner ascent from zeal to zealous dedication to God is nothing other than the revelation and appearance to our consciousness of God's work in us, or the working of our salvation and purification. The zealot becomes enlightened about this reality through frequent failures met in spite of all his efforts, and unexpected and great successes met without particularly trying. Mistakes and falls are especially enlightening as they bereave us of grace. All of these bring a man to the thought and belief that he is nothing, while God and His all-mighty grace are everything."[46]

Breadth and Length

Since Christian transformation touches every aspect of our lives, the task of spiritual formation, our intentional putting on and putting off, may be applied to any area of human experience (though not necessarily all at one time!). In *Renovation of the Heart: Putting on the Character of Christ*, Dallas Willard writes, regarding individual formation, "Now the simplicity of spiritual formation lies in its intention. Its aim is to bring every element in our being, working from inside out, into harmony with the will of God and the kingdom of God.

This is the simple focus." He goes on in the rest of this book to treat the application of spiritual formation to our thoughts, feelings, will, body, social relationships, and soul.[47] Just as Willard speaks of the "elements of our being" (and as John of the Cross speaks of "faculties" and John Wesley of "tempers"), we have explored human experience in terms of operational systems (cognitive, affective, volitional), stages (Being Aware, Experiencing, Understanding, Judging, Deciding/Acting, Integrating), a web of relationships (with self, others, nature, spiritual forces, and God), and the development and depth of human experience. The task of spiritual formation, as it involves the *breadth* of human experience, will apply the process of spiritual formation to a given area of life. As we apply steps of the process of spiritual formation (like identification, attention, and selection), we discern which areas of life may be touched by God's invitation and choose appropriate means to cooperate with God's transforming work in that area of life. Sometimes God invites us to put off a simple behavior (such as driving over the speed limit). Sometimes God touches our very core and invites us to put on a new way of looking at ourselves as a congregation (perhaps we have been thinking of church all wrong). Needless to say, the various steps of the process will be applied differently in each situation.

Similarly, there will be different kinds of putting off and putting on appropriate to the different stages—to the *length*—of Christian maturity. The task of spiritual formation for a new believer who is facing his own avarice in the active night of the senses will look different from the task for a mature believer who is facing her subtle attachments in the passive night of the spirit. Learning to stand requires different habits than learning to dance does. Thus (linking some of the steps of the process of spiritual formation outlined above to the stages of ongoing transformation outlined in the previous chapter), an *agent* of spiritual formation (self, spiritual friends, church community) might gain a *clear vision* for a community that is authentic to *this* community at *this* point in time. We cannot expect, for example, a house church of young believers within its first year to exhibit the same kind of familiarity with the ways of God's Spirit working in the community as one that has been together for ten years and is exploring the Christian life in a much broader way. As leaders of this younger community, then, our intentional formation should be geared toward helping them establish the basic habits of Christian life as individuals and as a group.

Likewise, the sense of *determination* will feel different for one who has already weathered some storms than for a young Christian, and the means used to encourage that determination will be different as well. The kinds of *community support* involved in the individual's formation will often vary depending on the maturity of the person. Similarly, a younger congregation needs an apostolic leader, church planter, denominational representative, or the like who will take initiative. A more mature congregation is better able to discern the movements of God in the congregation's life, but it still needs the support, guidance, and accountability of its leaders (and even outsiders) to assist in its ongoing formation into Christ. Steps of *identification, selection,* and *attention* will address patterns that are different for the younger than for the more mature community. For the group moving from crawling to standing to walking, one looks to see which basic truths of the Christian faith are lacking, which basic habits have not been established. For the group learning to climb, to dance, to journey, one looks not for the answers the group has but for the questions it has not asked. Later in life, a community must face questions (as must an individual) that did not need to be addressed earlier. And a good agent of spiritual formation selects means that will facilitate healthy navigation through these questions. And so the process goes through the various steps of spiritual formation and stages of transformation.

For both individuals and communities the task of spiritual formation requires unique reorientations and rehabituations for every dimension of human experience and every stage of growth (though, of course, growth never proceeds with nice, neat, textbook predictability). Different devotional skills, different ways of approaching the great themes of the Christian faith, different ways of considering our relationships—all must be lovingly and skillfully introduced at the right time to the right group (or individual). You can see why spiritual formation is such a delicate art.

The Means of Christian Spiritual Formation

Spiritual formation, as an intentional or semi-intentional process, involves the selection and application of *means*: activities, situations, relationships, and such that foster or express the transforming work of God in our lives. We learned in chapter 6 that God's pattern of initiation involves a kind of self-disclosure. God is present to us *as*—as the One who spoke to me, as the orderer of creation, as the one who identifies with the oppressed, and so on. God is also a presence *to*—God confronts another who receives that communication. Finally, God is present to us *through*. Analogies in the world point to aspects of God's character. Patterns in the world and events in our lives serve as indices of God's "having been there." Words in scripture and in Spirit speak the heart of God to us. More specifically, God's presence to us is communicated through *means*. As actively present to us in love, God initiates relationship with us by revealing himself, disclosing himself to us concretely by means of our own environment, and, through these disclosures, inviting us into relationship.

And just as God's presence to us is communicated to us through means, so our own assimilation to God is effected through means. Thus in spiritual formation God and human are communicated one to the other through signs, actions,

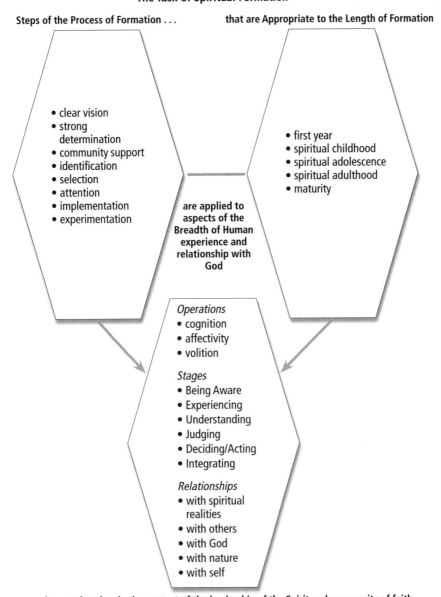

FIGURE 8.1
The Task of Spiritual Formation

Steps of the Process of Formation . . .   that are Appropriate to the Length of Formation

- clear vision
- strong determination
- community support
- identification
- selection
- attention
- implementation
- experimentation

are applied to aspects of the Breadth of Human experience and relationship with God

- first year
- spiritual childhood
- spiritual adolescence
- spiritual adulthood
- maturity

Operations
- cognition
- affectivity
- volition

Stages
- Being Aware
- Experiencing
- Understanding
- Judging
- Deciding/Acting
- Integrating

Relationships
- with spiritual realities
- with others
- with God
- with nature
- with self

. . . and are undertaken in the context of the leadership of the Spirit and community of faith.

words, and such: a "mutual adaptation." (God adapts himself to our thoughts, feelings, and such through revelation; and we adapt ourselves to God's thoughts and such through sanctification.) This mutual adaptation is also called a *mediated* relationship. Walter Brueggemann writes from the perspective of Old Testament theology, "It is daring of Israel to insist on relatedness with Yahweh. But to be specific about that relatedness requires that along with the daring of Israel's utterance, we pay attention, as best we can, to the practices that give the testimony *concrete embodiment*." He develops this notion of concrete embodiment further, speaking of "modes of mediation, whereby the fullness of Yahweh's sovereign, faithful self was genuinely available to Israel."[48] While Brueggemann admits that God can and does on occasion make

285

himself available to humans apart from any mediating agents, he devotes the bulk of his attention to the ways in which God is ordinarily present to Israel through torah, king, prophet, cult, and sage.

John Wesley spoke much of the "means of grace." In a sermon on the topic he defined the means of grace as "outward signs, words, or actions, ordained of God, and appointed for this end, to be the ordinary channels whereby he might convey to men, preventing, justifying, or sanctifying grace."[49] The "Large Minutes" of the Methodist Society distinguished between *instituted means* (prayer—private, family, public; searching scriptures—reading, meditating, hearing; the Lord's Supper; fasting; Christian conference, or fellowship) and *prudential means* (making use of particular rules for personal growth; attending class, band, or other meetings; watching against world, devil, and besetting sins; denying oneself useless pleasures and needless food or drink; taking up one's cross and willingly bearing whatever is grievous to our nature; and exercising the presence of God through always setting God before us).[50] We will explore the means of spiritual formation with a fourfold division: our experience of the Spirit, the circumstances of ordinary life, the community of believers, and the disciplines of the faith and ascetical practice.[51]

Experience of the Spirit

In one sense, human experience itself can be considered means of spiritual formation. Through the operations of human experience, we perceive the work of God's Spirit. Thus, to use experience as a *means*, we intentionally cultivate our own formation into Christ by placing ourselves (opening particular aspects of our experience) in the sphere of the Spirit's influence and attending to the Spirit's movements within our experience.

We have already learned, in our discussion of the Holy Spirit as an agent of spiritual formation, that one function of the Spirit's work is to stimulate aspects of human experience. Johannes Tauler writes that "some receive the Holy Spirit by way of their senses, through sensible images. Others receive Him in a loftier manner, by way of their higher powers. . . . The third group receives Him beyond mode or manner, within that hidden abyss, that secret realm."[52] We also learned that the Holy Spirit adds a supernatural dimension to ordinary human experience. The Spirit, for example, transforms our evangelistic efforts, our prayers for healing, our thoughts or feelings, our "relationshipping" into anointed encounters. Thus Paul states, "our message of the gospel came to you not in word only, but also in power and in the Holy Spirit and with full conviction" (1 Thessalonians 1:5). So also words of wisdom, expressions of tongues, prayers for healing, and such become manifestations of the Holy Spirit, infused with divine effect (1 Corinthians 12:1–11). By adding a supernatural dimension to natural human experience, our experience is reconfigured in light of God's reality.

Making use of the means of intentional spiritual formation, we encourage our experience of the Spirit in a variety of ways, exercising a variety of skills. We *prepare* for the coming of the Spirit: acquiring a clear understanding of the Spirit in scripture and tradition, fostering a passionate desire for the Spirit,[53] waiting for the Spirit with empty hands (we have a hard time receiving when our hands are already full with other things), going to where the Spirit is present (whether silent retreats or noisy revival meetings). We *open* ourselves to the experience of the Spirit, waiting in an attitude of expectant leisure (trust), ready to welcome and not to quench the Spirit no matter how the Spirit may manifest. We learn to *notice* the movements of the Spirit within experience: the fluctuations of thought or feeling, the demonstrations of signs and wonders, the manifestations of life through the gifted community. We develop an *appreciation* for the Spirit's presence in experience: a sense of wonder, anticipation, attentiveness. And finally we *respond* by letting go to the Spirit, yielding to the Spirit's touch, walking where the Spirit leads, taking that risk of obedience. Through these kinds of actions on our part, both as individuals and as communities, we facilitate experience of the Holy Spirit as a means of spiritual formation.

The Trials of Ordinary Life

My brothers and sisters, whenever you face trials of any kind, consider it nothing but joy, because you know that the testing of your faith produces endurance; and let endurance have its full effect, so that you may be mature and complete, lacking in nothing. (James 1:2–4)

The Holy Spirit is an agent, and experience of the Spirit is a means of spiritual formation, so the trials of life—indeed, life itself—are both *context* and *means* of our spiritual formation. As we learned above, we are at all times both already formed by and being formed by the forces that surround us. Thus the trials of ordinary life contribute to our formation, whether it is a spiritual formation or not. We can expect—as scripture and tradition both affirm—a variety of difficulties in life: obstacles (like a Red Sea), chastisements, tests, persecutions, "thorns in the flesh," temptations, and so on. The questions for us here are these: How do difficulties function to reorient or rehabituate us toward growth in Christlikeness? and What attitudes or actions can we undertake such that the trials of life (seemingly passively received) become an integrated part of intentional spiritual formation?

The trials of life serve to reorient or rehabituate our lives in a number of ways. They empty us of our self-sufficiency so that we are predisposed to receive from God. As author Philip Yancey summarizes the gifts of sufferers, "through no choice of their own—they may urgently wish otherwise—suffering and oppressed people find themselves in a posture that befits the grace of God. They are needy, dependent, and dissatisfied with life; for that reason they may welcome God's free gift of love."[54] Likewise, trials have the potential of drawing our attention from the superficial (and unpleasant) distractions of life to matters of eternal significance. The Christian practice of the consideration of the miseries of life is designed to accomplish just this kind of drawing of our thoughts to God.[55]

Furthermore, the trials of life introduce to us experiences that expand us. The consolation we receive in affliction, for example, enables us to better console others (see 2 Corinthians 1:1–7). Trials highlight salient features of events that perhaps were previously unnoticed; but when they are noticed in the context of trials, they become part of a valuable fund of wisdom and compassion. Trials also facilitate insight by forcing us to reframe experience. Research in problem solving suggests that one hindrance to solving a problem can be fixedness, the inability to see a situation from a fresh perspective. Trials have a way of putting our backs against the wall such that we are pressed to consider the situation anew. In this way trials serve to facilitate reorientation. Finally, trials have the potential to strengthen virtues and weaken vices. As gold is refined through fire, so the virtues of faith, hope, and love are made purer through the difficulties of

"Looks like Pastor White's going through another trial."

287

life, and our rehabituation to the things of God is reinforced.

So, knowing the value of the trials of life for spiritual formation, what attitudes or actions may we undertake such that the trials of life become an integrated part of intentional spiritual formation? First, trials of life become means of spiritual formation when we approach them with a *soft heart*. "As wax cannot take the imprint of a seal unless it is warmed or softened thoroughly," writes Diodochus of Photike, "so a man cannot receive the seal of God's holiness unless he is tested by labors and weaknesses."[56] If we allow trials to soften (rather than to harden) us, we begin to trust our life to God, lifting the container of our sufferings as a gift, to use Catherine of Siena's image, to be received by God and filled with the water of his grace.[57]

Second, trials of life become means of spiritual formation when we approach them with a *clear mind*. We have already learned of the need for attention in spiritual formation. By paying attention to the nature and character of our trials, we cultivate discerning spiritual formation: spiritual

---

Two "Celtic" Blessings

A Celtic Blessing for Harvesting Seaweed

> Produce of sea to land,
>   Produce of land to sea;
> He who doeth not in time,
>   Scant shall be his share.
> Seaweed being cast on shore
>   Bestow, Thou Being of bestowal;
> Fruitfulness being brought to wealth,
> O Christ, grant me my share![58]

A Celtic Blessing for Receiving Phone Calls

> Here is a child of God,
>   image of the Father,
>   redeemed by the Son,
>   invited by the Spirit,
> I welcome this person,
>   with the heart of Christ.

---

formation that is appropriate to the real conditions of one's life. Coming to our trials with a clear mind also means determining to learn from our trials. This is where a habit of self-examination is valuable, wherein we regularly account for the presence of God in the midst of the joys and trials of each day.[59]

Third, trials of life become means of spiritual formation when we approach them with a *strong will*. Having a strong will does not necessarily mean one has a *willfulness* toward the trials of life. At times our trials rather require a spirit of *willingness* in order to receive what they have to bring. Instead, the strong will encouraged here is a settled readiness to persevere through the thick of it. The New Testament is replete with encouragements to persevere. Indeed, it is characteristic of authentic Christian ongoing salvation.[60] Moses perseveres through the obstacle of the Red Sea, Job perseveres through his sufferings, Paul perseveres with his thorn, and so on. When we persevere through trials, they can have their full beneficial effect in our lives; reorientation and rehabituation can be completed and not cut short. This is the *willingness* of a strong will. Yet at times our trials (or the trials of others) are the result of injustice, or of spiritual or political oppressions, or of a deeply ingrained pattern of sin. In these cases, facing our trials with a strong will means a *willfulness*, girding up our loins and doing battle with the enemy.

Finally, here's a fun suggestion. Perhaps the trials of life can become means of grace when we remember God's presence in the details of our lives by *ritualizing* the activities of ordinary life. The Celtic tradition is especially rich in this aspect of spirituality. How would you write a blessing for the details of your day, to remind you of the presence of God?

The Community of the Faithful

A third means of grace in spiritual formation is the community of God's people. Just as the trials of life are both *context* and *means*, so too the community of the faithful is *context*, *agent*, *aim*, and *means*: context, insofar as we live *in* community and become who we are within the communities of our lives; agent, insofar as others within our communities exercise intention regarding our growth in maturity; aim, insofar as the purpose of God is to restore an embodied community of the Spirit; and means, insofar as the community of God's people mediate the things of God to one another.

But just how does the community of God mediate spiritual formation to individuals and to the community itself? Christian education specialist Susanne Johnson suggests a helpful fourfold division of the church's contributions to our initiation into the realm of God.[61] First, there is the "general guidance" the church provides simply by *being* church. Through the common prayer of liturgy, the common sharing of the charisms of the Spirit, the common reflection on our identity and history, and the interaction of life together, believers are formed into the faith.[62] This should never be minimized. We "catch" the gospel through repetition of the weekly Eucharist. We are welcomed into formation by the caring inquiries of members of our church family. Paul repeatedly uses family metaphors for the church (brother and sister, household of faith, and so on). The church as *familial* (informally sharing life) and as *sacramental* (formally sharing life) is itself a powerful force of spiritual formation.

Second, the "group guidance" of the church provides a place where spiritual formation can be addressed face-to-face with others. The format for group guidance may be identical with the primary gathering of the congregation, as in a house church setting. Other settings such as cell groups, Sunday school classes, golf fellowships, and such may also serve this function. John Wesley used three separate group settings (class meetings, bands, and select societies) in addition to the general meeting of the congregation to address the particular formation needs of people at different levels of maturity. The well-known monastic settlements on Mt. Athos in Greece have a similarly differentiated approach. In group guidance the church as *charismatic* reveals the ministry of the Spirit one to another. In group settings (again, both formal and informal) those who teach bring the truth, those who counsel bring comfort, those who prophesy bring a spontaneous word—and the whole body is built up.

"One-to-one guidance" is found in the ministries of pastoral care, spiritual direction, mentoring, discipling, coaching, counseling, tutoring, soul friendship, and the like. One-to-one guidance provides a degree of intimacy to the insight, accountability, encouragement, and support unavailable in group guidance. Within the commitment of a discipler, we learn the basics of the Christian faith. Within the safety of a soul friend, we bare our secrets. Within the wisdom of a spiritual director, we find the subtle nuances of the divine-human relationship noticed in the details of our lives.

Finally, we are formed through the "hidden guidance" of our communities. According to Johnson, hidden guidance is "the unspoken and the unconscious rules by which we socialize persons into the congregation"—rules created by "what is praised and noted as worthy of attention," by "those things in which the congregation invests itself," by "our life style."[63] Congregations foster rehabituation toward justice without saying a word, for example, by the mere presence in the congregation of groups dedicated to advocating justice in the world. Congregations foster Godward reorientation simply by the *fact* that we talk about God in our common meals.

Thus, with these four types of guidance—general, group, one-to-one, and hidden—the community of faith serves as a means through which spiritual formation is mediated. And we make use of these means insofar as we participate in a community of faith. We shall explore this more as we consider the life of care in chapter 10.

Figure 8.2
Outlines of Spiritual Disciplines in Selected Christian Literature

Celebration	Spirit of the Disciplines	Soul Feast	Spiritual Theology	Protestant Spiritual Exercises	Path to Salvation
Inward Disciplines meditation prayer fasting study *Outward Disciplines* simplicity solitude submission service *Corporate Disciplines* confession worship guidance celebration	*Abstinence* solitude silence fasting frugality chastity secrecy sacrifice *Engagement* study worship celebration service prayer fellowship confession submission	spiritual reading prayer common worship fasting self-examination confession awareness spiritual direction hospitality rule	*Fundamental Means* sacraments meritorious good works petitionary prayer *Aids to Growth* presence of God examination of conscience desire for perfection conformity to God's will fidelity to grace plan of life spiritual reading holy friendships spiritual direction	relaxation exercises rule of life four-stranded garland prayer of examen prayer for a new earth morn and eve prayer journal covenant group	*Rules for Preserving the Zeal for God* being within vision of another world remaining in feelings that lead to resolve *Exercises for Confirming the Believer in Goodness* Mind—read, study, ask, talk Will—submission to church, civil order, God, conscience . . . Heart—church, prayer, icons, holy customs Body—guarding senses, tongue, abstinence and fasting, moderate sleep . . . Outward ordering of life—abandon evil customs purge relationships and such determine new order rearrange duties to fit new life establish order in family Govenie completing ascetical labors receiving the Sacraments *Rule for War without the Passions* freely choosing and loving good reviewing our enemies rules of spiritual warfare

Richard Foster, *Celebration of Discipline: The Path to Spiritual Growth*, 20th Anniversary edition (San Francisco: Harper San Francisco, 1998).
Dallas Willard, *The Spirit of the Disciplines: Understanding How God Changes Lives* (San Francisco: Harper and Row, 1988).
Marjorie J. Thompson, *Soul Feast: An Invitation to the Christian Spiritual Life* (Louisville: Westminster John Knox, 1995).
Jordan Aumann, *Spiritual Theology* (London: Sheed and Ward, 1980).
Joseph D. Driskill, *Protestant Spiritual Exercises: Theology, History, Practice* (Harrisburg, PA: Morehouse, 1999).
Translated by Fr. Seraphim Rose, *The Path to Salvation: A Manual of Spiritual Transformation* (Platina, CA: St. Herman Press, 1998).

Spiritual Disciplines, Ascetical Practices

Our final category of means of spiritual formation is ascetical practice, also known as the application of the **disciplines** of the Christian faith. By these terms we refer to *"activities of mind and body purposefully undertaken, to bring our personality and total being into effective cooperation with the divine order."*[64] The *activities of mind and body*—our training exercises—include practices like solitude, fasting, study, journaling, and so on. There is no definitive list of spiritual disciplines; each contribution to the field has its own list of practices and its own way of organizing them.

Indeed, perhaps it is this interesting combination of features, their ambiguity and their particularity, that distinguishes ascetical practice for spiritual formation. On the one hand, almost *anything* can be-come a discipline of the spiritual life. There is no clearly specified program of practices that will facilitate unity with Christ for all. The boundaries of ascetical practice are necessarily vague. Yet at the same time, ascetical practice focuses energy on *this* practice effecting *these* aspects of life at *this* time. Thus, while the effects of a given practice may be somewhat uncertain, there is, nevertheless, an irreducible particularity to spiritual disciplines. This means that the motives, the means, the sphere-in-view, the effects, and so on will be unique to each practitioner and practice. As spiritual writer John Climacus (ca. 570–649) stated, "Similarly, the seething movement of our anger and of our other passions arises for many different reasons, so that the same cure cannot be offered for all of them. Hence I would propose that each sick man should very carefully look for his own particular cure, and the first step is the diagnosis of the disease. When this is known, the patients will get the right cure from the hands of God and from their spiritual doctors."[65] Thus for one person the spheres of physicality and personal embodiment may be central, whereas another may look to sociocultural impact for the significance of the same ascetical practice. Some practices are necessarily private (solitude), while others are corporate (celebration). Likewise, while the church has recognized the need for balance and wisdom in ascetical matters,[66] we must also recognize that one person's ascetical excess may be another person's balance. Spiritual disciplines are particular activities undertaken for particular circumstances.

The *personality and total being*, identified as the recipient of the effects of ascetical practice, can refer either to an individual or to a collective, since the *divine order* has both individual and corporate implications. Consequently, our ascetical practice can have either the restored individual or the restored society in view.[67] Furthermore, any dimension of human experience is potentially targeted for attention through ascetical practice (our "total being").[68] Some spiritual disciplines may be more external in focus (for example, fasting from red meat), while others may be more internal in focus (for example, regular meditation on heaven). Some may focus on the mind, others on the heart. In fact, some individuals or communities do not need a message of spiritual discipline at all. Some are so weighed down with life, or so confused with legalism or scruples, that encouragement toward the ascetical way hinders, rather than promotes, growth toward maturity. For some, the discipline of surviving the day is enough. Thus, while the ascetical way has often been conceived in terms of self-denial, we might do well at times to speak of an "asceticism of enjoyment," the discipline of gaining the most enjoyment out of every moment of life in the Spirit.

The activities of our ascetical practice are undertaken to bring us into *cooperation with the divine order*. The aim of spiritual formation is harmony with Christ. Other categories of means also served as context or aim. Spiritual disciplines, as part of spiritual "formation"—as training (*ascesis*)—are simply *means*. They facilitate spiritual formation. Thus Abba Moses (recorded by John Cassian) states, "Fasts and vigils, the study of Scripture, renouncing possessions and everything worldly are not in themselves perfection, as we have said; they are its tools. For perfection is not to be found in them; it is acquired through them."[69] Ascetical practices are means of grace; they are tools or vehicles through which formation is realized. The ultimate aim is perfection.

But promoting *effective cooperation* with the divine order means that personal spiritual maturity may not be the *only* goal of spiritual discipline. For example, historian Margaret Miles identifies four models of the methods and goals of ascetic practice: an asceticism of self-understanding (and transformation), an asceticism that seeks to model a counterculture, an asceticism that gathers and focuses energy toward God, and an asceticism that intensifies consciousness in order to free one for kingdom work.[70] The apostle Paul speaks of willingly enduring hardships so that the spread of the gospel might be facilitated. While not oriented toward personal spiritual maturity, this "functional asceticism" undertakes activities for the sake of *effective cooperation with the divine order*.[71] Similarly, Lorenzo Scupoli speaks about ascetical practices undertaken as part of "spiritual warfare."[72] Furthermore, spiritual disciplines serve not only to facilitate, but also to *express* transformation. The discipline of material simplicity, for example, may be undertaken as a way of expressing a new insight about our relationship with God, nature, and society. True, the discipline may foster still further insights. But the point is that the practice may be initially undertaken as a way of living out a transformation gained through other means (perhaps through a study of scripture). Sometimes spiritual disciplines are simply a matter of obedience.

Asceticism or Hedonism?

Hedonism is "the principle that happiness (defined in terms of pleasure) is the sole and proper aim of human action."[73] Ascetical practice has usually been identified with denying pleasures. Yet in recent years, author John Piper has advocated a spirituality founded on the principle of pleasure, calling it "Christian hedonism."[74] So which is it, asceticism or hedonism?

First, let's take a closer look at Piper's presentation of Christian hedonism. Piper begins with the character of God. God longs to display his glories to others, for he knows that in his glory all creation will find its greatest joy.[75] Conversion to Christ is the Spirit's implantation of a "new taste" for the glory of God, "a new longing, a new passion for the pleasure of God's presence."[76] It is "the creation of a Christian hedonist." For the Christian, then, the impulse toward God is not primarily one of principle or duty, but an impulse toward *pleasure*. The ramifications for spiritual formation are indicated at the close of Piper's chapter on love in his book *Desiring God*: "When the object of our delight is moral beauty, the longing to *behold* is inseparable from the longing to *be*. When the Holy Spirit awakens the heart of a person to delight in the holiness of God, an insatiable desire is born not only to *behold* that holiness but also to *be* holy as God is holy. . . . We don't want just to *see* the grace of God in all its beauty, saving sinners and

sanctifying saints. We want to share the power of that grace. We want to feel it saving."[77]

Piper calls this approach "faith in future grace."[78] Out of a longing to realize God's glory in our lives, in all of its pleasurable beauty, we willingly (and aggressively) battle with sin, making full use of the means of grace. (Piper's writings mention prayer, fasting, community life, and especially scripture memory as means to facilitate faith in future grace.) Such is Christian hedonism. Does this approach square with what we have learned of ascetical practice?

We have learned that paying attention to the *context* of our formation is important. Our perception of pleasure in God changes over time. Delight in God will look different for one in the second of Bernard's degrees of love for God (loving God for his own good) than for one in the third (loving God for God's sake). Moral beauty may appear different to one personality than to another. Piper is sensitive to the context of the young Evangelical believer raised to ignore feelings, and he offers an attractive alternative for such as these. But outside of this context, the principles of Christian hedonism could be misunderstood or misused. One must use Christian hedonism carefully.

We have learned that the *task* of spiritual formation is a reorientation and rehabituation into Christ. Christian hedonism advocates precisely

But how do spiritual disciplines function to facilitate the Godward reorientation and rehabituation of human experience, to *bring* us into cooperation with the divine order? To explore this we need to look at the way in which ascetical practice fits into the task of spiritual formation as a process in terms of our discussion of the steps involved in the process of spiritual

formation.[80] At the steps of gaining vision and determination, we acknowledge that each community transmits a fund of practices and proximate aims that shape the kinds of spiritual aspirations possible to a given individual or community.[81] The kind of community support enlisted serves to mediate one's tradition and to highlight aspects of ascetical practice uniquely grasped a massive reordering of our affections. "Grant me the future grace," the hedonist prays, "of strong influences on my heart to give me an appetite for your truth that breaks the power of my appetite for things."[79] Piper is suggesting neither a denial of pleasure, nor a naive pursuit of secular pleasure, but rather a reforming of our affective operational system itself such that it is driven by and oriented toward relationship with God.

This brings us to the question of the *aim* and *motive* of spiritual formation. Indeed, perhaps Piper's chief contribution is his legitimation of the motive of pleasure in view of the greater aim of God's glory. Ascetical practice has been often viewed in terms of negative self-denial. Piper has helped to reorient our views (and our practice) of spirituality in a valuable light. Yet we must be careful. As we have seen, the motives of spiritual formation are plural. Fear, reward, love, gratitude, identity, purpose, hope, and longing may all foster or express our spirituality. It may be dangerous to subsume all spiritual practice under the motive of pleasure. For instance, there are seasons of our lives, even for the mature believer, where the pleasure of Christian life, and even the sight of God's glory, dries up. We are drawn, by the Spirit, through dark nights. Through them we are purged of inadequate ways of perceiving both God and our own pleasure, and we become prepared to receive from God anew. In these times, the encouragement to "go for our delight" does not always work. Furthermore, as we mature, often the need for pleasure *from* God is set aside for the pleasure *of* God. And perhaps in the end one simply forgets oneself in the presence of the Other, and self-abandonment and self-fulfillment are united *in* God.

So, do we pursue asceticism or hedonism? Interestingly enough, when we take a refined understanding of both asceticism and Christian hedonism, we find that they are not all that far apart. Both point to the central thrust of Christian spiritual formation: intentional processes undertaken by believers aimed at bringing increasing conformity to Christ.

by that source of support. Then there is the step of identification, the "diagnosis of the passions," wherein disordered patterns of human experience are acknowledged in the light of the wisdom of the Spirit.

Using selection and attention, the genius of the ascetical way begins to show itself. Since the possibilities for spiritual disciplines are virtually endless, a good agent can tailor the treatment precisely to the needs of "the ascetic" (the individual or community seeking to use the disciplines), although one must always be aware that the sovereign grace of the Chief Agent has a way of accomplishing things that human agents had never considered when selecting means of grace. Implementation, the onset of a discipline, then begins, at times with a ritual celebration of that beginning. Then the warfare begins, for reorientation and rehabituation are usually preceded by an uncomfortable *disorientation* and *dishabituation*. Here we learn the fundamental virtue of the ascetical way, the virtue of detachment. As one settles into a discipline, one needs to give it enough time to accomplish its work. "Sit in your cell," demands Abba Moses, "and let your cell teach you!"[82] The Holy Spirit works with and through the discipline to reveal areas of newness. At times the areas of newness involve a certain strength fostered by the discipline. At other times we find ourselves face-to-face with our own fears, our shame, our unwillingness to change. We may be led into a time of healing, dealing with unknown family of origin influences or deeply rooted concerns. Ascetical practice leads to ongoing conversion. We persevere and experiment with our practice. Sometimes the practice becomes dead ritual. Gerald May, writing of dead ritual, says, "In my experience, all routines sooner or later become habits I begin to hide behind. I can take the best of spiritual disciplines—those that are most likely to really enable spacious presence—and turn them into doings. Then I go through the motions of the practice and escape the [holy] space altogether."[83] We watch, we revise, we persevere. Fifth-century ascetic Mother Syncletica, describing someone she knew, says that this woman, "when sitting in her cell, looked out for the introduction of thoughts; and she kept count of which was the first, which was the second, and for how much time each one of them held her; and whether she fell short of or exceeded the day before. Thus she knew accurately the grace of God and her own endurance as well as her power, in addition to the defeat of the enemy."[84]

Finally, we reach a settled place of increased reorientation or rehabituation. The experiments have led to disciplines that begin to show fruit in increased love for God and others. We have lived our visions and now reveal something more of the kingdom of God than before. The means have been used, and we have been the recipients of grace. We are ready to take the next step of growth.

Through the means of grace—Spirit, trials, community, and ascetical practice—the task of spiritual formation is put into action. We intend transformation through making use of means toward the aims of Christian perfection.

Questions

1. How have you been formed throughout your life? How have you been formed spiritually as a Christian?

2. The chapter only listed a few basic principles of Christian spiritual formation. What other principles might you derive from scripture? What other key passages might be used to summarize a biblical approach to spiritual formation? What key texts from Christian history might be used?

3. The emphasis on contexts in this and other chapters seems to make the application of the Christian faith relative to each individual or community. How (if at all) might you reconcile emphasis on the particular contexts of our formation with the Christian claim to absolute values?

4. Design a network of formal and informal agents of Christian spiritual formation for a small group, congregation, or ministry with whom you are involved. What factors must you consider in order to best link those who take initiative with those they encourage?

5. To which of the terms describing the ultimate aim of Christian spiritual formation are you most attracted? Why?

6. Link task and means by exploring a particular area of formation in your own life (or someone you know closely). See if you can include every one of the steps listed. Make particular selections of means. Implement the means for a while and see what happens. Revise and experiment. Then, after you have explored for a time, write up your conclusions. What have you learned from this exploration of the task and means of spiritual formation?

CHAPTER SUMMARY

1. Spiritual formation refers to the processes by which individuals and communities become more fully conformed and united to Christ, especially with regard to maturity of life and calling. Biblical formation does not focus on appearance, politics, or particulars. Rather, responding to the gracious work of God, it involves the intentional and ongoing Godward reorientation and rehabituation of human experience itself, expressed in the concrete realities of everyday life.

2. Christian spiritual formation is undertaken within contexts. Life itself acts as a context of spiritual formation, shaping the ways in which we perceive and receive form. There are also the specific contexts related to the settings in life wherein our spiritual life is nourished: solitude, home, spiritual guidance relationships, and congregational life. Each of these contexts offers unique contributions and challenges to our own growth in maturity. More specifically still, we give permission for some, the *agents* of spiritual formation, to take initiative in our lives with regard to our own formation. The Holy Spirit is our primary agent of spiritual formation, initiating encounters that facilitate transformation and provide a unique supernatural dimension to our experience. Human agents can be formally identified: spiritual directors, supervisors, and such. They can also be less formally recognized: a spiritual friend, a small group, one group that leads another, and so on.

3. The aim of Christian spiritual formation is conformity with Christ. Yet this aim can be described variously, leading to different emphases within our practice. Some speak of deification, others advocate holiness. One may talk about the personal realization of perfection, while another encourages the corporate realization of the kingdom of God. From day to day, however, our aim is simply *increase*—growth in mature likeness to Christ one step at a time.

4. The task of Christian spiritual formation is essentially a task of "putting off and putting on," a task of "practicing" the gospel. It generally includes, to some degree or another, a variety of steps along the way: gaining a clear vision of the end; cultivating determination; nurturing community support; identifying areas to be formed; selecting strategies and means; paying attention to context; implementing the transformation of life through practice, revision, and experimentation; and, finally, rehabituating life itself. It can touch every aspect of human experience: every operational system, every stage of experience, every relationship, from the shallows to the depths.

5. Spiritual formation involves the use of a variety of means—activities, situations, relationships—that cultivate growth in Christ. Our experience of the Holy Spirit itself can be a means of spiritual formation. We open ourselves to experience of the Spirit when we are prepared, open, attentive, appreciative, and responsive to the Spirit. The trials of life (both context and means) empty us and expand us. We encourage their work when we approach trials with a soft heart, a clear mind, and a strong will and when we ritualize the details of our lives. The community of Christ cultivates our formation through general guidance, group guidance, one-on-one guidance, and hidden guidance. Spiritual disciplines are activities of mind and body undertaken to bring our total being into cooperation with the divine order. They shape in specific ways each step of the process of spiritual formation.

Practicing Christian Spirituality

My Spiritual Agenda

The Problem

Many Christians today are longing for a deep and holy order in their lives. This longing for order is not simply the superficial desire for peace and quiet around the home. Beyond the wish that our computer would never freeze, that our kids would never fight, or that telephone solicitors would never interrupt us, there is a longing for something more. Most of us, at one time or another, have felt a longing (vague or clear, stimulated by growth or disappointment) for each of the elements of our life to have its proper attention. And these elements include not just the duties of life but especially the core elements of our personalities and histories. We long for the whole of our life to be somehow centered around our relationship with God.

A Practical Means

One tool that has been used by Christians through the centuries to promote lives ordered around relationship with God is some kind of written record of one's intentions. These written reflections have been called by various names. Puritan divines spoke of "resolutions" or "covenants." Methodists spoke of "instituted and prudential means of grace." Monastic communities spoke of "rules." Some Orthodox communities speak of "canons." Here we will speak of a *spiritual agenda*. Read the following and try one out for yourself.

What Is a Spiritual Agenda?

A *spiritual agenda* is a written reflection of one's specific spiritual practices—practices that one promises to keep and that are evaluated regularly, both individually and in the presence of a close spiritual friend.

What Are the Benefits of a Spiritual Agenda?

- A spiritual agenda provides a unifying focus for life.
- A spiritual agenda leads one toward spiritual development.
- A spiritual agenda provides a setting of unthreatening accountability.
- A spiritual agenda helps us to take charge of our time.

Sample Areas to Consider

Here are suggestions for areas you may wish to address in your agenda:

- your intention (such as a desire to love with sincerity or to seek God)
- your prayer life (such as specific devotional practices—worship, intercession, meditation—times, and places)
- your plans of study (such as reading, memorization, research, listening, and attitudes to take—diligence, openness, and so on)
- your family life (such as the time spent with family or the activities to share together)
- your fellowship or relationships (such as key relationships of focus, attitudes or actions to cultivate, meetings or activities in which to participate, or letters to write)
- your health (such as your exercise goals or your eating habits)
- your financial life (such as a record of income and expenses, a budget, lifestyle choices, and contributions)
- your community life (such as plans to read newspapers, to write letters on social issues, or to volunteer at organizations)

Sample Agenda

1. Prayer: Meditate on one psalm daily:
   S M T W T F S

2. Family: Spend quality time with my spouse three times a week (for at least two hours at a time)

   _____ _____ _____

3. Study: How diligent was I? (rank from 1 to 10)   _____

4. Did I show Christian love to others this week?

   _____

   _____

   _____

   _____

   Other comments:

   _____

   _____

   _____

   _____

LOOKING FURTHER

A number of works exploring the theme of spiritual formation are available. We might do best to divide resources loosely by our categories of practice (works that focus mainly on helping people to practice spiritual formation), dynamics (works that present a more general treatment or explore aspects of spiritual formation), and study (particular academic studies of spiritual formation within the field of Christian spirituality).

Practice

For resources on practice, see the following: Joseph D. Driskill, *Protestant Spiritual Exercises: Theology, History, and Practice* (Harrisburg, PA: Morehouse, 1999); Richard Foster, *Celebration of Discipline: The Path to Spiritual Growth*, 20th anniv. ed. (San Francisco: HarperSanFrancisco, 1998); Marjorie J. Thompson, *Soul Feast: An Invitation to the Christian Spiritual Life* (Louisville: Westminster John Knox, 1995); and Dallas Willard, *The Spirit of the Disciplines: Understanding How God Changes Lives* (San Francisco: Harper and Row, 1988).

Dynamics

The following three books address the dynamics of spiritual formation: Kenneth Boa, *Conformed to His Image: Biblical and Practical Approaches to Spiritual Formation* (Grand Rapids: Zondervan, 2001); Dallas Willard, *Renovation of the Heart: Putting on the Character of Christ* (Colorado Springs: NavPress, 2002); and Susanne Johnson, *Christian Spiritual Formation in the Church and Classroom* (Nashville: Abingdon, 1989).

Practice and Dynamics

For books that address both practice and dynamics, see Jordan Aumann's *Spiritual Theology* (London: Sheed and Ward, 1980) and Theophan the Recluse's *The Path to Salvation: A Manual of Spiritual Transformation,* trans. Fr. Seraphim Rose (Platina, CA: St. Herman Press, 1998).

Study

One topic related to the subject of spiritual formation has received significant academic attention, namely, asceticism. (Although it has not received much attention from social scientists, it has been the subject of study by scholars of antiquity, philosophy, and religion.) The Society of Biblical Literature for years sponsored a study group on asceticism. This group has published a few collections of essays relevant to the topic, including *Asceticism*, edited by Vincent L. Wimbush and Richard Valantasis (New York: Oxford University Press, 1995); and *Asceticism and the New Testament*, edited by Leif Vaage and Vincent L. Wimbush (New York: Routledge, 1999). The group has also stimulated the work of a number of individual authors. (See, for example, writings by Elizabeth Clark, Peter Brown, Richard Valantasis, Richard Wimbush, Edith Wyschogrod, Walter Kaelber, James Goehring, and others.) Perhaps the best entry into this literature is to review the essays in *Asceticism* and then to work out from there, exploring areas where interest leads.

The Life of Prayer

9

OBJECTIVES

In this chapter you will be introduced to the world of Christian prayer. You will learn something of the language of prayer: kinds of prayer, ways of prayer, settings of prayer, history of prayer. You will consider questions about the significance of God's character for prayer. You will hear stories of prayer and samples of prayer. You will also reflect on human experience, seeing how it is expressed in prayer. You will explore how Christian prayer exhibits dynamics of interpersonal relationship. You will review scientific inquiry regarding prayer. You will see how our own trans*formation* and our life of prayer develop together. Finally, you will explore designing a life of prayer for yourself.

After reading this chapter you should be able to

- define prayer, giving examples from a number of different types of prayer;
- list at least seven key figures, movements, or classics in the history of Christian prayer, briefly summarizing their contributions;
- introduce an individual or group to a number of different "ways" of doing prayer;
- identify the dimensions of human experience active in an example of a person's (or a congregation's) story of prayer, noting the significance of each dimension for the character of the prayer experience;
- illustrate how the dynamics of the divine-human relationship are played out in the life of prayer, giving concrete examples;
- summarize key issues regarding the theology of prayer and current "scientific" studies of prayer;
- design a strategy for your own maturation in prayer.

Introducing Christian Prayer

For many, Christian spirituality *is* prayer. Most of the books in the spirituality section of bookstores are about prayer (and there are legion). The most well-known classics of Christian spirituality have large sections devoted to prayer. Probably the most-memorized passage of the Bible is the Lord's Prayer. We lift our prayers in public; we cry out in private; we hear the whisper of the Spirit in life. And yet, we are not always sure just what prayer *is*.

Words for Prayer

The English word *prayer* comes from the Latin verb *precari*, meaning "to beg or entreat." While the word can be used with reference to other people ("I pray, tell me what is the o'clock?"), *prayer* is especially used with reference to God. Biblical terms for prayer (for example, *hitpallel* in Hebrew or *proseuche* in Greek) express entreaty or petition as well. Yet it has been understood from earliest Christian history that prayer means more than petition. First Timothy 2:1 recommends that "supplications, prayers, intercessions, and thanksgivings be made for everyone." Patristic theologians saw, in this passage, a reference to different types of prayer. The Lord's Prayer (Matthew 6:9–13; Luke 11:2–4), while structured in a series of petitions, has been seen to express adoration, confession, consecration, and more. Similarly, the Psalms have been seen, from the earliest Christian centuries, as an expansive resource for discovering and expressing "the stirrings and the equanimity of the soul appropriate to them." And certainly Paul's injunction that Christians "pray without ceasing" (1 Thessalonians 5:17) demands a broader view of prayer. Ultimately the term *prayer* has come to express both a specific meaning (petition) and a broader meaning (any expression of relationship with God).[1]

Communication with God

Broadly speaking, Christian prayer is communication with God. We have identified *communication* as meaningful, interactive self-disclosure. Communication takes something of one person's experience and brings it to another. In chapter 6 we examined communication in the context of *interpersonal* relationship, a mutual sharing that is informed by interest, expectations, and intimacy. *Interpersonal communication* involves three central elements: speaking (using verbal communication as a model), listening, and what can be called the space in between. We disclose to another. The other receives. There is silence between. The space in between speaking and listening is also the atmosphere of the relationship, which provides a kind of working understanding that guides the meaning of the speaking and listening. This structure of speaking, listening, and space is also present in the communication with God known as prayer. We "speak" to God. God "hears." (Or God speaks and we hear.) Both arise within the context of a silence and a relationship that give shape to the speech and the hearing. While Psalms, for example, records speeches we call prayers, the context of hearing and the space in between is assumed throughout.

Prayer is interpersonal communication *with God*. While prayer is a mutual self-disclosure, it is not a conversation between equals. Prayer is communication between created and Creator, between seeker and Savior. This distinction must always be retained, lest, in the excitement of interpersonal communication, we fail to regard God as *God*. Our worship, our thanksgiving, our meditation are all expressed before the Almighty One, who graces us with the very possibility of human-divine relationship. Prayer as petition reminds us, in all our prayers, that we have no rights before God. All is gift, and we are encouraged to ask.

Furthermore, whereas human-to-human communication is often conducted audibly, communication *with God*, who is spirit, does not need audible speech. God can hear our heart without the spoken words. We perceive God's self-disclosure with our spiritual—and not necessarily our physical—ears. "God knows your heart and is not so concerned with your words as He is with the attitude of your heart."[2] Thus "the essence of prayer is therefore the spiritual lifting of the heart towards God."[3] Nevertheless, we organize the lifting of our hearts to God often through words, either the words of a community or our own spontaneous, conversational prayers.

Types of Prayer

This leads us to the place where we can understand the different *types* of prayer. Adoration, worship, praise, thanksgiving, blessing, confession, petition, **supplication, intercession, aspiration**, consecration, meditation, **lament**, and so on are all different types of prayer. Each type of prayer expresses a different feeling or embodies a different "relational moment." You know how it is between people. One moment I am complaining to you about something, the next moment I am asking you for help, and then I am thanking you—lament, petition, thanksgiving. Or I ask you a question and you respond with another. Your question convicts me and I am in tears of repentance. You embrace me and I express myself not only in those tears of repentance, but also in tears of gratitude and joy. Another time we just sit quietly and muse together about this or that. Over time, a full relationship will experience a range of communication. Likewise, a healthy life of prayer will communicate a variety of different types of prayer. Indeed, when Jesus's disciples asked Jesus how to pray, he modeled this very variety with the different petitions of the Lord's Prayer.

Prayer, like human-to-human communication, can be looked at as a moment, as an event, or as a state. I complain to you—this is a *moment* of speaking. But our conversation—my complaint, your hearing and response, my asking for help

and your giving help, my thanking you, and so on—is an *event* of speaking (as in "I spoke yesterday to my friend about that"). Then we can go one step further and talk about the quality of our interpersonal communication itself. I might say, "We have reached a new state in our relationship. We talk about deeper things now, and we can just sit together without having to fill up the space with words." The same is true of communication with God. We speak of particular prayers (as in the *oratio* moment of *lectio divina*). We speak of a "time" of prayer (as we would in describing a full session of *lectio divina*). And we can also speak of prayer as a unique *state* of somewhat continual interpersonal relationship, due to God's presence with us at all times and his ability to communicate without

---

The Petitions of the Lord's Prayer[4]

• Hallowed be thy name	*worship*
• Thy kingdom come	*aspiration*
• Thy will be done	*surrender*
• Give us bread	*supplication*
• Forgive us	*confession*
• Deliver us	*warfare prayer*

---

audible words. Theophan the Recluse writes of this state and of the one whose prayer "continues within him in whatever he is doing, present when he talks and writes, speaking in his dreams, waking him up in the morning. Prayer in such a man is no longer a series of acts, but a state; and he has found the way to fulfill Paul's command, 'Pray without ceasing' (1 Thessalonians 5:17)."[5]

Communication with God can be expressed with or without the use of words, by an individual or a community. Spiritual writer Walter Hilton divided prayer into three simple categories in terms of the context and type of expression:

- spoken prayer ordained by God and the holy church ("**common**" or "public" prayer).
- spoken prayer expressing the stirrings of those who are in a state of devotion ("**conversational**" prayer).
- prayer in the heart alone and without speaking ("**contemplative**" prayer, broadly understood)[6]

We will use Hilton's basic division of common prayer, conversational prayer, and contemplative prayer as we survey, in the next section, the history of Christian prayer. We will explore the *meaning* of these types of prayer further as the chapter develops.

A Brief History of Christian Prayer

While we cannot fully reconstruct how individuals or communities prayed throughout Christian history, we can recover some bits and pieces, since we possess samples of people's prayers in written form along with literature from various periods instructing both individuals and communities how to pray (not to mention the resources we find in art, music, architecture, and so forth). A brief survey of this history will introduce us to the key figures, movements, and issues in Christian prayer.[7] Bernard McGinn divides the history of Western mysticism into three layers "in which earlier expressions live on into later periods to interact with new ideas, systems, and institutions to create ever more complex possibilities."[8] With a couple of adjustments we will explore common, conversational, and contemplative prayer following McGinn's divisions.

The first layer: 0–1200. Within this layer, Christianity grew from a Jewish sect into the dominant (and assumed) religion of Europe. Perhaps the most dramatic developments in prayer during this time were the changes seen in the practice of common, or liturgical, prayer. Within a single millennium, common prayer evolved from a loose, and highly participatory, mix of Jewish, Greco-Roman, and uniquely Christian elements (for example, the Christian understanding

of the ministry of the Holy Spirit, which was distinct from both Jewish and Greco-Roman religious traditions) into highly structured rituals, which were performed in the most elaborate buildings of the age. During this same period, understanding of conversational prayer began to accentuate the broader definition of prayer to the point where petition was minimized. This was due in part to a Greek understanding of God which was uncomfortable imagining God's specific involvement with individual embodied persons and which emphasized the goal of a unitive (and contemplative) vision of God. Celtic Christians of the same period spoke their blessings and petitions to the Trinitarian God in the forms of familiar cultural expressions (see the Celtic Eucharistic blessing below). During the latter half of this period, the prayers (petitions) of the laity were increasingly made within the context of the veneration of saints and the stories of miracles performed at the presence of sacred sites or sacred relics. The cross of Christ and the practice of penance became foci of personal prayer in early medieval Christian prayer. The Christian church also prayed contemplative prayer during this period, exploring the stages and skills of contemplation, especially its foundation in the character of God and the context of common worship.

The appearance of various movements compelled the church to wrestle with key ideas related to prayer. In the second century, a group gathered around the teachings of Montanus, who emphasized the ministry of the Holy Spirit and the role of prophetic utterance in the church. The discussions related to Montanism pressed the church to consider questions about listening to God. In the fourth and fifth centuries, a group called the Messalians, or Euchites, stressed the role of constant prayer in sanctification to the point of minimizing the sacraments and accountable relationships with the community of faith. The relationship between common, conversational, and contemplative prayer was explored in this controversy. In the eighth and ninth centuries, a

Figure 9.1
A Brief Summary of the History of Christian Prayer

	Context	Issues	Public Prayer		Private Prayer		
			Language	Participants	Focus	Process	Aim
First Layer							
100–600	church/home to monastic	Montanism (prophecy)	vernacular plus glossalalia	contributors	Spirit and scripture	pure, brief, frequent	*gnosis theoria contemplatio*
	persecuted to persecutors	Messalian (place of sacraments)					
			to				
600–1200	synthesis Dark Ages		vernacular Latin/Greek	participants	scripture saints (place, story relics) visions, life (Celtic)	*lectio divina* focus, not process	*contemplatio* = desire for heaven
	translation of Pseudo Dionysius	Iconoclast (role of imagery)					
			to				
Second Layer							
1200–1520	university, monastery	Hesychast (role of body, experience)	foreign Latin in West	observers	Devotions in vernacular	shift in "meditation"	*contemplatio* = higher state of consciousness
			to an				
Third Layer							
1520–present	expanding contexts	Reformation(s) (authority, structure)	ultimate return to vernacular	increasing participation (explosion of forms)	Variety - scripture - traditional forms - extemporaneous - reason	both simplification and experimentation	Each school or community sees a different aim in prayer - obedience to biblical command - self-improvement - intimacy with Spirit - and more
	New Globalism	Pentecostal	renewal of glossolalia				

battle waged over whether a picture (icon) was an appropriate focus point for prayer. Ultimately, the "iconoclast" controversy ruled in favor of the use of material reality as means through which devotion may be channeled. Central to the development of Christian prayer from the fourth century on was the institution of monasticism. Monastic communities provided an environment wherein Christian prayer could be practiced regularly and examined deeply.

A list of key figures who wrote on prayer during this period would surely include Origen, Augustine, Pseudo-Dionysius, and Bernard of Clairvaux. Origen's *On Prayer* was perhaps the first systematic theological treatise on Christian prayer. Origen considered what meaning prayer may have in light of a God who is omniscient; he commented on the Lord's Prayer; and he provided directions regarding the posture, preparation, and place of prayer. While Au-gustine did not write an extended treatise on prayer, the twelfth (and final) chapter of his commentary, *The Literal Meaning of Genesis*, articulates distinctions between various experiences of God that shaped the vocabulary of discussions about prayer from that time forward. A third work that was influential in shaping the Christian understanding of prayer was *The Mystical Theology*, published under the name of Paul's convert, Dionysius. This work laid the foundation for an apophatic perspective on Christian prayer which repeatedly appeared throughout history.[9] Bernard of Clairvaux, in a number of works, brought to the Western understanding of prayer a sense of rich, interpersonal feeling. One might also want to mention the work of Basil and Chrysostom in the East, who laid important foundations of liturgical prayer.[10]

The second layer: 1200–1520. The late-medieval period can be described as a time when prayer was "flowering".[11] While the first layer planted the seed of Christian prayer within an established community of faith and into a wide range of cultures and peoples, the second layer of the history of Christian prayer saw the flowering of that seed both in the experience of a wide range of lay movements in the West and with the victorious advance of Hesychast, or silent, prayer in the East. And yet at the same time, especially in the West, ecclesiastical structures became even more stratified and unwieldy. While the common prayer of the liturgy became more complicated (tending to distance people from access to God), developments regarding conversational and (to some extent) contemplative prayer made a wide variety of prayer types and methods available to the laity.

Three important figures in the thirteenth century were Gregory Palamas (1296–1359) in the East and Thomas Aquinas and Bonaventure in the West. Palamas wrote in the context of what is called the **Hesychast** controversy. The Greek word *hesuchia* literally means "quiet," and it frequently referred to those who had given themselves to a life of silent prayer. The Hesychast controversy addressed features of the practice of silent prayer common to a group of monks. Issues discussed in this controversy included the role of the body in prayer (is it legitimate to encourage the use of particular physical postures or practices in prayer?), the possibility of immediate contact with God (can God communicate himself to us apart from any particular rational concepts?), and the possibility of a vision of uncreated Light (can we experience Christ today as the disciples did at Jesus's Transfiguration?). Ultimately each of these points was affirmed. Nil Sorsky (d. 1508) brought Hesychast prayer into Russia. Aquinas, a Dominican, writing in the context of a great confusion regarding the definition of prayer, turned the focus once again to the idea of petition. Bonaventure, a Franciscan, wrote *The Soul's Journey into God*, which outlines a series of approaches to God through prayer.[12]

One of the most significant developments in the West was the explosion of writings on prayer by men *and women* of all walks of life in many languages. Here we find the so-called English mystics (Walter Hilton, Julian of Norwich, and the author of *The Cloud of Unknowing*) and the Italian spiritual writers (Catherine of Genoa, Catherine of Sienna, Angela of Foligno). We see the Beguines (for example, Hadewijch of Antwerp, Mechthild of Magdeburg, and Marguerite of Porete) and Teutonic mysticism (represented by Meister Eckhart, Johannes Tauler, Heinrich Suso). And we discover the *devotio moderna* (represented by John Ruusbroec, the author of *Theologia Germanica*, and Thomas á Kempis). All these and others brought to the West a wide range of practices and perspectives to Christian prayer.[13]

But "perhaps the most significant development in late medieval Christianity," writes Richard Kieckhefer, "was the rise of devotionalism."[14] Devotionalism can be identified with the rise of a host of practices that proliferated in the late Middle Ages: pilgrimages, veneration of relics, Marian devotions, meditations on the passion of Christ, penitential exercises, the saying of the rosary, veneration of the Eucharist and the Sacred Heart, and so on. Handbooks on devotions of these kinds circulated widely, as did the ivory panels, woodcuts, and paintings that were used in devotions. But while books and pictures were valuable, devotionalism was especially a prayer-centered movement of *action*. Devout Christians manifested their devotion by *doing* devotions: saying the rosary, going on pilgrimages, giving alms, walking the labyrinth (a winding path laid out on cathedral floors, which served as a poor person's substitute for pilgrimage), attending festivals, and so on. With key reflections on prayer, the expansion of spiritual writing, and the explosion of devotional practice, Christian prayer in the late-medieval West truly experienced a flowering.

The third layer: 1520–present. The Protestant Reformation rejected the hierarchy of

Roman common prayer (the late-medieval Latin Mass), the abuses of late-medieval conversational devotionalism, and the elitism of monastic contemplative prayer. In their place, the Reformers offered a radical simplification of prayer. The services of gathered prayer were reworked in the languages of the people, and congregational prayers and hymns were crafted to be both doctrinally Protestant and culturally appropriate. In place of the seven sacraments and myriad devotional practices, Reformers reduced the sacraments to two and encouraged meditation on the basic truths of the faith: the Lord's Prayer, the Apostles' Creed, the Ten Commandments, and the like. (See the sample from Martin Luther's "A Simple Way to Pray," below.) Family prayer was encouraged as a vehicle for both expressing prayer in small groups and instructing children in prayer. The struggle to articulate the relationship between scripture, reason, Spirit, and tradition resulted in tensions within various reforming communities (for example, the disputes in England between Anglicans, Congregationalists, and Quakers regarding the legitimacy of "spontaneous" prayer in congregational settings). Whereas the first generation of Reformers focused their energies on defending the fundamental availability of access to God, later generations of Pietists and Puritans explored the more nuanced dynamics of Christians' relationship with God in prayer. A number of classic works on prayer come from this period.[15] A final development regarding prayer from Protestant traditions is the establishment of united and corporate prayer for renewal and revival.[16]

Those in the West who remained loyal to Rome experienced their own developments regarding prayer. They established a greater uniformity of practice with regards to the Mass. Furthermore, the place of devotions was clarified such that they were more clearly and closely tied to the church. Those known as the Spanish mystics (for example, Ignatius of Loyola, Teresa of Avila, John of the Cross) advanced the understanding of the relationships between meditation and contemplation, each in their own way. (See the selection from Teresa of Avila's autobiography below.) The so-called French school and those associated with what became labeled Quietism (including Francis de Sales, Pierre de Bérulle, Brother Lawrence of the Resurrection, Madame Guyon, and Francis Fenelon) popularized many insights of the Spanish mystics, creating simple manuals for lay prayer. They also struggled with the question of the boundaries of human surrender (passivity, or "quiet") before God.[17]

In the East, prayer was perceived in traditional liturgical and monastic categories. And yet with the development of the figure of the *staretz* in Russia (a holy person who often offered counsel to the general public in person or in writing), the wisdom of the Hesychast tradition was made available to a wider audience. Tikhon of Zadonsk (1724–83) and Seraphim of Sarov (1759–1833) are good examples of this tradition.[18]

Through the nineteenth and twentieth centuries, Christian prayer both returned to its origins and pressed forward into the unknown. Developments in philosophy, biblical studies, and science challenged traditional views of God and humankind, forcing a rethinking of questions regarding the relationship of prayer and God's providence, along with other issues. The Pentecostal and charismatic movements brought the spontaneity of praying in tongues and other forms of participatory common prayer back into the church. (See the testimony from the Pentecostal revival at Azusa Street in Los Angeles below.) The Second Vatican Council brought a renewed biblical emphasis to the Mass, now offered in the language of the people. Monastic communities were encouraged both to recover their roots and to renew their forms of life (and prayer) for contemporary situations. The persecutions of Communist Russia became an unfortunate blessing to the world, as leaders of Eastern Orthodoxy fled to the West, bringing their wisdom to the rest of the world. Globalization has

Issues in the Historical and Theological Study of Prayer

- Should prayer be understood primarily as petition or in some broader way?
- Should prayer be addressed in some form to Mary or the saints as well as to God?
- How do we clarify the kind and importance of the various impressions that people experience during times of prayer?
- How should we accept the experiences perceived to be of the Spirit in prayer?
- Are there certain experiences in prayer that *ought* to be experienced?
- How important are the scriptures, sacraments, and other means of grace in relation to the value of private conversational or contemplative prayer?
- How legitimate or beneficial is it to use icons, imagination, bodily movements or positions, various devotions, and such to facilitate prayer or meditation?
- Should we emphasize the value of wordless (or "thoughtless") prayer?
- What meaning does petition have in light of the character of God (God's omniscience, God's responsiveness, God's relationship with time, and so on)?
- How appropriate is it to approach prayer with an analogy to marital love?
- Does (or *should*) our relationship with God in prayer develop in certain stages?
- What is the relationship between public and private prayer? between conversational and contemplative prayer?

forced Christianity to reflect on its life of prayer (for example, regarding the nature of Christian meditation in dialogue with Asia) in the context of a wide range of religious communities. Finally, new seeds of Christian expression are flowering in the third world, giving rise to entirely new expressions of common, conversational, and contemplative prayer.[19]

The Ways of Christian Prayer

Just as the art of human-to-human communication has its own skills and techniques, so too the life of Christian prayer has its own "ways." But because it is communication *with God*, distinct from human-to-human communication, prayer requires its own unique skills and techniques, appropriate both to the seasons of human life and to the character of the divine. As one introduction to the practice of prayer puts it, "Prayer is nothing more than conversation with a partner whose presence is elusive—God isn't here in material form, so we use all the resources at our disposal to enter into this conversation."[20] Even the disciples asked Jesus for a how-to lesson in prayer! Thus we can legitimately speak of the ways of prayer, or the practice of prayer, or of prayer exercises, methods, and techniques.[21]

The ways of prayer are those means that we use to structure our engagement with God or at least to bring us into a place where we can more easily communicate with God, or God with us, both personally and corporately. We arrange times of prayer that are not cluttered by other events. We secure places of prayer that facilitate attention to God. We make gestures and postures and actions that express the mood of prayer.[22] In both public and private prayer, we order our minds, our hearts, and our bodies to facilitate quality communication with the Word himself.

The Ways and Forms of Public Prayer

From the beginning, God's people have ordered their common encounter with God. The Lord gave, from Mt. Sinai, specific instructions regarding the rituals that would express Israel's relationship with God. (See, for example, Exodus 25–31.) Psalms were written to accompany many of these. By the time of Jesus, liturgical celebrations were used in temple, synagogue, and home. While the evidence is fragmentary, it is safe to say that both Jesus and the early apostles instituted basic elements of community worship, although these were probably expressed differently in different locations. Christians have been exploring

focus

Historical Portrait: Celtic Eucharistic Chant

Around 800, during the time of a reform of the Celtic church called the Céli Dé reform (*Céli Dé*, or Culdee, means "servant of God"), an order of worship known as the Stowe Missal was produced, giving directions for worship. Shortly thereafter, composer Moél Caích added chants to be used in the service. This particular chant was recited at the point in the Eucharist where the communion bread was "fractioned," that is, broken up into a number of pieces and arranged in the shape of a Celtic cross. This chant is from *Celtic Spirituality*, published by Paulist Press.[23]

> They recognized the Lord, Alleluia;
>> In the breaking of the bread, Alleluia (Luke 24:35).
>> For the bread that we break is the body of our Lord Jesus Christ, Alleluia;
>> The cup which we bless is the blood of our Lord Jesus Christ, Alleluia (1 Corinthians 10:16–17);
>> For the remission of our sins, Alleluia (Matthew 26:28).
>> O Lord, let your mercy come upon us, Alleluia;
>> For how have we hoped in you, Alleluia (Psalm 31:1).
>> They recognized the Lord, Alleluia;
>> In the breaking of the bread, Alleluia (Luke 24:35).
>> We believe, O Lord, we believe that in this breaking of your body and pouring out of your blood
> we become redeemed people;
>> We confess that by our sharing of this sacrament we are strengthened to endure in hope until we
> lay hold and enjoy its true fruits in the heavenly places.

ways of public or common prayer from then until now.

Author C. S. Lewis writes of the values and the dangers of the ways of common prayer in his *Letters to Malcolm Chiefly on Prayer*. "It is well to have specifically holy places, and things, and days, for, without these focal points or reminders, the belief that all is holy and 'big with God' will soon dwindle into a mere sentiment. But if these holy places, things, and days cease to remind us, if they obliterate our awareness that all ground is holy and every bush (could we but perceive it) a Burning Bush, then the hallows begin to do harm. Hence the necessity, and the perennial danger, of 'religion.'"[24] What Lewis calls "religion"—holy places, days, actions, and such—many discuss under the headings of "ritual" or "liturgy." While definitions of these terms vary, we may think of ritual and liturgy for our purposes here as structured acts, prayers, gestures, and such performed by communities as part of their common experience and expression of relationship with God.[25] Liturgy is a focal point, bringing the time, attention, and effort of a community together around a single event. A priest breaks bread as the congregation recites a chant, a small group of people pray together during the weekly common meal and house church meeting, an emerging church rehearses the story of Christ's passion and shares personal stories and prayers through poetry and art—all common, ordered, focused expressions of relationship with God.

Common prayer *names* the world we live in and *forms* us into that world. Our ritual provides a shared horizon of meaning that we celebrate in common and remember apart. We attend an Anglican service and we remember, through the responses in the

Eucharist, that we live in a world wherein Christ has died, Christ is risen, and Christ will come again. We attend a charismatic worship service and we discover, through the opportunities for spontaneous participation, that we live in a world wherein the Spirit of God is free to break in. The choices of how we arrange our common prayer— our forms and techniques—highlight key Christian themes, and in so doing they provide embodied means for learning. We live in a world shattered by the tragedy of human experience. We are, through Christ and the Spirit, reconciled to God, to one another, and to the world. We are sent out as agents of God's kingdom to the rest of the world. When we receive the cup, when we kneel, when we lay hands on another in prayer, we learn and live prayer in a way that is not possible in any other environment. Relationship with God is rehearsed in ritual, and through ritual the community participates in that relationship.

Liturgy—identifying the ways of common prayer—*structures* corporate relationship with God. Consequently, different spiritualities, different approaches to relationship with God, will be expressed through different liturgical forms. Thus,

Late at night in the gloom of his castle tower, the evil Dr. Mordrek composes new unsingable tunes for old favorite hymns.

the unique combination of words, images, music, gesture, and silence found in the Roman Mass enables the worshiper to "proclaim and enact the mystery of God incarnate in Jesus."[26] The fundamental symbols of Pentecostal and charismatic ritual (leadership, worship, word, gifts, ministry, and mission) facilitate "experience of God."[27] Chosen ways of common prayer (for example, should we encourage a quiet, reverent place of meeting, or should we facilitate the relationship-building work of casual conversation?) foster different skills and sensibilities in our common relationship with God. The times, places, postures, and forms of public prayer initiate us into the foundations of Christian prayer as passed on through the history of the church and as lived in concrete communities today.

Somewhere between common prayer and private prayer are family prayer and informal communal prayer. Like common prayer, family prayer draws different people around a single form (for example, as both adults and children join in the Lord's Prayer), yet like private prayer, fewer people and more intimate relationships can give greater freedom of "technique" involved in the prayer (for example, as time is given between each petition of the Lord's prayer for adult or child to offer an appropriate expression of prayer). As such, family and informal communal prayer can provide valuable bridges between the common life of church and the personal lives of individuals.[28]

The Ways and Forms of Private Prayer

Just as communities use their own ritualized ways to communicate with God, so too individuals make use of various techniques of prayer. We have so far, following Walter Hilton's lead, examined prayer within three primary categories: *common* (vocal and public or official), *conversational* (vocal and spontaneous), and *contemplation* (without words, usually private). Now we must refine these categories for the sake of exploring the ways of private prayer.

While conversation is generally vocal among two or more persons, between humans and God there is a kind of conversation that does not depend on audible words. We can *think* our prayers to God. We formulate sentences expressing our worship, our thanksgiving, our petitions, and so on to God. And God "listens." We can also think *about* God. We can read scripture (as in *lectio divina*), pondering the meaning of texts and being drawn through them into prayer. In this practice, thinking *about* God and thinking *to* God are mixed. We read as if God (the Spirit who illumines the written Word) is speaking to us. Thoughts and feelings arise as we read. We express things to God. Thought, feeling, imagination, and inclination all blend together in a time of listening and speaking with God, prayerfully reading scripture. Or perhaps we do not read scripture but gaze on a picture of Christ, an icon. We allow our thoughts to center on Christ, our heart to be drawn to Christ, as we look at the picture. Here we are not speaking so much of conversation but of *meditation*.[29]

After the eleventh century in the West, and in the context of the Hesychast controversy in the East (1336–51), increasing attention was given to the methods of Christian meditation and prayer. Many works on prayer from this period forward offer precise suggestions regarding ways that individuals can intentionally employ dimensions of their own experience in order to facilitate their attention or expression to God. Let us look at a few of these.

Repetition. Some techniques make use of *repetition* to focus attention, allowing individuals who are meditating or praying to bring ever more of themselves around a simple, but important center. Such is the way of the **Jesus Prayer**, common to Orthodox believers. The Jesus Prayer involves the repetition of the name of Jesus, or a phrase including this name. The most common phrase is *Lord Jesus Christ, Son of God, have mercy on me, a sinner.* While this phrase can be repeated anytime, a monk of the Eastern Church advises that beginners "do well to bind themselves to a certain regularity in their practice of the Prayer, choosing fixed times and solitary places." Then, "Having begun to pronounce the name with loving adoration, all that we have to do is to attach ourselves to it, cling to it, and to repeat it slowly, gently and quietly. . . . Little by little we are to concentrate our whole being around the name, allowing it like a drop of oil silently to penetrate and impregnate our soul."[30]

A similar use of the technique of repetition to focus and deepen attention to God is employed in what is currently known as **centering prayer**, wherein one repeats a single word (*God, love,* or the like) and allows that repetition to draw one below

---

Common prayer *names* the world we live in and *forms* us into that world.

---

surface thoughts and feelings into a deeper awareness of the presence of God.[31]

Body use. Other techniques use *bodily* positions or movements to facilitate communication with God. The Psalms speak of prostration, bowing, raising hands, and dancing before God. Standing, praying with hands outstretched in the form of a cross, and various genuflections were common in the early church. Using particular physical techniques to facilitate attention and expression was one of the concerns of the Hesychast controversy. For many today, bowing heads, folding hands, and kneeling are the only bodily movements used in prayer. In many circles the use of the body in prayer is receiving renewed emphasis. The Pentecostal and charismatic movements have stimulated a renewed appreciation for embodied praise in many forms. More recently, churches of all varieties have been reconsidering the role of the body in prayer.[32] Physical posture and movement engage unique ways of knowing and expression in the act of prayer.

Imagination. Still other techniques emphasize the role of our *imagination* to trigger thoughts and feelings in prayer. Ultimately, the iconoclast controversy (726–843) affirmed the legitimacy of images (icons) as vehicles for prayer, although the ways in which icons were used in the East did not generally encourage the active use of the imagination. In the eleventh century in the West, Aelred of Rivaulx, monastic reformer Peter Damian (1007–72), and others gave specific instructions or descriptions of the employment of imagination in order to "join" the biblical stories or other themes of the faith. In contrast to fellow reformer Andreas Bodenstein von Karlstadt, Martin Luther permitted the use of objects of art as means of focusing attention during meditation and prayer. The fourteenth-century *devotio moderna* movement—and, later, Roman Catholic Ignatius of Loyola and Puritan divine Richard Baxter (1615–91)—encouraged the intentional use of imagination to facilitate meditation. The renewal of Jesuit spirituality since Vatican II has stimulated interest in the role of imagination in prayer. Image often serves as a bridge between intellect and emotion. As such, image can serve a powerful function in facilitating our perception of God's self-communication and our own "speech" toward God.[33]

Contemplation as a way of prayer. Making sense of the term *contemplation* is a bit complicated. In early writings, contemplation described a moment or dimension within a larger event of prayer. Ignatius of Loyola uses the term *contemplation* to mean what others understand by *meditation.* By the sixteenth century, the term *contemplation* was regularly used to describe techniques of prayer that were different from either those used in the early church or those advocated by Ignatius. Thus far in this chapter we have defined contemplative prayer, with Hilton, simply as prayer from the heart, without words.

It is time for us to further explore the meaning of contemplation. Here we will look at contemplation as a "way" of prayer. Later we will explore contemplation as an "attitude" of prayer and as an "aim" of prayer.

Contemplation, as a means of prayer, involves not so much the *use* of means and operations but the intentional *non-use* of these. Here a monk of the Eastern Church reflects on the way of the "prayer of simplicity":

> The prayer of simplicity consists in placing yourself in the presence of God and maintaining yourself in his presence for a certain time, in an interior silence which is as complete as possible, while you concentrate upon the divine Object, reduce to unity the multiplicity of your thoughts and feelings, and endeavour to "keep yourself quiet" without words or arguments. This prayer of simplicity is the frontier and the most elementary degree of contemplation. It is not difficult. Anyone who is even to a slight degree accustomed to pray is sure to have experienced this form of contemplation for a few minutes at least.[34]

Devotions. The particular ways of employing our operations in prayer (repetition, body use, imagination, contemplation, and such), in conjunction with the precise foci of attention used to mediate God's presence, give rise to the innumerable kinds of **devotion** expressed in Christian prayer. Thus, repetition of key phrases is used in the recitation of the Rosary and in contemporary worship music. Bodily actions are used in ancient pilgrimage and contemporary use of the labyrinth. Imagination is employed in the adoration of the Sacred Heart and in recent approaches to the prayer of healing. The method of contemplation is used in the Jesus Prayer and in centering prayer. Devotional books, art, music, and more are all designed to stimulate the involvement of heart, mind, imagination, and body in communication with God.

Attention, Distraction, Awareness, and Depth

One function of the ways of prayer, both public and private, is to encourage communication with God that is attentive. One of the chief complaints regarding persons who fail to communicate is that "you're not paying attention." Our mind drifts, our speech becomes routine, we fail to notice the other, and communication falls short of its potential. The complaint is that "you're not aware of me" or "you're not being present with me," or we ask, "Do you even know I'm here?" While the art of being present, aware, or attentive with another human being is difficult, it is especially problematic when our partner in communication is invisible (no facial expressions) and audibly silent (no tone of voice). For some, prayer moves gradually into sleep as we become relaxed and attention dulls. For others, prayer is a chaos of distractions, with the mind jumping from one thought to another like a monkey jumping from branch to branch. Our rest, diet, and interest; the things going on around us; the physical setting of prayer; any special preparations—all these and more combine to create a kind of *situational mood* of prayer. Prayerful attention is shaped by this situational mood. For example, if we pray when we are most awake, we are more apt to notice things or to express ourselves more clearly than if we pray when we are sleepy. When prayer seems dull or distracted over time, it is wise to ask about the situations of prayer. As one master put it, "the essential, indispensable element is attention. Without attention there is no prayer."[35]

Distractions to prayer can come from a variety of sources, each requiring a different response. At times the forces of evil draw our minds away from prayer through temptation, accusation, or other wiles. The ways of prayer teach us to recognize the strategies of the enemy and to deny them ground. At times distraction is simply an unfortunate loss of attention. A bird flies by and our eyes (and mind) follow. We become aware of the distraction and return to our focus.

Techniques of prayer can help to guide our attention during these times. Repetition, imagination, study, bodily movements, and such can help to facilitate what writers on prayer have called "**recollection**," the re-collecting of ourselves before God in prayer.[36] At times, thoughts that keep coming to the surface may be indications of unexpressed feelings or unresolved concerns. They may be nudges from the Spirit. Here, the best response may not be to put our distractions aside but rather to give them a rightful place before God.[37] Finally, the condition of our mind wandering may not be "distraction" at all; it may instead be a kind of *sacred musing*, where we allow our mind to meander around this or that topic with God the way friends may allow the topic of conversation to wander. Here we open ourselves fully to God, sharing this and that, as God listens and shares with us.[38]

As we learned in chapter 3, *Being Aware* is an aspect of human experience that is subject to variables. Different ways of prayer require different kinds of awareness. Our awareness can be restricted in focus (as in attention to practicing a musical instrument, or in imaginative meditation on a specific biblical passage), or it can be open to a wide range of input (as in restfully listening to the noises of the springtime, or in contemplative prayer). Our awareness can be dulled (as when watching uninteresting television, or when saying routine prayers), or alert (as when watching for signs of danger while driving, or when looking for indications of the Spirit—or spirits—in ministry prayer). Some prayer is relaxed (like sitting with God on a bench in *sacred musing*). Other prayer requires a certain intensity (like corporate prayer for revival). The attention needed in prayer will change with each prayer. For this reason, the ways of prayer will vary from one moment, event, or state to another.

Similarly, different ways of prayer tend to facilitate different *depths* of communication, though there is no hard and fast rule for these matters.[39] Simple common

focus

Historical Portrait:
Martin Luther's "A Simple Way to Pray"

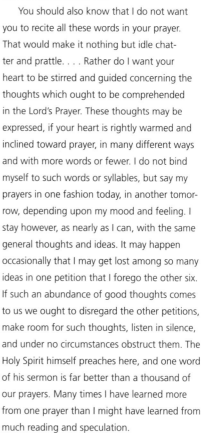

Here is a little introduction to prayer written by Martin Luther for his barber.

Dear Master Peter: I will tell you as best I can what I do personally when I pray. May our dear Lord grant to you and to everybody to do it better than I! Amen.

First, when I feel that I have become cool and joyless in prayer because of other tasks or thoughts (for the flesh and the devil always impede and obstruct prayer), I take my little psalter, hurry to my room, or, if it be the day and hour for it, to the church where a congregation is assembled and, as time permits, I say quietly to myself and word-for-word the Ten Commandments, the Creed, and, if I have time, some words of Christ or of Paul, or some psalms, just as a child might do. . . .

When your heart has been warmed by such recitation to yourself [of the Ten Commandments, the words of Christ, etc.] and is intent upon the matter, kneel or stand with your hands folded and your eyes toward heaven and speak or think as briefly as you can:

O Heavenly Father, dear God, I am a poor unworthy sinner. I do not deserve to raise my eyes or hands toward thee or to pray. But because thou hast commanded us all to pray and hast promised to hear us and through thy dear Son Jesus Christ hast taught us both how and what to pray, I come to thee in obedience to thy word, trusting in thy gracious promise. I pray in the name of my Lord Jesus Christ together with all thy saints and Christians on earth as he has taught us: Our Father who art, etc., through the whole prayer, word for word.

Then repeat one part or as much as you wish, perhaps the first petition: "Hallowed be thy name," and say: "Yes, Lord God, dear Father, hallowed be thy name, both in us and throughout the whole world. . . .

You should also know that I do not want you to recite all these words in your prayer. That would make it nothing but idle chatter and prattle. . . . Rather do I want your heart to be stirred and guided concerning the thoughts which ought to be comprehended in the Lord's Prayer. These thoughts may be expressed, if your heart is rightly warmed and inclined toward prayer, in many different ways and with more words or fewer. I do not bind myself to such words or syllables, but say my prayers in one fashion today, in another tomorrow, depending upon my mood and feeling. I stay however, as nearly as I can, with the same general thoughts and ideas. It may happen occasionally that I may get lost among so many ideas in one petition that I forego the other six. If such an abundance of good thoughts comes to us we ought to disregard the other petitions, make room for such thoughts, listen in silence, and under no circumstances obstruct them. The Holy Spirit himself preaches here, and one word of his sermon is far better than a thousand of our prayers. Many times I have learned more from one prayer than I might have learned from much reading and speculation.

This in short is the way I use the Lord's Prayer when I pray it. To this day I suckle at the Lord's Prayer like a child, and as an old man eat and drink from it and never get my fill.[40]

or conversational prayer easily expresses the level of thoughts, feelings, and choices. Prayer that addresses patterns of emotion, habits of living, or beliefs often requires a certain amount of meditation, facilitating the awareness of deeper levels of communication. Still further, at the level of worldview, core emotional concern, or lifestyle, we are sharing the central organizing principles of the self. Certain forms of healing prayer are designed to open these areas of life. Furthermore, three other forms of prayer—liturgical prayer that works its way into the soul over time, prayer in tongues (glossolalia, or praying in the Spirit), and the prayer of silence—seem to enable communication with God at the depths of our spirit.

Warning

- Another's ways of praying may be dangerous for you.
- Your own ways of praying may become dangerous for you.
- You can easily become trapped in the details of praying.
- You will become trapped if you reject the ways and means of prayer entirely.

Navigating the Ways of Prayer

While approaching communication with God according to ways or methods is both necessary and beneficial, it is not without its complications and dangers. Some of these will be addressed below as we explore prayer and the dynamics of relationship, but a few deserve mention here.

First, we must remember that relationship with God exhibits a wide range of *diversity*. So it is with prayer. Some groups can communicate with God more easily through formal liturgical ways. Others need a greater degree of spontaneity. Some individuals "find God" in prayer with others. Others are perfectly at home with God as they sit alone in a favorite chair in silent contemplation. Even our application of a single way of prayer might vary between individuals or groups. Thus, Evangelical author Jan Johnson writes of the practice of centering prayer, "Be aware that God may reveal to you your own method of centering. It would not be unlike God to see your uniqueness and lead you into abiding in Him in your own way."[41] Our natural tendencies in these areas become both our strengths and our weaknesses. It is one thing to nourish our communication with God in ways that are natural to us. It is another to harden ourselves against any other ways of receiving from God. Be warned, God has his ways of stretching our boundaries of communication.

Second, there is a perpetual danger, in exploring the ways of prayer, of mistaking the means for the ends. We get caught up during Mass in whether the sign of the cross moves from right to left or vice versa (a bodily motion that differs with tradition). We sense the need to share a prophetic utterance with the body but get lost in trying to word it just right. We spend our energies in personal devotions on perfecting the art of biblical imagination. Both individuals and communities are led astray as repetition becomes vain repetition, or as bodily expressions become dry routines, vehicles for show, or the like. There is wisdom in permitting a little boredom in our ways of prayer in order to allow things to settle into a pattern that runs deep. There is also the wisdom that recognizes when little real faith remains inside an empty shell of prayer performance.

And then there is the danger of rejecting ways and means of prayer altogether. It is quite possible, under the guise of "avoiding human religion" to deny oneself (whether one is an individual or a community) legitimate means of ordering and facilitating communication with God. This is the danger that surrounded the Messalian, or Euchite, heresy in the fifth century and the Quietist controversy in the seventeenth century. While overconcern with the methods of prayer can distract the one praying from authentic communication with God, the neglect of scripture, sacraments, or means of recollection can result in an unstable, unbalanced, or prideful faith.

The Dynamics of Christian Prayer

At the start of this chapter, we identified prayer as *communication*. As communication, prayer participates in all the dynamics of an interpersonal relationship, and yet it does so in a unique way, given that one of the "persons" is Almighty God. In chapter 6, we identified a fundamental pattern of the divine-human relationship: God initiates, we respond, and God responds to our response. In one sense prayer is our response to God's prior self-communication. Thus the Lord reveals to Julian of Norwich that "I am the foundation of your beseeching. First, it is my will that you would have it, and then I make you wish it, and then I make you beseech it. And if you beseech, how could it be that you would not have what you beseech?"[42] Yet in another sense prayer, as seen from the point of view of the person praying, exhibits a different pattern: *we* initiate (cry out, offer praise, complain), *God* responds (with "hearing" and "answering"), and then *we* respond again (with thanks).[43] Keeping both these perspectives in mind, we can explore the dynamics of prayer in terms of communication as summarized above: our speaking to God, our listening to God, and the space in between.

Our Speaking

We initiate communication with God. We open our mouths. Or we just plop ourselves down, wordless, on our knees. In either case, we are "speaking" to God, opening ourselves up in relationship. Understanding this opening of ourselves in prayer-speech requires examining a few features of the divine-human relationship.

The posture of initiation. Any time we initiate communication, we do so based on a certain *posture* of initiation; this way of approaching the other is rooted in assumptions about the other and about the state of our relationship. We measure our speech according to our understanding of those to whom we speak. I reveal myself more freely with my spouse, for example, assuming that she knows and loves me enough to absorb a few less-carefully considered comments here and there. The same is true of prayer. What do we think of God and of God's interest in our prayers? Karl Barth, for example, sees in the character of God reason for great confidence in prayer, stating that God is, "in a few words, the one whom we address not by our own initiative, but because we are invited, called to do so. We have the freedom to come to him. This freedom is given to us; it is not of ourselves, it is not natural."[44] Others reject this understanding of God and are, consequently, reticent about petitionary prayer.[45] Our understanding of God is central to our practice of prayer. What do we assume about God's experience of time? Do we think that God knows the future totally, or that God takes a risk in creation, or that our prayers change God's mind? What do we think about God's activity with regard to human freedom? Or more personally, what do *I* think about God's attitude toward *me*? Do I imagine God as an indulgent grandfather, as an angry policeman, or as a special friend?[46] Questions like these (answered consciously or unconsciously) shape the character of our *faith*. And our faith governs the posture of initiation, which is expressed in prayer.[47]

The content of communication. Speaking expresses *content*. We tell a story. We ask a question. We make a request. The types of prayer are determined by the kinds of content expressed. Praise and thanksgiving speak of our gratitude for who God is or what God has done. Confession and repentance speak of the breach in our relationship with God and our desire for that to be mended. Petition, supplication, and intercession make requests of God with regard to the lives of ourselves or others. As already mentioned, a healthy relationship requires the mutual expression of a range of content. The character of our relationship with God is, to some extent, reflected in the content of our prayers.

The disclosure of persons. Yet speaking is not only the communication of content, but also the disclosure of *persons*. Our petition may be not merely a request for help; it may also be a disclosure of fear. Our thanksgiving may be a statement of gratitude as well as a disclosure of relief. Our confession may also be desperation. And so on. We communicate our *selves* in prayer. Some prayer is verbal prayer, whereas other prayer is mental. We share voice and heart to God. Some prayer is with the mind; other prayer is in or with the spirit. Some prayer is affective, emphasizing the involvement of feelings. Other prayer is embodied, emphasizing the involvement of the body. We share with God our choices, our experiences, our inquiries, and our relationships. We share the mundane aspects of life and the depths of our hearts. All of human experience is open for communication.

There is a danger in understanding prayer as disclosure. It is that we can privilege certain operations or states of consciousness and, in so doing, inhibit communication with God. For example, a congregation may value emotional expression more than cognitive operations. Affective prayer is facilitated in the congregation, and analytical prayers are belittled (or vice versa). Or an individual reads a book that values imaginative prayer and begins to think that because he can't seem to picture things well and would rather just pray when he goes on walks "with God," he cannot enter into a vibrant relationship with God. There is the wisdom that supports the "real I" who struggles to speak in prayer.[48] There is also the folly of presuming who that "real I" is and how it is to be expressed to God in prayer. An intimate prayer life draws closer to God through an ever-increasing disclosure. Part of the disclosure of prayer is honestly admitting that we don't know who God is, that we don't know how to be honest (there are so many conflicting thoughts and feelings), but that we want to talk to God about it anyway.

Our Listening

Communication is not just a matter of speaking, but also a matter of *listening*. We have learned about God's free, gracious, Spirit-initiated, self-communication in chapter 6. We have also learned something of our perception of that communication: we perceive God both clearly and vaguely, we see God as both near and far, and we struggle between both true and false guilt. But let us now go deeper, for listening in prayer involves not just *perception* but *attention*, not just *attention* but *reception*. What is the difference between paying attention, as discussed earlier in this chapter, and listening? Paying attention is an act of human consciousness, whereas *listening is a part of human relationship*. Listening, like speaking, involves our understanding and expectations of the other. Listening includes our willingness to "hear" the other—to allow the other to be who he or she is, to move us, to shape us through his or her speech. Listening is not just about focus, though it does include this. It is more about receiving, about welcoming the other into our lives. And this kind of relational listening is what is needed in communication with God.

Contemplation as an attitude of prayer. Contemplation is not only a *way* of prayer; it is also an *attitude* that permeates our prayer. Just as there is a posture of initiation in our speaking, so also there is a posture of reception in our hearing. Contemplation as an attitude of prayer indicates both an *openness to perceive* and a relational *readiness to receive* God wherever he may want to make himself known. Perceptual openness and relational readiness are reflected in Eucharistic Prayer C in the Episcopal *Book of Common Prayer*: "Open our eyes to see your hand at work in the world about us." A contemplative attitude often involves *preparation*: we cultivate the desire to know God, release our preconceived notions of what God must appear like or how God must communicate himself, and purify ourselves so that we don't listen from the vantage point of our own misperceived needs. A contemplative attitude is not forced; instead, it is often referred to as a place of *leisure*, a kind of relaxed willingness to let God be God, and to open ourselves to who God is to us here

focus

Historical Portrait: An Experience of "Other Tongues"

Here is Jennie Evans Moore's account of her experience of Pentecostal prayer at the onset of the Azusa Street Revival in Los Angeles, California, 1906.

For years before this wonderful experience came to us, we as a family, were seeking to know the fullness of God, and He was filling us with His presence until we could hardly contain the power. I had never seen a vision in my life, but one day as we prayed there passed before me three white cards, each with two names thereon, and but for fear I could have given them, as I saw every letter distinctly. On April 9, 1906, I was praising the Lord from the depths of my heart at home, and when the evening came and we attended the meeting the power of God fell and I was baptized in the Holy Ghost and fire, with the evidence of speaking in tongues. During the day I had told the Father that although I wanted to sing under the power I was willing to do whatever He willed, and at the meeting when the power came on me I was reminded of the three cards which had passed [before] me in the vision months ago. As I thought thereon and looked to God, it seemed as if a vessel broke within me and water surged up through my being, which when it reached my mouth came out in a torrent of speech in the languages which God had given me. I remembered the names on the cards: French, Spanish, Latin, Greek, Hebrew, Hindustani. . . . [T]he Spirit led me to the piano, where I played and sang under inspiration, although I had not learned to play. In these ways God is continuing to use me to His glory ever since that wonderful day.[49]

and now.[50] A contemplative attitude exercises certain *skills*, such as being comfortable with solitude and silence, learning to notice small things, moving slowly, developing a sense of place, and so on. A contemplative attitude takes (as Walter Burghardt calls it) a "long, loving look at the Real," in which we are fully engaged in what is before us, losing ourselves in the Other, full of wonder and appreciation. Finally, a contemplative attitude is prepared to risk relationship with the world in responding to God.[51]

Signs of the Spirit. Listening is a *readiness for* the presence of the other, but it is also an active *discernment of* the presence of the other. In interpersonal communication this involves the sorting of verbal and nonverbal cues to determine what is actually being said. But since God is not present to us (often) through the same verbal and nonverbal cues as other people are, "listening" to God involves paying attention to other sorts of cues. Just as audible human speech ultimately stimulates thoughts or feelings in the mind of the listener that are not identical to a person's spoken words but that reflect them, so also the voice of the Spirit enlightens our minds or is poured into our hearts, stimulating thoughts and feelings in our experience, individually and corporately. Augustine and others refer to these thoughts, feelings, and inclinations as *impressions*. These impressions can be experienced as mere ideas, as visions, as "a sense of something," as intuitions, and so on.[52]

Listening for the voice and signs of the Spirit involves attending to these impressions, however subtle, especially (but not exclusively) within the context of those "places" where God makes himself known. We spoke of this in chapter 6 in terms of God being present *through* various arenas: nature, scripture, prophecy, the temple, Jesus.

God is present to us through the body of believers, through the sacraments, through our own stories, and through a variety of "windows of the soul."[53] The art of discerning the voice of the Spirit is that process whereby we, from the contexts wherein the impressions of God's voice are received, evaluate the character of the impressions to determine our response. But that is the topic of chapter 11.

The Space in Between

We speak. God listens, hears. God answers, speaks. We listen. And then there is the space in between the speaking and the listening. The first space in between is simply the *silence* between "words." There is the silence before we speak, wherein we gather ourselves together in order to express something (whether this speech is verbal or not). There is also the silence between our speech and God's "answer." Sometimes that silence lasts only a moment. Other times there is an extended delay between our communication and our perception of God's response ("Now about that item you mentioned the other day . . ."). If prayer is not merely our speech to God but is truly a mutual and ongoing interaction, we must admit that this first space—the space of silence—encompasses a fair amount of our communication.

The second kind of space in between is the atmosphere of the relationship itself. Just as we can speak of a *situational mood* of prayer formed by the environmental setting, our energy level, and the like, so we might also want to speak of a **relational mood**, which likewise shapes the character of our prayer at any given time. Our communication with God—like our communication with other people—is shaped by relational issues. We have already mentioned postures of speaking and listening. Our understanding of God (who God is and how God might relate to us) forms part of the relational mood of prayer. There is a very appropriate theological component to this. For example, the phrases *Our Father*,

---

A Few "Contemplative Beatitudes"

- Blessed are those who do not take life for granted, for they are within measurable distance of taking it as granted them by God.
- Blessed are those who learn to see the finger of God in the conspiracy of accidents that make up their lives; they shall be rewarded with daily miracles.
- Blessed are those who say yes to something higher than themselves; in that genuflection they will say the creed.
- Blessed are those whose discipleship includes the discipline of regular prayer; they shall know that it is in God that they live and move and have their being.
- Blessed are those who kiss a leper, who make the preferential option for the poor; for love and God will overwhelm them.
- And blessed are those who make this a life-long quest; they will make a good beginning.[54]

Hallowed be Thy name, and *Thy kingdom come* were given as models for our own relational moods. In these phrases we identify ourselves as children of a loving parent, we identify ourselves with the primary value of God's honor, and we identify with the struggle for righteousness visible here on earth.[55] We also bring our self-image to communication. For instance, some of us are intimidated (or cocky) around certain people. Our sense of self informs the relational mood of certain situations. The same is true in prayer. The relational mood of prayer is shaped both by our God-image and our self-image. It is also informed by our history of relationship with God. Recent (or prolonged) unconfessed sin, a long string of unanswered prayers (or a single significant one), a period of experienced dryness, or a recent awakening will shape our expectations of God and thus inform the character of the relational mood. The space in between speech is not only a space of silence. It is also a sense of the atmosphere of the relationship itself, of where we are with God. It is from this space that our speaking and listening arise.

In the silence and in the space of the relational mood, we gather ourselves together before God in prayer (as best we can). This act of gathering and placing is the bridge between the space and the speech. Prayer, seen as an event or a state, not merely as a moment, includes all of these: silence, gathering, placing, speech, listening, and answering. The Orthodox tradition, for example, speaks of gathering "the mind within the heart" or "being within" at the onset of prayer. This kind of gathered presence is not a *divided* prayer, where the mind is absent, wandering hither and thither. Yet it is also not mere intellectual prayer, where the mind thinks about the words but the affect is flat. Rather, prayer that brings the mind into the heart is integrated prayer, prayer that joins the whole person—from the integrative center of the human person out—into an undivided unity before God, awaiting the spark of God's Spirit.[56] Likewise the phenomena of "concerts of prayer" in some Protestant circles can be seen as a corporate example of gathering and plac-

ing in prayer. Just as we bring together the diverse operations and elements of our individual human experience in personal prayer, so we may also bring diverse groups and traditions together in corporate prayer, awaiting the spark of God's Spirit.[57]

Navigating the Dynamics of Prayer

The dynamics of relationship, like the ways or methods of prayer, pose their own complications for the life of prayer. According to authors William Barry and William Connolly, "Forming and developing any close relationship makes demands on a person's deepest resources of the heart and mind. The demand is no less rigorous when one of the two in the relationship is the mysterious Other we call God."[58]

Resistance. The first complication is that even though we desire relationship with God, we often resist it; in doing so, we often (consciously or unconsciously) avoid prayer. Spiritual directors see these dynamics exhibited through a variety of symptoms: exhibiting an emotionally unnuanced cheeriness about God, falling asleep during prayer, raising doubts about the faith, making excuses regarding lack of time for God, forgetting to pray about significant areas of concern, feeling animosity toward religious rules and authorities, searching for spiritual highs, determining to "work harder" at prayer, or going through the motions of prayer. Congregations exhibit these symptoms just as do individuals. While each of these is perfectly legitimate under many conditions, it is simply a fact that we use these patterns (and many others, for we are creative in relationships) to protect ourselves from intimacy with God.[59] Gerald May recounts the classic psychological defense mechanisms (repression, denial, projection, rationalization, intellectualization, isolation, displacement) and argues that we use these to avoid the implications of spiritual experience. Have you ever known someone whose pursuit of theology serves as a convenient way of appearing (and feeling) *in* relationship with

WHY MORE PASTORS DON'T PURSUE THE CONTEMPLATIVE LIFESTYLE...

IS SOMEBODY AROUND TO UNLOCK ROOM 217?

GOTTA CALL BOB.

CAN MY LAPEL MIKE BE FIXED?

IS EDITH WATSON'S SURGERY ON WEDNESDAY OR THURSDAY?

OOPS. WAS THERE A TRUSTEES' MEETING LAST NIGHT?

DID PHIL CHANGE THE OIL IN THE BUS?

HALL

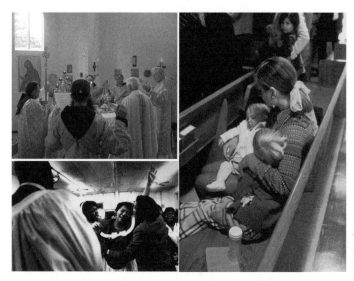

We pray, together: speaking, listening, and attending to the space-in-between.

God while, at the same time, actually *avoiding* authentic openness to the Spirit?[60]

The reasons for resistance to prayer are often perfectly understandable, given what we know of relationships. Indeed, as Barry and Connolly state, "Resistance in prayer is not something to be condemned or pitied but rather welcomed as an indication that the relationship with God is broadening and deepening."[61] Any relationship will involve change. Perhaps we have begun to ask new questions about God or we are beginning to see God in a new light. What will this mean for our expectations regarding spiritual experiences or answered prayers? The revelation of One to another can threaten the other. The other finds herself asking, "Can I handle *this* part of You?" Letting the novelty and the mystery of One lie bare before us can feel dangerous. And so we avoid getting too close. We are afraid of the things we love the most. And when the One is the Almighty God, there is also present at times a kind of fear of losing one's self, of being "swallowed up." And so we hesitate in our communication. We resist.

Dysfunction. We not only resist God in prayer; we also exhibit *dysfunctional "relationshipping"* with God in prayer. At times we "use" God for our own ends, thinking of prayer as a way to access a cosmic vending machine. At other times we bargain with

God or threaten to leave the relationship if God does not do what we want. We think we can manipulate God through our obedience, presuming that we deserve a certain response to a request because we have been good. Once again, these behaviors are perfectly normal (just examine the Psalms). God receives us as we are and will respond to us even if we fail to treat him as he really deserves to be treated. God seems to receive us in our combination of function and dysfunction. The issue more often is whether we will give ourselves the freedom to pursue God not only in the face of God's ambiguity, but in the midst of our *own* ambiguities.

Complications. And then there are those ordinary complications that arise in the middle of healthy relationship with God. God graces us with a powerful awakening, but it (unconsciously) feels like a bit too much, and so we withdraw for a season. Or we receive a grace from God and mistake the (deceiving) thoughts *following* that grace for the grace itself. Or the enemy appears to us disguised as an angel of light. (Have you ever had lofty, spiritual thoughts that ultimately were full of pride? Or seemingly humble thoughts that were full of self-condemnation?) The tensions in family life make it difficult to open up in prayer together. Our intimacy with or

319

longing for God can, at times, be experienced as sexual feelings during prayer, and we may not know what to make of these feelings. And then there are the common obstacles to open communication—unconfessed offense, unforgiveness, anger, greed, and the like. Prayer is full of ordinary complications.[62]

Seasons. Ultimately, we will experience the same kinds of seasons in our prayer life as we do in other relationships, only perhaps each season of prayer has the potential for being experienced more poignantly simply because it is experienced in relationship with the Source of life and relatedness. There are those seasons where prayer is open and free, when we are ready to share with God. There are other seasons of routinization, where our ways of communication become safe and perhaps mundane. In some seasons, the community plateaus and the congregation hesitates to take the next step of expressing or receiving. At times, we fixate on a certain image of God, a certain way of prayer, or a certain expectation for the relationship, and we are unable to move further in prayer. There are times of light and times of darkness, both given either by God or by the enemy. Our bodies, souls, minds, hearts, and relationships are all "at risk" in relationship with God. The joys and struggles of prayer attest to this vulnerability.

Psychologist Steve Duck, citing the research of others, summarizes a list of strategies that help to maintain satisfying interpersonal relationships through the seasons of life. This list includes communicative strategies (like "taking time to talk to one another about 'my day/your day'"), metacommunication ("talking about the way to handle a problem"), prosocial strategies (being especially nice, refraining from criticism), ceremonies (which remember or form the relationship in significant ways), and togetherness (just spending time together, just because you're together).[63] Could it be that such strategies might facilitate healthy communication with God? They are worth a try.

The Effects of Prayer

Prayer changes things. Again, prayer is not a dialogue between equals. Communication *with God* results in God-like responses. Prayer is not just about our speech; it is also about God's reply. Sometimes that reply is immediate. We go up to the sanctuary to complain, and we see things from a different perspective (Psalm 73:17). We cry to the Lord and are delivered from our distress (Psalm 107:6, 13, 19, 28). Other times, the reply is delayed and many prayers arise before an answer is perceived (Exodus 3:7; Luke 11:8). There is the reply of God's own communication, as when God speaks to the church at Antioch during a time of worship (Acts 13:2). There is the reply of God's action, as when the church in Jerusalem was shaken and filled with the Holy Spirit and boldness after a time of prayer (Acts 4:23–31). Again, to quote Barth, "Let us approach the subject from the given fact that God answers. God is not deaf, but listens; more than that, he acts."[64] Prayer changes things. It produces effects

Figure 9.2
Navigating the Dynamics of Prayer

Prayer involves

(1) hearing,

(2) speaking,

(3) the space in between

Reflect

• How might problems of communication work their way into a life of prayer (in hearing, speaking, or in the space in between)?

• How might you address communication problems when they begin to show up?

in the one who prays, in the divine-human relationship, and in the world.

Effects on the One Who Prays

Things happen when we pray—to us. Through worship, through confession, through petition, we ourselves who pray are affected in prayer. Even many who are cautious about the use of petitionary prayer will still affirm that "petitionary prayer is a means of grace whereby we grow and are sensitized to God's presence."[65] The act of prayer itself, at times, changes our way of Being Aware. Impulses and changes enter our experience either during prayer or as a result of prayer. Prayer also produces long-term effects on the health and life of those who pray. Let us explore each of these aspects in turn.

Prayer and awareness. We have learned that prayer is shaped by our Being Aware. Different ways of praying employ different kinds of Being Aware. Some prayer demands focused attention. Some prayer uses a more open kind of awareness. And in turn, our praying affects our Being Aware. This relationship between prayer and Being Aware has fascinated some scholars, especially those who study states of consciousness. The idea of altered states of Being Aware received a great deal of attention for a time. Physicians and psychologists examined different states of consciousness (like the active state known in cocaine use or the tranquil state known in daydreaming) and related them to types of spiritual activity. Roland Fischer, for example, developed a cartography of conscious states, moving from "ergotropic hyperarousal" (high energy, identified with schizophrenic states and mystical rapture), through normal arousal levels, to "trophotropic hypoarousal" (low energy, associated with meditation and yogic samadhi).[66] Others have explored the chemistry and neural structure of the brain in an effort to get at what is going on in spiritual experience, for example, pointing at a "transcendent function" of the brain.[67] This kind of research

reminds us that we are embodied creatures and that even the heights of prayer are experienced within the real-life context of the human brain.

Prayer also produces changes in awareness in a more general way. By bringing our mind repeatedly and appreciatively toward the things of God, we naturally (and by the work of grace) become more attuned to the things of God. Our Being Aware is shaped by our God-centered worldview and practice, which, over time, conditions the very patterns of our Being Aware. Consequently, we notice things we might not have noticed previously to this growth in awareness. We become conscious of subtleties that were once ignored.

The experience of prayer. The changes we experience are not only in our awareness. Indeed, the whole of human experience is subject to the effects of prayer. While some of these effects are experienced only over time, some are perceived during the event of prayer itself. How is God actively present to those who pray? This is the ministry of the Holy Spirit. We cannot seem to put our prayers into words and the Spirit of God assists as we express "sighs too deep for words" (Romans 8:26–27). We find ourselves calling out "Abba! Father!" inside, and our spirit bears witness with the Holy Spirit of our relationship with God (Romans 8:15–16; Galatians 4:6). We gather in prayer and God speaks to us through a prophetic utterance (1 Corinthians 14). We make our requests known to God and experience a peace (Philippians 4:6–7). We open ourselves to God and receive the impressions and the impulses of the Spirit. Thoughts, feelings, inclinations, intuitions, and such enter our experience, and we learn to recognize some of these as being of God. For example, a young man in a small, informal worship gathering is trying to express love to God. An image of young King Arthur and Merlyn, Arthur's mentor, enters his mind, associated with feelings like appreciation and respect. Perhaps he sees, in the image, a "word" from God: "*Here* is a model of love to which you

FIGURE 9.3
A Cartography of the Ecstatic and Meditative States

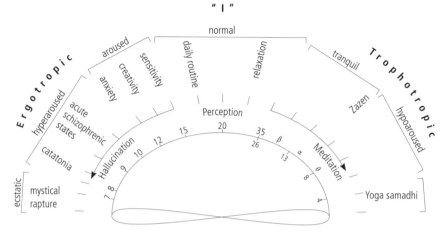

Varieties of conscious states mapped on a perception-hallucination continuum of increasing ergotropic arousal (left) and a perception-meditation continuum of increasing trophotropic arousal (right). These levels of hyper- and hypoarousal are interpreted by man as normal, creative, psychotic, and ecstatic states (left) and Zazen and samadhi (right). The loop connecting ecstasy and samadhi represents the rebound from ecstasy to samadhi, which is observed in response to intense ergotropic excitation. The numbers 35 to 7 on the perception-hallucination continuum are Goldstein's coefficient of variation (46), specifying the decrease in variability of the EEG amplitude with increasing ergotropic arousal. The numbers 26 to 4 on the perception-meditation continuum, on the other hand, refer to those beta, alpha, and theta EEG waves (measured in hertz) that predominate during, but are not specific to, these states (17).

From Roland Fischer, *Science*, 174, no. 4012, November 26, 1971: 898. Reprinted with permission from AAAS.

may relate." Some impressions or impulses are very subtle, and we wonder just what it was. Others are very strong, and we find ourselves limp or shaking under the power of the Spirit.

Certain impulses received during prayer play a significant role in the prayer itself—different impulses for different traditions. For example, masters of prayer in the Orthodox tradition speak about the importance of a kind of "warmth" experienced during prayer. Thus Theophan writes of bringing the mind into the heart:

> But when attention descends into the heart, it attracts all the powers of the soul and body into one point there. This concentration of all human life in one place is immediately reflected in the heart by a special sensation that is the beginning of future warmth. This sensation, faint at the beginning, becomes gradually stronger, firmer, deeper. . . . And so it comes about that, whereas in the initial stages the attention is kept in the heart by an effort of the will, in due course, this at-

tention, by its own vigour gives birth to warmth in the heart.[68]

Many from the Pentecostal and charismatic traditions have highlighted the experience of glossolalia, or speaking in tongues, during prayer as enabling an "enlarged capacity" for communication with God.[69] And finally, we experience the effects of prayer in the process of the act of prayer itself: our burden is lifted and we do not feel the need to continue in prayer or are strongly compelled to cry out in deeper prayer; or we find a particular direction in which to pursue prayer or an insight regarding God's character in terms of the particular matter about which we are praying. Thus prayer and experience shape each other moment to moment.

Long-term effects. Prayer makes us new. If, through deep, open, rich, communication with a loved one over a long period of time, we become different, more complete, simply because we have shared our life with this human being, how much more is this the case through our relationship with God!

Historical Portrait: Teresa of Avila's "Four Waters" from *The Book of Her Life*

It seems to me the garden can be watered in four ways. You may draw up water from a well (which is for us a lot of work). Or you may get it by means of a water wheel and aqueducts in such a way that it is obtained by turning the crank of the water wheel. (I have drawn it this way sometimes—the method involves less work than the other, and you get more water.) Or it may flow from a river or a stream. (The garden is watered much better by this means because the ground is more fully soaked and there is no need to water so frequently—and much less work for the gardener.) Or the water may be provided by a great deal of rain. (For the Lord waters the garden without any work on our part—and this way is incomparably better than all the others mentioned.)

Now, then, these four ways of drawing water in order to maintain the garden—because without water it will die—are what are important to me and have seemed applicable in explaining the four degrees of prayer in which the Lord in His goodness has sometimes placed my soul. . . .

Beginners in prayer, we can say, are those who draw water from the well. . . . They must tire themselves in trying to recollect their senses. Since they are accustomed to being distracted, this recollection requires much effort. . . .

Here [in the second manner—water wheel], the soul begins to be recollected and comes upon something supernatural because in no way can it acquire this prayer through any efforts it may make. True, at one time it seemingly got tired turning the crank, and working with the intellect, and filling the aqueducts. But here the water is higher, and so the labor is much less than that required in pulling it up from the well. I mean that the water is closer because grace is more clearly manifest to the soul. . . .

By this means [the third water—irrigation] the garden is irrigated with much less labor, although some labor is required to direct the flow of the water. The Lord so desires to help the gardener here that He Himself becomes practically the gardener and the one who does everything. This prayer is the sleep of the faculties: the faculties neither fail entirely to function nor understand how they function. The consolation, the sweetness, and the delight are incomparably greater than that experienced in the previous prayer. The water of grace rises up to the throat of the soul. . . .

In this fourth water [rain] the soul isn't in possession of its senses, but it rejoices without understanding what it is rejoicing in.[70]

The seasons and the years accumulate like many little streams that join to become a deep and powerful river. God has shared himself in relationship with us, even in the times when we have misunderstood who he is. And we know that. We have shared God's concerns for this or that over the years. We felt a hurt for the world and knew it to be God's hurt. And God knows that. We have shared together times when we have cried for the love of God—our love for God, God's love for us. We give our thoughts and feelings and hopes and dreams to God, and God gives us his thoughts and feelings and hopes and dreams. And over years of sharing in prayer with the Creator of the universe, prayer has its long-term effects. It is bound to. Likewise with communities— as the saying goes, the family that prays together stays together.

It appears that science is beginning to confirm the long-term effects of prayer. In particular, the relationship of prayer and spiritual life to health-related issues has become, in recent years, a topic of interest. Numerous empirical studies have been conducted to measure the effects of prayer and spirituality on health and well-being. And while the findings are not indisputable, "the increasing body of research suggests that when you pray for yourself, you are doing something medically wise."[71] Studies seem to show that those who pray have lower blood pressure, decreased depression, and a better ability to cope with stress. Furthermore, church attendance (which encompasses more than, but certainly includes, prayer) has been linked to longer life expectancy. The chance to cast our cares on One who cares for us, the opportunity to entrust ourselves to (and to rest in) the Almighty, the freedom to shake our fist at the Creator of it all—it is life-giving to communicate with the Lord of the earth.[72]

Effects on the Divine-Human Relationship

Prayer, as communication, is not only a matter of "us." It is also about our relationship with God. Consequently, prayer effects changes not only in us, but also in our relationship with God. We see this in our use of different types of prayer. The effects of prayer on the divine-human relationship is central with regard to the "mystical union," considered by many to be the final aim of Christian prayer.

Types and relationship. Some of our praying is more or less aimed at changes in ourselves (personal petitions). Some prayers anticipate changes in the world around us (intercessory prayer). Even in these kinds of prayer there is a navigation and development of relationship, as our cry to God meets the heart of God. Yet some types of prayer are especially designed to effect changes in our *relationship* with God. The prayer of confession is the most obvious example. The prayer of confession is about getting the relationship right again. This is the rhythm of the practice of *govenie* in the

Orthodox tradition. We strive to live a life of harmony with God. At the end of a season we look within to see where the harmony has been lost. We admit the out-of-tune moments to God and to another person. We celebrate our reunion with God at the Eucharist.[73] Confession brings us to a place of relational re*union*.

Other types of prayer are oriented to "relationshipping," as well. Think of praise and thanksgiving. These are not about changes in the world or about us. In praise and thanksgiving, we express appreciation and gratitude for who God is and what God has done. In so doing, we facilitate a stronger bonding between ourselves and God. Think of the prayer of commitment or surrender. While these aspects of prayer certainly involve us, it is really our response to God's invitation to relationship that is central. The prayers of commitment or surrender are a yes that permits God to come closer, enabling the relationship to develop. Christian meditation facilitates relationship as well. In meditation we bring ourselves before the means of God's self-communication (a passage of scripture, a walk in nature) and we attend. Christian meditation is not about exploring the depths of the human psyche. Rather it is a vehicle whereby human and divine can share quietly in an extended sitting. Sometimes meditation opens the depths, but at times there is simply a period of sacred musing that joins God and human being in pleasant conversation. In either case, as with many types of prayer, the communication simply brings the parties together.

"Mystical union": Contemplation as an aim of prayer. If the prayers of confession, thanksgiving, or meditation facilitate the divine-human relationship, the prayer of mystical union consummates the relationship. And herein lies a third sense in which the term *contemplation* is used. We have seen the term used to describe the simple, wordless *way* of prayer. We have also learned something about the contemplative *attitude* of prayer, an attitude of openness and receptivity. Yet *contemplation* is also

used to describe an aim—indeed *the* aim—of prayer. The term *contemplation* derives from the Latin *templum*, which referred to a space in earth or sky set apart for the sacred examination of animal entrails for indications of divine meaning. The Latin *contemplatio* was used to translate the Greek *theoria*, which in turn was used to refer to the recognition (vision) of the presence of God, either in created things (natural *theoria*) or in spiritual union (also called *theologia*). Greek thought valued the transforming vision of Truth, and this value was incorporated in early Christian reflection on prayer. Contemplation, as the conscious vision of the presence of God in as full a measure as possible here on earth, was thus seen as a high point of Christian prayer.

In the early medieval period, contemplation was but one element in the ordinary blend of prayerful reflection known as *lectio divina* (reading, meditation, expressed prayer, contemplation). Moments of wordless "sight" of God were expected within the communal life of the church or within private devotions. Later writings developed a hierarchical arrangement of these elements, transforming them into stages of prayer—moving from reading through meditation and prayer and culminating in contemplation, "when the mind is in some sort lifted up to God and held above itself, so that it tastes the joys of everlasting sweetness," when "all carnal motives are so conquered and drawn out of the soul that in no way is the flesh opposed to the spirit, and man becomes, as it were, wholly spiritual."[74] Others linked vision and contemplation with the ecstasy of intimacy, as the theoretical and the interpersonal were joined. Here contemplation was described not merely as transforming vision, but also as union and love. Commentaries on the Song of Songs emphasized the deep interpersonal sharing of God and human in contemplation. For example, Bernard of Clairvaux describes the "kiss on the lips" (Song of Songs 1:2) as "a wonderful and inseparable mingling of the light from above and the mind on which it is shed, which, when it is joined

with God is one spirit with him (1 Corinthians 6:17)."[75] Thus the notion of mystical union. Some described contemplation in terms of an incomprehensible darkness rather than a light.[76] Yet in virtually every case—whether a transforming vision of the beloved, an experience of Love, or a grasp of the incomprehensible mystery of the One in which we live—contemplative prayer was understood as a realization of divine-human *relationship*. It is still viewed as such by many today.[77] In this sense—as the realization, within the event of prayer, of the intimate sharing we were created to experience, insofar as this can be experienced on earth—contemplation can be understood not only as a *way* and an *attitude* of prayer, but also as an *aim* of prayer.

Effects on the World

But prayer, and especially petitionary prayer, aims to produce effects not merely

"We don't know what you're doing in here, but we've been waiting five minutes to talk to you about the broken hand dryer in the ladies' room."

Is Mysticism Biblical?

Like *contemplation*, the term *mysticism* is used to identify different things by different people. Indeed, the history of mysticism may document more the fascinations and fears of the Christians using the term than any objective phenomena. One of the uses of the term has been to contrast two ways of prayer: the mystical and the biblical. In this use, mysticism is associated with Greek philosophical influence, with techniques of solitude and silence (both verbal and mental silence), with particular states of consciousness, and with a dissolving of the self in union with God. Biblical or prophetic prayer, on the other hand, is identified with spontaneous petition offered in the context of a lively community of faith and ministry in the world.[78] The contrast usually favors biblical prayer, arguing that mysticism expresses or promotes a posture toward God that runs counter to central themes of the Christian faith. We may ask, "Can there be a convergence between these two types of spirituality?"[79]

I say yes! Indeed there *must* be a convergence of these two, if Christian prayer is to maintain a healthy balance. A convergence of this kind is comprehensible once we give careful attention to scripture and to the ways, the psychology, and the aims of prayer.

Unlike a contrast of biblical and mystical prayer, a convergence of biblical and mystical prayer sees forms of Christian mysticism as developments of the biblical foundations of key mystical themes. The theme of contemplation as a vision of Christ is foreshadowed, for example, in 1 Corinthians 13:12, where Paul identifies our state of glory as a "see[ing] face to face"; in the promise of sight to the pure in heart (Matthew 5:8); and in the progressive realization of the vision of God described in 2 Corinthians 3:17–18.[80] The New Testament writers were careful to affirm transcendent knowledge (*gnosis*) as the possession of Christians, but in doing so to distinguish it from mere pagan understandings of esoteric wisdom and experience. The knowledge of the Christian is a knowledge of love, a knowledge that transcends knowledge (Ephesians 3:16–19). Furthermore, the theme of union, so central to mystical writings throughout Christian history, is rooted in scripture. Again and again we hear of being "in Christ" and of the Spirit's "indwelling" (Galatians 2:19–20; 3:28; Romans 5:5). We are promised a share in the "divine nature" (2 Peter 1:4). Whereas sexual relations with prostitutes constitute an unholy union, we are "united" to the Lord in spirit (1 Corinthians 6:16–19; see also 2 Corinthians 6:16–18).[81] Thus, while Greek thought plays a role in the development of Christian mysticism, it is fair to say that "the issues that gave rise to Christian mysticism in the full sense were more the outcome of internal debates about the meaning of life in Jesus, the risen Lord, than importations from without."[82]

The ways or techniques of meditation and prayer, like the strategies of evangelism or politics, were never normatively specified in scripture. Hence, a convergence of the biblical and mystical is sensitive to the differences and the dangers of the various ways of prayer. We only catch glimpses in scripture of how prayer was conducted by different people. Jesus makes a habit of secluding himself for periods of time to be with God or to face temptation (Mark 6:46; Luke 5:16; 6:12; John 6:15; Matthew 4:1–11). The Psalms speak of "quieting my soul" or of "waiting in silence" (Psalm 131:1–3; 62:1, 5). We have learned the dangers of mistaking the means for the ends in prayer. A singular focus on apophatic prayer can become a means of isolating ourselves from the ministry of the community and the Word. But likewise, exposure to Word and community without silence can become a means of avoiding the ministry of the Spirit. Furthermore, as with all types of prayer, mystical ways of prayer need not become routine. Spontaneity happens in awesome or intimate silence just as with petitions.

The scripture acknowledges, but does not dwell on, alternate states of consciousness and powerful experiences. Enoch walks with God and "was no more" (Genesis 5:24). Moses is permitted special glimpses of God (Exodus 3:2–6; 19:16–25; 33:12–23; 34:6–7). Jesus is transfigured before the disciples (Matthew 17:1–9). Paul is taken up to a "third heaven" (2 Corinthians 12:1–6). John experiences things "in the spirit" (Revelation 1:10; 4:1–2). A convergence of biblical and mystical prayer recognizes that powerful experiences and different states of consciousness happen, but it does so without privileging any of them in a normative kind of way. We simply acknowledge that there are those times—whether in worship or in intercession or in meditation—when words fail us and, for some reason, the depths of our heart and the depths of God's heart are joined as never before.

Finally, a convergence of biblical and mystical prayer welcomes the widest and deepest pos-sible understanding of union with God as the aim of prayer and the spiritual life. Instead of focusing on the differences between the aim of mysticism ("possession of God") and that of biblical religion ("fellowship with God and the saints"),[83] we embrace the convergence of these prayer types and await, as the aim of the spiritual life, not only the transformation of our relationship with God, but also a reordering of all our relationships, involving a reunion with self, others, and nature itself. Mystical and biblical prayer ought to facilitate communication with God at both shallow and deep levels of our experience. Likewise, mystical and biblical prayer ought to drive us into greater involvement and care for the world (insofar as this involvement and care is appropriate for any given community or individual).[84]

Can there be a convergence between mystical and biblical prayer? Yes, there can and there must. When we are able to listen in absolute silence and to speak passionately, as both individuals and communities of Christ; when we strive for the clearest vision of God and the deepest union with God; when we reflect the great themes of the scriptures in the concrete realities of our lives today—only then will we live prayer in the fullness that was intended for us in the Spirit of Christ.

in those praying or in their relationship with God, but also in the earth. And indeed, these effects are produced. Scripture and history affirm these effects. As noted above, medical science is exploring the possibilities of healing prayer. And the relationship between contemplation and action suggests that the effects of prayer on those who pray, in turn, often produce their own effects in the world.

Scripture and history. Stories of answered prayer throughout history document the wide range of God's active presence as a part of prayerful communication. The course of nature and the course of battles are altered in response to prayer (Exodus 17:4–13; Joshua 10:12–13; 1 Samuel 7:7–11; James 5:16–18).[85] In answer to prayer, the hearts of kings and communities are softened (1 Kings 18:36–39; Nehemiah 1:1–2:8). Eyes and wombs are opened through prayer (1 Samuel 1:11–28; 2 Kings 6:17). The Lord answers prayer with healing, with guidance, with wisdom, and with provision (Judges 6:39–40; 1 Kings 3:3–14; 17:20–22; Acts 9:40–41; 28:8).[86] Scripture implies that prayer even effects changes in the mind of the Lord (Exodus 32:1–14; Deuteronomy 9:18–29). People call out to Jesus for healing or deliverance and find it (Matthew 8:2–3; 9:27–30; 15:21–28; Mark 5:21–42; Luke 9:37–43). Paul prays that his churches may receive unity, hope, knowledge of God's will, love, and peace (Romans 15:5–6, 13; Ephesians 3:14–21; Philippians 1:9–11; 1 Thessalonians 5:23–24; 2 Thessalonians 3:5, 16), and he gives thanks to God for seeing the same (Philippians 1:3–7; Colossians 1:3–5; 1 Thessalonians 1:2–3; Philemon 4–6). Not many years after the writing of the New Testament, Tertullian wrote this of prayer:

> And so it knows nothing save how to recall the souls of the departed from the very path of death, to transform the weak, to restore the sick, to purge the possessed, to open prison doors, to loose the bonds of the innocent. Likewise it washes away faults, repels temptations, extinguishes persecutions, consoles the faint-spirited, cheers the high-spirited, escorts travelers, appeases waves, makes robbers stand aghast, nourishes the poor, governs the rich, upraises the fallen, arrests the falling, confirms the standing. Prayer is the wall of faith: her arms and missiles against the foe, who keeps watch over us on all sides. And so never walk we unarmed.[87]

Broader still is the saying about the hermits and desert dwellers written around the fourth century: "Civilization, where lawlessness prevails, is sustained by their prayers. And the world, buried in sin, is preserved by their prayers."[88] While results are never guaranteed, the range of effects promised and produced through answered prayer is vast. Jesus's term is "whatever" (John 15:16; see also 15:7). There is no dimension of human experience outside the sovereignly responsive work of God. Through prayer emotions are softened, minds are enlightened, and wills are strengthened. Demons depart, self is encouraged, communities are reconciled, and nature is transformed, all in response to prayer.

Prayer and Medicine. Once again, contemporary medical science has taken an interest in prayer. We have already mentioned studies of the medical effects of prayer on the one who prays. But what about the effects of prayer on others for whom prayer is offered? "Scientific" studies of healing prayer have appeared since Francis Galton first challenged its effects in 1860. More recently, the popular review of studies, *Healing Words: The Power of Prayer and the Practice of Medicine*, and studies by Randolph Byrd, William Harris, Dale Matthews, Richard Davidson, and others appear to support the influence of prayer on healing.[89] In controlled experiments regarding coronary care, rheumatoid arthritis, AIDS, and other illnesses, a number of studies are beginning to suggest that prayer can have an influence on health. Others, such as Dr. Irwin Tessman, dispute the results.[90] Tessman argues that some experiments were not controlled properly and that others do not provide the extraordinary proof required to affirm the claims of the influence of prayer on health. Professor David Myers argues that other factors (unaccounted prayers, doubt, testing God) might call into question the results of *any* "scientific" experiment of intercessory prayer.[91] A massive study of the effects of intercessory prayer on heart patients, directed by Dr. Herbert Benson, concludes little.[92] While, as we saw above, the balance weighs slightly in favor of the impact of prayer upon the person praying, the jury is still out regarding the scientific demonstration of the effects of prayer for others.

Prayer and action. Finally, we find that prayer produces effects on the world *through* its influence on those who pray. The tension between a life of prayer and a life of action has often been symbolized throughout the history of the church through interpretations of Luke 10:38–42, the story of Mary (the "contemplative") and Martha (the "active"), with emphasis placed on one or the other figure.[93] A number of models for the integration of prayer and daily work have emerged over the centuries. There is the Benedictine rhythm of prayer and work (*ora et labora*). There is the Celtic prayer-

Issues in the Scientific Study of Prayer

With regard to our experience of prayer, we may ask,

- Are there any particular functions in the brain that correspond to perceptions of the transcendent?
- Do certain states of consciousness correspond to certain ways of prayer?
- By affecting a person's brain or body in some way (for example, chemically), can we induce spiritual experiences?
- What is the relationship between our modes of Being Aware and our sense of what is happening in prayer?

With regard to the long-term effects of prayer on those who pray, we may ask,

- What effect does a life of prayer have on the general health and well-being (for instance, life expectancy, depression, happiness) of those who pray?

With regard to prayers offered on behalf of others (within medical contexts), we may ask,[94]

- Was the patient's improvement a result of the prayer, or was it a chance correlation and a mere coincidence?
- If prayer actually caused the improvement, how did it do so? What constitutes the same amount of prayer applied to a given patient?
- How reliable is prayer? How is prayer to be defined operationally? Is one form of prayer more effective than another?
- If prayer does work, is it potent enough to be used alone, or should it be combined with therapies such as drugs or surgery? Do these therapies interfere with the action of prayer?
- Are some prayer strategies better than others? Is there a "best" way to pray?
- How about the skills of the people who pray—does a spectrum of talent exist?
- Can prayer ability be acquired, or is it innate?
- What conditions facilitate the effects of prayer and which retard them? How can we determine the effects of an outside person's prayers as distinct from the prayers of the patient him- or herself or those of others not associated with a scientific study?
- Is the effect of prayer always positive, or can it hurt as well as help?

ful ritualizing of daily activities. There is the Lutheran *vocation*, where God is found within the contexts of the activities and relationships of everyday life. There is the "practice of the presence of God" found in the kitchen work of Brother Lawrence. There is the Amish way of fully entering into the work of the community. In each of these, prayer brings the presence of God into the work and transforms the character of the work itself. Conversely, the work itself contributes in its own ways to the act of prayer. The results are manifest in the effects of the daily life of the Christian community within each sphere of influence.

Furthermore, through prayer, we ourselves are enabled to effect change in the world. One need only think of the retreats of Jesus (Luke 4:1–14), Paul (Galatians 1:15–18), and Antony of Egypt to see effects on the world that result from periods of prayerful retreat. We might also think of Peter Damian and Catherine of Siena, whose lives of prayer inspired active political involvement. Thomas Müntzer's advocacy of the Peasant War in Reformation Germany (1524–26) was directly tied to his spiritual doctrine and prayerful sense of the Holy Spirit's revelations. The twenty-four-hour vigil of the community at Herrnhutt (begun in 1722) inspired one of the largest missionary movements in Protestant history. Archbishop Oscar Romero's (1917–80) sharing of communal prayer with the poor of El Salvador softened his heart toward political advocacy. Through prayer, we hear the heart of God for the world and perhaps are moved to action. Our strategies for action are discerned through prayerful dialogue with God, with others, and with the structures and systems that constitute the world in which we live. And the power to persevere in action when it seems hopeless is often found in prayer.

A Life of Prayer

We are called, as Christians, into relationship with God. Hence, we are called into a life of communication with God, into a life of prayer (see Matthew 7:7; Luke 18:1; 21:36; Ephesians 6:18–20; Philippians 4:6; Colossians 4:2–3; 1 Thessalonians 5:17; 1 Timothy 2:1, 8). While the Christian life cannot be reduced to merely a life of prayer, it is safe to say that our communication with God, however expressed and experienced, plays a central role in the lived relationship with God that is our spirituality. We have learned that Christian spirituality is about lived *relationship* with God, an interactive relationship wherein one initiates and another responds and then one responds to that response. God invites us through the Word proclaimed in the gathered community. We respond by our attitude of reception after the Word is proclaimed. We come forward to receive prayer at the ministry time, we receive the Eucharistic elements with a renewed welcome, we offer testimony in the community's time of sharing. Is this prayer? Not necessarily, but prayer certainly plays a part of this event. Or we initiate by calling out to God on behalf of a loved one. The Spirit of God responds by stimulating us to certain acts of love toward that person. We, in turn, respond by acting. Is this prayer? It certainly started with prayer, but it involves much more.

We have also learned that relationship with God is a *transforming* relationship, a synergy of divine-human growth beginning at the cross and ending in the final restoration. While some have identified the stages of Christian transformation with particular ways or dynamics of prayer, we have suggested that it is best to identify stages of Christian growth more generally. Nonetheless, transformation from spiritual childhood to adulthood will involve a continuous deepening and broadening of one's disclosure to God along with an increasing perception of and response to God's own self-disclosures. And this will mean changes in our life of prayer. This is why we speak of seasons in our life of prayer. Ultimately, as we grow, we will increasingly feel as Christ might feel, we will see things as Christ might see them, we will be inclined to do things Christ might do. Our Being Aware, our Deciding, and our relationships are all affected by God's touch—from the shallows to the depths. Prayer cannot but play a central role in this transformation.

In the previous chapter we learned that, from the human point of view, this transforming relationship involves a degree of intentionality. This is the world of *spiritual formation*: a world where context, agent, aim, task, and means are all joined in a purposeful fostering of personal and corporate maturity. Prayer is involved at every point. My current history of prayer (experiences, unanswered prayers, and so on) informs the context within which my maturity is fostered. My agents of spiritual formation (for example, a spiritual director) may make intercessory prayer for me a part of his spiritual direction ministry. And while the aims of spiritual formation (an increase of deification, holiness, perfection, the kingdom of God) may not be directly tied to particular ways or experiences of prayer, one cannot help but see how the realization of these aims is ultimately caught up in an increasing breadth and depth of mutual sharing of heart, mind, and life with God. The task of spiritual formation involves my prayerful process of reorientation and rehabituation of life, paying attention to contexts, to choosing means, to evaluating results. Prayer can function as a means of formation (as with meditation on sin) or as a focus of formation (as we foster new aspects of praying).

Thus Christian spirituality, while not reducible to prayer, is inextricably caught up with prayer. Spirituality is lived relationship; prayer is communication. A mature relationship involves sharing of more of life together—sharing in a more sincere and integrated manner—and avoiding the traps that plague relationships. This is all about communication: the ways, the dynamics, and the effects of communication. We can mature into a life of prayer. Yet we cannot program this growth. God's ways are not our ways. Thus Theophan writes, "From experience in the spiritual life, it can be fairly concluded that he who has zeal to pray needs no teaching how to perfect himself in prayer. Patiently continued, the effort of prayer itself will lead us to prayer's very summit."[95]

Practicing Christian Spirituality

Designing a Time of Prayer

"Draw near to God, and he will draw near to you."
James 4:8

A time of prayer—whether we are talking about a regular time, or of a single retreat with God—is a special time. It is sacred time. For this reason, it is often helpful to plan for this time, much as one may plan a romantic evening with a lover.

The first thing you do when you plan is to think about your *relationship*. *How* are things between you and God? Just stop for a while and review the dynamics of your relationship. Where are the hopes, fears, tensions, miscommunications, confusions, or joys in your relationship with God? Having looked at this, ask yourself, What kind of a time do I need to spend with God? *Why* are we meeting? Is there an agenda that needs to be discussed? Are you thinking of a regular review of the day? Is this an extended time with no agenda at all in mind? Different kinds of prayer times might be appropriate to different relational moods. Begin to think of what kind of time might fit the mood.

Then consider the *place* of meeting. Is there a place where you often meet? Is this the kind of meeting where it might be wise to go to a different place, either to facilitate communication or to make the time special? Choose a place where you will be able to attend to the nuances of God's self communication with few unnecessary distractions and where you can feel free to express yourself to God fully. Some people need an environment where bodily movement is involved (for example, to take a walk together). Others need to sit still and talk eye to eye.

When will you meet? Sooner or later, when you plan a time together, you have to get out the calendar. How much time do you need to spend with God? How much time might God desire of you? When are you most ready for this kind of meeting? When are you likely to be called away elsewhere? Again, with some people, short and regular meetings keep the relationship healthy. Others may not need to meet as often, but the times they do meet are longer and deeper.

Then you consider *what* you will do in this time together. What are the ways of prayer that you and God do together? Do you want to explore a new way or means of communication? Will you use repetition, imagination, bodily gestures or postures, devotions? Do you expect to be noisy or silent? Will you need any resources for this meeting (say, a Bible, music, journal, food)? Prepare beforehand to have the necessary resources on hand (or on site) for your time together.

Having considered *how, why, where, when,* and *what*, you are ready for your time together. As you invest in drawing near to God, God will respond by drawing near to you.

CHAPTER SUMMARY

1. Christian prayer refers to our verbal entreaties to God and to much more. In a broader sense, Christian prayer encompasses communication with God of any kind, verbal or nonverbal, speaking, listening, and the space in between. Christian prayer can express many sentiments and therefore comes in many types: adoration, thanksgiving, surrender, confession, petition, complaint, and so on. Christian prayer can be public and vocal (common), private and vocal (conversational), or private and nonvocal (including both meditation and contemplation).

2. The church has understood and practiced prayer in a variety of ways throughout its history. Public prayer shifts at times from informal and very participatory to more formal and less participatory. Over time, emphasis moves from common to conversational to contemplative and back again (or from an interest in thinking to an interest in feeling). By the late Middle Ages, prayer is communicated in terms of precise stages and methods. A wide range of devotional practices made prayer more accessible to many throughout history. During the course of Christian history a number of key questions are raised with regard to prayer, and a number of key figures and movements model distinct approaches to Christian prayer.

3. Christian prayer, both public and private, is expressed and experienced in a number of different "ways." Public prayer involves the use of ritual or liturgy, structured actions embodying corporate communication with God. Liturgy identifies a common worldview and forms the community into that worldview. Christian prayer involves the use of a number of mechanisms to aid in communication with God: repetition, body use, imagination, or the intentional abstaining from means (contemplation as a *way*) of prayer. Devotions involve the combination of these elements. Frequently the ways of prayer help guide attention and facilitate communication with God at appropriate levels of depth. One must be careful, in making use of means, not to mistake means for ends or to pursue ends while rejecting appropriate use of means.

4. As communication with God, prayer involves us in all the necessary dynamics of interpersonal relationships. We speak to God from a posture of initiation rooted in our understanding and expectations of God. We disclose both content and person to God in prayer. Likewise, we listen to God's self-communication in the context of relational expectations and dynamics. Thus, we can conceive of contemplation also as an *attitude* of prayer. God's speech to us is often perceived by means of signs of the Spirit, impressions given through the various means of grace. Communication with God also involves the space in between speaking and listening, the sheer silence that encompasses the overt communication and the atmosphere of the relationship itself—the relational mood and "state of things between us" that shapes the character of our praying. It is from this space in between that we gather ourselves together and place ourselves before God in prayer. And as with other relationships, our communication with God will exhibit resistance, dysfunction, complications, seasonal changes, and the like.

5. Prayer changes things. It produces effects. Those who pray are changed in the praying itself both in terms of their state of awareness used in prayer and in their identification with the things of God. Those who pray receive experiences either during or after prayer, as the Spirit of God responds to our prayers. Some of these

experiences are more important to some groups than others. Prayer appears to facilitate well-being for many, as well. Prayer also has effects on the divine-human relationship itself. Different types of prayer are directed at shifts in the relationship as confession, for example, facilitates a new openness between the one praying and God. And as other forms of prayer facilitate divine-human relationship, mystical union consummates the relationship. In the deepest sharing of human and divine, contemplation can be understood also as an *aim* of prayer. Finally, prayer changes the world. Both scripture and history attest to the powerful acts of God in response to prayer. Medical science, however, is ambivalent about the empirical evidence for the effects of intercessory prayer for the sick. Nonetheless, prayer influences the world through the effects that it has on those who pray. While Christian spirituality cannot be reduced to prayer, communication with God plays a central part in our lived relationship with God.

LOOKING FURTHER

There are simply *far* too many excellent works on prayer to list. Here are a few books, divided loosely by practice, dynamics, and study.

Practice

These books introduce readers to the practice of prayer: Anthony Bloom, *Beginning to Pray* (New York: Paulist Press, 1982); Lawrence Cunningham, *Catholic Prayer* (New York: Crossroad, 1992); Anthony de Mello, *Sadhana, A Way to God: Christian Exercises in Eastern Form* (Garden City, NY: Image Doubleday, 1984); Richard Foster, *Prayer: Finding the Heart's True Home* (San Francisco: HarperSanFrancisco, 1992); Mark Link, *You: Prayer for Beginners and Those Who Have Forgotten How* (Niles, IL: Argus Communications, 1976); Kallistos Ware, *The Power of the Name: The Jesus Prayer in Orthodox Spirituality* (Oxford: SLG Press, 1986).

Dynamics

For books that discuss prayer more generally, see Karl Barth, *Prayer*, trans. Sara F. Terrien, 50th anniv. ed. (Louisville: Westminster John Knox, 2002); Igumen Chariton (comp.), *The Art of Prayer: An Orthodox Anthology*, trans. E. Kadloubavsky and E. M. Palmer (London: Faber and Faber, 1966); Ken Gire, ed. and comp., *Between Heaven and Earth: Prayers and Reflections that Celebrate an Intimate God* (New York: HarperCollins, 1997); Jack Hayford, *Prayer Is Invading the Impossible* (New York: Ballantine, 1983); C. S. Lewis, *Letters to Malcolm Chiefly on Prayer: Reflections on the Intimate Dialogue Between Man and God* (San Diego: Harcourt, 1964); Karl Rahner, *The Need and Blessing of Prayer*, trans. Bruce W. Gillette (Collegeville, MN: Liturgical Press, 1997); James Wilhoit, ed., *Nelson's Personal*

Handbook on Prayer (Nashville: Thomas Nelson, 2002); and Ann Ulanov and Barry Ulanov, *Primary Speech: A Psychology of Prayer* (Louisville: Westminster John Knox, 1982).

Study

The study of Christian spirituality and the study of prayer are deeply interlocked. Hence a review of the standard texts in the history of Christian spirituality and the standard journals in Christian spirituality will reveal a number of important studies of Christian prayer. Interdisciplinary academic study of Christian prayer has developed especially in two directions: the study of liturgy and the study of mysticism (drawing from theology, history, and the social sciences, and more).

For studies of liturgy, see, for example, *The Study of Liturgy*, edited by Cheslyn Jones, Geoffrey Wainwright, Edward Yarnold, and Paul Bradshaw (New York: Oxford University Press, 1986); Kevin W. Irwin, *Liturgy, Prayer, and Spirituality* (New York: Paulist Press, 1984); and Daniel E. Albrecht, *Rites in the Spirit: A Ritual Approach to Pentecostal/Charismatic Spirituality*, Journal of Pentecostal Theology Supplement Series (Sheffield, UK: Sheffield Academic Press, 1999).

For studies in mysticism, the best place to start is with Bernard McGinn's "Theoretical Foundations: The Modern Study of Mysticism," a review of theological, philosophical, and psychological studies of mysticism, in his book *The Foundations of Mysticism: Origins to the Fifth Century*, The Presence of God: A History of Western Christian Mysticism (New York: Crossroad, 1994). See also Peter Moore, "Recent Studies of Mysticism: A Critical Survey," *Religion* 3 (Autumn 1973): 146–56; and Bernard McGinn's "Quo Vadis? Reflections on the Current Study of Mysticism," *Christian Spirituality Bulletin* 6, vol. 1 (Spring 1998): 13–22. For a recent survey of psychological studies of prayer and mysticism, see also Ralph W. Hood Jr., Bernard Spilka, Bruce Hunsberger, and Richard Gorsuch, *The Psychology of Religion: An Empirical Approach*, 2nd ed. (New York: Guilford, 1996).

Questions

1. How do *you* define prayer? Review the words for prayer and types of prayer described in the Bible. Explore those historical figures and works that have emphasized petition and those that have emphasized other dimensions. Compare and contrast your definition with those found in scripture and history. How might your definition of prayer affect your practice of prayer?

2. Who or what are, for you, the most interesting figures or movements or controversies in the history of prayer? Why? Make a list of a few of these. Make a list of the questions you are most interested in asking regarding the theology or the scientific study of prayer. Summarize the contributions or questions briefly in your own words. Now create an initial list of resources on your own pursuit of prayer. Where might you go to learn more about these figures, movements, and questions?

3. Take a small group (or person) with whom you are involved as a "case study." Now evaluate their use of the *ways* of prayer. (You may have to interview them for this.) What are the contexts of their praying? What are the vehicles used (such as repetition, body, imagination, contemplation)? What resources are at hand (scripture, nature, and so on)? How do their ways of prayer function to facilitate attention, awareness, and appropriate depth? What recommendations might you make to them with regard to their *ways* of prayer?

4. Now take that same group (or person) and evaluate the *dynamics* of their prayer life. Summarize their posture of initiation, the habitual content of their prayers, the disclosure of persons you see in their praying. Explore their listening styles. They may not consciously apply habits of listening to their prayer life, but you may be able to determine their posture of listening, the skills of contemplation as an attitude of prayer that are used, or the signs of the Spirit that are most important to them. What are the key features of the space in between for them? Again, are there any recommendations you might make with regard to their *dynamics* of prayer?

5. This chapter has emphasized the diverse ways, traditions, and dynamics of prayer. Yet are there any normative "rules" for prayer in the Christian faith? What are they? How are they to be communicated and lived out in the diversity of the Christian community?

6. Review the effects of prayer you have seen in your life thus far: effects on yourself as the one praying, effects on your relationship with God, and effects on the world as a consequence of your praying. Where do you see the hand of God? Where do you see signs of difficulty or indications of an area to be addressed between you and God? How might you take the next step forward toward an effective life of prayer?

The Life of Care

OBJECTIVES

In this chapter you will be introduced to the world of Christian care. You will learn how a life of care is an essential part of Christian spirituality and discover the foundations of a life of care in the understanding of God, of human experience, and of restoration. You will probe the nature of care, looking at various terms that surround the notion of care. You will listen to a few stories of care, stories of how people have lived care in the flesh. You will examine the contexts within which a life of care is lived, discovering how care is expressed in these various worlds. You will explore a few dynamics that must be addressed in developing a spirituality of care. You will consider what effect a spirituality of care may have on one's approach to political action. Finally, you will consider the ways of Christian care, designing a plan of care for your own personal life.

After reading this chapter you should be able to

- summarize some of the foundational principles of a spirituality of care;
- define *care*, distinguishing it from other related terms;
- help another individual or group to identify their own "contexts" of care, suggesting ways in which a life of care may be lived within each context;
- distinguish between modalities and sodalities, describing the unique contributions each structure provides for the enrichment of an other;
- show how difference, power, and change must be addressed in a life of care, giving examples of each;
- describe the different elements of a life of care, showing how these elements are used in different situations.

The Character of Christian Care

Christian spirituality, at its most practical level, is the lived relationship between God and God's people. This relationship involves communication between God and people—a life of prayer. But it also involves our sharing and embodiment of the character and purposes of the One with whom we relate—a life of care. As we have discovered in chapters 3 and 6, appreciative sharing with another means that we find ourselves imitating the other, participating with the other in their purposes and ideals. Thus, communication and formation are partners in the dynamics of relationship. And, in terms of relationship with God, just as communication leads us into a life of prayer, formation leads us into a life of care. To abide in God's love we must love one another (John 15:9–13). Love God, love neighbor. Christian spirituality—as lived relationship—necessarily involves the expression of our care for others. A life of prayer involves the mutual self-*disclosure* and self-*communication* of two parties. A life of care goes further. A life of care requires the self-*involvement in* and self-*giving for* another. God has cared for us. We are to care for ourselves and others.

The Divine-Human Relationship

God is "care" supreme. As the divine Trinity, the Father provides for the Son, the Son glorifies the Father, and the Spirit expresses the Father to the Son and reveals the Son to God's people. This caring character of God is communicated further through the processions of the Son and the Spirit. Jesus's prayer for his disciples is that they may participate in the love that the Father has for the Son (John 17:20–23). The Creator provides for creation, nurturing its growth, being patient with its failures, giving of himself to restore it to its fullest potential. Care is not only part of what makes God God; care is also part of what makes humans human. We do not enter life absolutely neutral. Things matter to us. We care about things.[1] Human experience involves participation in a web of relationships—with our selves, others, nature, spiritual forces, and God. This very relatedness of human experience involves us, of necessity, not only in the corporate character of communication, but also in the mutual self-giving of care. As we relate to God, we relate as people of care to a God of care. The dynamics of care are central to Christian spirituality.

The Restoration of Human Experience

Furthermore, care is woven into the very purpose of human existence. As we have already learned in chapter 5, human beings have been placed on earth as vice-regents, as covenant partners with God, exercising a certain range of leadership (dominion) over the earth. The creation mandate for humanity is that we would "take care of" the earth (Genesis 2:15 NIV), a compassionate reign we will continue after the creation of the new heavens and the new earth (Revelation 22:5). The Mosaic law was given to form a people who would embody care on earth, who would facilitate appropriate order in the land among others, within themselves, and before God. Jesus called this the "kingdom of God," a reign of self-giving love for the sake of others. *Love* describes the manner of our life. *Care defines the mandate of our life.* While the tragedy of human experience is that we fail to live into our calling as caretakers of the earth, God, through Christ and the Spirit, enables humanity in the church to live the life necessary to fulfill our destiny. Whether we view Pentecost as the foundation of the church or as the anointing of the apostles for priestly ministry, the Holy Spirit came as the bringer of life, creating a community of care. Again, as we learned in chapter 5, the apostles saw the church as the new embodiment of Israel's calling to be a model of community and care: a "light to the nations," the "aroma of Christ," the "salt of the earth," the "leaven" of God in the world. The Holy Spirit inspires care, enables care, and brings forth the fruit of care from the people of God. Through love for God and others we are empowered to live out an authentic life of care, our calling from the beginning.

What Is Care?

Care, as we shall be exploring it here, can be defined as *intentional, loving, self-giving for the enrichment of another*. Caring, first, is an *intentional* activity. Caring moves beyond mutual communication to purposeful action. I share with a friend when I speak with her. I care for that friend when I intentionally bring her soup when she is sick. I intend that the soup would change her life, at least a little. Second, care is *loving*. It is expressed out of an interest in and personal involvement with another.[2] Unlike duty, which may involve self-giving activity on behalf of another, care is expressed out of a sincere appreciation for the other. Third, care is a *self-giving*. In care I offer something of myself to another. I offer time, energy, expressions of love, words of encouragement, possessions. I offer thoughts, feelings, actions. I give of some relationships to foster other relationships, for example, by sharing with you something of my relationship with my horse as you and I get to know each other. I give of my experience to another, for example, as I offer my understanding as a way of helping your quest for the truth. The ministries of healing and spiritual warfare are acts of care. In concern, I feel a kind of compassion for another; the other matters to me. In care, I express that concern with the gift of myself, by nurturing, protecting, providing, and attending to your needs through my self. Finally, care is *for the enrichment of another*. While few actions are done with entirely pure motives—and while determining just what really *is* caring for others is not always easy—an act of care involves the sense not merely of duty or profit, but also (and even more so) of the benefit of the one receiving our act. At times caring acts are "aimed" at one group "on behalf of" another, those for whom we intend

Beyond self-disclosure to self-giving,
smells of Trinity,
of humanness, for whom things matter.
We are placed on this earth to care.

to receive care (as when my small group advocates before government officials for justice on behalf of an oppressed segment of society). Whether the self-giving of care is offered directly to one (as when I offer soup to a sick friend) or indirectly through others (as in our political advocacy), the aim is some kind of enrichment to the life of others.

The Elements and Contexts of Christian Care

The life of care involves a number of elements. First, there is the *caregiver*, the self who is offering care (of course, this can be a corporate or individual self). A caregiver offers care on behalf of another self, the **recipient** (again, this can be an individual or corporate self—indeed the self receiving care might even be an inanimate

Historical Portrait: Sarah

The life of care is often a hidden life. Few become famous. Here is the story of one of those lesser-known people of care. Sarah lived during the Great Depression in the United States.[3]

At eighteen, Sarah married, moving in with her husband to a strange new life in the city. He set up a barber shop. Soon a son was born, then a daughter, then a second son. It was while still a toddler that her third child was diagnosed as having muscular dystrophy. The doctor told Sarah that the boy would not live to his fifth birthday. The Great Depression had struck and the barber shop was not doing well. Sarah took in laundry and when she found that that was not enough, she worked at other part-time jobs—cleaning houses, cooking in a high school cafeteria. She also began baking bread, dozens of loaves at a time. After school her daughter would load the still warm bread onto a small wagon to sell to stores and families in the neighborhood.

Her son required special care. She began going to daily Mass at six in the morning to pray for help for her son and strength for herself. Years later, an examining physician pronounced that her love had contributed greatly to her son's miraculously long life. He was fourteen when he died. After the funeral her husband returned home, took to bed, and did not leave it until he too died six months later. Now supporting herself and her two teenage children was entirely her responsibility. While continuing to work at her other jobs and caring for her family, Sarah began to go to beauty school in the evenings, learning hairdressing and eventually turning the small barber shop her husband operated in the front room of the house into a beauty shop.

She applied to become a foster parent and for many years following, years that stretched long after the time when her own children had left home and married, she had girls in their early teens come to live with her. Some stayed a few weeks; others stayed for years. And so began a pattern that would be hers for decades to follow. She rose at five in the morning, then walked to church for six o'clock Mass; she returned to make breakfast for those she cared for, meet her appointments for permanents or hairdos, make a quick lunch, and finally cook dinner. And not a day went by when she did not bake bread. She fit it in between her appointments and later on in the evening. She baked dozens of loaves at a time. But the time had long passed since she baked her bread for sale. Every loaf she made was given away. She baked for churches trying to raise money; she baked for soup kitchens serving food to the poor and homeless; she baked for her family and for the growing number of grandchildren; she baked for any of her neighbors whom she felt needed extra care or for anyone else she heard of who needed help.

Her philosophy was simple and direct. "God tells us to give what we have," she would say. "All I have to give is my bread." But she was giving much more than that. She was giving a special kind of love, a love that at once reached out to others while also making her life all of one piece, so that everything that she did, routine or ordinary as it might otherwise seem, came to express that love.

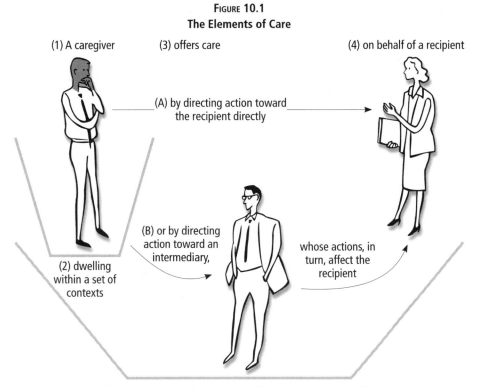

Figure 10.1
The Elements of Care

(1) A caregiver (3) offers care (4) on behalf of a recipient

(A) by directing action toward the recipient directly

(B) or by directing action toward an intermediary,

whose actions, in turn, affect the recipient

(2) dwelling within a set of contexts

Every element is conducted within a set of contexts, as is the whole process.

object, like a piece of property). At times (like when I offer you soup when you are sick), these two are the only parties involved in the caring relationship. At other times, however, a third party or self is involved: an **intermediary**. You may be so sick that I decide to call a doctor on your behalf; in this case, the doctor is intermediary and you are the recipient. Or, using another example, I may decide to write a letter to my congressperson, asking her to support a piece of legislation that would benefit starving children in another country or that would benefit local farmlands; in this case, my congressperson is the intermediary and the children or the farmlands are the recipients.

Each of these elements of care—caregiver, recipient, intermediary, and the act of offering care itself—is shaped by a variety of *contexts* of care. Just as we spoke in chapter 8 of the contexts of spiritual formation (those environments within which spiritual formation is lived out), so too there are

similar contexts of the life of care, environments within which our expressions of self-giving are discovered and expressed. By perceiving the context of each of the elements of care, we come to understand in greater measure the character of the caring act as a whole. Each context highlights different dimensions of human experience and calls on different aspects of our relationship with God. Particular expressions of a few of these contexts have become recognized institutions in Christian spirituality (for example, the ministry of spiritual direction in one-on-one relationships).

The Earth Itself

The most basic context of our life of care is the earth itself. We are placed *on* the earth to *care for* the earth. "The LORD God took the man and put him in the garden of Eden to till it and keep it" (Genesis 2:15). This keeping is a nurturing form of caring for another, implying concern for the other cared for. Thus our ecological context forms both a fundamental environment of care (it is where we are) and our most basic direction of care (responsible dominion over the earth). As Quaker leader John Woolman (1720–72) believed, a "spirit of tenderness" should accompany our attitude and actions "not only towards poor people but also towards all creatures of which we had the command."[4] We have only begun to reflect on the implications of our earthly embeddedness for a life of care. Perhaps, for example, our choices of technologies and lifestyles are not matters divorced from a life of care. And perhaps, by attending to the effects of our actions (our physical transformations of the earth—planting, building, changing, using, and such) on the ecosystem, we might act so as to enrich the lives of those species of life we were called to rule. Our life of care begins with the very ground on which we stand.[5]

Family Life

We are usually *first* aware of care in the context of family. Care is beautifully illustrated in the image of a mother holding and nursing her child: nurturing and providing, *self*-giving for the enrichment of the other. The family is the context in which our earliest and most fundamental needs—food, shelter, sleep, touch—are met. It is the context of our own realization as persons. As we usually have no choice in our family context, and as families can embody lack of care as well as care, this realization can be painful as well as nurturing. The family is also a critical context of care in our final season of life, when, as in infancy, we cannot care for ourselves. The care of family life invites us into a special *kenosis*, a self-emptying "that involves the reformation of the core of our beings, a radical expanding of the established contours of our hearts to include others in a permanent and life-altering way."[6] While the forms and expressions of family have varied somewhat throughout the centuries (tribal, extended, nuclear, alternative), the Christian church has recognized the importance of the family as an expression of the spirituality of care, speaking of marriage and family with terms such as *perichoresis* (the mutual interpenetration shared by the members of the Trinity), *nuptial priesthood*, and *domestic church*.[7]

Author Ernest Boyer portrays traditional monastic spirituality as "life on the edge" of society and ordinary life. In contrast family spirituality is "life in the center." Within the center of ordinary life, the family "sacrament of routine" brings a sense of sacredness to the most mundane of tasks. Likewise the "sacrament of the care of others" facilitates a unique set of virtues. "Courage, persistence, trust, forgiveness, and the ability to balance holding with letting go—these are the elements of the sacrament of the care of others."[8] The spirituality of care in the context of family requires a long-term perspective, carrying relationships through from birth to death. Activities like common work and common meals inform the kinds of care needed in family life. The vow of marriage, like the vow of holy orders, ushers us into a special form of a life of care, with its own unique trials and rewards. And the rewards are rich indeed: the compassionate touch, the vulnerability of love, the deep center of trust, and the mutual celebration of the ritual of the cycle of human life itself.[9]

Community Life

We live out a life of care in the midst of a variety of communities in addition to family. Some forms of community share relationship with God intentionally. Others are "secular" communities wherein common identity has less to do with relationship with God than with other factors. As we learned in chapter 3, we understand communities best when we come to understand patterns of self-disclosure, symbolic expression, communication, common and shared experience, roles and identities, governing structure, the sense of corporate identity, and culture. By understanding the leadership structure and common values of a local business, for example, one may be better able to exercise *care*ful (*care*-full) influence in that business for the sake of a suffering employee. And communities, as individuals, can perform acts of care, and they can receive acts of care performed either for the community or on behalf of another.

Christian communities (especially those who have some level of formal organization) can be divided into two types. Some communities comprise those young and old, mature in the faith and new in the faith, male and female. The local congregation and the broader denomination are examples of this type. And then there are communities of believers that seek to limit their membership to those who make a further commitment as adults and are often further delineated by age, sex, or marital status. Monasteries or missions organizations are examples of this type. Both types of communities have significantly influenced the history of the church. Each have their own ways of serving as a context for the life of care. Communities of the first type are known as *modalities*. Those of the second are known as *sodalities*.[10] Associations and small groups can have an intentional Christian component. Secular or mixed communities come in a variety of forms.

Christian Modalities. The wide range of membership in **modalities** (for example, in a congregation) means that we find ourselves caring for those we might not choose to care for and that the range of mutual enrichment of care is very wide. More than likely, you do not feel obligated to visit your sick employer, with whom you disagree so often. Yet it is simply part of church life to visit sick members, no matter who they may be. At the same time, during your own illness, you may receive a variety of expressions of care from the congregation: cards from the preschool class, visits from individuals, help with the chores at home, money from the mercy fund. The very breadth of modalities gives place for the widest expressions of care.

A congregation or a network of congregations is a nexus of common identity, vision, and life, constantly informed by—and informing—influences from within and without. Consider Acts 2:41–47:

> So those who welcomed his message were baptized, and that day about three thousand persons were added. They devoted themselves to the apostles' teaching and fellowship, to the breaking of bread and the prayers. Awe came upon everyone, because many wonders and signs were being done by the apostles. All who believed were together and had all things in common; they would sell their possessions and goods and distribute the proceeds to all, as any had need. Day by day, as they spent much time together in the temple, they broke bread at home and ate their food with glad and generous hearts, praising God and having the goodwill of all the people. And day by day the Lord added to their number those who were being saved.

This passage has been interpreted throughout the history of the church as a summary statement of ideal church life. And throughout the history of the church, various modalities have expressed sensitivity to some elements of this passage more than to others. Expanding popular use of the term *sensitive* (as in *seeker-sensitive*) we might suggest that some congregations are more *tradition-sensitive*, careful that the "breaking of bread and the prayers" are kept in harmony with the forms passed on through the history of the Christian faith. Others are more *scripture-sensitive*, insistent that the congregation must be devoted to "the apostles' teaching." Still others are *community-sensitive*, seeing church in rich "fellowship," in having "all things in common." Some congregations are indeed *seeker-sensitive*, especially conscious of the Lord's desire to "add to their number." Others are *society-sensitive*, aware that authentic Christian faith means living out alternative socioeconomic values such as "distributing" goods "to all, as any had need." Finally, some congregations are *Spirit-sensitive*, dependent on the pouring out of the Spirit of God (Acts 2:17) for the direction of their life.[11]

The presence of these unique sensitivities means that our expressions of self-giving for the enrichment of others will be fostered and received differently in different modalities. One congregation

---

And they who are well to do, and willing, give what each thinks fit; and what is collected is deposited with the president, who succors the orphans and widows and those who, through sickness or any other cause, are in want, and those who are in bonds and the strangers sojourning among us, and in a word takes care of all who are in need.

—First Apology of Justin (second century)[12]

---

may encourage the care of the intellectual development of youth through exposing them to the tough questions of life. Another congregation might not welcome challenging inquiry so eagerly, seeking instead to care for the youths' need for the regeneration of the Spirit. Thus the expression of sensitive care in the context of modalities involves not simply a choice for fellowship above liturgy, but rather an understanding attention to *how* we exercise fellowship or liturgy—the commitment to the enrichment of the body and the willingness to sacrifice for the body in every dimension of congregational life.[13]

Christian sodalities. **Sodalities**, as opposed to modalities, make explicit commitments to the kind of corporate identity, sensitivities, and distinctives they embody. These are expressed in terms of a Rule of life (if the sodality is some sort of monastic community), a mission statement, or some-

thing similar. Often these groups share not only common tasks and vision, but also a more developed mode of lifestyle involving common worship, meals, possessions, and so on. Protestant missiologist Ralph Winter defines sodalities as "a structured fellowship in which membership involves an adult second decision beyond modality membership, and is limited either by age or sex or marital status."[14] The Roman West tends to look at sodalities in terms of religious or consecrated life, with the particular groups identified as formal monastic societies, communities, or orders (such as the Society of Jesuits, the L'Arche Community, or the Order of Preachers). In the East, "there is only one order, the order of monks,"[15] with a great deal of flexibility between communities of monks.

Sodalities facilitate care by enforcing a high degree of intentionality, structure, and accountability. Some communities (such as the Sisters of Charity, founded by Mother Theresa of Calcutta) are explicitly designed to promote certain kinds of outreach care to others. For other communities (such as the Benedictines), care is expressed though the compassion of a somewhat cloistered communal life and through the hospitality to visitors. For many Orthodox monks, their structured life of prayer *is* their service to others. Sodalities structure activities and relationships to promote the care characteristic of a given community and the maturity of its members (or to allow the individual to find a place in the community to express care appropriately to individual and community life). Whereas order is harder to find in home and church, in the context of sodalities a life of care is carefully ordered to specific ends.

Associations. Care is also expressed within the context of voluntary societies or **associations**. Associations are usually organized around a particular compassionate cause or task: the abolition of slavery, the needs of urban orphans, the development of libraries, the plight of wilderness species, and so on. The Young Men's Christian Association in the United States, the Rhenish-Westphalian Deaconess Society in Germany, and the British and Foreign Bible Society in England are good examples of this kind of community. One strength of associations is that they can mobilize a wide range (and large number) of people for a particular cause. Some members devote their entire lives for the cause. Most sacrifice a briefer expenditure of time and energy (either regularly or within the context of a significant need) to an association. Associations can draw members from a variety of religious persuasions, resulting in believers and unbelievers of all kinds rubbing shoulders in the context of working together for a common compassionate cause. In recent decades, many have considered care once usually provided by associations to be the responsibility of national governments (and have transferred some of this responsibility *to* national governments). Consequently, in many circles energy for voluntary associations has floundered. This, and the ambiguity regarding the ability of large governmental structures to meet certain human needs, has led many to look again to the voluntary association as an important caregiver in the world.[16]

Small groups. The *small group* is a collection of approximately five to twenty people who meet regularly for some expression of care. Once again, emphases vary, even within Christian groups. Some gather for common worship. Others look forward to small groups for open sharing and accountability not available in a larger gathering. Some attend small groups for Bible study, in which intimacy permits questions and discussion. In many groups, the members care for each other. Other groups gather to plan and execute outreach, caring for those outside the group. Some groups are open groups, welcoming any and all who come. Others are closed groups, maintaining confidentiality within an established community. Some groups intentionally change members regularly. Other groups stay together for life. Small groups provide a

vehicle for greater attention to the needs of individuals within the group without resorting to a one-on-one relationship (though often significant one-on-one relationships develop from small-group connections). From the house churches of antiquity, to collections of monks in "sketes," to the *collegia pietas* of the Lutheran Pietists, to the bands and class meetings of Methodism, and beyond, small groups have frequently served as a mechanism of mutual care within the Christian church.[17]

Work. Our *work* also serves as a significant context of the life of care. Membership in work communities is related to the work itself. For this reason, a given work community may or may not be Christian in any sense. Likewise, a given work community may or may not be sensitive to care in any sense. Work might simply be about repainting apartments, manufacturing tennis shoes, or calculating balance sheets—in as efficient and professional a manner as possible under the circumstances.

Yet, as with all the contexts of life, opportunities for the expression of care (and even the intentional pursuit of a systematic lifestyle of care) are ever-present in the context of work. Just as the laws of the Pentateuch provided guidance for the production, use, and management of goods and services for the people of Israel, so today we can look to the scriptures, the Spirit, and the community of God's people in the context of our own situations to see what principles might govern our treatment of coworkers, natural resources, economic institutions, and so on. Benedictines, Lutherans, Amish, and others have thought long and deep about the relationship of faith to work. As we attend to the web of relationships—with nature, others, self, spiritual forces, and God—we transform our employment into *careful* vocation. We wisely consider the use of our bodies and the earth's resources. We encourage one another, nourishing the sense of the esprit de corps of the workforce. Insofar as possible, policies serve the people, rather than the reverse. God's presence is practiced.

Whether it looks or feels like it, through our work we tend the garden of the earth together with others. *How* we tend this garden is the question of a life of care.[18]

Polis. And then there is the *polis*, the formal structure of economic, political, and social organization. Our experience of relatedness with others implies relationships with the systems and structures of our world as well as interpersonal relationships with friends and acquaintances. We influence these structures for care in a variety of different ways. We pray for those in leadership locally, nationally, and globally. We involve ourselves in evangelistic ministry to those outside our small group, or we offer compassionate care for those in need. We persuade leaders to embrace policies of care through the spoken and written word or through symbolic actions. We educate ourselves about issues of care so that we may intelligently express care in a complex society. We model fresh and appropriate ways of living through our own lives as individuals and communities. We express desire for care through our economic choices, perhaps through avoiding the purchase of goods or services either produced by or contributing to unjust conditions of life. We involve ourselves directly in the political process: voting, collecting petitions for a referendum, or running for office. And as we cooperate together, the polis becomes not simply a recipient of care, but also an intermediary of care (we care for our city through caring for the parks) and a giver of care (the country cares for victims of violent crime by passing and enforcing federal laws).

Political involvement runs the danger of becoming a matter of my pet cause, apart from any larger sense of what may be best for the whole (as with involvement in other forms of care). Furthermore, the lessons of individual policies are often learned over a long period of time (for example, tracking the subtle effects of environmental policies). And to make matters worse, we live in a real (and tragic) world, in which values are, at times, in conflict. Do we choose to support the creation of jobs at the expense of environmental concerns? Is there a compromise? In light of these kinds of complications, political care is wisely pursued when it is tied to values rather than to particular measures. Our openness to hear different perspectives, our prayerful consideration of options, our deep rootedness in the heart of God revealed in the scriptures, and our willingness to risk and to sacrifice for the sake of a better town, nation, and world—these are the virtues of a life of care in the polis.[19]

One-on-One Relationships

The life of care is also lived out in one-on-one relationships, which come in a variety of forms: in mentorship, discipleship, evangelism, or counseling; with an acquaintance, a friend, a buddy, or a spouse. In some of these relationships (acquaintance, friend, spouse) there is an equality of giving and receiving of care. In others (mentor, counselor, evangelist) there is the sense of one more experienced offering a particular kind of care to one less experienced. The kinds of care given and received will vary with different kinds of relationships. As a volunteer with Meals on Wheels, I may bring a meal and a listening ear to an isolated senior citizen. As a psychiatrist, I may offer professional diagnosis to a suicidal adolescent.

One type of one-on-one relationship has received special attention among students of Christian spirituality: the relationship of spiritual guidance or **spiritual direction**. It is designed with special attention to the enrichment of another's relationship with God. From the desert fathers and mothers, to the Celtic *anamchara* (soul-friend), to the Reformed pastor, to the Jesuit facilitator of the Spiritual Exercises, to the contemporary spiritual friend, the ministry of spiritual direction has been a significant form of care expressed to those who want to grow in spiritual life. In spiritual direction, the directee simply reveals his life, and especially his life with God, to the director, who

	Friendship	Spiritual Direction	Evangelism	Mentoring	Counseling
1. Orientation of the relationship	"play"	"presence"	"position"	"plan"	"problem"
2. Goals of the relationship	mutuality	spiritual growth	spiritual life	spiritual/practical skill	psychological/ spiritual health
3. Means used in the relationship	varies	spiritual plus	varies	practical/spiritual	psychological plus
4. Mode of relating	sharing	being/watching	persuading/ demonstrating	equipping	restoring
5. Does one of the people come for help with a problem or a need?	both at times	not the focus	yes	yes	yes
6. Duration of the relationship	varies	long, varies	varies	varies	until problem ends
7. Frequency of meetings	often	varies	varies	varies	regular
8. Setting of the meetings	varies	carefully chosen	many	varies	usually office

listens and responds. The director notices the presence and work of the Spirit and brings the work of the Spirit to the awareness of the directee, encouraging him in his growth in response to the leading of the Spirit of God. Some traditions emphasize the place of confession or a "manifestation of thoughts" to the director. Some traditions emphasize the sharing of the life of prayer. Others look for the presence of God within the stories of ordinary life. Spiritual direction is a co-discernment of the active presence of God in the life of another, with director and directee listening and responding together.[20]

Intentional Solitude

Finally, the life of intentional solitude is itself a context for the life of care. Whether expressed in a temporary withdrawal and return to ministry, in the ministry of prayer, in the ministry of modeling alternative values, or in the ministry of spiritual direction, intentional solitude is not a removal from the life of care, but rather a unique *expression* of that life. As spiritual writer Evagrius Ponticus phrased it, a solitary life is "separated from all and in harmony [or united] with all."[21] The life of solitude gives greater freedom to think, to pray, and to explore *on behalf of others*. As expressed in the withdrawal of Elijah and John the Baptist, in the desert fathers and mothers, in the Celtic and Greek solitaries, in the renewal of the solitary life in the Carthusian and Camaldolese traditions, in the insertion of the solitary life into Russian soil through Sergius of Radonezh (ca. 1314–92) and Nils Sorsky, and in contemporary explorers of solitude such as Theophan the Recluse and Thomas Merton, the life of solitude has served as a rich expression of care to individuals and to the larger world. As A. Gordon Mursell writes about Guigo I (1083–1136) and his dual commitment to the solitary life and political action, Guigo's "vocation was not so much a flight *from* the world as a flight *for* it: the contemplative monk who addressed himself to secular concerns from his monastic solitude saw himself not as someone interfering in matters that did not concern him, but as someone who had the advantage of a clearer and surer perspective from which to view them."[22] While in some Christian traditions intentional solitude has been understood as a context of care for millennia, in other traditions the context of intentional solitude has yet to be explored.[23]

Contexts and Spiritualities

The configuration of contexts within which a given community or individual expresses a life of care results in a kind of

---

The Contexts of Care

- The Earth Itself
- Family Life
- Community Life
  - *Christian modalities* (all ages and commitments)
  - *Christian sodalities* (more specific ages and commitments)
  - *Associations* (those gathered for a specific cause)
  - *Small Groups* (a few who regularly meet for mutual care)
  - *Work* (communities of employment)
  - *Polis* (communities of location or government)
- One-on-One Relationships
- Intentional Solitude

Members of those communities which are totally dedicated to contemplation give themselves to God alone in solitude and silence and through constant prayer and ready penance. No matter how urgent may be the needs of the active apostolate, such communities will always have a distinguished part to play in Christ's Mystical Body, where "all members have not the same function" (Romans 12:4). For they offer God a choice sacrifice of praise. They brighten God's people with the richest splendors of sanctity. By their example they motivate this people; by imparting a hidden, apostolic fruitfulness, they make this people grow. Thus they are the glory of the Church and an overflowing fountain of heavenly graces.[24]

spirituality of care, a way that relationship with God is expressed in love to others. These spiritualities of care can be categorized into three primary groups: contemplative spiritualities, communal spiritualities, and apostolic spiritualities.

Contemplative spiritualities. First, there are **contemplative spiritualities**. Some express care primarily through means that do not require a great deal of contact with those who receive their care. While this kind of spirituality is often embodied by individuals, it need not be restricted to the solitary life. There are contemplative communities wherein the interaction between people is less significant to their sense of calling than the environment of contemplative reflection and prayer is. As we mentioned above regarding solitude, a contemplative life can be understood as a life of care. A life of solitude (whether lived privately or in community) can be devoted to intercessory prayer, to consideration of issues other people might not have the time or freedom to explore, or to a liturgical rhythm that incorporates the church at large into its purview. The "Decree on the Appropriate Renewal of the Religious Life" from the Second Vatican Council states it nicely:

Communal spiritualities. Others place most of their energies around relationships within a known community, whether family, modality, sodality, small group, or the like. Thus we can identify a separate **communal spirituality**. Whereas the *anchorite* (solitary monk) might see the rigors of ascetical practice as the central means of spiritual formation, softening the heart toward God and others, the *cenobite* (communal monk) sees life together itself as a central sanctifying influence and a primary context of the life of care. Jean Vanier, founder of the L'Arche communities, writes, "In community people care for each other and not just for the community in the abstract, as a whole, as an institution or as an ideal way of life. It is *people* that matter; to love and care for the people that are there, just as they are. It is to care for them in such a way that they may grow according to the plan of God and thus give much life."[25] Mennonite churches (modalities), Benedictine communities (sodalities), and many local small groups and congregations (unconsciously, at times) look within the community to direct a life of care. This is not to say that other contexts of care are ignored. (Indeed, some farming families may be very active in caring for the earth.) It is just that from the perspective of the caregiver, the bulk of their self-giving is directed within.

Apostolic spiritualities. A third group looks without to express care. Just as the apostles went out to proclaim and demonstrate the love of God to a people who had not heard and whom they did not know, so too **apostolic spiritualities** today place a premium on outreach. Outreach can take the form of evangelistic interest, compassionate assistance, or sociopolitical action. Apostolic spiritualities may look to the Great Commission found in Matthew 28:19–20 ("Go therefore and make disciples of all nations, baptizing them in the name of the Father and of the Son and of the Holy Spirit, and teaching them to obey everything that I have commanded you") or to the affirmation in Jeremiah 22:16 regarding king Josiah ("He judged the cause of the poor and needy; then it was well. Is not this to know me? says the LORD.") for inspiration. While some see their identity as an alternative community whether or not influence on the world is regarded as important, others see the need for a more active involvement in the lives of others. In any case, there is a sense of the importance of extending care to those who may be unknown or outside the community of reference. Franciscan friars, Evangelical churches, Jesuit communities, voluntary associations, and missionary organizations are all expressions of apostolic spiritualities. And, of course, some communities and individuals blend the contemplative, the communal, and the apostolic in various forms.

Living Care in Context

Deciding where to give and to receive care is often an act of discernment. In some cultures these decisions are largely a consequence of birth. One's family, land, congregation, and village mark out the reasonable boundaries of a life of care. For many in contemporary society, however, it is much more complicated. Congregations, associations, friendship circles, small groups, and political opportunities surround us like food at a buffet (or like swarms of flies).

Our sense of belonging (and, therefore, our sense of obligation or responsibility—who we are to care for) is weakened due to the mobility and fragmentation of our culture. The confusion of social and political rhetoric paralyzes us from involvement. We are left exhausted from going in too many directions at the same time, and we feel guilty for not doing enough. Our consumer culture inclines us toward low-investment, high yield relationships. The temptation is to retreat into the safety of some private sphere and to ignore care altogether. The challenge is to press into a life of care. Some channel their care through a single community, giving themselves to the community and through it to a larger world, receiving the rewards of a life lived together over time. Others piece together their context of giving and receiving care from a number of unrelated groups, *networking* their lives. Sociologist of religion Robert Wuthnow states that "such people may not be immersed in a single religious congregation, but they are linked generally to a variety of communities through their spiritual pursuits, their work, family, and friends."[26]

The life of care, for Christians, is a blend of freedom, responsibility, and calling. It involves *freedom* in that, as unique images and covenant partners of God, we offer uniquely creative expressions of care. This is how it was meant to be: humans imaginatively creating environments of nurture and enrichment, using that which God has created in harmony with the will and Spirit of God. In practice this means that a life

Pastoral Paralysis

of care is to be lived in a kind of joyful freedom to choose those expressions that best communicate our concern for others from our unique person and setting, those expressions that we may be really excited about. Yet our freedom is not separate from but rather blended with *responsibility*. We cannot neglect care for the environment simply because we are not interested and environmental politics are confusing. We have a God-given responsibility (domin-ion) for the earth. While the particulars are optional, the values that govern the particulars are not. Certain responsibilities may demand more of us during a given season of life (for example, with the care of young children or elderly parents). Nonetheless, our embeddedness in various layers of con-text is an embeddedness of response-ability (freedom) and responsibility (obligation). We must learn to navigate both. Finally, a life of care is a matter of *calling*. This is vocation in its deepest sense. Our life is not just about a job; rather it is about a blend of work, family, society, and more—a blend that, on prayerful consideration, offers the greatest possible gift to others and the greatest possible glory to God. Determining that calling is the work of discernment, the topic of our next chapter.

The Dynamics of Christian Care

A life of care, however, is not just about *what* we do (and certainly not about *how much* we do) but perhaps even more about *how* we do what we do. It is *how* we treat the forests, *how* we relate to our coworkers, *how* we provide for those in need. And this, in turn, brings us to the *dynamics* of care, certain aspects of the art of self-giving for the enrichment of others that must be ad-dressed if a life of care is to have its full im-pact. Whereas a knowledge of the dynamics of prayer (speaking, listening, the space in-between) facilitates a kind of sensitivity within, a knowledge of the dynamics of care facilitates a sensitivity without. This sensitivity without yields both a knowledge of the dynamics of the particular contexts

of that life (the unique dynamics of small groups, ecology, evangelism, political life, and so on) as well as of the general dynamics that govern the life of care *as such*. We will address three of these more general dynam-ics: differences, power, and change.

Difference and Contribution

To care is to offer something of myself to another. A nursing mother offers liter-ally something of herself to the child. A philanthropist offers finances to support a cause. A friend offers comfort when his comrade is down. In care we offer what we have—what the other does *not* have—for the enrichment of the other. In other words, care implies difference. Sometimes I need you to be firm with me. Other times I need you to be gentle. You provide what I am missing through your care. It is likewise with communities. My contribution of care to the community is what is unique to me. My care implies the gift of my difference. While care is often offered out of a false sense of self (the need to feel helpful, the need to be in control, and so on), by learning to understand my own self with my unique experience (or by understanding our "self," with our unique corporate identity, his-tory, and such) in comparison to the self for whom (recipient) or, in some cases, to whom (intermediary) I offer caring acts, I am (or we are) better able to channel care appropriate to each situation.

Spiritual gifts. This is precisely Paul's teaching on spiritual gifts. The one Spirit facilitates a variety of abilities, ministries, graces, and offices among the members of the church. By means of this variety, God builds up the body through that which is present in some and absent in others (1 Corinthians 12; Romans 12; Ephesians 4). Donald L. Gelpi suggests that the Pauline charisms of the Spirit transform each moment in the stages of human experience. Thus, the gifts of prayer and tongues transform Being Aware and Experiencing, gifts of teaching transform Understanding, prophecy and discernment transform Judging, healing and administration transform Deciding and Acting, and so on.[27] By looking at the work of the Spirit in this way we understand that the fullness of the mind of Christ is discovered and expressed in the mutual self-giving of the body of Christ. As Gelpi puts it, *"The mutual charismatic ministry of all Christians transforms their personal experience of faith into a shared, ecclesial experience."*[28] The fourth-century commentary on Romans attributed to the unknown Ambrosiaster states, "By using the example of the body, Paul teaches that it is impossible for any one of us to do everything on our own, for we are members of each other and need one another. For this reason we ought to behave toward one another with care, because we need each other's gifts."[29]

As we share what we have (who we are) out of love and with an eye to the needs of others, we enrich the body of Christ and cooperate with the work of the Spirit to bring the church into greater maturity and to spread the good news of Christ to the world.

Traditions. As we mentioned above, different modalities tend to gravitate toward different sensitivities with regard to their life as a Christian community (scripture-sensitive, seeker-sensitive, and so on). These various sensitivities combine, over time, with other dimensions of community life (especially in collectives of congregations) and lead to the development of traditions, each with their own character. We were introduced to traditions in chapter 2, locating traditions between informal relations and Christian history. What is important to notice here is that the types of care we have received from our traditions and our reactions to the types of care we have received (or have not received) influence what kinds of care we are apt to give others. For example, we may be inclined to give care out of a spontaneous sense of the Spirit because that is the tradition in which we were raised. On the other hand, if we have felt hurt by this tradition, we may avoid acting out of

spontaneity, choosing instead to care from a position of reason and caution.

And like spiritual gifts, different traditions tend to express different stages of human experience. Thus, using the names of the traditions presented in author Richard Foster's *Streams of Living Waters* (with two slight modifications) and imagining the corporate "mind" of the church of Christ, we might recognize various Contemplative traditions throughout history that have nourished the Being Aware of the body of Christ.[30] Charismatic traditions have enriched our Experiencing of God. Progressive traditions have posed important questions to the body of Christ, facilitating our Understanding of God. Evangelical traditions have kept us close to the center of our beliefs, fostering the church's Judging. Holiness traditions and Social Justice traditions have stressed practical life, nourishing our Deciding and Acting, either with regard to individual or social contexts. Finally, Sacramental traditions represent the whole through liturgy and art and life, serving the Integration of the corporate mind.

Just as some people are predisposed to one or another of the stages of human experience (some are thinkers, others are doers), so also some traditions tend to orient themselves around one or another way of living out relationship with God. And just as a human mind requires the cooperative integration of every stage of human experience for knowledge and life, so also the mind of the Church requires the cooperative integration of the various traditions for healthy knowledge and life in its relationship with God.

A life of care is aware of the dynamics of difference. Difference is both a threat and a gift. To offer something of our experience to another—an idea, a relationship, a tear—is to offer what that person may not have at the moment. The difference that we offer as individuals and as traditions may nourish a deep hunger. It may also shake a world. The art of care is the skill of knowing how and when to give and receive difference, a

Figure 10.3
Stages, Traditions, *Gifts*

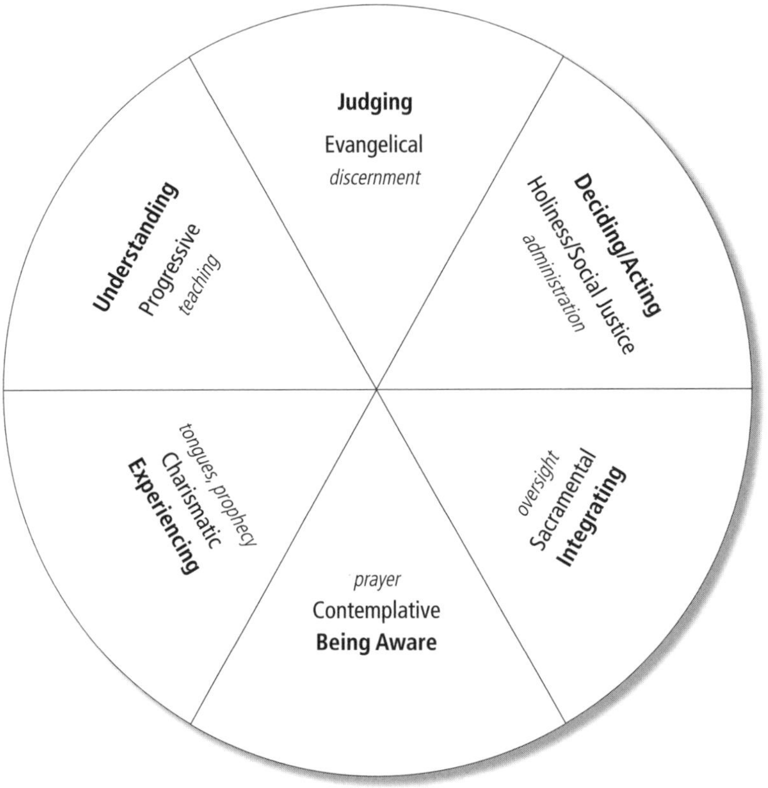

Judging
Evangelical
discernment

Deciding/Acting
Holiness/Social Justice
administration

Understanding
Progressive
teaching

Integrating
Sacramental
oversight

Experiencing
Charismatic
tongues, prophecy

Being Aware
Contemplative
prayer

skill that comes from knowing the differences deeply.

Power and Authority

The notion of difference brings us to a discussion of *power*. I have something you do not have and may even need. Out of care, I offer you of myself. And yet, because I have what you need, I have a certain power over you. I can withhold what you need or use what I have (and you need) to bargain for something I want. Furthermore, there is often a connection between power and *authority*, a position or right of rule. Local police have the authority to take people to jail because they care for the peace of a community. The police force has what we as individuals do not have: the power, by virtue of weapons and such, to maintain peace in a community in the face of great danger. A psychiatrist has authority to prescribe

medicines to treat people suffering from various maladies. The same psychiatrist also possesses power: the ability to interpret another's life. Advertising and information networks possess power, through identification with our wants and fears, to shape worldviews and actions. Power and authority are directed *to* others and *for* others. They can be used as an expression of care or not. Consider Ebenezer Scrooge's assessment of his former employer, Mr. Fezziwig, in Charles Dickens's well-known *A Christmas Carol*. When a party, sponsored by Fezziwig, is minimized as a mere expense of money, Scrooge replies, "It isn't that. He has the power to render us happy or unhappy; to make our service light or burdensome; a pleasure or a toil. Say that his power lies in words and looks; in things so slight and insignificant that it is impossible to add and count 'em up: what then?

The happiness he gives is quite as great as if it cost a fortune."[31]

The use and abuse of the power to care. The power to care is a valuable gift indeed. It comes in all kinds of forms. Power is the capacity to produce effects. Care is the production of certain kinds of effects (the enrichment of others). Parents possess coercive power, the ability to force someone to do something against his will. Usually we think of coercive power in a negative sense (as with bullies and evil dictatorships). Yet when a small child is preparing to step out in front of a car, the exercise of coercive power in pulling the child back is an important expression of care. Humans have physical power with relationship to soil. We can weed and till and support growth by the use of our power of movement. Some of us possess the power to offer reward or punishment. Teachers, for example, offer everything from encouragement to final grades as means of supporting the development of their students. Others possess legitimate power associated with a given role or position. A hotel owner in Rwanda, for example, can use his position to secure safe housing for thousands endangered in the midst of civil war.[32] Then there is the expression of referent power, the power of admiration and appreciation. I wield referent power for the sake of care when I, through modeling a life of care, draw others into the same kind of life or when I, as a person of charisma and recognition, notice the least on the social ladder, thereby functionally lifting that person up the ladder. (Consider Jesus's treatment of the woman with the hemorrhage in Matthew 9:19–22; Mark 5:25–34; and Luke 8:42–48.) There is the power of expertise, the sharing of knowledge or skill gained at much time and expense, that is shared freely and wisely with others. There is the power of prayer, wherein we identify ourselves with the power of God and repel the forces of evil. And we could go on. Ownership, access to control, social obligation, trust, and more can be seen as forms of power that can be used for the sake of care.[33] Every act

of self-giving is an expression of some form of power to produce effects in the world: effects in nature, in ourselves or other individuals, in the corporate structures and systems of our societies, or in the worlds of the transcendent and the divine. Consider, what effects can *you* produce? What effects can you produce that most others can't? Ask yourself, What kinds of power for care do I possess? What kinds of power does my nation possess? my church?

But quite often we hear about power not so much in terms of its use for care, but in terms of its *abuse*, its producing harm. An early stage of this arises through the *inattentive* use of power. I build a dam on my property not even considering what effects it might have on animal life or on my neighbor's garden. Even though my use of power is not malicious, it is still not *careful*, attentive to the needs of those around me. As we move from merely inattentive to self-serving or even exploitive uses of power, we begin to speak of *oppression*. There are at least five different verbal roots in the Hebrew scriptures used to designate oppression, with over eighty references in all. Withholding wages, unfair dealings, mistreating the weak, failure to sell at a fair price, leveraged buyouts, taking advantage of others through legal means, showing favoritism—all of these and others come under the biblical understanding of oppression. In sum, oppression is an unfair use of power that causes others who are less powerful to suffer in some fashion. Oppression, like inattentive uses of power, need not imply malicious intent to harm. Indeed, oppression may simply be the convenient consequence of an overly complex legal system in which some do not know how (or do not have the money) to defend themselves. Oppressive use of power in the church creates a climate of condemnation, as those who control segments of the community or institution maintain their position through misrepresenting others. The final stage of the misuse of power is *persecution*. Here there is intent to harm. Persecution ranges from the taunting of a

353

weak child in elementary school to systematic genocide. In each case power is aimed at harming others.

Humility and authority. The Christian alternative to the abuse of power is power exercised in humility. Humility sees with the eyes of Christ: it is keenly aware of our own tendencies toward self-justification, of the generous grace of God, and of the best in others. Humility hears with the ears of Christ, surrendering to God in response to his Word and listening to others with openness and vulnerability. Humility speaks with the mouth of Christ, honoring God in honest worship and honoring others by speaking at the right times (and by *not* speaking at the wrong times) and in the right manner. And humility acts with the hands of Christ, reaching out to touch, to give, and to nurture, and not to grasp or to crush. Humility is not weakness. It is strength, power wisely channeled where and how it can be best used. It is power that does not need recognition or position in order to serve. Or it is position and recognition that acts circumspectly, with the other in mind. William Law writes, in his *A Serious Call to a Devout and Holy Life*,

> When you have by such general reflections as these convinced your mind of the reasonableness of humility, you must not content yourself with this as if you was [sic] therefore humble because your mind acknowledges the reasonableness of humility, and declares against pride. But you must immediately enter yourself into the practice of this virtue like a young beginner that has all of it to learn, that can learn but little at a time, and with great difficulty. You must be content to proceed as a learner in it all your time, endeavoring after greater degrees of it and practicing every day acts of humility, as you every day practice acts of devotion.[34]

Power exercised in humility leads to a special kind of authority, and in this authority lies a special kind of power for care. This is especially true at the level of corporate experience. Consider first our model of the stages of human experience. At what stage is "truth"? Wherein do we find authority for our thought and action? From Experience (as the empiricists might say)? Understanding (as the rationalists might argue)? Action (as the pragmatists might affirm)? States of Being Aware (as some intuitivist philosophies might insist)? Does the presumed authority of our knowledge depend on our own frameworks of Integration (as some contemporary theorists might claim)? As we have explored this model, we have discovered that the power of human experience lies not in any single stage but in the cooperative integration of all operations, stages, and relationships. The authority of human experience is found in each part doing what it does best and in each part working together with the other parts properly. This kind of authority of mutuality is found only when Experiencing is humble before Understanding, when Understanding is sensitive to Being Aware, when heart is sensitive to mind, and so on.[35] And when this kind of authority is achieved, there is great confidence and freedom to act. (We call this wisdom.)

Now consider this more specifically at the level of the traditions of the church discussed above. Wherein may we find the wisdom of God? Where is the authority of the church? Is this authority to be found in the Contemplatives, or the Charismatics, or the Evangelicals, or the Social Gospelers? No, the wisdom of God is to be found in the combined gifts of the *whole* church insofar as each part is clearly and honestly surrendering and sharing and giving to each other. As we exercise power in humility—as we learn to embrace rather than exclude—a kind of mutual confidence arising from diversity in harmony is created.[36] Others see this harmony and confidence, won through painful sharing and self-giving, as representing the mutuality of many authorities, and they find in it a powerful authority worthy of deep loyalty. And indeed, against this kind of authority the gates of hell cannot prevail.[37]

Change and Care

The one who offers care—as the gift of one's difference, one's power, offered on behalf of another—walks with another through the changes of life. The one who offers care also intends change in the experience of the one who receives care. Care moves with the other—and *moves* the other—from what is to what may be. It enriches, nurtures, and provides both *through* change and *with* change. When we care, we intend for things to happen: oversight, provision, protection, correction of disorder, healing, reconciliation, and so on. And our caring actions introduce change *to* others (*recipients* and *intermediaries*), as when we plead with an abusive parent, seeking to change his or her mind (and behavior). Yet that caring action is also aimed at introducing a change *for* another (*recipient*), in that our hope is that the life of the abused child will be enriched through our advocacy. Thus, a life of care must come face-to-face with change. The desert fathers and mothers were artists in change, noticing the readiness for change in others and choosing just the right assignment to stimulate transformation. Catherine of Siena pleaded for change within the papal and governmental structures of her day. We are enmeshed in change today. Pastors care for their congregations, helping them through the ambiguities of contemporary church life. Stockholders care for the working conditions of employees, and so they ban together and propose that changes in these conditions be written into company policy. Parents care for their children, walking with them through the transitions from childhood to adulthood. Spiritual directors care for their directees, listening to them through transformation and suggesting changes when appropriate. Physical changes, personal changes, corporate changes—the dynamics of change are a part of nearly every act of care. Awareness of change is especially important as we navigate our way through the transitions of a postmodern culture.

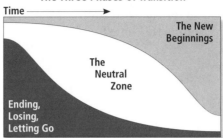

FIGURE 10.4
The Three Phases of Transition

All three phases of transition are present throughout the transition process. There is simply a shift where one phase dominates over the others until the process has ended and the losses and neutral zones remain as memories and the beginning is fully present.

We have mentioned change earlier in our discussion of transformation in chapter 7. We considered the images of heating sugar and of pilgrimage. In transformation, forces are introduced in a context where what was before is changed into something different. There is an ending, an in-between, and a new beginning. Since a life of care contributes to the Godward transformation of others, it will need to face each of these phases of change. Just as Moses led the people of Israel out of Egypt, through the wilderness, and into the promised land, so too we who offer care help others to leave behind what is lost, to navigate through the neutral zone, and to embrace new beginnings.[38]

Leaving behind. Care helps others through the **leaving behind** that is an essential part of change. At times we actually encourage "leaving behind," knowing that it will result in a sense of loss. Moses called God's people out of slavery, and sure enough, soon they were wishing they were back home in Egypt. There is a grief in change, even positive change. The adolescent leaves behind the security of concrete ways of thinking and the stability of a narrow family-oriented framework of values for a much wider world. True, there is excitement in this world, but there is also loss, even if it is not consciously expressed. The stockholders who lobby for new policy must realize that they are introducing loss to those who have followed certain procedures

355

**The following is a poem
of spiritual direction
by Antoinette Voûte Roeder.**[39]

The Witness
  When I witness transformation
  huge change in a moment of time
    a body riddled
    with angles and corners
    and edges so sharp
    they would surely cut;
    a throat so blackened
    a voice pulled tight
    and full of gravel
    (she sits as if
    the chair won't hold her
    hovers just above the seat)
Then
    a story told,
    a wound revealed,
    a breath of air
    (the Spirit passing)
    and eyes darken,
    the body sinks
    into the chair,
    edges soften,
    the voice clears,
    and all the angles melt into curves
  . . . when I am witness
  to transformation,
  words can't hold
  my gratitude.

for the company's life thus far—and some will certainly interpret this change as loss, rather than profit. The stockholders must be prepared for the resistance that comes from fear of loss. And the pastor who leads a congregation through the ambiguities of postmodernity must help the congregation to let go of the good old days when everybody knew what church was all about. A life of care gives compassion: sharing the grief, accepting reaction. It gives information: letting others know (insofar as you yourself know) just what will and will not change. And it gives respect, not dismissing, not

condemning what was for the sake of what is to come, but helping others integrate the past into their present and future.

The neutral zone. As we leave the past behind, we begin to enter a **neutral zone** where, "It's like being between trapezes. It's Linus when his blanket is in the dryer. There's nothing to hold on to."[40] It is symbolized in the Exodus story as the wilderness. The wilderness is both a very difficult and a very creative place. It is a difficult place. The teenager cries out, "I don't know who I am!" People looking to us for spiritual guidance speak of dryness or darkness, where familiar ways of relating to God do not work any longer. A congregation that knew itself in the era of few denominations now finds itself lost in a sea of home churches, megachurches, and emerging churches. Some will be confused and want to just go back to the way it was before. Others will want to rush ahead. Difficult indeed.

Yet the neutral zone is also a creative place. When you have set aside what was for a moment—and you are not quite sure of what will be—there is the freedom to try on a few new ideas. For the teenager, it may be literally a season of trying things on. One month it is a shaved head and black trench coat. Six months later it is long hair and handmade clothes. How else do you find out who you are? The corporation agrees to explore options for working conditions for its employees. Possibilities abound. The ministry of care honors the neutral zone, both its difficulties and its room for creativity. A *careful* use of change knows how to let time have its own way. A *careful* use of change learns to encourage enough experimentation to facilitate authentic discovery, yet not so much to disorient. A *careful* use of change gives space (and structure) to support the ambiguities of the neutral zone. A *careful* use of change loves the person or community *through* the darkness rather than by superficially trying to eliminate it.

New beginnings. Change ends with **new beginnings**: destination, the land of milk and honey, Camelot. A new beginning starts even as one begins to let go of the past. (It could never be otherwise.) In a healthy transition, it simply grows into place. The congregation gradually finds a new sense of purpose, one not necessarily opposed to the old, but a new one nonetheless. It pictures itself differently. Habits begin to change. After a time of experimentation, the corporation decides that there *is* a way that it can maintain a reasonable profit and improve working conditions, and both management and labor begin to settle into the new ways of life at work. The adolescent becomes an adult. And the person coming for spiritual direction watches the darkness of midnight gradually turn to day. Care paints the picture of the new beginning from the start of transition. Like Moses, we speak of the promise of God, of milk and honey, from the start. We walk people through change—and we introduce change—by giving them a sense (to the best of our knowledge) of what the other side is like. Yet at the same time, care does not force the new beginning but rather lets that beginning become what it will in the context of the person or community at hand. We may *think* it will look like *x*, but we may be surprised at the end that it looks like *y*. Our caring actions are directed at some element of another's experience (perhaps I want to comfort a depressed woman through giving time, listening, and a sincere smile), yet the *reception* of our acts may effect changes in other parts of another's experience (hence, I discover that my acts not only affected her mood but also stimulated an entire change of worldview). Finally, care celebrates the new beginning with those who begin, honoring the successful passage of transition.

The life of care travels through change with others. At times it introduces change to others, for their own sake. To care is to offer what we have—time, money, feelings, ideas, actions, difference, power—in the midst of others' changes so they might experience the change of an enriched life. Sometimes we offer the changes of tearing down; other times, the changes of build-ing up. We do this out of love, with an eye to timing, strategy, nuance. We minister change in tenderness, offering the right dose at the right time and place. We do so in cooperation with the transforming power of the Spirit of God.

The Ways of Christian Care

Just as there are ways and forms of the life of prayer, so there are also skills, means, attitudes and actions—a process—through which the life of care is experienced and expressed. And, like prayer, care cannot be reduced to an artificial formula. Care grows organically out of relationship with God and with others. It is a matter both of what we do and of how we do it. It is also a matter of who we are, modeling an authentic life to and for others. Thus, just as we can learn about prayer by attending to the ways in which we structure our self-communication with God, so we can also learn about Christian care by taking a look at how we structure our self-giving to others. We can summarize how care is expressed in four elements or steps: Care is prayerful. It grows out of sincere interest. It serves the needs of others. And it is often expressed in some form of structure.

Prayer

A life of Christian care both flowers from and produces the fruit of a life of Christian prayer. They feed on each other. The grace of God is active in spiritual formation, providing wisdom concerning what to address, guidance concerning how to address it, empowerment to see formation through, and the fruit of a changed life; so too, through prayer, by God's grace, we are both led into and led through care for others.

Consider as an example the life of John Woolman. Woolman was a Quaker leader. He lived in New Jersey and traveled throughout the American colonies, visiting Friends (fellow Quakers), sharing his concern both for slaves and for those who held them. Douglas Steere writes of

Historical Portrait: Beyond the Clinical Gaze

The Crisis of Care, edited by Susan S. Phillips and Patricia Benner, contains a number of narratives of faithful caregiving in various professions. In his essay "Beyond the Clinical Gaze," physician W. Thomas Boyce communicates the need for a depth of loving attention toward those for whom we care. He writes of the medical field that, "in our headlong efforts to bring into focus finer and more discriminating views of the lesions lying *beneath* the disease, we will have missed the opportunity to envision the person that lies *beyond* the disease." To illustrate this point, Boyce tells the story of an unsung hero of care.

A little more than a year ago during my month serving as the attending physician on the pediatrics ward of the University of California, San Francisco, I ran across a dying boy who, together with his mother, reminded me, as I often am reminded, of the troubled, myopic vision so characteristic of the medicine I have learned and practice. He was a relatively young boy (I will call him Blake), no more than seven years of age and afflicted with a terminal, disfiguring version of muculipidosis. . . . Over the years of Blake's short life, his disease had severely deformed and retarded him. His eyes were clouded and protruded from his face as did his tongue, like the overstuffed contents of a pastry shell too small to contain it. The gums surrounding his peg-like teeth were similarly engorged and frequently bled when disturbed. His massively swollen heart was failing, and he perennially threatened to drown in the secretions that flooded his airway. His chest and belly, glutted with a liver and spleen many times their normal sizes, had together become a single, reddened, congested globe from which four largely useless limbs projected. He was, in short, a small, grotesque tomato-of-a-boy whose appearance turned away even the most forgiving eyes.

Blake also was not overly grateful for the abundant, cutting edge medical care being provided for him. I think he somehow sensed that he was nearing the end of his time, and he had decided that the sticks and pokes and serial examinations did almost nothing to allay the other torments that his disease have long prolonged. So, the approach of doctors, nurses, technicians, and all the other assorted hospital personnel was greeted abruptly with a raspy incoherent grunt and a flailing motion of his arm that meant indisputably, "Get out of my face!" My own ability to humanly care for Blake also was compromised by the physical sight of him and by his stolid indifference or antagonism to my best efforts on his behalf.

One July evening, held in the hospital late by a series of unanticipated events, I approached Blake's room at an unaccustomed hour. His young, single mom, who was at her own place of work for the daylight hours of most days, was sitting on the edge of the bed, deeply immersed in conversation with Blake. I paused, and then settled at the door, transfixed by the scene before me in the darkened hospital room. Blake's mom was talking to him. In hushed and comforting tones she spoke of the day, wondering how things had gone, asking him about his new nurse, reviewing for him the events of her own day at work. As she spoke, leaning over her son, her hand stroked his forehead and hair in a mundane gesture that filled the room with her love for the boy.

Blake's eyes, moist and utterly devoid of his stern resistance, looked up into his mother's face, absorbing every moment, every piece of her presence there with him. Relaxed and more peaceful than I had ever seen him, Blake seemed to melt into his mother's eyes. She stroked his round swollen face and said to him, "Oh, my beautiful, little boy."

Suddenly I understood what I had not understood: When this mother gazed at her bloated, dying son, she *physically saw* a person I had never seen. Transformed by her eyes' willingness to see the child *beyond* the disease, Blake had become a different being, an individual no longer diseased and distorted, but a frightened child visibly changed by his mother's love.[41]

Woolman that "by the time of his early death in 1772 his faithfulness to his concern and the widespread support of those who associated themselves with him had opened the Quakers of colonial America to a new dimension of their responsibility to their black brothers and had all but cleared Quaker membership of the holding of slaves."[42] Woolman learned early the habit of waiting in silence in gatherings, hesitating to contribute to the meeting until the Spirit's leading was confirmed within him. He writes in his journal, "My understanding became more strengthened to distinguish the language of the pure Spirit which inwardly moves upon the heart and taught [me] to wait in silence sometimes many weeks together, until I felt that rise which prepares the creature to stand like a trumpet through which the Lord speaks to his flock."[43]

It is in the context of learning obedience to the Spirit that Woolman writes of his first encounter with the issue of slavery. His employer asked him to write a bill of sale for a slave. Woolman writes, "Through weakness I gave way and wrote it, but at executing it, I was so afflicted in my mind that I said before my master and the Friend who purchased the woman that I believed slavery to be a practice inconsistent with the Christian religion."[44] Care begins with sharing the heart of God for another, in this case the slave. Woolman's concern for those enslaved increased. He studied their condition. He waited in prayer. He spoke with others. In his essay, "On the Slave Trade," he writes, "The Lord in the Riches of his Goodness, is leading some unto the Feeling of the Condition of this People, who cannot rest without labouring as their Advocates; of which in some Measure I have had Experience: for, in the Movings of his Love in my Heart, these poor Sufferers have been brought near to me."[45]

And so Woolman began to express his care by means of advocacy throughout the Society of Friends (Quakers). Prayer not only guided Woolman into expressions of care, but also served to purify those expressions of care. The ministry of advocacy brings us face-to-face with our attitudes toward both those for whom we advocate and those at whom our advocacy is directed. Woolman observed of his visits with slave owners, "I often saw the necessity of keeping down to the root of where our concern proceeded, allowing the Lord to beget a spirit of sympathy and tenderness in me toward some who were grievously in the spirit of this world."[46] And again, "I have had renewed evidences that to be faithful to the Lord and content with his will is a most necessary and useful lesson for me to be learning, looking less at the effects of my labour than at the pure motion and reality of the concern as it arises from heavenly love."[47] Furthermore, a spirit of prayerful reflection informs the development of Woolman's conviction that what lay behind the evils of slavery was greed: "When our eyes are so single as to discern the selfish spirit clearly, we behold it the greatest of all tyrants."[48] Prayer guides not only the *what* of our care, but also the *how*, birthing in us the spirit appropriate to the situation and giving us insight concerning the nature of the situation itself.

Prayer also empowers us to persevere in care. For example, Woolman speaks of desires being "renewed in me" to be "inwardly acquainted with the hardships and difficulties of my fellow creatures and to labour in his love for the spreading of pure universal righteousness on earth."[49] Prayer also releases the power of God through intercession. Though he does not write specifically about his intercession for the slaves, one cannot imagine but that prayer was a part of Woolman's life of care in pleading to God on behalf of the slaves, bringing the power of God to bear on those for whom God's concern had been communicated to him. And in the end, the fruit of change is itself seen as grace—God's efforts working with our efforts to produce an expression of care beyond that which can be communicated by humans.

A life of care is a continual response to the initiation of God, who, in his own care for others, invites us to participate in his *care*ful oversight of creation. In turn, as we reach out in care for others, we are drawn into the heart of God and into communication with God. In so doing, we are led deeper and deeper into the life of care and prayer.

Interest

We learned about interest in our chapter on relationship, exploring how a sense of being drawn to the other shapes the formation and the quality of a relationship. Interest plays an important part in Christian care. Duty obliges acts of care out of conformity with a given rule or standard. Yet full-bodied Christian care moves beyond duty into expressing care from loving *interest*, from a genuine attraction to the other. The farming family lives on their land for years, and over the years they grow to love the land. They know the woodlots and the fields, how much water each section will need, how much harvest each will yield, what kind of care the land needs. The *care*ful farmer does not simply *use* the land but rather *takes care of* the land, attentive to generations of nourishment and development that give life to the earth. Likewise a pastor falls in love with a congregation—listening,

sharing, participating, relating—learning to feel excitement for those things that excite the others in the congregation. Similarly, counselors speak of the need for empathy, a genuine interest for and co-feeling with the one who comes to them for help.

Interest—born of natural attraction, of divine impulse, or simply of spending time together—shapes our openness to Experience. Just as the first-time parents of a newborn child are fascinated with and attentive to aspects of life previously ignored (for example, burping and bowel movements), interest in any relationship stimulates an attention to and a consciousness of hitherto unnoticed aspects of life. Interest makes us open to see again, from another point of view. And in this re-seeing, care is born and nurtured.

Service

As prayer and interest combine, we begin to see the needs of another from another's, and from God's, point of view. At this point, the natural impulse is simply to serve. We become aware of the particular and concrete "lostness" of our neighbor who is without knowledge of God, and we simply begin to share our own knowledge of God, not out of the duty to evangelize, but rather out of sincere interest in and love for that neighbor. We see the multitudes who have lost their homes in disaster and we are compelled to provide homes, not because we should do something, but because we care. We see a community losing its sense of itself, and we recover the memories and history of the community as an expression of care. And so we invest ourselves in the lives of others, simply meeting needs. This is the heart of Jesus, who went about doing good—feeding the hungry, healing the sick, freeing those oppressed by demons, sharing the good news. Serving was the heart of Saint Francis of Assisi, who was compelled to care for the lepers. Serving was the heart of Saint Dominic (1174–1221), who at the same time as Francis was compelled out of compassion to preach the gospel to those who had been led from orthodoxy into falsehood. Serving was the heart of Seraphim of Sarov who, after a time of withdrawal, received thousands of visitors who came to him for advice. We let the needs lead us, offering from ourselves what is needed. We till soil, listen to stories, build buildings, share memories, and perform operations simply in the act of meeting needs.

One must be careful these days, however, in encouraging service. The term *service* has been used (and abused) by systems and structures (even religious structures) that exercise power for the sake of self-preservation to the neglect of people's needs. Biblical scholar Joel Green writes of "a recognition that 'serving' today, and with it 'caring,' has become in many circles yet one more weapon in the arsenal of the control-oriented paradigm."[50] Green suggests that an appropriate understanding of service comes through a clear understanding of the biblical themes of our creation in the image of God, of the redemption of Israel as an invitation to become a new community of care, and of the Incarnation as a "judgment on those attitudes, those communities, those systems that support human reluctance to embrace caring service, which instead honor stories of escape from positions of giving service to positions of being served."[51] A life of Christian care is a life that goes to the other (Luke 10:34), that washes the feet of the other (John 13), that gives of itself to the other, simply serving.

Structure

Nevertheless, in time, the impulse of simply serving turns into a strategy, a plan, a structure. A program of care is born. Mother Theresa visits person after person dying on the streets of Calcutta, and she conceives a vision for a home for the dying. Pastor Bill Hybels is confronted with many people who have serious difficulties relating to traditional church structures, and he develops the seeker-sensitive model of church life. Members of Christian churches are burdened by the plight of many who are without food throughout the world, and together they design a political action network to support legislation that promotes fair and compassionate distribution of food to the hungry. Even the simple decision to *regularly* bring soup to a sick friend becomes a structured vehicle of care. Though structure is not always necessary, often when prayer, interest, and service coalesce in a certain direction, care becomes expressed through formal structures.

At this point the actions of following, sharing, and serving require further actions of leading, guiding, and directing. And with the creation of structure there is also the creation of mechanisms of power to facilitate and maintain the structure. Herein lies the strength of a structure of care: as a structured system of care, it can accomplish things that the spontaneous meeting of needs cannot. Yet conversely, therein lies the weakness of structures of care as well. The mechanisms of the structure can, if not wisely governed, undermine the very expressions of care intended. Those receiving care become mere patients, cases, or members, acknowledged merely for their place in the system rather than loved as people. In such times we encounter a "crisis of care."[52] A caring congregation is one where the programs serve the people and not the reverse. Structures that return frequently to the foundations of prayer, sincere interest, and serving allow the Spirit to give Christian care the mark of its special character. Through the coordination of heartfelt prayer, sincere interest, humble service, and creative structure, the community of God begins to embody the kind of covenant-partner reign for which we were designed.

A Life of Care

We are called into a *relationship* with a Triune God who is living Care: the Father who is Source and Provider, the Son who is Model, Savior, and Redeemer, the Spirit who is Sanctifier and Restorer of life. To be

Navigating Politics Today: Can a Spirituality of Care Help?

In previous generations we debated the question of whether the Christian community should focus its energies on evangelism or on political and social concerns. It appears that, for the most part, this debate has been settled. Many who fought on the side of evangelism are now raising funds for mission ventures *and* campaign politics. Some of those who argued for social concerns now see the church not simply as transformer of culture, but as witness to Jesus's gospel through liturgy and community life. And yet political issues confront Christians around the globe such that they are difficult to ignore.

The question that faces us today is *how*. How are we to navigate as Christians in the face of current political situations? Some propose an aggressive approach, citing the need for believers in political leadership or for policies that reflect Christian values. Others are cautious, suggesting that perhaps the best contribution the church can offer society is not support for social programs but the life of the church itself. The question of navigation is not a simple one; it touches our assessment of biblical values, our interpretation of history, our theology of salvation and the church, our sense of culture, and more. But if politics is about our relationships with others, and if a spirituality of care is about *how* we navigate our relationships with others, perhaps a spirituality of care may offer wisdom as we navigate ourselves through contemporary politics. What might we learn when we look at a spirituality of care?

By looking at the *character* of care we find that care—care for a wide range of relationships—is embedded in our very mandate as human beings. We are called to be covenant partners with God, to share in caring for this earth. As we live in relationship with others, so we are responsible (response-able) to live toward these others (nature, neighbors, systems and structures, and so on) in a *careful* manner. Political action is not about a utopian hope for a better society or about the need to make our viewpoint the controlling ideology. Perhaps it might help to look at the activities of politics as means of exercising care for those around whom we may have some influence.

By looking at the *contexts* of care we recognize the diversity with which authentic care is expressed. Politics are not the domain of the organizer-activist alone. The hermit has a unique contribution to offer the politics of the day. Local congregations, small informal communities, and faith-based associations all have something to offer the polis. Some may have a special concern for (and understanding of) single mothers. Others offer an understanding of the local ecosystem. Perhaps political wisdom (as opposed to political rhetoric) lies not in the dominance of one contextual representative over another, but rather in the faithful hearing of the whole through the whole for the sake of the whole, as best we can.

By looking at the *dynamics* of care we face our gifts and our limits. What we offer society is our difference. As a community of believers, for example, this means that we display our Trinitarian difference: we radically embody life together (polis). We embrace the marginalized; we reconcile our mutual hatreds. We explore the harmony of self, land, community, Spirit. We also, as individuals and communities, offer our own thoughts, feelings, time, possessions, and such. But, since the offer of care necessarily involves us in the dynamics of power, we acknowledge that there will be tensions, issues of control. A spirituality of care encourages us toward a bold humility of self-giving, knowing that as care is expressed both through change and by means of change, the problems of the past will, in time (perhaps in eschatological time), make way to a new beginning.

Finally, by looking at the *ways* of care, we discover a strategy for political action. Perhaps *careful* political action begins not in anger or guilt but in prayer and interest. This is part of the "insertion phase" of the Experience Cycle used by many spiritual directors to sensitize people to the societal dimensions of relationship with God.[53] Here we "insert" ourselves into a political structure or people group, seeking to find a heart of care. As interest begins to lead to

service, we find ourselves moving to the "social analysis" phase, wherein we investigate the way things are. This in turn leads to the "theological [and prayerful] reflection" phase of the cycle, wherein we discern the presence or concerns of God, either regarding this structure or group or regarding our relationship to this structure or group. Finally, as service leads to structure, we find ourselves in the "pastoral action" phase of the cycle, exploring concretely how care may be expressed in this situation at this time.

How do we navigate ourselves politically as Christians? We do so from a commitment to care: for nature, for others, for the world within which we live.

called into relationship with God is to be called into a life of care. Lived Christian spirituality takes us into a sphere wherein love for God and love for neighbor mutually support each other, bringing us into ever-increasing conformity with the character of the caring God. We have learned that Christian spirituality is a relationship lived out in response to God's invitation. As God invites, we follow him into a life of care. And we too initiate through prayer on behalf of those for whom we care.

We have also learned that relationship with God is a *transforming relationship*. As such we see, once again, that maturity in Christ is not simply about stages of prayer experience (although it may include this); maturity also implicates us in the transformation of our thoughts, feelings, actions, habits, relationships, and the like such that our lives embody in ever-increasing measure the kind of nurture for self, others, and nature that is characteristic of God himself. Transformation is transformation into care.

And we have learned that relationship with God involves not only transformation, but also intentional *spiritual formation*. We

press forward toward maturity, toward perfection, toward kingdom, toward the next step. We choose means within contexts to grow into that toward which God's Spirit invites. As we have mentioned above, such is the way of the life of care. We are led to those areas of care where our context, freedom, responsibilities, and calling point. We are guided by God into interest, into service, and into structure. We are refined through spiritual formation in the midst of care, finding again and again the need to repent of our own agendas and judgments so that we might care as Christ cares. Through Christ we are enabled to persevere in the life of care, for care can become full of trials and heaviness over time. We are led from depth into depth as we share increasingly the heart of God and the heart of others. To bring the body of Christ into an authentic expression of care is indeed a reorientation and rehabituation of life.

A variety of factors influence the effects of care. There may be unique features of the relationship between the *intermediary*, the self toward which my caring action is directed, and the *recipient*, the self on behalf of whom I am offering the caring ac-

Figure 10.5
The Christian Care Matrix

"Self" Giving Care	Dimension of Experience of "Self" Offered (difference)	"Self" Receiving Action (recipient)	Ways of Care (vehicle of offering gift)	Change Intended	"Self" Receiving Care (intermediary)
Whose power is offered?	Where is power located?	Where is power directed?	How is power exercised?	What is power trying to do?	On behalf of whom is power exercised?

• The earth itself
• Individual
• Family
• Small group
• Association
• Work community
• Sodality
• Modality
• Polis
  local
  provincial
  national
  global
• Spiritual realities
• God
	• Body
	• "Soul"
	• Time
	• Energy/intention
	• Thought
	• Feeling
	• Stages of experience
	• Web of relationships
	• Presence
	• Influence
	• Possessions
	• Change
	• Depths
		• The earth itself
		• Individual
		• Family
		• Small group
		• Association
		• Work community
		• Sodality
		• Modality
		• Polis
		  local
		  provincial
		  national
		  global
		• Spiritual realities
		• God
			• Life modeling
			• Prayer, meditation
			• Listening, attending
			• Sharing, participating
			• Communicating, relating
			• Following, serving
			• Giving, providing
			• Physical transformations (e.g., plant, build, surgery)
			• Leading, guiding, directing
			• Instructing, education
			• Proclamation, command
			• Advocacy (speak, write, act)
			• Public witness, protest
			• Participation/non-participation (e.g., through economic choices)
			• Political engagement (e.g., vote, lobby, petition, run for office)
			• Persevering in involvement
			• Withholding any of the above
				• Oversight
				• Provision, nurture
				• Protection
				• Direction, redirection
				• Ordering, correction of disorder
				• Strengthening, edifying
				• Healing, repairing, restoring
				• Connect, reconciling
				• Awakening, renewal, freshness
				• Freeing up
					• The earth itself
					• Individual
					• Family
					• Small group
					• Association
					• Work community
					• Sodality
					• Modality
					• Polis
					  local
					  provincial
					  national
					  global
					• Spiritual realities
					• God

Questions on Understanding the "Self" (giving care, receiving action, receiving care)	Factors Influencing Effect of Care	
• Self-disclosure • Symbolic expression • Communication • Comparison and imitation • Common and sharing note governing structure • Identity and roles • Corporate self/corporate identity • Community and culture	• Relationship of recipient and intermediary • Dynamics within giver (misunderstanding, unconscious) • Relationship between means and message/effect • Unforeseen events	• Changes are intended at both recipient and intermediary • When directed at "enemies" changes work reverse (e.g., tearing down rather than building)

tion. (For example, I may be unaware that a business owner has a vested interest in the unfair treatment of a worker.) There may be dynamics involving the *caregiver* (for instance, an association's effort to offer care by making a collection of food for the local needy may fail because of disorganization) or dynamics within the recipient or intermediary of care (say, relief sent to a foreign country may not get to those in need due to government corruption). Unforeseen happenings (like an electrical failure in the amplification equipment in an evangelistic event, or a financial crisis in the country exposing a deep spiritual hunger) may affect how an expression of care is re-

ceived. And then there is the relationship between the medium and the message of care. At times, mass-market expressions of care communicate not the sincere interest in others, but rather, *by the simple form of the communication*, that the other is merely another customer to be solicited.

Christian spirituality as lived relationship is both a life of prayer and a life of care. Through the life of prayer, we are invited into the very heart of God, free to share ourselves in openness with a God who cares. Through the life of care, we are invited to share the very life of God, a life of self-giving, creative nurture over self, others, and the very creation itself.

Practicing Christian Spirituality

A Six-Month Experiment in Christian Care

This assignment will not take you a half an hour or even a week. Finding our way into a life of care takes time, and this experiment will take you six full months. Be encouraged, however, for as you follow the leadings of the Spirit and try out your active sensitivity to others, you will reap rich rewards.

Determine the Recipient

First, choose who you will care for—the recipient (or recipients) of your care. This is done by evaluating a number of factors. Consider your *contexts*. Where do you live? What kinds of relationships are significant to you? What relationships are peripheral? Why? Look at your own contexts to get the range of possibilities for this experiment. Next, consider your *freedom*. Whom would you *like* to care for? When you were looking over your contexts, which "selves" struck your fancy? Take note, for in this experiment the self you care for can be anything from your garden, to a friend (or an enemy), to your nation. What might be a really creative exploration, a way of doing it that would really be *you*? But don't forget your *responsibilities*. Think about your place—on earth and in family, church, village, nation. What has God made clear to you regarding these areas of *your* life? Where do your own primary responsibilities lie at this time? What *must* be done? Finally, consider your sense of *calling*. Do you sense that God has been taking you in a certain direction? When you are at your best, to what are you inclined? Do those you respect agree with your assessment? After reviewing all these factors, make a choice and a commitment. For the next six months *this* will be the self you will care for.

Month One: Prayer and Interest

Once you have chosen the recipient of your care, you begin the first stage of the experiment of care: the cultivation of prayer and interest. Set a time to pray regularly with the other in mind. This is not simply a time of intercessory prayer, though it certainly can include that. Your aim is to begin to share God's heart for the other. Place the other before your mind during prayer. Think about his (or her) situation; let your mind wander. Perhaps you want to study his condition a bit, just as Woolman investigated the condition of the slaves. Invest prayerfully in his life. (Yes, you can do this on behalf of your garden. Farmers have been doing this for ages.) Cultivate an interest in the other. Spend time with the other. Hang out, participate, share, relate at whatever level simply gets you into the door of his life and facilitates your "falling in love" with the other. Keep a journal, and over the month record what you are seeing, what you are aware of that you might not have been aware of before.

Months Two and Three: Service

By now you have probably gotten a sense of some of the needs of the other. Perhaps you want to make a list of those needs. What changes might be in order for the other—encouragement, protection, redirection, strengthening, healing? And in what dimensions of her (or his) experience are these needed? Now look over that list and ask yourself, Which of these needs could *I* meet? How might *you* be able to serve the other? Is there some special gift you might have to offer the other? Begin to explore these questions in action. You need not settle on one need or one way of meeting her needs just yet. Just continue hanging out, growing in interest, and meeting needs in a free and open way. Record in your journal what you notice about yourself, about the other, about your relationship. What are you learning about a life of care?

Months Four and Five: Structure

Perhaps, by month four, you are ready to experiment with a particular expression of care, a regular commitment of some sort. Realistically determine what this expression of care will cost (time, money, energy, emotion, and so on). Adjust your schedule and margins to make room for this expression of care. Consider what kinds of activity it will involve. Will you need tools for physical transformations? Will you need skills in interpersonal relationships? Will you need connections for community development? Now is the time for prayerful, creative strategy. Acquire what you need and then begin to explore your new expression of care. Keep notes in your journal to give you guidance as the caring relationship matures.

Month Six: Review and Revise

After a brief time of exploring your experiment you will need to review. First review your own motives and attitudes. What is this all about to you? What factors have come to play on the inside as you pursue this expression of care? What have you heard from God as you have dwelt with the other in the context of the service and structure stages? Review your understanding of the others (the recipients and the intermediaries) of your experiment. Perhaps you want to review this in the context of a conversation with a mentor. Are there adjustments that need to be made in light of new information that you have gained over the months? Perhaps you need to revise your strategy of care. Get creative once again, and make necessary adjustments. Then go back to care and enjoy the final month within your revised version of this expression of care. When it is all over, summarize your experiment, for yourself and perhaps for another. What have you learned from this experiment of the other? of yourself? of the life of care?

CHAPTER SUMMARY

1. Human beings were created to care. Through care, we reflect the character of the Trinitarian God, and through care we express the compassionate dominion we were designed to embody. Just as the love of God expands outward from the members of the Trinity to encompass the earth, so also we naturally extend ourselves in concern for others.

2. Care is the intentional, loving, giving of ourselves for the enrichment of another. It involves a *caregiver*, who is the offerer of the gift of some dimension of the self's experience; a *recipient*, who is the "self" for whom or on behalf of whom the care is offered; and at times, an *intermediary*, who is a "self" toward which the caring act is offered on behalf of another. The caregiver offers care by performing *acts* toward the recipient or the intermediary. We may offer care on behalf of a single recipient through actions given to a number of intermediaries.

3. The elements of care exist within a variety of *contexts* within which care is expressed. The contexts of a life of care are present to us in a variety of forms. A fundamental context of human life is the earth itself, wherein we have our very being as physical persons. For most of us, family is the earliest-known context. It is the context where often the most private aspects of life are shared and where others experience us in the greatest need. Communities of various sorts also serve

as contexts of a life of care. Christian communities come in two primary varieties: *modalities*, which admit people of all ages, commitment levels, and such; and *sodalities*, which expect extra levels of commitment and are usually restricted in membership in other ways. Associations are communities that organize for a special purpose, and small groups gather to provide mutual or expressive care. Frequently these can have an explicitly Christian identity. The workplace and the polis, however, are usually mixed, bringing believers and unbelievers together to support a common geography, policy, or economy. Finally, one-on-one relationships and even a life of intentional solitude can provide contexts for a life of care. Settling oneself into a configuration of the contexts of care is often seen as the expression of a form of spirituality: contemplative, communal, or apostolic. A clear understanding of the character of the different contexts of the life of care gives acts of care a greater likelihood of effectiveness.

4. A life of care is expressed in the midst of a variety of dynamics that characterize the unique relationships involved. In addition to the dynamics unique to each of the specific contexts involved in a given act of care, three dynamics characteristic of care in general are worthy of note. First, care is the offer of an element of *difference*. An element of human experience not present in the recipient is provided by the caregiver. The Pauline understanding of spiritual gifts recognizes this dynamic wherein one offers what is unique for the enrichment of others, who in turn may possess different gifts to offer. Likewise, the history of the traditions of the Christian church reveals that various traditions have a tendency to contribute different gifts to the body of Christ at large. Sensitivity to these differences can help us to know how to offer quality care.

5. A second dynamic is that of power. In offering what is missing from another (be it knowledge, encouragement, money, physical transformations, or the like) we hold power with relation to the other. This power can be used for care with wonderful results, or it can be abused, preventing care even though it may be (mis)used in the name of care. In the history of Christian spirituality, humility is the virtue that moderates and directs our use of power such that it serves the other best. Through the humility of allowing the various aspects of human experience to inform each other, and through the humility of allowing the various traditions of the Christian church to inform each other, we come into an ever-fuller experience of God's fullness.

6. The third dynamic of a life of care is change. Care walks through change with people and introduces change for the sake of others. Changes are intended for both recipients and intermediaries. Our caring acts may provoke unforeseen changes, due to a number of circumstances. The "selves" of a life of care experience change in a threefold pattern, the knowledge of which enables us to provide care appropriate to the other. The first phase of change is "leaving behind," where we are especially conscious of what *was* prior to change. The second phase is "in between," wherein we are at a loss to identify ourselves and wherein a great deal of creativity is possible. The final stage of change is the "new beginning" that introduces us to what *is to come*.

7. The life of care is lived out in a process, and hence we can identify the *ways* of care. These can be summarized under four headings. First, care grows out of and leads into *prayer*. Prayer inspires the choice of care, guides the direction of care, empowers the perseverance in care, and, through grace, supplies the fruit of care. The second element is that of *interest*. Care takes loving interest in another, is drawn to the other, pays special attention to the details of the life of the other. Interest helps care to discover the other anew, to see the other from a fresh perspective. The third element is *service*, the simple act of meeting the needs of the other, without regard to plan or position. And the final element is *structure*, where prayer, interest, and service are directed to specific and programmed patterns of action on behalf of another.

Questions

1. While there are many books written about the life of prayer, there are few books written directly about the life of care. Why do you think this is? Do you think that a life of care is an appropriate theme of Christian spirituality? Is there an adequate foundation for the life of care as an integral part of Christian spirituality? How might it be framed differently?

2. The exploration of a spirituality of care within particular contexts of life might prove delightful. What might family spirituality as both prayer and care look like? How about creating a theology of volunteer associations? Or what would it look like to explore further how intentional solitude can be lived as an expression of care? What about the care of your own "self," or care of God? (Mother Theresa saw herself as caring for Christ in the poor.) Dig deeper. The possibilities are endless.

3. Consider your own local congregation or a group you are acquainted with. Characterize its spirituality and identity. Is it contemplative, communal, or apostolic? Is it a modality or a sodality? Does it emphasize evangelism or social concern? Now reflect and ask yourself how its style of spirituality affects its ability to give or to receive care. How might knowing the patterns of its spirituality affect your own relationship with this group? What do you have to offer? How might your offering be received?

4. We have, in this chapter, only discussed three primary dynamics of a life of care. Are there others that could be discussed? How might you analyze the dynamics of care? Play with it. Try to take into account a variety of factors that simultaneously affect your caring actions.

5. Examine an expression of Christian care close to you, one that you admire. What part has prayer played in this expression of care? How have prayer and care intersected? Has the element of interest been present? Does this care express service? Has there been a dimension of structure present? How have these combined (or not) uniquely within this expression of care? Are there other elements that could be mentioned?

LOOKING FURTHER

As we learned in our Questions, while there are many books written about the life of prayer, there are few books written directly about the life of care. We must simply read works that discuss spirituality within various contexts or works (which are not necessarily Christian) and explore the dynamics of care.

Sample Works from Different Contexts

The following list comprises works from different contexts and various perspectives: A. M. Allchin, ed., *Solitude and Communion: Papers on the Hermit Life Given at St. David's, Wales, in the Autumn of 1975* (Fairacres, UK: SLG Press, 1977); Wendell Berry, *The Art of the Commonplace: The Agrarian Essays of Wendell Berry*, ed. Norman Wirzba (Washington, DC: Shoemaker and Hoard, 2002); Ernst Boyer Jr., *Finding God at Home: Family Life as Spiritual Discipline* (San Francisco: Harper and Row, 1988); Margaret Guenther, *Holy Listening: The Art of Spiritual Direction* (Cambridge, MA: Cowley, 1992); Parker Palmer, *The Active Life: A Spirituality of Work, Creativity, and Caring* (San Francisco: Jossey-Bass, 1990); Susan S. Phillips and Patricia Benner, eds., *The Crisis of Care: Affirming and Restoring Caring Practices in the Helping Professions* (Washington, DC: Georgetown University Press, 1994); James Bryan Smith and Linda Graybeal, *A Spiritual Formation Workbook: Small-Group Resources for Nurturing Spiritual Growth* (San Francisco: HarperSanFrancisco, 1999); Jean Vanier, *Community and Growth* (New York: Paulist Press, 1982); John Woolman, *The Journal of John Woolman*, in *Quaker Spirituality*, ed. Douglas V. Steere, Classics of Western Spirituality (New York: Paulist Press, 1984), 159–237; and Robert Wuthnow, *Saving America? Faith Based Services and the Future of Civil Society* (Princeton: Princeton University Press, 2004).

A Few Works Related to the Dynamics of Care

These books more specifically address the dynamics of care: William Bridges, *Managing Transitions: Making the Most of Change* (Cambridge, MA: Da Capo, 2003); Richard Foster, *Streams of Living Water: Celebrating the Great Traditions of Christian Faith* (San Francisco: HarperSanFrancisco, 1998); and Miroslav Volf, *Exclusion and Embrace: A Theological Exploration of Identity, Otherness, and Reconciliation* (Nashville: Abingdon, 1996).

Christian Discernment

11

OBJECTIVES

In this chapter you will learn about the wisdom of Christian discernment, about how to tell what is from God and what is not. You will learn that discernment is grounded in our God, who desires to be known and followed. You will see how discernment flows from preparation: the preparation of the community or individual who is discerning, and practical preparations related to particular discernment situations. You will explore the process of discernment—from preparation to attention, to evaluation, to decision and action—learning skills at each step of the way. Finally, you will discover how discernment is ultimately expressed in confident action, leading to the transformation of ourselves and our world.

After reading this chapter you should be able to

- define Christian discernment;
- give examples of a number of different types of discernment from the history of the Christian church and from your own experience;
- situate a theology of discernment within the major themes of Christian theology;
- assist either an individual or a group through the various stages of the discerning process, with the hope of guiding them from a place of "not knowing" to a place of confidently taking the next step forward with regard to whatever discerning issue was confronting them;
- recognize the strengths and weaknesses of different "discerners," identifying how cultivation of the virtues of discernment (or lack thereof) might affect the discernment process;
- list key criteria of discernment appropriate to the different kinds of discerning situations you may encounter;
- describe three "times" for making an "election," or discerning choice, giving examples of each.

What Is Christian Discernment?

Let us begin by imagining a few case studies of discernment. While these are not "true stories," each of them presents an example of what discernment may look like for different individuals or communities.

Chris is unsure about the next step of life. Four years of college are almost over and all went well: a major in sociology and a minor in religious studies. A logical next step would be to take that job as a social worker with the state. With that kind of job, one could step right into a stable position and an opportunity to care for others. But Chris wonders, "Would I get a chance to integrate my faith into my work?" Perhaps the better option would be to attend seminary and use that training to develop a ministry to others. Chris's parents are eager to see their child in a stable career; peers are afraid Chris will get stuck in a meaningless routine of state paperwork. And then there is that *special* relationship. If Chris were to go away to seminary, there would be little hope of seeing where that relationship might go. Mostly Chris just wants to follow God. But with all the confusion of options and motives, how is one to find God's will?

The Alternative, a young congregation in the center of a large metropolis, is also thinking about its next step. The congregation was started three years ago with a vision for bringing together Evangelical theology, close community, charismatic and sacramental liturgy, and social justice. The community is growing, both in numbers and in depth, albeit with a few difficulties. The leadership is in solid agreement about the theology of the church. Everybody loves the worship. But while most of the congregation shares a common *commitment* to social justice, there is an increasing sense that they should take on some sort of common *expression*, some way of living out this commitment not just as individuals, but as a community. But what should the community do? The members of the community could just plug into the work of the food pantry and shelter down the block. Yet they also have this sense that the problems of their neighborhood are not just problems of food and shelter; these problems may involve relationships between the powerful and the powerless. How does the group go about investigating these issues with an ear for the leading of God? And then, how does the Alternative, *as a congregation*, go about making the critical decisions of what to do?

First Church of Midtown, Ghana, is both excited and concerned. Ever since this church first started as a mission outpost long ago, the members of the congregation have been praying that God's Spirit would be poured out on the land. And in the past few years they have witnessed an awakening the likes of which has never before happened in their country. People are coming to Christ by the hundreds. The joy expressed in the singing is contagious. People are confessing their sins. In times of difficulty, people are turning to Jesus more than the witch doctor. New life is breaking out all over. Yet the expressions of Christianity surrounding this awakening are different, even threatening. There is more emphasis on Jesus's conquering of evil spirits than on his atonement for sin. There is an excessive amount of emotion—people shriek and roll on the floor. Dreams and prophecies are proclaimed as if they were direct words from God. And rather than renouncing tribal customs, some are actually promoting them. The influence of this movement is really beginning to affect the church. The church is growing, but the newcomers want to do things the new way and the old-timers think the movement is more demonic than divine. So what should one recommend? How do you tell whether the movement is from God or not?

How do we take our next steps? How do we identify what comes from God and what does not? How do communities and individuals recognize and respond to the presence and activity of God in the seasons and transitions of life? These questions of discernment confront us again and again. What has God been doing in our lives?

What strategies would best foster our spiritual formation? How can we identify the spirits we may experience in prayer? How can we sort through all the myriad options for a life of care? These are not minor questions, for without good discernment, we might find ourselves shipwrecked in the faith—burned out after an overdose of spiritual disciplines, confused after mistaking a demonic vision for a divine one, enmeshed in power politics way over our heads. Desert father Abba Moses agrees: "You see, then," he says, "that the gift of discretion is no earthly or paltry matter but a very great bestowal of divine grace. Unless a monk has sought this grace with utter attentiveness and, with sure judgment, possesses discretion concerning the spirits that enter into him, it is inevitable that, like a person wandering in the dark of night and in deep shadows, he will not only fall into dangerous ditches and down steep slopes but will even frequently go astray on level and straight ways."[1] As we learned in our chapter on transformation, growth in discernment is one of the characteristics of maturity in Christ. It is also a common theme in the spiritual wisdom of the church.

A Few Basic Principles

The practice of Christian discernment is grounded in a few basic principles or assumptions.

God wants to be known. The first basic principle is that God wants to make himself known. We have seen this principle frequently. God is a self-communicating God. Through various means of revelation God displays himself and invites us into relationship. Discernment, therefore, involves the careful attention to God's self-revelation. For example, look over your past day and ask yourself, Where did I *find God*? You need not name anything special, but as you reflect and identify even the smallest indication of God's presence or action, you are noticing something of God's self-communicating character. This principle introduces us to ***appreciative discernment***. It is from our ordinary appreciative recognition of God and relationship with God that other discernments are conducted.[2]

We encounter ambiguity when identifying God's presence or activity. As you performed your exercise of looking over the day, were there any moments where you wondered whether this or that really *was* an instance of "finding God"? Even in the simplest acts, it can be difficult to identify what is or is not from God. God wants to be known. Yet our perception of God is ambiguous, somewhat beyond our knowing. And so we struggle. Although the Holy Spirit had been poured out on Jew and Gentile alike (God wants to be known), the early Christian community encountered difficulties determining just how to treat these converted Gentiles (Acts 15). Paul writes that the enemy appears disguised as an angel of light and that we must be on our guard (2 Corinthians 11:14). We confront trends and people that demand evaluation, and such evaluation is not always easy (see, for example, 3 John).

Thus, in addition to times of appreciative discernment when we simply recognize the presence and hand of God in the midst of life, there are crisis times, whether in personal crossroads or community confusion, when we struggle in ambiguity to determine what is of God. We might call these moments of ***situational discernment***, because in these moments, the situation seems to determine the kind of "knowing what is from God and what is not" we are after. Situational discernment is probably the kind of discernment we think about most when we talk about discernment. Somewhere between the general sensibility of appreciative discernment and the crisis moments of situational discernment is a kind of ongoing ***life discernment***, an assessment of the character, the stages, and the dynamics of relationship with God itself. We use life discernment when we ask ourselves (or others) the question, Where am I (are you) with God? Appreciative discernment, situational discernment, life discernment—each has its own kind of ambiguities.

Appreciative discernment notices God's presence and praises God.

Life discernment tries to see the presence or hand of God in the course of life.

Situational discernment struggles to find God in the ambiguous moment.

These ambiguities necessitate evaluation. Ultimately, the ambiguities of identifying what is of God force us to make some kind of evaluation. We have had a life-shattering dream and we simply cannot continue as we were before. The search committee of the church has two possible candidates for senior pastor and one of them needs a response within a month. The conflicts between Jew and Gentile reach the point where a gathering is necessary (Acts 15). The apostles encourage us to test the spirits in the congregation (1 Thessalonians 5:21; 1 John 4:1). Even in life discernment we are pressed to evaluate, in one case, whether the conflicts our community has experienced have really, over time, been an occasion of great grace from the Spirit or, in another case, whether we may be shifting spiritually into a period of dryness that requires a different way of navigating relationship with God.

This evaluation requires process. Although there are those moments where a difficulty is encountered and the answer is obvious, more often making an evaluation—determining what is from God and what is not—is a process: we need to set aside times and activities devoted to resolving this evaluation. We involve ourselves in clarifying the issue (Acts 15:5–6), gathering information (Acts 15:6–12), sharing wisdom (Acts 15:13–21), coming to decisions (Acts 15:22–29), and implementing a plan (Acts 15:30–35). Jesus spends time in prayerful reflection prior to choosing his key followers (Luke 6:12–16). Discerning evaluation often involves careful attention to process.

Discerning evaluation requires both gift and skill. There are two primary words in

the Greek New Testament used to express the idea of discernment. One (*diakrisis*) is used with reference to a grace of the Spirit for the discernment of spirits (1 Corinthians 12:10). The other (*dokimazo*) is used with reference to determining what is best (Philippians 1:10) and to testing everything (1 Thessalonians 5:21). There is a dimension of discernment that is simply the grace of God—a moment or a ministry of intuiting what is from God and what is not. Yet discernment is also discussed as a matter of skill in learning to test, to examine, to determine the best.

Defining Discernment

Discernment has been defined in a variety of ways, depending on whether it is seen as a gift or a virtue and depending on the context in which discernment is being examined. The well-known *Dictionnaire de Spiritualité* defines *discernment* as "the process by which we examine in the light of faith and in the connaturality of love, the nature of the spiritual states we experience in ourselves and in others. The purpose of such examination is to decide, as far as possible, which of the movements we experience lead to the Lord, and to a more perfect service of him and our brothers, and which deflect us from this goal."[3] An article titled "Pluralism and the Discernment of Spirits" defines *discernment* as "the question of recognizing the action of God in concrete situations in the universe and in the community of God's people, and responding appropriately to it."[4] According to the authors of a handbook on discerning call in community, "In classical spirituality, discernment means identifying what spirit is at work in a situation: the Spirit of God or some other spirit. Discernment is 'sifting through' our interior and exterior experiences to determine their origin. Discernment helps a person understand the source of a call, to whom it is directed, its content and what response is appropriate. Discernment also involves learning if one is dodging a call, is deaf to a call, or is rejecting a call."[5]

In an effort to see discernment from as broad a perspective as possible, we will explore Christian discernment as *the evaluation of inner and outer stuff in light of a relationship with God with a view to response*. First, Christian discernment addresses *stuff*, various phenomena arising either from within (such as voices, physical or emotional manifestations, changes in the mood of one's relationship with God, choices, decisions, or the like) or from without (prophetic words, manifestations in others, cultural trends, and so on). Although the term *discernment* has been used in regard to ethical choices (choices between right and wrong actions), generally the term refers to an evaluation of possibilities in which all options appear to be morally acceptable. I don't generally need to discern whether stealing cars is God's will for my life. Second, Christian discernment involves *evaluation*, the recognition and understanding of that stuff. In discernment, we often face something unknown that needs clarification or at least appreciative recognition. Christian discernment is an act of knowing. Third, Christian discernment involves evaluation *in light of one's relationship with God*. The discernment of a potential change in vocation is not simply an assessment of income potential or advancement possibilities. The question one must ask is, "What does *God* think about this decision?" Finally, Christian discernment moves toward a *response*. Discernment is not evaluation pursued as an academic exercise. Usually, we discern in order to *act*. Yet we must not imagine that discernment is merely an advice-securing technique. Discernment is really about relationship with God. As Ernest Larkin writes, "Discernment does not tell us what to do, since it moves on a different plane from the technical. But it does indicate whether or not we are moving in the right direction on the deepest level of our being, and in this way it enlightens our experiences, reinforces our decisions, and concretizes our desire to find God in all things."[6]

Types of Discernment

Recognizing that discernment is practiced within various common categories of situations, we can identify different kinds or *types* of discernment. As Jesuit scholar Jules Toner describes, "There are manifold kinds of spiritual discernment: discernment of true and false doctrine, of true and false prophecy, of true and false mystical experiences and of different degrees or stages of mystical experience, discernment of what is truly God's will for one's free choice among alternative courses of action, to name only a few."[7] There is the discernment of personal or communal guidance. There is the discernment of social and religious trends. There is the discernment of the experiences and stages of spiritual maturity as well as the discernment of strategies of spiritual formation appropriate to each. At times, discernment addresses the influence of divine or demonic spirits in individuals or groups. Appreciative discernment welcomes the presence of God. While the situations toward which discernment is pointed

"They're 'casting lots' to see who goes with the junior high kids to camp."

Practicing Christian Spirituality

Choosing a Discernment

In this chapter, we will do our practice of Christian spirituality in parts through the whole chapter, rather than in one single exercise all at the end (although you may choose to read through to the end and then work with the exercises later).[8] Now that you know something about what discernment is all about and have been introduced to the different types of discernment, perhaps you can think about a discerning situation in your own life. As you read this chapter, explore some issue of discernment, whether it be an upcoming decision, an experience you have had, a trend you want to evaluate, or a strategy for spiritual formation or evangelistic involvement—anything. So at this point in the chapter, all you need to do is to pick out your own discernment issue. Don't make it too large (should I marry this person?), because that might be difficult to resolve within the course of a chapter of reading. But it should not be too trivial

either (what kind of toothpaste should I use?). You may wish to explore, for example, involvement in a potential ministry or with a particular community, or an experience you recently had, or other discernments at this level. When you have thought of an issue, look at it in light of our discussion of the definition and types of discernment. What is the *stuff* you are to evaluate? Is it inner stuff or outer stuff? What is the *evaluation* about? What is the issue? Is this an appreciative discernment, a life discernment, or a situational discernment? In what ways might *God* be involved in this issue? What kinds of *response* might follow from different resolutions of the issue? What *type* of discernment is this, and how might that affect the discernment process? You might like to keep some kind of journal of your process through this practice in discernment. You may even wish to share it with a friend along the way.

---

are diverse, the actions performed within these circumstances are similar. Discernment, in each case, involves a coming to know in the light of faith a distinguishing of the presence or activity of God (or of "not-God"), with a view to living appropriately to what is learned.

Discernment among the People of God: A Brief History

Discernment changes with changing circumstances. Hence we can identify certain shifts in the understanding and practice of discernment as we review the history of discernment among the people of God.

The biblical period. Within the writings of the Old Testament, the question of community guidance was central. Should the

Hebrews go to battle or not? How should the nation conduct its affairs? At times God simply gave his people instructions. "Now this is the commandment—the statutes and the ordinances—that the LORD your God charged me to teach you to observe in the land," Moses declares to the nation of Israel (Deuteronomy 6:1). Because God is a God who acts and speaks, the interpretation of the deeds of God and the words of God (*torah*) has been—and continues to be—an important component of discernment among God's people. God's word came sometimes through a prophet, and determining which were truly God's prophets and which were false prophets itself became an issue of discernment.[9] At other times God's people (and especially the king) actively *sought* the guidance of the

Lord, "inquiring of God," either through a prophet or through the priestly class, who might discern God's hand through the use of the mysterious Urim and Thummim (1 Samuel 9:8–10; Numbers 27:21).

In the poetic and wisdom books, other dimensions of discernment are highlighted. The Psalms, for example, express a rich appreciative discernment, recognizing the presence and activity of God in creation, in the events of Israel's history, and in personal deliverance. In the notion of wisdom, the *skill* of discernment is developed. Wisdom is practical intelligence. It is the ability to make the choices of life that best correspond to the way things really are. It is "learned by discipline, interiorized in learning, and tested in processes of interaction."[10] The book of Proverbs is full of wise sayings that compare different choices, illustrating how the light of faith might influence the discernment of the everyday. To the one who seeks her, Wisdom is like a mother or a bride—she will feed the seeker with the bread of discernment (Sirach [Ecclesiasticus] 15:1–3).

The Gospels reveal a Jesus who is concerned with discernment and who is the ultimate criterion of discernment. Jesus consistently overturns common interpretations of *torah*, and in doing so he clarifies the criteria of well-discerned living. Jesus chides the religious leaders of his time for their failure to discern the signs of the times. Yet most significant is Jesus's pointing to himself as the living icon of God. "Whoever has seen me has seen the Father," Jesus states (John 14:9). If discernment is the evaluation of what is from God, then Jesus himself is the clearest sign of what "from God" might look like.

With the outpouring of the Holy Spirit on the followers of Jesus and the consequent establishment of Christian churches throughout the eastern Mediterranean, other dimensions of discernment are highlighted. The evaluation of prophetic utterance is revived, only now in the context of charismatic or sacramental gatherings (1 Thessalonians 5:20–21; see also 1 Corinthians 14). Affective dispositions such as hope, love, and peace—life-discerning signs of the work of God on individuals and communities—are recognized (Romans 5:1–5; Philippians 4:7). Believers need to evaluate trends, doctrines, and leaders in terms of their faithfulness to the message and life of the Christian faith (1 Corinthians 5; Revelation 2:12–17; 2 John 7–11). And the church needs to surrender distinctions of race, diet, and practice to more important concerns so it can, as James L. Jaquette phrases it, "discern what counts."[11]

The patristic period. The early church often saw discernment in terms of a discrimination between two ways: the way of light and the way of darkness. Both the *Didache* and the Shepherd of Hermas stress the need to be watchful lest one fall under the influence of evil. Origen, and later Athanasius (especially in his influential *Life of Antony*), portrayed the Christian life in terms of a struggle between good and evil spirits. Describing evil spirits' strategies in order to warn believers (and thus to inform their discernment and advance their growth in mature Christian living) was a common theme of the elders of the desert. Abba Agathon says, regarding prayer, that "every time a man wants to pray, his enemies, the demons, want to prevent him, for they know that it is only by turning him from prayer that they can hinder his journey."[12]

In the later patristic period, discernment was portrayed less in terms of a supernatural gift used to battle with spirits and more in terms of a virtue (indeed, often the *chief* virtue) used to maintain a prudent balance in life. John Cassian's second conference, a classic treatment of discernment in this fashion, gives the stories of four people who were seriously damaged due to lack of what Cassian calls "discretion."[13] The Eastern Church, through the works of figures like Evagrius Ponticus and Symeon the New Theologian, adapted the wisdom of the desert elders and retained it as a permanent synthesis of discernment wisdom. In the West, the final chapter of Augustine's *Literal Meaning of Genesis* pre-

Diodochus of Photike, *"On Spiritual Knowledge and Discernment"*

Those pursuing the spiritual way must always keep the mind free from agitation in order that the intellect, as it discriminates among the thoughts that pass through the mind, may store in the treasuries of its memory those thoughts which are good and have been sent by God, while casting out those which are evil and come from the devil. When the sea is calm, fishermen can scan its depths and therefore hardly any creature moving in the water escapes their notice. But when the sea is disturbed by the winds, it hides beneath its turbid and agitated waves what it was happy to reveal when it was smiling and calm; and then the fishermen's skill and cunning prove vain. The same thing happens with the contemplative power of the intellect, especially when it is unjust anger which disturbs the depths of the soul.[14]

sented a unique synthesis of the patristic wisdom on discernment, dealing especially with various impressions that Christians may experience. In this book, Augustine distinguished between bodily visions (an appearance of something really "out there" sensed by the body), spiritual visions (the "images" of bodily visions), and intellectual visions (the "seeing" of the truth or nature or meaning of a thing), and also between different states of consciousness: wakefulness, sleep, delirium, and ecstasy. Augustine went on to show how good and evil spirits influence human experience under different conditions, ultimately regarding intellectual visions as being least susceptible to deception.[15]

The medieval period. Medieval writings on discernment crystallized the late patristic emphases on prudent balance and intellectual vision. We see this in Bernard of Clairvaux and especially in Thomas Aquinas.[16] For Aquinas and others, prudence *points* us to the center of the balanced life. Discretion or discernment, then, determines how that center is to be reached in the particulars of the means of life.

But another development was taking place in the medieval understanding of discernment, the seeds of which were already planted in the patristic period. The desert elders had well perceived that humility was an important component of good discernment. It was often the proud, wannabe hermit who would venture off alone, only to succumb to deceptive impulses of the enemy. Thus humility—and the willingness to submit oneself to the wisdom and leadership of others—was frequently mentioned as an important component of discernment, even in the patristic period. But in the late-medieval period (1300–1500), and in the light of the flowering of lay devotional life, humility and submission were emphasized to the fullest. Indeed, the submissiveness of late-medieval (women) visionaries to their spiritual directors was made a central criterion or condition of the authenticity of spiritual experiences. Scholar and churchman Jean Gerson (1363–1429) wrote two classic works on discernment summarizing this late-medieval perspective.[17] On the one hand, the mutually understood hierarchical pattern of relationships and communication enabled some women—who might otherwise never have been heard—to give voice to the prophetic Spirit of God. On the other hand, the same discourse served as a means of keeping control over what some thought were "undesirable" elements in the church.[18]

The Reformation period. By the time of the Protestant Reformation, the principles of discernment had become an issue of authority. Rather than encouraging submissive response to ecclesial authority, many Protestant Reformers stressed the existential faith response to the Word of God. Rejecting what they saw as highly

Historical Portrait:
A Vision of Birgitta of Sweden (1303–73)

Birgitta of Sweden, known as the "Joan of Ark" of Sweden, was of royal blood. After her husband's death, she spent herself pleading for peace between France and England, pleading for the pope's return to Rome during the Avignon papacy, and giving words of wisdom to a variety of individuals. She was canonized as a saint in 1391. A later affirmation of this canonization was the stimulus behind Jean Gerson's second essay on discernment. In this excerpt from a "Life" of Birgitta, notice Birgitta's reticence to accept imaginative visions and her insistence on needing to submit her vision to a wise confessor. She speaks of herself, the bride of Christ, in the third person.

How she was sent to a teacher and how, after her husband's death, she was visited by the Spirit.

After some days, when the bride of Christ was worried about the change in her status and its bearing on her service of God, and while she was praying about this in her chapel, then she was caught up in spirit; and while she was in ecstasy, she saw a bright cloud; and from the cloud, she heard a voice saying to her: "Woman, hear me." And thoroughly terrified, fearing that it was an illusion, she fled to her chamber; and at once she confessed and then received the Body of Christ. When at last, after several days, she was at prayer in the same chapel, again that bright cloud appeared to her; and from the cloud, she heard again a voice uttering the words like those before, namely: "Woman, hear me." And then that lady, again thoroughly terrified, fled to her chamber; and having confessed she communicated as before, fearing that the voice was an illusion. Finally, after several days, when she was praying again in the same place, she was indeed caught up in spirit and again saw the bright cloud, and in it, the likeness of a human being, who said this: "Woman, hear me; I am your God, who wish to speak with you." Terrified, therefore, and thinking it was an illusion, she heard again: "Fear not," he said; "for I am the Creator of all, and not a deceiver. For I do not speak to you for your sake alone, but for the sake of the salvation of others. Hear the things that I speak; and go to Master Matthias, your confessor, who has experience in discerning the two types of spirit. Say to him on my behalf what I now say to you: you shall be my bride and my channel, and you shall hear and see spiritual things, and my Spirit shall remain with you even to your death."[19]

schematized mystical stages, unnecessary devotional practices, and an overcontrolling ecclesial hierarchy, Protestants desired that believers be free to discover discernment anew as the simple working out of a life of charity in the context of a settled position of faith and hope.[20] But it was not that simple. How was this Word of God to be interpreted, and by whom? Should not reason or tradition or the local community play some role? And if we are set free from the strictures of the church institution, are we not freed to respond to the spontaneous inclinations of the Spirit? Is not the Spirit of God, rather than a book, the Christian's authority and guide? The debates among the Socinians (reason), the Quakers (Spirit), the Catholics (tradition), the Reformers (scripture), the Anglicans (scripture, tradition, reason), the Anabaptists (scripture, Spirit, local community), the Puritans (scripture, Spirit), and the Methodists (scripture, tradition, reason, experience) were not ivory-tower feuds. They were also explorations of the sources of discernment. The church's and the believer's ability to navigate, both in ordinary times and in times of crisis, was at stake.

One of the chief figures of the Catholic reformation was Ignatius of Loyola. One of Ignatius's contributions to the church was his *Spiritual Exercises*, and the writings at the center of this retreat manual for spiritual growth and decision making are "Rules for the Discernment of Spirits" and "Times for the Making of an Election." Few documents have influenced the contemporary practice of discernment as much as Ignatius's brief comments on discernment and decision making. In his notes, Ignatius describes a few of the primary dynamics of the good and the evil spirits and outlines three different times when a well-discerned decision can be made. The French school of spirituality in the following centuries adapted Ignatian discernment for distribution and use among a wide audience. We will return to Ignatius later in this chapter.[21]

The modern period. All of the various nuances of discernment introduced in previous centuries returned in the following centuries, as did a few new twists characteristic of the modern period. Life discernment issues were often central. Protestants were concerned with discerning the signs of assurance, of sanctification, and of the empowerment of the Holy Spirit, especially in the context of revivals spreading throughout the church in Europe and America. How does the believer (or the minister receiving a candidate for communion) know that he or she has truly experienced an authentic rebirth? Should one look to a particular affective experience? A changed life? Or should one simply accept their transformation "by faith" in the fact of one's prayer for a new life? How is "entire sanctification" recognized? What are the certain signs of the baptism of the Holy Spirit? Roman Catholic manual spiritu-

ality integrated Origen's threefold stages of Christian growth (purgation, illumination, union), Augustine's division of the various kinds of visions, Ignatian insights, and the structures of Carmelite spirituality (drawing heavily from John of the Cross and Teresa of Avila) into a synthesis of life discernment within the context of a carefully monitored spiritual direction.

With the advent of modern political concerns (especially as framed by industrialism and Marxism), the concept of discernment was redeveloped in terms of embodying Jesus's radical kingdom life and selecting social strategies.[22] Furthermore, with the Second Vatican Council's encouragement for Roman Catholic religious to reappropriate the spirit of their founders, and with the rise of interest in all things spiritual in the late twentieth century more generally, we have seen a great deal of reflection on discernment in various contexts, resulting in the publication of a number of guides to discernment for the general public.[23] With the explosion of Christianity in the global South, there is every indication that discernment will continue to be a subject of interest in the years to come.

Preparation for Discernment

Whether we are simply appreciating the active presence of God in creation, or recognizing the subtle changes of life in the Spirit, or determining the will of God in the context of a critical situation, preparation helps. Discernment is a "coming to know," and we best come to know the presence and action of God when our faculties of spiritual knowing are in good working order, when we are open to the kinds of information appropriate to Christian discernment, and when we have readied ourselves for the rest of the discernment process. "Discernment cannot be reduced to any rules of thumb. Rather, the ability to discern develops from living the life of the Spirit, a process of growth involving an ever-greater integration of desires, feelings, reactions, and choices with a continuing commitment to

focus

Historical Portrait: Jonathan Edwards's *Distinguishing Signs of a Work of God*

Jonathan Edwards witnessed the best and the worst of America's Great Awakening. He wrote four essays describing and evaluating the nature of this movement. In this, his second essay, written in 1741, Edwards articulates signs by which one may determine whether a given trend or movement is a "work of God."

> The apostolical age, or the age in which the apostles lived and preached the Gospel, was an age of the greatest outpouring of the Spirit of God that ever was; and that both as the extraordinary influences and gifts of the Spirit, in inspiration and miracles, and also as to his ordinary operations, in convincing, converting, enlightening and sanctifying the souls of men. But as the influences of the true Spirit abounded, so counterfeits did also then abound: the Devil was abundant in mimicking both the ordinary and extraordinary influences of the Spirit of God, as is manifest by innumerable passages of the apostles' writings. This made it very necessary that the church of Christ should be furnished with some certain rules, and distinguishing and clear marks by which she might proceed safely in judging of spirits, and distinguish the true from the false, without danger of being imposed on. . . . My design therefore at this time is to shew what are the true, certain, and distinguishing evidences of a work of the Spirit of God, by which we may proceed safely in judging of any operation we find in ourselves, or see in others. . . .
>
> 1. When that spirit that is at work amongst a people is observed to operate after such a manner, as to raise their esteem of that Jesus that was born of a Virgin, and was crucified without the gates of Jerusalem; and seems more to confirm and establish their minds in the truth of what the Gospel declares to us of his being the Son of God and the Saviour of men; 'tis a sure sign that that spirit is the Spirit of God. . . .
> 2. When the spirit that is at work operates against the interest of Satan's kingdom, which lies in encouraging and establishing sin, and cherishing men's worldly lusts; this is a sure sign that 'tis a true, and not a false spirit. . . .
> 3. That spirit that operates in such a manner, as to cause in men a greater regard to the Holy Scriptures, and establishes them more in their truth and divinity, is certainly the Spirit of God. . . .
> 4. If by observing the manner of the operation of a spirit that is at work among a people, we see that it operates as a spirit of truth, leading persons to truth, convincing them of those things that are true, we may safely determine that 'tis a right and true spirit. . . .
> 5. If the spirit that is at work among a people operates as a spirit of love to God and man, 'tis a sure sign that 'tis the Spirit of God.[24]

abide in Christ."[25] Indeed, Theophan the Recluse writes, "The most effective means of cultivating true discernment in the soul of a child is to rear him carefully in the life of the Orthodox Church so that he will respect its teachings."[26] In one sense we prepare for discernment from the moment we are born. But there is also a more present and practical preparation for discernment in which we review the elements and process of discernment, we examine ourselves, and we cultivate the virtues that facilitate discernment. In situational discernment we learn about the situation at hand, and in community discernment those who are facilitating the process prepare for their work while the community prepares to gather and share wisdom.

The Elements of Discernment

As a first step of preparation for discernment, it is helpful to review the basic principles of discernment and to identify for *this* discernment who the basic players are and what the elements of the process might look like. Having covered the basic principles above, we now turn to these elements.

The "process" of discernment. As stated above, discernment is a coming to know. And as a coming to know, discernment will follow the ordinary stages of human experience: from Being Aware, to Experiencing, to Understanding and Judging, to Deciding and Acting, to Integrating, which again informs our Being Aware.[27] Thus a general description of the flow of discernment might move from preparation, which forms awareness, to the identification of various features of experience, which figure in this discernment, to the understanding and interpretation of those features. In communal (and often in individual) discernment this stage involves seasons of "sharing wisdom" where the community gathers and interprets together. Finally, a sense of "This is it!" (a judgment) is reached. As the process moves forward, the energy shifts toward planning and action; and as action is reviewed and revised, a new sense of integrative presence toward the discernment (and toward God) is welcomed.

The "discerner." Who discerns? For individual discernment, this might seem like an obvious question. *I* do, of course. But in some situations, even in individual discernment, it is not so simple. Perhaps it is best, at times, to release one's right to discern to the wisdom of another. In handing over our

fate to the leadership of another, we surrender our will to God in a way that can be very liberating. True, this kind of surrender can lead, and has led, to harmful abuse. We must learn, as individuals, to sense the times for *my* discernment, for *our* discernment, and for *your* discernment.

When the community discerns, similar questions are asked, but they are slightly different questions from those asked by individual discerners. Who discerns for the community? This is a debated issue both in theology and in practice. Joseph M. R. Belloso asks an interesting question: Who is capable of discerning? He suggests five possible options: the one who is placed closest to the problems, the one who is closest to God, the official leader, the community itself, or the experts.[28] Perhaps there are important roles for each to play in a given discernment. Or perhaps *this* discernment is the job of one or two of the above. There will be unique tensions in each case. Again, we must learn, as communities, to sense the times for each discerner.

The contexts of discernment. Just as there are contexts of spiritual formation, prayer, and care, so too there are contexts of discernment, and these shape the discernment process just as they shape the rest of our spiritual life. We must attend to our web of relationships. How are we related to nature? How does our geography affect us here and now? What part might animals, plants, weather, machines, medicines, or buildings play in this discernment? What about our relationship with ourselves? Discernment must address self-image, especially in transitions. What are our hopes or fears, and where do they originate? Look at the context of relationships with others. Theologian Mark McIntosh concludes his book *Discernment and Truth* with this beautiful doxology on the role of the community:

> From their first encounter with the crucified and risen Jesus, believers have been drawn into a worshiping community where truth has given itself to be known in the creation of a new life together. Spiritual

Figure 11.1
The Elements of Discernment

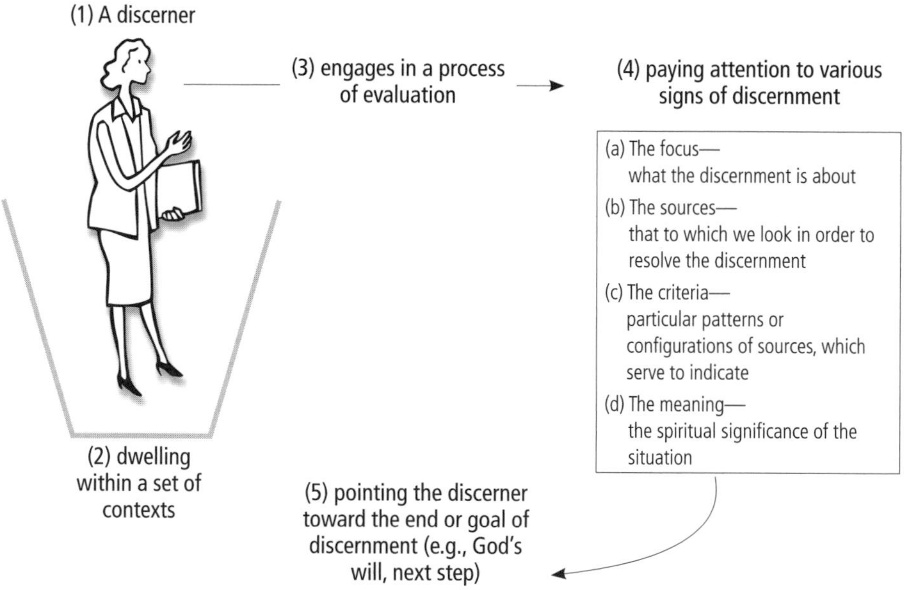

(1) A discerner

(3) engages in a process of evaluation →

(4) paying attention to various signs of discernment

> (a) The focus—
> what the discernment is about
>
> (b) The sources—
> that to which we look in order to resolve the discernment
>
> (c) The criteria—
> particular patterns or configurations of sources, which serve to indicate
>
> (d) The meaning—
> the spiritual significance of the situation

(2) dwelling within a set of contexts

(5) pointing the discerner toward the end or goal of discernment (e.g., God's will, next step) ←

discernment has arisen naturally and most necessarily for such a common life, because it reflects the pressure of a living truth—refusing partiality and bias, pushing beyond individual understanding, opening the discerning community to the creative, self-sharing life from which all truth springs. Discerning truth could never be a lonely form of life. The truth humanity hungers for seems far too large a feast for solitary diners. It requires a sharing far too joyful for any but the truly wise. For they alone discern the depth of thanks most justly due so great a giver. Knowing the giver in each gift, they are themselves set free from small desires and awake to God's desire in every thing; they discern the truth in praise.[29]

This brings us to the context of our relationship with God. Every discernment arises in the midst of a real, lived relationship with God, and it is *in light of* that relationship with God that discernment is weighed. Thus, as author Bob Mumford writes about the discernment of personal guidance, "Learning the skill of receiving guidance is learning to walk in intimate fellowship with God."[30]

The "signs" of discernment. When we speak of the signs of discernment, we indicate *what we pay attention to* when we discern. We look at signs for indications of God's presence and activity. We can name four separate kinds of signs of discernment, each of which play a role in the discernment process.[31]

- The *focus* of discernment is what I am discerning *about* (for example, a vocational decision).

- A *source* of discernment is that to which I look in order to resolve the discernment. (I may be looking to, among other things, my feelings in order to resolve my vocational decision.)

- A set of *criteria* for discernment is a configuration, or a way the sources look, indicating that a given criterion or condition of discernment is fulfilled. (For instance, I may look to a certain kind of sense of peace as an indication of God's guidance regarding this decision.)

- The *meaning* of the discernment is the spiritual significance toward which the fulfillment of the criteria points. (For instance, this peace may indicate a sign of God's presence or activity in my life as I move toward a particular vocational choice.)

The end or goal of discernment. We have discussed this above. While we might hope for a solid resolution and an answer to it all, we may not always find them. Sometimes God has other plans. We simply look for the next step forward. As Ladislas Orsy has written about community discernment, "Community discernment then is not a means to know the future. It has a different purpose: it helps the community to become aware of the next step and gives them the strength to take it, be it through the desert, be it in the battle, be it in carrying out the mandate of bringing the good news to all men."[32]

Preparation of Discerners

As we have mentioned, discernment is not merely a technique. Good discerners, those with the ability to distinguish the things that are from God, are attuned to the things of God. It is especially valuable to cultivate the following virtues in preparation for discernment:

Freedom in faith. Discernment begins in the trust that God loves us and has a wonderful plan for our lives. Wholehearted faith in God gives us the freedom to step forward, to risk, to make mistakes. Those walking in the freedom born of faith need not suffer anxiously in discernment, fearful that if we miss the will of God, our life might be ruined. Faith is a fundamental orientation toward a personal, loving, generous God. This basic orientation of faith lies beneath what Ignatius of Loyola calls "indifference." Indifference is not the state of having no preferences but rather the free, trusting release of our preferences to the greater wisdom and love of God.[33]

Commitment to obedience. Jesus said, "Anyone who resolves to do the will of God will know whether the teaching is from God or whether I am speaking on my own" (John 7:17). There is some connection between our predisposition to *follow* the guidance of God and our perception *of* that guidance. One way of probing this is to ask, "How do I respond to God's presence or guidance when it is made clear to me?" Patterns of blatant disobedience hinder discernment. Similarly, in communal discernment, making a mutual commitment to live with the well-discerned decision of the group before beginning the process makes a lot of difference in the quality of both the discernment process and the implementation of a discernment decision.

Shared concerns. As our relationship with another grows closer, we begin to share the other's concerns. We learn to love what he loves, even to feel as he might feel in a given situation. We know what the other might choose if he were to face what we face. It is the same with God. As we immerse ourselves in prayer and in scripture reading and in practicing our faith, we begin to have a sense of the kind of things God might like. We find God's will most clearly, in one sense, from this immersion in the thoughts, the commandments, and the values of God as revealed throughout scripture and history. And as we immerse ourselves in God, we begin to suspect what Jesus might do if he were in our shoes right now. This is a kind of presence and guidance in itself, a **connaturality** with God (a natural sharing with God of aspects of character and life) that shapes our perception and reception of God's active presence.[34]

Listening. We will not hear God if we are not listening. Conversely, those who learn to listen well can hear quite a bit. Discernment is often the fruit of the attitude of contemplation mentioned in chapter 9. As we cultivate a desire to see God; as we release our expectations; as we leisurely wait for God to communicate in any form he wishes; and as we acquaint ourselves with silence, solitude, and the other skills of contemplation, we open ourselves to "hear" God however God might speak. In communal discernment the virtue of listening includes a willingness to hear the voice of God through others. We learn to "hear another through," and through hearing the other, we learn to hear God for the group.

Humility. This brings us to humility. We touched on this earlier in our survey of history. Seekers who will not allow others to challenge their cherished perspectives or to step on their "rights" will be left alone, groping for God. John Climacus writes, "The sea is the source of the fountain, and humility is the source of discernment."[35] Humility is not a servile self-abnegation before one's superiors. With regard to discernment, pursuing humility is making room for God (and in communal discernment, a making room for God *through* others). "Discernment only works," writes Kees Waaijman, "if people unconditionally open themselves up before God, actually give shape to God's will in their everyday life, and in the process allow themselves increasingly to be questioned by God."[36] This is the humility that is the source of discernment.

Prayer. Prayer nourishes discernment in a number of ways. First, the attitude of contemplation shapes the "hearing" of the discerner. Second, the simple "asking" of prayer leads to receiving: "If any of you is lacking in wisdom, ask God, who gives to all generously and ungrudgingly, and it will be given you" (James 1:5). To the one who asks "in faith" (James 1:6), who rests confidently in God, God loves to give wisdom. So pray, that you might receive. We can also identify a third, more practical, dimension of prayer in discernment. There is kind of a rhythm in discernment (especially in situational discernment): out to do research, in to reflect; out to explore my own agendas, in to explore God's; out to talk to others, in to talk to God. Without intentionally creating space for prayer, discernment often gets caught up in the "doing." We must be courageous enough to ask for wisdom and patient enough to wait for it to be given.

Wisdom. When we are younger, we must discern this and that. When we are older and have seen how it goes with this and that, there is less need for intense situational discernment, for our sense of God's presence and activity and guidance has been informed by wisdom. Wisdom has seen God part the waters and has heard the still small voice. Wisdom knows how to distinguish fear of failure from responsible caution. Wisdom has felt the difference between the accusations of the enemy and the conviction of the Spirit. Wisdom has watched the group and knows its realistic possibilities and limits. Wisdom shapes the need of discernment and refines the process of discernment.

Love. Our last (in order, not in importance) virtue of discernment is love. A passionate love for God will settle for nothing less than wholehearted relationship through all the changes of life. An intimate love is sensitive to the least touch of the Beloved. A love for one another is found in communal discernment, desiring sincerely for the common good of the community and focusing on mutual support rather than some ideal of complete agreement. Love gives shape to all the other virtues of discernment, nourishing our faith at the start and empowering our follow-through at the end.

Preparation for Communal Gatherings

A special kind of preparation of the discerner is present when a community discerns together. Those who facilitate the sharing of wisdom and those who participate must adopt certain attitudes and agree to certain rules of the gathering.

The leader or facilitator of a discernment group plays a critical role. This person must guide and sense the spirit (or Spirit) of the group and its direction without directing the course of the process. The leader must know how to include the quiet and how to quiet the overincluded. The leader must know how to be a player-coach. The leader balances responsibility for the final outcome with the ministry of enabling and freeing people to grow. Different decisions require different wisdom. Some groups emphasize the role of one particular leader, a clerk or chairperson who guides the process through. This person may be in charge of setting the agenda, articulating the questions for the group, maintaining neutrality, judging what is irrelevant (when it is time to move on), or summarizing the sense of the meeting. Other groups divide leadership between a pastoral leader, who provides spiritual leadership and authority as a member of the group, and a group leader, who empowers the members, enables the process, and confronts dysfunctional behavior kindly, clearly, and consistently. In either case, it is important that any leader knows the group; focuses on God, not merely agreement; wisely judges the sense of the meeting; knows self-restraint; and acts with love and respect and, therefore, has earned the group's respect.

The group members gathering must also prepare to come together. Here are a few rules for gathering that many have found helpful:

Consider these times as holy moments. Take a prayerful attitude toward gathered discernment. Make a conscious commitment to the presence of the Spirit in an assembly, even of a small leadership team. Do not interrupt another. That person may be speaking the word

"I like to think of myself as the facilitator and enabler of this church rather than the senior pastor or chief executive officer."

of God. Learn to be humble enough to wait your turn in prayerful listening. Encourage an appropriate balance of speakers. Finally, be cautious of kibitzing (talking about what was discussed) between meetings. In these ways you respect the sacred character of the discerning community.

When you speak, disclose yourself in a simplicity that allows your story to unfold without inappropriate self-presentation. Express emotions honestly without manipulation or show. Give attention to matters in your real life, sharing ideas without needing to lecture.

When you listen, listen with self-discernment and self-criticism. (Ask yourself, Why am I responding this way to what is said?) Attend to the story being told, not to your imagined response. Be courageous enough to state opposition when needed. Remember, "Tacit approval of every voice, through fear of confrontation, will make the church lose its identity as quickly and surely as the rejection of every voice, through fear of change."[37]

Be willing to take the time necessary for discernment. Hasty discernment will be followed by ambiguous commitment. Quality discernment will be followed by solid commitment.

Be prepared to adjust. You may find, over time, that the question you initially asked is morphing into a new and more significant question.

Go where God leads. It's ultimately about God, not goals, anyway. Let go of the need to control, to win, to be right.

Be willing to leave the familiar and risk the unfamiliar.

Know how your community operates.

Preparation Regarding the Discernment Situation

Appreciative discernment does not require much work. Appreciative discernment is largely a matter of one's being present to notice God in the moment. The ongoing discernment of life requires a bit more work. We look back over this

Practicing Christian Spirituality

Preparing Yourself as a Discerner

Now it is time to get back to your own discernment. First, review the elements of discernment. What does the *process* of this discernment look like to you? Can you identify the *contexts*, the different *signs* of this discernment? What do you expect in the *end*? Does your discernment issue resemble any of the kinds mentioned in the history of discernment? Now, having looked again at your discernment more generally, it is time to look at yourself. Think of yourself as a discerner. As you face this particular discernment, examine the list of virtues. Which are your strongest virtues? Which are your weakest? How might your strengths and weaknesses affect this discernment process (or your discernment in general)? What might you do to address these strengths and weaknesses in *this* discernment? What might you do to facilitate your discernment in the future? Take a few notes if needed and get ready for the next step.

latest season of life. Perhaps we review our journals, or we talk to a few friends. We reflect on our relationship with God. This kind of review prepares us to see patterns and subtle shifts in the dynamics of our relationship with God. Situational discernment, however, can require a great deal of work. Consider our stories at the beginning of the chapter. Chris, the college student facing graduation and evaluating future career options, must weigh financial matters, potential relationships, personal dreams and fears, and life discernment itself as part of the determination of the next step of life. The Alternative, the emerging congregation, must, now that it is acquainted with its neighborhood, undertake some social analysis in an effort to discover what is going on there and some personal analysis to see what *it*, as a congregation, can do by way of corporately expressing care. Similarly the African congregation in the midst of a controversial revival must do the homework necessary to give this movement a fair evaluation. Its members need to visit meetings, review media, and interview people, not to mention doing the theological homework necessary for this kind of discernment. The leadership of the church also must conduct a corporate

life discernment, assessing whether participation in *this* trend might be wise for *this* congregation at *this* time. We will divide this kind of preparation into three steps:

Clarify the focus. The first step in preparing for situational discernment is making sure you know what your discernment is really about. It is one thing to wonder what your next step in life is going to be. It is another to assess whether or not you should accept this job offer. Two different kinds of consideration are involved. At one stage of clarification, it is time for brainstorming, for leaving all options open. At another stage, it is time for detailed analysis of a single option. Situational discernment can break down when an exciting specific opportunity distracts us from the life discernment required to assess true vision. Conversely, it can break down when we get so fascinated with all the open options that we never settle into any action. Situational discernment can also break down when we include too many ideas in our question. For example, the Alternative might propose that it start a legal aid clinic at the vacant office space down the street and hire people from within the church. But what if this particular office space becomes unavailable next week? Must they start the discernment process all over again? In this case, their focus—their stated question—was too narrow. One way of clarifying the focus is to ask, What is my (or our) *question*? Refinement of the question may be able to point you to the different signs (focus, source, criteria, meaning) toward which you may look for God's hand in the discernment process. Good clarification focuses discernment toward a question that is understandable and answerable by the discerner.

Acknowledge God's general concerns. It is at this time that we also weed out options that really are not options. If Chris discovered, for example, that there was something about the job offer to be a social worker for the state that would require a compromise of faith, Chris might have to reject further investigation of the job offer right up front. Or if, through a process of life discernment, members of the Alternative were convicted that they were getting too attached to property already, consuming so much of their time and money in building improvements that care for people was sidelined—they might find themselves re-evaluating the "clinic option" for living out social justice in light of this more general (and clear) concern for people over property. Acknowledging God's general concerns also leads us to distinguish between what matters and what doesn't matter. Whether our political involvement is understood or successful may not matter. Faithfulness to the gospel does.[38]

Gather information. Having clarified the question and eliminated false options, we must now gather information about the situation. One manual of communal discernment summarizes the essential principles of this step into four points:

- In communal discernment, the facts are essential. You need all the information necessary for any sound decision—this is what you take to prayer.
- The whole range of facts is required: people, energies, space, time, money,

needs, impacts, support systems, handicaps. The feelings and values held by the participants are also facts that are crucial.
- Everyone involved in the communal discernment must be able to assimilate all the necessary facts. The data, the time, and the ability to assimilate must be available and used.
- In a complex situation, research may need to be done by a committee, but the data must be communicated to the members and enough time allowed for personal reflection and assimilation.[39]

In the assessment of social justice alternatives, a fair amount of social analysis may need to be completed. The church would need to research the history of the neighborhood and its residents; to analyze the economic, political, cultural, and institutional structures in the neighborhood that shape the powerlessness that some people experience; to explore the various social divisions present in the neighborhood, which would affect the way the church's ministry may be received; and to distinguish between the different "levels" of issues involved: local issues, regional issues, national issues, and so on.[40] In the assessment of a revival movement or trend, however, a measure of theological work must be done. Proponents of different positions must be heard, and scriptures must be examined. A common hermeneutic must be established from which a recommendation for the congregation can be cogently given.[41] Even in personal situational discernment, a certain amount of information may need to be gathered.

A Note on Hindrances to Discernment

Somewhere in the process of discernment we look for traps: faulty assumptions or models that might hinder good discernment. These traps come in a variety of forms. Perhaps it is the voice that whines,

Practicing Christian Spirituality

Your Situation

If yours is a situational discernment, you will probably need to do a bit of preparing for the situation. Now is the time for that. First, clarify your focus. Is this a broad or a specific issue? Can you weed out unnecessary portions of the question? Can you identify the various signs in your discernment? Second, acknowledge God's concerns with relationship to your discernment. Are there any false options that show themselves? Can you distinguish things that matter or things that don't matter in your situation? Did you identify with any of the hindrances to discernment listed above? How might you improve discernment through a reunderstanding of yourself, of God, or of the process of discernment itself? You may not be able to gather all your information as you read this chapter, but perhaps you can list a few facts on this or that. What are the most important things you must explore in order to come to God informed appropriately for this discernment? Finally, spend some time in prayer once again, just surrendering your own concerns to God. Be honest with God. Tell God how you really feel about this situation. "Cast all your anxiety on him, because he cares for you" (1 Peter 5:7). Now you are ready for the formal process of discernment itself.

"God won't speak to me. I'm not spiritual enough," or the experience of having the circumstances confront us with such force that we are frozen still. It could be the expectation that God will speak to me every minute of the day or the assumption either that it's all in the Bible or that I must expect some prophetic or charismatic "word" to confirm my direction. It might also be the anxiety that I have to do this process just right or else I will miss God's will. Or I might be a self-deprecating loner ("they won't understand") or a self-aggrandizing loner ("I don't need their help").[42] These traps tend to be rooted in a false view of God or of ourselves. They reduce hearing God to a formula and tend to abdicate responsible decision making. We move beyond these traps when we view ourselves and God rightly (in faith and love), when hearing flows out of a living immersion in the Word and the Spirit of God, when we learn to pay attention to God where God is present, and when we hear God in the context of wisdom.

Recognizing the Presence and Action of God

We have prepared ourselves for discernment by clarifying the focus, gathering information, and recognizing God's and our own concerns. We are now ready to begin prayerful reflection on the issue at hand. But how do we listen for God's guidance? What are we to look for in this time of prayerful reflection? Where should we expect to sense the hand of God? And how do we assess what we perceive? These are the questions of recognition. And this recognition of God's active presence is born of various sensibilities that are found in various sources and assessed through various criteria.

Signs and Sensibilities

One way of illuminating the act of recognition is to take a closer look at the various signs of discernment.

The *focus* of discernment is what the discernment is about—a particular decision, a sense of where we are with God, an odd experience. Knowledge of the focus of discernment illuminates not only our problem, but something about the way to the answer as well. To know that the issue of discernment has to do with a career decision, for example, indicates that while my discernment of God's will may not *depend* on my life story, my schedule, or my financial situation, it will normally, in the end, be reconciled to those realities. Likewise, when we assess the character of a move of God, we may have to look at the effect of powerful experiences on people's lives.

As we reflect on the focus, then, we will find possibilities for the *sources* of discernment, that to which we look in order to resolve the discernment. As we will see below, we normally attend to a select number of sources while leaving others open to surprise us. For example, an examination of life story and the felt sense of direction may serve, along with a few practical considerations, as the primary sources of Chris's discernment. At the same time, if some overwhelming dream sheds light on the discernment, Chris is not apt to complain. But precisely what *about* a life story or feelings does one look for direction? Are we looking simply for some vague sense of peace about a decision?

This brings us to the *criteria* of discernment. A criterion is a particular configuration or pattern of the sources of discernment. Our assumption is that the Spirit of God is present and active in the process of discernment itself, communicating in a recognizable manner. (Remember, God wants to be known!) So Chris might look for a kind of settled confidence as Chris prayerfully considers a given option, not just for any vague sense of peace. Chris has learned to distinguish the character of the divinely sent peace, known as "consolation" and which comes from the Spirit of God, from the false peace, which just wants to get the decision over with.[43] Perhaps the practical step of conversation with others will help Chris distinguish and recognize this authentic peace. Similarly, First Church in Midtown, Ghana, might be looking for

indications that the leaders of this supposed move of God are proclaiming a gospel that is in substantial harmony with the biblical and historic church and that they are not unreasonably driven by the desire to create a following for themselves. As we shall see below, patterns observed in the sources of discernment indicate that certain *criteria* of discernment may be fulfilled.

Ultimately, the criteria of discernment give us a sense of the *meaning* of discernment—God's presence or activity or guidance in life.

We attend to all these signs of discernment, and to the omnipresent God, by a contemplative openness to the divine in all that surrounds us. And once again we are brought face-to-face with the importance of the sensibilities of a contemplative attitude. This attitude begins with belief that God is here, with wonder, and with appreciation. It takes a long, loving, look at the Real. It waits to interpret what it sees. First, it just sees. Discernment is, in one sense, appreciative awareness itself: waiting, anticipating, attending, noticing every sign for what it is.

Sources

The focus of discernment (what the discernment is *about*) points us to the *sources* of discernment. Throughout this text I have emphasized that God is a self-communicating God, desiring to make himself known. I have also noted that God communicates through a variety of means. God is revealed through history, through scripture, through Christ, and through the Spirit. Reason gives us access to God, as do tradition, local community, and human experience itself.[44] Here are examples of how a few of these sources might be used with relationship to discernment:

- *Scripture.* The course of ongoing study of scripture may secure a sense that God is concerned about a particular matter, which informs your discernment. At times a particular verse may jump out, as if sent from God. While reading scripture you may find yourself convicted about a wrong attitude regarding the discernment.

- *Experience.* While in a time of prayer, one member of the group may receive a mental image that summarizes the sense of the group regarding one aspect of the discernment. While at your spiritual best, you find yourself increasingly inclined to something, filled with deep feeling. The leaders of a congregation have a corporate intuition about a person they are dealing with.

- *Community.* A casual comment in a conversation strikes you, and you realize something about a discernment. Someone delivers a prophetic utterance during worship that powerfully reveals the heart of God for the church. Regular recitation of the Nicene Creed coincides with the sermon and the community is inspired to faithfulness.

- *Nature.* A walk through the forest reminds you of the cycles of life, and you realize that your own cycle is changing. You become aware of the geography of the neighborhood (which has very steep hills), and see that ministry to the community must address the transportation needs of the elderly.

- *Reason.* Your evaluation of one course of action reveals an unwarranted assumption that could affect the outcome of everything. Your analysis of the social systems of a community show that informal systems of power have repeatedly short-circuited the best decisions of the official leadership.

- *Circumstances.* On the one hand, fortuitous circumstances can be interpreted as sources (some use the term *signs*) of God's guiding work. Someone else is hired where Chris was offered a job, and Chris says, "God closed that door, and this is a sign to go on to seminary." The Alternative finds an open office

building nearby that would make a perfect space for a legal aid clinic, so this *must* be God's way of telling the congregation that this is his will. On the other hand, it actually might be the opposite. Perhaps God desires for Chris to press through (Chris has never taken much initiative) toward a better job with a clearer opportunity of integrating faith and work (not to mention pursuing that special relationship). Perhaps this opportunity to create a legal aid clinic is really a temptation from Satan to draw the young congregation away from a ministry of friendship to the neighborhood. Even in life discernment we can easily mistake the personal turmoil of life for a sign that something is wrong with us, when it might really express an unrest due to a partly unconscious desire for a new stage of growth. While God can communicate through circumstances, we must interpret them with caution and in harmony with the other sources of discernment.

We could go on to talk about angelic visitations, dreams, our own life trajectories, vision and hopes, media, and more. The sources of discernment are manifold, and the contributions they make to our discernment process are equally manifold. We pay attention to the sources of discernment, waiting to see what they may tell us. And as we listen, the Spirit speaks.

Criteria

After listening to the sources of discernment, we find ourselves with a store of **impressions**: thoughts, feelings, and such that may or may not be indications of God's presence or guidance. Before we share these impressions with the discerning community (or before the individual jumps to conclusions), it is helpful to sort them by exploring indications that a given impression really is from God. In the history of the church people have recognized the value of paying attention to certain clues or indicators that a given phenomenon may (or may not) be of God. Often they are worded in the form of conditions that, when met, serve to signify that something is (or is not) of God. We call these criteria of discernment. We can summarize a few of them as follows:[45]

1. Examine the *content* of the impression.

   - Is it in line with the scriptures and the traditions of the church?
   - Is it oriented toward the beauty and the holiness of God and not toward self (even subtly)?
   - Does it communicate the God of Christianity?
   - Are there pieces of the impression that are clearly from the flesh?
   - Over time, does it communicate a balance of speech or does it harp on one matter?

2. Examine the *spirit* of the impression.

   - Does it feel right? Does it come with the conviction of God?
   - Does it communicate and promote humble and Christlike character?
   - Does it have a discernible bearing on your present life situation?
   - What is the spiritual tone or effect? If it seems frightening, harsh, condemning, or critical, is it likely to be from the Holy Spirit?
   - Does it glorify Jesus?

3. Examine the *fruit* of the impression.

   - Have you known impressions of this sort (either in your life or in others') to produce, over time, growth in purity of doctrine, devotion, or conduct?

   - Is the impression attended by the comfort or conviction of God toward the development of godly fruit in your life?
   - Does this impression carry the power of God with it?

Once again, these signs are not guarantees of finding God's will. There are times when pieces of an impression are clearly from the flesh, but when you look at it you can see how God is present in the impression even though the flesh is there as well. Sometimes God reveals a side of himself that seems at odds with our normal way of perceiving God. We are seeking guidelines, not guarantees. It is often more fruitful to focus on the character of impressions than to try to sort out all the nuances of the source (what of this is from self, is from God, is demonic, and so on). Furthermore, God's revelation is often partial and periodic. We find clues from scripture at one point in time. This clue confirms another clue given later through conversation with a friend. And still later we ourselves find a strong inclination to pursue a particular avenue in concert with these clues. This is why it is good to recognize the presence and guidance of God not simply in the crisis of the moment, but in the ongoing maturity of life too. In this way you are filling the wells of discernment even before you start. Ultimately, at some point near the end of our evaluation of each impression, we synthesize the impressions as a whole, looking for agreement, complementarity, or conflicts. We see whether we are getting a sense of further direction, whether the question is being changed, whether we must return to some neglected aspect of gathering information, or whether we are ready to take the next step toward identifying God's will and taking action.

Discerning the Next Step: God's Will and the Movement to Action

Having learned about the principles of and the preparation for discernment, and

Practicing Christian Spirituality

Your Sources and Criteria

Now it is time to explore the sources and criteria of your own discernment. But first, review once again the sensibilities of your discernment. What attitudes do you need to perceive the guidance of God? Your knowledge about what the issue is about (your focus) will have guided you to a collection of sources to observe for signs of God's presence of guidance. To what sources have you primarily looked? What have you gained from scripture, community, nature, reason, feelings, or other experiences? Have there been other sources that have supplied significant contributions to your store of impressions? How do you see the set of circumstances that lie before you at present?

Now evaluate these impressions one by one according to the criteria of Christian discernment. Examine the content of these impressions. What does each impression gained from each source seem to say, and how does that statement ring with your sense of the faith? Check the spirit of each impression: its tone, bearing, and feel. Does the impression feel like it is from God? Check the fruit of each impression, one by one. Where have you seen this kind of impression lead? Does the impression carry God's power or conviction forward?

Now, having examined each impression one by one, pull them together as a whole. How do your various impressions interact with each other? How does what you gained from scripture interact with what you gained from others or from your own intuition? Do you sense unresolved conflicts? Is there an increasing sense of direction? Are there issues of gathering information to which you must return? Close this time again with a moment of surrender and trust, conscious that God is generous to offer wisdom when needed.

---

having gained familiarity with the practice of prayerful evaluation, we are now ready to enter the stage of establishing God's will and making decisions.

In communal discernment this is the stage of sharing wisdom, of bringing those impressions we deem relevant to the group and together moving from evaluation ultimately to action. There are a variety of models of how this might be accomplished. We might move from a time of *worship*, to a time of *intercession*, to a time of *open discussion*, to a time of *checking* for emerging consensus (a sense that "this" is from the Lord) that is finally *confirmed* by the power of the Spirit in action. Or we might begin with a time of *silence* followed by a *presentation of the problem* by a member of the group. Then we have a *preliminary discussion* where general questions and insights are offered and the waters are tested. If the discussion seems fruitful, then we conduct a time of *serious discussion*, where specific details and concerns are brought up. Prayerful consideration is given throughout this stage. Members of the group take *stands* on the issue at hand, taking care to balance their comments with the needs of the whole. Finally, the sense of the *whole* is weighed and, if there is sufficient reason to believe that God is glorified by a given option, implementation is considered. Another option for this stage, if the focus is clear (especially with a yes-or-no question) and if there is no profound sense of God's leading gained after a season of waiting and prayer, might be to encourage *presentations* by each member of reasons for each alternative and then against each alternative. (By having each member list reasons both for and against, all can think carefully about the alternatives and factions can be kept from developing.) Then after prayerful *reflection*, we allow the community to offer *evaluations*; then we have more *prayer*; then we have more sharing. Then perhaps we take a *vote* to get a sense of the whole.[46] Even in individual discernment, the process is not entirely clear. As author Frank Houdek writes, "Both the long tradition of teaching about discernment and my own personal experience tell me that there is no 'canonized' way to conduct spiritual discernment."[47]

Making a Decision

Most of what we do in discernment is waiting. We watch our sources, we evaluate impressions, we share wisdom, we integrate information, and we simply sit ourselves in the presence of God until it seems that a good decision can be made. Ignatius of Loyola outlines a set of three times for making a good decision (he calls it an "**election**"). Attention to these times can be very helpful for individuals and groups discerning the guidance of God.[48]

The "First Time": being blasted. "The First Time is an occasion when God our Lord moves and attracts the will in such a way that a devout person, without doubting or being able to doubt, carries out what is proposed."[49] We can call it getting *blasted*. There are times when God simply blasts us, and we have little doubt about what he said in that moment or what the appropriate evaluation of a situation is. We just know. This absolute clarity comes to us not merely with regard to matters of morality and sanctification (God is often quite clear on these points), but at times also with regard to some nonmoral choices. There are times when God's Spirit speaks to us about a decision in life, and it is crystal clear what God is revealing. Like Paul, we are knocked off our horse. Mother Theresa of Calcutta experienced such a time as she took a train ride. During the course of the ride she simply knew, without any doubt

in her mind, that she was to move out of her convent and into the poorest section of Calcutta to minister there. Yet even in these times choice is not circumvented. Even in these most extreme cases we are still left with responsibility (response-ability), a choice God freely gives us and a decision we freely make. We discern what we take to be strong evidence for divine preference, and we make a choice.

The "Second Time": being led. "The Second Time is present when sufficient clarity and knowledge are received from the experience of consolations and desolations, and from experience in the discernment of various spirits."[50] We can call this time being *led*. The context of the second time is the examination of the influences and the inclinations of the community or the individual. Follow the ups and downs of the process, asking, "What am I drawn to when I am at my best?" As you share wisdom with others, what do the movements of the Holy Spirit seem to indicate?

More often than not, God's revelation comes to us subtly; it's not often that we are blasted. This is a matter not only of our perception, but also of God's choice. There is a season of getting to know ourselves, our authenticity before various options, our honest fears, wants, and so on and of being transformed in things. And then, when all is done—when the "words" have been heard, when the feelings have been addressed, when counsel has been sought—there are times when, in our best moments, we perceive an inclination toward this or that. We may not have a clear sense of the future, but we have enough of a sense to take a next step forward. And that is all we need.

The "Third Time": being ignored. Ignatius provides instructions for making it "in this third time," in cases when "an election is not made in the first or second time."[51] We wait and observe and evaluate, and still there is no blasting. There is not even sufficient clarity to take the next step forward. We can call this being *ignored*—at least it feels like we're being ignored. Sometimes, we are presented with options and, after much spiritual gymnastics, we can discover no indication of what seems to be from the Lord. There is simply no spiritual movement to one or the other option. And in some of these situations we do not have the opportunity to wait around until greater confidence arises. Circumstances demand action. In other times, God himself may be pressing us to take greater personal responsibility. So we place ourselves before his presence and reaffirm our commitment to serve God above all. We also reaffirm our trust in God, aware that God loves us more than we do ourselves, and that no matter where we find ourselves, we are always in God's care. And then, in a time of "tranquility," having "considered the end for which I was born," we simply "elect a life or state of life within the bounds of the Church." We weigh the pros and cons. We consider what others might do in our situation.[52] We take the information collected and we evaluate the situation, always attentive to feelings and reasons. And again, when all is said and done, we simply make a rational choice and trust ourselves to God.

We may hear God's voice and God says, "My will for you in this case is for you to decide on your own." Or we may hear nothing and feel abandoned. And still we choose. After the choice is made, we may look for confirmations in a sense of the Spirit and in life in general, but the signs in the midst of a "Third Time" election will have more to do with God's work in our reasonable evaluation. Then we live with the decision, just as we do in the other times of election. We think and pray and trust that God is present with our ordinary reasoning, and we simply decide.

Implementation, Communication, and Review

This is the step of follow through. You simply make the decision. In Chris's situation, as an individual, the process is easy. Chris simply makes the decision and takes the necessary steps to live out this next career stage. For communal discernment, however, a bit more is involved. After the early church decided that Gentiles were to be allowed into the community of faith without requiring their obedience to the law (given a few stipulations), the leaders were careful to communicate and implement this decision appropriately (Acts 15:22–29). But whether you are making a community decision or an individual decision, clarity and charity are vital if a well-discerned decision is also to be a well-received decision. For this reason a few points are worth noting:

Formal approval. Here is where the relationship between authority and discerning community comes into play. An individual decision simply needs to receive approval from appropriate people (family, community, authorities) in order for the individual to move forward. In communal discernment, the structures relevant to the group must begin by agreeing on how decisions are to be made from the start of the process (for example, determining what is to happen if there is no consensus or if other complications arise). Some groups separate discernment meetings and formal business meetings, taking the results of a discernment process to the formal approval structures. Yet there are dangers if key structural authorities have not shared in the discernment process. Different forms of government will have to find their own way in these matters. In any case, appropriate formal approval secures the wisdom gained through discernment and translates it into a realizable plan.

Communication. The communication of discerned decisions is not a light matter. Including the right people at the right times is very important in order to have a decision that is well received. Good communication insures that all those involved in any way are informed in an appropriate manner and time and by the appropriate people. Decisions are not simply *presented.* Often they are pastorally *imparted,* with consideration of the needs of each recipient of information. (This is true even for an individual decision: individuals should think in advance about *how* well-discerned decisions are communicated.) Wisdom lies not only in hearing the voice of God *for* the body, but also in facilitating the work of God *in* the body. Once again, both clarity and charity are vital to well-implemented decisions.

Administration. Though less significant for individual discernment, administration is important in communal discernment to the life of the decision. While the discernment team or the decision makers need not administrate a decision, it is still necessary during the discernment process to designate those people who *will* take the next step. Knowledge of the implementing body can shape the character of the discernment process itself. Or perhaps a special implementing body can be named after the discernment process and decision. Much will depend on the government and culture of a given community. It is helpful at times (even for an individual) to establish a time frame for when tasks are to be accomplished. Those who implement may need these kinds of guidelines in order to enact the character of a decision as discerned by a leadership team.

Evaluation and review. While communication and administration can be performed by others, evaluation and review of the discernment process must include the discerners themselves. Again, evaluation and review are valuable not only for groups, but for individuals as well. At some point in time, simply for the sake of the ongoing maturity of the discerner, it is valuable to look back at discerning processes with a critical eye. These few questions—which can be reworded as needed for an individual—will help those who review the process step by step:

- Was every member of the discerning community thoroughly acquainted with all the relevant facts?
- Were we sufficiently learned and versed in the subject matter of the discernment?

- Were we given ample time for reflection and for developing original insights, or did we labor under pressure?
- Were we peaceful, quiet, and receptive? Were there any virtues that needed cultivation?
- Was the climate prayerful?
- What sources were used? What criteria were most significant? How did each play a part? Was our evaluation and integration of these sources and criteria fair?
- Was the final decision making and implementation appropriate for this discernment?
- What have we noticed since the decision?

The end or goal. Simply (and hopefully) put, by the end of discernment a clarity appears—about one's situation, oneself, and one's God. And often this awareness is accompanied by feelings and motion toward activity. But note that though we may have clarity, we might not experience certainty. And the clarity we have may not even be about the stuff or the situation. Indeed, at times, our understanding of these matters may be left quite vague. Yet along with this uncertainty we find an awareness of one's own freedom to choose, to move forward in life, free from anxiety, in the context of God's care. Again, discernment is not about methods and techniques. Discernment is a matter of a relationship. Techniques are there to help cultivate and comprehend the nature of the relationship. If we substitute religious procedure for relational process, we will be missing the point of discernment.

At times in discernment, the issue is not the issue. We move to discern an issue that may seem critical to us. *God's* point in our discerning, however, may be to get us to face ourself (or one another) in ways we have not done before, or God may be facilitating a new humility or love or listening. We need to be prepared, in discernment, to allow God to face us with what is on

Practicing Christian Spirituality

Your Decision and Action

Now is the time to consider making a decision of life. Have you waited enough yet? What have you noticed as the time has rolled by? Was there a time of being *blasted*, a time when you received some guidance that is almost beyond doubt? Are you feeling *led*, sufficiently guided by the indications given through the various sources and evaluations to take at least the next step forward? Or are you *ignored*, still wondering when (or *if*) God will even show up? Are you compelled to decide in spite of your lack of guidance? In any case, remind yourself of the character of God: God loves you and has a wonderful plan for your life. Consider those aspects where you have felt clarity and those where you have not. What is left to explore? Consider those places where you have experienced the transform-ing touch of God in the midst of the process. To what new aspects of relationship might God be inviting you through this discernment?

And then consider your next step. Given this process, what do I do now? Don't predict your future; just decide your next step. Leave the future to God. What precisely are you going to do? Does this decision need some kind of approval by someone? Who needs to know about this? Ask yourself how you will implement this decision. Do you need a list of things to do or a timeline to help this implementation? Do you need a community of accountability and support to help you? How will this decision be administrated over the long haul? Finally, go back and review the process as a whole. Ask a few of the review questions listed above. What have you learned from this process?

God's mind for us in the situation. The clarity reached may be different from what we had expected. In discernment we allow God to clarify our motives, our perspectives, and our healings or to initiate new options never considered.

Furthermore, a sense of calling is not necessarily a guarantee of success. All we know in discernment is the wisdom (or freedom) of taking the next step forward. Often the apostle Paul took a next step into persecution. We *know* that if we are following God we will encounter trials and difficulties. We need not question a well-discerned decision simply because it leads us into difficulty. We discern, we choose, and we leave the results up to God.

The Life of Discernment

Christian spirituality is about relationship with God. A life of discernment— appreciating God in the ordinary, watching the hand of God over time in our lives, and determining the guiding presence of God in key situations—is the means by which that relationship is navigated. As part of relationship with God, discernment involves both divine and human actions. God initiates, inviting us to the next step of life, effecting transformations that lead to new decisions, showing us bits and pieces of his character (and showing us our own character, as well).

In turn, we struggle to perceive, to recognize, to interpret God's initiation and then to respond in faith and obedience. We are human, so our discernment will be characterized by the ordinary operations of human experience. For example, discernment is a process of categorization (distinguishing what is of God from what is not of God). As a process of human categorization, discernment will exhibit features of natural human categorization tendencies. We will tend to give greater attention to a single notable impression (the public prophetic "word," for example) to the neglect of other less notable ones. Our discernment categorization improves with the acquisition of "expertise" in the things of God. Furthermore, because discernment is a human process, our affective operations are involved. Our emotional history influences how we recognize (or deny) moments of the Spirit's touch. Attention to the patterns in a group's mood reveals a sense of God's activity in the community. As we have noted, as a process of coming to know, discernment will follow the normal stages of human experience (from Being Aware, to Experiencing, and so on). Discernment will involve each of our relationships (with nature, self, others, spiritual forces, God) and will, at different times, touch us at different levels of depth. Sometimes responding to God's will is a simple act of obedience. At other times it involves an overhaul of our lifestyle. As with other aspects of Christian spirituality, discernment involves the entirety of human experience.[53]

As we have stated, discernment is the means by which our relationship with God is navigated. This is true of every aspect of our relationship with God. Discerning

transformation is a critical part of Christian life; it is life discernment itself. Where are we with God right now? What dynamics of ongoing salvation are central? Am I shifting stages of maturity? Where, in the breadth of transformation, does God's attention appear to be focused? Discerning elements of *spiritual formation* is a normal part of Christian life. Is this trial permitted by God as a means of formation? How should we respond? Was that experience an invitation of the Spirit to a new way of seeing and relating to God? What particular ascetical practices would best promote authentic growth in relationship? *Prayer*, as communication with God, requires discernment constantly. The attitude of contemplation developed in our chapter on prayer is a central attitude in discernment as well. We discern the dynamics of prayer, the experiences of prayer, the forms of prayer, and the effects of prayer. Likewise, the life of *care* is bound up with discernment. How do we know—in the here and now, with all the competing demands of life—specifically how I (or we) are to express care? Discernment forms the perceptive link between God's initiation and our response. Perhaps it is at this point that the tension of the divine-human relationship is most clearly grasped.

CHAPTER SUMMARY

1. Christian discernment is the evaluation of inner and outer stuff in light of a relationship with God with a view to response. It is rooted in a few basic principles: God desires to be known, we encounter ambiguity in our knowing, and resolving that ambiguity necessitates a process of evaluation involving both gift and skill. Discernment is of many types. Appreciative discernment celebrates the presence of God in the ordinary moment. Life discernment acknowledges the hand of God present through the course of time. And situational discernment evaluates the presence or action of God in a number of life situations: evaluating various trends in the church or society, determining God's will for vocational decisions, assessing the character of

movements of various spirits experienced in spiritual life, selecting sociopolitical or evangelistic strategy, and so on.

2. Discernment has been a topic of discussion throughout the history of the church. In the Old Testament the focus was on the *torah*, on the evaluation of prophets, and on the value of wisdom. Jesus came as the living icon of what "from God" looks like, the ultimate criterion of discernment, while the epistles show the tests necessary to distinguish the Spirit of Christ from false spirits. The desert elders understood discernment especially as distinguishing between various spirits, although over time discernment became increasingly associated with the virtue of prudence. In the late Middle Ages, discernment issues became central in light of the need to authenticate visions and prophecies. An emphasis on the criterion of humility, interpreted as submission to authority, both empowered and controlled those who wished to discern their experience. While the Protestant Reformation freed the populace from controlling strictures, it resulted in a debate regarding various sources of discernment. In both Protestant and Catholic circles, discerning the signs of advancing stages of life was emphasized. Recent interest in discernment has applied wisdom to a variety of areas of personal and corporate life.

3. The process of discernment starts with preparation. Preparation for discernment begins by reviewing the elements of discernment in a given case: reflecting on the process, the discerner, the context, the signs, and the end or goal of a given discernment. Discernment also involves a preparation of the discerner, the facilitation of key virtues that promote awareness, recognition, and response to the activity of God. In situational discernment, preparation necessary includes knowing the situation. In communal discernment, it is valuable to be aware of the roles and the rules of facilitators and participants in the gathered communal discernment process.

4. Discernment draws prayerful attention to a variety of sources. Assuming that God desires to be known and that God communicates through a variety of means, we look to those means to notice God's active presence. Scripture, reason, local community, tradition, personal history, current experience, and more can all serve as sources of discernment.

5. We observe these sources, seeing "how they look," watching for patterns or clues that may indicate that certain criteria of discernment have been met. We assess the impressions we receive from the sources of discernment in light of wise criteria of discernment, which have been passed down through the church. We examine the content of impressions in light of the truth of the Christian faith. We examine the spirit of impressions in light of how they affect our faith. We examine the fruit of impressions in light of the impact of the faith. We integrate our sense of the impressions as the process develops.

6. Ultimately, Christian discernment involves a season of waiting. We trust, observe, interpret, and evaluate until the right time for a response. Three times for making a choice of life can be identified. The first is when God moves so strongly that we have no doubt what to do. We are *blasted*. The second is when we have sufficient indication from the integration of information gained from the various sources to take the next step forward. We are *led*. In the third, we feel *ignored*. There is no blasting or leading, and we must simply commit ourselves to God, trust that God loves us, and make a responsible decision with the wisdom we possess.

7. A well-discerned decision is embodied in implementation. When we implement discernment we identify who will carry out the decision and how the decision will be carried out. We gain formal approval for the decision if necessary. We communicate the decision with those who need to know in a manner that is appropriate to each. We establish guidelines to ensure the administration of the decision. And we evaluate the process of discernment itself.

Questions

1. We have defined discernment as an evaluation *in light of relationship with God*. Is there the possibility of a *secular* discernment, where the evaluation is not made in light of relationship with God? What would that look like? What do you learn about Christian discernment by comparing it with, for example, materialist or Buddhist discernment?

2. List all the types of discernment you can think of. What kinds of situations do people discern about? Now look at the list. How does discernment differ based on the situations involved? How is it the same in all these cases?

3. Select one figure or movement from the history of the church and explore his or her ideas regarding discernment in greater detail. How does their historical context shape their concerns regarding discernment? What do you learn about your own discernment process from investigating that of another?

4. Can you think of any other virtues to add to the list of those valuable for cultivating quality discernment? Identify these virtues and explain how they facilitate Christian discernment.

5. Evaluate the preparation of a difficult group decision with which you are familiar. Identify the strengths and weakness of the preparation of the discerners, their awareness of the process, the preparation regarding the situation, and the preparation of the facilitator and the participants. Were there any points at which problems in the preparation were evident? What might have been done in advance to address these problems? What might you remember from this review as a leader of groups for your own ministry with groups?

6. What are your favorite sources of discernment? Why are they your favorite sources? What sources to you tend to avoid, and why? How do you respond to changes in circumstances and their bearing on discernment? What does all this reveal about your relationship with God?

7. Select a trend in the church with which you are familiar. Briefly collect your impressions about this trend. Now evaluate these impressions according to the criteria of discernment. Examine the content, the spirit, and the fruit of this trend. Now integrate your insights. What might you recommend to another (invent this person) regarding that trend based on your evaluation?

8. Doesn't all this talk about sources, evaluation, criteria, approval, implementation, and such make discernment just one more institutional procedure? Isn't it too complicated? How do we (or, even, *can* we) integrate all this with an understanding of Christianity as a simple relationship with God?

LOOKING FURTHER

Perhaps the best way of suggesting resources from the many available on Christian discernment is to divide loosely between practice, dynamics, and study. Again, various perspectives are represented.

Practice

The following works are aimed at helping the reader start a practice of discernment: Suzanne G. Farnham, Joseph P. Gill, and R. Taylor McLean, *Listening Hearts: Discerning Call in Community* (Harrisburg, PA: Morehouse, 1991); Debra K. Farrington, *Hearing with the Heart: A Gentle Guide for Discerning God's Will for Your Life* (San Francisco: Jossey-Bass, 2003); J. B. Libânio, *Spiritual Discernment and Politics: Guidelines for Religious Communities*, trans. Theodore Morrow (Eugene, OR: Wipf and Stock, 2003); James Ryle, *Hippo in the Garden: A Non-Religious Approach to Having a Conversation with God* (Orlando, FL: Creation House, 1993); Dallas Willard, *Hearing God: Developing a Conversational Relationship with God* (Downers Grove, IL: InterVarsity Press, 1999).

Dynamics

The works listed here, some of which are classics from the history of spirituality on discernment, explore or illumine the character of Christian discernment: Saint Diodochus of Photike, "On Spiritual Knowledge and Discernment: One Hundred Texts," in *The Philokalia: The Complete Text*, comp. Saint Nikodimos of the Holy Mountain and Saint Makarios of Corinth, trans. G. E. H. Palmer, Philip Sherrard, and Kallistos Ware (London: Faber and Faber, 1979); Jonathan Edwards, *The Distinguishing Marks of a Work of the Spirit of God* and *Religious Affections*, in *The Great Awakening*, ed. C. G. Goen, vol. 4, The Works of Jonathan Edwards (New Haven: Yale University Press, 1972), 213–88; Jean Gerson, "On Distinguishing True from False Revelations," in *Jean Gerson: Early Works*, trans. Brian Patrick McGuire, Classics of Western Spirituality (New York: Paulist Press, 1998), 334–64; Luke Timothy Johnson, *Scripture and Discernment: Decision Making in the Early Church* (Nashville: Abingdon, 1996); Ignatius of Loyola, *Spiritual Exercises*, in *Ignatius of Loyola: The Spiritual Exercises and Selected Works*, ed. George E. Ganss, Classics of Western Spirituality (New York: Paulist Press, 1991), 113–214; and Michael Sheeran, *Beyond Majority Rule: Voteless Decisions in the Religious Society of Friends* (Philadelphia: Philadelphia Yearly Meeting, 1983).

Study

For books that explore discernment more technically from the perspective of the academic field of spirituality, see Evan B. Howard, *Affirming the Touch of God: A Psychological and Philosophical Exploration of Christian Discernment* (Lanham, NJ: University Press of America, 2000); Edward Maletesta, ed., *Discernment of Spirits* (Collegeville, MN: Liturgical Press, 1970); Mark McIntosh, *Discernment and Truth: The Spirituality and Theology of Knowledge* (New York: Herder and Herder, 2004); Jules J. Toner, *A Commentary on Saint Ignatius' Rules for the Discernment of Spirits* (St. Louis: Institute of Jesuit Sources, 1982); Jules J. Toner, *Discerning God's Will: Ignatius of Loyola's Teaching on Christian Decision Making* (St. Louis: Institute of Jesuit Sources, 1991); and Kees Waaijman, *Spirituality: Forms, Foundations, Methods*, trans. John Vriend (Leuven, Belgium: Peeters, 2002), esp. 483–515.

The Renewal
of Christian Spirituality

12

OBJECTIVES

In this chapter you will put together all you have learned in the previous chapters while exploring renewal, the bringing of new life into relationship with God. You will discover the foundations of Christian renewal within the transforming divine-human relationship. You will see cycles of renewal in scripture and in the history of the church. You will explore various dynamics of renewal—how things act when renewal happens or when it doesn't. And you will take a peek into the future, asking what Christian spirituality might look like in the years ahead. By the end of the chapter you should be able to

- define *renewal*, comparing this term to other related terms;
- describe the foundations of Christian renewal, using what you have learned in the previous chapters;
- illustrate some of the significant features of renewal from scripture and the history of the church;
- recognize signs of renewal in a variety of settings, using the model of human experience presented in this book as a resource;
- identify some of the various dynamics of renewal both in history and in contemporary situations;
- locate the trajectory of your own relationship with God (or that of your community) in terms of a variety of trends shaping the future of Christian spirituality.

Imagine the rough setting of Jerusalem in 600 BC. It is a world where "justice never prevails" (Habakkuk 1:4). Destruction and violence are rampant. Strife and contention are the norm. "The wicked surround the righteous—therefore judgment comes forth perverted" (Habakkuk 1:4). And, as many of us might, the prophet Habakkuk complains to God about this state of affairs. "How long shall I cry for help, and you will not listen?" (Habakkuk 1:2). Why does God just let this kind of thing happen? Shouldn't God do *something* about it?

God responds. "I am rousing the Chaldeans" (Habakkuk 1:6). This fierce nation will itself be the instrument of God's correction of injustice, "with faces pressing forward; they gather captives like sand" (Habakkuk 1:9). God will use the violence of one nation to punish the wrongs of another.

But this is little comfort for Habakkuk. Would God permit the victories of the evil Chaldeans, whose "own might is their god" (Habakkuk 1:11) to be used to judge others? "Why do you look on the treacherous," cries Habakkuk, "and are silent when the wicked swallow those more righteous than they?" (Habakkuk 1:13). God's plan of salvation seems more unjust than the conditions from which Habakkuk desires to be saved.

Again God responds. Their time will come. "If it seems to tarry, wait for it; it will surely come, it will not delay" (Habakkuk 2:3). While the proud approach these conditions with a wrong spirit, the righteous will live by faith (Habakkuk 2:4). God issues a series of woes (each beginning, "Alas...") for those who deserve judgment: those who heap up what is not their own, who get evil gain for their houses, who build towns by bloodshed, who pour wrath on their neighbors, who worship idols. Their judgment will come. "But the LORD is in his holy temple; let all the earth keep silence before him!" (Habakkuk 2:20).

The final chapter of Habakkuk is a prayer of faith. Habakkuk first looks back to God's active presence in the past. "I have heard of your renown, and I stand in awe, O LORD, of your work." His desire is to see the same work in the present. "In our own time revive it" (Habakkuk 3:2). Revive it. Here is the longing for renewal—a cry that brings God's past into the present for the sake of a new future. Revive! Habakkuk cries for a renewal of the manifest presence of God, who brought life to his community once before. God answers Habakkuk's cry with a vision of his powerful, saving intervention. And Habakkuk responds to God with faith. "Though the fig tree does not blossom, and no fruit is on the vines; ... though the flock is cut off from the fold and there is no herd in the stalls, yet I will rejoice in the Lord; I will exult in the God of my salvation" (Habakkuk 3:17–18).

The longing for renewal, the faith that waits for it, and the response to it when it comes are important to Christian spirituality. Indeed, renewal is so important that we will conclude our exploration of Christian spirituality with this theme. God is interested in restoration, a big restoration—ultimately a new heavens and a new earth. This is a restoration *of* relationship and a restoration realized *through* relationship. In Christian *transformation* we see this restoration realized in the lives of individuals and communities, in humans cultivating spiritual *formation*, and in the Spirit working a new creation. This ever-being-restored relationship with God is expressed in a life of *prayer* and in a life of *care*, navigated through the subtleties of Christian *discernment*. Yet every change, every step of growth, points us toward something more. And every awareness of our lack points us to the same more. We long to see the hand of God active not merely in select individuals or in isolated communities, but over whole regions, initiating widespread movements, transforming the church as a whole. We desire greater intensity, greater scope, greater consequences. The cry for renewal is the plea that Christian spirituality would be actualized on an ever-larger scale. And throughout the history of the church there have been tastes of this renewal. Those tastes keep us longing for more.

The Language of Christian Renewal

We have been using the word *renewal* to identify this theme, but Christians know this theme by a variety of terms. Let's review a few of these terms in route to defining renewal and its significance for Christian spirituality.

Words for Renewal

Richard Lovelace, at the outset of his *Dynamics of Spiritual Life: An Evangelical Theology of Renewal*, surveys a few of these terms. He traces *renewal, revival*, and *awakening* back to biblical metaphors for the infusion of spiritual life, "used synonymously for broad scale movements of the Holy Spirit's work in renewing spiritual vitality in the church and in fostering its expansion in mission and evangelism."[1] Scholars tend to use the term *awakening* to refer to two movements in North America. The first of these (the Great Awakening, or the First Awakening) spread from New England throughout the American colonies from around 1740 to 1745 and had its own influence on movements in England and the continent; the second (the Second Awakening, or the Second Great Awakening) was a network of predominantly American movements from around 1780 to 1830. The term *awakening* is also used in Germany (*Erweckung*) to refer to movements of renewal especially within the eighteenth and nineteenth centuries.[2] Awakening is used to speak of the church (predominantly the Protestant church of the Enlightenment) *awakening* from its slumber, increasing in numbers, and growing in interest in and liveliness toward the things of God.

The term *revival* is also generally used with regard to Protestant movements. A wide range of movements are identified with this term: the evangelical revival in England, the Welsh revival of 1904, the *Reveil*

in France, the revivals led by Charles Finney (1792–1875) in the United States, the great prayer revival of 1858, and so on. Due to the linking of certain techniques (means of grace) with the term *revival*, it is also common to speak of *revivalism*, a particular approach to relationship with God and the expansion of the church that relies heavily on the techniques developed in the midst of the nineteenth-century revivals. The term *revival* speaks of a coming alive, of a church that was "dead" exhibiting growth, excitement, and movement once again.

The term **renewal** has a generally broader reference, especially in this century. We think of the charismatic renewal and of the Roman Catholic Second Vatican Council and Pope John Paul II's "sources of renewal." We speak of liturgical renewal and the renewal of religious life. A young organization promoting spiritual formation calls itself Renovaré (Latin for *renewal*). Evangelical Protestants recall the renewal movement in church structure in the 1970s. While not excluding the concept of numerical growth, renewal has generally referred to a season when new leaders, forms, ideas, structures and such arise within the church.

A few other related words may be mentioned as well. Lovelace states that *reformation* "refers to the purifying of doctrine and structures in the church, but implies also a component of spiritual revitalization."[3] We speak of the Gregorian reform of the

I think our church is on the verge of renewal—they wanted to sing the third verse of a hymn last Sunday!

What Do You Call Renewal?

Term	Definition	Example
awakening	a season in which the church of God rises from its slumber, increases in numbers, and grows in liveliness	the Great Awakening
revival	a season in which a "dead" church comes alive and exhibits growth, excitement, and movement	the Welsh Revival
renewal	a season in which new leaders, ideas, forms, structures, and such arise within the church	the charismatic renewal
reformation	a season in which the fundamental doctrines or structures of church life are organized in new and different ways	the Protestant Reformation
revitalization	a season in which a culture is reconfigured around new leaders, ideas, or forms of life	tribal revitalizations
movement	the collection of peoples influenced by or associated with renewal	the Keswick movement

More generally, renewal refers to any or all
of these large-scale patterns of relationship with God.

Roman church, the Clunaic or Studite reforms of monastic life, the Protestant Reformation, and so on. The term *revitalization* is less common within the Christian church, but it is often used by anthropologists to describe similar phenomena among various cultures. Thus, a revitalization is a process of cultural re-configuration around new leaders, ideas, and forms. The concepts anthropologists use to explore change in so-called primitive peoples can be used to explore changes in Christian spirituality.[4] Finally, there is the **movement**. Whereas renewal or revival speaks of the event of new life, a renewal movement speaks of the collection of peoples, structures (however loose), energies, and such that are associated with the renewal.

Defining Renewal

We shall, in this text, use each of these terms to refer to the patterns of religious life commonly associated with it (hence, the Great *Awakening*, the Azusa Street *revival*, the Pentecostal *movement*). Nevertheless, we will use *renewal* to refer in a more general way to any or all of these large-scale patterns of relationship with God: where the church experiences a fresh sense of life or vitality, where there is some powerful manifestation of God's active presence, where significant change is experienced (such as growth in numbers or the pioneering of new forms or structures), where the world itself is transformed through the church's witness, or other similar phenomena.

Note that in speaking of renewal we do not use the word *repeat*. Renewal is not a mere repetition of something that has happened before. Rather, some dynamic of the past is uniquely experienced here and now. Renewal is a reappropriation of God's Spirit, pulling together past, present, and future. In renewal, we look to the past—to when God did something special, to when things were alive, or further back to the creative character of God's Spirit. We also look to the present: to where the needs are felt, to where God's creative Spirit must be manifest and renewal must be embodied. And we look to the future as well: to when "what was" will be transformed into "what may be," or perhaps further, as all hope for renewal is ultimately a hope for the eschaton.

Foundations of the Renewal of Christian Spirituality

The foundations of renewal are to be found in the nature of Christian spirituality itself: the divine-human relationship,

FIGURE 12.1
The Foundations of the Renewal of Christian Spirituality

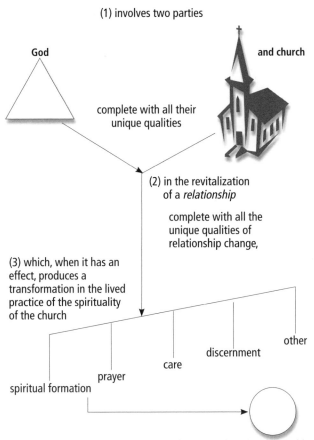

The renewal of Christian spirituality

(1) involves two parties

God   **and church**

complete with all their
unique qualities

(2) in the revitalization
of a *relationship*

complete with all the
unique qualities of
relationship change,

(3) which, when it has an
effect, produces a
transformation in the lived
practice of the spirituality
of the church

other

discernment

care

prayer

spiritual formation

(4) and in turn, effects a manifestation of God in the world

the dynamics of that relationship, and the character of the practice of that relationship. In other words, providing the foundations for understanding Christian renewal means simply reviewing the material we have already covered.

The God-Human Relationship

Renewal is the revitalization of a *relationship*, and as such it is governed by the character of the parties involved in the relationship. Christian renewal, the renewal of spirituality, is the revitalization of the relationship between humans (individuals and communities) and the Christian God. The possibility of renewal on the human side is found in our capacity to perceive the touch of God and to receive it, to hear God's voice and to respond. Likewise, Christian renewal assumes the active presence of God—a God who chooses, at times, to intervene in history and to make himself known. Thus we return to the themes of chapters 3 and 4. Renewal is God entering into human experience once again, reopening our hearts, reconfiguring our minds, reintegrating our lives, reconciling our relationships. As we shall see, different times of renewal will touch different aspects of human experience. And renewal is human experience confronted with the Christian God. As the Christian God is both known and unknown, times of renewal will exhibit both clarity and mystery. As the Christian God is known through names and images, times of renewal will bring to the surface different names or metaphors of God and God's activity. As the divine-human relationship is a covenant of love, Christian renewal will restore the church in love, love for God and for others.

Furthermore, because renewal is the experience of God in the midst of the realities of human experience, all renewal will exhibit the greatness of human experience and the tragedy of human experience we learned about in chapter 5. Revivals can combine precious healings with excessive showmanship. Awakenings can give rise to rapid growth and contentious strife. Reformation births newly adapted structures, which can become the power hierarchies of tomorrow. All renewal involves the restoration of human experience. Renewal *is* restoration—partially realized but always pointing toward the ultimate restoration of human (and cosmic) experience in the eschaton.

The Dynamics of Christian Spirituality

Because Christian renewal is rooted in relationship, it will exhibit the characteristic *dynamics* of the interpersonal relationship of God and humans. Renewal, for example, results in a rise of *interest* in God. Jonathan Edwards, for instance, writing about the onset of the Great Awakening in Northampton, Massachusetts, says that "a great and earnest concern about the great things of religion and the eternal world became universal in all parts of the town. . . . All the conversation in all companies and upon all occasions, was upon these things only."[5] Similarly, renewal comes from the *invitation* of God and demands our *response*. Powerful waves of the Spirit are often invitations, where God (to use the language of Revelation 3:20) knocks loudly on our door and waits for the response of our faith, our openness, our obedience. And as invitation leads to response, renewal brings a broad range of transformations—transformation of individuals, of communities, and of the surrounding world.

The Practice of Christian Spirituality

Finally, as a revitalization of *lived* relationship, Christian renewal flows both from and into the concrete *practice* of spirituality. Much has been said, for example, about the important role that the practice of intercessory prayer plays in facilitating seasons of revival. Powerful movements have often been preceded by prevailing prayer. Yet renewal also leads the church into prayer, such as when, through the Pentecostal revivals of the early twentieth century, many were introduced to the prayer of speaking in tongues. Exploration with regard to expressions of care (styles of preaching or evangelism, for example) have led the way into awakening, just as new expressions of care have followed the awakening itself (such as the growth of voluntary societies following the Second Great Awakening). Similarly, using the means of spiritual formation has led the church into renewal (such as when ascetical practices were explored in the desert traditions or when suffering was central to many during the fourteenth century), just as renewal has also fostered innovations in the means of grace (such as the Methodist development of classes and bands to shepherd the multitudes that were coming to Christ).

Thus we see that an exploration of Christian renewal is really nothing more than a case study in the principles and dynamics of Christian spirituality itself, albeit on a larger scale. God invites us into relationship. We hesitate, or we advance into that invitation. And we are changed.

A Select History of Christian Renewal

If, indeed, the exploration of Christian renewal is a case study in Christian spirituality, then a review of the history of

Christian renewal can offer an interesting window into models and perspectives of Christian spirituality. We can only present a few examples here.

Scripture and Renewal

One of the clearest summaries of the cycle of spiritual decline and renewal is found in Judges 2. It describes the Israelites as they enter the promised land:

> The people worshiped the LORD all the days of Joshua, and all the days of the elders who outlived Joshua, who had seen the great work that the LORD had done for Israel. ... And another generation grew up after them, who did not know the LORD or the work that he had done for Israel. ...
>
> Then the Israelites did what was evil in the sight of the LORD and worshiped the Baals; and they abandoned the LORD ... and they provoked the LORD to anger. ... So the anger of the LORD was kindled against Israel, and he gave them over to plunderers who plundered them, ... and they were in great distress.
>
> Then the LORD raised up judges, who delivered them out of the power of those who plundered them. (Judges 2:7–16)

As we shall see, this pattern is identifiable throughout history: renewal, distance, decline, difficulty, despair, and renewal again. Though the form of decline, despair, and renewal may change from situation to situation, the basic pattern is the same. Sociologists have discussed such themes as the routinization of a charismatic movement, the establishment of hierarchy, the shift from inspirational ideas into normative ideology, and the transformation of these through the revitalization of leadership, idea, and practice. Essentially these same dynamics can be observed in ancient Israel here in the book of Judges.

Another example of renewal in Israelite history comes under the reign of king Josiah of Judah (around 622 BC). Elements of foreign (and inappropriate) religion had crept into the Israelite worship of Yahweh. Indeed, shrines and altars to other gods dotted the landscape of Judah. Local priests facilitated this idolatry, while the temple of the Lord remained in disrepair and the Torah of Yahweh was forgotten. Second Kings 22–23 records how, under the rule of Josiah, the law of the Lord was rediscovered. This discovery brought great conviction on the ruling party. Consequently, a thorough reform was instituted: shrines and altars were destroyed, priests were deposed, Passover was celebrated, the poor and needy were defended (see Jeremiah 22:16), and the law of God was made the law of the land. Yet in spite of all these reforms, "the LORD did not turn from the fierceness of his great wrath" (2 Kings 23:26). In the next two chapters we hear of the besieging of Jerusalem and the exile of the people to Babylon.

Perhaps the most well-known story of renewal in the New Testament is that of Pentecost. Jesus had died, risen, and ascended. His followers were "all together in one place" (Acts 2:1). They became "filled with the Holy Spirit" and found themselves speaking in other languages "as the Spirit gave them ability" (Acts 2:4). Visitors to Jerusalem heard them praising God in their own languages and wondered what was going on. One of Jesus's followers, Peter, gave an inspired speech, identifying this event with the fulfillment of the Old Testament promise of restoration. He gave an invitation and about three thousand responded positively to this message. From this point on there was growth upon growth. There was renewal of individual experience ("awe came upon everyone," Acts 2:43) and of corporate life ("all who believed were together and had all things in common," Acts 2:44). And although, as a reading of the book of Acts reveals, they faced divisions from within and persecutions from without, still "day by day the Lord added to their number those who were being saved" (Acts 2:47).

Monastic Renewals

The renewal of the people of God through the Pentecostal ministry of the

And so, from then on, there were monasteries in the mountains, and the desert was made a city by monks, who left their own people and registered themselves for the citizenship in the heavens.

—Athanasius[6]

Holy Spirit stimulated the formation of both modalities (communities that welcomed all ages, genders, and commitment levels—for example, the "church" in a city) and sodalities (groups that required further levels of commitment or strictures regarding gender and such—for example, the Pauline mission team or the enrolled widows). One vehicle of renewal and expansion during the first thousand years of Christian history was what we now call monasticism; then it was simply a collection of sodalities. The story of Pachomius (292–346) and the development of Egyptian communal (coenobitic) monasticism is a good example. Converted through the hospitality of believers who cared for him in prison, Pachomius committed himself to the service of God and the love of others. He learned something of the disciplined life from a solitary named Palamon. Fasting, long prayer vigils, study of the Scriptures, and manual labor became his rhythm of life. On discovering a deserted village, he sensed God leading him to form a monastic community, "for," a voice said, "many will come to thee to become monks."[7] Indeed, many came. Between Pachomius's first foundation at Tabennesis (the deserted village) and his death in 346, he founded or incorporated over ten different monasteries numbering around 5,200 monks, all of them committed to a life of withdrawal from the world, prayer, ascetical practice, and meditation on the scriptures. While Pachomius's monastic foundations were not necessarily the first or the only foundations of their kind, they were pivotal in shaping the course of monasticism for the centuries to come.

Whereas the Pachomian sodalities were communities of "withdrawal" (although they continued to interact with each other and with the world on a limited scale), the renewal that began with fifth-century Saint Patrick of Ireland was a movement of "advance." Patrick, a nominal British Christian, came into the vibrancy of faith while a captured slave of the Irish. After an escape and some years in England and Gaul, Patrick again left for Ireland as a monk and bishop to be a fisher of men and ambassador among the Irish. What did this mission achieve? Patrick himself mentions that he baptized "all those thousands," that he "ordained clergy everywhere," and that the people of Ireland became "a prepared people of the Lord."[8] Indeed, "an ancient document called the *Annals of the Four Masters* reports that Patrick's mission planted about 700 churches, and that Patrick ordained perhaps 1000 priests. Within his lifetime, 30 to 40 (or more) of Ireland's 150 tribes became substantially Christian."[9] Following Patrick's lead, people like Columba (521–97, also known as Colum Cille), Columbanus (d. 615), and Aidan (d. 651) evangelized the Picts (Scotland), the Anglo-Saxons, and into Europe, "saving civilization," as author Thomas Cahill claims, and creating a society ordered around monastic life.[10]

Monastic renewals fed the revitalization of the church through the development of sodalic forms of life, groups of people who made special commitments to Christianity that were above and beyond the ordinary. Some sodalic renewals (like the Pachomian foundations or the renewal of Orthodox monastic life in the Studite reform of the eighth century) primarily touched those within the community of believers. Others (such as the development of mendicant orders in the twelfth century or the Moravian missions thrust in the eighteenth) had a significant apostolic dimension.

Reformations of the Sixteenth and Seventeenth Centuries

The Christian church experienced reforms of one sort and another from the beginning. We can see, for example, the council in Acts 15 as a reform of policy regarding the treatment of Gentile converts. Similarly, reforms under Gregory the Great (ca. 540–604) centralized the leadership and specified the practice of the church.

Nonetheless, when we hear the word *reformation*, we usually think of the Protestant and Catholic Reformations of the sixteenth century. The reform movements of this period resulted in wide, sweeping changes in modality and sodality alike. Within Protestant modalities, for example, sacraments were reduced from seven to two, the place of congregational singing and preaching was elevated, and the emphasis in congregational meetings shifted from the clergy's performance of liturgical duties, distant from the language and location of the congregation, to full congregational participation. The small catechism was invented for the sake of fostering the faith of children. Monastic sodalities were either eliminated or, in the case of many Anabaptist communities, reconstituted in a wholly new configuration. Furthermore, we must remember, the Protestant Reformation of the sixteenth and seventeenth centuries was not the establishment of a single new form of church. Rather, it was the spontaneous birth of a number of diverse forms of church life, from Lutheran to Anglican to Quaker to Mennonite and more. Each of these groups modeled distinct forms of modality. Within the Roman Church, reform movements resulted in a clarification of the moral standards of the clergy (for example, as communicated in the papal reform commission's *Concerning the Reform of the Church*, published in 1537), in the foundation of the missionary-minded Jesuit order, and in the calling of the Council of Trent, which improved ecclesial organization, removed abuses of power, reaffirmed the authority of Rome, and clarified controversial doctrine.

Renewal and reformation, the altering of the doctrinal and ecclesial framework of the church—especially when carried out as thoroughly as was done in the sixteenth and seventeenth centuries—results

> There was first the reform which began within the Catholic Church itself and was underway by the end of the fifteenth century; . . . a second reform was carried out under the direction of the political authorities in protest against Catholicism. . . . Alongside these two [there was] a third group of reformers which . . . can be conveniently classified into four groups: Revolutionaries, Anabaptists, Mystical Spiritualists, and Rationalists.
>
> —Peter Erb[11]

in a transformation of community identity. Common history, vision, leadership, and such shift as people see themselves on different sides of the reforming impulse. Consequently, we identify ourselves after such a reformation as Lutheran or Mennonite or Roman Catholic, rather than simply as Christian.[12] Yet at the same time the component of spiritual revitalization present in such reforms draws people to God as each grows to see God anew. Such times can bring out the best and the worst in human experience. Though we use the term *reform* to describe significant changes in segments of the church, seldom do we speak of a "reformation" of the church as such (outside the transformation of the Western church during the sixteenth and seventeenth centuries). But as we shall see, some have begun to speak of a "new reformation" in our time.

Awakenings and Revivals in the Eighteenth and Nineteenth Centuries

"In religious usage, the word 'revival' first appeared in the language in 1702," writes revival historian J. Edwin Orr, "when a powerful spiritual awakening claimed the public attention." In the summer of 1727, Count Nicholaus Ludwig von Zinzendorf and a community of diverse settlers living with him experienced a powerful touch of the Holy Spirit in their midst. The love of God overpowered them and Lutheran, Brethren, Catholic, and Anabaptist alike were reconciled to unity in Christ. And as their love expanded, so did their numbers through the Great Moravian missionary movement. In the same year, Theodore Frelinghuysen (1691–1748) preached a message of conversion to his Dutch Reformed congregation in New Jersey and witnessed a revival among the community. Nearby Presbyterian pastor Gilbert Tennant (1673–1746) also began to experience stirrings in his congregation.

Then, in 1734, Jonathan Edwards experienced a remarkable transformation, not only of his congregation, but of the entire region around Northampton, Massachusetts. He documented this event in *A Faithful Narrative of the Surprising Work of God in the Conversion of Many Hundreds of Souls in Northampton and the Neighboring Towns and Villages of the County of Hampshire, in the Province of the Massachusetts Bay in New England,* first published in 1737. Edwards's account helped to communicate abroad what word of mouth had already spread around the American colonies: God's Spirit was moving. Soon after this (1738), in England, John Wesley, inspired in part by the Moravians, received his "Aldersgate experience," and the Methodist revival in England took a leap forward. Wesley's friend and fellow street-preacher George Whitefield traveled to Georgia in 1738 and then throughout the colonies. Church attendance exploded everywhere. The travels of Whitefield and others, along with the exchange of ideas and leadership, helped galvanize many local

revivals into a single Great Awakening. Historian Sydney Ahlstrom summarizes the results of the Great Awakening in the American colonies as follows:

> Flamboyant and highly emotional preaching made its first appearance in the Puritan churches (though by no means in all), and under its impact there was a great increase in the number and intensity of bodily effects of conversion—fainting, weeping, shrieking, etc. But we capture the meaning of the revival only if we remember that many congregations in New England were stirred from a staid and routine formalism in which experiential faith had been a reality to only a scattered few. . . . Preaching, praying, devotional reading, and individual "exhorting" [spiritual direction] took on new life. In spite of far more demanding requirements, the increase in church membership is estimated variously between twenty and fifty thousand.[13]

Awakenings and revivals followed the First Great Awakening one after another. The Second Great Awakening inspired the birth of many volunteer associations, such as the British and Foreign Bible Society (1804), the American Home Missionary Society (1826), the German *Das Rauhe Haus* (Rough House) for the care of neglected children (1833), and the Young Men's Christian Association (1855). The missionary and humanitarian interest flowering from the Second Great Awakening inspired historian Kenneth Scott Latourette to call the nineteenth century the "Great Century" in the history of the church. The revival efforts of Charles Grandison Finney (1792–1875) stimulated debates concerning the place of various new measures for cultivating renewal in the lives of individuals and congregations, such as the use of protracted meetings, advertising, and the "anxious bench" (a bench at the front of the church where people came to consider the state of their souls and to counsel with those who might help them). In 1858, New York City businessmen turned to prayer during their lunch

Historical Portrait: The Prayer Meeting Revival of 1858

Most histories of revival highlight the extravagant behaviors of the frontier camp meetings. Yet many revivals were not characterized by excess. Here is a description of the typical lunch-hour gathering that served as a vehicle for God's grace setting aflame the "Event of the Century."

At 11:55 A.M. the room began to fill up rapidly and three minutes later a leader took his place at the desk. At the first stroke of twelve, the leader arose and read the opening verses of a familiar hymn. The people sang heartily. The leader offered a short prayer, then read a brief portion of Scripture.

Meanwhile, many requests for prayer had been sent up to the desk. Every nook and cranny was filled, while an overflow meeting was under way upstairs. The leader stood up, with slips of paper in both hands, and announced: "This meeting is now open for prayer. Brethren from a distance are especially invited to take part." The first request was read aloud, "A son in North Carolina desires the fervent and effectual prayers of the righteous of this congregation for the immediate conversion of his mother in Connecticut."

Immediately a father arose and requested the prayers of all the meeting for two sons and

a daughter. In deep emotion, he sat down and laid his head on the back of the seat before him, and a Christian man arose and poured out his intercession for the mother, the two sons and daughter. The next request was for the conversion of the two brothers of the lady making the request. Request after request, prayer after prayer followed in quick succession. Then the company sang

> There is a fountain filled with blood
> > Drawn from Immanuel's veins,
> And sinners plunged beneath that flood
> > Lose all their guilty stains.

Forty-five minutes had passed. The Chairman, still reading the requests, added one of his own for the feeble church in which his lot was cast, also for the thirty churches of the Presbytery in Virginia, being among the few reported unvisited with the showers of grace. Other requests followed. The meeting closed promptly at 1 P.M. with a benediction until next day's meeting for prayer in that place.[14]

hour. Soon converts were being reported at ten thousand a week, which stimulated an awakening that spread around the world. The Holiness movement, under the leadership of Phoebe Palmer and others, inspired thousands within and without Methodism to a fuller surrender to and experience of God's love. Through the eighteenth and nineteenth centuries renewal and revival fed the church as never before.

Twentieth-Century Renewal Movements

In this past century the church has experienced many powerful waves of renewal. We have already described the transforming results of the Welsh revival (1904) in chapter 7, and have heard a story from the Azusa Street revival (1906) in our chapter on prayer. These were only the beginning. North America has felt the impact of Pentecostal revivals, the Latter Rain movement, the Evangelical awakening, the charismatic movement, the Jesus Movement, and more.[15] Here we will look at two expressions of renewal that have their origin outside North America.

When Angelo Roncalli was installed as Pope John XXIII on November 4, 1958, everyone was expecting his to be a brief, uneventful pontificate. Yet, as historian

---

From 1966 to 1979, institutional Christianity was completely eradicated in China. Bibles were burned, and many pastors and converts were sent to prison. However, a few Christians continued to meet secretly in their homes, especially in the countryside. The house churches grew in size and in number in the late 1970s. . . . Christianity experienced a great revival under Socialism in the 1980s and 1990s and developed notable Chinese characteristics.

—Leung Ka-Lun
and the China Group[16]

Eamon Duffy states, "Human calculation has seldom been more spectacularly mistaken." Less than three months after his election, Pope John XXIII announced the calling of a general council of the church. And "the council he had called, with no very clear notion of what it might do, proved to be the most revolutionary Christian event since the Reformation."[17] The first session of this council opened on October 11, 1962, and three more sessions followed in the three following years. The aim of the council, which drew together the world's three thousand bishops and a number of observers from outside the Roman community, was *aggiornamento* (inculturation, renewal), the updating of the church for the present age.

And update the church it did. The council produced guidelines for liturgical renewal (for example, holding Mass in the language of the people) and for fostering relationships with non-Catholics (for example, soon after the second session Pope Paul VI met and embraced Athenagoras, the chief Orthodox Patriarch of the East, taking a significant step toward healing one thousand years of division between East and West). The third session produced the central document of the council, the *Dogmatic Constitution on the Church* (*Lumen Gentium*), a masterful and thoroughly biblical presentation of the church as the people of God. The council also addressed the renewal of the life of sodalities in the *Decree on the Appropriate Renewal of the Religious Life* (*Perfectae Caritatis*). Virtually every aspect of the life of the Roman Catholic Church was affected by Vatican II: priestly formation, development of the laity, missions, education, and relations with non-Christian all were discussed in this council. While questions still linger concerning the appropriate application of the recommendations of the council, nearly all will agree that the second Vatican Council brought a fresh wave of renewal into the Roman Catholic Church around the world, facilitating the church's adaptation to the contemporary context.

Similarly, when missionary relationships with China were eliminated at the birth of the People's Republic of China in 1949, many feared for the health of the Chinese Christian church. Few had any hopes for growth. But once again, the world was caught off guard to discover, when the country opened in the 1980s, what has been perhaps the most rapid church growth in the history of Christianity. One author calls this growth "the China miracle."[18] Four separate times the West brought Christianity to China (the Nestorian mission around 635, the Franciscan missions around 1300, the Jesuit mission around 1600, and the Protestant missions beginning in 1807), and four times the missionaries were evicted from the country. China tasted of revival, especially from 1900 to 1920 under the ministry of Jonathan Goforth and Chinese revivalists such as Ding Limei, but anti-Christian and anti-Western sentiment, especially after the Communist victory over the Nationalists in 1949, won the day.

The policy under the government of the People's Republic was one of local rule. Religion and politics were too interrelated to allow Western imperialists to control the former. The government established the Three-Self Patriotic Movement Committee (TSPM) and the Chinese Catholic Patriotic Association (CPA) in 1954 and 1956. All churches were required to register with the TSPM/CPA, and those who opposed were arrested as counterrevolutionaries. During the Cultural Revolution (1966–79), things got even worse. Institutional Christianity was virtually eradicated from the country. "However," writes scholar Leung Ka-Lun, "a few Christians continued to meet secretly in their homes, especially in the countryside. The house churches gradually grew in size and number in the late 1970s."[19] This is an understatement. Philip Jenkins, documenting the growth of the church worldwide, finds it reasonable to conclude that China now has "ten times as many Christians as it did when Mao Zedong's forces seized control of the country in 1949. In absolute terms, there are more Christians in the People's Republic of China than in either France or Great Britain."[20] The revival of Christianity in China, especially within the house churches, has both grown from and given birth to fervent prayer, passionate evangelism, extended meetings, respect for those who suffer for the faith, healings, and other signs and wonders.

The Breadth of Christian Renewal

Throughout this textbook we have explored the breadth of Christian spirituality by examining how relationship with

God involves all of human experience. We have seen how Christian transformation, spiritual formation, prayer, care, and discernment unite heart to God here and head to God there. We have seen how our operations, stages, relationships, levels of depth, and more are all present before the fullness of the God present to us. For example, since we exist "in relationship," Christian spirituality cannot but involve our relationships with self, others, nature, spiritual forces, and God. Furthermore, Christian spirituality is about communities, not just about individuals, so we speak of the mind of the people, the prayer life of the congregation, and the like. Although God does not generally reach the whole of human experience at any single season, through the duration of our individual or corporate lives we will find different aspects of our experience functioning in different seasons as unique focal points of relationship with God.

It is no different with renewal. And this is important. For while it is natural, for example, to pray for revival, with clear expectation of what that revival may look like (given some impression from a few salient events in the past), we find that in fact God's revival will look very different from one situation to the next. Christian renewal reveals the same range of diversity, and touches the same breadth of experience, as every other aspect of Christian spirituality—basic patterns, wide range of diversity.

Operations and Systems

We have learned that human experience is constituted by the somewhat integrated rise of various mental-biological operations or systems of operations. We identified two key systems of operations, cognitive and affective (thinking and feeling, head and heart), and a third, volition (willing), which functions to move each of the other two forward. Throughout the text we have observed the subtle interplay of these systems of operation in terms of our relationship with God as individuals and as communities. For example, our sense of basic relational freedom before God is shaped both by our understanding of God (cognitive) and by our history of hurts or healings related to God (affective). Similarly, our approach to care for a particular group of others is shaped by our understanding of this group (and of God's thoughts toward them), by our developing affective interest in the group, and by our choices and actions toward this group (volition).

Christian renewal—the powerful manifestation of God's Spirit, the fresh sense of vitality or of profound change in the church—touches the head and the heart uniquely in each season. The massive transformation of Greece and Rome in late antiquity from predominantly pagan to predominantly Christian civilizations was more than a matter of numbers of conversions. It was also an awakening of the mind of the culture. One need only read the stories of Justin Martyr (d. ca. 165) or of Augustine to observe the hand of God enlightening the minds not only of a few leaders, but of an entire culture to see the truth of the Christian worldview in the midst of a diverse religious and philosophical culture. Likewise, cognitive matters were front and center during the Protestant Reformation and the Second Vatican Council.

In the Great Awakening, however, affectivity was prominent. The church was being called out from dead orthodoxy to a living faith, and for this, God had to touch the heart. And when the heart is touched deeply, the body joins in. (Have you ever shouted for joy at a sports event or cried over a lost love?) Crying, shouting, and swooning were common expressions during these events. Should we be surprised that the premiere work of the Great Awakening was Jonathan Edwards's *Treatise on Religious Affections*? Edwards's contemporaries John Wesley and George Whitefield also witnessed strong expressions of emotions as they preached throughout America and England. Affectivity also played an important role in the Pentecostal revivals

and in the more recent Toronto Blessing (1994 and after). It is very present in renewal movements outside of Europe and America today.

Stages

We have also learned that human experience ordinarily proceeds in generally definable stages: Being Aware, Experiencing, Understanding, Judging, Deciding and Acting, and Integrating. We have learned that the restoration of human experience intended by Christ aims at all of these stages: opening our Awareness of God, awakening our Experience of God, enlightening our Understanding of God, and so on. We saw, in our chapter on care, that various gifts of the Spirit and various streams of the church can be comprehended as an expression of one or another of these stages of human experience. Thus, for instance, the gift of teaching (or the Progressive stream of Christianity) facilitates or expresses our Understanding of God, the gift of prophecy (or the Charismatic stream) brings the church a more direct Experience of God, and the gift of administration (or the Social Justice and Holiness streams) fosters the Decisions and Actions of God.

God's Spirit blows where it will, renewing the church uniquely in each time and place, touching every stage of our experience. Withdrawal into the desert creates an environment for watchfulness, for Being Aware of the presence of God. Signs and wonders at biblical Pentecost or in contemporary China bring the church a powerful Experience of God. Just as the Dominican branch of the mendicant revival of the early twelfth century gave birth, in later centuries, to many creative thinkers, those eager to Understand and to communicate the gospel in the context of their day, so too the Franciscan branch gave birth to many powerful doers who led the church into compassionate Action for others. Reforms under Josiah (described above) and Martin Luther brought a new framework of Judging truth within the community of God's people. And the "protests" in the Reformation of the sixteenth and seventeenth centuries of those who reunderstood, rejudged, and re-acted their own existence led to a number of different Integrations of Christianity, each with their own institutional and liturgical expressions.

Relationships

We have also learned that human experience is an experience *in relationship*. We are not who we are apart from our relationships—with self, others, nature, spiritual forces, and God. And we have learned that relationship with God is lived out in the context of all these relationships, some more present at one time and others more present at another. God may lead us into a transformed self-understanding at one season of life and a transformed relationship with creation a few years later. The fullness of God's restoration is seldom revealed to us in one moment. Rather we walk into the breadth of God's reconciliation step by step.

And so it is with the renewal of the church. One dimension of the Celtic expansion was a renewal of the Hebraic sense of relationship with nature (largely neglected in the church). "Hail to you, glorious Lord!" a Welsh poem proclaims. "May plain and hillside praise you, ... May darkness and light praise you, / The cedar and the sweet fruit tree."[21] Renewals of relationship with others were experienced, for example, in the Second Great Awakening, in the nineteenth-century German *Erweckung*, and in the Studite reform of Orthodox monasticism. The Second Great Awakening and the German Awakening both gave birth to a deep sense of responsibility for the needs of others, both spiritual and material. This in turn gave rise to a number of associations to meet those needs. The Studite reform sought to bring a renewed order and life to the monastic communities for its own time. Theodore the Studite (759–826) reorganized the monastery at Constantinople, which quickly became

the center of monastic life in the East. He reworked the Rule of Basil of Caesarea, addressing such matters as the saying of the office, common meals, and appropriate clothing. The Protestant Reformation transformed the spirituality of *families* all over Europe. A renewed sense of relationship with self was present in the Holiness revivals, for example, with their emphasis on self-review and surrender. And a renewed consciousness of the relationship with spiritual forces (for example, dealings with the demonic) has been prominent in the recent awakenings in Africa and China.

Depth and Development

Finally, we have learned that human experience—and relationship with God—is lived at various levels of depth and at different stages of development. Sometimes God speaks to a simple thought, a surface feeling, a single act. Other times the Spirit may address a belief, an emotional pattern, a habit. And then there are those times when God goes further and reworks our worldview, our core emotional concerns, or our lifestyle. Generally, seasons of renewal touch us deeply. Revivals, almost by definition, are events that bring renewed vitality to the core of the life of the church. One or another dimension of this model may be more present in one event than another, but generally renewal touches us deeply. Nonetheless, there are times when the *application* of renewal can result in a shallow *reception* of renewal. Take, for example, Josiah's reform. We read less about the transforming conversion of the people to Josiah's reform ideas and more about the imposition of these ideas on the nation. God's wrath was not changed. Perhaps this renewal was only skin deep. Likewise, much of the application of Reformation ideas was decided by kings and princes. Perhaps this affected the depth of the reception of the gospel and stimulated the need, for example, of the Pietist impulse to renew the German Lutheran Church itself.

We have also observed that human experience—and relationship with God—

417

Renewal of Christian spirituality can affect every area:
- our thoughts and our feelings
- each step of our experience
- our closest relationships
- both young and old
- at every season of our lives

develops, changing in fundamental ways over the course of its existence. A child's cognitive capabilities (and understanding of God) are different from those of a middle-aged adult. God reveals himself to a community or person insofar as she or he is able to receive him. And it is possible to identify a developmental dimension to the history of renewal. The First Great Awakening, for example, brought the church out of a staid formalism into a vital relationship with God. The Second Great Awakening went a step further, inspiring those who had relationship with God into meaningful ministry with others. Similarly, the interest in power for a changed life, characteristic of the Holiness movement, led naturally into concern with power for ministry, which was strong in the Pentecostal movement.

Christian renewal is as rich as the character of God and the fullness of human experience. At one moment God's hand is on the church and we feel the shallowness of our commitment. We renew practices of simplicity, devotion, and community. We shun worldly entertainments. At another season God's Spirit is poured out and the church, sensing its distance from God, is led into ever-deepened worship. New songs are written, new ways of prayer are explored, and the church is consumed with the desire to be before the presence of God. Still another season may bring a sense of our misunderstanding of God. We have repeated doctrinal formulas and debated theological disputes, but we find that we have been missing the point. And we find ourselves reexamining scripture and tradition all over again. What does renewal look like? It looks like the grace of God, reaching down to his people, inviting us to new life, touching us when and where we need it most. What does renewal look like? Who can say? God's mercies are new every morning.

The Dynamics of Christian Renewal

To explore the dynamics of Christian renewal is to look at the way things happen, to examine the tendencies of the ways of God with humans and of humans with God. We have already examined dynamics of the divine-human relationship as such (fundamental patterns of initiation, perception, and response), dynamics of initial and ongoing salvation (a work of God, humans, the body of Christ), dynamics of prayer (speaking, listening, the space in between, resistance, and so on), and dynamics of care (difference, power, change). Here we will consider six tendencies of the ways of God with the church in the context of seasons of renewal.

A Divine-Human Affair

First, we must acknowledge the dynamic that has been characteristic of all of Christian spirituality: renewal—as with all other dimensions of Christian spirituality—is a *divine-human affair*. Renewal is a work of

God and a tendency of human experience. And to understand renewal we must appreciate both.

The fact of renewal. Consider the fact of renewal itself. Is the presence of renewal in a given time and place a matter of the outpouring of God's spirit? Or is it a function of social situation or mass psychology? J. Edwin Orr writes, "Outpourings of the Spirit are exclusively the work of God; but revivals are the work of God with the response of the people; awakenings are the work of God with the response of the people."[22] The work of God, the response of the people. Perhaps, for our purposes, it might be better stated that *renewal is the work of God in the experience of the people.* For renewal involves not only the response of humans, but also the human socioeconomic-philosophical climate that shapes the character of a given renewal and the actions of humans that facilitate the presence and character of a given renewal. Take, for example, the "event of the century" associated with the prayer revival of 1858–59. Some will argue that this event was simply a natural sociological response to the anomie caused by the bank panic of the year before. Yet signs of life were being seen in prayer meetings throughout America months before the panic. And the widespread influence of this revival from city to country and from the United States to the rest of the world reveals a simple "bank panic" explanation to be insufficient. Did the bank panic strike fear in the hearts of many and remind them of other, perhaps more important, matters of life? Certainly! But the conversion of millions throughout the world in the context of very orderly prayer meetings must be seen as the human experience of a simple *move of God.*

Similarly, the mass exodus to the desert in the fourth century has been described as a natural human response to the dangers of persecution, the chaos of the collapsing Roman Empire, and the superficiality of a growing church. Certainly each of these factors played a part in the hearts and minds of some who withdrew to the desert. Nonetheless, the writings of the desert elders talk more about the desire to live a life fully responsive to God's Word and of the need to seek God wholeheartedly. The facts of monastic history simply do not warrant simple naturalistic explanations of the desert renewal. Rather, we see the ascetic impulse (present in the church from the beginning and itself an expression of deep divine-human dynamics) giving rise, in the very human conditions of late antiquity, to a unique human response to a unique divine invitation. And monasticism was born.[23]

The shape of renewal. And just as the *fact* of renewal is a divine-human affair, so also is the *shape* of renewal. It is touching to read, for example, personal accounts of mass revivals like the Great Awakening or the Welsh revival and to see how individuals in the same meeting can receive very different and personalized experiences of God. God invites and blesses the body and each of its members at the same time. Both the general character and specific events within a given renewal are directed by the movement of the Spirit. Even significant shifts of worldview, such as those of the Reformation, are appropriated uniquely by individuals and particular communities as the Spirit leads.

Yet this invitation and this blessing are given to humans, who perceive and respond to the Spirit as humans. Consider, for example, the variety of human affectivity surrounding a group of individuals as they enter an evening Pentecostal renewal meeting. One may come to the meeting as a Pentecostal habitual experiencer, an "experience junkie," as some say. Another comes for the first time, uncertain but expectant. Another comes for the second time; the previous night he was "zapped" by the Spirit. Another comes in caution, because the last time she came to a meeting like this, she had a negative experience. Still another has been coming for weeks and still has yet to experience anything of significance. Nonetheless, he is sincere about his desire to pursue God and doesn't

FIGURE 12.2
The Cycles of Renewal

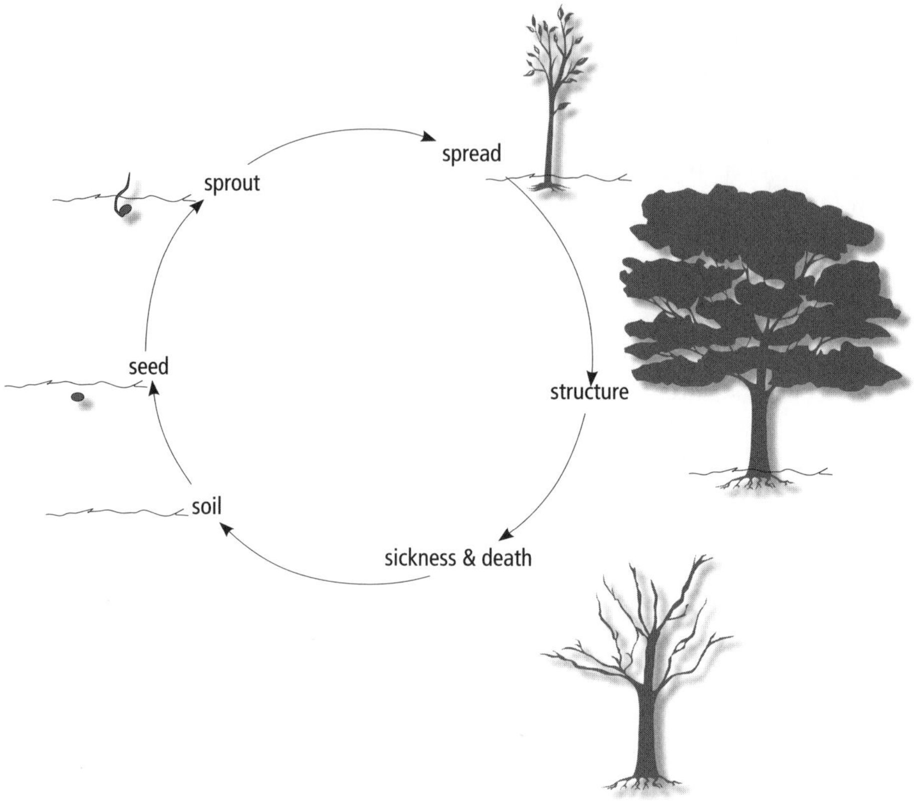

want to miss the opportunity for something more. Still another comes having felt something slightly the night before, though she didn't "go with it" because she was very self-conscious, aware of the other people around her. She doesn't want to fake it, but she also feels that in order to actually make contact with God, she needs to press in. Still another just wants to fit in with the crowd, to fit in with all the excitement that is going on. He wants experience; he wants the relationship with God that the others are talking so much about. Another is an introvert, shy of big groups, of loud noise, and of unpredictability, so meetings like these are unpleasant or fear inducing. And this is just the *entrance* to the meeting! Consider the range of experience *during* the meeting.

Renewal will express the loving touch of God and the human grasp of power. This is true of both a Pentecostal revival and

an awakening of simplicity and humility. Vicious factions broke out among the Franciscans even before Francis died. Renewal will be comprehended within the limited understandings of people. Some Roman bishops misperceived the Celtic evangelism strategy as a dangerous innovation, misunderstanding both the worldview of the Celts and the *aggiornamento* (inculturation) applied by the evangelists. And renewal will be both facilitated and manipulated by human leaders. George Whitefield, one of the most powerful communicators of the Great Awakening, received correction more than once for manipulating his crowds. Renewal is both a divine and a human affair.

Cycles of Renewal

Second, it appears that renewal *comes and goes in cycles*. We have touched on this already as we observed how the book of

420

Judges summarizes the cycles of decline and renewal among the Hebrews: renewal, distance, decline, difficulty, despair, and renewal again. Peter O'Dwyer writes, regarding monastic life, that "it is an unwritten law in monastic history that Orders need a reform at least every two centuries."[24] Social scientists and students of missions have studied patterns of decline and renewal in human collectives and have identified similar stages of change.[25] For our purposes, these stages can be summarized (by analogy to the growth and death of a tree) as follows.

Soil. A tree is first planted in soil; and the tree of renewal is planted in the soil of tension. The tension can be a physical tension of the hardships of the environment itself, a social tension of conflicts or anomie, a spiritual tension where a people feel dry and in need of a sense of the presence of God, or an intellectual tension wherein old ideas do not explain existing circumstances anymore. Social scientists speak of "pre-revitalization conditions." Here the sense of longing is high. (Remember the continuum of longing and contentment from chapter 6?) We cry out to God. We look for answers. We wait in emptiness.

Waiting for renewal is what the season of Advent is all about: preparation for God's coming. We open ourselves to God. We confess our sins and address those areas of repentance that need to be addressed. We wait, open to whatever form of coming God may choose yet (in light of the breadth of God's renewals) not presuming what that coming may look like. Waiting, longing, and praying for renewal is anticipating the arrival of a mysterious, but honored loved one. Waiting for renewal is embodying a contemplative attitude. It is Advent.

Seed. A seed is planted in the soil. The seed will become the tree, though it looks very different from the tree it will be, and one cannot see the tree in the seed. But it is the planting of the seed in the soil that brings the tree. And it is the planting of the seed of renewal into the soil of tension that births renewal into the church. The seed of renewal can be any of a number of things or events. It can be a single experience, like the outpouring of the Spirit at Pentecost. It can be the appearance of a key leader (like Martin Luther or Patrick of Ireland) who either identifies or communicates a new "big idea." It may even be a scheduled meeting (like Vatican II). Some seeds are easy to recognize (like Pentecost). Others are difficult to identify (what is the seed of the recent China miracle?). Yet whether it is a person, an event, or an idea, whether it is easy or hard to identify, one has a sense (often after the renewal) that *here* is where it began.

Sprout. The seed sprouts. At times a seed remains in the soil for a while before it sprouts, but when it sprouts, a tree is born. Something has taken root and begun to grow. And when the seed of renewal begins to sprout, we can see new life in the church. People begin to flock to the desert. Church attendance soars. People are healed, delivered, touched by God. Psalm 126:1–3 recalls,

> When the LORD restored the fortunes of Zion,
> we were like those who dream.
> Then our mouth was filled with laughter,
> and our tongue with shouts of joy;
> then it was said among the nations,
> "The LORD has done great things for them."
> The LORD has done great things for us,
> and we rejoiced.

Here contentment is high. The movement is born and begins to grow. Renewal is beginning to be felt by many. The ideas are beginning to take hold outside the founding circle. It is clear to some, at this stage, that God's hand is on us.

Spread. As the sprout begins to grow, roots deepen, branches begin to spread, and leaves reach out to catch the sun. The tree grows tall and wide. Renewal spreads too. An account of the Great Awakening is read and others want to experience the same. Word of mouth reaches one community that something is going on in another, and people check it out. The Toronto Blessing was a unique renewal movement in the twentieth century in that communication of testimony and interpretation was spread through the medium of the Internet, resulting in a rapid and wide spreading. At this stage transformation is visible and organization begins to take shape. Here people outside the renewal begin to acknowledge that something is happening.

Structure. One feature of a maturing tree is its structure. Roots go down deep to meet the increasing need for nourishment. The trunk and key branches solidify and bear the weight of others. The tree begins to take on a definable shape. So also with renewal. Whether monastic foundations or reforms recommended by a Vatican council, whether a matter of Pentecostal experience or congregational community, structure appears sooner or later. The structure bears the weight of the circumstances surrounding the renewal, giving the renewal a more defined shape. The seed and the sprout themselves indicate certain directions for structuring. Some practices are natural in light of this renewal; others are less. Some ways of looking at community relationships are highlighted and others ignored. Some leaders rise to the top of the renewal movement and others do not. Structure clarifies the renewal, articulating its distinctives and protecting the renewal itself against aberrations. Thus structure serves valuable functions.

Yet structure can also mark a transition from vibrancy and maturity to decline and old age. Social scientists speak of the "routinization" of revitalization. As structure becomes increasingly rigid, vital functions of modality and sodality become regimented duties, and structure begins to kill life rather than support it.

Sickness and death. Ultimately trees die. They grow old and dry and are subject to fires. They get sick, and the leaves fall off the branches or the trunk decays from the roots. And so it is with renewal movements. The forms of liturgy no longer mediate the faith either to or through the people of God. They are merely dead rituals. Leadership is now a matter of power and prestige rather than of gifts and needs. Sickness enters the movement, and factions or excess affect the community. And things get dry once again. Author John White speaks of "spiritual drought": "Secret sin abounds in times of spiritual drought. Coldness and formality replace living faith. Ecclesiastical power moves into the vacuum created by the absence of spiritual power. The church grows cold, worldly and sinful while in the world iniquity and lawlessness grow more and more."[26]

At this point (degeneration), the renewal movement can either appropriate its own renewal once again in light of its current circumstances (and perhaps experience re-renewal) or die. It is only natural for movements to come and go. At times wisdom teaches that renewal is best served by allowing one expression to die so as to give rise to another (or to wait for another) that God may bring.

Historian Richard Lovelace suggests that perhaps there are factors that might promote the "continuous renewal" of the church. He identifies the preconditions of continuous renewal as the awareness of the holiness of God and the depth of our sin. A vision of the Ideal and of the realities of our life draw us to seek God for more. The primary elements of ongoing renewal involve a "depth presentation" of the gospel: the message of justification (you are accepted), sanctification (you are free from bondage to sin), the indwelling Spirit (you are not alone), and authority in spiritual conflict (you have authority over the enemy). Insofar as these themes are continually presented in depth in the church, the church opens itself to promote and recognize God's renewing work as it is revealed in scripture and in our midst. Secondary elements of renewal, which express the outworking of the gospel in the life of the church, are an orientation to mission, a life of dependent prayer, a deepened sense of community, and a practice of theological integration. As these expressions are habitually embodied in the church, the church lives in harmony with the values Christ loves to renew.[27] Is Lovelace right? Is continuous renewal possible, given the right preparation? It is certainly a hypothesis worth testing.

Discerning Renewal

Third, authentic renewal is *recognized like any other touch of God*. When renewal happens (or when some *think* renewal happens), there is always the question, Is this from God or not? Some see a fresh wave of the Spirit and others see emotional excess. Some see a Spirit-filled reform of the church and others see rebellion against legitimate authority. And, as we know, renewal is *both* human and divine. At times a great deal is at stake in the question. How do we evaluate?

The question of evaluation takes us right back to the topic of our previous chapter: discernment, the evaluation of inner and outer stuff in light of relationship with God with a view to response. Without repeating all that we learned there, let us explore three questions specifically with regard to discerning renewal movements: Who discerns? How do we prepare for the discernment of renewal movements? And what are the various signs involved in discerning renewal movements?[28]

The discerner. In the previous chapter we raised the issue of who discerns best in a given situation. There we learned that often others are involved in the discernment process, even if an individual decision is in view. So what about the evaluation of perceived renewal movements? (At this point in our discussion, whether or not a movement is an *authentic* renewal movement depends on the results of the discernment process.) On the one hand, there is the individual question, "Do *I* go to the meeting (or flee to the desert, or move to Germany where the Protestants are, or join the Chinese house church, or whatever) or not?" But often other people's interests are involved in the assessment. Is the question posed by the leadership of a wide range of congregations as a means of evaluating the movement *in general*? Is this an evaluation by the leadership of a single community for the purpose of determining whether to recommend participation in the perceived renewal? Different factors must be considered, and consequently a different configuration of discerners may be appropriate, in each case.

If this is a discernment for the sake of a particular community, then appropriate authority should be involved in the discernment at some level. But in general, in keeping with our model of human experience, there is great wisdom in gathering a team of "experts" to conduct the evaluation. A leadership body may simply gather to discern. Or a decision-making body might appoint a discernment team, and the team, in turn, may invite a wide range of outside participants to contribute to certain stages of the discernment, though not participate in the final recommendation. A number of configurations are possible. The discernment team should draw from people who have had experience in renewal movements, preferably renewal movements of different types, so that they will not be subject to the "all renewal looks alike" fallacy. The team should include those who know the needs of those asking for discernment and who are open and sensitive to the active presence of God. Because of the emotional attachments people often make with regard to renewal movements (either for or against), it is wise to select a team composed of people with a range of opinion coming into the discernment process. Including those who are sensitive to spiritual experiences, those who are action oriented, those who integrate different aspects well, and those who are oriented around different types of relationships will enable this diverse group to notice things that would bypass a homogeneous group. The Roman Catholic Church has modeled this type of discernment for some time, drawing commissions together to evaluate such issues as the sainthood of individuals, the advisability of political strategies, and the character of charismatic renewal.

Preparation for discernment. The first part of preparing for discernment is the preparation of the discerners. Again, in light of the significant changes introduced by renewal movements—and in light of the attachments we bring into discernment—it is difficult for discerners to be indifferent. It is important that discerners prepare thoroughly and prayerfully. We need room to openly admit prejudices and power issues that may contribute to a faulty discernment of the work of God. We need to soak ourselves in the Word of God and in the history of the work of God, developing a connatural sense of God's character and God's invitations. We need to open ourselves to honest collaboration with believers from all sides, welcoming, as best we can, the wisdom that each has to bring. The attitudes of listening, prayer, humility, and love are especially important in this kind of discernment. Finally, the special and careful preparations for the gathering of discerners—which involves establishing rules for communication, decision making, and implementation—ensure that the group communicates well and that a well-discerned decision is not compromised by lack of planning.

The signs of discernment. In the previous chapter we identified four separate signs of discernment: the *focus* (what the discernment is *about*), the *sources* (what we look at in order to discern), and the *criteria* (the way the sources of discernment look), which ultimately indicate the *meaning* of discernment (a sense of the active presence of God). Determining these signs is vital to the evaluation of renewal movements. Determining the focus of a renewal movement involves a clarification of the question. For example, Jonathan Edwards wrote an early assessment of the Great Awakening as a movement in general. His evaluation was published as *The Distinguishing Marks of a Work of the Spirit of God* (1741). Having accomplished this general assessment,

he later wrote a treatise dealing with the discernment of particular experiences encountered *in the context* of the Awakening. This evaluation was published as *A Treatise Concerning Religious Affections . . . Shewing What Are Distinguishing Signs of Truly Gracious and Holy Affections* (1746).[29] An evaluation of *the work in general* and an assessment of *experiences encountered within a work* are entirely different. A work of God may be subject to all kinds of distortion and excess here and there and yet still exhibit the character of an authentic work of God. Yet for an individual in the midst of this setting (and again, this applies not only to Protestant revivals, but to Hesychast renewal and the implementation of Vatican recommendations as well), evaluating particular experiences is a distinctly different matter. Clarifying the focus of renewal helps us know what we are discerning and points us to the sources of discernment.

In order to evaluate a renewal movement in general, we look to the sources of movement. We examine the teachings, the practices, the relationships, and the effects of the movement on the lives of individuals and communities. (Edwards speaks of "operations.") Interviews are taken, observations are made, and studies are conducted, through which the discernment team gets a sense of the renewal in question.

Yet the team looks at these sources for particular patterns, tendencies, and ways of being for indications that this movement reflects the character of the transforming work of God. (Edwards speaks of the "manner" of the operations.) It is here that we begin to think of the *criteria* (or "distinguishing marks," as Edwards calls them) of discernment. Some criteria will be more appropriate to the evaluation of the expansion of Christianity among sixth-century Celts than to the evaluation of the twentieth-century Chinese expansion. Yet some criteria will remain the same, as God's work among people bears the stamp of his character. We saw Edwards's distinguishing marks of a work of God in general in the previous chapter.

Ultimately, through the prayerful analysis of the sources of discernment—comparing observations of the perceived renewal with criteria known in scripture and tradition—and through the sharing of wisdom among its members, a discernment team comes to a sense that this *is* (or is *not*) a work of God (or, perhaps, that it is a work of God, but that for this community at present the team does not recommend heavy participation in the activities of this movement). We identify the meaning of discernment, recognizing the touch of God in renewal movements, just as we recognize the touch of God in any aspect of life.

Wonderful and Difficult

Fourth, renewal is *wonderful for some and difficult for others*. We may wish that renewal would be precious for all, but it isn't. As mentioned, renewal movements stimulate wide, sweeping changes and intense emotional reactions. For reasons both divine and human, some find it easier to receive from a given renewal, while others find it hard to receive. God may be doing something special in the life of one through a time of solitude, right in the middle of a noisy renewal among her community in general. Another may find it difficult to receive because of relational issues with God (resistance, avoidance, fear of being overwhelmed by God, or the like). Perhaps God *is* doing something and the person does not notice it. Perhaps some are put off by the leadership or the style of the renewal, and this makes it hard to receive. Perhaps the environment of the renewal (the emptiness of the desert, or the chaos of Pentecostal meetings) is disorienting. Perhaps a person has pragmatic problems regarding the renewal (he just can't seem to figure out what to *do* in order to receive). Individual reception of a general invitation of God is a complex affair.

Even for those who *do* find it easy to receive, there are a couple of dynamics that need to be noted. First, there is the danger of mistaking God's *invitation* for his *transformation*. The crowds who followed Jesus exhibited the tendency to do just this. Jesus reached out in healing, inviting people to come. Yet for many who were healed, there was no permanent transformation of divine-human relationship. Many who were healed abandoned Jesus. Associating with the movement or having a powerful experience at a meeting does not mean one is thereby transformed. The transformation of life is part of an interactive relationship with God, where God initiates and we respond. Powerful experiences are no certain sign of new life. They may simply indicate that God has to knock very hard on the door to get our attention. Similarly, one must be careful of the impulses experienced in the moment *after* receiving from renewal. It is common for the enemy to attempt to undo the work of God (to steal the seed right from the path, Matthew 13:3–9) by introducing dangerous thoughts into our minds in the context of a renewal.[30]

Critics and Counterfeits

Furthermore, renewal *gives birth to critics and counterfeits*. While the apostle Peter argued that what happened on Pentecost was not a result of drunkenness but was rather an outpouring of the Holy Spirit, perhaps there were some who still thought they were drunk (despite thousands believing his message; see Acts 2). Shortly after (Acts 4), Peter was arrested. Yet when Simon Magus sees the manifestation of the Spirit, he wants to market the ministry (see Acts 8:14–24). We find critics and counterfeits. Early monasticism was accompanied by Encratites, Messalians, Montanists, Eustathians, Euchites, and other non-orthodox groups. While we have learned about Edwards's contribution to the Great Awakening, his contributions cannot be understood apart from the critiques of the Awakening given by Charles Chauncy or apart from the excesses promoted by James Davenport. There were critics of the Protestant Reformation, and there were critics of the Second Vatican Council.

425

Frequently, critics and counterfeits alike have bought into one or more myths about renewal. Critics often fall prey to the "nothing buttery" fallacy we discussed in chapter 2. Secular critics go beyond the acknowledgement that psychological and social factors are enmeshed in renewal movements to the conclusion that renewal movements are nothing but mass psychology or a function of social forces. Religious critics go beyond the acknowledgement that the enemy has his hand even in the midst of the work of God to the conclusion that the renewal is nothing but a demonic deception; or they go beyond the acknowledgement that human emotionalism may be present to the conclusion that a renewal is nothing but emotionalism. But counterfeits have their own set of myths: they believe that renewal always looks the same, that receiving from the renewal (with appropriate signs) is an identity marker of God's favor, that association with those who are not following the renewal results in being out of God's will, and so on.

Perhaps we can explore the dynamics of renewal by considering various approaches to water. First, we are thirsty and weak. There is a drought, and we long for water. Some deal with their thirst by telling stories of the good-old days when water was plenty. They sing the old songs and remember how the water tasted, and that helps somewhat. Indeed, perhaps they are not even aware of their own thirst. Some go water hunting. They hear rumors that there is a downpour over here or over there and they travel from place to place—from retreat to retreat, from trend to trend. Others attempt to squeeze the last drop of water out of the vessels that used to provide water before. They continue to offer the "anxious bench" long after there is any real spiritual anxiety, hoping that someone will respond. At these moments, it is easy for the means of grace to become the manipulations of grace. Others, desiring some evidence of renewal, latch on to whatever appears like water, manufacturing (consciously or unconsciously) the manifestations, practices, and forms characteristic of a given renewal. This can be dangerous, for H_2O_2 is not that different from H_2O. Others, having a little water, occupy their time with tasting wars. ("My water tastes better than your water.") Some give up hope for drink. Yet still others spend their time mending their cisterns, digging wells, or sharing what water they have.

Unions and Divisions

Finally, renewal *leads to unions and divisions*. We have reason to rejoice—and to grieve. The Jesus who prayed "that they may be one, as we are one" (John 17:11) is the same Jesus who said, "I have not come to bring peace, but a sword," dividing mother from daughter and so on (Matthew 10:34–36). The Pentecost that brought into being a group of believers who "were of one heart and soul" (Acts 4:32) was the same Pentecost that resulted in a significant group who were "enraged and wanted to kill" the believers (Acts 5:33). We find unions and divisions. The Celtic expansion brought a great union of believers among the loose association of monasteries connected with the expansion. The same expansion brought tensions with Rome. The Great Awakening gave rise to an interdenominational union hitherto unseen. It also gave rise to tensions between New Lights (who supported the Awakening) and Old Lights (who did not). Even the generous steps toward unity initiated through the reforms of the Second Vatican Council stimulated the formation of Tridentine and other Latin rite groups.

We have a dream, and rightfully so, that renewal will bring universal peace, that Christians of various stripes will see, in *this* renewal, the invitation of the Spirit to enter together into the work of God. But, as we have seen, while renewal is wonderful for some, it is difficult for others—and this at times through no fault of their own. While renewal brings a fresh vibrancy of faith, it also brings critics and counterfeits. Furthermore, the natural differences within human experience make some renewals dif-

The Dynamics of Renewal

- Renewal is a divine-human affair.
- Renewal comes and goes in cycles.
- Renewal is recognized like any other touch of God.
- Renewal is wonderful for some and difficult for others.
- Renewal gives birth to critics and counterfeits.
- Renewal leads to unions and divisions.

Are you ready for renewal?

ficult for others to accept. A contemplative renewal may seem, to some evangelistic or social-action types, to declaw the gospel of Christ. Some who are sincerely concerned about adequately recognizing the human element in spirituality may separate from African or Chinese expressions of renewal, wherein there is more attention to the demonic. Those in Progressive streams, who ask questions, and those in Evangelical streams, who require solid answers, each assess renewal movements in light of their own concerns. In the midst of renewal we find both the longing of God for restoration and the tragedy of human experience. And when we enter sympathetically into both sides of a division, we find that contempt is not a possibility. We can only cry the tears of God.

Consequently, those who lead renewal must allow space for those who leave. And those who leave renewal expressions (perhaps doubting whether they are authentic renewal expressions) must respect those who follow renewal. Again, this is hard, for renewal stimulates significant change in worldview and in practice. While renewal will draw together those who have been longing for and sensing the coming changes into a richness and freshness that can only come from the Spirit of God, others may perceive the changes as heresy. (Indeed, some expressions *are* heresy.) Nonetheless, in spite of the difficulties, we may have

hope, for, as Orr affirms, "neither denomination nor organization, nor pastor nor evangelist, can organize [or disorganize] an outpouring of the Spirit."[31]

The Renewal of Christian Spirituality: Looking Forward

Having explored a few of the dynamics of Christian renewal, and having considered what we have learned in this text under the heading of renewal, we may now reflect for a moment on the future of Christian spirituality. In chapter 1, we outlined a few trends characteristic of the current approach to Christian spirituality primarily as an academic field of study. We tend to approach relationship with God *descriptively* rather than prescriptively. We tend to emphasize *experience*, whatever this may mean. We are increasingly making room for things *corporate*, seeing relationship with God not simply in terms of individual interiority, but also in terms of community life. We see the study of spirituality as a *somewhat engaged* activity, involving tension and cooperation between lived faith commitment and careful scholarship. And finally, we are increasingly approaching spirituality from an *interdisciplinary* perspective, drawing on varied insights to provide wisdom regarding the character of relationship with God. Now we must step beyond these trends to consider the future shape of Christian spirituality as a whole—as lived relationship with God, as a network of approaches to relationship with God, and as an academic discipline.

Lived Relationship

We have described Christian spirituality at three levels: the level of practice, the level of dynamics, and the level of academic discipline. At the first level we examined Christian spirituality in terms of the actually lived (practiced) relationships with God of individuals and communities. How do people conduct their relationship with God through Jesus Christ? Throughout the

427

book we have discovered that Christians of different places and times have lived their faith differently. Congregational liturgy and private devotions, personal spiritual formation and social transformation—all exhibit the character of their own setting. So having considered a number of renewals of lived relationship in Christian history, what renewals might lie ahead for the Body of Christ?

The "global South." Certainly the largest and most significant renewal of Christianity is taking place in what is called the "global South." South America, Asia, and Africa are experiencing massive religious transformation. The population—and perhaps, power—centers of Christendom, are shifting to the South and the East. There are, for example, nearly twice the number of Presbyterians in Korea than in the United States. There are more active members of Anglican churches in Nigeria than in England. Slightly over half of the world's Roman Catholics live in Latin America. The Orthodox Church is rapidly expanding in areas like Uganda and Zaire.[32] Furthermore, many in these new centers of faith are feeling the need to shed much of the baggage of Western culture that has been transmitted along with the Christian faith, and they are discovering their own lived spirituality. Asian churches, for example, have pioneered daybreak prayer meetings, houses of prayer, and corporate prayer composed of simultaneous individual vocal expression. Together, this pioneering spirit, the numbers of conversions to Christianity, the variety of forms of Christianity being explored, and the complex political settings surrounding the renewals produce a very dynamic but unstable environment. (Such is the case with many renewals.) We can expect this to continue.

Furthermore, Christian renewal in the global South is affecting the church, the culture, and the conflicts of the rest of the world. The boundaries of orthodoxy, syncretism, and heresy are being explored as, for example, African prophets and theologians reestablish a Christology without Greco-Roman philosophical categories as well as a notion of salvation that addresses the character of our victory over the demonic more than pardon from sin. The spectacular and supernatural elements of renewal are greater in the South. And, for this reason, the principles of the discernment of renewal are especially needed. Likewise, where Christianity is growing, it is expressing influence over the educational, social, and political institutions of local cultures. The Constantinian question of what a "Christian" town or country might look like is being asked again in new settings, as believers feel what it is to be in the numerical majority and to have political power for the first time. And, as renewal brings both unions and conflicts, the same is found in the global South. Some of these conflicts are especially violent, as rapid growth occurs in environments that have been hostile to Christianity or as developing forms of Christianity in a given setting appear irreconcilably disparate.

The issue of the relationship between Christianity and other religions is critical to the developing spiritualities of the global South and East. From questions of our God-image (is it appropriate in India to speak of God as *Brahman*?), to spiritual ministry (is some kind of synthesis of Christian healing prayer and African shamanic ritual possible?), to community life (what can be learned of sodalic practice from the ancient Buddhist Sangha?), the intersection between the Christian's lived relationship with God and the practice of the surrounding religious pluralism must be addressed. I have not addressed this issue in the present text in an effort to focus on Christian spirituality as viewed from within the historical tradition itself. Nonetheless, comparative approaches to Christian spirituality may have much to contribute in light of the renewal of Christianity worldwide.

The "West." Although the most spectacular renewal of Christian spirituality is that being manifest in the global South, the West—Europe, North America, Australia—are not without their own renewals.

Indeed, as we navigate our way out of a modern Western culture and into a postmodern culture (and further into what lies beyond the in-between of postmodernism), the Western church itself is creating a new spectrum of options for lived spirituality.

Perhaps the most obvious change is the proliferation of ecclesial or *modalic* options. It is not, despite predictions to the contrary, the case that traditional churches—which own buildings, are part of formal denominations, and hire pastors—have served their purpose and are doomed to extinction. Indeed, just as there was renewal within the community of those faithful to Rome even as the Protestant Reformation was transforming the face of early modern modalic options, so too there are signs of renewal within traditional churches even as we face a new reconfiguration of modality in the postmodern West. Eastern Orthodoxy is gaining new converts in record numbers even as they struggle to retain many who have been raised in the tradition. It is likely that Pope Benedict XVI will pay close attention to the renewal of Roman Catholicism in the West, bringing a fresh appreciation of scripture and early tradition to liturgy, education, and more. Protestant churches of all stripes are exploring church once again, experimenting with purpose-driven, emerging, and seeker-sensitive models, even as others reappropriate their own liturgical and communal heritage for a postmodern world.[33]

Nonetheless, the spectrum of modalic options is widening. Whereas most people in the mid-1900s would have had a fairly accurate sense of what going to church looked like, that is no longer true today. And all indications show that this will be increasingly the case in the future. Thousands flock to full-service megachurches that offer advanced degrees, social service management, and athletic leagues. Emerging churches of one style or another are popping up throughout the West, integrating gospel narrative with community life, traditional liturgy, and social action. Cell or house churches continue to multiply through-out the West, offering a simple version of church, drawing a few people together in homes. And so on, and so on.[34]

The consequences of these shifts for ecclesial spirituality are vast. For example, the dynamics of the corporate experience of the Eucharist vary greatly among a megachurch service of two thousand, a traditional church of two hundred, an emerging church of fifty, and a house church of twelve. Each of these models will understand (and mediate) relationship with God differently, both to the individuals present and as a community. For one community, the Lord's Supper may be a time of securing the commitment of new believers. For another, the Eucharist may be a time of connecting with the historic beliefs and practices of the church. For yet another, Communion may be a time of testimony, of hearing how Christ's body is broken day by day on the streets. For another, the Lord's Supper may simply be a shared meal with symbolic meaning. Spiritual formation, prayer, care, discernment—each of these will be navigated differently in each of these different contexts of modalic life.

There are also signs of *sodalic* renewal. Monasteries in Russia in the 1990s grew rapidly. The famed Orthodox monastery on Mt. Athos is flourishing. Although many Catholic religious communities have struggled in the past half century, religious life has experienced revitalization through various renewal movements and through the formation of new communities. Pope Benedict XVI has a deep regard for the consecrated life. (Note that when inaugurated as pope, Josef Alois Ratzinger took the name Benedict, recalling Saint Benedict, one of the founders of Western monasticism.) It remains to be seen what renewals or reforms may appear in the next season. One of the most interesting developments in sodalic renewal is the emergence of a "new monasticism" among inner-city Protestant communities. These communities integrate such values as simplicity of life, hospitality to the stranger, relocation to areas of need, intentional spiritual formation, community living, and contemplative reflection; and they seek to live as renewed communities of committed believers in the midst of the world's hardship. Some of these communities call themselves "orders" or are experimenting with a common Rule of Life, modeling themselves after historic monastic movements.[35]

Finally, we may speak of a new spectrum of *personal* options for lived relationship with God. Interest in spiritual formation is still on the rise, and while conferences on spiritual formation are beginning to take notice of corporate spirituality, plenty of attention is still given to personal spiritual growth. In terms of resources available, there has been no time like the present for personal spiritual practice. We are also seeing a renewed interest in areas such as community, art, and hospitality.[36] Furthermore, we can choose from among a wide array of options with regard to spiritual practices themselves, and we can also identify a range of *ways of living out* personal relationship with God. Robert Wuthnow, in his study of spirituality in America since the 1950s, distinguishes between dwelling, seeking, and practicing. Some see their relationship with God as *dwelling* within a stable sacred presence: the places, the people, the ideas, and the practices transmitted through geography and community and lived in the present. Others are *seeking*—comparing ideas, communities, and activities and expressing the freedom to find God on their own. Still others are *practicing*—integrating personal search, interpersonal commitments, and intentional disciplines into a tailor-made spirituality.[37] Well-known pollster George Barna predicts a growth of "revolutionaries" who live out a devout Christian spirituality largely disconnected from traditional church structures.[38] Some Christians see themselves simply as members of a local community. Others see themselves as nontraditional revolutionaries, living the deeper life apart from what is perceived as a shallow church and culture. Still others are just trying to put the pieces of life with God together, drawing from this com-munity, this program, this friendship, this Web site. Once again, our notions of prayer, discernment, and such will vary depending on the way we live out our relationship with God.

Schools and Approaches

We have spoken of Christian spirituality not only as actual lived (practiced) relationship with God, but also as a *formulation of a teaching about* or an *"approach" to* the lived reality. As we have learned, this way of speaking about spirituality identifies examples like Ignatian or Lutheran spiritualities, which refer not to Ignatius of Loyola's or Martin Luther's own lived experience, but rather to the teachings, the examples, and the encouragements that dominated their approaches to the spiritual life and that have become patterns for their followers. We found that the exploration of this level of Christian spirituality often involves the creation of models of understanding the dynamics of relationship with God, of how relationship with God works. Formulations about or approaches to relationship with God are often developed in what Kees Waaijman calls "schools" and "countermovements" of spirituality.[39] These schools and counter-movements collect people around a way of understanding and living relationship with God and, over time, take on something of a life of their own. Thus we might speak of revivalism as an approach to relationship with God, complete with its own heroes, theological assumptions, and characteristic practices. Is it possible to identify any emerging schools, countermovements, or more generalized approaches to relationship with God as we examine the horizons of the Christian spirituality?

Identifiable approaches to Christian spirituality arise from communities-in-context and from the interplay of ideas. Certainly the developing Christian communities-in-context of the global South are producing distinct spiritualities. Just as we speak of the Rhineland mystics or the "modern devotion," so might we speak of Korean mysticism or Latin American devotions as well. Likewise, just as we speak of mendicant spirituality (speaking largely in terms of Dominican and Franciscan movements), perhaps someday we will be able to speak of a distinct "new monastic" or "new friar" spirituality, as young communities in the inner cities of the world share values, practices, and leadership. It is likely that there will develop distinct house-church approaches to relationship with God (just as Brethren or Amish congregational forms have produced unique approaches to spirituality), emphasizing those features characteristic of house-church life (informality, fellowship, mutual ministry, and the like). Perhaps, with enough adherents, we might even speak of "network" spirituality as a distinct approach—designing one's relationship with God from an array of personal practices, meetings, relationships, Web sites, podcasts, and so on. Here a loose (very loose) community-in-context might develop an identifiable approach to relationship with God apart from key events, leaders, or formal "schools"—a truly twenty-first-century folk spirituality.

It may be harder to predict the influence of theological trends on the rise of schools or approaches to Christian spirituality. For example, while process theology has had a significant impact on certain spirituality-relevant questions (like the question of our God-image or the problem of evil), we have not seen a distinct "process" school of spirituality arise. Nonetheless, a few trends may be noted. First, with regards to Roman Catholic spirituality, while the flowering of Christian spirituality after Vatican II was nourished heavily by the theology of Karl Rahner, there has been, of late, increasing interest in the aesthetic theology of Hans Urs von Balthasar, a comparable theologian of the same era. Perhaps we may begin to see discussion of spirituality informed by Balthasarian theological assumptions, just as we have seen treatments of spirituality governed by a Rahnerian view of things.[40] Second, there appears to be distinct schools

of theology, if not spirituality, forming around what might be called revisionist and postliberal or postconservative theologies.[41] On the one hand, there are those who see many of the traditional doctrines of the Christian faith (such as Jesus's divinity, the Trinity, atonement) as inadequate foundations for a contemporary spirituality. These theologians wish to re-vision Christianity for the twenty-first century, rebuilding not only our understanding, for example, of the nature of the historical Jesus, but also our understanding of prayer and spiritual practice.[42] On the other hand, there are those who, rather than reconceiving Christianity according to modern exegetical or philosophical trends (whether liberal or conservative), are increasingly content to find themselves within the narrative of the traditional Christian story and to live the values and liturgical life of the historic Christian church.[43] Finally, in reaction to these trends, we may identify various communities of Christians who wish to separate from contemporary denominations, academic institutions, and liturgical practices, forging unique, strictly "biblical" spiritualities.[44]

An Academic Discipline

Finally, we have spoken about Christian spirituality as a formal "academic discipline" of study, wherein people engage in a systematic investigation of the lived relationship or formulated teachings about relationship with God. We have also taken a look at some recent trends within this discipline, trends that show every sign of continuing (those that take a descriptive approach, those that are experience oriented, those that make room for the corporate, those that are somewhat engaged, and those that are interdisciplinary). Yet perhaps a few additional comments may be offered regarding the future of the discipline.

First, let us attend to the ecumenical character of the study of Christian spirituality. Bernard McGinn, in his address at the celebration of the twenty-fifth anniversary of the Classics of Western Spirituality series (CWS), specifically notes the need for the discipline of spirituality to be ecumenical, drawing attention to the fact that the CWS has published a wide range of classics from Christianity, Judaism, and Islam.[45] The range could even be wider yet, even within Christian spirituality. There is much work to be done in terms of recovering spiritual texts and wisdom, especially within Protestant traditions. There is a host of rich literature from the "Spiritual Reformers" of the sixteenth century that have never been translated into English. The Pietists deserve much greater attention than they have received. We have only begun to peek into the storehouse of Puritan spirituality. And while CWS recently published a volume of samples from the German Awakening, the Great Awakenings and revivals of the West have received little treatment as subjects of the study of spirituality. It might also be interesting to see a volume of indigenous spiritual classics, a compilation of works written by and recognized by local communities as classics of Christian spirituality.

Second, we can address the place of the corporate dimension in the study of Christian spirituality. While there has been expressed interest in this dimension (in particular those aspects of corporate life involving justice or political issues), there has been little serious exploration of corporate spirituality—relationship with God *as communities*. Edward Howells, taking stock of the state of the discipline via a review of a recent compilation of essays by members of the Society for the Study of Christian Spirituality, states that "the communal dimension of spirituality is insufficiently explored."[46] We have only begun to make use of the social sciences in our interdisciplinary exploration of relationship with God. If scholars of Christian spirituality are to step out of modern individualism—and to serve not only interested individuals, but communities of inquirers too—then it will be necessary to give increasing attention to the corporate dimensions of Christian spirituality.

Mention of who is served by the study of Christian spirituality brings us to the issue of the location of scholars of Christian spirituality. Howells speaks to members of the Society for the Study of Christian Spirituality of a "confusion over whether we—those engaged in the academic study of spirituality—are in a church or a university." While admitting that scholars of Christian spirituality often live in both worlds, Howells urges his readers to recognize that "the university is not a church and cannot make itself the forum for spiritual formation."[47] On the other hand, Mary Frohlich, teaching in a school of ministry, suggests that the subject of spirituality requires attention to formation, to one's own appropriation of meaning. Rather than an academic discipline in the modern sense, simply requiring technical skills of concept and communication, the discipline of spirituality, she suggests, might serve to incorporate spiritual exercises, contemplation, and personal transformation.[48]

Our location as scholars of Christian spirituality makes a difference. A professor in a state university must maintain a semblance of neutrality with regard to transformational exercises designed to form people into a tradition. Yet an instructor in a church-related graduate school of ministry is encouraged to facilitate student formation into the faith. Indeed, it is precisely this aspect of formation into ministry that has been neglected in past decades and is so appreciated by students and denominational leaders alike. Other scholars of Christian spirituality are not in academic settings at all. Some are spiritual directors or pastors or serve in some apostolic ministry. Some are monastics, either solitary or in communities. For some, scholarship in Christian spirituality will be an independent exploration of Christian's relationship with God, somewhat removed from the locations of a community of faith. Others, however, will undertake scholarship in Christian spirituality *as representatives of* a community of faith and *for the sake of* a community of faith. Both our professional locations and our personal sense of location will govern the character of our teaching and writing. The task for us will be to acknowledge and celebrate this rich variety of scholars and approaches to the act of scholarship (a variety unlike that found in most fields).

Finally, the exploration of Christian spirituality—as lived relationship, formulated approach, academic discipline—is lived out in a tension between affirmation and negation. McGinn also draws attention to this issue in his CWS anniversary address. He argues that "affirming, understanding, utilizing created realities, the downward

procession of all things from God, is just as necessary, if not as final, as the uplifting return that unsays all things to eventually pass beyond both affirmation and negation and the height of the trajectory aimed at the unknown God."[49] God is both the One we can never know as well as the One we cannot help but know. God is both *Deus revelatus* and *Deus absconditus*, the revealed God and the hidden God. Navigating a relationship with God in Christ is the adventure of entering into this known-unknown. Neither the known nor the unknown must be sole guide. The mystery of the divine-human relationship itself is the guide of Christian spirituality. It always has been, and so it will be into eternity.

Questions

1. Recall a renewal you have witnessed. Would you call it an awakening, a revival, a revitalization, or a reform, or would you use some other term? Why would you call it this?

2. We covered the theological and spiritual foundations of renewal in terms of relationship with God. We spent less time with the sociological foundations of renewal. What do the human sciences have to say about why renewals appear or why they look the way they do?

3. Similarly, while we gave a few examples of the history of renewal, much was left untreated. Here is your chance to go deeper. Perhaps you would like to identify a renewal from your own tradition and explore further. To what did this renewal draw attention? Where do you see the hand of God in this renewal? What conflicts or problems arose? How did this renewal shape the character of your tradition?

4. Or you might want to interview a number of people who have experienced renewal of one kind or another. What characterizes their experiences as a whole? What distinguishes some from others? What do you learn from this informal research that you did not gain through reading the chapter?

5. What other dynamics of renewal might be explored? For example, how does leadership function in various stages of renewal? How does one's understanding of care differ in a time of renewal from other times? What does spiritual warfare look like in the various stages of renewal? What are some other questions you might ask?

6. Consider the projections regarding the future of Christian spirituality. How might individuals and communities be conducting relationship with God in your neighborhood in the near future? How might the renewals and changes affecting spirituality worldwide affect the ways in which your own community lives out its relationship with God? How might they affect your own personal relationship with God?

Practicing Christian Spirituality

What If?

In this final exercise we are going to play a little imaginative game. Throughout this chapter we have been talking about renewal: reform, revival, awakening, and the like. In some traditions people talk about an end-time revival, a revival where the fullness of the knowledge of God spreads throughout the whole earth in great power and glory, a near completion of the purpose of history here on earth. Given what we have learned about the fullness of knowledge and the nature of renewal in the church, let us take some time here to reflect on what an end-time revival might look like. First, imagine the whole earth. Consider each continent, one by one. Think about race, culture, government. Think about how a family conducts life there and there. Think of individuals, families, communities, cities, nations. Think of the whole earth.

Now imagine what it might be like for people to begin to experience a renewing of their *minds* or cognition. Imagine people all over the world learning to think the way that God thinks about things. See the spread of truth throughout the globe. How does this renewal of knowledge affect this group, that community? Imagine what it might be like for the world to experience a massive revival of the *heart*, the affective side of human experience. See God touching the core concerns of people's lives, bringing healing and restoration to suffering communities and wounded individuals. Now picture God renewing the depths of our *volition*, transforming our choices, habits, and lifestyles, bringing us into intimate conformity with God's own excellency. How does the world begin to act in the end times revival?

Now imagine the *fullness* of the knowledge of God spread throughout the world, taking as your guide our outline of the stages of Christian experience and the streams of the church. What might it be like to experience a renewal of *both* awareness of God and experience of God? What would a contemplative *and* charismatic revival look like? Think of a revival that opens the church to sincere inquiry (Understanding) and commitment to true judgment (Judgment). Think of an awakening of Action and Integration, of holiness, social justice, and sacrament. Put it all together. Imagine what a real end-time revival might feel like. What would you do in the midst of a revival of power and humility, in the midst of a growth of conversions and of authentic sanctification?

Now consider the web of relationships. Imagine a powerful work of God among individuals and communities that stimulates a renewed sense of themselves. See the twisted misconceptions and damaged images falling aside. See the face of Christ re-creating the face of the church. Experience the Spirit poured out on our relationships with one another. Witness the reconciliation of person to person, group to group. Picture the restoration of family life. Watch forgiveness reign and welcome rule. See embrace after embrace. Now picture a restoration of our relationship with spiritual forces. Celebrate the victories as Satan is defeated again and again, as the people of God become a people governed by life rather than by death. Imagine the reconciliation of humans and nature. How might an end-time revival affect our own sense of our bodies, of our relationship with the land, of scientific discovery? And finally, see the fullness of union with God, believers throughout the whole earth becoming one with the God who made the earth. See the bride coming to meet the bridegroom.

Consider what spirituality as lived relationship might look like within such a renewal. What would our practice of relationship with God, as individuals and communities, be like? How would we approach spiritual formation? What would our prayer life be like? What kinds of expressions of care might we see? How might the church confront the world, the flesh, and the devil in an end-time revival? How would our approach to discerning the presence and action of God be affected? Can you imagine any new schools of spirituality or fresh approaches to relationship with God arising? And what about the study of Christian spirituality? Is there a future for the academic discipline of Christian spirituality in the midst of an end-time revival?

When you have finished exploring the big picture, return to yourself. Where do *you* fit into this end-time revival? In light of your glimpse of the end, the fulfillment of history, what might renewal mean for you today?

CHAPTER SUMMARY

1. We speak of renewal with various terms: *revival*, *awakening*, *reformation*, and *revitalization*. *Revival* and *awakening* have been used synonymously, though each refers to specific events of significance in the church. *Reformation* usually refers to large changes in structure and worldview, most often to changes in the church that took place in the sixteenth century. *Revitalization* is used by social scientists to refer to the reordering of cultures of all types. The term *renewal* tends to have the broadest reference, identifying large-scale patterns of relationship with God where the church experiences a fresh sense of life or vitality, where there is some powerful manifestation of God's active presence, where significant change is experienced (such as growth in numbers or the pioneering of new forms or structures), where the world itself is transformed through the church's witness, or other similar phenomena. While *renewal*, *revival*, and such refer to the event or process of transformation, *movement* identifies the people directly involved in the transformation.

2. The foundations of Christian renewal are found in the principles of the divine-human relationship presented throughout the book. The actively-present, self-communicating *God* initiates relationship with his people. And people respond. And God responds. Renewal is a renewal of *human* experience, involving all of the dimensions that human experience exhibits. Renewal is a moment of restoration, a transforming anticipation of the final restoration, even though in the midst of renewal elements of human greatness and human tragedy are exhibited. Renewal is a renewal of *relationship*, rekindling interest, communication, and other interpersonal dynamics. Renewal can affect any area of Christian spiritual practice: spiritual formation, prayer, care, discernment, and more.

3. We can identify examples of renewal throughout the history of God's people. God continually brought renewal to his people in the time recorded in the book of Judges as they repeatedly fell away from devotion to God until difficulty brought them to desperation and to God. King Josiah initiated a reform of the Hebrew religion.

God poured out his Spirit on the church at Pentecost. Renewals have stimulated changes in sodalities through, for example, the development of monasticism in Egypt or the formation of Celtic evangelist-monks who evangelized the British Isles and Europe. Renewals have also stimulated changes in modalities, like the various forms of church that emerged from the Protestant Reformation. Awakenings in the nineteenth century touched dry hearts and encouraged Christians to act on behalf of others. And in the twentieth century, a variety of renewals have been experienced, such as the sweeping reforms stimulated by the Second Vatican Council and the explosion of Christianity in China.

4. A review of renewal in scripture and history demonstrates how broad the renewing hand of God really is. Every dimension of human experience is subject to the Spirit's touch. Christ renews our minds, enabling God's people to understand God anew. God softens our hearts, helping us to feel God's love truly and deeply. God energizes our will, moving us to choose the things of God in our lives and lifestyles. Every stage of human experience has been touched by God, giving rise to various movements of new life in the church: Contemplative, Charismatic, Progressive, and so on. At times God renews our relationship with others, and a wave of reconciliation and forgiveness spreads across the body of Christ. At other times God addresses our relationship with nature, and we come to repent of our mistreatment of creation and our bodies. All of us, as individuals and as communities, are the recipients of the gracious renewing work of God.

5. As an aspect of divine-human relationship, renewal exhibits a number of ordinary relational dynamics. Renewal generally arises and falls in cycles, much like the life cycle of trees (soil, seed, sprout, spread, structure, sickness and death). Renewal is recognized like any other touch of God; we pay careful attention to who is discerning, to preparation for discernment, and to the various signs of discernment. For a variety of reasons, renewal is wonderful for some and difficult for others. It produces both critics and counterfeits, unions and divisions.

6. Finally, Christian spirituality is likely to experience renewal in a number of areas in the future. As lived relationship with God, Christian spirituality is being birthed into the global South as never before. Both numbers of believers and development of various forms of relationship with God will have a renewing effect on Christianity as a whole. The West is experiencing change and renewal as well, with an opening up of a new spectrum of modalic options (renewal in traditional forms; growth of cell churches, seeker-sensitive churches, emerging churches, and the like), sodalic options (for example, in Russia and in the development of a new monasticism in the Protestant West), and personal options. New approaches to Christian spirituality will grow out of the different communities-in-context of postmodern Christiandom, along with changes in theological perspective. As an academic discipline, Christian spirituality shows signs of an increasing ecumenicity, a continuing attention to the communal dimension, a wrestling with our location as scholars of spirituality, and a struggle with the balance of affirmation and negation.

LOOKING FURTHER

Below are listed a few classic stories of renewal along with a few works that document or explore aspects of renewal. See the notes for sources on specific historic or contemporary renewal expressions.

Classics

For accounts of classic renewals, see *The Spirituality of the German Awakening*, trans. David Crowner and Gerald Christianson (Mahwah, NJ: Paulist Press, 2003); Jonathan Edwards, *A Faithful Narrative of the Surprising Work of God*, in *The Great Awakening*, ed. C. G. Goen, vol. 4, The Works of Jonathan Edwards (New Haven: Yale University Press, 1972), 128–211; and *The Documents of Vatican II* (New York: Guild, 1966).

Documentation and Exploration

The following works provide accounts and evaluations of renewal in various times and places: Thomas Cahill, *How the Irish Saved Civilization: The Untold Story of Ireland's Heroic Role from the Fall of Rome to the Rise of Medieval Europe* (New York: Doubleday, 1995); Derwas J. Chitty, *The Desert a City: An Introduction to the Study of Egyptian and Palestinian Monasticism under the Christian Empire* (Crestwood, NY: St. Vladimir's Seminary Press, 1966); Philip Jenkins, *The Next Christendom: The Coming of Global Christianity* (New York: Oxford University Press, 2002); Richard Lovelace, *Dynamics of Spiritual Life: An Evangelical Theology of Renewal* (Downers Grove, IL: InterVarsity Press, 1979); William G. McLoughlin, *Revivals, Awakenings, and Reform: An Essay on Religion and Change in America, 1607–1977* (Chicago: University of Chicago Press, 1978); and Richard M. Riss, *A Survey of 20th Century Revival Movements in North America* (Peabody, MA: Hendrickson, 1988). J. Edwin Orr has written a number of lesser known but very well documented historical studies of revivals: see, for example, *The Eager Feet: Evangelical Awakenings, 1790–1830* (Chicago: Moody, 1975); *The Second Evangelical Awakening in America* (London: Marshall, Morgon, and Scott, 1952); *The Light of the Nations: Evangelical Renewal and Advance in the Nineteenth Century* (Grand Rapids: Eerdmans, 1965); *The Event of the Century: The 1857–1858 Awakening* (Wheaton: International Awakening Press, 1989); *The Fervent Prayer: The Worldwide Impact of the Great Awakening of 1858* (Chicago: Moody, 1974); *Campus Aflame: Evangelical Awakenings in Collegiate Communities* (Glendale, CA: Regal Books, 1971); and *The Flaming Tongue: The Impact of Twentieth-Century Revivals* (Chicago: Moody, 1973).

Notes

Chapter 1

1. Condensed from William Faulkner's *The Sound and the Fury* (New York: Random House, 1929), 369–71.

2. Bernard McGinn, "The Letter and the Spirit: Spirituality as an Academic Discipline," *Christian Spirituality Bulletin* 1, no. 2 (Fall 1993): 4.

3. See Jean Leclercq, "Spiritualitas," *Studi Medievali* 3 (1962): 273–96; Jon Alexander, "What Do Recent Writers Mean by Spirituality?" *Spirituality Today* 32 (1980): 247–56; Philip Sheldrake, *Spirituality and Theology: Christian Living and the Doctrine of God* (Maryknoll, NY: Orbis, 1998), 40–64; McGinn, "The Letter and the Spirit."

4. With regard to the level of practice, see, for example, Richard Foster, *Celebration of Discipline: The Path to Spiritual Growth*, 20th anniv. ed. (San Francisco: HarperSanFrancisco, 1998); Joan Chittester, *Wisdom Distilled from the Daily: Living the Rule of St. Benedict Today* (San Francisco: HarperSanFrancisco, 1990); St. Theophan the Recluse, *The Path to Salvation: A Manual of Spiritual Transformation*, trans. Fr. Seraphim Rose (Platina, CA: St. Herman Press, 1998). Examples of literature written with regard to the level of dynamics include Richard Lovelace, *Dynamics of Spiritual Life: An Evangelical Theology of Renewal* (Downers Grove, IL: InterVarsity Press, 1979); and Vladimir Lossky, *The Mystical Theology of the Eastern Church* (Crestwood, NY: St. Vladimir's Press, 1998). For the level of academic discipline, see Michael Downey, *Understanding Christian Spirituality* (New York: Paulist Press, 1997); or the collection of essays found in Kenneth J. Collins, ed., *Exploring Christian Spirituality: An Ecumenical Reader* (Grand Rapids: Baker, 2000). For Principe's model, see Walter Principe, "Toward Defining Spirituality," *Studies in Religion* 12, no. 2 (1983): 127–41.

5. See, for example, the massive collection in the Classics of Western Spirituality series published by Paulist Press. The ongoing translation and publication of *The Philokalia* by Faber and Faber serves a similar purpose for the Orthodox traditions. Four of five volumes are published currently; see G. E. H. Palmer, Philip Sherrard, and Kallistos Ware, trans. and eds., *The Philoka-*lia: *The Complete Text* (London: Faber and Faber, 1979–1955).

6. For examples of single-volume anthologies, see Louis Dupré and James A. Wiseman, *Light from Light: An Anthology of Christian Mysticism* (New York: Paulist Press, 1988); Richard J. Foster and James Bryan Smith, eds., *Devotional Classics: Selected Readings for Individuals and Groups* (San Francisco: HarperSanFrancisco, 1993); and Richard J. Foster and Emilie Griffin, eds., *Spiritual Classics: Selected Readings for Individuals and Groups on the Twelve Spiritual Disciplines* (San Francisco: HarperSanFrancisco, 2000).

7. See the historical surveys in Cheslyn Jones, Geoffrey Wainwright, and Edward Yarnold, eds., *The Study of Spirituality* (New York: Oxford University Press, 1986); in the three volumes devoted to Christianity (vols. 16–18) of *World Spirituality: An Encyclopedic History of the Religious Quest*, gen. ed. Ewert Cousins (New York: Crossroad, 1989); James M. Gordon, *Evangelical Spirituality: From the Wesleys to John Stott* (London: SPCK, 1991); and the outline of traditions presented in Frank Senn, ed., *Protestant Spiritual Traditions* (New York: Paulist Press, 1986), and in Collins, *Exploring Christian Spirituality*, 93–226. Good examples of extended explorations of particular historical models are Martin Thornton, *English Spirituality: An Outline of Ascetical Theology According to the English Pastoral Tradition* (Cambridge, MA: Cowley Publications, 1986), and Howard L. Rice, *Reformed Spirituality: An Introduction for Believers* (Louisville: Westminster John Knox, 1991).

8. A superb example of this can be found in Bernard McGinn's projected five-volume historical exploration of mysticism, The Presence of God: A History of Western Christian Mysticism (of which four have been published to date): *The Foundations of Mysticism: Origins to the Fifth Century* (New York: Crossroad, 1991); *The Growth of Mysticism: Gregory the Great through the 12th Century* (New York: Crossroad, 1994); *The Flowering of Mysticism: Men and Women in the New Mysticism, 1200–1350* (New York: Crossroad, 1998); and *The Harvest of Mysticism in Medieval Germany* (New York: Crossroad/Herder and Herder, 2005).

9. Taken from Bernard of Clairvaux, "On Loving God," in *Bernard of Clairvaux: Selected Works*, G. R. Evans, trans., The Classics of Western Spirituality (Mahwah, NJ: Paulist Press, 1987), 186–96.

10. See Andrew Louth, "Mysticism," in *The Westminster Dictionary of Christian Spirituality*, ed. Gordon S. Wakefield (Philadelphia: Westminster Press, 1983), 272–74.

11. In the East, within the Orthodox traditions, mystical theology and mysticism have retained, for the most part, the close connection of the objective and subjective dimensions. Doctrine, sacrament, and Spirit were tightly linked in the writings of the spiritual fathers and mothers of the East. For this reason, the use of the term *mysticism* in Orthodox writings does not reflect the interests of Western discussion.

12. See William James, *The Varieties of Religious Experience* (New York: Simon and Schuster, 1997); Baron Friedrich von Hügel, *The Mystical Element of Religion as Studied in Saint Catherine of Genoa and Her Friends* (London: James Clarke, 1961); Evelyn Underhill, *Mysticism: A Study in the Nature and Development of Man's Spiritual Consciousness* (New York: Meridian Books, 1955); Rudolf Otto, *The Idea of the Holy: An Inquiry into the Non-Rational Factor in the Idea of the Divine and Its Relation to the Rational*, trans. John W. Harvey, 2nd ed. (New York: Oxford University Press, 1958); and Joseph Maréchal, *Studies in the Psychology of the Mystics*, trans. Algar Thorold (London: Burns, Oates, and Washbourne, 1927).

13. McGinn, *Foundations of Mysticism*, xvii.

14. Jordan Aumann, *Spiritual Theology* (London: Sheed and Ward, 1980), 22. Simon Chan, in his recently published *Spiritual Theology: A Systematic Study of the Christian Life* (Downers Grove, IL: InterVarsity Press, 1998), adopts this definition as the core of his own treatment of the spiritual life.

15. See Chan, *Spiritual Theology*, 17; and Bradley C. Hanson, "Spirituality as Spiritual Theology," in *Modern Christian Spirituality: Methodological and Historical Essays*, ed. Bradley C. Hanson (Atlanta: Scholars Press, 1990), 50.

16. On Christian spirituality as a self-implicating discipline, see Sandra M.

Schneiders, "Spirituality in the Academy," in *Exploring Christian Spirituality: An Ecumenical Reader*, ed. Ken Collins (Grand Rapids: Baker, 2000), 249–69.

17. Charles André Bernard, "The Nature of Spiritual Theology," in *Exploring Christian Spirituality: An Ecumenical Reader*, ed. Ken Collins (Grand Rapids: Baker, 2000), 238.

18. Philip Sheldrake, *Spirituality and History: Questions of Interpretation and Method* (Maryknoll, NY: Orbis, 1998), 58.

19. Adolphe Tanquerey, *The Spiritual Life: A Treatise on Ascetical and Mystical Theology*, trans. Herman Branderis, 2nd and rev. ed. (Tournai, Belgium: Desclée, 1930), 3–4.

20. This attention to broader concerns and connections is reflected in the topics discussed in recent gatherings of the Society for the Study of Christian Spirituality.

21. See Ninian Smart, *The Religious Experience of Mankind* (New York: Scribner, 1984).

22. Gerald May, *Care of Mind, Care of Spirit: Psychiatric Dimensions of Spiritual Direction* (San Francisco: Harper and Row, 1983), 6–7. These terms are, in turn, to be distinguished from *discipleship* as it is understood within the Protestant Evangelical community. I will address these distinctions more fully in my chapter on spiritual formation.

23. See Alister E. McGrath, *Christian Spirituality: An Introduction* (Oxford: Blackwell, 1999), 8–24.

24. See Kees Waaijman, *Spirituality: Forms, Foundations, Methods*, trans. John Vriend (Leuven, Belgium: Peeters, 2002), 9–304.

25. Geoffrey Wainwright, "Types of Spirituality," in *The Study of Spirituality*, ed. Cheslyn Jones, Geoffrey Wainwright, and Edward Yarnold (New York: Oxford University Press, 1986), 592–605; McGrath, *Christian Spirituality*, 19–24.

26. Downey, *Understanding Christian Spirituality*, 124–31.

27. Bruce Demarest, *Satisfy Your Soul: Restoring the Heart of Christian Spirituality* (Colorado Springs: NavPress, 1999), 74–79.

28. Samuel M. Powell, *A Theology of Christian Spirituality* (Nashville: Abingdon, 2005), 12–13.

29. Sheldrake, *Spirituality and History*, 60.

30. Dave Hunt and T. A. McMahon, *The Seduction of Christianity* (Eugene, OR: Harvest House, 1985), 9. This sentiment is reiterated in Hunt's more recent critique of the Renovaré *Spiritual Formation Study Bible* (San Francisco: HarperSanFrancisco, 2005), available at www.thebereancall.org.

31. Demarest, *Satisfy Your Soul*, 70–72; Downey, *Understanding Christian Spirituality*, 146–50; Chan, *Spiritual Theology*, 25–39.

Chapter 2

1. Good defenses for the use of interdisciplinarity can be found in J. Wentzel van Huyssteen, *The Shaping of Rationality: Toward Interdisciplinarity in Theology and Science* (Grand Rapids: Eerdmans, 1999); N. T. Wright, *The New Testament and the People of God*, vol. 1, Christian Origins and the Question of God (Minneapolis: Fortress, 1992); and Donald L. Gelpi, *Inculturating North American Theology: An Experiment in Foundational Method* (Atlanta:

Scholars Press, 1988). An interdisciplinary approach to Christian spirituality is presented in Sandra M. Schneiders, "The Letter and the Spirit: Spirituality as an Academic Discipline," *Christian Spirituality Bulletin* 1, no. 2 (Fall 1993): 10–15; and Kees Waaijman, *Spirituality: Forms, Foundations, Methods*, trans. John Vriend (Leuven, Belgium: Peeters, 2002).

2. I have adapted my categories slightly from those found in Gelpi, *Inculturating*, 151–53; and Donald L. Gelpi, *To Hope in Jesus Christ*, vol. 1, The Firstborn of Many: A Christology for Converting Christians (Milwaukee: Marquette University Press, 2000), 97. My thanks to Terese M. Howard, who supplied the final option for treating opposition presented here.

3. I have chosen to treat the disciplines of theology and philosophy together. First, they share important unifying and critical thinking functions. Second, while the relationship between theology and spirituality has been much discussed among current scholars in Christian spirituality, the place of philosophy has seldom been mentioned. For this reason I have chosen briefly to address philosophical aims and methods at the close of the section on theology.

4. Needless to say, these six fields of study are by no means the *only* fields which have application to Christian spirituality. The six areas of study are not a comprehensive list of possible fields of integration. Literature, art, and the natural sciences have all been explored in terms of integration with Christian spirituality. The study of world religions offers a number of insights through which Christians can better understand relationship with God. One can even think about the study of physiology and kinesthetics with regard to how humans embody relationship with God in worship and life. I have chosen these six because these have received significant discussion in secondary literature and because both space and my own limited expertise prevent me from attempting more.

5. For more on the asceticism of interpretation, see Geoffrey Galt Harpham, *The Ascetic Imperative in Culture and Criticism* (Chicago: University of Chicago Press, 1987).

6. A case in point in this regard is found in the study of Puritan spirituality. If we limit ourselves to written texts, Puritan spirituality is worked out in the sermons, treatises, devotional manuals, *and* diaries of the Puritan divines. To neglect any of these diverse genres is to disregard an important source of the Puritan spiritual integration. On Puritan spiritual practice, see Charles Hambrick-Stowe, *The Practice of Piety: Puritan Devotional Disciplines in Seventeenth-Century New England* (Chapel Hill: University of North Carolina Press, 1982); and Richard Lovelace, "The Anatomy of Puritan Piety: English Puritan Devotional Literature, 1600–1640," in *Christian Spirituality: Post-Reformation and Modern*, ed. Louis Dupré and Don E. Saliers, vol. 18, World Spirituality: An Encyclopedic History of the Religious Quest (New York: Crossroad, 1989), 294–323.

7. Athanasius, *On the Incarnation*, trans. and ed. by a religious of CSMV, intro. C. S. Lewis (London: A. R. Mowbray, 1944; repr. 1975), 57.3, 96. See also Abba Philemon's comment on theology in "A Discourse on Abba Philemon," in *The Philokalia: The Complete Text*, comp. Saint Nikodimos of the Holy Mountain and Saint Makarios of Corinth, trans. G. E. H. Palmer, Philip Sherrard, and Kallistos Ware (London: Faber

and Faber, 1981), 2:355; John Meyendorff, *Byzantine Theology: Historical Trends and Doctrinal Themes* (New York: Fordham University Press, 1979), 14; and the discussion of the integration of personal experience and theology in Dumitru Staniloae, *The Experience of God: Orthodox Dogmatic Theology*, trans. Ioan Ionita and Robert Barringer, 2 vols. (Brookline, MA: Holy Cross Orthodox Press, 1994), 1:87.

8. On this issue of experiential components in the spirituality classroom, see the discussions by Bernard McGinn and Sandra M. Schneiders in *Christian Spirituality Bulletin* 1, no. 2 (Fall 1993); the various articles in *Christian Spirituality Bulletin* 7, no. 2 (Fall–Winter 1999); and especially Elizabeth Liebert's presidential address to the Society for the Study of Christian Spirituality, "The Role of Practice in the Study of Christian Spirituality," *Spiritus: A Journal of Christian Spirituality* 2, no. 1 (Spring 2002): 30–49.

9. A good model of this kind of integration of personal experience and research in Christian spirituality may be found in Belden Lane, *The Solace of Fierce Landscapes: Exploring Desert and Mountain Spirituality* (New York: Oxford University Press, 1998).

10. Sandra M. Schneiders, "Biblical Spirituality: Life, Literature, and Learning," in *Doors of Understanding: Conversations in Global Spirituality in Honor of Ewert Cousins*, ed. Steven Chase (Quincy, IL: Franciscan, 1997), 62.

11. John Paul II, *Catechism of the Catholic Church* (Washington, DC: United States Catholic Conference, 1994), no. 104.

12. For these two dimensions of the relationship between scripture and spirituality, see Sandra M. Schneiders, "Scripture and Spirituality," in *Christian Spirituality: Origins to the Twelfth Century*, ed. Bernard McGinn, John Meyendorff, and Jean Leclercq, vol. 16 World Spirituality: An Encyclopedic History of the Religious Quest (New York: Crossroad, 1985), 2–4; and Steven Katz, *Mysticism and Sacred Scripture* (Oxford: Oxford University Press, 2000).

13. For a suggestive illustration on the authority of scripture, see, for example, Wright, *New Testament and the People of God*, 140–43.

14. For the relationship of interpretation to spirituality, see, for example, Christopher A. Hall, *Reading Scripture with the Church Fathers* (Downers Grove, IL: InterVarsity Press, 1998); Douglas Burton-Christie, *The Word in the Desert: Scripture and the Quest for Holiness in Early Christian Monasticism* (New York: Oxford University Press, 1993); Elizabeth A. Clark, *Reading Renunciation: Asceticism and Scripture in Early Christianity* (Princeton: Princeton University Press, 1999); Walter Wink, *The Bible in Human Transformation: Toward a New Paradigm for Biblical Study* (Philadelphia: Fortress, 1973); M. Robert Mulholland Jr., *Shaped by the Word: The Power of Scripture in Spiritual Formation* (Nashville: Upper Room, 1985); Sandra M. Schneiders, *The Revelatory Text: Interpreting the New Testament as Sacred Scripture*, 2nd ed. (Collegeville, MN: Liturgical Press, 1999); Evan B. Howard, *Praying the Scriptures: A Field Guide for Your Spiritual Journey* (Downers Grove, IL: InterVarsity Press, 1999); David Steinmetz, "The Superiority of Pre-Critical Exegesis," *Theology Today* 37 (April 1980–January 1981): 27–38; Andrew Louth, *Discerning the Mystery: An Essay on the Nature of Theology* (Oxford: Clarendon, 1983); Rick Joyner, "Fundamentals of Biblical Interpretation," *Morning Star Journal* 1 (1985): 38–49

(www.morningstarministries.org); Sandra M. Schneiders, "Scripture and Spirituality," 16–19; and Bonnie Thurston's review of trends in New Testament Studies, "The Study of the New Testament and the Study of Christian Spirituality: Some Reflections," *Christian Spirituality Bulletin* 8, no. 2 (Fall–Winter 2000): 3–6.

15. A chiasm is a form of poetry common in the Bible within which thoughts are placed in a form such as A, B, C, D, C′, B′, A′. A and A′ are somewhat parallel in idea. B and B′ are parallel, and so on.

16. Ralph W. Hood Jr., Bernard Spilka, Bruce Hunsberger, and Richard Gorsuch, eds., *The Psychology of Religion: An Empirical Approach*, 2nd ed. (New York: Guilford Press, 1996), 74.

17. See John Cassian, *The Conferences*, trans. and ann. Boniface Ramsey, Ancient Christian Writers, vol. 57 (New York: Newman Press, 1997), 511–16; and John Cassian, *The Monastic Institutes*, trans. Jerome Bertram (London: The Saint Austin Press, 1999), 169.

18. *The Rule of St. Benedict*, trans. Anthony C. Meisel and M. L. del Mastro (New York: Image Doubleday, 1975), 48.1.

19. Jean Leclercq, "Prayer and Contemplation: II. Western," in *Christian Spirituality: Origins to the Twelfth Century*, ed. Bernard McGinn, John Meyendorff, and Jean Leclercq, vol. 16, World Spirituality: An Encyclopedic History of the Religious Quest (New York: Crossroad, 1985), 420.

20. Bernard McGinn, *The Growth of Mysticism: Gregory the Great through the 12th Century*, vol. 2, The Presence of God: A History of Western Christian Mysticism (New York: Crossroad, 1994), 139. I will discuss contemplation in greater detail in chapter 9.

21. See Mariano Magrassi, *Praying the Bible: An Introduction to Lectio Divina*, trans. Edward Hagman (Collegeville, MN: Liturgical Press, 1998); M. Basil Pennington, *Lectio Divina: Renewing the Ancient Practice of Praying the Scriptures* (New York: Crossroad, 1998); Thelma Hall, *Too Deep for Words: Rediscovering Lectio Divina* (New York: Paulist Press, 1988). My own suggestions for integrating scripture and prayer can be found in Howard, *Praying the Scriptures*.

22. Aelred of Rievaulx, *Spiritual Friendship*, trans. Mary Eugene Laker (Kalamazoo, MI: Cistercian Publications, 1977), 3.103.

23. Cicero, *On Friendship*, cited in William J. Bennett, ed., *The Book of Virtues: A Treasury of Great Moral Stories* (New York: Simon and Schuster, 1993), 334. See also Cicero, *De Amicitia*, vii.23 in *Cicero: De Senectute, De Amicitia, De Divinatione*, trans. William Armistead Falconer, Loeb Classical Library, vol. 154 (Cambridge: Harvard University Press, 1923), 133.

24. Of course, some Christians widen the spectrum even further, joining history and informal relationship, to include the larger "communion of saints."

25. Rowan Williams, *The Wound of Knowledge: A Theological History from the New Testament to Luther and St. John of the Cross* (Eugene, OR: Wipf and Stock, 1998), 1.

26. See Barsanuphius and John, *Guidance Toward Spiritual Life: Answers to the Questions of Disciples*, trans. Fr. Seraphim Rose (Platina, CA: St. Herman Press, 1990).

27. For more detail on this see Philip Sheldrake, *Spirituality and History: Questions of Interpretation and Method* (Maryknoll, NY: Orbis, 1998).

28. See Sheldrake's critique of previous histories of Christian spirituality in ibid., 98–101.

29. On this see ibid., 65–90, and Gustavo Gutierrez, *We Drink from Our Own Wells: The Spiritual Journey of a People*, trans. Matthew J. O'Connell (Maryknoll, NY: Orbis, 1984).

30. Bernard McGinn, *The Foundations of Mysticism: Origins to the Fifth Century*, vol. 1, The Presence of God: A History of Western Christian Mysticism (New York: Crossroad, 1991), xii.

31. Philip Yancey, *Reaching for the Invisible God* (Grand Rapids: Zondervan, 2000), 230–31.

32. See, for example, Andrew Walls, "Christianity," in *A New Handbook of Living Religions*, ed. John R. Hinnells (Oxford: Blackwell, 1997), 55–161; Philip Jenkins, *The Next Christendom: The Coming of Global Christianity* (New York: Oxford University Press, 2002).

33. This history is presented in greater detail in Philip Sheldrake, *Spirituality and Theology: Christian Living and the Doctrine of God* (Maryknoll, NY: Orbis, 1998), 33–64.

34. With regards to the relationship of theology to spirituality see, for example, Lawrence S. Cunningham, "*Extra Arcam Noe*: Criteria for Christian Spirituality," *Christian Spirituality Bulletin* 3, no. 1 (Spring 1995): 6–9; J. Matthew Ashley, "The Turn to Spirituality? The Relationship between Theology and Spirituality," *Christian Spirituality Bulletin* 3, no. 2 (Fall 1995): 13–18; Simon Chan, *Spiritual Theology: A Systematic Study of the Christian Life* (Downers Grove, IL: InterVarsity Press, 1998), 25–34; Andrew Louth, *Theology and Spirituality*, rev. ed. (Fairacres, UK: SLG Press, 1978), 5–6; Sheldrake, *Spirituality and Theology*, 35, 53–54; Bradley Hanson, "Theological Approaches to Spirituality: A Lutheran Perspective," *Christian Spirituality Bulletin* 2, no. 1 (Spring 1994): 6; Sandra M. Schneiders, "Theology and Spirituality: Strangers, Rivals, or Partners?" *Horizons* 13 (Fall 1986): 253–74; and Samuel M. Powell, *A Theology of Christian Spirituality* (Nashville: Abingdon, 2005).

35. One might mention Orthodox theologians such as Kallistos Ware, Vladimir Lossky, John Meyendorff, and Dumitru Staniloae; Roman Catholic theologians such as Karl Rahner, Bernard Lonergan, Hans Urs von Balthasar, Gustavo Gutierrez, Donald L. Gelpi, and Elizabeth Ann Johnson; and Protestant theologians such as Paul Tillich, Jürgen Moltmann, Wolfhart Pannenburg, George Lindbeck, Stanley Hauerwas, Alister McGrath, Donald Bloesch, Thomas Oden, and Bruce Demarest.

36. See Louth, *Theology and Spirituality*, 8, 10; and Mark McIntosh, *Mystical Theology: The Integrity of Spirituality and Theology* (Malden, MA: Blackwell, 1998), 33.

37. See Ellen T. Charry, *By the Renewing of Your Minds: The Pastoral Function of Doctrine* (New York: Oxford University Press, 1997).

38. We must remember, of course, that spirituality also shapes the task of theology: shaping the heart and perspective of the theologian, introducing new texts (spiritual writings) that can be included as theologically relevant, providing to an overly formulaic interpretation of the faith stimulating symbols for theological use, helping to define the atmosphere within which theology is done, and more. See Louth, *Theology and Spirituality*, 12–14; McIntosh, *Mystical Theology*, 14–15; Sheldrake, *Spirituality and History*, 22; Ashley, "Turn to Spirituality?"; and the essays in *Spirituality and Theology: Essays in Honor of Diogenes Allen*, ed. Eric O. Springsted (Louisville: Westminster John Knox, 1998).

39. Evagrius Ponticus, *Chapters on Prayer* 60, in *The Praktikos and Chapters on Prayer*, trans. John Eudes Bamberger (Kalamazoo, MI: Cistercian Publications, 1981), 65.

40. See Nicholas Wolterstorff, *Reason within the Bounds of Religion* (Grand Rapids: Eerdmans, 1976), and Philip Endean, "Theology Out of Spirituality: The Approach of Karl Rahner," *Christian Spirituality Bulletin* 3, no. 2 (Fall 1995): 7–8.

41. For an example of how spirituality might look different given different theological emphases see, for example, the comparison of theologians Karl Rahner and Hans Urs von Balthasar in McIntosh, *Mystical Theology*, 90–118, and the review of contemporary theologians in Sheldrake, *Spirituality and Theology*, 66–75.

42. Jonathan Edwards's works on revivals provide classic examples of this kind of use of theology for spirituality. For the use of theological categories in the evaluation of corporate experience (the authenticity of a work of God in general), see Jonathan Edwards, *The Great Awakening*, ed. C. G. Goen, vol. 4, The Works of Jonathan Edwards (New Haven: Yale University Press, 1972). For the same with regard to the evaluation of individual experience (the authenticity of one's personal experience in the context of revival events), see Jonathan Edwards, *Religious Affections*, ed. John E. Smith, vol. 2, The Works of Jonathan Edwards (New Haven: Yale University Press, 1959). The evaluative function of theology for spirituality is also discussed in Sandra M. Schneiders, "Theology and Spirituality," 270–71; Walter Principe, "Spirituality, Christian," in *The New Dictionary of Catholic Spirituality*, ed. Michael Downey (Collegeville, MN: Liturgical Press, 1993), 931–38; Sheldrake, *Spirituality and History*, 65–95; Bruce Demarest, *Satisfy Your Soul: Restoring the Heart of Christian Spirituality* (Colorado Springs: NavPress, 1999); Chan, *Spiritual Theology*; and McIntosh, *Mystical Theology*.

43. Gelpi, *To Hope in Jesus Christ*, 98.

44. Needless to say, the dialogue of spirituality with the theology of, for example, Karl Rahner brings with it a necessarily philosophical component. Likewise, mention of an "interpretive" or "hermeneutical" approach to the study of spirituality—borrowing from the thought of, for example, Paul Ricoeur or Clifford Geertz—can be comprehended only within the context of contemporary philosophical discourse. Yet within the study of spirituality so far, scholars have tended toward historical, theological, or social-critical analysis, leaving the specifically philosophical dimensions of spirituality relatively unaddressed.

45. See, for example, Pierre Hadot, *Philosophy as a Way of Life*, trans. Michael Chase (Oxford: Blackwell, 1995).

46. See the review of philosophical analysis of mysticism in McGinn, *Foundations of Mysticism*, 291–325, and the review of William Alston's *Perceiving God: The Epistemology of Religious Experience* in *Christian Spirituality Bulletin* 2/1 (Spring 1994): 27–28. I will review this issue in greater detail in the chapter on prayer.

47. See the philosophical defense for asceticism in Peter Van Ness, *Spirituality, Diversion*

and Decadence: The Contemporary Predicament (Albany, NY: State University of New York Press, 1992), and in Peter Van Ness, ed., *Spirituality and the Secular Quest*, vol. 22, World Spirituality: An Encyclopedic History of the Religious Quest (New York: Crossroad, 1996), 1–17; see also the reviews of *Spirituality and the Secular Quest* and Alston's *Perceiving God* in *Christian Spirituality Bulletin* 2/1 (Spring 1994): 27–30; and Peter Van Ness's own reflections in *Christian Spirituality Bulletin* 5/1 (Spring 1997): 16–18. See also Bernard McGinn's review of developments in the philosophy of mysticism in McGinn, *Foundations of Mysticism*, 291–326; chaps. 4 and 5 of Evan B. Howard, *Affirming the Touch of God: A Psychological and Philosophical Exploration of Christian Discernment* (Lanham, NJ: University Press of America, 2000), 235–90; and Kees Waaijman's discussion of phenomenology in Waaijman, *Spirituality*.

48. For a more detailed review of models of integrating psychology and Christian theology, see Hendrika Vande Kemp, "Psychology and Christian Spirituality: Explorations of the Inner World," *Journal of Psychology and Christianity* 15, no. 2 (1996): 161–74, and Eric L. Johnson and Stanton L. Jones, eds., *Psychology and Christianity* (Downers Grove, IL: InterVarsity Press, 2000). Unfortunately, although the term *spirituality* is used increasingly in the titles of psychological articles, serious understanding of the texts, terms, and development of Christian spirituality (especially as an academic discipline) is lacking in some articles claiming to relate spirituality and psychology.

49. See, for example, Ana-Maria Rizzuto, *Birth of the Living God: A Psychoanalytic Study* (Chicago: University of Chicago Press, 1979); Francis Kelly Nemek and Marie Theresa Coombs, *The Spiritual Journey: Critical Thresholds and Stages of Adult Spiritual Genesis* (Wilmington, DE: Michael Glazier, 1987); Morton T. Kelsey, *Encounter with God: A Theology of Christian Experience* (Minneapolis: Bethany Fellowship, 1972); and the use of temperament models (especially popular are the Myers-Briggs analysis and the Sufi Enneagram) as frameworks to understand differences in personal approach to relationship with God. Larger conceptual models of integration can be found in the writings of Morton T. Kelsey, Gerald May, Adrian Van Kaam, Bernard Tyrrell, Han F. de Wit, Larry Crabb, and Gary Collins. The School of Psychology at Fuller Seminary in Pasadena, California, places a special emphasis on integration of Christian theology and psychological insights and models. A wide variety of psychological approaches to religious experience in general (not necessarily Christian) can be found in Ralph W. Hood Jr., ed., *Handbook of Religious Experience* (Birmingham: Religious Education Press, 1995).

50. For psychological interpretations of figures in the history of Christian spirituality, see, for example, Erik H. Erikson, *Young Man Luther: A Study in Psychoanalysis and History* (New York: W. W. Norton, 1958), and W. W. Meissner, *Ignatius of Loyola: The Psychology of a Saint* (New Haven: Yale University Press, 1992). For the psychology of mystical experience and the psychology of the mystics, see William James, *The Varieties of Religious Experience* (New York: Library Classics of the United States, 1987), and Joseph Maréchal, *Studies in the Psychology of the Mystics*, trans. Algar Thorold (London: Burns, Oates, and Washbourne, 1927). For psychology

and asceticism, see Bruce J. Malina, "Power, Pain and Personhood: Ascetic Behavior in the Ancient Mediterranean," in *Asceticism*, ed. Vincent L. Wimbush and Richard Valantasis (New York: Oxford University Press, 1995), 162–77, and other studies in this volume. Some also seek to redesign the frameworks of psychology itself such that the field is fundamentally informed by the wisdom of classical spiritual writings. For different approaches to "contemplative psychology," see the articles in *Christian Spirituality Bulletin* 1/2 (Fall 1993) on or by Han F. de Wit; and Gerald G. May, *Will and Spirit: A Contemplative Psychology* (San Francisco: Harper and Row, 1982).

51. On operationalizing spirituality, see Richard L. Gorsuch and William R. Miller, "Assessing Spirituality," in *Integrating Spirituality into Treatment*, ed. William R. Miller (Washington, DC: American Psychological Association, 1999), 47–64, and other essays in this volume.

52. For an example of the use of the psychology of categorization and emotion, see Howard, *Affirming the Touch of God*, 177–224. A survey of psychological approaches to mysticism is found in McGinn, *Foundations of Mysticism*, 331–43. For the use of developmental psychology see Elizabeth Liebert, *Changing Life Patterns: Adult Development in Spiritual Direction* (New York: Paulist Press, 1992). On dreams, see Morton T. Kelsey, *Dreams: The Dark Speech of the Spirit* (New York: Doubleday, 1968). On empirical approaches to the psychology of religion in general, see the survey in Hood et al., eds., *Psychology of Religion*.

53. William Barry uses insights from interpersonal psychology in his numerous writings on spiritual direction and spirituality. Lynn Bridgers explores the psychology of trauma and Christian spirituality in Lynn Bridgers, "Beyond Recognition: Trauma, Spirituality and Pedagogy for the Prophetic," paper presented to the American Academy of Religion Spirituality Group, Denver, November 17–20, 2001). Environmental psychology and urban spirituality have been explored in Sally A. Kenel, "Urban Psychology and Spirituality," *Journal of Psychology and Theology* 15, no. 4 (1987): 300–307. For studies regarding conversion, mysticism, religious organizations, coping, and mental disorders, see the appropriate chapters in Hood et al., eds., *Psychology of Religion*.

54. See, for example, Gerald May, *Care of Mind, Care of Spirit: Psychiatric Dimensions of Spiritual Direction* (San Francisco: Harper and Row, 1983) and James D. Whitehead and Evelyn Eaton Whitehead, *Shadows of the Heart: A Spirituality of the Painful Emotions* (New York: Crossroad, 1996). I will be addressing spiritual direction in greater detail in chapter 10.

55. For general reflections on corporate spirituality, see, for example, Dietrich Bonhoeffer, *Life Together*, trans. John W. Doberstein (San Francisco: HarperSanFrancisco, 1954); Jean Vanier, *Community and Growth* (New York: Paulist Press, 1982); J. Heinrich Arnold, *Discipleship*, comp. and ed. the Hutterian Brethren (Farmington, PA: Plough Publishing House, 1994); and John D. Zizioulas, *Being as Communion: Studies in Personhood and the Church* (Crestwood, NY: St. Vladimir's Seminary Press, 1985). The wealth of missiological literature on "people movements" is valuable for the exploration of corporate conversion. For an example of the use of ritual stud-

ies to illumine our understanding of corporate Christian worship, see Daniel E. Albrecht, *Rites in the Spirit: A Ritual Approach to Pentecostal/Charismatic Spirituality*, Journal of Pentecostal Theology Supplement Series (Sheffield, UK: Sheffield Academic Press, 1999).

56. See, for example, John R. Sommerfeldt, *Abba: Guides to Holiness East and West* (Kalamazoo, MI: Cistercian Publications, 1982); John T. McNeill, *A History of the Cure of Souls* (New York: Harper and Row, 1951). The social function of the role of prophetic women is discussed in Caroline Walker Bynum, "Religious Women in the Later Middle Ages," in *Christian Spirituality: High Middle Ages and Reformation*, ed. Jill Raitt, Bernard McGinn, and John Meyendorff, vol. 17, *World Spirituality: An Encyclopedic History of the Religious Quest* (New York: Crossroad, 1987), 121–39. Sociological contexts of Christian spirituality are discussed in Anthony Russell, "Sociology and the Study of Christian Spirituality," in *The Study of Spirituality*, ed. Cheslyn Jones, Geoffrey Wainwright, and Edward Yarnold (New York: Oxford University Press, 1986), 33–38. The various "types" of spirituality are discussed in the standard historical introductions to Christian spirituality. For an application of H. Richard Niebuhr's five categories of "Christ and culture" to spirituality, see Geoffrey Wainwright, "Types of Spirituality," in *The Study of Spirituality*, ed. Cheslyn Jones, Geoffrey Wainwright, and Edward Yarnold (New York: Oxford, 1986), 592–605.

57. See, for example, Joann Wolski Conn, ed., *Women's Spirituality: Resources for Christian Development*, 2nd ed. (New York: Paulist Press, 1996); Richard Rohr and Joseph Martos, *The Wild Man's Journey: Reflections on Male Spirituality* (Cincinnati: St. Anthony's Messenger Press, 1996); Flora Wilson Bridges, *Resurrection Song: African-American Spirituality* (Maryknoll, NY: Orbis, 2001); Robert Wuthnow, *After Heaven: Spirituality in America since the 1950s* (Berkeley and Los Angeles: University of California Press, 1998). For inquiries specifically regarding postmodernism and Christian spirituality, see discussions in *Christian Spirituality Bulletin* 5/1 (Spring 1997).

58. Ronald J. Sider, *Rich Christians in an Age of Hunger: Moving from Affluence to Generosity*, 20th anniv. ed. (Nashville: Word, 1997), 138. The linking, through the use of social sciences, of spirituality to the outward thrust of social action is clearly expressed in Joe Holland and Peter Henriot, *Social Analysis: Linking Faith and Justice* (Maryknoll, NY: Orbis, 1983); Joe Holland, "Linking Social Analysis and Theological Reflection: The Place of Root Metaphors in Social and Religious Experience," in *Tracing the Spirit: Communities, Social Action, and Theological Reflection*, ed. James E. Hug (New York: Paulist Press, 1983), 170–91; and Elizabeth Liebert, "Linking Faith and Justice: Working with Systems and Structures as a Spiritual Discipline," *Christian Spirituality Bulletin* 5, no. 1 (Spring 1997): 19–21.

59. For an Orthodox approach to psychology, see Metropolitan of Nafpaktos Hierotheos, *Orthodox Psychotherapy: The Science of the Fathers*, trans. Esther Williams (Levadia, Greece: Birth of the Theotokos Monastery, 1997). A helpful and practical response to concerns for the conservative Protestant is found in Demarest's *Satisfy Your Soul*, 219–54.

60. See Malcolm Jeeves, *Psychology and Christianity: The View Both Ways* (Downers Grove, IL: InterVarsity Press, 1976), especially pp. 83–84.

61. See also Gelpi's summary of the functions of psychological insights. In his books *Inculturating* and *To Hope in Jesus Christ*, Gelpi mentions validation and amplification only. In an earlier draft of the second book, he specifically lists three positive tasks, identifying interpretation and illumination as a third task.

62. For helpful summaries see, Stephen Kosslyn, *Image and Mind* (Cambridge: Harvard University Press, 1980); Anees A. Sheikh, ed., *Imagery: Current Theory, Research, Application* (New York: John Wiley and Sons, 1983); Ronald Finke, *Principles of Mental Imagery* (Cambridge, MA: MIT Press, 1989); Margaret W. Matlin, *Cognition*, 3rd ed. (Fort Worth: Harcourt Brace, 1994), 172–211. For further information see the studies published in the *Journal of Mental Imagery*.

Chapter 3

1. In order to facilitate recognition of the categories presented in this chapter, the terms for the elements of experience (Quality/Evaluation, Force/Act, Tendency/Habit) and the stages of human experience (Being Aware, Experiencing, Understanding, Judging, Deciding/Acting, Integrating) are capitalized throughout the text when specifically drawing attention to those elements or stages.

2. See, for example, Michael Downey, *Understanding Christian Spirituality* (New York: Paulist Press, 1997), 118–31; Mary Frohlich, "Spiritual Discipline, Discipline of Spirituality: Revisiting Questions of Definition and Method," *Spiritus* 1, no. 1 (Spring 2001): 69–70; Edward Howells, "Review of *Minding the Spirit: The Study of Christian Spirituality*," *Spiritus* 5, no. 2 (Fall 2005): 223–27.

3. See, generally, John E. Smith, "The Reconception of Experience in Peirce, James and Dewey" in *America's Philosophical Vision* (Chicago: University of Chicago Press, 1992), 17–35. The various distinctions of the term *experience* are also developed in Donald L. Gelpi, *The Turn to Experience in Contemporary Theology* (Mahwah, NJ: Paulist, 1994), 1–8. The most recent summary of Gelpi's own metaphysics of experience can be found in Donald L. Gelpi, *The Gracing of Human Experience: Rethinking the Relationship Between Nature and Grace* (Collegeville, MN: Liturgical Press, 2001), 263–314.

4. Following, for the most part, the leads of Charles S. Peirce more generally, and Donald L. Gelpi more specifically. See Gelpi's *Turn to Experience* and *Gracing of Human Experience*, 263–314.

5. Again following Charles S. Peirce. For a brief summary of Peirce's triadic system, see Douglas R. Anderson, *Strands of System: The Philosophy of Charles Peirce* (West Lafayette, IN: Purdue University Press, 1995).

6. Certain body schemas, once learned, do not require the kind of intellectual processing used in ordinary thinking. The act (or sequence of acts) is simply available within the nervous system when triggered by key events. Some of these body memories may actually bypass processing through the cortex of the brain.

7. See, for example, S. L. Frank, *Man's Soul: An Introductory Essay in Philosophical Psychology* (Athens: Ohio University Press, 1993); Heinrich Zimmer, *Philosophies of India*, ed. Joseph Campbell, Bollingen Series 26 (Princeton: Princeton University Press, 1951), 355–78; David J. Kalupahana, *A History of Buddhist Philosophy: Continuities and Discontinuities* (Delhi: Motilal Banarsidass, 1994), 68–77; Kelly A. Parker, *The Continuity of Peirce's Thought* (Nashville: Vanderbilt University Press, 1998), 122–27; and Smith, *America's Philosophical Vision*, 121–92. For a review of psychological theories, see Calvin S. Hall, Gardner Lindzey, and John B. Campbell, *Theories of Personality*, 4th ed. (New York: John Wiley and Sons, 1998). Interesting contemporary discussions can be found in Francisco J. Varela, Evan Thompson, and Eleanor Rosch, *The Embodied Mind: Cognitive Science and Human Experience* (Cambridge, MA: MIT Press, 1991); Charles Taylor, *The Sources of the Self: The Making of Modern Identity* (Cambridge, MA: Harvard University Press, 1989); and Calvin O. Schrag, *The Self after Postmodernity* (New Haven, CT: Yale University Press, 1997).

8. This last statement is taken from Varela, Thompson, and Rosch, *Embodied Mind*, 124.

9. Suzanne Noffke, "Soul," in *The New Dictionary of Catholic Spirituality*, ed. Michael Downey (Collegeville, MN: Liturgical Press, 1993), 908.

10. It was the work of Maurice Merleau-Ponty that brought human embodiment to the attention of the philosophical community. More recently, see especially the philosophical work of Mark Johnson, who finds a bodily basis for all kinds of aspects of human life and thought. In the field of intellectual history, Michel Foucault has pioneered attention to the body. More directly related to the history of Christian spirituality, see especially Peter Brown, *The Body and Society: Men, Women, and Sexual Renunciation in Early Christianity* (New York: Columbia University Press, 1988); Margaret R. Miles, *Augustine on the Body* (Missoula, MT: Scholars Press, 1979); Margaret R. Miles, *Plotinus on Body and Beauty: Society, Philosophy and Religion in Third-Century Rome* (Oxford: Blackwell, 1999); and Caroline Walker Bynum, *Holy Feast and Holy Fast: The Religious Significance of Food to Medieval Women* (Berkeley and Los Angeles: University of California Press, 1987). See also the reflections on body, spouse, and land in Wendell Berry, "The Body and the Earth," in *The Unsettling of America: Culture and Agriculture* (1977; San Francisco: Sierra Club Books, 1986), 97–140. More practical presentations relevant to Christian spirituality can be found in David R. Ellingson, *My Body, My Life* (Minneapolis: Augsburg, 1981); Margaret R. Miles, *Fullness of Life: Historical Foundations for a New Asceticism* (Eugene, OR: Wipf and Stock, 2000); Dallas Willard, *The Spirit of the Disciplines: Understanding How God Changes Lives* (San Francisco: Harper and Row, 1988), 75–129; Dallas Willard, *Renovation of the Heart: Putting on the Character of Christ* (Colorado Springs: NavPress, 2002), 159–77; Stephanie Paulsell, *Honoring the Body: Meditations on a Christian Practice* (San Francisco: Jossey-Bass, 2002); and Rodney Clapp, *Tortured Wonders: Christian Spirituality for People, Not Angels* (Grand Rapids: Brazos, 2004).

11. For a full (and fascinating) treatment of the dynamics of human visual experience, see Stephen Palmer, *Vision Science: Photons to Phenomenology* (Cambridge, MA: MIT Press, 1999).

12. Oliver Sacks, *The Man Who Mistook His Wife for a Hat and Other Clinical Tales* (New York: HarperPerennial, 1987), 157.

13. Ibid., 157.

14. Maurice Merleau-Ponty, *Phenomenology of Perception*, trans. Colin Smith (London: Routledge, 1962), 179.

15. See, for example, Brown, *Body and Society*.

16. An entire field of cognitive psychology explores various aspects of cognitive operations and the cognitive system. See, for example, Margaret Matlin, *Cognition*, 3rd ed. (Fort Worth: Harcourt Brace, 1994), and J. R. Anderson, *Cognitive Psychology and Its Implication*, 4th ed. (New York: W. H. Freeman, 1995). Philosophy addresses these matters in terms of "reason" or of "the intellect." Many of the classic works of philosophy address the nature of human cognition (Aristotle's *Organon*, John Locke's and Thomas Reid's *Essays*, David Hume's *Enquiry*, Immanuel Kant's first *Critique*, Georg Wilhelm Friedrich Hegel's *Philosophy of the Mind*, and so on). I have treated one aspect of cognition (categorization) with relationship to Christian spirituality (specifically the issue of discernment) in Evan B. Howard, *Affirming the Touch of God: A Psychological and Philosophical Exploration of Christian Discernment* (Lanham, NJ: University Press of America, 2000), 139–77.

17. For a historical survey of philosophical reflection on the emotions, see H. M. Gardiner, Ruth Clark Metcalf, and John G. Beebe-Center, *Feeling and Emotion: A History of Theories* (New York: American Book Company, 1937). A helpful survey of important contemporary empirical theories of emotion is Randolph R. Cornelius, *The Science of Emotion: Research and Tradition in the Psychology of Emotion* (Upper Saddle River, NJ: Prentice Hall, 1996). For a treatment of emotions in greater detail insofar as they are relevant to Christian spirituality (specifically the issue of discernment), see Howard, *Affirming the Touch of God*, 177–233.

18. For a survey of philosophical views concerning volition and "the will," see "Willing," pt. 2 of Hannah Arendt, *The Life of the Mind* (San Diego: Harcourt Brace, 1971). The psychology of volition, popular in the early twentieth century, has been recently, for the most part, subsumed under various subcategories: the psychology of choice and decision making (often connected with shopping and such), the psychology of motivation (often connected with learning theory and behavior), or the psychology of habit and habit breaking (often connected with smoking, dieting, and such). For the distinction, by psychologists, of volition as a potential third system, see Nico H. Frijda, *The Emotions*, Studies in Emotion and Social Interaction (Cambridge: Cambridge University Press, 1986), 388; Nico H. Frijda, "The Laws of Emotions," *American Psychologist* 43, no. 5 (May 1988): 357; Richard Lazarus, *Emotion and Adaptation* (New York: Oxford University Press, 1991), 171–72; and Howard Leventhal, "Toward a Comprehensive Theory of Emotion," in *Advances in Experimental Psychology*, ed. Leonard Berkowitz (New York: Academic Press, 1980), 13:168.

19. Willard, *Renovation of the Heart*, 34.

20. See John of the Cross, *The Ascent of Mount Carmel*, in *The Collected Works of John of the Cross*, trans. Kieran Kavanaugh and Otilio

Rodriguez (Washington, DC: Institute of Carmelite Studies, 1979); Johann Arndt, *Johann Arndt: True Christianity*, trans. Peter Erb, Classics of Western Spirituality (New York: Paulist Press, 1979), 37; Saint Theophan the Recluse, *The Path to Salvation: A Manual of Spiritual Transformation*, trans. Fr. Seraphim Rose (Platina, CA: St. Herman Press, 1998), 204.

21. An excellent summary of Adrian Van Kamm's model can be found in Susan Muto, "Formative Spirituality," *Epiphany International* 6, no. 1 (Spring 2000): 8–16. Elizabeth Liebert and Nancy Wiens's "Experience Circle" is described in Elizabeth Liebert, "Supervision as Widening the Horizons," in *Supervision of Spiritual Directors: Engaging in Holy Mystery*, ed. Mary Rose Bumpus and Rebecca Bradburn Langer (Harrisburg, PA: Morehouse, 2005), 125–45. For Dallas Willard's model, see Willard, *Renovation of the Heart*.

22. The labels for the second through fifth stages (Experiencing, Understanding, Judging, Deciding/Acting) are taken from Bernard Lonergan, *Insight: A Study of Human Understanding* (New York: Harper and Row, 1958). The first and last stages have been added to account for aspects of the process of human experience and knowing not fully developed by Lonergan's model.

23. I have adapted these categories from Gerald G. May, *Will and Spirit: A Contemplative Psychology* (San Francisco: Harper and Row, 1982), 37–51, 218–20.

24. This is emphasized philosophically in Charles Hartshorne, *The Philosophy and Psychology of Sensation* (Chicago: University of Chicago Press, 1945), and Merleau-Ponty, *Phenomenology of Perception*. Cognitive psychology has increasingly drawn attention to the integration of top-down with bottom-up constraints in pattern recognition and perception in general. These constraints are treated in detail in Stephen Palmer's treatment of visual perception. See the central chapters of Palmer, *Vision Science*.

25. A delightful account of the movement from inquiry to understanding is found in the PBS interview with physicist Richard Feynman. For a transcription of this interview, see Clark McKowen, *Thinking about Thinking: A Fifth-Generational Approach to Deliberate Thought* (Los Altos, CA: William Kaufmann, 1986), 218–33. See also John Dewey, *Logic: The Theory of Inquiry* (New York: Henry Holt, 1938). For an account of affect and understanding from the perspective of therapeutic relationships, see Donna Orange, *Emotional Understanding: Studies in Psychoanalytic Epistemology* (New York: Guilford, 1995).

26. The philosophical literature on logic and judgment is vast, encompassing entire systems of approach from historical period to historical period. On the distinctions between abduction, deduction, and induction, see Douglas R. Anderson, *Strands of System*.

27. See, for example, the appropriate chapters in J. R. Anderson, *Cognitive Psychology*, and Matlin, *Cognition*.

28. Along with the voluntarist philosophers after Immanuel Kant, pragmatists and pragmaticists tend to emphasize this stage of Decision and Action, but in different ways. For a historical account of critical schools of pragmatism, see H. O. Mounce, *The Two Pragmatisms: From Peirce to Rorty* (London: Routledge, 1997). A couple of works from the psychological side that cover Judging and Deciding are Daniel Kahneman,

Paul Slovic, and Amos Tversky, eds., *Judgment under Uncertainty: Heuristics and Biases* (Cambridge: Cambridge University Press, 1982), and Robyn M. Dawes, *Rational Choice in an Uncertain World* (Fort Worth: Harcourt Brace, 1988).

29. See, for example, Japanese philosopher Kitaro Nishida's shift of emphasis from his early voluntarism to an approach that more clearly emphasizes the standpoint from which one perceives in Kitaro Nishida, *An Inquiry into the Good*, trans. Masao Abe and Christopher Ives (New Haven: Yale University Press, 1990), and Kitaro Nishida, *Last Writings*, trans. David Dilworth (Honolulu: University of Hawaii Press, 1987). Compare also Martin Heidegger's attention to the relationship between "Being" and "being-in" a world in Martin Heidegger, *Being and Time*, trans. John Macquarrie and Edward Robinson (San Francisco: HarperSanFrancisco, 1962); and Jonathan Edwards's philosophical interpretation of Christian conversion in Jonathan Edwards, *Religious Affections*, ed. J. E. Smith, vol. 2, *The Works of Jonathan Edwards* (New Haven: Yale University Press, 1959), and Perry Miller, "Jonathan Edwards on the Sense of the Heart," *Harvard Theological Review* 41, no. 2 (April 1948): 123–46.

30. The essential relatedness of human experience is emphasized in myriad fields. For the essential relatedness of human experience in the thought of Confucius, see Ch'u Chai and Winberg Chai, *The Sacred Books of Confucius and Other Confucian Classics* (New York: Bantam, 1965). For the essential relatedness of human experience in Navajo philosophy, see John R. Farella, *The Main Stalk: A Synthesis of Navajo Philosophy* (Tuscon: University of Arizona Press, 1984), and Gary Witherspoon, *Language and Art in the Navajo Universe* (Ann Arbor: University of Michigan Press, 1977). For Edmund Husserl's notion of "intersubjectivity," see Edmund Husserl, *Cartesian Meditations: An Introduction to Phenomenology* (Dordrecht, Netherlands: Kluwer Academic, 1995), 89–157, and Joseph J. Kockelmans, *Edmund Husserl's Phenomenology* (West Lafayette, IN: Purdue University Press, 1994), 277–99. For Martin Heidegger's emphasis on our being embedded within *das Mann*, see Heidegger, *Being and Time*. For an introduction to Emmanuel Levinas's later thought, see Adriaan Peperzak, *To the Other: An Introduction to the Philosophy of Emmanuel Levinas* (West Lafayette, IN: Purdue University Press, 1993). For the essential relatedness of human experience in the thought of John Macmurray, see John Macmurray, *Persons in Relation* (Atlantic Highlands, NJ: Humanities Press, 1961). And for the essential relatedness of human experience in the thought of American philosophers Josiah Royce and George Herbert Mead, see Josiah Royce, *The Sources of Religious Insight* (Washington, DC: Catholic University of America Press, 2001); Josiah Royce, *The Problem of Christianity* (Washington, DC: Catholic University Press of America, 2001); and George Herbert Mead, *Mind, Self, and Society: From the Standpoint of a Social Behaviorist*, ed. Charles W. Morris, vol. 1, The Works of George Herbert Mead (Chicago: University of Chicago Press, 1967).

31. In addition to the philosophical sources mentioned in the previous note, one might point to the thought of (the later) Wittgenstein, Francois Lyotard, and Michel Foucault. On the social theory of emotions, see James Averill, "A Constructivist View of Emotion," in vol. 1 of

Theories of Emotion, ed. Robert Plutchik and Henry Kellerman, Emotion: Theory, Research, and Experience (New York: Academic Press, 1980), 305–39. A standard introduction to social psychology is Elliot Aronson, *The Social Animal*, 6th ed. (New York: W. H. Freeman, 1992). See also the wealth of material contained within the fields of sociology, anthropology, political science, economics, and the like.

32. A classic work on indigenous perspectives toward spiritual realities is Mircea Eliade, *Shamanism: Archaic Techniques of Ecstasy*, trans. Willard R. Trask (New York: Bollingen Foundation, 1964).

33. Of course, there are a variety of reasons and motivations for taking interest in spiritual forces, and a variety of factors affect perception of these realities.

34. Royce, *Sources of Religious Insight*, 58.

35. Augustine, *City of God*, trans. Henry Bettenson (London: Penguin, 1972), 10.7, p. 381.

36. In philosophy this is expressed by saying that relationships are fundamentally "semiotic." On semiosis, see, for example, David Savan, *An Introduction to C. S. Peirce's Full System of Semeiotic*, Monograph series of the Toronto Semiotic Circle, no. 1 (Toronto: Toronto Semiotic Circle, 1989); James Jakób Liszka, *A General Introduction to the Semiotic of Charles Sanders Peirce* (Bloomington, IN: Indiana University Press, 1996); T. L. Short, "The Development of Peirce's Theory of Signs," in *The Cambridge Companion to Peirce*, ed. C. J. Misak (New York: Cambridge University Press, 2004), 214–40. In religion and anthropology we see an emphasis on the semiotic nature of community in the research of Clifford Geertz. See Clifford Geertz, *The Interpretation of Cultures: Selected Essays* (New York: Basic, 1973). The heritage of George Herbert Mead and the sociological school of "symbolic interactionism" gives a similar emphasis from the perspective of sociology.

37. Emmanuel Levinas emphasizes this dimension of interpersonal relationship. We are confronted by the other who enters our experience, and this confrontation obligates us to respond. See, for example, Levinas's reflections on facing another human face in Emmanuel Levinas, *Totality and Infinity: An Essay on Exteriority*, trans. Alphonso Lingis (Pittsburgh: Duquesne University Press, 1969), 187–247.

38. One interpreter of Christianity who has made comparison and imitation central to his thought is René Girard. See, for example, René Girard, *The Girard Reader*, ed. James G. Williams (New York: Crossroad, 2002), and Gil Bailie, *Violence Unveiled: Humanity at the Crossroads* (New York: Crossroad, 1995).

39. Steve Duck, *Understanding Relationships* (New York: Guilford, 1991), 13. A similar emphasis on sharing in relationships is found in John Stewart's notion of interpersonal communication as a meeting *between* persons. See John Stewart, "Interpersonal Communication: A Meeting between Persons," in *Understanding Relationships: Selected Readings in Interpersonal Communication*, ed. Benjamin J. Broome (Dubuque, IA: Kendall/Hunt, 1986), 5–21.

40. Martin Buber, *I and Thou*, trans. Walter Kaufmann (New York: Charles Scribner's Sons, 1970), 67. If we want to explore the Trinitarian God as a "corporate experience," we might want to reflect on the mutuality of the sharing between the members of the Godhead.

In patristic theology this aspect of Trinitarian relations is known as *perichoresis*. Catherine Mowry LaCugna writes of *perichoresis*, "Each divine person is irresistibly drawn to the other, taking his/her existence from the other, containing the other in him/herself, while at the same time pouring self out into the other." Catherine Mowry LaCugna, *God for Us: The Trinity and Christian Life* (New York: HarperCollins, 1991), 271. See also Donald L. Gelpi, *The Divine Mother: A Trinitarian Theology of the Holy Spirit* (Lanham, MD: University Press of America, 1984), 42, 132–37.

41. See Royce, *Problem of Christianity*, 229–71, 321–42.

42. On lifestyle enclaves, see Robert N. Bellah et al., *Habits of the Heart: Individualism and Commitment in American Life* (New York: Harper and Row, 1985), 71–75.

43. On common place, see Wendell Berry, *The Art of the Commonplace: The Agrarian Essays of Wendell Berry*, ed. Norman Wirzba (Washington, DC: Shoemaker and Hoard, 2002).

44. Mead, *Mind, Self, and Society*, 255. Mead speaks of the acquisition of the self through a process of role taking, which forms a constant navigation between the "Me" (the organized set of attitudes of others which one assumes) and the "I" (the response of the organism to the attitudes of others). See ibid., 173–78, 253–60. We might also speak here of Heidegger's notion of Being (*Dasein*) as Being-with and of Royce's understanding of the self as being established through position within loyalty to a cause and a community.

45. These issues are developed from a Christian perspective in Miroslav Volf, *Exclusion and Embrace: A Theological Exploration of Identity, Otherness, and Reconciliation* (Nashville: Abingdon, 1996). See also Anselm Min, *The Solidarity of Others in a Divided World* (Edinburgh: T and T Clark, 2004).

46. Robert E. Park, *Society* (New York: Free Press, 1955), 285–86; cited in Lewis A. Coser, *Masters of Sociological Thought: Ideas of Historical and Social Context*, 2nd ed. (New York: Harcourt Brace Jovanovich, 1977), 365.

47. Plato, *The Collected Dialogues of Plato*, ed. Edith Hamilton and Huntington Cairns, Bollingen Series (Princeton: Princeton University Press, 1989), *Republic*, book 4.

48. See Confucius, *The Analects of Confucius*, trans. Arthur Waley (New York: Vintage, 1938); Bellah et al., *Habits of the Heart*.

49. As above, see Muto, "Formative Spirituality"; Liebert, "Supervision as Widening the Horizons"; Willard, *Renovation of the Heart*.

50. See Robert Kastenbaum, ed., *Encyclopedia of Adult Development* (Phoenix: Oryx, 1993). For spiritual development, see James W. Fowler, *Stages of Faith: The Psychology of Human Development and the Quest for Meaning* (San Francisco: Harper and Row, 1981). For a more contemporary assessment of development in terms of postmodern culture, see Friedrich L. Schweitzer, *The Postmodern Life Cycle: Challenges for Church and Theology* (St. Louis: Chalice, 2004).

Chapter 4

1. See for example, Catherine Mowry LaCugna, "The Practical Trinity," in *Exploring Christian Spirituality*, ed. Kenneth Collins

(Grand Rapids: Baker, 2000), 273–82; Catherine Mowry LaCugna, *God for Us: The Trinity and Christian Life* (New York: HarperCollins, 1991); Sallie McFague, *Models of God: Theology for an Ecological, Nuclear Age* (Philadelphia: Fortress, 1988); and Clark Pinnock et al., *The Openness of God: A Biblical Challenge to the Traditional Understanding of God* (Downers Grove, IL: InterVarsity Press, 1994). Another work joining spiritual and theological reflection around the theme of God is Philip Sheldrake, *Spirituality and Theology: Christian Living and the Doctrine of God* (Maryknoll, NY: Orbis, 1998). As mentioned in the last chapter, the Orthodox traditions have more consistently linked theological reflection and spirituality. For Orthodox discussion of God, see, for example, Dumitru Staniloae, *The Experience of God*, trans. Ioan Ionita and Robert Barringer, vol. 1: Revelation and Knowledge of the Triune God (Brookline, MA: Holy Cross Orthodox Press, 1994); and Kallistos Ware, *The Orthodox Way* (Crestwood, NY: St. Vladimir's Seminary Press, 1995). See also the treatments of God in standard texts in Christian spirituality: Bernard McGinn, John Meyendorff, and Jean Leclercq, eds., *Christian Spirituality: Origins to the Twelfth Century*, vol. 16, World Spirituality: An Encyclopedic History of the Religious Quest (New York: Crossroad, 1985), 231–90; Simon Chan, *Spiritual Theology: A Systematic Study of the Christian Life* (Downers Grove, IL: InterVarsity Press, 1998), 40–55; Alister E. McGrath, *Christian Spirituality: An Introduction* (Oxford: Blackwell, 1999), 36–40, 47–54.

2. See, for example, Karen Armstrong, *A History of God* (New York: Ballantine, 1993); McFague, *Models of God*; Marvin Harris, *Cows, Pigs, Wars, and Witches: The Riddles of Culture* (New York: Vintage, 1974); and Fritjof Capra, *The Web of Life: A New Scientific Understanding of Living Systems* (New York: Anchor, 1996). Sample expressions of the concern with regard to exclusivity within the Christian religion—what is sometimes called the "pluralist" concern—can be found in John Hick and Paul F. Knitter, eds., *The Myth of Christian Uniqueness: Toward a Pluralistic Theology of Religions* (Maryknoll, NY: Orbis, 1989).

3. Pseudo-Dionysius, *The Divine Names*, in *Pseudo-Dionysius: The Complete Works*, trans. Colm Luibheid, Classics of Western Spirituality (New York: Paulist Press, 1987), 872a. See also Vladimir Lossky, *The Mystical Theology of the Eastern Church* (Crestwood, NY: St. Vladimir's Press, 1998), 23–43; and Sheldrake, *Spirituality and Theology*.

4. On the ways of speaking of God, see Harry Austryn Wolfson, "St. Thomas on Divine Attributes," in *Studies in Maimonides and St. Thomas Aquinas*, ed. Jacob I. Dienstag (Jersey City, NJ: KTAV Publishing House, 1975), 29–49; Thomas Aquinas, *Summa Theologica*, trans. Fathers of the English Dominican Province (Westminster, MD: Christian Classics, 1981), 1.Q13; Bernard McGinn, "Meister Eckhart on Speaking about God," in *Meister Eckhart: Teacher and Preacher*, ed. Bernard McGinn, Classics of Western Spirituality (New York: Paulist Press, 1986), 15–30; and Thomas C. Oden, *The Living God* (Peabody, MA: Prince, 1998), 35. For a more devotional approach to the ways of speaking of God, see Bonaventure's *The Soul's Journey to God*, in *Bonaventure: The Soul's Journey into God; The Tree of Life; The Life of St. Francis*, trans. Ewert

Cousins, Classics of Western Spirituality (New York: Paulist Press, 1978), 51–116.

5. See Ana-Maria Rizzuto, *Birth of the Living God: A Psychoanalytic Study* (Chicago: University of Chicago Press, 1979); James W. Fowler, *Stages of Faith: The Psychology of Human Development and the Quest for Meaning* (San Francisco: Harper and Row, 1981); Gerald May, *Care of Mind, Care of Spirit: Psychiatric Dimensions of Spiritual Direction* (San Francisco: Harper and Row, 1983), 60–67. Note that one's God-image is not simply an intellectual model, but also a set of affective predispositions associated with matters of ultimate concern.

6. To this extent I share the concerns of Armstrong, *History of God*; and Harris, *Cows, Pigs, Wars*. See also Peter L. Berger, *The Sacred Canopy: Elements of a Sociological Theory of Religion* (New York: Anchor, 1969).

7. On assimilation and accommodation, see the works of developmental psychologist Jean Piaget: for example, Jean Piaget, *The Origins of Intelligence in Children* (New York: Norton, 1952); Jean Piaget, *The Construction of Reality in the Child* (New York: Basic, 1954); Jean Piaget and B. Inhelder, *The Psychology of the Child* (New York: Basic, 1969).

8. As a student of Christian spirituality, I am keenly aware of the motives of pride, security, and advancement in the theological enterprise. I know the temptation of being on the cutting edge, or on the opposite end, of closing my eyes to truth out of blind loyalty to my ecclesial heritage. We cannot pretend that these motives do not affect our research and the pictures of God we form as the result of our research. We feel the pressures of dominance and marginalization even within the theological community. Reflection on God thus becomes something of an act of spiritual self-examination.

9. A. W. Tozer, *The Pursuit of God* (Harrisburg, PA: Christian Publications, 1948), 36–39.

10. For a summary of Old Testament understanding of God, see Walter Brueggemann, *Theology of the Old Testament: Testimony, Dispute, Advocacy* (Minneapolis: Fortress, 1997). For the Christian adoption and revision of Jewish monotheism, see especially N. T. Wright, *The New Testament and the People of God*, vol. 1, Christian Origins and the Question of God (Minneapolis: Fortress, 1992), 248–52, 456–58; and N. T. Wright, *The Climax of the Covenant: Christ and the Law in Pauline Theology* (Minneapolis: Fortress, 1993), 120–36.

11. See also Isaiah 44:6–20; Romans 1:20–23; 1 Timothy 6:16. See also Athanagoras, *Plea* 8, in *The Ante-Nicene Fathers*, vol. 2, ed. Alexander Roberts and James Donaldson, American reprint of the Edinburgh edition, accessed through the Ages Digital Library Collections, version 2.0 (Albany, OR: The Master Christian Library Ages Software, 1997).

12. Catherine of Siena, *The Dialogue*, no. 135, trans. Suzanne Noffke (New York: Paulist Press, 1980), 277.

13. For example, consider the European philosophy of Georg Wilhelm Friedric Hegel, the Asian philosophy of Kitaro Nishida, and the process philosophy of Alfred North Whitehead.

14. The term *panentheism* is sometimes used to account for God's simultaneous distinction from (or God's being more than) creation and intimate omnipresence toward and with creation. See, for example, Charles Hartshorne, "Panthe-

ism, Panentheism," in *Encyclopedia of Religion*, ed. Mircea Eliade (New York: Macmillan, 1987), 165–71; John L. Gresham Jr., *The God We Never Knew: Beyond a Dogmatic Religion to a More Authentic Contemporary Faith* (San Francisco: HarperSanFrancisco, 1997), 32–54; Sallie McFague, *The Body of God: An Ecological Theology* (Minneapolis: Fortress, 1993); Donald L. Gelpi, *The Divine Mother: A Trinitarian Theology of the Holy Spirit* (Lanham, MD: University Press of America, 1984), 95–101.

15. For exegetical considerations on this text, see John I. Durham, *Exodus*, Word Biblical Commentary 3 (Dallas: Word, 1987), contra Armstrong, *History of God*, 21–22.

16. Bernard McGinn, introduction to *Christian Spirituality*, ed. McGinn, Meyendorff, and Leclercq, xxi.

17. LaCugna, *God for Us*, 1. I would modify her statement slightly from "ultimately not" to "not merely."

18. For sample treatments of Christology of the New Testament, see Aloys Grillmeier, *Christ in Christian Tradition*, vol. 1, *From the Apostolic Age to Chalcedon (451)*, trans. John Bowden, 2nd and rev. ed. (Atlanta: John Knox, 1975), 9–32; Donald L. Gelpi, *The Firstborn of Many: A Christology for Converting Christians*, 3 vols. (Milwaukee: Marquette University Press, 2000–2001).

19. For material related to the deity of the Holy Spirit, see Yves Congar, *I Believe in the Holy Spirit*, trans. David Smith (New York: Crossroad, 1997); Gordon Fee, *God's Empowering Presence: The Holy Spirit in the Letters of Paul* (Peabody, MA: Hendrickson, 1994), 827–45; Thomas C. Oden, *Life in the Spirit* (Peabody, MA: Prince, 1998), 15–78; Gelpi, *Divine Mother*.

20. See 1 Corinthians 12:4–6; 2 Corinthians 1:21–22; 2 Thessalonians 2:13–14; Titus 3:4–6; 1 Peter 1:2. Of special note are the Trinitarian blessing found in 2 Corinthians 13:13 and the baptismal command found in Matthew 28:19.

21. These models were not meant as definitive statements of who God as Trinity *is*. Rather they were suggestive paradigms designed to facilitate understanding and to act at protective boundaries governing our thought and life toward God such that Christians do not begin to think or act toward God as God is *not*. See John Meyendorff, *Byzantine Theology: Historical Trends and Doctrinal Themes* (New York: Fordham University Press, 1979), 168–79; and more generally LaCugna, *God for Us*.

22. Thomas Hopko, "The Trinity in the Cappadocians," in *Christian Spirituality: Origins to the Twelfth Century*, ed. Bernard McGinn, John Meyendorff, and Jean Leclercq, vol. 16, World Spirituality: An Encyclopedic History of the Religious Quest (New York: Crossroad, 1985), 266. Another way of understanding the Cappadocian emphasis is that for the Cappadocians, the notion of "person" comes first and reflection on the attributes of energies follows. A social view of the Trinity can also be found in the work of twelfth-century Latin theologian Richard of St. Victor.

23. For more on the models of the Trinity and the spiritualities that develop from them, see Hopko, "Trinity in the Cappadocians"; Mary T. Clark, "The Trinity in Latin Christianity," in *Christian Spirituality: Origins to the Twelfth Century*, ed. Bernard McGinn, John Meyendorff, and Jean Leclercq, vol. 16, World Spirituality: An Encyclopedic History of the Religious Quest

(New York: Crossroad, 1985), 276–90; John L. Gresham Jr., "Three Trinitarian Spiritualities," in *Exploring Christian Spirituality*, ed. Kenneth J. Collins (Grand Rapids: Baker, 2000), 283–95; and Sheldrake, *Spirituality and Theology*.

24. For the strengths and weaknesses of spiritualities of the Father, Son, and Spirit, see Chan, *Spiritual Theology*, 45–50.

25. Ewert H. Cousins, "What Is Christian Spirituality?" in *Modern Christian Spirituality: Methodological and Historical Essays*, ed. Bradley C. Hanson (Atlanta: Scholars Press, 1990), 44.

26. Oden, *Living God*, 88.

27. James B. Torrance, "Contemplating the Trinitarian Mystery of Christ," in *Exploring Christian Spirituality: An Ecumenical Reader*, ed. Kenneth J. Collins (Grand Rapids: Baker, 2000), 301.

28. For further discussion of God's infinity in the early church see Oden, *Living God*, 58–64, and the references contained therein. For current discussion on timelessness and temporality in God, see William Lane Craig, *Time and Eternity: Exploring God's Relationship to Time* (Wheaton: Crossway, 2001); John S. Feinberg, *No One Like Him: The Doctrine of God* (Wheaton: Crossway, 2001); and the essays in Gregory E. Ganssle, ed., *God and Time: Four Views* (Downers Grove, IL: InterVarsity Press, 2001).

29. Jean Daniélou, *God and the Ways of Knowing*, trans. Walter Roberts (San Francisco: Ignatius, 1957), 39.

30. On conceiving God as simultaneously outside and inside time, see, for example, Donald M. MacKay, *The Open Mind and Other Essays* (Downers Grove, IL: InterVarsity Press, 1988), 184–96; John Houghton, *Does God Play Dice?* (Downers Grove, IL: InterVarsity Press, 1988); John Polkinghorne, *Science and Providence* (London: SPCK, 1989); and John Polkinghorne, *The Faith of a Physicist: Reflections of a Bottom-Up Thinker* (Minneapolis: Fortress, 1996), 59–63.

31. The presence of God is a much-used notion not only in the classics of Christian spirituality, but also in the Christian scriptures. The notion of the presence of God is especially common in the book of Psalms. See Psalm 14:5; 16:8, 11; 17:15; 18:12; 21:6; 23:6; 27:4; 34:18; 41:12; 46:4; 61:4; 84:1–4; 113:5–7; 132:1–8; and 139:7–10.

32. Oden, *Living God*, 68–69.

33. See Tozer, *The Pursuit of God*, 35.

34. See Brother Lawrence, *The Practice of the Presence of God* (Springdale, PA: Whitaker House, 1982); Jean-Pierre de Caussade, *The Sacrament of the Present Moment*, trans. Kitty Muggeridge (San Francisco: HarperSanFrancisco, 1981). For watchfulness and attentiveness in Orthodox thought, see the references in the indices throughout the volumes of the *Philokalia*. See *The Philokalia: The Complete Text*, comp. Saint Nikodimos of the Holy Mountain and Saint Makarios of Corinth, trans. G. E. H. Palmer, Philip Sherrard, and Kallistos Ware (London: Faber and Faber, 1979).

35. For more on the God of the Old Testament as fundamentally active, see Brueggemann, *Theology of the Old Testament*, 122–26.

36. For example, the classic statement of the "ontological argument for the existence of God" in Archbishop of Canterbury Anselm's *Monologion* (written in 1078–79) is written as a prayer. Pseudo-Dionysius's "positive theology,"

contained in his *Divine Names*, is essentially an analysis finding God as the cause behind the presence of good, being, wisdom, power, and more. Jonathan Edwards's exploration of the "book of nature," recorded in his *Scientific and Philosophical Writings* and in his *Typological Writings*, constantly vacillates between scientific investigation, application of the ways of causation and analogy, and devotional reflection. See also the progression in Bonaventure's *Soul's Journey into God*.

37. Daniélou, *God and the Ways of Knowing*, 121.

38. Karl Rahner, *Foundations of Christian Faith: An Introduction to the Idea of Christianity*, trans. William V. Dych (New York: Crossroad, 1987), 22.

39. For a collection of Rahner's writings related to spirituality see Karl Rahner, *The Practice of Faith: A Handbook of Contemporary Spirituality*, ed. Karl Lehmann and Albert Raffelt (New York: Crossroad, 1992). For an example of the spirituality that flows from Rahner's approach, see the numerous works of Thomas Green and Harvey D. Egan. A similar approach to relationship with God may be found in the works reflecting the thought of Bernard Lonergan.

40. Karl Barth, *The Doctrine of the Word of God*, ed. G. W. Bromiley and T. F. Torrance, *Church Dogmatics* (Edinburgh: T and T Clark, 1956), I.2, 44.

41. See Karl Barth, *Church Dogmatics*, 14 vols., ed. G. W. Bromiley and T. F. Torrance (Edinburgh: T and T Clark, 1956–75). For a sample of Barth's approach to spirituality, see Karl Barth, *Prayer*, trans. Sara F. Terrien, 50th anniv. ed. (Louisville: Westminster John Knox, 2002). For another approach that bears similarity to that of Karl Barth, see Donald Bloesch, *God the Almighty: Power, Wisdom, Holiness, Love* (Downers Grove, IL: InterVarsity Press, 1995). Bloesch has developed a spirituality along these lines in a number of books, most particularly in Donald Bloesch, *The Crisis of Piety* (1968; reprint, Colorado Springs: Helmers and Howard, 1988); Donald Bloesch, *The Struggle of Prayer* (New York: Harper and Row, 1980); and Donald Bloesch, *Faith and Its Counterfeits* (Downers Grove, IL: InterVarsity Press, 1981). One might also want to look at the recovery of Protestant reformation spirituality found in the works of Alister McGrath, especially those related to Christian spirituality. See Alister McGrath, *Spirituality in an Age of Change: Rediscovering the Spirit of the Reformers* (Grand Rapids: Zondervan, 1994); Alister McGrath, *Beyond the Quiet Time: Practical Evangelical Spirituality* (Grand Rapids: Baker, 1995); and McGrath, *Christian Spirituality*.

42. Donald L. Gelpi, *Grace as Transmuted Experience and Social Process, and Other Essays in North American Theology* (Lanham, NJ: University Press of America, 1988), 91.

43. Donald L. Gelpi, *Charism and Sacrament: A Theology of Christian Conversion* (New York: Paulist Press, 1976), 16; Donald L. Gelpi, *The Turn to Experience in Contemporary Theology* (Mahwah, NJ: Paulist Press, 1994), 134.

44. Aspects of Gelpi's spirituality can be found in Donald L. Gelpi, *Committed Worship: A Sacramental Theology for Converting Christians* (Minneapolis: Liturgical Press, 1993); Donald L. Gelpi, *Functional Asceticism: A Guideline for American Religious* (New York: Sheed and Ward, 1966); Donald L. Gelpi, *Experiencing God: A*

Theology of Human Emergence (Lanham, MD: University Press of America, 1987); and Donald L. Gelpi, *Pentecostalism: A Theological Viewpoint* (New York: Paulist Press, 1971). Another approach to spirituality that gives emphasis to the role of the Spirit can be found in the works of Morton T. Kelsey. The most comprehensive presentation of Kelsey's overall approach is found in Morton T. Kelsey, *Encounter with God: A Theology of Christian Experience* (Minneapolis: Bethany Fellowship, 1972); Morton T. Kelsey, *Discernment: A Study in Ecstasy and Evil* (New York: Paulist Press, 1978); Morton T. Kelsey, *Companions on the Inner Way: The Art of Spiritual Guidance* (New York: Crossroad, 1983). Examples of his application of this model regarding aspects of spirituality can be found in Morton T. Kelsey, *The Other Side of Silence: A Guide to Christian Meditation* (New York: Paulist Press, 1976); Morton T. Kelsey, *Discernment*; and Kelsey, *Companions on the Inner Way*.

45. Daniélou, *God and the Ways of Knowing*, 88.

46. The statement is a summary of many found in Catherine of Siena's dialogue on divine providence. See Catherine of Siena, *Dialogue*, no. 135–53, pp. 277–326.

47. Oden, *Living God*, 121.

48. Though we will use the term *operations* under the heading of the way of analogy, the Eastern view of the operations or energies of God does not see them as merely analogical ways of analyzing God's activity, but should perhaps more correctly be considered as ways in which God is communicated to us. For discussions of essence, energies, and operations in the Eastern Church, see Staniloae, *Experience of God*, 1:125–244; Lossky, *Mystical Theology*, 67–90; and Meyendorff, *Byzantine Theology*, 186–88. Surveys of God's attributes are found in most treatments of the doctrine of God in Western theologies. See, for example, Herman Bavinck, *The Doctrine of God*, trans. William Hendriksen (Grand Rapids: Baker, 1951), 115–254; Feinberg, *No One Like Him*, 233–374. The *Catechism of the Catholic Church* treats the attributes of God in their relationship to the affirmations of the Creed. See also the rethinking of God's attributes reflected in the treatment of God by Langdon Gilkey in his contribution to *Christian Theology: An Introduction to Its Traditions and Tasks*, ed. Peter C. Hodgson and Robert H. King (Minneapolis: Fortress, 1994), 88–113.

49. Jonathan Edwards states that "if we should suppose the faculties of a created spirit to be enlarged infinitely, there would be the Deity, to all intents and purposes." See Jonathan Edwards, "The Mind," in *Scientific and Philosophical Writing*, ed. Wallace E. Anderson, vol. 6, The Works of Jonathan Edwards (New Haven: Yale University Press, 1980), 363n5.

50. See, for example, Origen, *Contra Celsus*, 2.20; Origen, *On Prayer*, 5–6; Augustine, *City of God*, 5.9ff; Aquinas, *Summa Theologica*, 1.Q14. A13. For contemporary discussion, see Gregory A. Boyd, *God of the Possible: A Biblical Introduction to the Open View of God* (Grand Rapids: Baker, 2000); Bruce A. Ware, *God's Lesser Glory: The Diminished God of Open Theism* (Wheaton, IL: Crossway, 2000); and Feinberg, *No One Like Him*, 735–75. For a discussion of these issues with regard to prayer, see Terrance Tiessen, *Providence and Prayer: How Does God Work in the World?* (Downers Grove, IL: InterVarsity Press, 2000).

51. In my personal review of the scriptures, I have found only three significant emotions not mentioned of God: fear, surprise, and hope. If we were to speak simply of the five basic emotions listed in emotions texts (happiness, sadness, anxiety or fear, anger, disgust), the only emotion missing would be anxiety or fear. Yet to be fair to the differing views among those who research emotions, I have enlarged the list. That these three are not expressed of God's experience supports, to my mind, the inclusion of a cognitive element in the emotional system—God's unique way of knowing prescinds the possibility of possessing the cognitive elements necessary for fear, surprise, and hope. For more on basic emotions, see Keith Oatley and P. N. Johnson-Laird, "Toward a Cognitive Theory of Emotions," *Cognition and Emotion* 1, no. 1 (1987): 29–50; Nico H. Frijda, "Comment on Oatley and Johnson-Laird's 'Toward a Cognitive Theory of Emotions,'" *Cognition and Emotion* 1, no. 1 (1987): 51–58; and Andrew Ortony and T. J. Turner, "What's So Basic about Basic Emotions?" *Psychological Review* 97, no. 3 (1990): 315–31. For an excellent presentation of the affectivity of God in the prophetic literature, see Abraham J. Heschel, *The Prophets* (New York: Harper and Row, 1962).

52. Tertullian, *Against Marcion*, 16. See also Lactantius, *A Treatise on the Anger of God*.

53. One cannot read the literature, for example, of Richard Rolle, Bernard of Clairvaux, Catherine of Siena, Johann Arndt, or Jonathan Edwards without recognizing their clear experience of the affectivity of God.

54. See, for example, Gordon R. Lewis and Bruce A. Demarest, *Integrative Theology*, 3 vols. (Grand Rapids: Zondervan, 1987–94), 1:235–37.

55. Origen (*On Prayer*, 6.3–5) and John Cassian (*Conference 13*) present interesting samples of what God's dynamic sovereignty might look like with relationship to human freedom.

56. Saint Peter of Damaskos, in *The Philokalia: The Complete Text*, comp. Saint Nikodimos of the Holy Mountain and Saint Makarios of Corinth, trans. G. E. H. Palmer, Philip Sherrard, and Kallistos Ware (London: Faber and Faber, 1984), 3:255. The notes immediately following are also taken from this edition, which is the standard English translation. I will indicate author, volume in collection, and page number.

57. Saint Theognostos in *Philokalia*, 2:371; see also Saint Makarios of Egypt in *Philokalia*, 3:314–15.

58. Saint Isaiah the Solitary in *Philokalia*, 1:22ff.

59. Nikitas Stithatos in *Philokalia*, 4:114, 118.

60. Nikitas Stithatos in *Philokalia*, 4:111, 113.

61. Saint Maximos the Confessor in *Philokalia*, 2:166.

62. Saint John Cassian in *Philokalia*, 1:96–97; Saint Theodoros the Great Ascetic in *Philokalia*, 2:38.

63. McFague, *Models of God*, xi.

64. See, for example, Borg, *The God We Never Knew*, 57–107; John Shelby Spong, *Why Christianity Must Change or Die: A Bishop Speaks to Believers in Exile* (San Francisco: HarperSanFrancisco, 1998), 56–70.

65. See chapter 10 for more about spiritual direction.

66. On this, see Sheldrake, *Spirituality and Theology*, 118–21. Julian of Norwich also spoke of Jesus as "Mother."

67. See, for example, the nuanced discussion of women's responses to the imagery of Ignatius of Loyola's *Spiritual Exercises* in Katherine Dyckman, Mary Garvin, and Elizabeth Liebert, *The Spiritual Exercises Reclaimed: Uncovering Liberating Possibilities for Women* (New York: Paulist Press, 2001).

68. Maximos the Confessor in *Philokalia*, 2:185.

69. Nikitas Stithatos in *Philokalia*, 4:139–40; see also Saint Gregory Palamas in *Philokalia*, 4:358–63.

70. Maximos the Confessor in *Philokalia*, 2:123.

71. Maximos the Confessor, "Second Century on Theology," no. 39, in *The Philokalia: The Complete Text*, comp. Saint Nikodimos of the Holy Mountain and Saint Makarios of Corinth, trans. G. E. H. Palmer, Philip Sherrard, and Kallistos Ware (London: Faber and Faber, 1981), 2:147. Progression from the positive to the negative approach is sometimes considered a function of spiritual maturity.

72. Harvey D. Egan, "Affirmative Way," in *The New Dictionary of Catholic Spirituality*, ed. Michael Downey (Collegeville, MN: Liturgical Press, 1993), 15.

73. On *Deus absconditus* and *Deus revelatus*, see Bloesch, *God the Almighty*, 49, 59–65. Walter Brueggemann addresses the complexities of God's self-communication in the Old Testament by means of the image of a courtroom with testimony and countertestimony. See Brueggemann, *Theology of the Old Testament*.

74. Philip Yancey, *Reaching for the Invisible God* (Grand Rapids: Zondervan, 2000), 112.

75. See ibid., 113–22.

76. Wendell Berry, *Jayber Crow: A Novel* (Washington, DC: Counterpoint, 2000), 52.

77. Daniélou, *God and the Ways of Knowing*, 55.

78. Gregory of Nyssa, *Gregory of Nyssa: The Life of Moses*, trans. Abraham J. Malherbe and Everett Ferguson, Classics of Western Spirituality (New York: Paulist Press, 1978), 2.163.

79. Pseudo-Dionysius, *The Mystical Theology*, in *Pseudo-Dionysius: The Complete Works*, trans. Colm Luibheid, Classics of Western Spirituality (New York: Paulist Press, 1987), 3.1033B.

80. Ibid., 5.1048B. See also John of Damascus's *On the Orthodox Faith* (ed. Philip Schaff [Albany, OR: Ages Software, 2000]), for another example of an apophatic approach to God.

81. Daniélou, *God and the Ways of Knowing*, 210.

82. See Mark McIntosh, *Mystical Theology: The Integrity of Spirituality and Theology* (Malden, MA: Blackwell, 1998), 123–26. For Augustine's comments on the utter fullness of divinity, see Mary T. Clark, introductory note to *Augustine of Hippo: Selected Writings*, trans. Mary T. Clark, Classics of Western Spirituality (New York: Paulist Press, 1984), 363.

83. John Meyendorff, introduction to *Gregory Palamas: The Triads*, Classics of Western Spirituality (Mahwah, NJ: Paulist Press, 1983), 14.

84. Samples of theological meditation can be found in Bonaventure's *Soul's Journey to God* and in the great Puritan classic of Lewis Bayly, *The Practice of Piety: Directing a Christian How to Walk, That He May Please God* (London:

Danel Midwinter, 1714). A modern version of this practice can be found in McGrath, *Beyond the Quiet Time*. See also Evan B. Howard, *Praying the Scriptures: A Field Guide for Your Spiritual Journey* (Downers Grove, IL: InterVarsity Press, 1999), 48–51.

Chapter 5

1. This point—the impossibility of grasping the human without comprehending the divine-human relationship, and the divine itself as initiator of relationship—is what fueled Karl Barth's critique of "religion" and the liberal theology of his time, and we should be warned today against any theology of human experience or spirituality that does not take seriously the priority of God's self-revelation. For a brief summary of this aspect of Barth's thought, see Robert W. Jenson, "Karl Barth," in *The Modern Theologians*, ed. David F. Ford, 2 vols. (Oxford: Blackwell, 1989), 1:23–49.

2. See Adolphe Tanquerey, *The Spiritual Life: A Treatise on Ascetical and Mystical Theology*, trans. Herman Branderis, 2nd and rev. ed. (Tournai, Belgium: Desclée, 1930), 28–45.

3. See Walter Brueggemann, *Theology of the Old Testament: Testimony, Dispute, Advocacy* (Minneapolis: Fortress, 1997), 552–64. He also uses terms like a forming or choosing in the context of God's generosity; an experience of scattering or becoming subject to exile, chaos and death; and a restoration to hope, rule, blessing and love.

4. See, for example, Vladimir Lossky, *The Mystical Theology of the Eastern Church* (Crestwood, NY: St. Vladimir's Press, 1998), 114–73; Dumitru Staniloae, *The World: Creation and Deification*, trans. Ioan Ionita and Robert Barringer, vol. 2, The Experience of God: Orthodox Dogmatic Theology (Brookline, MA: Holy Cross Orthodox Press, 2000), 65–103; Johann Arndt, *True Christianity*, trans. Peter Erb, Classics of Western Spirituality (New York: Paulist Press, 1979); and Bernard McGinn, "Human Persons as Image of God: Western Christianity," in *Christian Spirituality: Origins to the Twelfth Century*, ed. Bernard McGinn, John Meyendorff, and Jean Leclercq, vol. 16, World Spirituality: An Encyclopedic History of the Religious Quest (New York: Crossroad, 1985), 328.

5. George Herbert, "Easter Wings," in *George Herbert: The Country Parson, the Temple*, ed. John N. Wall Jr., Classics of Western Spirituality (New York: Paulist Press, 1981), 157. To "imp," in falconry, is to engraft feathers in a damaged wing, so as to improve or restore damaged powers of flight.

6. The Apostles' Creed confesses that the Father Almighty is "Creator of heaven and earth." The Nicene Creed affirms that God is creator of "all that is seen and unseen." The Westminster Confession states that "after God had made all other creatures, he created man, male and female" (4.2). The Presbyterian Confession of 1967 affirms that "God has created man in a personal relation with himself that man may respond to the love of the Creator" (1.B). The *Catechism of the Catholic Church* (1994) speaks of "man, himself created in the 'image of God' and called to a personal relationship with God" (299). For a quick survey of contemporary positions regarding faith and origins, see J. P. Moreland and John

Mark Reynolds, eds., *Three Views on Creation and Evolution* (Grand Rapids: Zondervan, 1999). It is worth noting that Howard J. Van Till, contributor of the "theistic evolution" portion of *Three Views on Creation and Evolution*, is emphatic about calling his position *not* "theistic evolution" (in spite of the editors' choice), but "fully gifted creation." Van Till clearly desires the affirmation of God's hand in creation to be at the center of his position.

7. John Meyendorff, *Byzantine Theology: Historical Trends and Doctrinal Themes* (New York: Fordham University Press, 1979), 129, 131.

8. Karl Rahner, *Foundations of Christian Faith: An Introduction to the Idea of Christianity*, trans. William V. Dych (New York: Crossroad, 1987), 42, 43.

9. The phrase "getting along with nature" comes from Wendell Berry, "Getting Along with Nature," in *Home Economics* (New York: North Point Press, 1987), 6–20.

10. Excerpted from "The Loves of Taliesin," in *Celtic Spirituality*, trans. Oliver Davies (New York: Paulist Press, 1999), 283–85.

11. Peter Lombard, *Sentences*, 2.16.3. See *The Books of Opinions of Peter Lombard*, private typescript, trans. Robert E. O'Brien (1970), 401, held in the library of the Graduate Theological Union.

12. These options (and still others) are reviewed in Gordon R. Lewis and Bruce A. Demarest, *Integrative Theology*, 3 vols. (Grand Rapids: Zondervan, 1987–94), 2:124–34; Gordon Wenham, *Genesis 1–15*, Word Biblical Commentary (Dallas: Word, 1987), esp. commentary on Genesis 1:27; and Stanley J. Grenz, *The Social God and the Relational Self: A Trinitarian Theology of the Imago Dei* (Louisville: Westminster John Knox, 2001), 141–82, 192–203.

13. Grenz, *Social God and the Relational Self*, 202.

14. Walter Hilton, *Toward a Perfect Love: The Spiritual Counsel of Walter Hilton*, trans. and intro. David L. Jeffrey (Portland: Multnomah, 1985), 64–65. Later (pp. 65–66, 99–103) he goes on to explain how the faculties of this "created trinity" are muddied by sin and restored by Christ. See also the edition of Walter Hilton's *Scale of Perfection* in the Classics of Western Spirituality series (Mahwah, NJ: Paulist Press, 1991).

15. Brueggemann, *Theology of the Old Testament*, 451.

16. Ibid., 459. His development of the disciplines and implications flowing from such a view of humankind (pp. 460–91) are well worth prayerful meditation.

17. Grenz, *Social God and the Relational Self*, 202.

18. For a succinct summary of this evidence, see, N. T. Wright, *The Climax of the Covenant: Christ and the Law in Pauline Theology* (Minneapolis: Fortress, 1993), 24. See also N. T. Wright, *The New Testament and the People of God*, vol. 1, Christian Origins and the Question of God (Minneapolis: Fortress, 1992), 262–68.

19. Grenz, *Social God and the Relational Self*, 210.

20. Wright, *Climax of the Covenant*, 40.

21. Our share in Christ's eschatological rule is indicated in such passages as Daniel 7; Matthew 19:28 par. Luke 22:28–30; 1 Corinthians 6:3; Romans 5:17; 2 Timothy 2:11–12; Revelation 2:26; 3:21; 5:9–10; 20:4; 22:1–5.

22. Ralph P. Martin, *2 Corinthians*, vol. 40, The Word Biblical Commentary, ed. David A. Hubbard, Glen W. Barker, and Ralph P. Martin (Waco: Word, 1986), 72. The notion of humanity as a "microcosm" and "mediator" of the universe—created with both earthly and heavenly dimensions and called to effect a harmonious union of these spheres—common to the Orthodox Church, unites in a similar manner both the "creational" and the "eschatological" dimensions of the concept of the *imago dei*. See Lars Thunberg, "The Human Person as Image of God: Eastern Christianity," in *Christian Spirituality: Origins to the Twelfth Century*, ed. Bernard McGinn, John Meyendorff, and Jean Leclercq, vol. 16, World Spirituality: An Encyclopedic History of the Religious Quest (New York: Crossroad, 1985), 291–312; Kallistos Ware, *The Orthodox Way* (Crestwood, NY: St. Vladimir's Seminary Press, 1995), 49–50.

23. Lossky, *Mystical Theology*, 114.

24. Brueggemann, *Theology of the Old Testament*, 461.

25. Ibid., 461. See also ibid., 466, for his comments on wisdom.

26. Steven Harper, "Old Testament Spirituality," in *Exploring Christian Spirituality: An Ecumenical Reader*, ed. Kenneth J. Collins (Grand Rapids: Baker, 2000), 317.

27. Thus medieval writer Johannes Tauler speaks of a "Grund" of our soul wherein God is specially present, while contemporary theologian Paul Tillich speaks of God as the "ground of being." Early Quakers speak of the "inner word" present in every human person, while contemporary theologian Karl Rahner speaks of humans as "hearers of the word," a word that is given fundamentally in the very structure of the human spirit. Others speak of a "spark" or an "inner light" within the human person.

28. McGinn, "Human Persons as Image of God," 323.

29. Robert R. Williams, "Sin and Evil," in *Christian Theology: An Introduction to Its Traditions and Tasks*, ed. Peter C. Hodgson and Robert H. King (Minneapolis: Fortress, 1994), 196.

30. Hildegard of Bingen, *Hildegard of Bingen: Scivias*, trans. Mother Columba Hart and Jane Bishop, Classics of Western Spirituality (New York: Paulist Press, 1990), 149–50, 153.

31. Robin C. Cover, "Sin, Sinners (OT)," in *The Anchor Bible Dictionary*, ed. David Noel Freedman, 6 vols. (New York: Doubleday, 1992), 6:31.

32. Thunberg, "Human Person as Image of God," 307.

33. Wenham speaks of Adam and Eve being presented "as both paradigmatic and protohistorical." See his explanation of Genesis 2:4–3:24 in Wenham, *Genesis 1–15*.

34. Gil Bailie, *Violence Unveiled: Humanity at the Crossroads* (New York: Crossroad, 1995), 137.

35. Henri Blocher, *Original Sin: Illuminating the Riddle*, New Studies in Biblical Theology (Grand Rapids: Eerdmans, 1997), 20.

36. John Wesley, *Original Sin*, in vol. 9, The Works of John Wesley (Peabody, MA: Hendrickson Publishers, 1984), 238.

37. For comment on the emphasis on the primacy of death for the tragedy of human experience in 1 Corinthians 15:22, see Meyendorff, *Byzantine Theology*, 144.

38. Blocher identifies four points as characteristic of the doctrine of original sin: "First,

original sin is *universal sinfulness*,... Secondly, it belongs to the *nature* of human beings.... Thirdly, ... it is *inherited*; ... Fourthly, it *stems from Adam*." Blocher, *Original Sin*, 18 (italics in original).

39. Ware, *Orthodox Way*, 59.

40. Staniloae, *The World*, 170.

41. The distinction between natural and disordered drives and affections—their roots in creation, their deformation through the fall, and their restoration through Christ—is developed nicely in Etienne Gilson's treatment of *necessitas* and *cupidas* in the thought of Bernard of Clairvaux. See Etienne Gilson, *The Mystical Theology of Saint Bernard*, trans. A. H. C. Downes (Kalamazoo: Cistercian Publishers, 1990), 42–45.

42. Gregory of Sinai, "On Commandments and Doctrines, Warnings and Promises; on Thoughts, Passions and Virtues, and also on Stillness and Prayer: One Hundred and Thirty-Seven Texts," no. 2, in *The Philokalia: The Complete Text*, comp. Saint Nikodimos of the Holy Mountain and Saint Makarios of Corinth, trans. G. E. H. Palmer, Philip Sherrard, and Kallistos Ware (London: Faber and Faber, 1979), 4.213.

43. See, for example, Michel Foucault, *Power and Knowledge: Selected Interviews and Other Writings 1972–1977*, ed. Colin Gordon (New York: Pantheon Books, 1980), and Miroslav Volf's response to Foucault concerning the relationship of power and knowledge in Miroslav Volf, *Exclusion and Embrace: A Theological Exploration of Identity, Otherness, and Reconciliation* (Nashville: Abingdon, 1996), 233–73.

44. On this see, for example, William McNamara, *Mystical Passion* (New York: Paulist Press, 1977).

45. Elmer A. Martens, *God's Design: A Focus on Old Testament Theology* (Grand Rapids: Baker, 1981), 30.

46. On this see, for example, Valerie Saiving Goldstein, "The Human Situation: A Feminine View," *Journal of Religion* 40 (1960): 100–12; Susan Nelson Dunfee, "The Sin of Hiding: A Feminist Critique of Reinhold Niebuhr's Account of the Sin of Pride," *Soundings* 65 (1982): 316–27; Carol Lakey Hess, *Caretakers of Our Common House: Women's Development in Communities of Faith* (Nashville: Abingdon, 1997), 31–54.

47. Because human sinfulness is grasped most clearly in meditation, the discipline of self-examen has been central to Christians of all traditions: Orthodox monks, Ignatian exercitants, Puritan divines, and so on.

48. Bernard Lonergan, *Insight: A Study of Human Understanding* (New York: Harper and Row, 1958), 223.

49. See René Girard, *The Girard Reader*, ed. James G. Williams (New York: Crossroad, 2002). See also Bailie, *Violence Unveiled*, and the material from Girard reviewed there. For a sample of a more strictly sociological analysis of the institutionalization of the darker side of human experience, see Peter L. Berger and Thomas Luckmann, *The Social Construction of Reality: A Treatise in the Sociology of Knowledge* (Garden City, NY: Doubleday Anchor, 1966).

50. Charles Dickens, *A Christmas Carol* (New York: Weathervane Books, 1977), 33.

51. John Painter, "World," in *Dictionary of Jesus and the Gospels*, ed. Joel Green and Scott McKnight (Downers Grove, IL: InterVarsity Press, 1992), 883.

52. See, for example, the analysis of structural evil in Ron Sider, *Rich Christians in an Age of Hunger: Moving from Affluence to Generosity*, 20th anniv. ed. (Nashville: Word Publishing, 1997), 109–24.

53. See Reinhold Niebuhr, *Moral Man and Immoral Society: A Study in Ethics and Politics* (New York: Charles Scribner's Sons, 1960); and M. Scott Peck, *People of the Lie: The Hope for Healing Human Evil* (New York: Simon and Schuster, 1983), 212–53.

54. Boniface Ramsey, "Martyrdom," in *The New Dictionary of Catholic Spirituality*, ed. Michael Downey (Collegeville, MN: Liturgical Press, 1993), 634. See also John McGuckin, "The Early Church Fathers," in *The Story of Christian Spirituality: Two Thousand Years from East to West*, ed. Gordon Mursell (Philadelphia: Fortress, 2001), 50–54.

55. Benedicta Ward, trans., *The Sayings of the Desert Fathers: The Alphabetical Collection* (Kalamazoo, MI: Cistercian Publishers, 1975), 5.

56. See Meyendorff, *Byzantine Theology*, 136; Staniloae, *The World*, 116–32; Lewis and Demarest, *Integrative Theology*, 2:102–3; Thomas C. Oden, *The Living God* (Peabody, MA: Prince, 1998), 240–41. See also the systematic treatments of John Calvin, Lewis Berkhof, and H. Orton Wiley. Ware's summary of Orthodox theology places discussion of demonology at the very start of his treatment of evil and sin. See Ware, *Orthodox Way*, 57–58.

57. On the notion of "warfare mentality," see Gregory A. Boyd, *God at War: The Bible and Spiritual Conflict* (Downers Grove, IL: InterVarsity Press, 1997).

58. Satan, angels, demons, and such may also be included in discussions of theories of the atonement. See, for example, Williams, "Sin and Evil"; and Donald G. Bloesch, *God, Authority, and Salvation*, Essentials of Evangelical Theology (Peabody, MA: Prince, 1998), 108–9. Karl Barth, in his *Church Dogmatics*, treats angels and demons at the very close of his treatment of the doctrine of creation (after the creation of humanity) and immediately prior to his treatment of fall and reconciliation. See Barth, *Church Dogmatics*, trans. G. W. Bromiley, R. J. Ehrlich, ed. G. W. Bromiley, T. F. Torrence (Edinburgh: T and T Clark, 1960), 3.3.51. Barth's "brief look" at the demonic (3.3.522) is, perhaps, an intentional rejection of the kind of warfare mentality Boyd advocates.

59. For more information from various perspectives, see, for example, Boyd, *God at War*; Gregory A. Boyd, *Satan and the Problem of Evil: Constructing a Trinitarian Warfare Theodicy* (Downers Grove, IL: InterVarsity Press, 2001); Walter Wink, *Naming the Powers: The Language of Power in the New Testament* (Philadelphia: Fortress, 1984); Walter Wink, *Engaging the Powers: Discernment and Resistance in a World of Domination* (Philadelphia: Fortress, 1992); Walter Wink, *Unmasking the Powers: The Invisible Forces that Determine Human Existence* (Philadelphia: Fortress, 1986); Edward F. Murphey, *The Handbook for Spiritual Warfare* (Nashville: Thomas Nelson, 1992); Staniloae, *The World*, 147–62; Tremper Longman and Daniel Reid, *God Is a Warrior*, Studies in Old Testament Biblical Theology (Grand Rapids: Zondervan, 1995).

60. Matthew Fox, *Original Blessing: A Primer in Creation Spirituality Presented in Four Paths, Twenty-Six Themes, and Two Questions* (Santa Fe, NM: Bear, 1983), 9.

61. Other themed sections in ibid. include "Humility as Earthiness," "Panentheism," "Cosmic, Universalist," "Emptying," "Being Emptied," "Art as Meditation," "Dialectical, Trinitarian," "God as Mother," "The New Creation," "Compassion," and "Sin and Salvation."

62. For example, the thematic section of the first volume of Crossroad's Christian Spirituality series offers chapters on Christ as savior and on the human person as the image of God, but it does not have a separate chapter on sin or evil. See Bernard McGinn, John Meyendorff, and Jean Leclercq, eds., *Christian Spirituality: Origins to the Twelfth Century*, vol. 16, World Spirituality: An Encyclopedic History of the Religious Quest (New York: Crossroad, 1985), 231–59, 291–330. Richard Lovelace's *Dynamics of Spiritual Life* and Simon Chan's *Spiritual Theology*, however, make only the briefest comments about humans in God's image but have extended discussions about sin and redemption. See Richard Lovelace, *Dynamics of Spiritual Life: An Evangelical Theology of Renewal* (Downers Grove, IL: InterVarsity Press, 1979), 81–144, and Simon Chan, *Spiritual Theology: A Systematic Study of the Christian Life* (Downers Grove, IL: InterVarsity Press, 1998), 56–101.

63. On the view that God's division of the human race into male-female anticipates the fall, or that human sexuality and sexual reproduction is somehow tainted from creation, see Grenz, *Social God and the Relational Self*, 267–303.

64. Lewis Bayly, *The Practice of Piety: Directing a Christian How to Walk that He May Please God* (London: Daniel Midwinter, 1714), 2 (italics added).

65. Fox sets these against one another in the appendices of *Original Blessing*.

66. Boyd, *God at War*, 166. See also Longman and Reid, *God Is a Warrior*.

67. See, for example, Torleif Elgvin, "Belial, Beliar, Devil, Satan," in *Dictionary of New Testament Background*, ed. Craig Evans and Stanley Porter (Downers Grove, IL: InterVarsity Press, 2000).

68. Athanasius, *Athanasius: The Life of Antony and the Letter to Marcellinus*, trans. Robert C. Gregg, Classics of Western Spirituality (New York: Paulist Press, 1980), 78.

69. On the theme of cosmic conflict in the New Testament, see N. T. Wright, *Jesus and the Victory of God*, vol. 2, Christian Origins and the Question of God (Philadelphia: Fortress, 1996), 451–63; Boyd, *God at War*, 171–293; Longman and Reid, *God Is a Warrior*, 91–192.

70. Irenaeus, *Against Heresies*, 2.32.4.

71. See the examples in Davies, *Celtic Spirituality*.

72. Thomas Aquinas, *Summa Theologica*, 1.Q64.A4.

73. For reflections on Ignatius's belief in the demonic and the relevance of Ignatius's rules in a contemporary setting, see Jules J. Toner, *A Commentary on Saint Ignatius' Rules for the Discernment of Spirits* (St. Louis: Institute of Jesuit Sources, 1982), 260–70.

74. John Calvin, *Institutes*, 1.14.19.

75. See William Gurnall, *The Christian in Complete Armour* (Edinburgh: Banner of Truth, 1986), and Lorenzo Scupoli, *Unseen Warfare: The Spiritual Combat and Path to Paradise of Lorenzo Scupoli, Edited by Nicodemus of the Holy Mountain and Revised by Theophan the Recluse*, trans. E. Kadloubovsky and G. E. H. Palmer (Crestwood, NY: St. Vladimir's Seminary Press, 1987).

76. See Kenneth Leech, *Soul Friend: The Practice of Christian Spirituality* (San Francisco: Harper and Row, 1977), 127–34; Gerald May, *Care of Mind, Care of Spirit: Psychiatric Dimensions of Spiritual Direction* (San Francisco: Harper and Row, 1983), 21; Lovelace, *Dynamics of Spiritual Life*, 133–44.

77. See, for example, Murphey, *Handbook for Spiritual Warfare*, and Thomas B. White, *The Believer's Guide to Spiritual Warfare* (Ann Arbor, MI: Servant, 1990). For a more academic approach from the same community, see the collection of essays in C. Peter Wagner and F. Douglas Pennoyer, eds., *Wrestling with Dark Angels: Toward a Deeper Understanding of the Supernatural Forces in Spiritual Warfare* (Ventura, CA: Regal Books, 1990).

78. See Ari Kiev, ed., *Magic, Faith, and Healing: Studies in Primitive Psychiatry Today* (New York: Free Press, 1964); Peck, *People of the Lie*; Kurt Koch, *Christian Counseling and Occultism* (Grand Rapids: Kregal, 1972); Morton T. Kelsey, *Encounter with God: A Theology of Christian Experience* (Minneapolis: Bethany Fellowship, 1972); and Morton T. Kelsey, *Discernment: A Study in Ecstasy and Evil* (New York: Paulist Press, 1978).

79. For another example of reconceptualizing the demonic, see Wink, *Naming the Powers*.

80. This is the point of Boyd's critique of Wink in Boyd, *God at War*, 273–76.

81. The debates on issues such as whether demons can "possess" Christians and whether they can dwell "within" believers illustrate the degree of influence of the demonic. On this, see C. Fred Dickason, *Demon Possession and the Christian* (Chicago: Moody, 1987). With regards to a different issue, Boyd argues in *God at War* and in *Satan and the Problem of Evil* that demonic forces have a great deal of freedom, not only in terms of human experience, but also in terms of their effect on God's experience. Others, such as Don Carson, disagree with Boyd, emphasizing the context of demonic freedom within the sovereignty of God. See Don A. Carson, "God, the Bible and Spiritual Warfare: A Review Article," *Journal of the Evangelical Theological Society* 42, no. 2 (June 1999): 251–70.

82. See, for example, Mark 1:39; 3:10–12; 9:14–29; Matthew 12:22 par. Luke 11:14; Luke 13:32; along with Peter H. Davids, "Sickness and Suffering in the New Testament," in *Wrestling with Dark Angels: Toward a Deeper Understanding of the Supernatural Forces in Spiritual Warfare*, ed. C. Peter Wagner and F. Douglas Pennoyer (Ventura, CA: Regal Books, 1990), 215–47. For another example of embodiment and spiritual forces, see 1 Corinthians 5:5.

83. See also 2 Corinthians 10:5; 11:14; and 1 Timothy 4:1. For an exploration of the corporate expression of lies—the perpetuation of false, self-serving beliefs linking systems of power, information, and public opinion—see Walter Wink, *Engaging the Powers*, on propaganda.

84. See also 1 Chronicles 21:1; 1 Timothy 5:14–15; 6:9–10.

85. Walter Wink, "The Powers Behind the Throne," *Sojourners*, September 1984, 24. On territorial spirits, see Walter Wink, *Unmasking the Powers*; C. Peter Wagner, "Territorial Spirits," in *Wrestling with Dark Angels: Toward a Deeper Understanding of the Supernatural Forces in Spiritual Warfare*, ed. C. Peter Wagner and F. Douglas Pennoyer (Ventura, CA: Regal Books,

1990), 73–92, and the response following. See also the discussion of national spiritualities in Alexander Solzhenitsyn, *From Under the Rubble*, trans. Michael Scammel (New York: Bantam, 1976).

86. Staniloae, *The World*, 149.

87. Depending on how one takes the chronological relationship between creation, the "fall" of Satan, and the "fall" of humans, one might also posit the possibility of additional aspects of the tragedy of human experience, namely, aspects of nature that are not directly caused by human or demonic rebellion. The cycle of seasons, the existence of bacteria and parasites, the cycle of decay and growth, the presence of carnivores, the cooling of the earth (which necessitates earthquakes and volcanoes), clouds and weather conditions (which cause lightning), and so on. Are we to understand all of these as consequences of a "fall" (either human or angelic), or are they the natural dynamics of a universe created to support human life and into which a host of other "unnatural" tragedies are to be added?

88. See, for example, the notion of counterfactuals in Eleanor Rosch, "The Environment of Minds: Toward a Noetic and Hedonic Ecology," in *Cognitive Ecology*, ed. Morton P. Friedman and Edward C. Carterette (San Diego: Academic Press, 1996), 17.

89. On satisfaction, see Alfred North Whitehead, *Process and Reality: An Essay in Cosmology* (New York: Free Press, 1929), and Donald L. Gelpi, *Experiencing God: A Theology of Human Emergence* (Lanham, MD: University Press of America, 1987).

90. Augustine, *Confessions* I.i (1).

91. Blaise Pascal, *Pascal's Pensees*, trans. H. F. Stewart (New York: Modern Library, 1947), no. 250, 143.

92. Brueggemann, *Theology of the Old Testament*, 561. He articulates four aspects of this hope in pp. 479–85.

93. Wright, *Jesus and the Victory of God*, 96. For Wright's account of the hope of second-temple Judaism, see his *New Testament and the People of God*, 280–338.

94. Thomas Oden writes of the inclusion of this phrase in the Apostle's Creed that "Christian teaching differs radically from pagan deliverance myths in that its salvation event is the only one with a historical date." Thomas C. Oden, *The Word of Life* (Peabody, MA: Prince, 1998), 327.

95. On this, see, for example, the discussions in Marcus J. Borg, *Jesus: A New Vision*; *Spirit, Culture, and the Life of Discipleship* (San Francisco: HarperSanFrancisco, 1987); Wright, *Jesus and the Victory of God*; and Donald L. Gelpi, *To Hope in Jesus Christ*, vol. 1, The Firstborn of Many: A Christology for Converting Christians (Milwaukee: Marquette University Press, 2000), 115–332. Gelpi's "multidisciplinary portrait" of Jesus is complemented in his subsequent volume by three separate "narrative Christologies" outlining the portrait of Jesus presented in each of the Synoptics, viewed as coherent narratives. See Donald L. Gelpi, *Synoptic Narrative Christology*, vol. 2, The Firstborn of Many: A Christology for Converting Christians (Milwaukee: Marquette University Press, 2000).

96. Consider, for example the many portraits of Jesus presented in the Jesus literature today. Jesus is presented as a prophet, a sage, a shaman, a revitalization-movement founder and

more. Yet Jesus seems to transcend each of our pigeonholes, encompassing all that we can say of him and more. See the portraits presented in Borg, *Jesus: A New Vision*; Philip Yancey, *The Jesus I Never Knew* (Grand Rapids: Zondervan, 1995); Luke Timothy Johnson, *The Real Jesus: The Misguided Quest for the Historical Jesus and the Truth of the Traditional Gospels* (San Francisco: HarperSanFrancisco, 1995); and Wright, *Jesus and the Victory of God*. For a review of the work of Jesus in the context of Jewish apocalyptic, see especially Wright, *Jesus and the Victory of God*, 576–611.

97. Anthony de Mello, *Sadhana: A Way to God; Christian Exercises in Eastern Form* (Garden City, NY: Image Doubleday, 1984), 80–82.

98. This theme is developed in George T. Montague, *The Holy Spirit: Growth of a Biblical Tradition* (New York: Paulist Press, 1976), 286–87.

99. Walter Lowe, "Christ and Salvation," in *Christian Theology: An Introduction to Its Traditions and Tasks*, ed. Peter C. Hodgson and Robert H. King (Minneapolis: Fortress, 1994), 224–25.

100. Joseph A. Fitzmyer, *According to Paul: Studies in the Theology of the Apostle* (New York: Paulist Press, 1993), 11–16.

101. Generally these matters are discussed in theology under the heading of the doctrine of "salvation." Yet while the doctrine of salvation generally treats all aspects of God's saving work (election, grace, regeneration, and so on), here we will focus on the ways in which human experience is affected by the work of Christ. And while most treatments of the Christ-event's effect on human experience emphasize the meaning of the *death* of Christ, we will explore ways in which the whole of the Christ-event (birth, life, teachings, death, resurrection, ascension, sending of the Spirit) affects human experience.

102. Irenaeus, *Against Heresies*, 5.21.1.

103. For these categories, see Eugene TeSelle, *Augustine the Theologian* (London: Burns and Oates, 1970), 165ff.

104. See Maximos the Confessor, *Ambigua*, no. 41 (1305B), in *Maximos the Confessor*, trans. Andrew Louth, The Early Church Fathers (London: Routledge, 1996), 157.

105. Bruce Demarest, *The Cross and Salvation: The Doctrine of Salvation*, Foundations of Evangelical Theology (Wheaton: Crossway, 1997), 153.

106. Angela of Foligno, *Angela of Foligno: Complete Works*, trans. Paul Lachance, Classics of Western Spirituality (New York: Paulist Press, 1993), 288. A similar spirit can be found in the sermons of Johannes Tauler and in the classic *Imitation of Christ* by Gerhard Groote. A contempary example of the appeal to Christ's death as an example for our life can be found in Volf, *Exclusion and Embrace*.

107. Lossky, *Mystical Theology*, 215. John Meyendorff writes, "Communion in the risen body of Christ; participation in divine life; sanctification through the energy of God, which penetrates true humanity and restores it to its 'natural' state; . . . these are at the center of Byzantine understanding of the Christian Gospel." Meyendorff, *Byzantine Theology*, 146. See also Nicholas Cabasilas, *The Life in Christ* (Crestwood, NY: St. Vladimir's Press, 1997).

108. See Oden, *Word of Life*, 411.

109. Athanasius, *Life of Antony*, no. 30, 54.

110. Contemporary examples of this kind of spirituality can be seen in efforts toward the liberation of the poor or disenfranchised, in recovery ministries of various shapes and sizes, and in various expressions of "spiritual warfare" in Protestant Evangelicalism.

111. On this, see the discussion of the Greek preposition *hyper* in Demarest, *Cross and Salvation*, 133–34, and in Murray J. Harris, "Prepositions and Theology in the Greek New Testament," in *New International Dictionary of New Testament Theology*, ed. Colin Brown, 3 vols. (Grand Rapids: Zondervan, 1979), 3:1196–98.

112. Martin Luther, *A Commentary on St. Paul's Epistle to the Galatians* (Cambridge: James Clarke, 1953), 179–80.

113. "The Cleansing Wave," words by Phoebe Palmer, music by her daughter, Phoebe Palmer Knapp. "The Cleansing Wave" appeared in Wesleyan Methodist, Free Methodist, and Pilgrim Holiness hymnbooks into the 1960s. It has been carried in hymnals published by the Church of the Nazarene from its beginning. *Sing to the Lord*, issued in 1993, included it. See also Charles Edward White, *Beauty of Holiness: Phoebe Palmer as Theologian, Revivalist, Feminist, and Humanitarian* (Grand Rapids: Zondervan, 1986), 132.

114. Meyendorff, *Byzantine Theology*, 162.

115. Oden, *Word of Life*, 355.

116. Barth, *Church Dogmatics*, IV.1, 67. Along with this theme, one must include the theme of forgiveness.

117. Hans Küng, *The Church* (New York: Image Doubleday, 1976), 162.

118. Kallistos Ware, *How Are We Saved? The Understanding of Salvation in the Orthodox Tradition* (Minneapolis: Light and Life, 1996), 68. Perhaps we might amend this to read "salvation is *social* and *communal*, not *merely* personal and individual."

119. John Ruusbroec, *The Spiritual Espousals and Other Works*, trans. James A. Wiseman, Classics of Western Spirituality (New York: Paulist Press, 1985), 41–42.

120. Ware, *How are We Saved?* 64.

121. Staniloae, *The World*, 162.

122. William Law, *William Law: A Serious Call to a Devout and Holy Life*, in *William Law: A Serious Call to a Devout and Holy Life; the Spirit of Love*, ed. Paul G. Stanwood, Classics of Western Spirituality (New York: Paulist Press, 1978), 328–29.

Chapter 6

1. For similar notions in philosophy, see Alfred North Whitehead's understanding of "concrescence," Charles S. Peirce's "logic of relations," and the synthesis of North American philosophy and theology found in the work of Donald L. Gelpi.

2. Consider also the breadth and intimacy of the Hebrew verb yada, "to know."

3. See, for example, Steve Duck, *Understanding Relationships* (New York: Guilford Press, 1991), 29–60; Benjamin Beit-Hallahmi, "Object Relations Theory and Religious Experience," in *Handbook of Religious Experience*, ed. Ralph W. Hood (Birmingham: Religious Education Press, 1995), 254–68.

4. On consent in Jonathan Edwards see, for example, Jonathan Edwards, "True Virtue"

in *Ethical Writings*, ed. Paul Ramsey, vol. 8, *The Works of Jonathan Edwards* (New Haven: Yale University Press, 1989), 540–48; Roland André Delattre, *Beauty and Sensibility in the Thought of Jonathan Edwards* (New Haven: Yale University Press, 1968), 21ff.; and Stephen H. Daniel, *The Philosophy of Jonathan Edwards* (Bloomington, IN: Indiana University Press, 1994), 180–87.

5. Catherine Mowry LaCugna, *God for Us: The Trinity and Christian Life* (New York: HarperCollins, 1991), 270–71. The notion of other-orientation is also found in discussion of emotion theory and in the philosophies of John Macmurray and Emmanuel Levinas; see John Macmurray, *Persons in Relation* (Atlantic Highlands, NJ: Humanities Press, 1961); Adriaan Peperzak, *To the Other: An Introduction to the Philosophy of Emmanuel Levinas*, Purdue Series in the History of Philosophy (West Lafayette, IN: Purdue University Press, 1993).

6. Duck, *Understanding Relationships*, 61–130; Macmurray, *Persons in Relation*, 86–105.

7. Duck, *Understanding Relationships*, 3.

8. Donald L. Gelpi, *The Divine Mother: A Trinitarian Theology of the Holy Spirit* (Lanham, MD: University Press of America, 1984), 138.

9. Walter Brueggemann, summarizing 500 pages of his *Old Testament Theology*, writes, "Everywhere in Israel's testimony about Yahweh, the God to which Israel bears witness is Yahweh-in-relation." Walter Brueggemann, *Theology of the Old Testament: Testimony, Dispute, Advocacy* (Minneapolis: Fortress, 1997), 567.

10. For an account of the effect of this cultural shift on American spirituality, see Robert Wuthnow, *After Heaven: Spirituality in America Since the 1950s* (Berkeley and Los Angeles: University of California Press, 1998).

11. See Luke Timothy Johnson, *Religious Experience in Earliest Christianity* (Philadelphia: Fortress, 1998).

12. John of the Cross, *The Ascent of Mount Carmel*, in *The Collected Works of John of the Cross*, trans. Kieran Kavanaugh and Otilio Rodriguez (Washington, DC: Institute of Carmelite Studies, 1979), bks. 2–3.

13. See William James, *The Varieties of Religious Experience* (New York: Simon and Schuster, 1997), and the response to James by his colleague Josiah Royce in Josiah Royce, *The Sources of Religious Insight* (Washington, DC: Catholic University of America Press, 2001).

14. See the summary chart of the work of the Alister Hardy Centre in Ralph W. Hood Jr., Bernard Spilka, Bruce Hunsberger, and Richard Gorsuch, eds., *The Psychology of Religion: An Empirical Approach*, 2nd ed. (New York: Guilford Press, 1996), 186–87, and more generally, the entire chapter on religious experience. A presentation of the variety of religious experiences in the context of spiritual direction can be found in Gerald May, *Care of Mind, Care of Spirit: Psychiatric Dimensions of Spiritual Direction* (San Francisco: Harper and Row, 1983), 27–41.

15. See, for example, Catherine Bell, *Ritual: Perspectives and Dimensions* (New York: Oxford University Press, 1997), 164.

16. James Houston, *The Transforming Friendship: A Guide to Prayer* (Oxford: Lion Books, 1989), 130.

17. See, for example, Chester P. Michael and Marie C. Norrisey, *Prayer and Temperament: Different Prayer Forms for Different Personality Types* (Charlottesville, VA: Open Door, 1984);

Suzanne Zuercher, *Enneagram Spirituality: From Compulsion to Contemplation* (Notre Dame, IN: Ave Maria Press, 1992); Gary Thomas, *Sacred Pathways: Discover Your Soul's Path to God* (Nashville: Thomas Nelson, 1996).

18. For reflections on development and spirituality, see, for example, James W. Fowler, *Stages of Faith: The Psychology of Human Development and the Quest for Meaning* (San Francisco: Harper and Row, 1981); Raymond Studzinski, *Spiritual Direction and Midlife Development* (Chicago: Loyola University Press, 1985); Francis Kelly Nemek and Marie Theresa Coombs, *The Spiritual Journey: Critical Thresholds and Stages of Adult Spiritual Genesis* (Wilmington, DE: Michael Glazier, 1987); Robert Coles, *The Spiritual Life of Children* (Boston: Houghton Mifflin, 1990); Hood et al., eds., *Psychology of Religion*, 44–182; and Elizabeth Liebert, *Changing Life Patterns: Adult Development in Spiritual Direction* (St. Louis: Chalice, 2000). Friedrich L. Schweitzer reflects on the significance, for theology and church, of development and historical cultural setting in a postmodern context. See Friedrich L. Schweitzer, *The Postmodern Life Cycle: Challenges for Church and Theology* (St. Louis: Chalice, 2004).

19. Liebert, *Changing Life Patterns*, 106.

20. Wendy Wright, "Woman-Body, Man-Body: Knowing God," in *Women's Spirituality: Resources for Christian Development*, 2nd ed. (New York: Paulist Press, 1996), 83.

21. Carol Gilligan, *In a Different Voice: Psychological Theory and Women's Development* (Cambridge: Harvard University Press, 1993), 6. For further reflection on women's spirituality, see, for example, Joann Wolski Conn, ed., *Women's Spirituality: Resources for Christian Development*, 2nd ed. (New York: Paulist Press, 1996); Kathleen Fischer, *Women at the Well: Feminist Perspectives on Spiritual Direction* (New York: Paulist Press, 1988); Katherine Dyckman, Mary Garvin, and Elizabeth Liebert, *The Spiritual Exercises Reclaimed: Uncovering Liberating Possibilities for Women* (New York: Paulist Press, 2001). For sample perspectives on men's spirituality, see Richard Rohr and Joseph Martos, *The Wild Man's Journey: Reflections on Male Spirituality* (Cincinnati: St. Anthony's Messenger Press, 1996); Philip Leroy Culbertson, *New Adam: The Future of Masculine Spirituality* (Minneapolis: Fortress, 1992); and John Eldredge, *Wild at Heart: Discovering the Secret of a Man's Soul* (Nashville: Thomas Nelson, 2001).

22. For examples of studies in African-American spirituality, see Theophus H. Smith, "The Spirituality of Afro-American Traditions," in *Christian Spirituality: Post-Reformation and Modern*, ed. Louis Dupré and Don E. Saliers, vol. 18, World Spirituality: An Encyclopedic History of the Religious Quest (New York: Crossroad, 1989), 372–414; Carlyle Fielding Stewart III, *Black Spirituality, Black Consciousness: Soul Force, Culture, and Freedom and the African-American Experience* (Trenton: Africa World Press, 1999); and Flora Wilson Bridges, *Resurrection Song: African-American Spirituality* (Maryknoll, NY: Orbis, 2001). For Hispanic spirituality, see Yolanda Tarango, Consuelo Covarrubias, and Ada-Maria Isasi-Diaz, eds., *Así Es: Stories of Hispanic Spirituality* (Collegeville, MN: Liturgical Press, 1994). For Asian spirituality, see Basil Pennington with Simon Chan, "Spirituality, Christian," in *A Dictionary of Asian Christianity*, ed. Scott

W. Sundquist (Grand Rapids: Eerdmans, 2001), 790–94, and other entries in the volume.

23. Ann Ulanov and Barry Ulanov, *Primary Speech: A Psychology of Prayer* (Atlanta: John Knox, 1982), 29–32.

24. For surveys of different traditions in addition to the historical surveys of Christian spirituality, see Kenneth J. Collins, ed., *Exploring Christian Spirituality: An Ecumenical Reader* (Grand Rapids: Baker, 2000), and Frank Senn, ed., *Protestant Spiritual Traditions* (New York: Paulist Press, 1986). On Pentecostal and charismatic spirituality, see Daniel E. Albrecht, *Rites in the Spirit: A Ritual Approach to Pentecostal/Charismatic Spirituality*, Journal of Pentecostal Theology Supplement Series (Sheffield, UK: Sheffield Academic Press, 1999).

25. Johnson, *Religious Experience*, 184.

26. For examples, see Brueggemann, *Theology of the Old Testament*, 267–313, and Hood et al., eds., *Psychology of Religion*, 183–223.

27. John Cassian, *Conferences*, trans. Colm Luibheid (New York: Paulist Press, 1985), conference 3.12, page 93.

28. Ibid., conference 3.19, page 97. See also the extended conversation detailing the dynamics of God's creative and appropriate responses to our responses to God's invitations in conference 13 (which is not published in the Paulist edition but is available in other editions of the Conferences).

29. Donald Bloesch, *God the Almighty: Power, Wisdom, Holiness, Love* (Downers Grove, IL: InterVarsity Press, 1995), 95; Thomas C. Oden, *The Living God* (Peabody, MA: Prince, 1998), 112. The authors of *The Openness of God* write, "The Christian life involves a genuine interaction between God and human beings. We respond to God's gracious initiatives and God responds to our responses . . . and on it goes." See Clark Pinnock et al., *The Openness of God: A Biblical Challenge to the Traditional Understanding of God* (Downers Grove, IL: InterVarsity Press, 1994), 7.

30. John Ruusbroec, *John Ruusbroec: The Spiritual Espousals and Other Works*, trans. James A. Wiseman, Classics of Western Spirituality (New York: Paulist Press, 1985), 54.

31. Relevant surveys of the theology of grace can be found in Bruce Demarest, *The Cross and Salvation*, Foundations of Evangelical Theology (Wheaton: Crossway, 1997), 49–96; Roger Haight, "Grace," in *The New Dictionary of Catholic Spirituality*, ed. Michael Downey (Collegeville, MN: Liturgical Press, 1993), 452–64; Kenneth J. Collins, *The Scripture Way of Salvation: The Heart of John Wesley's Theology* (Nashville: Abingdon, 1997), 19–25, and the structure of the rest of the book; and Donald L. Gelpi, *The Gracing of Human Experience: Rethinking the Relationship Between Nature and Grace* (Collegeville, MN: Liturgical Press, 2001). The theme is also woven throughout Vladimir Lossky, *The Mystical Theology of the Eastern Church* (Crestwood, NY: St. Vladimir's Press, 1998).

32. See the notion of grace as supernatural in Karl Rahner, "Concerning the Relationship of Nature and Grace," in *Theological Investigations*, 23 vols. (Baltimore: Helicon Press, 1961), 1:297–318.

33. Credit for insight into this aspect of grace belongs to a message by Dallas Willard entitled "My Grace Is Sufficient for You" (Renovaré regional conference, Denver, October 5, 2001).

34. An account of grace similar to this is presented in much greater detail in Donald L. Gelpi, *Grace as Transmuted Experience and Social Process, and Other Essays in North American Theology* (Lanham, NJ: University Press of America, 1988), 41–96; and Donald L. Gelpi, *Gracing of Human Experience*, 315–59.

35. Dietrich Bonhoeffer, *The Cost of Discipleship* (New York: Macmillan, 1963), 49.

36. N. T. Wright, *The Resurrection of the Son of God*, vol. 3, Christian Origins and the Question of God (Philadelphia: Fortress, 2003), 456.

37. For a treatment of these four elements of gospel transformation, see Richard Lovelace's classic *Dynamics of Spiritual Life: An Evangelical Theology of Renewal* (Downers Grove, IL: InterVarsity Press, 1979), 95–144; and Richard Lovelace, *Renewal as a Way of Life* (Downers Grove, IL: InterVarsity Press, 1985), 131–57.

38. Lars Thunberg, *Man and the Cosmos: The Vision of St. Maximus the Confessor* (Crestwood, NY: St. Vladimir's Seminary Press, 1885), 42.

39. See Genesis 1:2; 2:7; 6:3; see also Paul's reference to these passages in his speech to the Gentiles at Athens in Acts 17:25.

40. See Wisdom of Solomon 12:1–2; see also 1:6–7. That these passages refer to the Spirit's work among the nations in general, and not simply the people of God, is seen by the reference to the Canaanites in the verses that follow and in the parallel to God's judgment "little by little" in Wisdom of Solomon 12:10. (The Wisdom of Solomon is canonical for Orthodox and Roman Catholic traditions but not for Protestant traditions.)

41. Once again, this is no place to present a survey of the theology of the Holy Spirit. For examples of more comprehensive treatments, see George T. Montague, *The Holy Spirit: Growth of a Biblical Tradition* (New York: Paulist Press, 1976); Gordon Fee, *God's Empowering Presence: The Holy Spirit in the Letters of Paul* (Peabody, MA: Hendrickson, 1994); Abraham Kuyper, *The Work of the Holy Spirit*, trans. Henri de Vries (Grand Rapids: Eerdmans, 1979); Jürgen Moltmann, *The Spirit of Life: A Universal Affirmation*, trans. Margaret Kohl (Minneapolis: Fortress, 1992); Yves Congar, *I Believe in the Holy Spirit*, three vols. David Smith (New York: Crossroad, 1997); Clark H. Pinnock, *Flame of Love: A Theology of the Holy Spirit* (Downers Grove, IL: InterVarsity Press, 1996); Donald L. Gelpi, *Divine Mother*; Lossky, *Mystical Theology*, 156–73; and John Meyendorff, *Byzantine Theology: Historical Trends and Doctrinal Themes* (New York: Fordham University Press, 1979), 168–79.

42. John Owen, *The Work of the Spirit*, in *The Works of John Owen*, 16 vols. (Edinburgh: Banner of Truth, 1967), 3:283.

43. Ignatius of Loyola, *Spiritual Exercises*, in *Ignatius of Loyola: The Spiritual Exercises and Selected Works*, ed. George E. Ganss (New York: Paulist Press, 1991), sec. 314–15. Note: I will designate the sections of the *Spiritual Exercises* by placing them in square brackets [314–15].

44. See, for example, Erving Goffman, "The Presentation of Self to Others," in *Understanding Relationships: Selected Readings in Interpersonal Communication*, ed. Benjamin J. Broome (Dubuque: Kendall/Hunt, 1986), 59–70; Duck, *Understanding Relationships*, 55–71.

45. Compare, for example, some of the stories found in Kevin Orlin Johnson, *Apparitions: Mystic Phenomena and What They Mean*

(Dallas: Pangaeus, 1995), with the story of novelist Frederick Buechner found in Philip Yancey, *Reaching for the Invisible God* (Grand Rapids: Zondervan, 2000), 32.

46. A fine treatment of the themes of ambiguity and darkness (see below) is Kenneth Leech, "God of Cloud and Darkness," in *Experiencing God: Theology as Spirituality* (San Francisco: Harper and Row, 1985), 162–98.

47. Paul Hinnebusch, "The Need for Discernment," *Catholic Charismatic*, June–July 1978, 4.

48. William Barry, *Spiritual Direction and the Encounter with God: A Theological Inquiry* (Mahwah, NJ: Paulist Press, 1992), 34.

49. Houston, *Transforming Friendship*, 218. See also 100.

50. Symeon the New Theologian, *Symeon the New Theologian: The Discourses*, trans. C. J. de Catanzaro, Classics of Western Spirituality (New York: Paulist Press, 1980), 200–201. The theme of light is also strong in the *Theologia Germanica* (a late-medieval work influential to Martin Luther) and in the works of Quaker spirituality. See Bengt Hoffman, ed., *The Theologia Germanica of Martin Luther*, Classics of Western Spirituality (New York: Paulist Press, 1980); Douglas V. Steere, ed., *Quaker Spirituality: Selected Writings*, Classics of Western Spirituality (New York: Paulist Press, 1984); and Leech, *Experiencing God*, 93. For the themes of absence, darkness, and dryness see John of the Cross, *The Dark Night of the Cross*, in *The Collected Works of John of the Cross*, trans. Kieran Kavanaugh and Otilio Rodriguez (Washington, DC: Institute of Carmelite Studies, 1979); Thomas Green, *When the Well Runs Dry: Prayer Beyond the Beginnings*, rev. ed. (Notre Dame, IN: Ave Maria Press, 1998); and Belden Lane, *The Solace of Fierce Landscapes: Exploring Desert and Mountain Spirituality* (New York: Oxford University Press, 1998).

51. William Barry and William Connolly address many of these interpersonal dynamics of spirituality in their classic, *The Practice of Spiritual Direction* (New York: Seabury, 1982).

52. Joseph F. Delany, "Scruple," *The Catholic Encyclopedia*, http://www.newadvent.org/cathen/13640a.htm.

53. See also Ignatius of Loyola, *Spiritual Exercises* [sec. 345–51].

54. For example, see the treatment of original sin (sec. 396–409) and personal sin (sec. 1846–76) in *Catechism of the Catholic Church* (Washington, DC: United States Catholic Conference, 1994).

55. Ignatius of Loyola begins his Spiritual Exercises with a week of attention to our forms of resisting God. See Ignatius of Loyola, *Spiritual Exercises* [sec. 23–90]. Historical theologian Richard Lovelace, following the lead of the Puritan divines, proclaims in his *Dynamics of Spiritual Life* that one of the keys to Christian spiritual renewal is a profound awareness of sin. See Lovelace, *Dynamics of Spiritual Life*, 81–94.

56. Gerald May rehearses a number of ways that we avoid the implications of spiritual experience in terms of the classic psychological defense mechanisms. His treatment is a brilliant analysis of the ways in which human beings avoid response to God's gracious invitations. See Gerald May, *Care of Mind, Care of Spirit*, 70–73. He discusses other kinds of resistance on pp. 74–77.

57. Lorenzo Scupoli, *Unseen Warfare: The Spiritual Combat and Path to Paradise of Lorenzo*

Scupoli, ed. Nicodemus of the Holy Mountain and rev. Theophan the Recluse, trans. E. Kadloubovsky and G. E. H. Palmer (Crestwood, NY: St. Vladimir's Seminary Press, 1987), 159–60.

58. George R. Beasley-Murray, *John*, Word Biblical Commentary (Dallas: Word, 1987), 12.

59. Gregory of Sinai, "On Commandments and Doctrines, Warnings and Promises; on Thoughts, Passions and Virtues, and Also on Stillness and Prayer: One Hundred and Thirty-Seven Texts," in *The Philokalia: The Complete Text*, comp. Saint Nikodimos of the Holy Mountain and Saint Makarios of Corinth, trans. G. E. H. Palmer, Philip Sherrard, and Kallistos Ware (London: Faber and Faber, 1979–), sec. 107, 4:235–36.

60. John Calvin, *Institutes of the Christian Religion*, trans. Henry Beveridge (Grand Rapids: Eerdmans, 1953), 3.3.14. Calvin uses the terms obedience and obedient 255 times in this work.

61. Peter Walpot, "True Yieldedness and the Christian Community of Goods," in *Early Anabaptist Spirituality*, ed. Daniel Liechty, Classics of Western Spirituality (New York: Paulist Press, 1994), 147. I am grateful to professor Ron Sider for translations of some of the writings of Andreas Bodenstein von Karlstadt. *Gelassenheit* is found in the *Theologia Germanica* and in the works of Meister Eckhart, Johannes Tauler, Andreas Bodenstein von Karlstadt, Hans Denck, Peter Walpot, and others. See also contemporary psychiatrist and spiritual writer Gerald May's distinction between willfulness and willingness in Gerald May, *Will and Spirit: A Contemplative Psychology* (San Francisco: Harper and Row, 1982). Similar to the notion of yieldedness is the concept of "docility" to the Spirit of God. On this see, Donald L. Gelpi, *Discerning the Spirit: Foundations and Futures of Religious Life* (New York: Sheed and Ward, 1970), 310; and Donald L. Gelpi, "Discernment and the Varieties of Conversion" (paper presented at Catholic Charismatic Renewal Conference, 1996), 11.

62. Duck, *Understanding Relationships*, 71.

63. *The Cloud of Unknowing*, ed. James Walsh (New York: Paulist Press, 1981), chap. 54, p. 225. Note how this passage echoes Jesus's own condemnations of religiosity in Matthew 6. Other examples may be found in *Symeon the New Theologian, Discourses*, 210–12, and in William Wilberforce's portrayals of "inadequate conceptions of Christianity" found in William Wilberforce, *Real Christianity Contrasted with the Prevailing Religious System*, Classics of Faith and Devotion (Portland, OR: Multnomah, 1982).

64. Many scholars divide the Psalms into "praise" and "lament" psalms. Walter Brueggemann speaks of psalms expressing orientation, dis-orientation, and new-orientation. See, for example, his *The Message of the Psalms: A Theological Commentary* (Minneapolis: Augsburg, 1984). Both situation and the fundamental dynamics of the divine-human relationship are involved in all these kinds of distinctions.

65. Thomas à Kempis, *The Imitation of Christ*, trans. William Creasy (Notre Dame, IN: Ave Maria Press, 1989), book 3, chap. 21, p. 109.

66. Hannah Whitall Smith, *The Christian's Secret of a Holy Life*, Ages Christian Online Library, The Master Christian Library Ages Software, 2000.

67. Augustine, Homily on the Epistles of John, 4.6, cited in Andrew Louth, "Augustine," in *The Study of Spirituality*, ed. Cheslyn Jones, Geoffrey Wainwright, and Edward Yarnold (New York: Oxford University Press, 1986), 140.

68. Mike Bickle, *Passion for Jesus: Perfecting Extravagant Love for God* (Orlando, FL: Creation House, 1993), 72.

69. William Stringfellow, *My People Is the Enemy* (New York: Holt, Rinehart and Winston, 1964), 3, quoted in John M. Gessel, "Stringfellow and the Law," in *Prophet of Justice, Prophet of Life: Essays on William Stringfellow*, ed. Robert Boak Slocum (New York: Church Publishing, 1997), 106.

70. Bickle, *Passion for Jesus*, 103.

71. Ronald Sider, *Andreas Bodenstein von Karlstadt: The Development of His Thought 1517–1525*, Studies in Medieval and Reformation Thought (Leiden, Netherlands: Brill, 1974), 303.

72. Kent Harold Richards, "Bless/Blessing," in *The Anchor Bible Dictionary*, 6 vols., ed. David Noel Freedman (New York: Doubleday, 1992), 1:754.

73. May speaks of our need to welcome our deep uneasiness with life—rather than to attempt to eliminate through therapy—and to allow it to draw us to God. He urges us to remember "that our most basic dis-ease may not be a disorder at all. Instead it may be our finest hope." See May, *Care of Mind, Care of Spirit*, 50.

74. Francis de Sales, *Oeuvres*, 4: Treatise, 2, 8, cited in Francis de Sales and Jane de Chantal, *Francis de Sales, Jane de Chantal: Letters of Spiritual Direction*, trans. Péronne Marie Thibert, Classics of Western Spirituality (New York: Paulist Press, 1988), 35.

75. G. C. Berkouwer, *Sin*, Studies in Dogmatics (Grand Rapids: Eerdmans, 1971), 383.

76. See, for example, the fifth exercise of the first week of Ignatius of Loyola's Spiritual Exercises; the example of Cotton Mather's manual on the spiritual life in Charles Hambrick-Stowe, *The Practice of Piety: Puritan Devotional Disciplines in Seventeenth-Century New England* (Chapel Hill: University of North Carolina Press, 1982), 223; and Tikhon of Zadonsk, *Journey to Heaven: Counsels on the Particular Duties of Every Christian*, trans. George D. Lardas (Jordanville, NY: Holy Trinity Monastery, 1991), 174–81.

Chapter 7

1. Classic portraits of Christian spirituality in the image of a journey can be found in such works as Gregory of Nyssa's (330–95) *Life of Moses*, John Comenius's *The Labyrinth of the World and the Paradise of the Heart*, and John Bunyan's *Pilgrim's Progress*. For a Jungian approach to the image of pilgrimage in spirituality, see Jean Dalby Clift and Wallace B. Clift, *The Archetype of Pilgrimage: Outer Action with Inner Meaning* (Mahwah, NJ: Paulist Press, 1996).

2. Emilie Griffin, *Turning: Reflections on the Experience of Conversion* (Garden City, NY: Image, 1982), 171.

3. Billy Crockett, "Carrier," on *Carrier* (Word Records, 1984).

4. For philosophical discussions of this kind of reorientation (not necessarily referring to *Christian* transformation), see, for example, Thomas S. Kuhn, *The Structure of Scientific Revo-*

lutions (Chicago: University of Chicago Press, 1962); Nancey Murphey, *Theology in the Age of Scientific Reasoning*, Cornell Studies in the Philosophy of Religion (Ithaca, NY: Cornell University Press, 1990); Kitaro Nishida, *An Inquiry into the Good*, trans. Masao Abe and Christopher Ives (New Haven: Yale University Press, 1990) and other works of Nishida. Jonathan Edwards also speaks of a transformation of standpoint in a similar manner in his philosophical and theological works.

5. On this, see A. D. Nock's distinction between "adhesion" and Christian "conversion" in A. D. Nock, *Conversion: The Old and the New in Religion from Alexander the Great to Augustine of Hippo* (London: Oxford University Press, 1933).

6. See Richard Peace, *Conversion in the New Testament: Paul and the Twelve* (Grand Rapids: Eerdmans, 1999), esp. 123–25. See also Gordon Smith's summary of biblical images of conversion in Gordon Smith, *Beginning Well: Christian Conversion and Authentic Transformation* (Downers Grove, IL: InterVarsity Press, 2001), 107–35. For Eckhart, see *Meister Eckhart: The Essential Sermons, Commentaries, Treatises, and Defense*, trans. and intro. by Edmund College and Bernard McGinn, Classics of Western Spirituality (New York: Paulist Press, 1981), 55–57, and the passages cited in *Meister Eckhart: Teacher and Preacher*, ed. Bernard McGinn, Classics of Western Spirituality (New York: Paulist Press, 1986), 401. For Tauler, see sermon 1 (Christmas) in *Johannes Tauler: Sermons*, trans. Maria Shrady (New York: Paulist Press, 1985), 35–40.

7. Dorothy Day, *The Long Loneliness: The Autobiography of Dorothy Day* (New York: Harper, 1952), 132–33.

8. Ignatius of Loyola, *The Autobiography*, in *Ignatius of Loyola: The Spiritual Exercises and Selected Works*, ed. George E. Ganss, Classics of Western Spirituality (New York: Paulist Press, 1991), 70–71.

9. Jackie Pullinger, with Andrew Quicke, *Chasing the Dragon* (Ann Arbor, MI: Servant Books, 1980), 25.

10. A good review of the psychology of conversion can be found in Ralph W. Hood Jr., Bernard Spilka, Bruce Hunsberger, and Richard Gorsuch, eds., *The Psychology of Religion: An Empirical Approach*, 2nd ed. (New York: Guilford, 1996), 273–99; see the earlier chapters for a review of religion in the various developmental stages of life. Both psychological and social factors are addressed in Lewis R. Rambo, *Understanding Religious Conversion* (New Haven: Yale University Press, 1993). An exploration of the influence of political factors in religious transformation may be found in Gauri Viswanathan, *Outside the Fold: Conversion, Modernity, and Belief* (Princeton: Princeton University Press, 1998).

11. For the difficulties involved in human choice, see Robyn M. Dawes, *Rational Choice in an Uncertain World* (Fort Worth: Harcourt Brace, 1988).

12. Steve Duck, *Understanding Relationships* (New York: Guilford, 1991), 64; see the rest of the book for further treatment of these and other dynamics.

13. Smith, *Beginning Well*, 28.

14. Melvin E. Deiter et al., *Five Views on Sanctification* (Grand Rapids: Zondervan, 1987), 7.

15. This division—and the use of the term *salvation*—reflects the use of the term *sozo/soteria* (saved, salvation) in the Greek New Testament. The term is used in past, present, and future tenses to refer to our transforming appropriation of God's gracious action.

16. John Murray, *Redemption Accomplished and Applied* (Grand Rapids: Eerdmans, 1955).

17. Karl Barth, *The Doctrine of God*, ed. G. W. Bromiley and T. F. Torrance, trans. T. H. L. Parker, W. B. Johnston, Harold Knight, J. L. M. Heine, vol. 1, Church Dogmatics (Edinburgh: T and T Clark, 1957), I.1, 154. In his discussion of sanctification, Barth writes that "the exaltation of man, which in defiance of his reluctance has been achieved in the death and declared in the resurrection of Jesus Christ, is as such the creation of his new form of existence as the faithful covenant-partner of God." Karl Barth, *The Doctrine of Reconciliation*, edited by G. W. Bromiley and T. F. Torrance, vol. 4, Church Dogmatics (Edinburgh: T and T Clark, 1958), IV.2, 499.

18. Rambo, *Understanding Religious Conversion*, 176.

19. See, for example, Kenneth J. Collins and John H. Tyson, eds., *Conversion in the Wesleyan Tradition* (Nashville: Abingdon, 2001); and Bruce Demarest, *The Cross and Salvation*, Foundations of Evangelical Theology (Wheaton: Crossway, 1997), 235–76.

20. See Saint Theophan the Recluse, *The Path to Salvation: A Manual of Spiritual Transformation*, trans. Fr. Seraphim Rose (Platina, CA: St. Herman Press, 1998), 105–23.

21. Smith, *Beginning Well*, 35.

22. Luke and Paul use the same words with reference to the Spirit with different emphases: Luke uses these terms to describe the events of the Holy Spirit's work; Paul uses them to communicate theological truth concerning the work of the Spirit. On Luke's use of metaphor with reference to the Spirit, see M. M. B. Turner, "Spirit Endowment in Luke-Acts: Some Linguistic Considerations," *Vox Evangelica* 12 (1981): 45–63.

23. See Demarest, *Cross and Salvation*, 252–61.

24. See Hood et al., eds., *Psychology of Religion*, 273–99.

25. This wisdom can be collected from a survey of the classics of Christian spirituality. See, for example, Bernard of Clairvaux, "On Conversion," in *Bernard of Clairvaux: Selected Works*, trans. G. R. Evans (New York: Paulist Press, 1987), 65–97; Jonathan Edwards, *Religious Affections*. vol. 2, *The Works of Jonathan Edwards*, ed. John E. Smith (New Haven: Yale University Press, 1959); Theophan the Recluse, "The Usual Order of the Gift of Awakening Grace" and "Ascent to the Resolve to Abandon Sin and Dedicate One's Life to Pleasing God" in Theophan the Recluse, *The Path to Salvation*. A more recent example is Os Guinness, *In Two Minds: The Problem of Doubt and How to Resolve It* (Downers Grove, IL: InterVarsity Press, 1976). Exploration of the juncture of spirituality and evangelism could prove to be a fascinating field for future research.

26. See Luke Timothy Johnson, *Religious Experience in Earliest Christianity* (Philadelphia: Fortress, 1998), 69–103.

27. For a discussion of the implications of seeing the church as the midwife of conversion, see Smith, *Beginning Well*, 227–32.

28. Theophan the Recluse, *Path to Salvation*, 65.

29. Klaus Issler, "Biblical Perspectives on Developmental Grace for Nurturing Children's Spirituality," in *Children's Spirituality: Christian Perspectives, Research, and Applications*, ed. Donald Ratcliff (Eugene, OR: Cascade Books, 2004), 54–71.

30. Francis Newman, *The Soul: Its Sorrows and Aspirations*, 3rd ed. (London: Chapman, 1852), 89, 91, quoted in William James, *The Varieties of Religious Experience*, in *William James: Writings, 1902–1910*, The Library of America (New York: Literary Classics of the United States, 1987), 79; see also 77–120.

31. See James, *Varieties of Religious Experience*, 121–238.

32. See, for example, Griffin, *Turning*, 33–34; John Wimber, *Power Evangelism* (San Francisco: Harper and Row, 1986), 56; Lelan Harris, "Spiritual Formation Stage Models: Some Implications for Evangelism" (unpublished paper, 2003); and Peace, *Conversion in the New Testament*. These modern examples develop from the point of view of the human sciences that Protestant theologians have long discussed under the rubric of the *ordo salutis*, or order of salvation, encompassing both initial and ongoing salvation.

33. See Rambo, *Understanding Religious Conversion*. This schema structures his entire book, and we will be drawing heavily from his book throughout this section. A summary chart may be found on pp. 168–69 of Rambo's book.

34. This is adapted with permission from ibid., fig. 6.

35. Gerald May, *The Awakened Heart: Opening Yourself to the Love You Need* (San Francisco: HarperSanFrancisco, 1993), 54.

36. Griffin, *Turning*, 53–54, 57.

37. This is adapted with permission from Rambo, *Understanding Religious Conversion*, fig. 8.

38. This is adapted with permission from ibid., fig. 10.

39. Griffin, *Turning*., 141–42.

40. See Smith, *Beginning Well*, 79–106.

41. On this, see, for example, Donald L. Gelpi, *Committed Worship: A Sacramental Theology for Converting Christians*, 2 vols. (Minneapolis: Liturgical Press, 1993).

42. May, *Awakened Heart*, 64, 49.

43. Griffin, *Turning*, 148.

44. On testimony and spiritual autobiography, see Rambo, *Understanding Religious Conversion*, 137–39; Smith, *Beginning Well*, 219–27.

45. J. Edwin Orr, *The Flaming Tongue: The Impact of Twentieth-Century Revivals* (Chicago: Moody, 1973), 17. For the conversion of families see William Thompson, "Evangelization of Whole Families Report," in *Let the Earth Hear His Voice: International Congress on World Evangelization; Lausanne, Switzerland*, ed. J. D. Douglas (Minneapolis: World Wide Publications, 1975), 974–76. For stories of the transformation of cities, see, for example, the video *Transformations*, directed by George Otis Jr. (Lynwood, WA: Sentinel Group, 2001), and the sequels.

46. Griffin, *Turning*, 175. For a wonderful treatment of a few psychodynamic and social consequences of Christian transformation, see Gerald May, *Care of Mind, Care of Spirit: Psychiatric Dimensions of Spiritual Direction* (San Francisco: Harper and Row, 1983), 77–83.

47. This list forms the structure of Smith's *Beginning Well*.

48. Griffin, *Turning*, 34.

49. Demarest, *Cross and Salvation*, 271.

50. Bernard McGinn, "Human Persons as Image of God: Western Christianity," in *Christian Spirituality: Origins to the Twelfth Century*, ed. Bernard McGinn, John Meyendorff, and Jean Leclercq, vol. 16, World Spirituality: An Encyclopedic History of the Religious Quest (New York: Crossroad, 1985), 318.

51. A few classic summaries of the commandments of the scriptures can be found in Exodus 20:1–17; Deuteronomy 5–28; Romans 12–15; Galatians 5–6; Ephesians 4–6; Colossians 2:6–4:6; and many other places.

52. Irénée Hausherr, *Penthos: The Doctrine of Compunction in the Christian East*, trans. Anselm Hufstader (Kalamazoo, MI: Cistercian Publications, 1982), 18.

53. John D. Zizioulas, *Being as Communion: Studies in Personhood and the Church* (Crestwood, NY: St. Vladimir's Seminary Press, 1985), 114.

54. Pullinger, *Chasing the Dragon*, 61–63.

55. Andrew Louth, *The Origins of the Christian Mystical Tradition: From Plato to Denys* (Oxford: Clarendon, 1981), 59. In chapter 1, we mentioned the Western model of the threefold way of purgation, illumination, and union. For Origen's expression, see Origen, *The Song of Songs: Commentary and Homilies*, trans. R. P. Lawson, Ancient Christian Writers (London: Longmans, Green, 1957), 21–58. For more on Origen's approach to spiritual maturity, see Henri Crouzel, *Origen*, trans. A. S. Worrall (San Francisco: Harper and Row, 1985), 99–133. See also chap. 4 of Maximus the Confessor, "The Church's Mystagogy," in *Maximus Confessor: Selected Writings*, trans. George C. Berthold, Classics of Western Spirituality (New York: Paulist Press, 1985), for Maximus the Confessor's (ca. 580–662) use of these categories by way of an analogy between the design of a church building and the spiritual life. Both East and West were influenced by Gregory of Nyssa's (330–95) *The Life of Moses*, in which he interprets the life of Moses as a model for Christian growth through a progression from purification toward union. See *Gregory of Nyssa: the Life of Moses*, trans. Abraham J. Malherbe and Everett Ferguson, Classics of Western Spirituality (New York: Paulist Press, 1978). For other examples of the Western development of the threefold way regarding Augustine, see James Mohler, *Late Have I Loved You: An Interpretation of Saint Augustine on Human and Divine Relationships* (New York: New City Press, 1991), 33–34; regarding Bonaventure, see Pierre Pourrat, *Christian Spirituality in the Middle Ages*, trans. S. P. Jacques, Christian Spirituality (Westminster, MD: Newman Press, 1927), 177–80; and Bernard McGinn, *The Flowering of Mysticism: Men and Women in the New Mysticism, 1200–1350*, The Presence of God: A History of Western Christian Mysticism (New York: Crossroad, 1998), 102–5.

56. Guigo II, "The Ladder of Monks: A Letter on the Contemplative Life," in *The Ladder of Monks and Twelve Meditations*, trans. Edmund Colledge and James Walsh, vol. 48, Cistercian Studies Series (Kalamazoo, MI: Cistercian Publications, 1979), 79–80.

57. For Bonaventure, see "The Triple Way" in *The Works of Bonaventure*, ed. I. Mystical Opscula, trans. José de Vinck (Patterson, NJ: St.

Anthony Guild Press, 1960), 63–94. For the Dominicans, see Simon Tugwell, "A Dominican Theology of Prayer," *Dominican Ashram* 1, no. 3 (September 1982): 128–44; Albert the Great and Thomas Aquinas, *Albert and Thomas: Selected Writings*, trans. Simon Tugwell, Classics of Western Spirituality (New York: Paulist Press, 1988).

58. See, for example, Roland H. Bainton, *The Reformation of the Sixteenth Century* (Boston: Beacon, 1952); the chapters on Lutheran and Reformed spiritualities in Kenneth J. Collins, ed., *Exploring Christian Spirituality: An Ecumenical Reader* (Grand Rapids: Baker, 2000); Dennis E. Tamburello, *Union with Christ: John Calvin and the Mysticism of St. Bernard*, Columbia Series in Reformed Theology (Louisville: Westminster John Knox, 1994); Peter C. Erb, "Anabaptist Spirituality," in *Protestant Spiritual Traditions*, ed. Frank C. Senn (New York: Paulist Press, 1986), 80–124.

59. Richard Lovelace, *The American Pietism of Cotton Mather: Origins of American Evangelicalism* (Grand Rapids: Eerdmans, 1979), 177. For Pietism and the *ordo salutis*, see Peter C. Erb, introduction to *Pietists: Selected Writings*, ed. Peter C. Erb, Classics of Western Spirituality (New York: Paulist Press, 1983), 6 (and Erb's references). For a discussion of preparationist schemes with relation to American Puritanism, see David Laurence, "Jonathan Edwards, Solomon Stoddard, and the Preparationist Model of Conversion," *Harvard Theological Review* 72, no. 3–4 (July–October 1979): 267–83.

60. On Ignatius's "weeks," see Ignatius of Loyola, *Spiritual Exercises*, in *Ignatius of Loyola: The Spiritual Exercises and Selected Works*, ed. George E. Ganss, Classics of Western Spirituality (New York: Paulist Press, 1991), 113–214; and David L. Fleming, ed., *Notes on the Spiritual Exercises of Ignatius of Loyola* (St. Louis: Review for Religious, 1989). For a brief introduction to Carmelite spirituality, see Keith J. Egan, "Carmelite Spirituality," in *Exploring Christian Spirituality: An Ecumenical Reader*, ed. Kenneth J. Collins (Grand Rapids: Baker, 2000), 97–107.

61. On Holiness, Pentecostal, and Keswick models of spiritual growth, see George M. Marsden, *Fundamentalism and American Culture: The Shaping of Twentieth-Century Evangelicalism, 1870–1925* (Oxford: Oxford University Press, 1980), 77–101; and Vinson Synan, *The Holiness-Pentecostal Tradition: Charismatic Movements in the Twentieth Century*, 2nd ed. (Grand Rapids: Eerdmans, 1997). For samples of the threefold way in Roman Catholic manual spirituality, see Adolphe Tanquerey, *The Spiritual Life: A Treatise on Ascetical and Mystical Theology*, trans. Herman Branderis, 2nd and rev. ed. (Tournai, Belgium: Desclée, 1930); and Joseph de Guibert, *The Theology of the Spiritual Life*, trans. Paul Barrett (New York: Sheed and Ward, 1953). A more contemporary expression of this may be found in Jordan Aumann, *Spiritual Theology* (London: Sheed and Ward, 1980).

62. James W. Fowler, *Stages of Faith: The Psychology of Human Development and the Quest for Meaning* (San Francisco: Harper and Row, 1981).

63. Francis Kelly Nemek and Marie Theresa Coombs, *The Spiritual Journey: Critical Thresholds and Stages of Adult Spiritual Genesis* (Wilmington, DE: Michael Glazier, 1987); and Elizabeth Liebert, *Changing Life Patterns: Adult Development in Spiritual Direction* (New York: Paulist Press, 1992).

64. Janet Hagberg and Robert Guelich, *The Critical Journey: Stages in the Life of Faith*, rev. ed. (Salem, WI: Sheffield, 2005).

65. See, for example, Friedrich L. Schweitzer, *The Postmodern Life Cycle: Challenges for Church and Theology* (St. Louis: Chalice, 2004).

66. Again, I think there is a difference between *normative* and *descriptive* schemas here. For example, Jonathan Edwards's tensions with the preparationist models were based not only on reflection on scripture, but also on his first-hand observations of the transformations taking place during the First Great Awakening. He saw development of authentic conversions that did not go through the "prescribed" stages.

67. See Rick Warren, *The Purpose-Driven Church: Growth without Compromising Your Message and Mission* (Grand Rapids: Zondervan, 1995); and Hagberg and Guelich, *Critical Journey*, 186–214.

68. I wonder, could there be something of an application of Abraham Maslow's "hierarchy of needs" to an understanding of stages of spiritual growth? Perhaps stages of spiritual growth are constrained by our sense of need, such that we generally first address the spiritual issues related to basic physiological needs; we then address in turn those related to our sense of safety (temporal or eternal), to our sense of belonging and love, and to issues of esteem and actualization. If so, this may give some support for the general direction of the traditional movement from outward to inward.

69. Ralph Martin, *Philippians*, New Century Bible Commentary (Grand Rapids: Eerdmans, 1976), 135.

70. Bengt Hoffman, ed., *The Theologia Germanica of Martin Luther*, Classics of Western Spirituality (New York: Paulist Press, 1980), 120.

71. Vladimir Lossky, *The Mystical Theology of the Eastern Church* (Crestwood, NY: St. Vladimir's Press, 1998), 196. The theme of divinization is common in the writings of late-medieval Roman Catholic spiritual writers and of early Anabaptists such as Andreas Bodenstein von Karlstadt and Hans Denck. It is especially important to the Orthodox tradition from Maximus through Gregory Palamas and up to Lossky and others in the present. We will treat the subject of deification in greater detail in the following chapter.

72. For the story of the Dani, see John Dekker, *Torches of Joy* (Seattle: YWAM Publishing, 1992).

73. Bruce Demarest speaks of authentic repentance as having intellectual, emotional, and volitional aspects. See Demarest, *Cross and Salvation*, 254.

74. Thomas Merton letter published in *Information Catholiques Internationale*, April 1973, back cover, quoted in Griffin, *Turning*, 196.

75. Donald L. Gelpi has discussed the forms of conversion in a number of works. See especially Gelpi, *Committed Worship*, and Donald L. Gelpi, *The Conversion Experience: A Reflective Process for RCIA Participants and Others* (Mahwah, NJ: Paulist Press, 1998). For other similar accounts of forms of conversion, see Bernard Lonergan, *Method in Theology* (Minneapolis: Seabury, 1972), 237–44; Robert Doran, *Subject and Psyche: Ricoeur, Jung and the Search for Foundations* (Washington, DC: University Press of America, 1977); and Bernard J. Tyrrell,

Christotherapy II: The Fasting and the Feasting Heart (New York: Paulist Press, 1982). In what follows, I am drawing a great deal from Gelpi's work, although, unlike Gelpi, I am considering conversion strictly *within* the context of Christian life. For a treatment of Gelpi's theology, see Evan B. Howard, *Affirming the Touch of God: A Psychological and Philosophical Exploration of Christian Discernment* (Lanham, NJ: University Press of America, 2000), 235–90.

76. Jonathan Edwards, *Religious Affections*, 95.

77. Gelpi, *Committed Worship*, 1:26.

78. This is not to say that feeling more emotions is necessarily better. Gerald May wisely notes that "in some cases people are too fearful to let the feelings come to consciousness, but I also assume it is just not God's way for many people. Romantic passion is but one of many ways of loving God. It may appear dramatic and enticing, but it might not be what love is inviting. Never assume that your spiritual life is less deep or valuable because it seems less colorful than someone else's. Evelyn Underhill, the great twentieth-century student of spiritual passion, put it strongly: 'Do not make the mistake of thinking if you feel cold and dead, that you do not know how to love.' The question is not whether one way is better or more attractive than another. The question is what God is inviting." May, *Awakened Heart*, 175.

79. Griffin, *Turning*, 65.

80. Gelpi, *Conversion Experience*, 33–34.

81. See Wendell Berry, "Getting Along with Nature," in *Home Economics: Fourteen Essays by Wendell Berry* (New York: North Point Press, 1987), 6–20.

82. May discusses this aspect of relationship with God with his characteristic wisdom in May, *Care of Mind, Care of Spirit*, 77–80.

83. For more detail on these dynamics of conversion see Gelpi, *Committed Worship*, 1:33–55.

84. J. Sidlow Baxter, *His Deeper Work in Us: A Further Enquiry Into New Testament Teaching on the Subject of Christian Holiness* (Grand Rapids: Zondervan, 1967), 167. For more on this trend in Protestantism, see Marsden, *Fundamentalism and American Culture*, 72–101. For a contemporary presentation of what the author calls "exchanged life" spirituality, see Kenneth Boa, *Conformed to His Image: Biblical and Practical Approaches to Spiritual Formation* (Grand Rapids: Zondervan, 2001), 110–23.

85. Hootie and the Blowfish, "Deeper Side," on *Hootie and the Blowfish* (Atlantic, 2003).

86. Duck, *Understanding Relationships*, 79–84.

87. I suspect questions of this sort, and the difficulty of resolving them, lie behind some of the "Lordship salvation" debates among Evangelical Protestants. For a summary of this debate, see Demarest, *Cross and Salvation*, 265–70.

88. On intensification, see Rambo, *Understanding Religious Conversion*, 13. On sensitivity to the gaps in relationship with God in the context of spiritual direction, see William A. Barry and William J. Connolly, *The Practice of Spiritual Direction* (New York: Seabury, 1982), 31–45. We will discuss renewal and revival in chapter 12.

89. Suzanne G. Farnham, Joseph P. Gill, and R. Taylor McLean, *Listening Hearts: Discerning Call in Community* (Harrisburg, PA: Morehouse, 1991), 40, quoting Esther de Waal, *Seeking God:*

The Way of St. Benedict (Collegeville, MN: Liturgical Press, 1984), 73.

90. This tool is an adaptation of Gordon Smith's discussion of spiritual autobiography found in Smith, *Beginning Well*, 219–27.

Chapter 8

1. The term *ascesis* ("training," "discipline," from whence we get *asceticism, ascetic*, and such) has been used by the Eastern church and Roman Catholicism, although recent Catholic writings have tended to restrain the use of *asceticism* to avoid negative stereotypical perceptions. The phrase *spiritual disciplines* is more well known in Protestant circles, especially within the past few decades. For the most part, I will use these terms interchangeably. See below in the section on the means of Christian spiritual formation for further discussion.

2. Gordon Smith, *Beginning Well: Christian Conversion and Authentic Transformation* (Downers Grove, IL: InterVarsity Press, 2001), 153.

3. For example, the terms *formation* and *spiritual formation* are not listed in the indexes to the Crossroad three-volume series on Christian spirituality; Oxford University Press's *The Study of Christian Spirituality*; *The Westminster Dictionary of Christian Spirituality*; Frank N. Magill and Ian P. McNeal's review of the Christian classics; Pierre Pourrat's four volume series on the history of Christian spirituality; Richard Woods's *Christian Spirituality: God's Presence Through the Ages*; or Bernard McGinn's volumes on the history of Western Christian mysticism. I did not find these terms in the classic manuals of Adolphe Tanquerey or Joseph de Guibert or in Réginald Garrigou-Lagrange's classic *Christian Perfection and Contemplation*. Neither did I find them in the indexes to the Rules of Augustine or Benedict or to the works of Jean Gerson, Francis of Assisi, or John Wesley. The *New Dictionary of Catholic Spirituality* has a listing under "formation, spiritual," in which it refers the reader to other articles. An important defining essay on spiritual formation is the article by Bernard-Marie Chevignard on "spirituelle formation" in the *Dictionnaire de Spiritualité Ascetique et Mystique*. The primary headings of the present chapter have been drawn from Chevignard's article.

See Ewert Cousins, gen. ed., *World Spirituality: An Encyclopedic History of the Religious Quest*, vols. 16–18 (New York: Crossroad, 1985–89); Cheslyn Jones, Geoffrey Wainwright, Edward Yarnold, eds., *The Study of Christian Spirituality* (Oxford: Oxford University Press, 1986); Gordon S. Wakefield, ed., *The Westminster Dictionary of Christian Spirituality* (Atlanta: The Westminster Press, 1983); Frank N. Magill and Ian P. McGreal, *Christian Spirituality: The Essential Guide to the Most Influential Spiritual Writings of the Christian Tradition* (San Francisco: HarperSanFrancisco, 1988); Pierre Pourrat, *Christian Spirituality*, 4 vols. (Westminister, MD: Newman, 1927–55); Richard Woods, *Christian Spirituality: God's Presence through the Ages* (Chicago: Thomas Moore Press, 1989); Bernard McGinn, *The Foundations of Mysticism: Origins to the Fifth Century*; *The Growth of Mysticism: Gregory the Great through the 12th Century*; and *The Flowering of Mysticism: Men and Women in the New Mysticism, 1200–1350*, vols. 1–3 of The Presence of God: A History of Western Christian Mysticism (New York: Crossroad, 1994–98); Adolphe Tanquerey, *The Spiritual Life: A Treatise on Ascetical and Mystical Theology*, trans. Herman Branderis, 2nd and rev. ed. (Tournai, Belgium: Desclée, 1930); Joseph de Guibert, *The Theology of the Spiritual Life*, trans. Paul Barrett (New York: Sheed and Ward, 1953); Réginald Garrigou-Lagrange, *Christian Perfection and Contemplation, According to St. Thomas Aquinas and St. John of the Cross*. (St. Louis: Herder, 1937); St. Augustine, *The Monastic Rules*, trans. Sister Agatha Mary and Gerald Bonner, The Augustine Series, vol. 4 (Hyde Park, NY: New City Press, 2004); *The Rule of St. Benedict*, trans. Anthony C. Meisel and M. L. de Mastro (New York: Image Doubleday, 1975); Jean Gerson, *Jean Gerson: Early Works*, trans. Brian Patrick McGuire, Classics of Western Spirituality (New York: Paulist Press, 1998); Marion A. Habig, ed., *St. Francis of Assisi, Writings and Early Biographies: English Omnibus of the Sources for the Life of St. Francis* (Chicago: Franciscan Herald Press, 1983); John Wesley, *The Works of John Wesley*, vols. (Peabody, MA: Hendrickson, 1984); "Formation, Spiritual," in *The New Dictionary of Catholic Spirituality*, ed. Michael Downey (Collegeville, MN: Liturgical Press, 1993); Bernard-Marie Chevignard, "Formation, Spirituelle," in the *Dictionnaire de Spiritualité Ascetique et Mystique*, 17 vols. (Paris: Beauchesne, 1964), 5:699–716.

4. John W. Padberg, ed., *The Constitutions of the Society of Jesus and Their Complementary Norms* (St. Louis: Institute of Jesuit Sources, 1996), norms 4.66.1. See also "Decree on Priestly Formation" 4.8, in *The Documents of Vatican II* (New York: Guild Press, 1966).

5. Evan B. Howard, "Three Temptations of Spiritual Formation," *Christianity Today*, December 9, 2002, 46–49. Other similar definitions can also be found in Gerald May, *Care of Mind, Care of Spirit: Psychiatric Dimensions of Spiritual Direction* (San Francisco: Harper and Row, 1983), 6; M. Robert Mulholland Jr., *Invitation to a Journey: A Road Map for Spiritual Formation* (Downers Grove, IL: InterVarsity Press, 1993), 15; Kenneth Boa, *Conformed to His Image: Biblical and Practical Approaches to Spiritual Formation* (Grand Rapids: Zondervan, 2001), 515; Dallas Willard, *Renovation of the Heart: Putting on the Character of Christ* (Colorado Springs: NavPress, 2002), 22.

6. Note also how Paul's use of the aorist tense in Colossians 3, emphasizing the decisive transfer from old to new, is balanced by his use of the present in Romans 8, emphasizing the ongoing nature of Christian transformation. See also the motif of the athletic contest in 1 Corinthians 9:24–27 and elsewhere.

7. By "intentional" and even "aggressive," I do not mean to imply anxious "striving" or "trying." Rather it might be helpful to think of an intentional "willingness" (recall the idea of "yieldedness" from chapter 6) as opposed to a harsh "willfulness." See Gerald G. May, *Will and Spirit: A Contemplative Psychology* (San Francisco: Harper and Row, 1982), 5–7.

8. Note the similarities between these basic principles and Willard's outline of *vision, intention*, and *means* presented in *Renovation of the Heart*.

9. David Lowes Watson, "Methodist Spirituality," in *Exploring Christian Spirituality*, ed. Kenneth J. Collins (Grand Rapids: Baker, 2000), 174–75.

10. A full list of questions can be found in the "Rules of the Band Societies," drawn up December 25, 1738. See John Wesley, "Rules of the Band Societies," in vol. 8, The Works of John Wesley (Peabody, MA: Hendrickson, 1984), 272–73.

11. Watson, "Methodist Spirituality," 176.

12. For the wider context of human formation, see especially the works of Adrian van Kamm. A clear summary of his thought on this matter can be found in Susan Muto, "Formative Spirituality," *Epiphany International* 6, no. 1 (Spring 2000): 8–18.

13. See, for example, Chevignard's division of the contexts (*milieux*) of spiritual formation in Chevignard, "Formation, Spirituelle."

14. Prologue to *The Rule of St. Benedict*, trans. Anthony C. Meisel and M. L. de Mastro (New York: Image Doubleday, 1975), 45.

15. Susanne Johnson, *Christian Spiritual Formation in the Church and Classroom* (Nashville: Abingdon, 1989), 86.

16. See Donald L. Gelpi, *Committed Worship: A Sacramental Theology for Converting Christians*, 2 vols. (Minneapolis: Liturgical Press, 1993), 1:52.

17. Vladimir Lossky, *The Mystical Theology of the Eastern Church* (Crestwood, NY: St. Vladimir's Press, 1998), 171.

18. For a survey of various kinds of formative relationships, see Paul D. Stanley and J. Robert Clinton, *Connecting: The Mentoring Relationships You Need to Succeed in Life* (Colorado Springs: NavPress, 1992). We will address some of these relationships in greater detail in chapter 10.

19. Andrew T. Lincoln, comments on Ephesians 1:11, in *Ephesians*, vol. 42, *Word Biblical Commentary*, CD-ROM (Dallas: Word, 1998), 33.

20. Jonathan Edwards speaks of "the glory of God" as the ultimate aim of human existence and the ground beneath true virtue. See Jonathan Edwards, *Ethical Writings*, ed. Paul Ramsey, vol. 8, Works of Jonathan Edwards (New Haven: Yale University Press, 1989), 399–629. We might also include the term *union* to name the aim of spiritual formation. On union, see Thomas D. McGonigle, "Union, Unitive Way," in *The New Dictionary of Catholic Spirituality*, ed. Michael Downey (Collegeville, MN: Liturgical Press, 1993), 987–88.

21. John Meyendorff, *Byzantine Theology: Historical Trends and Doctrinal Themes* (New York: Fordham University Press, 1979), 165.

22. Kallistos Ware, *How Are We Saved? The Understanding of Salvation in the Orthodox Tradition* (Minneapolis: Light and Life, 1996), 64.

23. See, for example, Irenaeus, preface to book 5 of *Against Heresies*; Athanasius, *On the Incarnation*, chap. 54. For other references see Lossky, *Mystical Theology*, 134.

24. Lossky, *Mystical Theology*, 196.

25. Jonathan Edwards, "Miscellany a: Holiness," in *The "Miscellanies": a–500*, ed. Thomas A. Schafer, vol. 13, Works of Jonathan Edwards (New Haven: Yale University Press, 1994), 163–64.

26. On this, see, for example, Peter Brown's discussion of holiness in the Encratite tradition in Peter Brown, *The Body and Society: Men, Women, and Sexual Renunciation in Early Christianity* (New York: Columbia University Press, 1988), 96–97, and elsewhere. On the personal and political forces involved in the definition

of holiness, especially with regard to sexuality, see Elizabeth A. Clark, *Reading Renunciation: Asceticism and Scripture in Early Christianity* (Princeton: Princeton University Press, 1999); and Susanna Elm, *Virgins of God: The Making of Asceticism in Late Antiquity* (Oxford: Oxford University Press, 1994).

27. See Tanquerey, *The Spiritual Life*; and Garrigou-Lagrange, *Christian Perfection and Contemplation*. Garrigou-Lagrange differed from Tanquerey somewhat in his characterization of mysticism in order to make his point. Nonetheless, it would appear that chap. 5 of the Dogmatic Constitution on the Church of Documents of the Second Vatican Council, entitled "The Call of the Whole Church to Holiness," settled the issue for Roman Catholics in the direction of Garrigou-Lagrange.

28. This question is posed most insightfully in Louis Beirnaert, "Does Sanctification Depend on Psychic Structure?" *Cross Currents* 2 (Winter 1951): 39–43.

29. *Telos* and *teleo* in Greek are translated both "mature" and "perfect" in English.

30. This distinction between different levels of calling to holiness is foreshadowed biblically in Matthew 19:11, 21 and in the early church document *Didache* 6.2 ("For if you can bear the whole yoke of the Lord, you will be perfect; but if you cannot, do what you can"). These, in turn, have become the basis for the "evangelical counsels," or "counsels of perfection," which eventually identified the vows of poverty, chastity, and obedience as possessing special value in forming one toward perfection in Christ.

31. Richard Hays asserts, as one of his three primary focal images to guide New Testament ethics, the theme of community: "Thus, the primary sphere of moral concern is not the character of the character of the individual but the corporate obedience of the church. . . . The coherence of the New Testament's ethical mandate will come into focus only when we understand that mandate in *ecclesial* terms, when we seek God's will not by asking first, 'What should *I* do,' but 'What should *we* do?'" Richard B. Hays, *The Moral Vision of the New Testament: Community, Cross, New Creation* (San Francisco: HarperSanFrancisco, 1996), 196–97.

32. J. Heinrich Arnold, *Discipleship*, comp. and ed. the Hutterian Brethren (Farmington, PA: Plough Publishing House, 1994), 272–73.

33. Howard A. Snyder, *The Community of the King* (Downers Grove, IL: InterVarsity Press, 1977), 96. The kingdom of God is not to be identified with the church. "The Church is the community of the Kingdom but never the Kingdom itself." George Eldon Ladd, *A Theology of the New Testament* (Grand Rapids: Eerdmans, 1974), 111. Rather the church is the community of the King, and members of this community act as the primary subjects and agents of the kingdom; a kingdom that reaches beyond the boundaries of these subjects and agents.

34. This aspect of the realm of God as realized through corporate spiritual formation is discussed in Johnson, *Christian Spiritual Formation*, 43–54.

35. This tension of relationship to mystery and formation can be sensed in the differences between mystery-oriented spiritual direction as it has developed in the past twenty years and the practice of goal- or increase-oriented "coaching" as it is being applied to spiritual formation. The

tension between mastery and Mystery is to be maintained.

36. Bernard of Clairvaux, "On Loving God," in *Bernard of Clairvaux: Selected Works*, trans. G. R. Evans, Classics of Western Spirituality (New York: Paulist Press, 1987), 292–97.

37. Bengt Hoffman, ed., *The Theologia Germanica of Martin Luther*, Classics of Western Spirituality (New York: Paulist Press, 1980), 113.

38. William James, *The Varieties of Religious Experience* in *William James: Writings (1902–1910)* (New York: Library Classics of the United States, 1997), 272. He explores these motives in a survey of case studies.

39. Tanquerey, *The Spiritual Life*, no. 349, p. 174.

40. Boa, *Conformed to His Image*, 125–50.

41. Emilio Castro, "Your Kingdom Come: A Missionary Perspective," in *Your Kingdom Come, Mission Perspectives: Report on the World Conference on Mission and Evangelism* (Geneva: World Council of Churches, 1980), 29.

42. These are outlined in John of the Cross's *Ascent of Mount Carmel* and *Dark Night of the Soul*. See John of the Cross, *The Collected Works of John of the Cross*, trans. Kieran Kavanaugh and Otilio Rodriguez (Washington, DC: Institute of Carmelite Studies, 1979).

43. Dallas Willard, *The Spirit of the Disciplines: Understanding How God Changes Lives* (San Francisco: Harper and Row, 1988), 156–92.

44. Robert Wuthnow, *After Heaven: Spirituality in America since the 1950s* (Berkeley and Los Angeles: University of California Press, 1998), 169.

45. Walter Brueggemann, *Theology of the Old Testament: Testimony, Dispute, Advocacy* (Minneapolis: Fortress, 1997), 701 (italics in original). The notion of spirituality as embodied practice has become increasingly popular, especially in light of the influence of the thought of anthropologist Clifford Geertz. See especially Clifford Geertz, *The Interpretation of Cultures: Selected Essays* (New York: Basic, 1973).

46. Saint Theophan the Recluse, *The Path to Salvation: A Manual of Spiritual Transformation*, trans. Fr. Seraphim Rose (Platina, CA: St. Herman Press, 1998), 317. On healing of hindrances to spiritual formation, see Leanne Payne, *Restoring the Christian Soul: Overcoming Barriers to Completion in Christ through Healing Prayer* (Grand Rapids: Baker, 1991).

47. Willard, *Renovation of the Heart*, 93. See also Boa, *Conformed to His Image*, 202, and Boa's treatment of the "quadrants" of relationship with God (comprehending our life of prayer, Bible study, and our image of God), relationship with self (our inner life, our hobbies and such, and our image of self), relationship with the body (church, family, ministry), and relationship with the world (the things, people, and systems of the world).

48. Brueggemann, *Theology of the Old Testament*, 568.

49. John Wesley, "The Means of Grace," in vol. 5, *The Works of John Wesley* (Peabody, MA: Hendrickson Publishers, 1984), 187.

50. John Wesley, "Minutes of Several Conversations between the Rev. Mr. John Wesley and Others," in vol. 8, *The Works of John Wesley* (Peabody, MA: Hendrickson Publishers, 1984), 322–24. Compare Wesley's list with the summary of American Puritan devotional practices in Charles Hambrick-Stowe, *The Practice of Piety: Puritan Devotional Disciplines in Sev-

enteenth-Century New England* (Chapel Hill: University of North Carolina Press, 1982).

51. See also Dallas Willard, who speaks of a "golden triangle" of spiritual growth: the action of the Holy Spirit, ordinary events of life, and planned disciplines. See Dallas Willard, *The Divine Conspiracy: Rediscovering Our Hidden Life in God* (San Francisco: HarperSanFrancisco, 1998), 347–64.

52. Johannes Tauler, *Johannes Tauler: Sermons*, trans. Maria Shrady, Classics of Western Spirituality (New York: Paulist Press, 1985), 80.

53. Note that the most common prayer addressed to the Holy Spirit in the history of liturgy is *Veni Sanctus Spiritus*, "Come, Holy Spirit."

54. Philip Yancey, *Where Is God When It Hurts* (Grand Rapids: Zondervan, 1990), 146.

55. For this exercise, see, for example, Jeremy Taylor, *Holy Living and Holy Dying*, in *Jeremy Taylor: Selected Works*, ed Thomas K. Carroll, Classics of Western Spirituality (New York: Paulist Press, 1990), 486–94.

56. Diodochus of Photike, "On Spiritual Knowledge and Discrimination: One Hundred Texts," no. 94, in *The Philokalia: The Complete Text*, compiled by Saint Nikodimos of the Holy Mountain and Saint Makarios of Corinth, trans. G. E. H. Palmer, Philip Sherrard, and Kallistos Ware (London: Faber and Faber, 1979), 1:291.

57. See Catherine of Siena, *Catherine of Siena: The Dialogue*, trans. Suzanne Noffke, Classics of Western Spirituality (New York: Paulist Press, 1980), dialogue 12, p. 46.

58. Alexander Carmichael, ed., *Carmina Gadelica* (Edinburgh: Floris Books, 1992), 333; *Celtic Spirituality*, trans. Oliver Davies, Classics of Western Spirituality (New York: Paulist Press, 1999), and many other titles document historic Celtic blessings or give similar blessings in a Celtic fashion.

59. See the "Practicing Christian Spirituality" exercise at the end of chapter 5.

60. See, for example, Matthew 13:21–22; Mark 13:13; Luke 9:62; 21:19, 36; Acts 11:22–23; 20:24; 1 Corinthians 1:8; 11:2; 15:2; Galatians 1:6; 1 Thessalonians 3:2; 2 Thessalonians 1:4; 2:15; 3:4; Hebrews 10:35–39; James 1:12; Revelation 2:2–19.

61. Johnson, *Christian Spiritual Formation*, 121–35. I will use Johnson's general outline, adding my own perspective here and there.

62. Ibid., 124.

63. Ibid., 132, 133.

64. Willard, *Spirit of the Disciplines*, 68, italics added. Willard is here giving a definition of "the spiritual disciplines." Similarly, *The New Dictionary of Catholic Spirituality* defines *asceticism* as "a training program that conditions individuals for the attainment of a spiritual goal," as " the willingness to make whatever efforts are necessary to fulfill God's will, no matter what the cost, so that at the end of life the Christian may join St. Paul in saying, 'I have competed well, I have finished the race, I have kept the faith' (2 Tim 4:7).'" See Kenneth C. Russell, "Asceticism," in *The New Dictionary of Catholic Spirituality*, ed. Michael Downey (Collegeville, MN: Liturgical Press, 1993), 63–65. See also Orthodox theologian Kallistos Ware's discussion of the essence of asceticism in Kallistos Ware, "The Way of the Ascetics: Negative or Affirmative," in *Asceticism*, ed. Vincent L. Wimbush and Richard Valantasis (New York: Oxford University

Press, 1995), 3–15. The definition of *asceticism* has come under intense scrutiny recently. For a range of perspectives on this discussion see, for example, Walter O. Kaelber, "Asceticism," in *The Encyclopedia of Religion*, ed. Mircea Eliade (New York: Macmillan, 1986), 441–45; Elizabeth A. Clark, "The Ascetic Impulse in Religious Life: A General Response," in *Asceticism*, ed. Vincent L. Wimbush and Richard Valantasis (New York: Oxford University Press, 1995), 505–12; Richard Valantasis, "Constructions of Power in Asceticism," *Journal of the American Academy of Religion* 63, no. 4 (Winter 1995): 775–821; Anthony J. Saldarini, "Asceticism in the Gospel of Matthew," in *Asceticism and the New Testament*, ed. Leif E. Vaage and Vincent L. Wimbush (New York: Routledge, 1999), 11–28; and David Rensberger, "Asceticism in the Gospel of John," in *Asceticism and the New Testament*, ed. Leif E. Vaage and Vincent L. Wimbush (New York: Routledge, 1999), 127–48.

65. John Climacus, *John Climacus: The Ladder of Divine Ascent*, trans. Colm Luibheid and Norman Russell, Classics of Western Spirituality (New York: Paulist Press, 1982), step 8, p. 150.

66. See, for example, the discussion of the Encratites in Giulia Sfameni Gasparro, "Asceticism and Anthropology: *Encrateia* and 'Double Creation' in Early Christianity," in *Asceticism*, ed. Vincent L. Wimbush and Richard Valantasis (New York: Oxford University Press, 1995), 127–46; and the canons from the council of Gangra (ca. 355) in O. Larry Yarbrough, "Canons from the Council of Gangra," in *Ascetic Behavior in Graeco-Roman Antiquity: A Sourcebook*, ed. Vincent L. Wimbush (Minneapolis: Fortress, 1990), 448–55.

67. Discussion of asceticism has tended to vacillate between looking at ascetical practice in terms of facilitating transformation of the individual and seeing asceticism in terms of expressing a transformed society. See, for example, discussion concerning the backgrounds and origins of Christian asceticism in Derwas J. Chitty, *The Desert a City: An Introduction to the Study of Egyptian and Palestinian Monasticism under the Christian Empire* (Crestwood, NY: St. Vladimir's Seminary Press, 1966); Brown, *Body and Society*; Vincent L. Wimbush, ed., *Ascetic Behavior in Graeco-Roman Antiquity: A Sourcebook* (Minneapolis: Fortress, 1990); Vincent L. Wimbush and Richard Valantasis, eds., *Asceticism* (New York: Oxford University Press, 1995); Leif E. Vaage and Vincent L. Wimbush, *Asceticism and the New Testament* (New York: Routledge, 1999); James E. Goehring, *Ascetics, Society, and the Desert: Studies in Early Egyptian Monasticism* (Harrisburg, PA: Trinity Press International, 1999).

68. For example, concerning the significance of food for medieval women, see Caroline Walker Bynum, *Holy Feast and Holy Fast: The Religious Significance of Food to Medieval Women* (Berkeley and Los Angeles: University of California Press, 1987); on the adaptations of the ascetic tradition in the Reformation period, see Kenneth Ronald Davis, *Anabaptism and Asceticism: A Study in Intellectual Origins*, Studies in Anabaptist and Mennonite History (Scottsdale, PA: Herald Press, 1974). With the understanding of the fivefold web of relationships presented in this text, it is possible to see ascetical practice exploring change in relationships with the spiritual forces, others, self, God, and nature simultaneously.

69. John Cassian, "On the Holy Fathers of Sketis and on Discrimination," in *The Philokalia: The Complete Text*, comp. Saint Nikodimos of the Holy Mountain and Saint Makarios of Corinth, trans. G. E. H. Palmer, Philip Sherrard, and Kallistos Ware (London: Faber and Faber, 1979), 1:96.

70. Margaret R. Miles, *Fullness of Life: Historical Foundations for a New Asceticism* (Eugene, OR: Wipf and Stock, 2000), 135–54.

71. On functional asceticism, see Donald L. Gelpi, *Functional Asceticism: A Guideline for American Religious* (New York: Sheed and Ward, 1966).

72. Lorenzo Scupoli, *Unseen Warfare: The Spiritual Combat and Path to Paradise of Lorenzo Scupoli Edited by Nicodemus of the Holy Mountain and Revised by Theophan the Recluse*, trans. E. Kadloubovsky and G. E. H. Palmer (Crestwood, NY: St. Vladimir's Seminary Press, 1987), 105.

73. Antony Flew, ed., *A Dictionary of Philosophy* (New York: St. Martin's Press, 1979), 128.

74. John Piper, *Desiring God: Meditations of a Christian Hedonist* (Sisters, OR: Multnomah, 1996).

75. Ibid., 33–50.

76. Ibid., 69–70.

77. Ibid., 119.

78. See John Piper, *Future Grace: The Purifying Power of Living by Faith in Future Grace* (Sisters, OR: Multnomah, 1995).

79. Ibid., 227.

80. Although asceticism has been explored historically, anthropologically, and more recently, biblically, there is little recent psychological research on the topic. While mysticism has received a great deal of attention, asceticism is not indexed in *The Psychology of Religion: An Empirical Approach*, in the massive *Handbook of Religious Experience*, or many other texts in psychology or psychology of religion. A key-word search through the PsychInfo database under "ascetic*" yielded no results. See Bruce Hunsberger, and Richard Gorsuch, eds., *The Psychology of Religion: An Empirical Approach*, 2nd ed. (New York: Guilford, 1996); and Ralph W. Hood Jr., ed., *Handbook of Religious Experience* (Birmingham: Religious Education Press, 1995). Paul Pruyser, in *A Dynamic Psychology of Religion*, presents a chapter exploring how religious attitudes toward such things as possessions, time and space, work and play, authority, and such function in human emotion and cognition. See Paul Pruyser, *A Dynamic Psychology of Religion* (New York: Harper and Row, 1968). It appears that while scholarship has followed William James's lead in the exploration of the psychology of mysticism, it has not followed his lead in matters of asceticism. James encouraged that "a more careful consideration of the whole matter, distinguishing between the general good intention of asceticism and the uselessness of some of the particular acts of which it may be guilty, ought to rehabilitate it in our esteem." James, *Varieties of Religious Experience*, 329; see also 251, 272–84, 327–31.

81. Thus Edith Wyschogrod speaks of culturally shaped "epistemes" that condition the conceptual frameworks within which ascetical practice is conceived. Edith Wyschogrod, "The Howl of Oedipus, the Cry of Héloïse: From Asceticism to Postmodern Ethics," in *Asceticism*, ed. Vincent L. Wimbush and Richard Valantasis (New York: Oxford University Press,

1995), 16–30. Walter O. Kaelber speaks factors that affect the ascetic's "vision of wholeness, plenitude, and perfection." Walter O. Kaelber, "Understanding Asceticism: Testing a Typology," in *Asceticism*, ed. Vincent L. Wimbush and Richard Valantasis (New York: Oxford University Press, 1995), 321–22.

82. Benedicta Ward, trans., *The Sayings of the Desert Fathers: The Alphabetical Collection* (Kalamazoo, MI: Cistercian Publishers, 1975), 139.

83. Gerald May, *The Awakened Heart: Opening Yourself to the Love You Need* (San Francisco: HarperSanFrancisco, 1991), 106–7.

84. In Elizabeth A. Castilli, "Pseudo-Athanasius: Life and Activity of Syncletica," in *Ascetic Behavior in Graeco-Roman Antiquity: A Sourcebook*, ed. Vincent L. Wimbush (Minneapolis: Fortress, 1990), 302.

Chapter 9

1. See Origen, *On Prayer*, 14.2; John Cassian, *Conferences*, 9.9; Tertullian, *On Prayer*, chaps. 2–8; and Athanasius, *Letter to Marcellinus on the Interpretation of the Psalms*. For a review of this history, see Simon Tugwell, "Thomas Aquinas: Introduction," in Albert the Great and Thomas Aquinas, *Albert and Thomas: Selected Writings*, trans. and ed. Simon Tugwell, Classics of Western Spirituality (New York: Paulist Press, 1988), 273–78.

2. Bill Bright, *The Four Spiritual Laws* (San Bernardino, CA: Campus Crusade for Christ International, 1965), 10.

3. Saint Theophan the Recluse in Igumen Chariton, comp., *The Art of Prayer: An Orthodox Anthology*, trans. E. Kadloubavsky and E. M. Palmer (London: Faber and Faber, 1966), 53.

4. Adapted from Evan B. Howard, *Praying the Scriptures: A Field Guide for Your Spiritual Journey* (Downers Grove, IL: InterVarsity Press, 1999), 26–32, 111–12.

5. Saint Theophan the Recluse, in Chariton, comp., *The Art of Prayer*, 23.

6. Walter Hilton, *Walter Hilton: The Scale of Perfection*, trans. John P. H. Clark and Rosemary Dorward, Classics of Western Spirituality (Mahwah, NJ: Paulist Press, 1991), bk. 1, secs. 27–31.

7. For greater detail, see the standard treatments of the history of spirituality in, for example, Bradley Holt, *Thirsty for God: A Brief History of Christian Spirituality* (Minneapolis: Augsburg, 1993); Gordon Mursell, ed., *The Story of Christian Spirituality: Two Thousand Years from East to West* (Minneapolis: Fortress, 2001); Cheslyn Jones, Geoffrey Wainwright, and Edward Yarnold, eds., *The Study of Spirituality*, rev. ed. (New York: Oxford University Press, 1986); and the three volumes on Christian spirituality in Crossroad's World Spirituality series. See Ewert Cousins, gen. ed., *World Spirituality: An Encyclopedic History of the Religious Quest*, vols. 16–18 (New York: Crossroad, 1987–91). Bernard McGinn specifically addresses the history of mystical prayer (into the fourteenth century thus far) in his series The Presence of God: A History of Western Christian Mysticism; see Bernard McGinn, *The Foundations of Mysticism: Origins to the Fifth Century*; *The Growth of Mysticism: Gregory the Great through the 12th Century*; *The Flowering of Mysticism: Men and*

Women in the New Mysticism, 1200–1350; and *The Harvest of Mysticism in Medieval Germany*, vols. 1–4 of *The Presence of God: A History of Western Christian Mysticism* (New York: Crossroad, 1991–2005). For a brief history of contemplative prayer in the Roman Catholic tradition, see Thomas Keating, "Contemplative Prayer in the Christian Tradition," in *Finding Grace at the Center: The Beginning of Centering Prayer*, by M. Basil Pennington, Thomas Keating, and Thomas E. Clarke (Petersham, MA: St. Bede's Publications, 1985), 35–47.

8. McGinn, *Foundations of Mysticism*, 131.

9. See the section in chapter 4 regarding the way of negation for more on the apophatic approach to God.

10. A number of editions of these works are available. See, for example, Origen, *Origen: An Exhortation to Martyrdom; Prayer; First Principles: Book IV; Prologue to the Commentary on the Song of Songs; Homily XXVII on Numbers*, trans. Rowan A. Greer, Classics of Western Spirituality (New York: Paulist Press, 1979); Augustine, *On Genesis: A Refutation of the Manichees; Unfinished Literal Commentary on Genesis; The Literal Meaning of Genesis*, trans. Edmund Hill, The Works of Saint Augustine: A Translation for the 21st Century (Hyde Park, NY: New City Press, 2002); Pseudo-Dionysius, *The Mystical Theology*, in *Pseudo-Dionysius: The Complete Works*, trans. Colm Luibheid, Classics of Western Spirituality (New York: Paulist Press, 1987), 133–42; and Bernard of Clairvaux, *Bernard of Clairvaux: Selected Works*, trans. G. R. Evans, Classics of Western Spirituality (New York: Paulist Press, 1987).

11. Thus the title of McGinn's *The Flowering of Mysticism: Men and Women in the New Mysticism, 1200–1350*.

12. See Albert the Great and Thomas Aquinas, *Albert and Thomas: Selected Writings*, Classics of Western Spirituality (New York: Paulist Press, 1988); and Bonaventure, *Bonaventure: The Soul's Journey into God; The Tree of Life; The Life of St. Francis*, trans. Ewert Cousins, Classics of Western Spirituality (New York: Paulist Press, 1978).

13. Key works of each of these figures may be found in the Classics of Western Spirituality series (published by Paulist), with the exception of Thomas á Kempis, whose classic *The Imitation of Christ* can be found in numerous editions. See also the volume on *devotio moderna* in the Classics of Western Spirituality series.

14. Richard Kieckhefer, "Major Currents in Late Medieval Devotion," in *Christian Spirituality: High Middle Ages and Reformation*, ed. Jill Raitt, Bernard McGinn, and John Meyendorff (New York: Crossroad, 1987), 75.

15. For an example of a Puritan work, see Richard Baxter, *The Saint's Everlasting Rest*, in *The Doubleday Devotional Classics*, ed. E. Glen Hinson (Garden City, NY: Doubleday, 1978), 1:1–196. For an example of a Pietist work, see Johann Arndt, *True Christianity*, in Johann Arndt, *True Christianity: A Treatise on Sincere Repentance, True Faith, the Holy Walk of the True Christian, Etc.*, trans. A. W. Boehm (Philadelphia: General Council Publication House, 1910), bk. 2, chap. 34, pp. 269–85.

16. For example, one might consider the twenty-four-hour "prayer watch" of the Pietist community at Hernhutt. See also Jonathan Edwards, *An Humble Attempt to Promote Explicit Agreement and Visible Union of God's People in Extraordinary Prayer for the Revival of Religion*,

in Jonathan Edwards, *Apocalyptic Writings*, ed. Stephen J. Stein, vol. 5, The Works of Jonathan Edwards (New Haven: Yale University Press, 1980), 307–436.

17. Again, each of these figures are represented in the Classics of Western Spirituality series with the exception of Madame Guyon, Francis Fenelon, and Brother Lawrence, whose central works are available in a number of editions.

18. See, for example, Tikhon of Zadonsk, *Journey to Heaven: Counsels on the Particular Duties of Every Christian*, trans. George D. Lardas (Jordanville, NY: Holy Trinity Monastery, 1991); and Helen Kontzevitch, *Saint Seraphim: Wonderworker of Sarov and His Spiritual Inheritance*, trans. St. Xenia Skete (Wildwood, CA: St. Xenia Skete, 2004).

19. Key figures regarding prayer during this period might include Theophan the Recluse, Andrew Murray, R. Garrigou-Lagrange, Karl Barth, John Baillie, Thomas Merton, and Vladimir Lossky, though many others could be mentioned. For a survey of Pentecostal teaching regarding tongues, see Gary McGee, ed., *Initial Evidence: Historical and Biblical Perspectives on the Pentecostal Doctrine of Spirit Baptism* (Peabody, MA: Hendrickson, 1991).

20. Daniel Wolpert, *Creating a Life with God: The Call of Ancient Prayer Practices* (Nashville: Upper Room Books, 2003), 20.

21. See, for example, Richard Foster, *Prayer: Finding the Heart's True Home* (San Francisco: HarperSanFrancisco, 1992); Anthony de Mello, *Sadhana, a Way to God: Christian Exercises in Eastern Form* (Garden City, NY: Image Doubleday, 1984); Wolpert, *Creating a Life with God*; and Chariton, comp., *Art of Prayer*.

22. On time, place, and posture, see, for example, Mark Link, *You: Prayer for Beginners and Those Who Have Forgotten How* (Niles, IL: Argus Communications, 1976); and Gabriel Bunge, *Earthen Vessels: The Practice of Personal Prayer According to the Patristic Tradition* (San Francisco: Ignatius, 2002).

23. Oliver Davies, trans., *Celtic Spirituality* (New York: Paulist Press, 1999), 314.

24. C. S. Lewis, *Letters to Malcolm Chiefly on Prayer: Reflections on the Intimate Dialogue between Man and God* (San Diego: Harcourt, 1964), 75.

25. See, for example, Ronald L. Grimes, *Beginnings in Ritual Studies* (Lanham, MD: University Press of America, 1982); Catherine Bell, *Ritual: Perspectives and Dimensions* (New York: Oxford University Press, 1997), 267; Mark Searle, "Ritual," in *The Study of Liturgy*, ed. Cheslyn Jones, Geoffrey Wainwright, Edward Yarnold, and Paul Bradshaw, rev. ed. (New York: Oxford University Press, 1992), 51–58; and Kevin W. Irwin, *Liturgy, Prayer, and Spirituality* (New York: Paulist Press, 1984), 15.

26. Irwin, *Liturgy, Prayer and Spirituality*, 272; see 258–72.

27. Daniel E. Albrecht, *Rites in the Spirit: A Ritual Approach to Pentecostal/Charismatic Spirituality*, Journal of Pentecostal Theology Supplement Series (Sheffield, UK: Sheffield Academic Press, 1999), 238; see 218–51.

28. See, for example, Rosalind Rinker, *How to Have Family Prayers* (Grand Rapids: Zondervan Publishers, 1977); David Robinson, *The Christian Family Toolbox: 52 Benedictine Activities for the Home* (New York: Crossroad, 2001); Jeffrey Arnold, *The Big Book on Small*

Groups (Downers Grove, IL: InterVarsity Press, 1992), 147–60.

29. Meditation can even be somewhat vocal, as our thought wanders around a phrase that we repeat again and again. The biblical words for meditation express this idea of muttering or quietly repeating. Consider the Hebrew practice of memorization, which incorporates reflection on meaning as well as the mere repetition of words.

30. A Monk of the Eastern Church, *The Jesus Prayer*, rev. ed. (Crestwood, NY: St. Vladimir's Seminary Press, 1997), 93, 94. A common-prayer use of repetition can be found, for example, in the ninth-hour prayer of the Orthodox monastic prayer book. Here the phrase *Lord, have mercy* is repeated forty times. See *The Great Horologion: Or Book of Hours*, trans. Holy Transfiguration Monastery (Brookline, MA: Holy Transfiguration Monastery, 1997), 170, and elsewhere. For a brief introduction to the Jesus Prayer, see Irma Zaleski, *Living the Jesus Prayer* (New York: Novalis Continuum, 2003); and Kallistos Ware, *The Power of the Name: The Jesus Prayer in Orthodox Spirituality* (Oxford: SLG Press, 1986).

31. See, for example, Thomas Keating, *Open Mind, Open Heart: The Contemplative Dimension of the Gospel* (New York: Continuum, 1998).

32. See Lawrence S. Cunningham, *Catholic Prayer* (New York: Crossroad, 1992), 49–68; Jane E. Vennard, *Praying with Body and Soul: A Way to Intimacy with God* (Minneapolis: Fortress, 1998); and Rodney Clapp, *Tortured Wonders: Christian Spirituality for People, Not Angels* (Grand Rapids: Brazos, 2004).

33. A well-known introduction to the use of imagination in meditation is Morton T. Kelsey, *The Other Side of Silence: A Guide to Christian Meditation* (New York: Paulist Press, 1976). For the theology of icons in the Orthodox tradition, see Leonid Ouspensky and Vladimir Lossky, *The Meaning of Icons*, trans. G. E. H Palmer and E. Kadloubovsky (Crestwood, NY: St. Vladimir's Press, 1999).

34. A Monk of the Eastern Church, "The Essentials of Orthodox Spirituality," in *Exploring Christian Spirituality*, ed. Kenneth J. Collins (Grand Rapids: Baker, 2000), 112. See also Bernard McGinn's description of the "practical meaning of silence" in Bernard McGinn, *Growth of Mysticism*, 131. For an account of something close from Methodist history, see John Wesley, "A Plain Account of Christian Perfection," in vol. 11 of The Works of John Wesley (Peabody, MA: Hendrickson, 1984), 412.

35. Bishop Ignatii, in Chariton, *Art of Prayer*, 104.

36. See, for example, the treatment on disturbed prayer in Kenneth Leech, *Soul Friend: The Practice of Christian Spirituality* (San Francisco: Harper and Row, 1977), 181–84. Augustine gives a delightful confession of his own distractions in Augustine, *The Confessions*, trans. Henry Chadwick (Oxford: Oxford University Press, 1991), 10.35, p. 57.

37. See the treatment in Ann Ulanov and Barry Ulanov, *Primary Speech: A Psychology of Prayer* (Atlanta: John Knox, 1982), 27–43.

38. See, for example, David Hansen, *Long Wandering Prayer: An Invitation to Walk with God* (Downers Grove, IL: InterVarsity Press, 2001).

39. See the summary of Bishop Ignatii Brianchaninov of Russia (1807–67), in Chariton, comp., *Art of Prayer*, 188.

40. Martin Luther, *Devotional Writings II*, ed. Jaroslav Pelikan, Hilton C. Oswald, and Helmut T. Lehmann, vol. 43, Luther's Works (Philadelphia: Fortress, 1999), 200.

41. Jan Johnson, *When the Soul Listens: Finding Rest and Direction in Contemplative Prayer* (Colorado Springs: NavPress, 1999), 95.

42. Julian of Norwich, *Showings*, trans. Edmund Colledge and James Walsh, Classics of Western Spirituality (New York: Paulist Press, 1978), short text, chap. 19, p. 157. Similarly, author Eugene Peterson titles his book on the Psalms *Answering God*. See Eugene Peterson, *Answering God: The Psalms as Tools for Prayer* (San Francisco: HarperSanFrancisco, 1989).

43. For this pattern, see Patrick D. Miller, *They Cried to the Lord: The Form and Theology of Biblical Prayer* (Minneapolis: Fortress, 1994), 3, 55–232.

44. Karl Barth, *Prayer*, trans. Sara F. Terrien, 50th anniv. ed. (Louisville: Westminster John Knox, 2002), 26.

45. See, for example, John Shelby Spong, *Why Christianity Must Change or Die: A Bishop Speaks to Believers in Exile* (San Francisco: HarperSanFrancisco, 1998), 139, 140.

46. Andrew Murray brings together the biblical or theological and the personal (as well as bringing together our posture of life and our posture of prayer) in his encouragement that "when we pray thus" (as one who lives as a child to a Father, as one who lives as a friend to God), we can expect the responses of a Father to a child or a Friend to a friend. See Andrew Murray, *With Christ in the School of Prayer* (Old Tappan, NJ: Fleming H. Revell, 1965), 37, 47.

47. For an examination of ten different approaches to the relationship between our understanding of God's sovereignty and petitionary prayer, see Terrance Tiessen, *Providence and Prayer: How Does God Work in the World?* (Downers Grove, IL: InterVarsity Press, 2000).

48. See Lewis, *Letters to Malcolm*, 77–82.

49. *Apostolic Faith*, May 1907, p. 3, as quoted in Douglas J. Nelson, "For Such a Time as This: The Story of Bishop William J. Seymour and the Azuza Street Revival" (PhD diss., University of Birmingham, England, 1981), 226–27; and cited in Richard Foster, *Streams of Living Water: Celebrating the Great Traditions of Christian Faith* (San Francisco: HarperSanFrancisco, 1998), 393.

50. Take, for example, C. S. Lewis's approach to seeing pleasures—*every* pleasure—as "shafts of glory striking our sensibilities." See Lewis, *Letters to Malcolm*, 88–93.

51. See, for example, Thomas Merton, *Contemplative Prayer* (New York: Doubleday, 1996); William A. Barry and William J. Connolly, *The Practice of Spiritual Direction* (New York: Seabury, 1982), 46–64; Walter J. Burghardt, "Contemplation: A Long, Loving Look at the Real," *Church*, Winter 1989, 14–18; Douglas Burton-Christie, "Learning to See: Epiphany in the Ordinary," *Weavings* 11, no. 6 (November–December 1996): 6–16; and Johnson, *When the Soul Listens*.

52. For a variety of treatments, see Augustine, *On Genesis*, 12; John of the Cross, *The Ascent of Mount Carmel*, in *The Collected Works of John of the Cross*, trans. Kieran Kavanaugh and Otilio Rodriguez (Washington, DC: Institute of Carmelite Studies, 1979), bk. 2; and Jonathan Edwards, *Religious Affections*, ed. J. E. Smith,

vol. 2, The Works of Jonathan Edwards (New Haven: Yale University Press, 1959).

53. See Ken Gire, *Windows of the Soul: Experiencing God in New Ways* (Grand Rapids: Zondervan, 1996).

54. Ronald Rolheiser, *The Shattered Lantern: Rediscovering a Felt Presence of God* (New York: Crossroad, 2001), 204.

55. See the review of Karl Barth's writings on the Lord's Prayer in Donald K. McKim, "Karl Barth on the Lord's Prayer," in Karl Barth, *Prayer*, trans. by Sara F. Terrien, 50th anniv. ed. (Louisville: Westminster John Knox, 2002), 114–34.

56. See, for example, the discussions in Chariton, comp., *Art of Prayer*, and in Saint Theophan the Recluse, *The Path to Salvation: A Manual of Spiritual Transformation*, trans. Fr. Seraphim Rose (Platina, CA: St. Herman Press, 1998).

57. See, for example, Edwards, *An Humble Attempt*; and David Bryant, *Concerts of Prayer: Christians Join for Spiritual Awakening and World Evangelism* (Ventura, CA: Regal Books, 1984).

58. Barry and Connolly, *Practice of Spiritual Direction*, 82.

59. See ibid., 81–83; and Gerald May, *Care of Mind, Care of Spirit: Psychiatric Dimensions of Spiritual Direction* (San Francisco: Harper and Row, 1983), 74–76.

60. See May, *Care of Mind*, 70–77.

61. Barry and Connolly, *Practice of Spiritual Direction*, 89.

62. These (and more) are treated in texts on discernment and spiritual direction. See, for example, Benedicta Ward, trans., *The Sayings of the Desert Fathers: The Alphabetical Collection* (Kalamazoo, MI: Cistercian Publishers, 1975); Ignatius of Loyola, *Spiritual Exercises*, in *Ignatius of Loyola: The Spiritual Exercises and Selected Works*, ed. George E. Ganss, Classics of Western Spirituality (New York: Paulist Press, 1991), 113–214; Edwards, *Religious Affections*; and Leech, *Soul Friend*, 168–73. On sexuality in spiritual direction, see Samuel Hamilton-Poore, "The Given and the Gift: Sexuality and God's Eros in Direction and Supervision," in *Supervision of Spiritual Directors: Engaging in Holy Mystery*, ed. Mary Rose Bumpus and Rebecca Bradburn Langer (Harrisburg, PA: Morehouse, 2005), 83–103.

63. Steve Duck, *Understanding Relationships* (New York: Guilford, 1991), 123.

64. Barth, *Prayer*, 13.

65. David G. Myers, "Is Prayer Clinically Effective?" *Reformed Review* 53, no. 2 (2000): 95–102. See also the early chapters of Tiessen, *Providence and Prayer*.

66. See Roland Fischer, "A Cartography of Understanding Mysticism," *Science*, November 26, 1971, 897–904, and fig. 9.3.

67. See, for example, Virginia Ross, "The Transcendent Function of the Bilateral Brain," *Zygon* 21, no. 2 (June 1986): 233–46; and Colwyn Travarthen, "Brain Science and the Human Spirit," *Zygon* 21, no. 2 (June 1986): 161–200.

68. Theophan the Recluse, in Chariton, comp., *Art of Prayer*, 94.

69. Jack W. Hayford, *Prayer Is Invading the Impossible* (New York: Ballantine, 1983), 103–12.

70. Teresa of Avila, *The Book of Her Life*, in *The Collected Works of St. Teresa of Avila*, vol. 1, trans. Kieran Kavanaugh and Otilio Rodriguez

(Washington, DC: Institute of Carmelite Studies, 1976), 81, 97, 108, 116.

71. Greg Easterbrook, "Can You Pray Your Way to Health?" http://www.beliefnet.com/story/69/story_6991_4.html.

72. See, for example, John R. Finney and H. Newton Maloney Jr., "Empirical Studies of Christian Prayer: A Review of the Literature," *Journal of Psychology and Theology* 13, no. 2 (1985): 104–15; Stephen Kiesling and T. George Harris, "The Prayer War," *Psychology Today* 23, no. 10 (October 1989): 65–66; David G. Myers, "On Assessing Prayer, Faith, and Health," *Reformed Review* 23, no. 2 (2000): 119–26; Claudia Kalb, "Faith and Healing," *Newsweek*, November 10, 2003, 44–56.

73. On *govenie*, see Theophan the Recluse, *Path to Salvation*, 244, 269–79. Theophan imagines here a seasonal rhythm, with the great fasts as the times of preparation for confession. Yet the same can be accomplished in a weekly rhythm—striving through the week, self-examination and confession on Friday or Saturday, and Eucharist on Sunday.

74. Guigo II, "The Ladder of Monks: A Letter on the Contemplative Life," in *The Ladder of Monks and Twelve Meditations*, trans. Edmund Colledge and James Walsh, vol. 48, Cistercian Studies Series (Kalamazoo, MI: Cistercian Publications, 1979), 68, 74.

75. Bernard of Clairvaux, "Sermon 2 on the Song of Songs," in Bernard of Clairvaux, *Selected Works*, 216.

76. Examples can be found in Gregory of Nyssa, *Gregory of Nyssa: The Life of Moses*, trans. Abraham J. Malherbe and Everett Ferguson, Classics of Western Spirituality (New York: Paulist Press, 1978); Pseudo-Dionysius, *Mystical Theology*; *The Cloud of Unknowing*, ed. James Walsh, Classics of Western Spirituality (New York: Paulist Press, 1981); John of the Cross, *The Dark Night of the Soul*, in *The Collected Works of John of the Cross*, trans. Kieran Kavanaugh and Otilio Rodriguez (Washington, DC: Institute of Carmelite Studies, 1979). See also Lutheran mystic Jacob Boehme's description of the "abyss" of God in Jacob Boehme, *Jacob Boehme: The Way to Christ*, trans. Peter Erb, Classics of Western Spirituality (New York: Paulist Press, 1978), 194–226.

77. See, for example, Thomas Merton, *The Inner Experience: Notes on Contemplation* (San Francisco: HarperSanFrancisco, 2003); Keating, *Open Mind, Open Heart*; Vladimir Lossky, *The Mystical Theology of the Eastern Church* (Crestwood, NY: St. Vladimir's Press, 1998); Foster, *Prayer*, 155–66.

78. Two examples of this use can be found in Friedrich Heiler, *Prayer: A Study in the History and Psychology of Religion*, trans. Samuel McComb (London: Oxford University Press, 1932) and Donald Bloesch, *The Struggle of Prayer* (New York: Harper and Row, 1980).

79. Bloesch, *Struggle of Prayer*, 117.

80. See also the Johannine theme of seeing God in Christ presented throughout John's Gospel and in other writings as well (esp. 1 John 3:2). A discussion of this is found in McGinn, *Foundations*, 76.

81. See also the discussions of "fellowship" with the Lord. Again, for Johannine theology of union, see McGinn, *Foundations*, 78.

82. Ibid., 83. See also 183–85.

83. See Bloesch, *Struggle of Prayer*, 154.

84. See Teresa of Avila's discussion of love *after* her treatment of the seventh and final mansion in Teresa of Avila, *The Interior Castle*, in vol. 2, *The Collected Works of St. Teresa of Avila*, trans. Kieran Kavanaugh and Otilio Rodriguez (Washington, DC: Institute of Carmelite Studies, 1976), 7.4, 12–13. See also Lossky, *Mystical Theology*, 212–16.

85. See also the stories of prayer during the Second World War in Norman Grubb, *Rees Howells: Intercessor* (Fort Washington, PA: Christian Literature Crusade, 1952).

86. For stories and models of healing prayer, see Ronald Kydd, *Healing through the Centuries* (Peabody, MA: Hendrickson, 1998). On prayers for provision, see A. E. C. Brooks, comp., *Answers to Prayer from George Muller's Narratives* (Chicago: Moody, n.d.).

87. Tertullian, *On Prayer*, chap. 29.

88. Joseph P. Amar, "On Hermits and Desert Dwellers," in *Ascetic Behavior in Graeco-Roman Antiquity: A Sourcebook*, ed. Vincent L. Wimbush (Minneapolis: Fortress, 1990), #501, p. 69.

89. See Randolph Byrd, "Positive Therapeutic Effects of Intercessory Prayer in a Coronary Care Unit Population," *Southern Medical Journal* 81, no. 7 (July 1988): 826–29; William Harris et al., "A Randomized, Controlled Trial of the Effects of Remote, Intercessory Prayer on Outcomes in Patients Admitted to the Coronary Care Unit," *Archives of Internal Medicine* 159 (October 1999): 2273–77; Dale Matthews, Sally M. Marlowe, and Francis S. MacNutt, "Effects of Intercessory Prayer on Patients with Rheumatoid Arthritis," *Southern Medical Journal* 93, no. 2 (December 2000): 1177–86; R. J. Davidson et al., "Alterations in Brain and Immune Function Produced by Mindfulness Meditation," *Psychosomatic Medicine* 65 (2003): 564–70; and Larry Dossey, *Healing Words: The Power of Prayer and the Practice of Medicine* (New York: HarperCollins, 1993).

90. See the debate between Irwin Tessman and William Harris, "Is There Scientific Evidence that Intercessory Prayer Speeds Medical Recovery? A Debate," March 13, 2001, University of Missouri, Columbia, transcript, http://www.csicop.org/articles/20010810-prayer.

91. Myers, "Is Prayer Clinically Effective?" This is also available at www.davidmyers.org.

92. See Herbert Benson et al., "Study of the Therapeutic Effects of Intercessory Prayer (STEP) in Cardiac Bypass Patients: A Multicenter Randomized Trial of Uncertainty and Certainty of Receiving Intercessory Prayer," *American Heart Journal* 151, no. 4 (2006): 934. (A PDF of the revised version of the report presented to the primary funding organization, the Templeton Foundation, can be found under "Press Releases" at http://www.templeton.org.) This study has received a great deal of attention in the media, once again stimulating discussion of the issues of the scientific study of prayer.

93. See, for example, the discussions in Mary Rose Bumpus, "The Story of Martha and Mary and the Potential for Transformative Engagement: Luke 10:38–42" (PhD diss., Graduate Theological Union, 2000); and J. Matthew Ashley, "Contemplation in Prophetic Action," *Christian Spirituality Bulletin* 8, no. 1 (Spring–Summer 2000): 6–13.

94. These questions are largely taken from Dossey, *Healing Words*, 9.

95. Theophan the Recluse, in Chariton, comp., *Art of Prayer*, 90.

Chapter 10

1. See, for example, Martin Heidegger's insistence that "care" (*Sorge*) is an intrinsic component of human Being-in-the-world. Martin Heidegger, *Being and Time*, trans. John Macquarrie and Edward Robinson (New York: Harper Collins, 1962), 225–73. Similarly, author Susan Phillips speaks of a person as "constituted by what is cared for." Susan S. Phillips, introduction to *The Crisis of Care*, ed. Susan S. Phillips and Patricia Benner (Washington, DC: Georgetown University Press, 1994), 7.

2. On various dimensions of love, see, for example, Anders Nygren, *Agape and Eros* (Philadelphia: Muhlenberg, 1953); C. S. Lewis, *The Four Loves* (San Diego: Harcourt, 1960); Leon Morris, *Testaments of Love* (Grand Rapids: Eerdmans, 1981).

3. This story is adapted from Ernest Boyer Jr., *Finding God at Home: Family Life as Spiritual Discipline* (San Francisco: Harper and Row, 1988), 45–50.

4. John Woolman, *The Journal of John Woolman*, in *Quaker Spirituality*, ed. Douglas V. Steere, Classics of Western Spirituality (New York: Paulist Press, 1984), 173.

5. For different approaches to caring for the earth, see, for example, Anthony Campolo, *How to Rescue the Earth without Worshiping Nature: A Christian's Call to Save Creation* (Nashville: Thomas Nelson, 1992); Sallie McFague, *Super, Natural Christians: How We Should Love Nature* (Philadelphia: Fortress, 1997); and Wendell Berry, *The Art of the Commonplace: The Agrarian Essays of Wendell Berry*, ed. Norman Wirzba (Washington, DC: Shoemaker and Hoard, 2002). Orthodox Patriarch Bartholomew has expressed concern regarding ecological sensitivity in Protocol No. 756, which is available at http://www.cerkiew.pl/en/news.php?id=5.

6. Wendy M. Wright, *Sacred Dwelling: A Spirituality of Family Life* (Leavenworth, KS: Forest of Peace Publishing, 1994), 28. For the idea of marriage as kenosis, see Paul Evdokimov, *The Sacrament of Love*, trans. Anthony P. Gythiel and Victoria Steadman (Crestwood, NY: St. Vladimir's Seminary Press, 2001), 70.

7. See, for example, Evdokimov, *Sacrament of Love*, 32, 89, 116, 121; Wright, *Sacred Dwelling*, 23. See also the images of family presented in Edith Schaeffer, *What Is a Family?* (Old Tappan, NJ: Fleming Revell, 1975), and the treatment of lay spirituality in Kees Waaijman, *Spirituality: Forms, Foundations, Methods*, trans. John Vriend (Leuven, Belgium: Peeters, 2002).

8. Boyer, *Finding God at Home*, 68; see 3–36, 58–94 for Boyer's treatment of these themes. For a historical study of the family as an expression of order, see Edmund S. Morgan, *The Puritan Family: Religion and Domestic Relations in Seventeenth-Century New England* (New York: Harper and Row, 1966).

9. For treatments of family life in comparison to the Rule of Benedict, see Larry Spears, "A Rule for Families of Faith," *American Benedictine Review* 40, no. 2 (June 1989): 142–69; and David Robinson, *The Family Cloister: Benedictine Wisdom for the Home* (New York: Crossroad, 2000). For the rewards of family spirituality see Boyer, *Finding God at Home*, 106–9.

10. For the distinction between modalities and sodalities, see Ralph D. Winter, "The Two Structures of God's Redemptive Mission," in *Perspectives on the World Christian Movement:* *A Reader*, ed. Ralph D. Winter and Steven C. Hawthorne, rev. ed. (Pasadena, CA: William Carey Library, 1992), B-45–57.

11. Sodalities also manifest these differences of orientation. The distinction between sodalities and modalities, however, is that sodalities can consciously *limit* their membership based on a conscious choice to focus on one or another aspect.

12. *First Apology of Justin*, chap. 67.

13. See, for example, Jean Vanier, *Community and Growth* (New York: Paulist Press, 1982); and Tod E. Bolsinger, *It Takes a Church to Raise a Christian: How the Community of God Transforms Lives* (Grand Rapids: Brazos, 2004).

14. Winter, "Two Structures," B-50.

15. Donald Allchin, "Eastern Orthodox Monasticism," *London Quarterly and Holborn Review* 189 (January 1964): 23. See also N. F. Robinson, *Monasticism in the Orthodox Churches: Being an Introduction to the Study of Modern Hellenic and Slavonic Monachism* (London: Cope and Fenwick, 1916).

16. For this sentiment expressed from a North American perspective, see Robert N. Bellah et al., *Habits of the Heart: Individualism and Commitment in American Life* (New York: Harper and Row, 1985), 167–95, 258–62, 282. While the connections between Christian spirituality and voluntary associations have yet to be explored, history suggests that a dig into these connections might yield rich treasure. See also Robert Wuthnow, *Saving America? Faith-Based Services and the Future of Civil Society* (Princeton: Princeton University Press, 2004).

17. For an introduction to the structure and dynamics of small groups, see Jeffrey Arnold, *The Big Book on Small Groups* (Downers Grove, IL: InterVarsity Press, 1992). For small groups in the context of spiritual direction and formation, see Rose Mary Dougherty, *Group Spiritual Direction: Community for Discernment* (New York: Paulist Press, 1995); Larry Crabb, *Connecting: Healing Ourselves and Our Relationships* (Nashville: Word, 1997); and James Bryan Smith and Linda Graybeal, *A Spiritual Formation Workbook: Small-Group Resources for Nurturing Spiritual Growth* (San Francisco: HarperSanFrancisco, 1999).

18. For various treatments of the spirituality of work, see Sue Bender, *Plain and Simple: A Woman's Journey to the Amish* (San Francisco: HarperSanFrancisco, 1989); Joan Chittester, *Wisdom Distilled from the Daily: Living the Rule of St. Benedict Today* (San Francisco: HarperSanFrancisco, 1990), 80–94; Parker Palmer, *The Active Life: A Spirituality of Work, Creativity, and Caring* (San Francisco: Jossey-Bass, 1990); and Matthew Fox, *The Reinvention of Work: A New Vision of Livelihood for Our Time* (San Francisco: HarperSanFrancisco, 1994).

19. For different approaches to sociopolitical action see, for example, Jim Wallis, *God's Politics: Why the Right Gets It Wrong and the Left Doesn't Get It* (San Francisco: HarperSanFrancisco, 2005); Paul B. Henry, *Politics for Evangelicals* (Valley Forge, PA: Judson, 1974); Ronald J. Sider, *Rich Christians in an Age of Hunger: Moving from Affluence to Generosity*, 20th anniv. ed. (Nashville: Word, 1997); Joe Holland and Peter Henriot, *Social Analysis: Linking Faith and Justice* (Maryknoll, NY: Orbis, 1983); and Walter Wink, *Engaging the Powers: Discernment and Resistance in a World of Domination* (Philadelphia: Fortress, 1992). For an approach to strate-

gies of compassionate care, see Bryant L. Myers, *Walking with the Poor: Principles and Practices of Transformational Development* (Maryknoll, NY: Orbis, 1999).

20. On spiritual direction, see Kallistos Ware, "The Spiritual Father in Orthodox Christianity," in *Spiritual Direction: Contemporary Readings*, ed. Kevin G. Culligan (Locust Valley, NY: Living Flame Press, 1983), 20–40; Kenneth Leech, *Soul Friend: The Practice of Christian Spirituality* (San Francisco: Harper and Row, 1977); William A. Barry and William J. Connolly, *The Practice of Spiritual Direction* (New York: Seabury, 1982); Gerald May, *Care of Mind, Care of Spirit: Psychiatric Dimensions of Spiritual Direction* (San Francisco: Harper and Row, 1983); Margaret Guenther, *Holy Listening: The Art of Spiritual Direction* (Cambridge, MA: Cowley, 1992); and Bruce Demarest, *Soul Guide: Following Jesus as Spiritual Director* (Colorado Springs: NavPress, 2003). The organization Spiritual Directors International serves the interests of all kinds of spiritual directors.

21. Evagrius Ponticus, "Chapters on Prayer," in *The Praktikos and Chapters on Prayer*, trans. John Eudes Bamberger (Kalamazoo, MI: Cistercian Publications, 1981), no. 124, p. 76.

22. A. Gordon Mursell, introduction to *The Meditations of Guigo I: Prior of the Charterhouse*, trans. A. Gordon Mursell (Kalamazoo, MI: Cistercian Publications, 1995), 14.

23. On intentional solitude, see, for example, Thomas Merton, *Disputed Questions* (New York: New American Library, 1960), 139–59; Thomas Merton, *Contemplation in a World of Action* (New York: Doubleday, 1971), 297–330 (note that the more recent edition of this book does not include Merton's essays on the eremitical life); and A. M. Allchin, *Solitude and Communion: Papers on the Hermit Life Given at St. David's, Wales, in the Autumn of 1975* (Fairacres, UK: SLG Press, 1977). You'll find an interesting collection of resources on the solitary life at www.hermitary.com.

24. "Decree on the Appropriate Renewal of the Religious Life," no. 7, in *The Documents of Vatican II* (New York: Guild, 1966), 471.

25. Vanier, *Community and Growth*, 20.

26. Robert Wuthnow, *After Heaven: Spirituality in America Since the 1950s* (Berkeley and Los Angeles: University of California Press, 1998), 181.

27. I am adapting ideas found in Donald L. Gelpi, *Committed Worship: A Sacramental Theology for Converting Christians*, 2 vols. (Minneapolis: Liturgical Press, 1993), 1:125–35.

28. Ibid., 1:141, italics in original.

29. Cited in Gerald Bray, ed., *Romans*, Ancient Christian Commentary on Scripture (Downers Grove, IL: InterVarsity Press, 1998), 310.

30. See Richard Foster, *Streams of Living Water: Celebrating the Great Traditions of Christian Faith* (San Francisco: HarperSanFrancisco, 1998). I have replaced the term Incarnational with Sacramental (Foster uses Incarnational to describe the sacramental life), and I have also added what I call the Progressive traditions, perhaps embodied in groups of Socinians, freethinkers, liberals, and such.

31. Charles Dickens, *A Christmas Carol* (New York: Weathervane Books, 1977), 56–57.

32. See the movie *Hotel Rwanda*, directed by Terry George (United Artists and Lions Gate International, 2004).

33. See, for example, J. P. R. French Jr. and B. Raven, "The Bases of Social Power," in *Group Dynamics*, ed. D. Cartwright and A. Zander (New York: Harper and Row, 1960), 607–23; R. J. Rummel, *The Conflict Helix* (Beverly Hills: Sage, 1976).

34. William Law, *A Serious Call to a Devout and Holy Life*, in *William Law: A Serious Call to a Devout and Holy Life; The Spirit of Love*, ed. Paul G. Stanwood, Classics of Western Spirituality (New York: Paulist Press, 1978), 233. On humility and the use of power, see Richard Foster, *Money, Sex, and Power: The Challenge of the Disciplined Life* (San Francisco: HarperSanFrancisco, 1985), 196–227; George Maloney, *On the Road to Perfection: Christian Humility in Modern Society* (Hyde Park, NY: New City Press, 1995).

35. For a similar approach to cognitive or epistemological authority, see Alvin Plantinga, *Warrant and Proper Function* (New York: Oxford University Press, 1993).

36. See Miroslav Volf, *Exclusion and Embrace: A Theological Exploration of Identity, Otherness, and Reconciliation* (Nashville: Abingdon, 1996), especially pp. 233–74 with regard to "truth."

37. For an interesting program for exercising power in humility, see the Institute for Servant Leadership's "A Twelve-Step Discipline for Practicing a Life-Giving Use of Power," http://www.servleader.org/articles/12steps.htm.

38. These categories, and the illustration of Moses, can be found in William Bridges, *Managing Transitions: Making the Most of Change* (Cambridge, MA: Da Capo, 2003). See also John Hayes's application of similar stages to New Monastic communities (labeled *ideal*, *ordeal*, and *new deal*) in *Sub-merge: Living Deep in a Shallow World* (Ventura, CA: Regal, 2006).

39. Antoinette Voûte Roeder, "The Witness," in *Presence: An International Journal of Spiritual Direction* 11, no. 1 (February 2005): 56.

40. Marilyn Ferguson, cited in Bridges, *Managing Transitions*, 39.

41. W. Thomas Boyce, "Beyond the Clinical Gaze," in *The Crisis of Care: Affirming and Restoring Caring Practices in the Helping Professions*, ed. Susan S. Phillips and Patricia Benner (Washington, DC: Georgetown University Press, 1994), 144–48.

42. Douglas V. Steere, ed., *Quaker Spirituality: Selected Writings*, Classics of Western Spirituality (New York: Paulist Press, 1984), 162.

43. John Woolman, *The Journal of John Woolman*, in *Quaker Spirituality*, ed. Douglas V. Steere, Classics of Western Spirituality (New York: Paulist Press, 1984), 167–68.

44. Ibid., 169.

45. John Woolman, "On the Slave Trade," available at http://www.qhpress.org/texts/oldqwhp/wool-496.htm.

46. Woolman, *Journal*, 191.

47. Ibid., 186.

48. John Woolman, *The Journal of John Woolman and a Plea for the Poor* (New York: Corinth Books, 1961), 238.

49. Woolman, *Journal*, in *Quaker Spirituality*, 227.

50. Joel Green, "Caring as Gift and Goal: Biblical and Theological Reflections," in *The Crisis of Care: Affirming and Restoring Caring Practices in the Helping Professions*, ed. Susan S. Phillips and Patricia Benner (Washington, DC: Georgetown University Press, 1994), 150.

51. Ibid., 164.

52. See Susan S. Phillips and Patricia Benner, eds., *The Crisis of Care: Affirming and Restoring Caring Practices in the Helping Professions* (Washington, DC: Georgetown University Press, 1994).

53. See, for example Miriam Cleary, "A Societal Context for Supervision," *Presence: The Journal of Spiritual Directors International* 4, no. 2 (May 1998): 26–31.

Chapter 11

1. In John Cassian, *The Conferences*, trans. Boniface Ramsey, Ancient Christian Writers (New York: Newman Press, 1997), 2.1.4, p. 84.

2. The appreciative dimension of discernment is highlighted in Mark McIntosh, *Discernment and Truth: The Spirituality and Theology of Knowledge* (New York: Herder and Herder, 2004).

3. Edward Malatesta, ed., *Discernment of Spirits* (Collegeville, MN: Liturgical Press, 1970), 9. This book is an English translation of the valuable article from the *Dictionaire de Spiritualité* on discernment.

4. J. S. Upkong, "Pluralism and the Discernment of Spirits," *Ecumenical Review* 41 (1989): 416.

5. Suzanne G. Farnham, Joseph P. Gill, and R. Taylor McLean, *Listening Hearts: Discerning Call in Community* (Harrisburg, PA: Morehouse, 1991), 23.

6. Ernest Larkin, *Silent Presence: Discernment as Process and Problem* (Denville, NJ: Dimension, 1981), 58.

7. Jules J. Toner, *Spirit of Light or Darkness? A Casebook for Studying Discernment of Spirits* (St. Louis: Institute of Jesuit Sources, 1995), 11.

8. The practice in this chapter was originally inspired by a retreat led by Elizabeth Liebert, titled "Discerning God's Will in Daily Life."

9. On discernment criteria related to the prophetic community, see Malatesta, *Discernment of Spirits*, 21–25.

10. Kees Waaijman, *Spirituality: Forms, Foundations, Methods*, trans. John Vriend (Leuven, Belgium: Peeters, 2002), 502.

11. See James L. Jacquette, *Discerning What Counts: The Function of the Adiaphora Topos in Paul's Letters*, SBL Dissertation Series (Atlanta: Scholars Press, 1995).

12. Benedicta Ward, trans., *The Sayings of the Desert Fathers: The Alphabetical Collection* (Kalamazoo, MI: Cistercian Publishers, 1975), Abba Agathon no. 10, 22.

13. Cassian, *The Conferences*, 77–112. On the shift from discernment as a gift to discernment as a virtue in the patristic period more generally, see Joseph Lienhard, "On Discernment of Spirits in the Early Church," *Theological Studies* 41 (Spring 1980): 505–29.

14. Saint Diodochus of Photike, "On Spiritual Knowledge and Discernment: One Hundred Texts," no. 26, in *The Philokalia: The Complete Text*, comp. Saint Nikodimos of the Holy Mountain and Saint Makarios of Corinth, trans. G. E. H. Palmer, Philip Sherrard, and Kallistos Ware (London: Faber and Faber, 1979), 1:259–60.

15. See Augustine, *On Genesis: A Refutation of the Manichees; Unfinished Literal Commentary*

on Genesis; *The Literal Meaning of Genesis*, trans. Edmund Hill, *The Works of Saint Augustine: A Translation for the 21st Century* (Hyde Park, NY: New City Press, 2002), 474–79.

16. Kees Waaijman writes of Thomas Aquinas, "Thomas subsumed *discretio* under *prudentia*, which gives to all virtues the *form* of the good because it 'seeks the mean' in the concrete circumstances of the particular act. . . . *Discretio* is the application of the correct middle in the order of the means." Waaijman, *Spirituality*, 505.

17. See Jean Gerson, "On Distinguishing True from False Revelations," in *Jean Gerson: Early Works*, trans. Brian Patrick McGuire, Classics of Western Spirituality (New York: Paulist Press, 1998), 334–64; Paschal Boland, *The Concept of Discretio Spirituum in John Gerson's "De Probatione Spirituum" and "De Distinctione Verarum Visionum a Falsis,"* Catholic University of America Studies in Sacred Theology, 2nd ser. (Washington, DC: Catholic University of America Press, 1959).

18. On this development, see Rosalynn Voaden, *God's Words, Women's Voices: The Discernment of Spirits in the Writing of Late-Medieval Women Visionaries* (Woodbridge, UK: York University Press, 1999).

19. Prior Peter and Master Peter, "The Life of Blessed Birgitta," in *Birgitta of Sweden: Life and Selected Revelations*, trans. Albert Ryle Kezel, Classics of Western Spirituality (New York: Paulist Press, 1990), no. 26, pp. 77–78.

20. Yet Protestant Reformers and Catholic reformers were not entirely separate in their approach to faith. For a comparison of Martin Luther and Ignatius of Loyola on this point, see Michael Proterra, *Homo Spiritualis Nititur Fide: Martin Luther and Ignatius of Loyola; An Analytical and Comparative Study of a Hermeneutic Based on the Heuristic Structure of Discretio* (Washington, DC: University Press of America, 1983).

21. On Ignatius, see, for example, J. C. Futrell, "Ignatian Discernment," *Studies in the Spirituality of Jesuits* 2, no. 2 (April 1970): 1–88; Jules J. Toner, *A Commentary on Saint Ignatius' Rules for the Discernment of Spirits* (St. Louis: Institute of Jesuit Sources, 1982); Jules J. Toner, *Discerning God's Will: Ignatius of Loyola's Teaching on Christian Decision Making* (St. Louis: Institute of Jesuit Sources, 1991); Dean Brackley, *The Call to Discernment in Troubled Times: New Perspectives on the Transformative Wisdom of Ignatius of Loyola* (New York: Crossroad, 2004).

22. See, for example, J. B. Libânio, *Spiritual Discernment and Politics: Guidelines for Religious Communities*, trans. Theodore Morrow (Eugene, OR: Wipf and Stock, 2003); Jon Sobrino, "Following Jesus as Discernment," in *Discernment of the Spirit and of Spirits*, ed. Casiano Floristan and Christian Duquoc (New York: Seabury, 1979), 14–22; Elizabeth Liebert, "Linking Faith and Justice: Working with Systems and Structures as a Spiritual Discipline," *Christian Spirituality Bulletin* 5, no. 1 (Spring 1997): 19–21; and Walter Wink, *Engaging the Powers: Discernment and Resistance in a World of Domination* (Philadelphia: Fortress, 1992).

23. Here is a small sample of recent books on discernment: Thomas Green, *Weeds among the Wheat: Discernment; Where Prayer and Action Meet* (Notre Dame, IN: Ave Maria Press, 1984); Dallas Willard, *Hearing God: Developing a Conversational Relationship with God* (Downers Grove, IL: InterVarsity Press, 1999); Farnham, Gill,

and McLean, *Listening Hearts*; Ben Campbell Johnson, *Discerning God's Will* (Louisville: Westminster John Knox, 1990); James Ryle, *Hippo in the Garden: A Non-Religious Approach to Having a Conversation with God* (Orlando, FL: Creation House, 1993); Maureen Conroy, *The Discerning Heart: Discovering a Personal God* (Chicago: Loyola Press, 1993); A Carthusian, *The Call of Silent Love: Vocation and Discernment*, Carthusian Novice Conferences (Kalamazoo, MI: Cistercian Publications, 1995); Gordon Smith, *Listening to God in Times of Choice* (Downers Grove, IL: InterVarsity Press, 1997); Debra K. Farrington, *Hearing with the Heart: A Gentle Guide for Discerning God's Will for Your Life* (San Francisco: Jossey-Bass, 2003).

24. See Jonathan Edwards, *The Distinguishing Marks of a Work of the Spirit of God*, in *The Great Awakening*, ed. C. G. Goen, vol. 4, Works of Jonathan Edwards (New Haven: Yale University Press, 1972), 213–88.

25. Farnham, Gill, and McLean, *Listening Hearts*, 25.

26. Saint Theophan the Recluse, *The Heart of Salvation: The Life and Teachings of Russia's Saint Theophan the Recluse*, trans. Esther Williams (Newbury, MA: Praxis Institute Press, n.d.), 8.

27. Mark McIntosh has enumerated five aspects, or phases, of discernment, moving from the contemplative to the active and back to the contemplative once again: (1) the foundation of Faith, (2) the identification of Impulses, (3) the wisdom of Discretion, (4) the determination of the Divine Will, and (5) the Illumination of relationship with God. These can be set alongside our model of human experience as follows: from Being Aware (Faith as the framework of awareness), to Experiencing (and perceiving Impulses), to Understanding and Judging (Discretion), to Deciding and Acting (in consonance with the Will of God), to Integrating (through the Illumination of God). See McIntosh, *Discernment and Truth*, 5–22.

28. See Joseph M. Rovira Belloso, "Who Is Capable of Discerning?" in *Discernment of the Spirit and of Spirits*, ed. Casiano Floristan and Christian DuQuoc (New York: Seabury, 1979), 84–94.

29. McIntosh, *Discernment and Truth*, 255.

30. Bob Mumford, *Take Another Look at Guidance: A Study of Divine Guidance* (Plainfield, NJ: Logos International, 1971), 33.

31. I have adapted these categories from Robert M. Gay, *Vocation et Discernment Des Esprits* (Montreal: Fides, 1959), 67–74. See also Waaijman's discussion of the discernment of form in Waaijman, *Spirituality*, esp. 423–24.

32. Ladislas Orsy, *Probing the Spirit: A Theological Evaluation of Communal Discernment* (Denville, NJ: Dimension Books, 1976), 44.

33. See Ignatius of Loyola, *Spiritual Exercises*, in *Ignatius of Loyola: The Spiritual Exercises and Selected Works*, ed. George E. Ganss (New York: Paulist Press, 1991), no. 23.

34. Ignatius's exercises of the kingdom of Christ (ibid., nos. 91–100) and of the "Two Standards" (ibid., nos. 136–48) and the appreciative contemplation of the life of Jesus in the Second Week of the Spiritual Exercises are designed to foster such shared concerns and to help us gain a vision for the things of Christ. For another treatment of finding God's will through the scriptures, see Gary Friesen, *Decision Making and the Will of*

God: A Biblical Alternative to the Traditional View (Portland, OR: Multnomah, 1980).

35. John Climacus, *The Ladder of Divine Ascent*, trans. Colm Luibheid and Norman Russell, Classics of Western Spirituality (New York: Paulist Press, 1982), 228.

36. Waaijman, *Spirituality*, 496.

37. Luke Timothy Johnson, *Scripture and Discernment: Decision Making in the Early Church* (Nashville: Abingdon, 1996), 139.

38. For more on discerning what matters, see Jacquette, *Discerning What Counts*.

39. Sisters of the Holy Names of Jesus and Mary, *Momentum* (St. Anthony-on-Hudson, Rensselaer, NY: privately printed, 1991), 8–9.

40. On the elements of social analysis, see Joe Holland and Peter Henriot, *Social Analysis: Linking Faith and Justice* (Maryknoll, NY: Orbis, 1983), 21–29.

41. This kind of information gathering is like that used for clarifying issues such as the blessing of same-sex unions, the admission of public tongues-speaking, or a congregation's hiring of a "Christian-Jungian" therapist to the counseling staff.

42. For a treatment of hindrances, see, for example, Willard, *Hearing God*, 86–116.

43. On consolation (and desolation), see Ignatius of Loyola, *Spiritual Exercises*, nos. 316–17 with accompanying footnotes.

44. An exploration of Paul's journeys, as recorded in the book of Acts and in his letters, reveals the source of Paul's discernment as a combination of reason (strategic planning), experience, dreams, prophetic utterances, advice of others, circumstances, and more.

45. For other contemporary lists of discernment criteria, see, for example, Mumford, *Take Another Look*, 65–74, 119–25; Sobrino, "Following Jesus as Discernment," 19–20; Susan Rakoczy, "The Structures of Discernment Processes and the Meaning of Discernment Language in Published U.S. Catholic Literature 1965–1978," (PhD diss., Catholic University of America, 1980), 150–84: William A. Barry and William J. Connolly, *The Practice of Spiritual Direction* (New York: Seabury, 1982), 101–17; Michael Sheeran, *Beyond Majority Rule: Voteless Decisions in the Religious Society of Friends* (Philadelphia: Philadelphia Yearly Meeting, 1983), 24–30; McIntosh, *Discernment and Truth*, 91–114.

46. For various models of the communal discernment process, see Jules J. Toner, "A Method for Communal Discernment of God's Will," *Studies in the Spirituality of Jesuits* 3, no. 4 (September 1971): 121–52; William C. Spohn, "Charismatic Communal Discernment and Ignatian Communities," *The Way: Supplement* 20 (Autumn 1973): 38–54; Sheeran, *Beyond Majority Rule*; Mary Benet McKinney, *Sharing Wisdom: A Process for Group Decision Making* (Allen, TX: Tabor Publishing, 1987); Danny E. Morris and Charles M. Olsen, *Discerning God's Will Together: A Spiritual Practice for the Church* (Bethesda, MD: Alban, 1997).

47. Frank J. Houdek, *Guided by the Spirit: A Jesuit Perspective on Spiritual Direction* (Chicago: Loyola Press, 1996), 115.

48. The terms *blasted*, *led*, and *ignored* are my own terms for Ignatius's first, second, and third times for making an election. On the three times for making an election see Ignatius of Loyola, *Spiritual Exercises*, nos. 175–88. See also Toner, *Discerning God's Will*.

49. Ignatius of Loyola, *Spiritual Exercises* [sec. 175].

50. Ibid., [sec. 176].

51. Ibid., [sec. 178].

52. Ibid., [secs. 177, 178–88].

53. For more detail on this, see Evan B. Howard, *Affirming the Touch of God: A Psychological and Philosophical Exploration of Christian Discernment* (Lanham, NJ: University Press of America, 2000).

Chapter 12

1. Richard Lovelace, *Dynamics of Spiritual Life: An Evangelical Theology of Renewal* (Downers Grove, IL: InterVarsity Press, 1979), 21–22. J. Edwin Orr (a historian of revival) distinguishes between nuances in the use of *revival* (renewal of believers), and *awakening* (renewal of community). J. Edwin Orr, *The Re-Study of Revival and Revivalism* (Pasadena, CA: School of World Mission, 1981), iv. For a discussion of the use of terms and of the basic understanding of renewal and revival, it is helpful to compare the works of Lovelace and those of Orr with those of William G. McLoughlin. See, for example, McLoughlin's *Revivals, Awakenings, and Reforms: An Essay on Religion and Social Change in America 1607–1977* (Chicago: University of Chicago Press, 1978).

2. For a discussion of the interplay of the terms *awakening* and *revival* with reference to movements throughout Europe and America, see *The Spirituality of the German Awakening*, trans. David Crowner and Gerald Christianson, Classics of Western Spirituality (Mahwah, NJ: Paulist Press, 2003), 5–7.

3. Lovelace, *Dynamics of Spiritual Life*, 22.

4. For an application of these ideas, see William G. McLoughlin, *Revivals, Awakenings, and Reform: An Essay on Religion and Social Change in America 1607–1977* (Chicago: University of Chicago Press, 1978).

5. Jonathan Edwards, *A Faithful Narrative of the Surprising Work of God*, in *The Great Awakening*, editor C. G. Goen, vol. 4, Works of Jonathan Edwards (New Haven: Yale University Press, 1972), 149–50.

6. Athanasius, *The Life of Antony and the Letter to Marcellinus*, trans. Robert C. Gregg, Classics of Western Spirituality (New York: Paulist Press, 1980), no. 14.

7. *The Life of Pachomius*, cited in Derwas J. Chitty, *The Desert a City: An Introduction to the Study of Egyptian and Palestinian Monasticism under the Christian Empire* (Crestwood, NY: St. Vladimir's Seminary Press, 1966), 10.

8. "Patrick's Declaration of the Great Works of God" in Oliver Davies, trans., *Celtic Spirituality* (New York: Paulist Press, 1999), 78, 80.

9. George G. Hunter III, *The Celtic Way of Evangelism: How Christianity Can Win the West . . . Again* (Nashville: Abingdon, 2000), 23.

10. See Thomas Cahill, *How the Irish Saved Civilization: The Untold Story of Ireland's Heroic Role from the Fall of Rome to the Rise of Medieval Europe* (New York: Doubleday, 1995).

11. Peter C. Erb, "Anabaptist Spirituality," in *Protestant Spiritual Traditions*, ed. Frank C. Senn (New York: Paulist Press, 1986), 80, 82.

12. Yet during the sixteenth and seventeenth centuries in the West, one's religious affiliation was also often subject to the choices of political rulers. One ruler would declare that a given country (or city) was Lutheran, and so the people would be Lutheran—or else. Yet even in these cases, the designations were made according to the lines set by the Reformation disputes. Here we see how spiritual renewal and reform arise within the all-too-human realities of social and political life.

13. Sydney E. Ahlstrom, *A Religious History of the American People* (New Haven: Yale University Press, 1972), 286–87.

14. Taken from J. Edwin Orr, *The Event of the Century: The 1857–1858 Awakening* (Wheaton: International Awakening Press, 1989), 283.

15. For a review of these, see Richard M. Riss, *A Survey of 20th-Century Revival Movements in North America* (Peabody, MA: Hendrickson, 1988).

16. Leung Ka-Lun and the China Group, with contributions from Xu Ru Lei, "China," trans. Tung Lun-Hsien and Dufresse Chang, in *A Dictionary of Asian Christianity*, ed. Scott W. Sunquist (Grand Rapids: Eerdmans, 2001), 145.

17. Eamon Duffy, *Saints and Sinners: A History of the Popes* (New Haven: Yale University Press, 1997), 269, 273.

18. Arthur Wallis, *China Miracle: A Silent Explosion* (Columbia, MO: Cityhill, 1986).

19. Ka-Lun et al., "China," 145.

20. Philip Jenkins, *The Next Christendom: The Coming of Global Christianity* (New York: Oxford University Press, 2002), 70.

21. In Davies, trans., *Celtic Spirituality*, 267.

22. J. Edwin Orr, "The Outpouring of the Spirit in Revival and Awakening and Its Issue in Church Growth" (Pasadena, CA: Privately distributed paper, 1984), 5.

23. See, for example, Douglas Burton-Christie, *The Word in the Desert: Scripture and the Quest for Holiness in Early Christian Monasticism* (New York: Oxford University Press, 1993).

24. Peter O'Dwyer, "Celtic Monks and the Culdee Reform," in *An Introduction to Celtic Christianity*, ed. James P. Mackey (Edinburgh: T and T Clark, 1995), 141.

25. I have benefited greatly from two surveys of studies of movements: Daniel E. Albrecht, "An Investigation of the Sociocultural Characteristics and Dynamics of Wallace's 'Revitalization Movements': A Comparative Analysis of the Works of Four Social Scientists" (unpublished paper, 1989); and J. Robert Clinton, *Bridging Strategies: Leadership Strategies for Introducing Change* (Altadena, CA: Barnabas Publishing, 1992). See also Steve Addison, "Movement Dynamics: Keys to the Expansion and Renewal of the Church in Mission" (unpublished paper, 2003).

26. John White, *When the Spirit Comes in Power: Signs and Wonders among God's People* (Downers Grove, IL: InterVarsity Press, 1988), 236.

27. See Lovelace, *Dynamics of Spiritual Life*; and Richard F. Lovelace, *Renewal as a Way of Life* (Downers Grove, IL: InterVarsity Press, 1985).

28. For greater detail on the evaluation of revival or affective trends, see Evan B. Howard, *Affirming the Touch of God: A Psychological and Philosophical Exploration of Christian Discernment* (Lanham, NJ: University Press of America, 2000), 349–72.

29. For a review of Edward's treatment of discernment in each of these two works, see Howard, *Affirming the Touch*, 85–132.

30. See, for example, Ignatius of Loyola's comments regarding this. Ignatius of Loyola, *Spiritual Exercises*, in *Ignatius of Loyola: The Spiritual Exercises and Selected Works*, ed. George E. Ganss, Classics of Western Spirituality (New York: Paulist Press, 1991), [sec. 336].

31. Orr, "Outpouring of the Spirit," 4.

32. See Jenkins, *Next Christiandom*, 71; and George Weigel, *God's Choice: Pope Benedict XVI and the Future of the Catholic Church* (New York: HarperCollins, 2005), 256. For statistics regarding church attendance worldwide, see www.adherents.com.

33. See, for example, Theodore G. Stylianopoulos, *The Way of Christ: Gospel, Spiritual Life and Renewal in Orthodoxy* (Brookline, MA: Holy Cross Orthodox Press, 2002); Weigel, *God's Choice*; Rick Warren, *The Purpose-Driven Church: Growth without Compromising Your Message and Mission* (Grand Rapids: Zondervan, 1995); Cynthia Woolever and Deborah Bruce, *Beyond the Ordinary: Ten Strengths of U.S. Congregations* (Louisville: Westminster John Knox, 2004); Robert E. Webber, *The Younger Evangelicals: Facing the Challenges of the New World* (Grand Rapids: Baker, 2002); and Marva Dawn, *Reaching Out without Dumbing Down: A Theology of Worship for This Urgent Time* (Grand Rapids: Eerdmans, 1995).

34. Warren's *Purpose-Driven Church* presents the model of one megachurch. For essays on the emerging church model, see Leonard Sweet, ed., *The Church in Emerging Culture* (Grand Rapids: Zondervan, 2003). For models of missional and emerging churches, see Darrell L. Guder, *The Missional Church: A Vision for the Sending of the Church in North America* (Grand Rapids: Eerdmans, 1998); and Michael Frost and Alan Hirsch, *The Shaping of Things to Come: Innovation and Mission for the 21st Century Church* (Peabody, MA: Hendrickson, 2003). For samples of the house church model, see Robert Banks and Julia Banks, *The Church Comes Home* (Peabody, MA: Hendrickson, 1998); and Larry Kreider, *House Church Networks: A Church for a New Generation* (Ephrata, PA: House to House Publications, 2001). It is also helpful to explore a few Web sites. See, for example, "Megachurches Today 2000: Summary of Data from the Faith Communities Today 2000 Project," a 2000 report by the Hartford Institute for Religious Research at http://hirr.hartsem.edu/org/faith_megachurches_FACTsummary.html; the collection of links at http://www.emergingchurch.info; and the site for House2House, an organization that encourages home-based churches, at http://www.house2house.net.

35. On new monasticism, see, for example, Jason Byassee, "The New Monastics," *Christian Century*, October 18, 2005, 38–47; The Rutba House, *School(s) for Conversion: Twelve Marks of a New Monasticism* (Eugene, OR: Cascade, 2005); Shane Claiborne, *The Irresistible Revolution* (Grand Rapids: Zondervan, 2006); Scott Bessenecker, *The New Friars: The Emerging Movement Serving the World's Poor* (Downers Grove, IL: InterVarsity Press, 2006); and John Hayes, *Sub-merge: Living Deep in a Shallow World* (Ventura, CA: Regal, 2006).

36. See, for example, Marjorie J. Thompson, *Soul Feast: An Invitation to the Christian Spiritual Life* (Louisville: Westminster John Knox, 1995); Ben Pasely, *Enter the Worship Circle* (Lake Mary, FL: Relevant Books, 2001); Rodney Clapp, *Tortured Wonders: Christian Spirituality for People, Not Angels* (Grand Rapids: Brazos, 2004).

37. Robert Wuthnow, *After Heaven: Spirituality in America Since the 1950s* (Berkeley and Los Angeles: University of California Press, 1998).

38. George Barna, *Revolution* (Wheaton: Tyndale House, 2005).

39. See Kees Waaijman, *Spirituality: Forms, Foundations, Methods*, trans. John Vriend (Leuven, Belgium: Peeters, 2002), 116–303.

40. For a first step, see Mark McIntosh's comparison between Rahner and Balthasar in Mark McIntosh, *Mystical Theology: The Integrity of Spirituality and Theology* (Malden, MA: Blackwell, 1998), 90–118.

41. Samuel M. Powell, *A Theology of Christian Spirituality* (Nashville: Abingdon, 2005).

42. See, for example, John Shelby Spong, *Why Christianity Must Change or Die: A Bishop Speaks to Believers in Exile* (San Francisco: HarperSanFrancisco, 1998); Karen Armstrong et al., *The Once and Future Faith* (Santa Rosa, CA: Polebridge Press, 2001); and Marcus J. Borg, *The Heart of Christianity: Rediscovering a Life of Faith* (San Francisco: HarperSanFrancisco, 2004).

43. One may discover hints of what a postliberal, postconservative spirituality might look like in Powell, *Theology of Christian Spirituality*; George A. Lindbeck, *The Church in a Postliberal Age*, ed. James J. Buckley (Grand Rapids: Eerdmans, 2002); Stanley Hauerwas, *A Better Hope: Resources for a Church Confronting Capitalism, Democracy, and Postmodernity* (Grand Rapids: Brazos, 2000); and Clapp, *Tortured Wonders*.

44. This pattern is evident among representatives of the house-church movement, of "river" churches in the West and many charismatic movements in the global South, and in Calvary Chapel churches and other conservative Evangelical groups.

45. This address is published in Bernard McGinn, "Spirituality Confronts Its Future," *Spiritus* 5, no. 1 (Spring 2005): 88–96.

46. Edward Howells, "Review of *Minding the Spirit: The Study of Christian Spirituality*," *Spiritus* 5, no. 2 (Fall 2005): 224.

47. Ibid., 226.

48. Mary Frohlich, "Spiritual Discipline, Discipline of Spirituality: Revisiting Questions of Definition and Method," *Spiritus* 1, no. 1 (Spring 2001): 65–78.

49. McGinn, "Spirituality Confronts Its Future," 94.

Image Permissions

Unless otherwise noted, all figures created by Evan Howard.

18 Bernard of Clairvaux, used by permission of Sally Barto.

20 Taken from *Church is Stranger than Fiction* by Mary Chambers. Copyright © Mary Chambers. Used with permission of InterVarsity Press, PO Box 1400, Downers Grove, IL 60515. www.ivpress.com.

25 House, used by permission of Nick Parish and Jennifer Parish.

25 Abundant Life Tabernacle, used by permission of Joyce Jackson and the Louisiana Folklife Program. www.louisianafolklife.org.

25 Calvary Baptist Church in Washington DC, courtesy of the National Photo Company Collection at the Library of Congress. www.loc.gov.

25 Willow Creek Community Church, © 2006 Willow Creek Community Church. Photography by McShane-Fleming Studios. Used by permission. www.willowcreek.org.

34 Transforming power . . . , by Doug Hall, used by permission.

49 Other interpretations . . . , by Don Pegoda, used by permission. First published by *Leadership Journal*, www.leadershipjournal.net.

52 "Lectio" by Albrect Dürer, courtesy of Dover Pictorial Archive Series.

62 Theological issue . . . , by Doug Hall, used by permission.

64 Church and psychology . . . , by Johnny Hawkins, used by permission. First published by *Leadership Journal*, www.leadershipjournal.net.

84 "Vitruvian Man" by Leonardo daVinci, public domain.

84 "Alessandro del Borro" by Velasquez (disputed), public domain.

84 Woman chin-up, used by permission of Nick Parish and Jennifer Parish.

94 Pastor Billingsley . . . , by Don Pegoda, used by permission. First published by *Leadership Journal*, www.leadershipjournal.net.

99 People singing in a prayerful pose by Wendell Jones, detail of a larger painting on the post office in Grandville, Ohio, public domain.

117 A. W. Tozer, used with permission of the National Archives of The Christian and Missionary Alliance. www.cmalliance.org.

120 "Trinity" by Andrej Rublëv, public domain.

120 Shamrock, used by permission of Nick Parish and Jennifer Parish.

120 Trinitarian diagram, used by permission of Nick Parish and Jennifer Parish.

128 While You Were Out . . . , by Doug Hall, used by permission.

129 Analogy making . . . , by Don Pegoda, used by permission. First published by *Leadership Journal*, www.leadershipjournal.net.

150 Walter Hilton, used by permission of Nick Parish and Jennifer Parish.

153 Great Pyramid of the Cheops, courtesy of the Library of Congress. www.loc.gov.

153 Sluggish clod, courtesy of the Library of Congress. www.loc.gov.

153 Brain surgery, public domain.

156 Hildegard of Bingen, used by permission of Krystan Bruce.

159 Original Sin . . . , by Doug Hall, used by permission.

170 Antony of Egypt, used by permission of Sally Barto.

174 Disabled veteran, public domain.

174 "Smash the Prostitution Racket, 1941–1945," courtesy of the National Archives. www.archives.gov.

174 Labor altercation, courtesy of the FDR Library. www.fdrlibrary.marist.edu.

180 Resurrection icon, image compliments of St. Isaac of Syria Skete. www.skete.com.

182 Angela of Foligno, used by permission of Krystan Bruce.

184 Phoebe Palmer, used by permission of Sally Barto.

186 John Ruusbroec, used by permission of Krystan Bruce

188 Band-Aid, used by permission of Nick Parish and Jennifer Parish.

188   Restoring furniture, used by permission of Nick Parish and Jennifer Parish.

188   "Peace Treaty," by Warren K. Leffler, courtesy of the Library of Congress. www.loc.gov.

200   Burning bush . . . , by Doug Hall, used by permission.

206   Hosea and Gomer, used by permission of Terese M. Howard.

219   Open door, used by permission of Nick Parish and Jennifer Parish.

219   Folded arms, used by permission of Nick Parish and Jennifer Parish.

222   Reading in lounge chair, used by permission of Nick Parish and Jennifer Parish.

222   Reaching for the cookie jar, used by permission of Nick Parish and Jennifer Parish.

233   Dorothy Day, courtesy of The Catholic Worker. www.catholicworker.org.

234   Ignatius of Loyola, used by permission of Sally Barto.

235   Jackie Pullinger-To, used by permission of Krystan Bruce.

240   "Just As I Am," taken from *Church Is Stranger than Fiction* by Mary Chambers. Copyright © Mary Chambers. Used by permission of InterVarsity Press, PO Box 1400, Downers Grove, IL 60515. www.ivpress.com.

241   "A Sequential Stage Model" (fig. 7.1) by Lewis Rambo in *Understanding Religious Conversion*. Used with permission of Yale University Press.

242   "Contours of Crisis" (fig. 7.2) by Lewis Rambo in *Understanding Religious Conversion*. Used with permission of Yale University Press.

243   "Modes of Response" (fig. 7.3) by Lewis Rambo in *Understanding Religious Conversion*. Used with permission of Yale University Press.

243   "Prescriptions and Proscriptions of the Advocate" (fig. 7.4) by Lewis Rambo in *Understanding Religious Conversion*. Used with permission of Yale University Press.

244   Good ol' days . . . © Rob Portlock. Used by permission.

245   Sidney Evans, used by permission of Llyfregell Genedlaethol Cymru/The National Library of Wales. www.llgc.org.uk

247   Ejection seat . . . , by Johnny Hawkins, used by permission. First published by *Leadership Journal*, www.leadershipjournal.net.

257   "What Might Conversion Look Like?" used by permission of Nick Parish and Jennifer Parish.

271   John and Charles Wesley, used by permission of Sally Barto.

273   Strangely warmed . . . , used by permission of Ed Koehler.

277   Freeze-dried locusts . . . , by Frank Cotham, used by permission. First published by *Leadership Journal*, www.leadershipjournal.net.

280   John of the Cross, used by permission of Krystan Bruce.

282   Dirty shoes, used by permission of Nick Parish and Jennifer Parish.

282   Clean shoes, used by permission of Nick Parish and Jennifer Parish.

282   Dancing shoes, used by permission of Nick Parish and Jennifer Parish.

287   Another trial . . . , © Rob Portlock, used by permission. First published by *Leadership Journal*, www.leadershipjournal.net.

307   Celtic cross, used by permission of Nick Parish and Jennifer Parish.

308   Late at night . . . , by Doug Hall, used by permission.

312   "Martin Luther" by Lucas Cranach the Elder, public domain.

316   Jennie Evans Moore, used by permission of Sally Barto.

318   Why pastors don't . . . , by Doug Hall, used by permission.

319   "Pentecostal Prayer," by Mark Graham, used with permission.

319   "Young Woman Sitting at Church," by David Stroble, used with permission.

319   Orthodox liturgy, used by permission of Holy Transfiguration Skete. www.society stjohn.com.

322   "A Cartography of the Ecstatic and Meditative States" (fig. 9.3) by Roland Fischer in *Science*. Used by permission of AAAS. www.aaas.org.

323   "Teresa of Avila" by Peter Paul Rubens, public domain.

325   We've been waiting . . . , © Rob Portlock, used by permission. First published by *Leadership Journal*, www.leadershipjournal.net.

339   Mom caring for child, used by permission of Nick Parish and Jennifer Parish.

349   Pastoral paralysis . . . by Dik LaPine, used by permission. First published by *Leadership Journal*, www.leadershipjournal.net.

355   "The Three Phases of Transition" (fig. 10.4). From *Managing Transitions* by William Bridges. Reprinted by permission of Da Capo Press, a member of Perseus Books Group.

375   Casting lots . . . , © Larry Thomas, used by permission. First published by *Leadership Journal*, www.leadershipjournal.net.

378   Diodochus of Photike, used by permission of Sally Barto.

379   Birgitta of Sweden, public domain.

381   Jonathon Edwards, public domain.

386   The Facilitator . . . © Rob Portlock, used by permission. First published by *Leadership Journal*, www.leadershipjournal.net.

405   Taken from *Church Is Stranger than Fiction* by Mary Chambers. Copyright © Mary Chambers. Used by permission of InterVarsity Press, PO Box 1400, Downers Grove, IL 60515. www.ivpress.com.

413   "Prayer during revival meeting. Pentecostal church, Cambria, Illinois," by Arthur Rothstein. Courtesy of the Library of Congress. www.loc.gov.

418   Hot drink time, used by permission of Nick Parish and Jennifer Parish.

418   Story time, used by permission of Nick Parish and Jennifer Parish.

418   Holding hands, used by permission of Nick Parish and Jennifer Parish.

Glossary

Act—See *Force*.

Acting—See *Deciding/Acting*.

affective—The *affective* operations or operational system are those acts of human experience that exhibit a special sensitivity to the meaning of our environment-person relationship and more heavily involve physiological processes (like hormonal activity, increased heart rate, and the like). We also use the words *feeling* and *emotion* to refer to this system.

affective conversion—A form of transformation that emphasizes the reordering of our moods, emotional concerns, and feelings.

affirmation, the way of—This approach to understanding God attends especially to what can be stated positively from scripture and tradition.

agent—An *agent* of spiritual formation is one who takes initiative in the discernment, guidance, or accountable support for an individual or community's formation.

agreement—Information from sources *agree* when they say the same thing about the same topic.

analogy, the way of—This approach to understanding God discovers something of God's character by noticing similarities and differences to things of our world.

antinomianism—A laxity of approach to relationship with God and in particular the commandments of God.

apophatic—This way of approaching God, and relationship with God, intentionally avoids use of ideas, images, feelings, and the like.

apostolic spirituality—A way of expressing Christian care that is oriented toward reaching outside one's own community.

appreciative discernment—The noticing and identifying of God's presence in the midst of the most ordinary aspects of life.

ascetic, asceticism—Literally, "training." *Asceticism* refers to the self-discipline, the self-restraint, or the use of intentional means to facilitate conformity with God (see chap. 8). Metaphorically speaking, an asceticism of scholarship refers to a kind of self-restraint from pet ideas and such in order to foster openness to truth.

aspiration—A type of prayer that expresses longing for God or for some expression of God's character or work.

associations—Voluntary *associations* are collectives of people who gather around a particular (often compassionate) cause.

attention—With regard to spiritual formation, the watchful observation of one's own habits of thought and life, taking note of how situations and contexts affect the dynamics of one's own relationship with God.

awakening—With reference to the renewal of the church, *awakening* indicates the coming to life of the church, especially in the increase in numbers and interest in the things of God.

Being Aware—This is a stage of the process of human experience (usually considered first) whereby we activate a general capacity to evaluate within a certain range of possibilities, an intensity of focus, a degree of energy, and a level of consciousness. At times, the term *consciousness* is used to identify this stage or state of experience in general.

blessing—A pattern of God's response to us whereby God generously provides as part of the interactive relationship.

care—Intentional, loving self-giving for the enrichment of another.

causation, the way of—This approach to understanding God learns, from what is caused around us, something of the nature of the One who caused it all.

centering prayer—A type of prayer that makes use of the repetition of a word or phrase as a means of bringing a person before God.

cognitive—The *cognitive* operations or operational system are those acts of human experience that exhibit a special sensitivity to the structure of our environment: for example, inquiry, insight deduction, comparison, synthesis, and the like. We often use the word *thinking* to describe this system of experience.

cognitive model—A model of the Christian Trinity that likens the Trinity to the unity of mental operations in a single "mind."

commitment—A stage in the process of initial salvation in which one makes a decision to follow the Christian faith and formalizes this in some manner.

common prayer—Spoken prayer ordained by the church.

communal spirituality—A way of living out relationship with God, and expressing Christian care, that is centered for the most part around one's community life.

compatibility—Information from sources are *compatible* when they say different things about the same reality or when they say true things about different but interrelated realities.

concupiscence—The movement of drives, modes, emotions, and other more embodied operations,

468

inclining persons away from harmony with God.

connaturality—A natural kinship of thought, feeling, and life that develops through time with God and familiarity with God. The natural sharing with God of aspects of character and life, which facilitates our sensing the presence, activity, and will of God in particular situations.

consequences—A stage in the process of initial salvation in which the new believer experiences the concrete results of the new commitment in life.

contemplative, contemplation—The term *contemplation* generally refers to a Christian's awareness of God through love. As a *way* of prayer, it refers to prayer undertaken intentionally without the use of words or other means; as an *attitude* of prayer, it refers to the quieting and opening of our souls to receive from God; as an *aim* of prayer, it refers to the union of person and God in the prayerful vision of the presence of God (see chap. 9).

contemplative spirituality—A way of living out relationship with God, and expressing Christian care, that is centered around acts of prayer and reflection.

contentment—A dynamic of relationship with God wherein we sense a degree of satisfaction, comfort, or fit in that relationship. See also *longing*.

context—The milieu in which and through which relationship with God is encountered and lived. This includes general contexts of geography, culture, and history as well as the specific contexts of congregation, spiritual direction, relationships, and particular ministries. *Context* is also the first stage of initial salvation. (See chaps. 7, 8, 10.)

conversational prayer—Spoken prayer following the stirrings of one's own heart.

coordinate—Methods of research or insights provided by different realms of experience are *coordinated* within a single exploration when the contributions of each are made to relate meaningfully within the whole.

corporate evil—The dimension of the tragedy of human experience characterized by social forces, as corporate units, that act contrary to God, attack God's community, and attract some away from God's heart.

covenant—A term describing the character of the divine-human relationship as one that involves initiation and response of both God and humanity.

covenant partner—Term used to refer to our created place as co-rulers with God (in relationship or agreement with God) over this world.

covenant unfaithfulness—Identifies the failure of our partnership and relationship with God, our not living up to our own commitments with God.

creation—One aspect of the greatness of human experience is our place in creation: as distinct from God, as dependent on God, and as participants with the rest of the created order.

crisis—A stage of initial salvation in which we confront our need or desire for something more.

criteria—Clues, conditions, or indications used to point to the presence or activity of God.

Deciding/Acting—This is a stage of the process of human experience (usually considered fifth) whereby we are involved in expressing our evaluative process. Decision making, choosing, deliberating, acting, and such are primary in this stage. Here we ask, "What do we do about it?"

deification—The participation in the divine nature that Christians receive through the process of maturity in Christ.

demon, demonic, Satan—Identifies a network of spiritual forces, beings, or powers that form a part of the cosmic conflict within which the gospel is realized and, more specifically, that subject human experience to tragedy.

depth dimension—The *depth dimension* of human experience names the tendencies we have toward various levels of significance within our experience: for example, a more surface level in which feelings, thoughts, and actions interact with the trivialities of daily life; a deeper level in which beliefs, emotions, and habits exhibit stable patterns of relating to and encountering our environment; a still deeper level in which worldviews, nuclear emotive concerns, and lifestyles ground our lives in fundamental orderings; and perhaps a still deeper and more mysterious center where all our faculties converge (or wherein they are all transcended).

descriptive—An approach to relationship with God that is most interested in describing or exploring how relationship with God is actually experienced.

desert elders—The desert fathers and mothers who, around the fourth century, withdrew from ordinary civic life in the cities to live alone or in Christian community (most notably in the deserts of Egypt). These elders became famous for their austere and holy lives and for their expressions of divine power and wisdom.

devotions—Regular employment of repetition, body movements, imagination,

or other means for the sake of mediating the presence of God.

discernment—The evaluation of inner and outer stuff in light of a relationship with God with a view to a response.

disciplines, spiritual—Activities of mind and body undertaken in order to facilitate or express formation into Christ.

dynamics—The characteristic ways that relationship with God is lived and explored, the nuanced patterns of give-and-take involved in our experience of God and of God's communication with communities and individuals.

ecological conversion—A form of transformation that emphasizes the reordering of our sense of relatedness to nature.

election—The process by which we, having determined the presence or action of God, make a decision, or a choice of life (nothing to do with election in the Calvinist sense).

embodied—Humans are *embodied* in that we experience ourselves, for the most part, as bodied, physical, enfleshed creatures. Our bodies both shape and are shaped by the nonphysical dimension of our experience.

eminence, the way of—This approach to understanding God sees God as the supreme model of the highest values that surround human experience.

encounter—A stage in initial salvation in which we come to meet ourselves, another representative of the faith, and ultimately the divine invitation.

enrichment—The benefit of the one receiving care; the expansion of life for another.

Evaluation—See *Quality*.

experience, Experiencing—These related terms refer to a variety of things. *Experience* refers to one's exposure to some aspect of life (one's "experience" of something). *Experiencing* refers to a stage of human life that includes sensation, perception, and such but is generally prior to analysis and understanding. In a broader sense, *experience* can refer to reality as such—a confluence of Evaluation, Force, and Tendency. (Thus we speak of human "experience" rather than a human "being.")

faith—A way of describing positive response to God: assent to the truth of God and entrustment to the person of God.

final (or eschatological) salvation—The transformation of the individual or community that will take place in the context of the final restoration.

flesh—A special term used by the apostle Paul to describe human experience insofar as it is oriented away from consensual relationship with God.

469

focus—The focus of a discernment process is that which one is discerning *about*.

Force—A fundamental element of experience, corresponding to Charles S. Peirce's category of Secondness, *Force* identifies a confrontation with otherness, resistance, reaction. The term *Act* is also used to refer to this element.

forms—A *form* of spirituality is a particular lived expression of spirituality characteristic of an individual or a collective.

foundation—The *foundation* of Christian spirituality refers to the fundamental principles on which relationship with God has been understood and experienced, presented as a unified structure or whole.

gospel—The presentation of the story and offer of God through Christ.

grace—That characteristic of God (and of those who share with God) wherein God offers favor and relationship uncompelled and unearned, and full of power.

greatness—A term used to describe those features of human experience that are, by the design of God, unique, special, and somewhat exalted above other creatures.

Habit—See *Tendency*.

hedonism—An orientation to life that emphasizes the role of pleasure.

Hesychast—Literally, "quiet," a style of prayer that emphasizes silence, the use of a brief phrase (see *Jesus Prayer*), and the direct experience of God.

historical salvation—Our real (though not necessarily realized) transformation effected by the work of Christ.

holiness—As an aim of spiritual formation, *holiness* refers to a life uniquely set apart with Christ, exhibiting the special character of the divine in thought, word, and deed.

hope—An expectation of synthesis or satisfaction. With regard to the Christian faith, hope anticipates the complete restoration of human experience.

identification—A part of the process of spiritual formation whereby we distinguish particular areas of concern of divine initiative that need response or intentional action on our part.

image of God, of Christ—A term used both in scripture and in tradition to describe our similarity to God or Christ in form and purpose.

imitation of Christ—A kind of spirituality paying special attention to the ways in which our actions or thoughts conform to those of Jesus as seen in the Gospels.

immanence—God's closeness or "withness" to human experience in terms of space and time.

impressions—Thoughts, feelings, noticings, and such that may or may not be indications of God's presence or guidance.

initial salvation—The transformation (or conversion) of the community or individual by means of a beginning commitment to Christ or an entering into relationship with Christ.

initiation—A disclosing self-presentation that functions as the starting point of a relational encounter, characteristically seen in the ways of God with humans (initiation, response, response).

insiders—Those who come to relationship with God from within the context of being raised in a Christian community.

Integrating—This is a stage of the process of human experience (usually considered sixth) whereby we are involved in self-transformation as a part of the evaluative process. Reinforcement, adjustment, paradigm shifts, feedback, and other similar functions are usually present in this stage. Here we ask, "Who am I in light of what is?" and "To what am I inclined now?"

intellectual conversion—A form of transformation that emphasizes the reordering of our thoughts, beliefs, and worldviews.

interaction—A stage in the process of initial salvation in which we engage with (and perhaps struggle with) the objects we encounter in our religious quest prior to making a new commitment to faith.

intercession—A type of prayer that brings requests to God on behalf of others or brings the heart of God concerning others back to God in prayer.

interdisciplinary—An *interdisciplinary* study employs the methods of exploration or integrates the insights of a variety of academic disciplines or informal realms of experience within a single study.

intermediary—A "third party" toward whom acts of care are, at times, offered in order to facilitate benefit for a separate recipient who is related to the intermediary.

interpersonal relationship—The mutual experience of another along with the shared knowledge of that experience.

Jesus Prayer—The repetition of a phrase such as *Lord Jesus Christ, Son of God, have mercy on me, a sinner* as a focus of prayer.

Judging—This is a stage of the process of human experience (usually considered fourth) whereby we are involved in completing an evaluative process. Verification, demonstration, deduction, induction, and conclusion are primary in this stage. Here we ask, "Is it?" or "Is it the case?"

judgment—A dynamic of God's response to us whereby God, out of faithfulness both to us and to God's own concerns, initiates harm to others.

kataphatic—This way of approaching God, and relationship with God, makes intentional use of ideas, images, feelings, and the like.

kingdom of God—This term indicates both an eschatological promise of a new order of humanity and, as such, an aim of spiritual formation: the goal of realizing and *becoming* a new community of the King, ordered around his leadership of love.

lament—A type of prayer that bemoans or complains to God regarding one's (or another's) circumstances.

leaving behind—A stage or state of change in which one is especially sensitive to loss.

lectio divina—Literally, "sacred reading." *Lectio divina* refers to a method of prayerful reading of scripture or some other text usually involving some combination of *lectio* (reading), *meditatio* (meditation on the reading), *oratio* (expressed prayer about what arises during the reading process), and *contemplatio* (simply being present with God).

life discernment—The assessment of the character, stages, and dynamics of one's relationship with God in general, especially with a view to summarizing that relationship up to the present.

longing—A dynamic of relationship with God wherein we sense a degree of dissatisfaction, unrest, or incompleteness in that relationship. See also *contentment*.

means—The *means* of grace or *means* of spiritual formation are those activities, situations, relationships, and such that foster or express the transforming work of God in our lives.

meditation—A means of prayer where thought and feeling *about* God and thought and feeling *toward* God are joined.

mercy—A dynamic of God's response to us whereby God expresses kindness, hesitates to inflict pain, even when we may resist.

mind—This word (along with *soul*, *spirit*, and *self*) most generally refers to the nonphysical dimension of human experience. The term also has special reference to our cognitive operations.

modality—Communities of believers including people of all ages, maturity, or commitment levels and such.

model—Informal relationships and Christian history provide the student of Christian spirituality with *models*: particular samples of embodied relationship with God, examples of the lived spirituality concretely manifest. A *model* can also refer to a pattern or way of looking at a set of ideas or realities, like a *model* of human experience.

monk, monastic, monastery—*Monastic* originally referred to one who went alone (*monos*, literally, "alone") to live in communion with God. Over time, however, the word came to refer to those given to a life of special commitment to God, whether living alone (for example, Carthusian monks) or in community (as Benedictine monks); whether more contemplative or stable in character (as Cistercian monks) or more active or apostolic in character (thus we sometimes hear of Franciscan monks, though friars is the more correct term); whether male (*monk*) or female (*nun*). A *monastery* is the place (especially the stable communities) where monks or nuns reside and serve.

moral conversion—A form of transformation that emphasizes the reordering of our choices, acts, habits, and lifestyle.

movement—With relationship to the renewal of the church, a *movement* speaks of the collection of peoples, structures, energies, and such that are associated with the renewal.

mysticism—That part of the belief and practices of Christianity concerning encounter with the direct presence of God.

negation, the way of—This approach to understanding God learns of God by paying attention to the ways in which God is *not* like human experience.

neutral zone—A stage or state of change in which one is between and without identity, facilitating confusion and experimentation.

new beginnings—A stage or state of change in which one is beginning to see or to realize what one might become.

normative—An approach to relationship with God that is most interested in presenting a framework of understanding and pursuing God considered standard to a given Christian tradition. Also known as *prescriptive*.

nun—See monk, monastic, monastery.

obedience—A way of describing positive response to God: bringing our lives in conformity with the demands of God's presence

omni-passionate—This term refers to God insofar as God reveals and exhibits feelings in an absolutely perfect manner.

once-born—Those who, even though they might not have been raised in a Christian environment, perceive themselves as having always been in positive relationship with God.

ongoing salvation—The transformation of relationship with God that arises through the day-to-day interaction with the Spirit.

openness—A way of describing positive response to God: vulnerable receptivity to the personal and mutual self-giving between ourselves and God.

operation, operational system—*Operations* are sets of Tendencies, patterns of habits of evaluating, responding, and adapting to that which appears around us. A single operation might be identified as perception. An *operational system* involves a somewhat integrated network of operations (as when comparison, definition or clarification, and synthesis are all involved in the cognitive system).

opposition—Information from sources are *opposed* when they appear to contradict each other.

outsiders—Those who come to relationship with God from outside the context of being raised in a Christian community.

perfection—As an aim of spiritual formation, *perfection* refers to the complete maturity of a believer in love.

perspective—Informal relationships and Christian history provide the student of Christian spirituality with *perspectives*: ways of looking at things, concepts and terms to name things, frameworks by which things are comprehended together, unique emphases that highlight things, and the like.

practice—In spirituality, *practice* speaks of the ways in which Christians live out relationship with God in the concrete details of daily life.

prescriptive—See *normative*.

psychological conversion—A form of transformation that emphasizes the reordering of our understanding and experience of our self.

Quality—A fundamental element of experience, corresponding to Charles S. Peirce's category of Firstness, *Quality* identifies a movement toward evaluation, a suchness, or a feeling or thought. The term *Evaluation* is also used to refer to this element.

quest—A stage in initial salvation in which there is an intentional pursuit of something more.

recapitulation—A summing up of the whole of human experience through the life and death of Christ, accomplishing what Adam was created to accomplish and failed.

recipient—The one who receives the benefit of care; the self on behalf of whom care is offered.

recollection—The "bringing together" of oneself in attention toward God in prayer.

reconciliation—The bringing of estranged parties together. In Christian spirituality we speak of reconciliation as Christ's work of rejoining human beings with God and with one another.

rehabituation—A transformation of the patterns of emotions, conducts, thoughts, and such that characterize our experience.

relational mood—The atmosphere of prayer created by the state of our relationship with God as cultivated and perceived at any given time.

religion—The confluence, in concrete collectives of human beings, of myth, institution, doctrine, experience, ethics, ritual, and physical culture regarding matters of ultimacy within human civilization.

religiosity—A way of describing a response to God that appears to be positive to others but is, in reality, a way of avoiding or resisting the invitation of the Spirit. Also called *spiritual pride*.

religious conversion—A form of transformation that emphasizes the reordering of our relationship with God.

renewal—The bringing of new life to the church, generally referring to the arising of new leaders, forms, ideas, structures, or other large-scale patterns of relationship with God.

reorientation—A change in the way a community or individual sees itself in terms of that which surrounds it. A *reorientation* of our relationship with God means that our perspective changes, that we find our bearings with regard to God and human experience differently as a result of relationship with God.

resistance—Patterns of distancing ourselves from or responding negatively to God's initiation.

restoration—The work of God through history, Christ, and the Spirit that brings human experience into holiness and wholeness.

revival—With reference to the renewal of the church, *revival* speaks of new excitement, growth, significant fresh expressions, or other similar phenomena.

sacred musing—A prayerful practice of allowing the mind to wander freely as one spends time with God.

sanctification—The doctrine of the work of God and human participation leading to growth in Christian holiness.

satisfaction—A harmonious or appropriate bringing together of elements of human experience into an experience of integration.

scruple—Unfounded obsession with acts or patterns of life that one considers (falsely) to be sinful.

selection—A part of the process of spiritual formation whereby we choose appropriate means or strategies for intentional progress in maturity.

self—This word (along with *soul*, *mind*, and *spirit*) most generally refers to the nonphysical dimension of human experience. This word also draws attention to the individual person or community as an integrated whole.

self-examen, self-examination—The Christian discipline whereby believers prayerfully look within themselves after a time of activity (at the end of a day, a week, or a season) to reflect on the character of their own relationship with God or the quality of their own thoughts, habits, and feelings. See the "Practicing Christian Spirituality" exercise at the end of chapter 5.

self-existent—God is *self-existent* in that God's existence, God's being, is not dependent on anything outside of God; rather God arises from God's *self*. God makes his own existence happen.

sin—A term used to summarize human experience as separated or alienated from God.

situational discernment—The evaluation of circumstances in the midst of particular (and often difficult) junctions of life in order to determine God's presence or activity.

situational mood—The atmosphere of prayer created by the surroundings, our physical energy, the setting (public or private), and other similar kinds of factors.

social conversion—A form of transformation that emphasizes the reordering of our relationships with others (including both small, informal social relationships as well as larger structural relationships).

social model—A model of the Christian Trinity that likens the Trinity to a unity of distinct persons in social relationship.

sodality—Communities of believers who tend to limit themselves by commitment level and by age, sex, or other characteristics.

soul—This word (along with *mind*, *spirit*, and *self*) most generally refers to the nonphysical dimension of human experience. *Soul*, along with *spirit*, has at times identified a kind of core or center of the human personality.

sources—The sources of discernment are those areas of experience toward which one looks to find indications of God's presence or guidance.

spirit—This word (along with *soul*, *mind*, and *self*) most generally refers to the nonphysical dimension of human experience. *Spirit*, along with *soul*, has at times identified a kind of core or center of the human personality. In particular, *spirit* has been used to refer to that dimension of human experience through which we are especially related to God.

spiritual direction—A relationship of care wherein one (a director) attends especially to the active presence of God and the response of another (the directee).

spiritual formation—Christian *spiritual formation* in general refers to the intentional and semi-intentional processes by which believers become more fully conformed and united to Christ, especially with regard to maturity of life and calling. As a field of study, *spiritual formation* explores particularly the means by which growth toward maturity is fostered in Christian life.

spiritual pride—See *religiosity*.

spiritual theology—That part of theology defining the nature of the supernatural life and describing the process of the advancement of Christians toward full perfection.

spiritual warfare—A perspective or approach to spiritual life that recognizes the existence of evil spiritual powers at work against human experience and that seeks to oppose these forces.

spirituality—Christian *spirituality* refers to relationship with God as lived in practice, as dynamics are formulated within a given approach to lived relationship, and as the lived practice and dynamics are explored through formal study.

supplication—A type of prayer that pleads with God on behalf of oneself or another.

Tendency—A fundamental element of experience, corresponding to Charles S. Peirce's category of Thirdness. *Tendency* identifies a recognition of pattern, a sign, or a law of behavior. The term *Habit* is also used to refer to this element.

tragedy—A term used to describe human experience insofar as it is kept from fulfilling its character and purpose by forces or factors within and without.

transcendence—God's distance or "otherness" from human experience of space and time.

transformation—A change in the form or the character of something or some experience. In Christian spirituality it refers to the changes in our experience that follow from relationship with God.

twice-born—Those who enter relationship with God through the context of a significant season or event that serves as a fundamental transforming pivot toward the faith.

Understanding—This is a stage of the process of human experience (usually considered third) whereby we are involved in an active evaluative process. Inquiry, insight, image, hypothesis, and such usually are present in this stage. Here we ask, "What is it?" or "What is the case?"

volition—The *volitional* operations or operational system are those acts of human experience that exhibit a special sensitivity to intentionality, to our initiation of change within either thought or feeling. We also use the term *will* to refer to this system.

welcome—Patterns of drawing ourselves toward or responding positively to God's initiation.

world—A special term used by the apostle John to describe the corporate dimension of humanity oriented away from God.

yieldedness—From the German *Gelassenheit*; a way of describing positive response to God: the letting go of ourselves to the presence and guidance of God.

Bibliography

Addison, Steve. "Movement Dynamics: Keys to the Expansion and Renewal of the Church in Mission." Unpublished paper, 2003.

Aelred of Rievaulx. *Spiritual Friendship.* Translated by Mary Eugene Laker. Kalamazoo, MI: Cistercian Publications, 1977.

Ahlstrom, Sydney E. *A Religious History of the American People.* New Haven: Yale University Press, 1972.

Albert the Great and Thomas Aquinas. *Albert and Thomas: Selected Writings.* Translated by Simon Tugwell. Classics of Western Spirituality. New York: Paulist Press, 1988.

Albrecht, Daniel E. "An Investigation of the Sociocultural Characteristics and Dynamics of Wallace's 'Revitalization Movements': A Comparative Analysis of the Works of Four Social Scientists." Unpublished paper, 1989.

———. *Rites in the Spirit: A Ritual Approach to Pentecostal/Charismatic Spirituality.* Journal of Pentecostal Theology Supplement Series. Sheffield, UK: Sheffield Academic Press, 1999.

Alexander, Jon. "What Do Recent Writers Mean by Spirituality?" *Spirituality Today* 32 (1980): 247–56.

Allchin, A. M., ed. *Solitude and Communion: Papers on the Hermit Life Given at St. David's, Wales, in the Autumn of 1975.* Fairacres, UK: SLG Press, 1977.

Allchin, Donald. "Eastern Orthodox Monasticism." *London Quarterly and Holborn Review* 189 (January 1964): 22–26.

Alston, William. *Perceiving God: The Epistemology of Religious Experience.* Ithaca and London: Cornell University Press, 1991.

Amar, Joseph P. "On Hermits and Desert Dwellers." In *Ascetic Behavior in Graeco-Roman Antiquity: A Sourcebook,* edited by Vincent L. Wimbush, 66–80. Minneapolis: Fortress, 1990.

Anderson, Douglas R. *Strands of System: The Philosophy of Charles Peirce.* West Lafayette, IN: Purdue University Press, 1995.

Anderson, J. R. *Cognitive Psychology and Its Implication.* 4th ed. New York: W. H. Freeman, 1995.

Angela of Foligno. *Angela of Foligno: Complete Works.* Translated by Paul Lachance. Classics of Western Spirituality. New York: Paulist Press, 1993.

Anselm of Canterbury. *Monologium.* In *St. Anselm: Basic Writings.* 2nd ed. Translated by S. N. Deane, 81–190. LaSalle, IL: Open Court Publishing Company, 1962.

Aquinas, Thomas. *Summa Theologica.* Translated by Fathers of the English Dominican Province. Westminster, MD: Christian Classics, 1981.

Arendt, Hannah. *The Life of the Mind.* San Diego: Harcourt Brace, 1971.

Armstrong, Karen. *A History of God.* New York: Ballantine, 1993.

Armstrong, Karen, Don Cupitt, Robert W. Funk, Lloyd Geering et al. *The Once and Future Faith.* Santa Rosa, CA: Polebridge, 2001.

Arndt, Johann. *Johann Arndt: True Christianity.* Translated by Peter Erb. Classics of Western Spirituality. New York: Paulist Press, 1979.

———. *True Christianity: A Treatise on Sincere Repentance, True Faith, the Holy Walk of the True Christian, Etc.* Translated by A. W. Boehm. Philadelphia: General Council Publication House, 1910.

Arnold, J. Heinrich. *Discipleship.* Compiled and edited by the Hutterian Brethren. Farmington, PA: Plough Publishing House, 1994.

Arnold, Jeffrey. *The Big Book on Small Groups.* Downers Grove, IL: InterVarsity Press, 1992.

Aronson, Elliot. *The Social Animal.* 6th ed. New York: W. H. Freeman, 1992.

Ashley, J. Matthew. "Contemplation in Prophetic Action." *Christian Spirituality Bulletin* 8, no. 1 (Spring–Summer 2000): 6–13.

———. "The Turn to Spirituality? The Relationship between Theology and Spirituality." *Christian Spirituality Bulletin* 3, no. 2 (Fall 1995): 13–18.

Athanasius. *Athanasius: The Life of Antony and the Letter to Marcellinus.* Translated by Robert C. Gregg. Classics of Western Spirituality. New York: Paulist Press, 1980.

———. *On the Incarnation.* Translated and edited by a religious of CSMV with an introduction by C. S. Lewis. London: Mowbray, 1975.

Athenagoras. "A Plea for the Christians," and "On the Resurrection of the Dead." In *The Ante-Nicene Fathers,* Vol 2. Edited by A. Roberts and J. Donaldson. Albany, OR: Ages Software, 2000.

Augustine of Hippo. *City of God.* Translated by Henry Bettenson. London: Penguin, 1972.

———. *The Confessions.* Translated by Henry Chadwick. Oxford: Oxford University Press, 1991.

———. *On Genesis: A Refutation of the Manichees; Unfinished Literal Commentary on Genesis; The Literal Meaning of Genesis.* Translated by Edmund Hill. The Works of Saint Augustine: A Translation for the 21st Century. Hyde Park, NY: New City Press, 2002.

———. *The Monastic Rules.* Translated by Sister Agatha Mary and Gerald Bonner. The Augustine Series, Vol 4. Hyde Park, NY: New City Press, 2004.

Aumann, Jordan. *Spiritual Theology.* London: Sheed and Ward, 1980.

Averill, James. "A Constructivist View of Emotion." In vol. 1 of *Theories of Emo-*

tion, edited by Robert Plutchik and Henry Kellerman. Emotion: Theory, Research, and Experience, 305–39. New York: Academic Press, 1980.

Bailie, Gil. Violence Unveiled: Humanity at the Crossroads. New York: Crossroad, 1995.

Bainton, Roland H. The Reformation of the Sixteenth Century. Boston: Beacon, 1952.

Banks, Robert, and Julia Banks. The Church Comes Home. Peabody, MA: Hendrickson, 1998.

Barna, George. Revolution. Wheaton: Tyndale House, 2005.

Barry, William A., and William J. Connolly. The Practice of Spiritual Direction. New York: Seabury, 1982.

———. Spiritual Direction and the Encounter with God: A Theological Inquiry. Mahwah, NJ: Paulist Press, 1992.

Barsanuphius and John. Guidance Toward Spiritual Life: Answers to the Questions of Disciples. Translated by Fr. Seraphim Rose. Platina, CA: St. Herman Press, 1990.

Barth, Karl. Church Dogmatics. Edited by G. W. Bromiley and T. F. Torrance. 14 vols. Edinburgh: T and T Clark, 1956–75.

———. Prayer. Translated by Sara F. Terrien. 50th anniv. ed. Louisville: Westminster John Knox, 2002.

Bavinck, Herman. The Doctrine of God. Translated by William Hendriksen. Grand Rapids: Baker, 1951.

Baxter, J. Sidlow. Going Deeper. Grand Rapids: Zondervan, 1959.

———. His Deeper Work in Us: A Further Enquiry into New Testament Teaching on the Subject of Christian Holiness. Grand Rapids: Zondervan, 1967.

Bayly, Lewis. The Practice of Piety: Directing a Christian How to Walk that He May Please God. London: Daniel Midwinter, 1714.

Beasley-Murray, George R. John. Word Biblical Commentary. Dallas: Word, 1987.

Beirnaert, Louis. "Does Sanctification Depend on Psychic Structure?" Cross Currents 2 (Winter 1951): 39–43.

Beit-Hallahmi, Benjamin. "Object Relations Theory and Religious Experience." In Handbook of Religious Experience, edited by Ralph W. Hood Jr., 254–68. Birmingham, AL: Religious Education Press, 1995.

Bell, Catherine. Ritual: Perspectives and Dimensions. New York: Oxford University Press, 1997.

Bellah, Robert N., Richard Madsen, William M. Sullivan, Ann Swidler, and Steven M. Tipton. Habits of the Heart: Individualism and Commitment in American Life. New York: Harper and Row, 1985.

Belloso, Joseph M. Rovira. "Who Is Capable of Discerning?" In Discernment of the Spirit and of Spirits, edited by Casiano Floristan and Christian DuQuoc, 84–94. New York: Seabury, 1979.

Bender, Sue. Plain and Simple: A Woman's Journey to the Amish. San Francisco: HarperSanFrancisco, 1989.

Benedict of Nursia. The Rule of St. Benedict. Translated by Anthony C. Meisel and M. L. del Mastro. New York: Image Doubleday, 1975.

Bennett, William J., ed., The Book of Virtues: A Treasury of Great Moral Stories. New York: Simon and Schuster, 1993.

Benson, Herbert, et al. "Study of the Therapeutic Effects of Intercessory Prayer (STEP) in Cardiac Bypass Patients: A Multicenter Randomized Trial of Uncertainty and Certainty of Receiving Intercessory Prayer." American Heart Journal 151, no. 4 (2006): 934.

Berger, Peter L. The Sacred Canopy: Elements of a Sociological Theory of Religion. New York: Anchor, 1969.

Berger, Peter L., and Thomas Luckmann. The Social Construction of Reality: A Treatise in the Sociology of Knowledge. Garden City, NY: Doubleday Anchor, 1966.

Berkouwer, G. C. Sin. Studies in Dogmatics. Grand Rapids: Eerdmans, 1971.

Bernard, Charles André. "The Nature of Spiritual Theology." In Exploring Christian Spirituality: An Ecumenical Reader, edited by Ken Collins, 227–41. Grand Rapids: Baker, 2000.

Bernard of Clairvaux. Bernard of Clairvaux: Selected Works. Translated by G. R. Evans. Classics of Western Spirituality. Mahwah, NJ: Paulist Press, 1987.

Berry, Wendell. The Art of the Commonplace: The Agrarian Essays of Wendell Berry. Edited by Norman Wirzba. Washington, DC: Shoemaker and Hoard, 2002.

———. "The Body and the Earth." In The Unsettling of America: Culture and Agriculture, 97–140. San Francisco: Sierra Club Books, 1986.

———. "Getting Along with Nature." In Home Economics: Fourteen Essays by Wendell Berry, 6–20. New York: North Point, 1987.

———. Home Economics: Fourteen Essays by Wendell Berry. New York: North Point, 1987.

———. Jayber Crow: A Novel. Washington, DC: Counterpoint, 2000.

Bessenecker, Scott. The New Friars: The Emerging Movement Serving the World's Poor. Downers Grove, IL: InterVarsity Press, 2006.

Bickle, Mike. Passion for Jesus: Perfecting Extravagant Love for God. Orlando, FL: Creation House, 1993.

Blocher, Henri. Original Sin: Illuminating the Riddle. New Studies in Biblical Theology. Grand Rapids: Eerdmans, 1997.

Bloesch, Donald. The Crisis of Piety. Colorado Springs: Helmers and Howard, 1988.

———. Faith and Its Counterfeits. Downers Grove, IL: InterVarsity Press, 1981.

———. God, Authority, and Salvation. Essentials of Evangelical Theology. Peabody, MA: Prince, 1998.

———. God the Almighty: Power, Wisdom, Holiness, Love. Downers Grove, IL: InterVarsity Press, 1995.

———. The Struggle of Prayer. New York: Harper and Row, 1980.

Bloom, Anthony. Beginning to Pray. New York: Paulist Press, 1970.

Boa, Kenneth. Conformed to His Image: Biblical and Practical Approaches to Spiritual Formation. Grand Rapids: Zondervan, 2001.

Boehme, Jacob. Jacob Boehme: The Way to Christ. Translated by Peter Erb. Classics of Western Spirituality. New York: Paulist Press, 1978.

Boland, Paschal. The Concept of Discretio Spirituum in John Gerson's "De Probatione Spirituum" and "De Distinctione Verarum Visionum a Falsis." Catholic University of America Studies in Sacred Theology, 2nd ser. Washington, DC: Catholic University of America Press, 1959.

Bolsinger, Tod E. It Takes a Church to Raise a Christian: How the Community of God Transforms Lives. Grand Rapids: Brazos, 2004.

Bonaventure. Bonaventure: The Soul's Journey into God; The Tree of Life; The Life of St. Francis. Classics of Western Spirituality. New York: Paulist Press, 1978.

———. The Triple Way. In The Works of Bonaventure I: Mystical Opscula. Translated by Jose de Vinck. Patterson, NJ: St. Anthony Guild Press, 1960.

Bonhoeffer, Dietrich. The Cost of Discipleship. New York: Macmillan, 1963.

———. Life Together. Translated by John W. Doberstein. San Francisco: Harper SanFrancisco, 1954.

Borg, Marcus J. The God We Never Knew: Beyond a Dogmatic Religion to a More Authentic Contemporary Faith. San Francisco: HarperSanFrancisco, 1997.

———. The Heart of Christianity: Rediscovering a Life of Faith. San Francisco: HarperSanFrancisco, 2004.

———. Jesus: A New Vision; Spirit, Culture, and the Life of Discipleship.

San Francisco: HarperSanFrancisco, 1987.

Boyce, W. Thomas. "Beyond the Clinical Gaze." In *The Crisis of Care: Affirming and Restoring Caring Practices in the Helping Professions*, edited by Susan S. Phillips and Patricia Benner, 144–48. Washington, DC: Georgetown University Press, 1994.

Boyd, Gregory A. *God at War: The Bible and Spiritual Conflict*. Downers Grove, IL: InterVarsity Press, 1997.

———. *God of the Possible: A Biblical Introduction to the Open View of God*. Grand Rapids: Baker, 2000.

———. *Satan and the Problem of Evil: Constructing a Trinitarian Warfare Theodicy*. Downers Grove, IL: InterVarsity Press, 2001.

Boyer, Ernest, Jr. *Finding God at Home: Family Life as Spiritual Discipline*. San Francisco: Harper and Row, 1988.

Brackley, Dean. *The Call to Discernment in Troubled Times: New Perspectives on the Transformative Wisdom of Ignatius of Loyola*. New York: Crossroad, 2004.

Bray, Gerald, ed. *Romans*. Ancient Christian Commentary on Scripture. Downers Grove, IL: InterVarsity Press, 1998.

Bridgers, Lynn. "Beyond Recognition: Trauma, Spirituality and Pedagogy for the Prophetic." Paper presented to the American Academy of Religion Spirituality Group, Denver, November 17–20, 2001.

Bridges, Flora Wilson. *Resurrection Song: African-American Spirituality*. Maryknoll, NY: Orbis, 2001.

Bridges, William. *Managing Transitions: Making the Most of Change*. Cambridge, MA: Da Capo, 2003.

Bright, Bill. *The Four Spiritual Laws*. San Bernardino, CA: Campus Crusade for Christ International, 1965.

Brooks, A. E. C., comp. *Answers to Prayer from George Muller's Narratives*. Chicago: Moody, n.d.

Broome, Benjamin J., ed. *Understanding Relationships: Selected Readings in Interpersonal Communication*, Dubuque, IA: Kendall/Hunt, 1986.

Brother Lawrence. *The Practice of the Presence of God*. Springdale, PA: Whitaker House, 1982.

Brown, Peter. *The Body and Society: Men, Women, and Sexual Renunciation in Early Christianity*. New York: Columbia University Press, 1988.

Brueggemann, Walter. *The Message of the Psalms: A Theological Commentary*. Minneapolis: Augsburg, 1984.

———. *Theology of the Old Testament: Testimony, Dispute, Advocacy*. Minneapolis: Fortress, 1997.

Bryant, David. *Concerts of Prayer: Christians Join for Spiritual Awakening and World Evangelism*. Ventura, CA: Regal Books, 1984.

Buber, Martin. *I and Thou*. Translated by Walter Kaufmann. New York: Charles Scribner's Sons, 1970.

Bumpus, Mary Rose. "The Story of Martha and Mary and the Potential for Transformative Engagement: Luke 10:38–42." PhD diss. Graduate Theological Union, 2000.

Bunge, Gabriel. *Earthen Vessels: The Practice of Personal Prayer According to the Patristic Tradition*. San Francisco: Ignatius, 2002.

Bunyan, John. *The Pilgrim's Progress: From This World to That Which is to Come*. Uhrichsville, OH: Barbour and Company, 1993.

Burghardt, Walter J. "Contemplation: A Long, Loving Look at the Real." *Church* (Winter 1989): 14–18.

Burton-Christie, Douglas. "Learning to See: Epiphany in the Ordinary." *Weavings* (November–December 1996): 6–16.

———. *The Word in the Desert: Scripture and the Quest for Holiness in Early Christian Monasticism*. New York: Oxford University Press, 1993.

Byassee, Jason. "The New Monastics." *Christian Century*, October 18, 2005, 38–47.

Bynum, Caroline Walker. *Holy Feast and Holy Fast: The Religious Significance of Food to Medieval Women*. Berkeley and Los Angeles: University of California Press, 1987.

———. "Religious Women in the Later Middle Ages." In *Christian Spirituality: High Middle Ages and Reformation*, edited by Jill Raitt, Bernard McGinn, and John Meyendorff. Vol. 17 of *World Spirituality: An Encyclopedic History of the Religious Quest*, 121–39. New York: Crossroad, 1987.

Byrd, Randolph. "Positive Therapeutic Effects of Intercessory Prayer in a Coronary Care Unit Population." *Southern Medical Journal* 81, no. 7 (July 1988): 826–29.

Cabasilas, Nicholas. *The Life in Christ*. Crestwood, NY: St. Vladimir's Press, 1997.

Cahill, Thomas. *How the Irish Saved Civilization: The Untold Story of Ireland's Heroic Role from the Fall of Rome to the Rise of Medieval Europe*. New York: Doubleday, 1995.

Calvin, John. *Institutes of the Christian Religion*. Translated by Henry Beveridge. Grand Rapids: Eerdmans, 1953.

Campolo, Anthony. *How to Rescue the Earth without Worshiping Nature: A*

Christian's Call to Save Creation. Nashville: Thomas Nelson, 1992.

Capra, Fritjof. *The Web of Life: A New Scientific Understanding of Living Systems*. New York: Anchor, 1996.

Carmichael, Alexander, ed. *Carmina Gadelica*. Edinburgh: Floris Books, 1992.

Carson, Don A. "God, the Bible and Spiritual Warfare: A Review Article." *Journal of the Evangelical Theological Society* 42, no. 2 (June 1999): 251–70.

A Carthusian. *The Call of Silent Love: Vocation and Discernment*. Carthusian Novice Conferences. Kalamazoo, MI: Cistercian Publications, 1995.

Cassian, John. *Conferences*. Translated by Colm Luibheid. Classics of Western Spirituality. New York: Paulist Press, 1985.

———. *John Cassian: The Conferences*. Translated and annotated by Boniface Ramsey. Ancient Christian Writers, Vol. 57. New York: Newman Press, 1997.

———. *The Monastic Institutes*. Translated by Jerome Bertram. London: The Saint Austin Press, 1999.

Castilli, Elizabeth A. "Pseudo-Athanasius: Life and Activity of Syncletica." In *Ascetic Behavior in Graeco-Roman Antiquity: A Sourcebook*, edited by Vincent L. Wimbush, 265–311. Minneapolis: Fortress, 1990.

Castro, Emilio. "Your Kingdom Come: A Missionary Perspective." In *Your Kingdom Come, Mission Perspectives: Report on the World Conference on Mission and Evangelism*, 26–36. Geneva: World Council of Churches, 1980.

Catechism of the Catholic Church. Second edition. Washington, DC: Libraria Editrice Vaticana/United States Catholic Conference, 1994.

Catherine of Siena. *Catherine of Siena: The Dialogue*. Translated by Suzanne Noffke. Classics of Western Spirituality. New York: Paulist Press, 1980.

Chai, Ch'u, and Winberg Chai. *The Sacred Books of Confucius and Other Confucian Classics*. New York: Bantam, 1965.

Chan, Simon. *Spiritual Theology: A Systematic Study of the Christian Life*. Downers Grove, IL: InterVarsity Press, 1998.

Chariton, Igumen, comp. *The Art of Prayer: An Orthodox Anthology*. Translated by E. Kadloubavsky and E. M. Palmer. London: Faber and Faber, 1966.

Charry, Ellen T. *By the Renewing of Your Minds: The Pastoral Function of Doctrine*. New York: Oxford University Press, 1997.

Chevignard, Bernard-Marie. "Formation, Spirituelle." In *Dictionnaire de*

Spiritualité Ascetique et Mystique, edited by M. Viller, F. Cavallera, and J. de Guibert, Vol. 5, cols. 699–716. Paris: Beauchesne, 1964.

Chittester, Joan. *Wisdom Distilled from the Daily: Living the Rule of St. Benedict Today*. San Francisco: HarperSanFrancisco, 1990.

Chitty, Derwas J. *The Desert a City: An Introduction to the Study of Egyptian and Palestinian Monasticism under the Christian Empire*. Crestwood, NY: St. Vladimir's Seminary Press, 1966.

Cicero. *De Amicitia*. In *Cicero: De Senectute, De Amicitia, De Divinatione*. Translated by William Armistead Falconer. Loeb Classical Library, Vol. 154. Cambridge: Harvard University Press, 1923.

Claiborne, Shane. *The Irresistible Revolution*. Grand Rapids: Zondervan, 2006.

Clapp, Rodney. *Tortured Wonders: Christian Spirituality for People, Not Angels*. Grand Rapids: Brazos, 2004.

Clark, Elizabeth A. "The Ascetic Impulse in Religious Life: A General Response." In *Asceticism*, edited by Vincent L. Wimbush and Richard Valantasis, 505–12. New York: Oxford University Press, 1995.

———. *Reading Renunciation: Asceticism and Scripture in Early Christianity*. Princeton: Princeton University Press, 1999.

Clark, Mary T. Introductory note to *Augustine of Hippo: Selected Writings*, translated by Mary T. Clark. Classics of Western Spirituality, 363–64. New York: Paulist Press, 1984.

———. "The Trinity in Latin Christianity." In *Christian Spirituality: Origins to the Twelfth Century*, edited by Bernard McGinn, John Meyendorff, and Jean Leclercq. Vol. 16, World Spirituality: An Encyclopedic History of the Religious Quest, 276–90. New York: Crossroad, 1985.

Cleary, Miriam. "A Societal Context for Supervision." *Presence: The Journal of Spiritual Directors International* 4, no. 2 (May 1998): 26–31.

Clift, Jean Dalby, and Wallace B. Clift. *The Archetype of Pilgrimage: Outer Action with Inner Meaning*. Mahwah, NJ: Paulist Press, 1996.

Climacus, John. *John Climacus: The Ladder of Divine Ascent*. Translated by Colm Luibheid and Norman Russell. Classics of Western Spirituality. New York: Paulist Press, 1982.

Clinton, J. Robert. *Bridging Strategies: Leadership Strategies for Introducing Change*. Altadena, CA: Barnabas Publishing, 1992.

The Cloud of Unknowing. Edited by James Walsh. Classics of Western Spirituality. New York: Paulist Press, 1981.

Coles, Robert. *The Spiritual Life of Children*. Boston: Houghton Mifflin, 1990.

Collins, Kenneth J. *The Scripture Way of Salvation: The Heart of John Wesley's Theology*. Nashville: Abingdon, 1997.

Collins, Kenneth J., ed. *Exploring Christian Spirituality: An Ecumenical Reader*. Grand Rapids: Baker, 2000.

Collins, Kenneth J., and John H. Tyson, eds. *Conversion in the Wesleyan Tradition*. Nashville: Abingdon, 2001.

Confucius. *The Analects of Confucius*. Translated by Arthur Waley. New York: Vintage, 1938.

Congar, Yves. *I Believe in the Holy Spirit*. Translated by David Smith. New York: Crossroad, 1997.

Conn, Joann Wolski, ed. *Women's Spirituality: Resources for Christian Development*. 2nd ed. New York: Paulist Press, 1996.

Conroy, Maureen. *The Discerning Heart: Discovering a Personal God*. Chicago: Loyola Press, 1993.

Cornelius, Randolph R. *The Science of Emotion: Research and Tradition in the Psychology of Emotion*. Upper Saddle River, NJ: Prentice Hall, 1996.

Coser, Lewis A. *Masters of Sociological Thought: Ideas of Historical and Social Context*. 2nd ed. New York: Harcourt Brace Jovanovich, 1977.

Cousins, Ewert H. "What Is Christian Spirituality?" In *Modern Christian Spirituality: Methodological and Historical Essays*, edited by Bradley C. Hanson, 39–44. Atlanta: Scholars Press, 1990.

Cousins, Ewert, gen. ed. *World Spirituality: An Encyclopedic History of the Religious Quest*. New York: Crossroad, 1989–.

Cover, Robin C. "Sin, Sinners (OT)." In *The Anchor Bible Dictionary*, edited by David Noel Freedman, 6 vols., 6:31–40. New York: Doubleday, 1992.

Crabb, Larry. *Connecting: Healing Ourselves and Our Relationships*. Nashville: Word, 1997.

Craig, William Lane. *Time and Eternity: Exploring God's Relationship to Time*. Wheaton: Crossway, 2001.

Crockett, Billy. "Carrier." On *Carrier*. Word Records, 1984.

Crouzel, Henri. *Origen*. Translated by A. S. Worrall. San Francisco: Harper and Row, 1985.

Crowner, David, and Gerald Christianson, trans. *The Spirituality of the German Awakening*, Classics of Western

Spirituality. Mahwah, NJ: Paulist Press, 2003.

Culbertson, Philip Leroy. *New Adam: The Future of Masculine Spirituality*. Minneapolis: Fortress, 1992.

Cunningham, Lawrence S. *Catholic Prayer*. New York: Crossroad, 1992.

———. "*Extra Arcam Noe*: Criteria for Christian Spirituality." *Christian Spirituality Bulletin* 3, no. 1 (Spring 1995): 6–9.

Daniel, Stephen H. *The Philosophy of Jonathan Edwards*. Bloomington, IN: Indiana University Press, 1994.

Daniélou, Jean. *God and the Ways of Knowing*. Translated by Walter Roberts. San Francisco: Ignatius, 1957.

Davids, Peter H. "Sickness and Suffering in the New Testament." In *Wrestling with Dark Angels: Toward a Deeper Understanding of the Supernatural Forces in Spiritual Warfare*, edited by C. Peter Wagner and F. Douglas Pennoyer, 215–47. Ventura, CA: Regal Books, 1990.

Davidson, R. J., et al. "Alterations in Brain and Immune Function Produced by Mindfulness Meditation." *Psychosomatic Medicine* 65 (2003): 564–70.

Davies, Oliver, trans. *Celtic Spirituality*. Classics of Western Spirituality. New York: Paulist Press, 1999.

Davis, Kenneth Ronald. *Anabaptism and Asceticism: A Study in Intellectual Origins*. Studies in Anabaptist and Mennonite History. Scottsdale, PA: Herald Press, 1974.

Dawes, Robyn M. *Rational Choice in an Uncertain World*. Fort Worth: Harcourt Brace, 1988.

Dawn, Marva. *Reaching Out without Dumbing Down: A Theology of Worship for This Urgent Time*. Grand Rapids: Eerdmans, 1995.

Day, Dorothy. *The Long Loneliness: The Autobiography of Dorothy Day*. San Francisco: HarperCollins, 1952.

de Caussade, Jean-Pierre. *The Sacrament of the Present Moment*. Translated by Kitty Muggeridge. San Francisco: HarperSanFrancisco, 1981.

de Guibert, Joseph. *The Theology of the Spiritual Life*. Translated by Paul Barrett. New York: Sheed and Ward, 1953.

de Mello, Anthony. *Sadhana, a Way to God: Christian Exercises in Eastern Form*. Garden City, NY: Image Doubleday, 1984.

de Sales, Francis, and Jane de Chantal. *Francis de Sales, Jane de Chantal: Letters of Spiritual Direction*. Translated by Péronne Marie Thibert. Classics of Western Spirituality. New York: Paulist Press, 1988.

de Wit, Han F. "Contemplative Psychology: Uncovering the Field." In

Christian Spirituality Bulletin 1, no. 2 (Fall 1993):23–25.

Deiter, Melvin E., Anthony A. Hoekema, Stanley M. Horton, J. Robertson McQuilkin, and John F. Walvoord. *Five Views on Sanctification.* Grand Rapids: Zondervan, 1987.

Dekker, John. *Torches of Joy.* Seattle: YWAM Publishing, 1992.

Delattre, Roland André. *Beauty and Sensibility in the Thought of Jonathan Edwards.* New Haven: Yale University Press, 1968.

Demarest, Bruce. *The Cross and Salvation: The Doctrine of Salvation.* Foundations of Evangelical Theology. Wheaton: Crossway, 1997.

———. *Satisfy Your Soul: Restoring the Heart of Christian Spirituality.* Colorado Springs: NavPress, 1999.

———. *Soul Guide: Following Jesus as Spiritual Director.* Colorado Springs: NavPress, 2003.

Dewey, John. *Logic: The Theory of Inquiry.* New York: Henry Holt, 1938.

Dickason, C. Fred. *Demon Possession and the Christian.* Chicago: Moody, 1987.

Dickens, Charles. *A Christmas Carol.* New York: Weathervane Books, 1977.

The Documents of Vatican II. New York: Guild, 1966.

Doran, Robert. *Subject and Psyche: Ricoeur, Jung and the Search for Foundations.* Washington, DC: University Press of America, 1977.

Dossey, Larry. *Healing Words: The Power of Prayer and the Practice of Medicine.* New York: HarperCollins, 1993.

Dougherty, Rose Mary. *Group Spiritual Direction: Community for Discernment.* New York: Paulist Press, 1995.

Downey, Michael. *Understanding Christian Spirituality.* New York: Paulist Press, 1997.

Downey, Michael, ed. *The New Dictionary of Catholic Spirituality.* Collegeville, MN: Liturgical Press, 1993.

Driskill, Joseph D. *Protestant Spiritual Exercises: Theology, History, and Practice.* Harrisburg, PA: Morehouse, 1999.

Duck, Steve. *Understanding Relationships.* New York: Guilford, 1991.

Duffy, Eamon. *Saints and Sinners: A History of the Popes.* New Haven: Yale University Press, 1997.

Dunfee, Susan Nelson. "The Sin of Hiding: A Feminist Critique of Reinhold Niebuhr's Account of the Sin of Pride." *Soundings* 65 (Fall 1982): 316–27.

Dupré, Louis, and James A. Wiseman. *Light from Light: An Anthology of Christian Mysticism.* New York: Paulist Press, 1988.

Durham, John I. *Exodus.* Word Biblical Commentary 3. Dallas: Word, 1987.

Dyckman, Katherine, Mary Garvin, and Elizabeth Liebert. *The Spiritual Exercises Reclaimed; Uncovering Liberating Possibilities for Women.* New York: Paulist Press, 2001.

Easterbrook, Greg. "Can You Pray Your Way to Health?" http://www.belief net.com/story/69/story_6991_4 .html.

Eckhart, Meister. *Meister Eckhart: The Essential Sermons, Commentaries, Treatises and Defence.* Translated by Edmund College and Bernard McGinn. Classics of Western Spirituality. New York: Paulist Press, 1986.

———. *Meister Eckhart: Teacher and Preacher.* Edited by Bernard McGinn. Classics of Western Spirituality. New York: Paulist Press, 1986.

Edwards, Jonathan. *The Works of Jonathan Edwards.* 24 Vols. New Haven: Yale University Press, 1957–2006.

Egan, Harvey D. "Affirmative Way." In *The New Dictionary of Catholic Spirituality,* edited by Michael Downey, 14–17. Collegeville, MN: Liturgical Press, 1993.

Egan, Keith J. "Carmelite Spirituality." In *Exploring Christian Spirituality: An Ecumenical Reader,* edited by Kenneth J. Collins, 97–107. Grand Rapids: Baker, 2000.

Eldredge, John. *Wild at Heart: Discovering the Secret of a Man's Soul.* Nashville: Thomas Nelson, 2001.

Elgvin, Torleif. "Belial, Beliar, Devil, Satan." In *Dictionary of New Testament Background,* edited by Craig Evans and Stanley Porter. Downers Grove, IL: InterVarsity Press, 2000.

Eliade, Mircea. *Shamanism: Archaic Techniques of Ecstasy.* Translated by Willard R. Trask. New York: Bollingen Foundation, 1964.

Ellingson, David R. *My Body, My Life.* Minneapolis: Augsburg, 1981.

Elm, Susanna. *Virgins of God: The Making of Asceticism in Late Antiquity.* Oxford Classical Monographs. Oxford: Clarendon/Oxford University Press, 1994.

Endean, Philip. "Theology Out of Spirituality: The Approach of Karl Rahner." *Christian Spirituality Bulletin* 3, no. 2 (Fall 1995): 6–8.

Erb, Peter C. "Anabaptist Spirituality." In *Protestant Spiritual Traditions,* edited by Frank C. Senn, 80–124. New York: Paulist Press, 1986.

———. Introduction to *Pietists: Selected Writings.* Edited by Peter C. Erb. Classics of Western Spirituality. New York: Paulist Press, 1983.

Erikson, Erik H. *Young Man Luther: A Study in Psychoanalysis and History.* New York: W. W. Norton, 1958.

Evagrius Ponticus. "Chapters on Prayer." In *The Praktikos and Chapters on Prayer,* translated by John Eudes Bamberger, 43–80. Kalamazoo, MI: Cistercian Publications, 1981.

Evdokimov, Paul. *The Sacrament of Love.* Translated by Anthony P. Gythiel and Victoria Steadman. Crestwood, NY: St. Vladimir's Seminary Press, 2001.

Farella, John R. *The Main Stalk: A Synthesis of Navajo Philosophy.* Tuscon: University of Arizona Press, 1984.

Farnham, Suzanne G., Joseph P. Gill, and R. Taylor McLean. *Listening Hearts: Discerning Call in Community.* Harrisburg, PA: Morehouse, 1991.

Farrington, Debra K. *Hearing with the Heart: A Gentle Guide for Discerning God's Will for Your Life.* San Francisco: Jossey-Bass, 2003.

Faulkner, William. *The Sound and the Fury.* New York: Random House, 1929.

Fee, Gordon. *God's Empowering Presence: The Holy Spirit in the Letters of Paul.* Peabody, MA: Hendrickson, 1994.

Feinberg, John S. *No One Like Him: The Doctrine of God.* Wheaton: Crossway, 2001.

Finke, Ronald. *Principles of Mental Imagery.* Cambridge, MA: MIT Press, 1989.

Finney, John R., and H. Newton Maloney Jr. "Empirical Studies of Christian Prayer: A Review of the Literature." *Journal of Psychology and Theology* 13, no. 2 (1985): 104–15.

Fischer, Kathleen. *Women at the Well: Feminist Perspectives on Spiritual Direction.* New York: Paulist Press, 1988.

Fischer, Roland. "A Cartography of Understanding Mysticism." *Science,* November 26, 1971, 897–904.

Fitzmyer, Joseph A. *According to Paul: Studies in the Theology of the Apostle.* New York: Paulist Press, 1993.

Fleming, David L., ed. *Notes on the Spiritual Exercises of Ignatius of Loyola.* St. Louis: Review for Religious, 1989.

Flew, Antony, ed. *A Dictionary of Philosophy.* New York: St. Martin's Press, 1979.

Foster, Richard. *Celebration of Discipline: The Path to Spiritual Growth.* 20th anniv. ed. San Francisco: HarperSanFrancisco, 1998.

———. *Money, Sex, and Power: The Challenge of the Disciplined Life.* San Francisco: HarperSanFrancisco, 1985.

———. *Prayer: Finding the Heart's True Home.* San Francisco: HarperSanFrancisco, 1992.

―――. *Streams of Living Water: Celebrating the Great Traditions of Christian Faith*. San Francisco: HarperSanFrancisco, 1998.

Foster, Richard, ed. *The Renovaré Spiritual Formation Bible*. San Francisco: HarperSanFrancisco, 2005.

Foster, Richard J., and Emilie Griffin, eds. *Spiritual Classics: Selected Readings for Individuals and Groups on the Twelve Spiritual Disciplines*. San Francisco: HarperSanFrancisco, 2000.

Foster, Richard J., and James Bryan Smith, eds. *Devotional Classics: Selected Readings for Individuals and Groups*. San Francisco: HarperSanFrancisco, 1993.

Foucault, Michel. *Power and Knowledge: Selected Interviews and Other Writings, 1972–1977*. Edited by Colin Gordon. New York: Pantheon Books, 1980.

Fowler, James W. *Stages of Faith: The Psychology of Human Development and the Quest for Meaning*. San Francisco: Harper and Row, 1981.

Fox, Matthew. *Original Blessing: A Primer in Creation Spirituality Presented in Four Paths, Twenty-Six Themes, and Two Questions*. Santa Fe, NM: Bear, 1983.

―――. *The Reinvention of Work: A New Vision of Livelihood for Our Time*. San Francisco: HarperSanFrancisco, 1994.

Frank, S. L. *Man's Soul: An Introductory Essay in Philosophical Psychology*. Athens: Ohio University Press, 1993.

French, J. P. R., Jr., and B. Raven. "The Bases of Social Power." In *Group Dynamics*, edited by D. Cartwright and A. Zander, 607–23. New York: Harper and Row, 1960.

Friesen, Gary. *Decision Making and the Will of God: A Biblical Alternative to the Traditional View*. Portland, OR: Multnomah, 1980.

Frijda, Nico H. "Comment on Oatley and Johnson-Laird's 'Toward a Cognitive Theory of Emotions.'" *Cognition and Emotion* 1, no. 1 (1987): 51–58.

―――. *The Emotions*. Studies in Emotion and Social Interaction. Cambridge: Cambridge University Press, 1986.

―――. "The Laws of Emotions." *American Psychologist* 43, no. 5 (May 1988): 349–58.

Frohlich, Mary. "Spiritual Discipline, Discipline of Spirituality: Revisiting Questions of Definition and Method." *Spiritus* 1, no. 1 (Spring 2001): 65–78.

Frost, Michael, and Alan Hirsch. *The Shaping of Things to Come: Innovation and Mission for the 21st-Century Church*. Peabody, MA: Hendrickson, 2003.

Futrell, J. C. "Ignatian Discernment." *Studies in the Spirituality of Jesuits* 2, no. 2 (April 1970): 1–88.

Ganssle, Gregory E., ed. *God and Time: Four Views*. Downers Grove, IL: InterVarsity Press, 2001.

Gardiner, H. M., Ruth Clark Metcalf, and John G. Beebe-Center. *Feeling and Emotion: A History of Theories*. New York: American Book Company, 1937.

Garrigou-Lagrange, Réginald. *Christian Perfection and Contemplation, According to St. Thomas Aquinas and St. John of the Cross*. St. Louis: Herder, 1937.

Gasparro, Giulia Sfameni. "Asceticism and Anthropology: *Encrateia* and 'Double Creation' in Early Christianity." In *Asceticism*, edited by Vincent L. Wimbush and Richard Valantasis, 127–46. New York: Oxford University Press, 1995.

Gay, Robert M. *Vocation et Discernment Des Esprits*. Montreal: Fides, 1959.

Geertz, Clifford. *The Interpretation of Cultures: Selected Essays*. New York: Basic, 1973.

Gelpi, Donald L. *Charism and Sacrament: A Theology of Christian Conversion*. New York: Paulist Press, 1976.

―――. *Committed Worship: A Sacramental Theology for Converting Christians*. 2 vols. Minneapolis: Liturgical Press, 1993.

―――. *The Conversion Experience: A Reflective Process for RCIA Participants and Others*. Mahwah, NJ: Paulist Press, 1998.

―――. *Discerning the Spirit: Foundations and Futures of Religious Life*. New York: Sheed and Ward, 1970.

―――. "Discernment and the Varieties of Conversion." Paper presented at Catholic Charismatic Renewal Conference, n.p., 1996.

―――. *The Divine Mother: A Trinitarian Theology of the Holy Spirit*. Lanham, MD: University Press of America, 1984.

―――. *Experiencing God: A Theology of Human Emergence*. Lanham, MD: University Press of America, 1987.

―――. *The Firstborn of Many: A Christology for Converting Christians*. 3 vols. Milwaukee: Marquette University Press, 2000–2001.

―――. *Functional Asceticism: A Guideline for American Religious*. New York: Sheed and Ward, 1966.

―――. *Grace as Transmuted Experience and Social Process, and Other Essays in North American Theology*. Lanham, NJ: University Press of America, 1988.

―――. *The Gracing of Human Experience: Rethinking the Relationship Between Nature and Grace*. Collegeville, MN: Liturgical Press, 2001.

―――. *Inculturating North American Theology: An Experiment in Foundational Method*. Atlanta: Scholars Press, 1988.

―――. *Pentecostalism: A Theological Viewpoint*. New York: Paulist Press, 1971.

―――. *Synoptic Narrative Christology*. Vol. 2, The Firstborn of Many: A Christology for Converting Christians. Milwaukee: Marquette University Press, 2000.

―――. *To Hope in Jesus Christ*. Vol. 1, The Firstborn of Many: A Christology for Converting Christians. Milwaukee: Marquette University Press, 2000.

―――. *The Turn to Experience in Contemporary Theology*. Mahwah, NJ: Paulist Press, 1994.

Gerson, Jean. "On Distinguishing True from False Revelations." In *Jean Gerson: Early Works*. Translated by Brian Patrick McGuire, 334–64. Classics of Western Spirituality. New York: Paulist Press, 1998.

Gessel, John M. "Stringfellow and the Law." In *Prophet of Justice, Prophet of Life: Essays on William Stringfellow*, edited by Robert Boak Slocum, 100–117. New York: Church Publishing, 1997.

Gilligan, Carol. *In a Different Voice: Psychological Theory and Women's Development*. Cambridge: Harvard University Press, 1993.

Gilson, Etienne. *The Mystical Theology of Saint Bernard*. Translated by A. H. C. Downes. Kalamazoo, MI: Cistercian Publishers, 1990.

Girard, René. *The Girard Reader*. Edited by James G. Williams. New York: Crossroad, 2002.

Gire, Ken. *Windows of the Soul: Experiencing God in New Ways*. Grand Rapids: Zondervan, 1996.

Gire, Ken, comp. and ed. *Between Heaven and Earth: Prayers and Reflections that Celebrate an Intimate God*. New York: HarperCollins, 1997.

Goehring, James E. *Ascetics, Society, and the Desert: Studies in Early Egyptian Monasticism*. Harrisburg, PA: Trinity Press International, 1999.

Goffman, Erving. "The Presentation of Self to Others." In *Understanding Relationships: Selected Readings in Interpersonal Communication*, edited by Benjamin J. Broome, 59–70. Dubuque, IA: Kendall/Hunt, 1986.

Goldstein, Valerie Saiving. "The Human Situation: A Feminine View." *Journal of Religion* 40, no. 2 (April 1960): 100–112.

Gordon, James M. *Evangelical Spirituality: From the Wesleys to John Stott*. London: SPCK, 1991.

Gorsuch, Richard L., and William R. Miller. "Assessing Spirituality." In *Integrating Spirituality into Treatment*, edited by William R. Miller, 47–64. Washington, DC: American Psychological Association, 1999.

Green, Joel. "Caring as Gift and Goal: Biblical and Theological Reflections." In *The Crisis of Care: Affirming and Restoring Caring Practices in the Helping Professions*, edited by Susan S. Phillips and Patricia Benner, 149–67. Washington, DC: Georgetown University Press, 1994.

Green, Thomas. *Weeds among the Wheat: Discernment; Where Prayer and Action Meet*. Notre Dame, IN: Ave Maria Press, 1984.

———. *When the Well Runs Dry: Prayer Beyond the Beginnings*. Rev. ed. Notre Dame, IN: Ave Maria Press, 1998.

Gregory of Nyssa. *Gregory of Nyssa: The Life of Moses*. Translated by Abraham J. Malherbe and Everett Ferguson. Classics of Western Spirituality. New York: Paulist Press, 1978.

Grenz, Stanley J. *The Social God and the Relational Self: A Trinitarian Theology of the Imago Dei*. Louisville: Westminster John Knox, 2001.

Gresham, John L., Jr. "Three Trinitarian Spiritualities." In *Exploring Christian Spirituality: An Ecumenical Reader*, edited by Kenneth J. Collins, 283–95. Grand Rapids: Baker, 2000.

Griffin, Emilie. *Turning: Reflections on the Experience of Conversion*. Garden City, NY: Image, 1982.

Grillmeier, Aloys. *Christ in Christian Tradition, Volume One: From the Apostolic Age to Chalcedon (451)*. Translated by John Bowden. 2nd and rev. ed. Atlanta: John Knox, 1975.

Grimes, Ronald L. *Beginnings in Ritual Studies*. Lanham, MD: University Press of America, 1982.

Grubb, Norman. *Rees Howells: Intercessor*. Fort Washington, PA: Christian Literature Crusade, 1952.

Guder, Darrell L. *The Missional Church: A Vision for the Sending of the Church in North America*. Grand Rapids: Eerdmans, 1998.

Guenther, Margaret. *Holy Listening: The Art of Spiritual Direction*. Cambridge, MA: Cowley, 1992.

Guigo II. "The Ladder of Monks: A Letter on the Contemplative Life." In *The Ladder of Monks and Twelve Meditations*, translated by Edmund Colledge and James Walsh. Vol. 48, Cistercian Studies Series, 11–37. Kalamazoo, MI: Cistercian Publications, 1979.

Guinness, Os. *In Two Minds: The Problem of Doubt and How to Resolve It*. Downers Grove, IL: InterVarsity Press, 1976.

Gurnall, William. *The Christian in Complete Armour*. Edinburgh: Banner of Truth, 1986.

Gutierrez, Gustavo. *We Drink from Our Own Wells: The Spiritual Journey of a People*. Translated by Matthew J. O'Connell. Maryknoll, NY: Orbis, 1984.

Habig, Marion, ed. *St. Francis of Assisi: Writings and Early Biographies: English Omnibus of the Sources for the Life of St. Francis*. Chicago: Franciscan Herald Press, 1983.

Hadewijch, *Hadewijch: The Complete Works*. Translated by Mother Columba Hart. Classics of Western Spirituality. Mahwah, NJ: Paulist Press, 1980.

Hadot, Pierre. *Philosophy as a Way of Life*. Translated by Michael Chase. Oxford: Blackwell, 1995.

Hagberg, Janet, and Robert Guelich. *The Critical Journey: Stages in the Life of Faith*. Rev. ed. Salem, WI: Sheffield, 2005.

Haight, Roger. "Grace." In *The New Dictionary of Catholic Spirituality*, edited by Michael Downey, 452–64. Collegeville, MN: Liturgical Press, 1993.

Hall, Calvin S., Gardner Lindzey, and John B. Campbell. *Theories of Personality*. 4th ed. New York: John Wiley and Sons, 1998.

Hall, Christopher A. *Reading Scripture with the Church Fathers*. Downers Grove, IL: InterVarsity Press, 1998.

Hall, Thelma. *Too Deep for Words: Rediscovering Lectio Divina*. New York: Paulist Press, 1988.

Hambrick-Stowe, Charles. *The Practice of Piety: Puritan Devotional Disciplines in Seventeenth-Century New England*. Chapel Hill: University of North Carolina Press, 1982.

Hamilton-Poore, Samuel. "The Given and the Gift: Sexuality and God's Eros in Direction and Supervision." In *Supervision of Spiritual Directors: Engaging in Holy Mystery*, edited by Mary Rose Bumpus and Rebecca Bradburn Langer, 83–103. Harrisburg, PA: Morehouse, 2005.

Hansen, David. *Long Wandering Prayer: An Invitation to Walk with God*. Downers Grove, IL: InterVarsity Press, 2001.

Hanson, Bradley C. "Spirituality as Spiritual Theology." In *Modern Christian Spirituality: Methodological and Historical Essays*, edited by Bradley C. Hanson, 45–52. Atlanta: Scholars Press, 1990.

———. "Theological Approaches to Spirituality: A Lutheran Perspective." *Christian Spirituality Bulletin* 2, no. 1 (Spring 1994): 5–8.

Harper, Steven. "Old Testament Spirituality." In *Exploring Christian Spirituality: An Ecumenical Reader*. Edited by Kenneth J. Collins. Grand Rapids: Baker, 2000.

Harpham, Geoffrey Galt. *The Ascetic Imperative in Culture and Criticism*. Chicago: University of Chicago Press, 1987.

Harris, Lelan. "Spiritual Formation Stage Models: Some Implications for Evangelism." Unpublished paper, 2003.

Harris, Marvin. *Cows, Pigs, Wars, and Witches: The Riddles of Culture*. New York: Vintage, 1974.

Harris, Murray J. "Prepositions and Theology in the Greek New Testament." In *New International Dictionary of New Testament Theology*, edited by Colin Brown, 3 vols., 3:1171–215. Grand Rapids: Zondervan, 1979.

Harris, William, et al. "A Randomized, Controlled Trial of the Effects of Remote, Intercessory Prayer on Outcomes in Patients Admitted to the Coronary Care Unit." *Archives of Internal Medicine* 159 (October 25, 1999): 2273–77.

Hartshorne, Charles. "Pantheism, Panentheism." In *Encyclopedia of Religion*, edited by Mircea Eliade, 165–71. New York: Macmillan, 1987.

———. *The Philosophy and Psychology of Sensation*. Chicago: University of Chicago Press, 1945.

Hauerwas, Stanley. *A Better Hope: Resources for a Church Confronting Capitalism, Democracy, and Postmodernity*. Grand Rapids: Brazos, 2000.

Hausherr, Irénée. *Penthos: The Doctrine of Compunction in the Christian East*. Translated by Anselm Hufstader. Kalamazoo, MI: Cistercian Publications, 1982.

Hayes, John. *Sub-merge: Living Deep in a Shallow World*. Ventura, CA: Regal, 2006.

Hayford, Jack W. *Prayer Is Invading the Impossible*. New York: Ballantine, 1983.

Hays, Richard B. *The Moral Vision of the New Testament: Community, Cross, New Creation*. San Francisco: HarperSanFrancisco, 1996.

Heidegger, Martin. *Being and Time*. Translated by John Macquarrie and Edward Robinson. San Francisco: HarperSanFrancisco, 1962.

Heiler, Friedrich. *Prayer: A Study in the History and Psychology of Religion*. Translated by Samuel McComb. London: Oxford University Press, 1932.

Henry, Paul B. *Politics for Evangelicals*. Valley Forge, PA: Judson, 1974.

Herbert, George. *George Herbert: The Country Parson, the Temple*. Edited by John N. Wall Jr. Classics of Western

Spirituality. New York: Paulist Press, 1981.

Heschel, Abraham J. *The Prophets*. New York: Harper and Row, 1962.

Hess, Carol Lakey. *Caretakers of Our Common House: Women's Development in Communities of Faith*. Nashville: Abingdon, 1997.

Hick, John, and Paul F. Knitter, eds. *The Myth of Christian Uniqueness: Toward a Pluralistic Theology of Religions*. Maryknoll, NY: Orbis, 1989.

Hildegard of Bingen. *Hildegard of Bingen: Scivias*. Translated by Mother Columba Hart and Jane Bishop. Classics of Western Spirituality. New York: Paulist Press, 1990.

Hilton, Walter. *Toward a Perfect Love: The Spiritual Counsel of Walter Hilton*. Translated and introduced by David L. Jeffrey. Portland, OR: Multnomah Press, 1985.

———. *Walter Hilton: The Scale of Perfection*. Translated by John P. H. Clark and Rosemary Dorward. Classics of Western Spirituality. Mahwah, NJ: Paulist Press, 1991.

Hinnebusch, Paul. "The Need for Discernment." *Catholic Charismatic* 3, no. 2 (June–July 1978): 4–9.

Hinson, E. Glen, ed. *The Doubleday Devotional Classics*. Garden City, NY: Doubleday, 1978.

Hodgson, Peter C., and Robert H. King, eds. *Christian Theology: An Introduction to Its Traditions and Tasks*. Minneapolis: Fortress, 1994.

Hoffman, Bengt, ed. *The Theologia Germanica of Martin Luther*. Classics of Western Spirituality. New York: Paulist Press, 1980.

Holland, Joe. "Linking Social Analysis and Theological Reflection: The Place of Root Metaphors in Social and Religious Experience." In *Tracing the Spirit: Communities, Social Action, and Theological Reflection*, edited by James E. Hug, 170–91. New York: Paulist Press, 1983.

Holland, Joe, and Peter Henriot. *Social Analysis: Linking Faith and Justice*. Maryknoll, NY: Orbis, 1983.

Holt, Bradley. *Thirsty for God: A Brief History of Christian Spirituality*. Minneapolis: Augsburg, 1993.

Holy Transfiguration Monastery, trans. *The Great Horologion: Or Book of Hours*. Brookline, MA: Holy Transfiguration Monastery, 1997.

Hood, Ralph W., Jr., ed. *Handbook of Religious Experience*. Birmingham, AL: Religious Education Press, 1995.

Hood, Ralph W., Jr., Bernard Spilka, Bruce Hunsberger, and Richard Gorsuch, eds. *The Psychology of Religion: An Empirical Approach*. 2nd ed. New York: Guilford, 1996.

Hootie and the Blowfish. "Deeper Side," on *Hootie and the Blowfish*. Atlantic, 2003.

Hopko, Thomas. "The Trinity in the Cappadocians." In *Christian Spirituality: Origins to the Twelfth Century*, edited by Bernard McGinn, John Meyendorff, and Jean Leclercq. Vol. 16, World Spirituality: An Encyclopedic History of the Religious Quest, 260–76. New York: Crossroad, 1985.

Houdek, Frank J. *Guided by the Spirit: A Jesuit Perspective on Spiritual Direction*. Chicago: Loyola Press, 1996.

Houghton, John. *Does God Play Dice?* Downers Grove, IL: InterVarsity Press, 1988.

Houston, James. *The Transforming Friendship: A Guide to Prayer*. Oxford: Lion Books, 1989.

Howard, Evan B. *Affirming the Touch of God: A Psychological and Philosophical Exploration of Christian Discernment*. Lanham, NJ: University Press of America, 2000.

———. *Praying the Scriptures: A Field Guide for Your Spiritual Journey*. Downers Grove, IL: InterVarsity Press, 1999.

———. "Three Temptations of Spiritual Formation." *Christianity Today*, December 9, 2002, 46–49.

Howells, Edward. "Review of *Minding the Spirit: The Study of Christian Spirituality*." *Spiritus* 5, no. 2 (Fall 2005): 223–27.

Hunsberger, Bruce, and Richard Gorsuch, eds. *The Psychology of Religion: An Empirical Approach*. 2nd edition. New York: Guilford, 1996.

Hunt, Dave, and T. A. McMahon. *The Seduction of Christianity*. Eugene, OR: Harvest House, 1985.

Hunter, George G., III. *The Celtic Way of Evangelism: How Christianity Can Win the West . . . Again*. Nashville: Abingdon, 2000.

Husserl, Edmund. *Cartesian Meditations: An Introduction to Phenomenology*. Dordrecht, Netherlands: Kluwer Academic, 1995.

Ignatius of Loyola. *Ignatius of Loyola: The Spiritual Exercises and Selected Works*, edited by George E. Ganss. Classics of Western Spirituality. New York: Paulist Press, 1991.

Irenaeus. *Against Heresies*. In *The Ante-Nicene Fathers*, edited by A. Roberts and J. Donaldson. Albany, OR: Ages Software, 2000.

Irwin, Kevin W. *Liturgy, Prayer, and Spirituality*. New York: Paulist Press, 1984.

Issler, Klaus. "Biblical Perspectives on Developmental Grace for Nurturing Children's Spirituality." In *Children's Spirituality: Christian Perspectives,*

Research, and Applications, edited by Donald Ratcliff, 54–71. Eugene, OR: Cascade Books, 2004.

Jacquette, James L. *Discerning What Counts: The Function of the Adiaphora Topos in Paul's Letters*. SBL Dissertation Series. Atlanta: Scholars Press, 1995.

James, William. *The Varieties of Religious Experience*. In *William James: Writings 1902–1910*. The Library of America. New York: Library Classics of the United States, 1987.

Jeeves, Malcolm. *Psychology and Christianity: The View Both Ways*. Downers Grove, IL: InterVarsity Press, 1976.

Jenkins, Philip. *The Next Christendom: The Coming of Global Christianity*. New York: Oxford University Press, 2002.

Jenson, Robert W. "Karl Barth." In *The Modern Theologians*, edited by David F. Ford, 2 vols., 1:23–49. Oxford: Blackwell, 1989.

John Climacus. *John Climacus: The Ladder of Divine Ascent*. Translated by Colm Luibheid and Norman Russell. Classics of Western Spirituality. New York: Paulist Press, 1982.

John of Damascus. *On the Orthodox Faith*. In *The Nicene and Post-Nicene Fathers, Second Series*. Vol. 9. Edited by Philip Schaff. Albany, OR: Ages Software, 2000.

John of the Cross. *The Collected Works of John of the Cross*. Translated by Kieran Kavanaugh and Otilio Rodriguez. Washington, DC: Institute of Carmelite Studies, 1979.

Johnson, Ben Campbell. *Discerning God's Will*. Louisville: Westminster John Knox, 1990.

Johnson, Eric L., and Stanton L. Jones, eds. *Psychology and Christianity*. Downers Grove, IL: InterVarsity Press, 2000.

Johnson, Jan. *When the Soul Listens: Finding Rest and Direction in Contemplative Prayer*. Colorado Springs: NavPress, 1999.

Johnson, Kevin Orlin. *Apparitions: Mystic Phenomena and What They Mean*. Dallas: Pangaeus, 1995.

Johnson, Luke Timothy. *The Real Jesus: The Misguided Quest for the Historical Jesus and the Truth of the Traditional Gospels*. San Francisco: HarperSanFrancisco, 1995.

———. *Religious Experience in Earliest Christianity*. Philadelphia: Fortress, 1998.

———. *Scripture and Discernment: Decision Making in the Early Church*. Nashville: Abingdon, 1996.

Johnson, Susanne. *Christian Spiritual Formation in the Church and Classroom*. Nashville: Abingdon, 1989.

Jones, Cheslyn, Geoffrey Wainwright, and Edward Yarnold, eds. *The Study of Spirituality*. New York: Oxford University Press, 1986.

Joyner, Rick. "Fundamentals of Biblical Interpretation." *Morning Star Journal* 1 (1985): 38–49.

Julian of Norwich. *Julian of Norwich: Showings*. Translated by Edmund Colledge and James Walsh. Classics of Western Spirituality. New York: Paulist Press, 1978.

Justin Martyr. *First Apology*. In *The Ante-Nicene Fathers*, Vol. 1. Edited by A. Roberts and J. Donaldson. Albany, OR: Ages Software, 2000.

Kaelber, Walter O. "Asceticism." In *The Encyclopedia of Religion*, edited by Mircea Eliade, 441–45. New York: Macmillan, 1986.

———. "Understanding Asceticism: Testing a Typology." In *Asceticism*, edited by Vincent L. Wimbush and Richard Valantasis, 320–28. New York: Oxford University Press, 1995.

Kahneman, Daniel, Paul Slovic, and Amos Tversky, eds. *Judgment under Uncertainty: Heuristics and Biases*. Cambridge: Cambridge University Press, 1982.

Kalb, Claudia. "Faith and Healing." *Newsweek*, November 10, 2003, 44–56.

Ka-Lun, Leung, and the China Group, with contributions from Xu Ru Lei. "China." Translated by Tung Lun-Hsien and Dufresse Chang. In *A Dictionary of Asian Christianity*, edited by Scott W. Sunquist. Grand Rapids: Eerdmans, 2001.

Kalupahana, David J. *A History of Buddhist Philosophy: Continuities and Discontinuities*. Delhi: Motilal Banarsidass, 1994.

Kastenbaum, Robert, ed. *Encyclopedia of Adult Development*. Phoenix: Oryx, 1993.

Katz, Steven. *Mysticism and Sacred Scripture*. Oxford: Oxford University Press, 2000.

Keating, Thomas. "Contemplative Prayer in the Christian Tradition." In *Finding Grace at the Center: The Beginning of Centering Prayer*, by M. Basil Pennington, Thomas Keating, and Thomas E. Clarke, 35–47. Petersham, MA: St. Bede's Publications, 1985.

———. *Open Mind, Open Heart: The Contemplative Dimension of the Gospel*. New York: Continuum, 1998.

Kelsey, Morton T. *Companions on the Inner Way: The Art of Spiritual Guidance*. New York: Crossroad, 1983.

———. *Discernment: A Study in Ecstasy and Evil*. New York: Paulist Press, 1978.

———. *Dreams: The Dark Speech of the Spirit*. New York: Doubleday, 1968.

———. *Encounter with God: A Theology of Christian Experience*. Minneapolis: Bethany Fellowship, 1972.

———. *The Other Side of Silence: A Guide to Christian Meditation*. New York: Paulist, 1976.

Kenel, Sally A. "Urban Psychology and Spirituality." *Journal of Psychology and Theology* 15, no. 4 (1987): 300–307.

Kieckhefer, Richard. "Major Currents in Late Medieval Devotion." In *Christian Spirituality: High Middle Ages and Reformation*, edited by Jill Raitt, Bernard McGinn, and John Meyendorff, 75–108. New York: Crossroad, 1987.

Kiesling, Stephen, and T. George Harris. "The Prayer War." *Psychology Today* 23, no.10 (October 1989): 65–66.

Kiev, Ari, ed. *Magic, Faith, and Healing: Studies in Primitive Psychiatry Today*. New York: Free Press, 1964.

Koch, Kurt. *Christian Counseling and Occultism*. Grand Rapids: Kregal, 1972.

Kockelmans, Joseph J. *Edmund Husserl's Phenomenology*. West Lafayette, IN: Purdue University Press, 1994.

Kontzevitch, Helen. *St. Seraphim: Wonderworker of Sarov and His Spiritual Inheritance*. Translated by St. Xenia Skete, 2004.

Kosslyn, Stephen. *Image and Mind*. Cambridge: Harvard University Press, 1980.

Kreider, Larry. *House Church Networks: A Church for a New Generation*. Ephrata, PA: House to House Publications, 2001.

Kuhn, Thomas S. *The Structure of Scientific Revolutions*. Chicago: University of Chicago Press, 1962.

Küng, Hans. *The Church*. New York: Image Doubleday, 1976.

Kuyper, Abraham. *The Work of the Holy Spirit*. Translated by Henri de Vries. Grand Rapids: Eerdmans, 1979.

Kydd, Ronald. *Healing through the Centuries*. Peabody, MA: Hendrickson, 1998.

Lactantius. *On the Anger of God*. In *The Ante-Nicene Fathers*, Vol. 7. Edited by A. Roberts and J. Donaldson. Albany, OR: Ages Software, 2000.

LaCugna, Catherine Mowry. *God for Us: The Trinity and Christian Life*. New York: HarperCollins, 1991.

———. "The Practical Trinity." In *Exploring Christian Spirituality: An Ecumenical Reader*, edited by Kenneth Collins, 273–82. Grand Rapids: Baker, 2000.

Ladd, George Eldon. *A Theology of the New Testament*. Grand Rapids: Eerdmans, 1974.

Lane, Belden. *The Solace of Fierce Landscapes: Exploring Desert and Mountain Spirituality*. New York: Oxford University Press, 1998.

Larkin, Ernest. *Silent Presence: Discernment as Process and Problem*. Denville, NJ: Dimension, 1981.

Laurence, David. "Jonathan Edwards, Solomon Stoddard, and the Preparationist Model of Conversion." *Harvard Theological Review* 72, no. 3–4 (July–October 1979): 267–83.

Law, William. *A Serious Call to a Devout and Holy Life*. In *William Law: A Serious Call to a Devout and Holy Life; The Spirit of Love*, edited by Paul G. Stanwood. Classics of Western Spirituality. New York: Paulist Press, 1978.

Lazarus, Richard. *Emotion and Adaptation*. New York: Oxford University Press, 1991.

Leclercq, Jean. "Prayer and Contemplation: II. Western." In *Christian Spirituality: Origins to the Twelfth Century*, edited by Bernard McGinn, John Meyendorff, and Jean Leclercq. Vol. 16, World Spirituality: An Encyclopedic History of the Religious Quest, 415–26. New York: Crossroad, 1985.

———. "Spiritualitas." *Studi Medievali* 3 (1962): 273–96.

Leech, Kenneth. *Experiencing God: Theology as Spirituality*. San Francisco: Harper and Row, 1985.

———. *Soul Friend: The Practice of Christian Spirituality*. San Francisco: Harper and Row, 1977.

Leventhal, Howard. "Toward a Comprehensive Theory of Emotion." In *Advances in Experimental Psychology*, edited by Leonard Berkowitz, 13:139–207. New York: Academic Press, 1980.

Levinas, Emmanuel. *Entre Nous: On Thinking-of-the-Other*. Translated by Michael B. Smith and Barbara Harshav. New York: Columbia University Press, 1998.

———. *Totality and Infinity: An Essay on Exteriority*. Translated by Alphonso Lingis. Pittsburgh: Duquesne University Press, 1969.

Lewis, C. S. *The Four Loves*. San Diego: Harcourt, 1960.

———. *Letters to Malcolm Chiefly on Prayer: Reflections on the Intimate Dialogue between Man and God*. San Diego: Harcourt, 1964.

Lewis, Gordon R., and Bruce A. Demarest. *Integrative Theology*. 3 vols. Grand Rapids: Zondervan, 1987–94.

Libânio, J. B. *Spiritual Discernment and Politics: Guidelines for Religious Communities*. Translated by Theodore Morrow. Eugene, OR: Wipf and Stock, 2003.

Liebert, Elizabeth. *Changing Life Patterns: Adult Development in Spiritual*

Direction. St. Louis: Chalice, 2000; previously published by New York: Paulist Press, 1992.

———. "Linking Faith and Justice: Working with Systems and Structures as a Spiritual Discipline." *Christian Spirituality Bulletin* 5, no. 1 (Spring 1997): 19–21.

———. "Supervision as Widening the Horizons." In *Supervision of Spiritual Directors: Engaging in Holy Mystery*, edited by Mary Rose Bumpus and Rebecca Bradburn Langer, 125–45. Harrisburg, PA: Morehouse, 2005.

Lienhard, Joseph. "On Discernment of Spirits in the Early Church." *Theological Studies* 41 (Spring 1980): 505–29.

Lindbeck, George A. *The Church in a Postliberal Age*. Edited by James J. Buckley. Grand Rapids: Eerdmans, 2002.

Link, Mark. *You: Prayer for Beginners and Those Who Have Forgotten How*. Niles, IL: Argus Communications, 1976.

Liszka, James Jakób. *A General Introduction to the Semiotic of Charles Sanders Peirce*. Bloomington, IN: Indiana University Press, 1996.

Lonergan, Bernard. *Insight: A Study of Human Understanding*. New York: Harper and Row, 1958.

———. *Method in Theology*. Minneapolis: Seabury, 1972.

Longman, Tremper, and Daniel Reid. *God Is a Warrior*. Studies in Old Testament Biblical Theology. Grand Rapids: Zondervan, 1995.

Lossky, Vladimir. *In the Image and Likeness of God*. Crestwood, NY: St. Vladimir's Press, 1974.

———. *The Mystical Theology of the Eastern Church*. Crestwood, NY: St. Vladimir's Press, 1998.

Louth, Andrew. "Augustine." In *The Study of Spirituality*, edited by Cheslyn Jones, Geoffrey Wainwright, and Edward Yarnold, 134–44. New York: Oxford University Press, 1986.

———. *Discerning the Mystery: An Essay on the Nature of Theology*. Oxford: Clarendon, 1983.

———. "Mysticism." In *The Westminster Dictionary of Christian Spirituality*, edited by Gordon S. Wakefield, 272–74. Philadelphia: Westminster Press, 1983.

———. *The Origins of the Christian Mystical Tradition: From Plato to Denys*. Oxford: Clarendon, 1981.

———. *Theology and Spirituality*. Rev. ed. Fairacres, UK: SLG Press, 1978.

Lovelace, Richard. *The American Pietism of Cotton Mather: Origins of American Evangelicalism*. Grand Rapids: Eerdmans, 1979.

———. "The Anatomy of Puritan Piety: English Puritan Devotional Literature, 1600–1640." In *Christian Spirituality: Post-Reformation and Modern*, edited by Louis Dupré and Don E. Saliers. Vol. 18, World Spirituality: An Encyclopedic History of the Religious Quest, 294–323. New York: Crossroad, 1989.

———. *Dynamics of Spiritual Life: An Evangelical Theology of Renewal*. Downers Grove, IL: InterVarsity Press, 1979.

———. *Renewal as a Way of Life*. Downers Grove, IL: InterVarsity Press, 1985.

Lowe, Walter. "Christ and Salvation." In *Christian Theology: An Introduction to Its Traditions and Tasks*, edited by Peter C. Hodgson and Robert H. King, 222–48. Minneapolis: Fortress, 1994.

Luther, Martin. *A Commentary on St. Paul's Epistle to the Galatians*. Cambridge: James Clarke, 1953.

———. *Luther's Works on CD-ROM*. 55 volumes. Edited by Jaroslav Pelekan and Helmut T. Lehmann. n.p.: Fortress Press and Concordia Publishing House, 1999.

MacKay, Donald M. *The Open Mind and Other Essays*. Downers Grove, IL: InterVarsity Press, 1988.

Macmurray, John. *Persons in Relation*. Atlantic Highlands, NJ: Humanities Press, 1961.

Magill, Frank N., and Ian P. McGreal. *Christian Spirituality: The Essential Guide to the Most Influential Spiritual Writings of the Christian Tradition*. San Francisco: HarperSanFrancisco, 1988.

Magrassi, Mariano. *Praying the Bible: An Introduction to Lectio Divina*. Trans. Edward Hagman. Collegeville, MN: Liturgical Press, 1998.

Malatesta, Edward, ed. *Discernment of Spirits*. Collegeville, MN: Liturgical Press, 1970.

Malina, Bruce J. "Power, Pain and Personhood: Ascetic Behavior in the Ancient Mediterranean." In *Asceticism*, edited by Vincent L. Wimbush and Richard Valantasis, 162–77. New York: Oxford University Press, 1995.

Maloney, George. *On the Road to Perfection: Christian Humility in Modern Society*. Hyde Park, NY: New City Press, 1995.

Maréchal, Joseph. *Studies in the Psychology of the Mystics*. Translated by Algar Thorold. London: Burns, Oates, and Washbourne, 1927.

Marsden, George M. *Fundamentalism and American Culture: The Shaping of Twentieth-Century Evangelicalism, 1870–1925*. Oxford: Oxford University Press, 1980.

Martens, Elmer A. *God's Design: A Focus on Old Testament Theology*. Grand Rapids: Baker, 1981.

Martin, Ralph. *2 Corinthians*. Vol. 40, The Word Biblical Commentary. Edited by David Hubbard, Glen W. Barker, and Ralph P. Martin. Waco: Word, 1986.

———. *Philippians*. New Century Bible Commentary. Grand Rapids: Eerdmans, 1976.

Matlin, Margaret W. *Cognition*. 3rd ed. Fort Worth: Harcourt Brace, 1994.

Matthews, Dale, Sally M. Marlowe, and Francis S. MacNutt. "Effects of Intercessory Prayer on Patients with Rheumatoid Arthritis." *Southern Medical Journal* 93, no. 2 (December 2000): 1177–86.

Maximus the Confessor. "The Church's Mystagogy." In *Maximus Confessor: Selected Writings*, translated by George C. Berthold. Classics of Western Spirituality, 181–225. New York: Paulist Press, 1985.

———. *Maximus the Confessor*. Translated by Andrew Louth. The Early Church Fathers. London: Routledge, 1996.

May, Gerald G. *The Awakened Heart: Opening Yourself to the Love You Need*. San Francisco: HarperSanFrancisco, 1991.

———. *Care of Mind, Care of Spirit: Psychiatric Dimensions of Spiritual Direction*. San Francisco: Harper and Row, 1983.

———. *Will and Spirit: A Contemplative Psychology*. San Francisco: Harper and Row, 1982.

McFague, Sallie. *The Body of God: An Ecological Theology*. Minneapolis: Fortress, 1993.

———. *Models of God: Theology for an Ecological, Nuclear Age*. Philadelphia: Fortress, 1988.

———. *Super, Natural Christians: How We Should Love Nature*. Philadelphia: Fortress, 1997.

McGee, Gary, ed. *Initial Evidence: Historical and Biblical Perspectives on the Pentecostal Doctrine of Spirit Baptism*. Peabody, MA: Hendrickson, 1991.

McGinn, Bernard. *The Flowering of Mysticism: Men and Women in the New Mysticism, 1200–1350*. Vol. 3, The Presence of God: A History of Western Christian Mysticism. New York: Crossroad, 1998.

———. *The Foundations of Mysticism: Origins to the Fifth Century*. Vol. 1, The Presence of God: A History of Western Christian Mysticism. New York: Crossroad, 1991.

———. *The Growth of Mysticism: Gregory the Great through the 12th Century*.

Vol. 2, The Presence of God: A History of Western Christian Mysticism. New York: Crossroad, 1994.

———. The Harvest of Mysticism in Medieval Germany. Vol. 4, The Presence of God: A History of Western Christian Mysticism. New York: Crosroad/Herder, 2005.

———. "Human Persons as Image of God: Western Christianity." In Christian Spirituality: Origins to the Twelfth Century, edited by Bernard McGinn, John Meyendorff, and Jean Leclercq. Vol. 16, World Spirituality: An Encyclopedic History of the Religious Quest, 312–30. New York: Crossroad, 1985.

———. "The Letter and the Spirit: Spirituality as an Academic Discipline." Christian Spirituality Bulletin 1, no. 2 (Fall 1993): 1–10.

———. "Meister Eckhart on Speaking about God." In Meister Eckhart: Teacher and Preacher, edited by Bernard McGinn. Classics of Western Spirituality, 15–30. New York: Paulist Press, 1986.

———. "Quo Vadis? Reflections on the Current Study of Mysticism," Christian Spirituality Bulletin 6/1 (Spring 1998): 13–22.

———. "Spirituality Confronts Its Future." Spiritus 5, no. 1 (Spring 2005): 88–96.

McGinn, Bernard, John Meyendorff, and Jean Leclercq, eds. Christian Spirituality: Origins to the Twelfth Century. Vol. 16, World Spirituality: An Encyclopedic History of the Religious Quest. New York: Crossroad, 1985.

McGonigle, Thomas D. "Union, Unitive Way." In The New Dictionary of Catholic Spirituality, edited by Michael Downey, 987–88. Collegeville, MN: Liturgical Press, 1993.

McGrath, Alister E. Beyond the Quiet Time: Practical Evangelical Spirituality. Grand Rapids: Baker, 1995.

———. Christian Spirituality: An Introduction. Oxford: Blackwell, 1999.

———. Spirituality in an Age of Change: Rediscovering the Spirit of the Reformers. Grand Rapids: Zondervan, 1994.

McGuckin, John. "The Early Church Fathers." In The Story of Christian Spirituality: Two Thousand Years from East to West, edited by Gordon Mursell, 31–72. Philadelphia: Fortress, 2001.

McIntosh, Mark. Discernment and Truth: The Spirituality and Theology of Knowledge. New York: Herder and Herder, 2004.

———. Mystical Theology: The Integrity of Spirituality and Theology. Malden, MA: Blackwell, 1998.

McKim, Donald K. "Karl Barth on the Lord's Prayer." In Prayer, by Karl Barth, translated by Sara F. Terrien. 50th anniv. ed., 114–34. Louisville: Westminster John Knox, 2002.

McKinney, Mary Benet. Sharing Wisdom: A Process for Group Decision Making. Allen, TX: Tabor Publishing, 1987.

McKowen, Clark. Thinking about Thinking: A Fifth-Generational Approach to Deliberate Thought. Los Altos, CA: William Kaufmann, 1986.

McLoughlin, William G. Revivals, Awakenings, and Reform: An Essay on Religion and Social Change in America, 1607–1977. Chicago: University of Chicago Press, 1978.

McNamara, William. Mystical Passion. New York: Paulist Press, 1977.

McNeill, John T. A History of the Cure of Souls. New York: Harper and Row, 1951.

Mead, George Herbert. Mind, Self, and Society: From the Standpoint of a Social Behaviorist. Vol. 1, The Works of George Herbert Mead, edited by Charles W. Morris. Chicago: University of Chicago Press, 1967.

Meissner, W. W. Ignatius of Loyola: The Psychology of a Saint. New Haven: Yale University Press, 1992.

Merleau-Ponty, Maurice. Phenomenology of Perception. Translated by Colin Smith. London: Routledge, 1962.

Merton, Thomas. Contemplation in a World of Action. New York: Doubleday, 1971.

———. Contemplative Prayer. New York: Doubleday, 1996.

———. Disputed Questions. New York: New American Library, 1960.

———. The Inner Experience: Notes on Contemplation. San Francisco: HarperSanFrancisco, 2003.

Metropolitan of Nafpaktos Hierotheos. Orthodox Psychotherapy: The Science of the Fathers. Translated by Esther Williams. Levadia, Greece: Birth of the Theotokos Monastery, 1997.

Meyendorff, John. Byzantine Theology: Historical Trends and Doctrinal Themes. New York: Fordham University Press, 1979.

———. Introduction to Gregory Palamas: The Triads. Classics of Western Spirituality, 1–22. Mahwah, NJ: Paulist Press, 1983.

Meyendorff, John, and Tobias, Robert, eds. Salvation in Christ: A Lutheran-Orthodox Dialogue. Minneapolis: Augsburg, 1992.

Michael, Chester P., and Marie C. Norrisey. Prayer and Temperament: Different Prayer Forms for Different Personality Types. Charlottesville, VA: The Open Door, 1984.

Miles, Margaret R. Augustine on the Body. Missoula, MT: Scholars Press, 1979.

———. Fullness of Life: Historical Foundations for a New Asceticism. Eugene, OR: Wipf and Stock, 2000.

———. Plotinus on Body and Beauty: Society, Philosophy and Religion in Third-Century Rome. Oxford: Blackwell, 1999.

Miller, Patrick D. They Cried to the Lord: The Form and Theology of Biblical Prayer. Minneapolis: Fortress, 1994.

Miller, Perry. "Jonathan Edwards on the Sense of the Heart." Harvard Theological Review 41, no. 2 (April 1948): 123–46.

Min, Anselm. The Solidarity of Others in a Divided World. Edinburgh: T and T Clark, 2004.

Mohler, James. Late Have I Loved You: An Interpretation of Saint Augustine on Human and Divine Relationships. New York: New City Press, 1991.

Moltmann, Jürgen. The Spirit of Life: A Universal Affirmation. Translated by Margaret Kohl. Minneapolis: Fortress, 1992.

A Monk of the Eastern Church. "The Essentials of Orthodox Spirituality." In Exploring Christian Spirituality: An Ecumenical Reader, edited by Kenneth J. Collins, 108–21. Grand Rapids: Baker, 2000.

———. The Jesus Prayer. Rev. ed. Crestwood, NY: St. Vladimir's Seminary Press, 1997.

———. Orthodox Spirituality: An Outline of the Ascetical and Mystical Traditions. 2nd edition. Crestwood, NY: St. Vladimir's Press, 1978.

Montague, George T. The Holy Spirit: Growth of a Biblical Tradition. New York: Paulist Press, 1976.

Moore, Peter. "Recent Studies of Mysticism: A Critical Survey," Religion 3 (Autumn 1973): 146–56.

Moreland, J. P., and John Mark Reynolds, eds. Three Views on Creation and Evolution. Grand Rapids: Zondervan, 1999.

Morgan, Edmund S. The Puritan Family: Religion and Domestic Relations in Seventeenth-Century New England. New York: Harper and Row, 1966.

Morris, Danny E., and Charles M. Olsen. Discerning God's Will Together: A Spiritual Practice for the Church. Bethesda, MD: Alban, 1997.

Morris, Leon. Testaments of Love. Grand Rapids: Eerdmans, 1981.

Mounce, H. O. The Two Pragmatisms: From Peirce to Rorty. London: Routledge, 1997.

Mulholland, M. Robert, Jr. Invitation to a Journey: A Road Map for Spiritual Formation. Downers Grove, IL: InterVarsity Press, 1993.

———. *Shaped by the Word: The Power of Scripture in Spiritual Formation.* Nashville: Upper Room, 1985.

Mumford, Bob. *Take Another Look at Guidance: A Study of Divine Guidance.* Plainfield, NJ: Logos International, 1971.

Murphey, Edward F. *The Handbook for Spiritual Warfare.* Nashville: Thomas Nelson, 1992.

Murphey, Nancey. *Theology in the Age of Scientific Reasoning.* Cornell Studies in the Philosophy of Religion. Ithaca: Cornell University Press, 1990.

Murray, Andrew. *With Christ in the School of Prayer.* Old Tappan, NJ: Fleming H. Revell, 1965.

Murray, John. *Redemption Accomplished and Applied.* Grand Rapids: Eerdmans, 1955.

Mursell, A. Gordon. Introduction to *The Meditations of Guigo I: Prior of the Charterhouse,* translated by A. Gordon Mursell, 7–60. Kalamazoo, MI: Cistercian Publications, 1995.

Mursell, Gordon, ed. *The Story of Christian Spirituality: Two Thousand Years from East to West.* Minneapolis: Fortress, 2001.

Muto, Susan. "Formative Spirituality." *Epiphany International* 6, no. 1 (Spring 2000): 8–16.

Myers, Bryant L. *Walking with the Poor: Principles and Practices of Transformational Development.* Maryknoll, NY: Orbis, 1999.

Myers, David G. "Is Prayer Clinically Effective?" *Reformed Review* 53, no. 2 (2000): 95–102.

———. "On Assessing Prayer, Faith, and Health." *Reformed Review* 53, no. 2 (2000): 119–26.

Nemek, Francis Kelly, and Marie Theresa Coombs. *The Spiritual Journey: Critical Thresholds and Stages of Adult Spiritual Genesis.* Wilmington, DE: Michael Glazier, 1987.

Nicodemus of the Holy Mountain. *Nicodemus of the Holy Mountain: A Handbook of Spiritual Counsel.* Translated by Peter A. Chamberas. Classics of Western Spirituality. New York: Paulist Press, 1989.

Niebuhr, Reinhold. *Moral Man and Immoral Society: A Study in Ethics and Politics.* New York: Charles Scribner's Sons, 1960.

Nishida, Kitaro. *An Inquiry into the Good.* Translated by Masao Abe and Christopher Ives. New Haven: Yale University Press, 1990.

———. *Last Writings.* Translated by David Dilworth. Honolulu: University of Hawaii Press, 1987.

Nock, A. D. *Conversion: The Old and the New in Religion from Alexander the Great to Augustine of Hippo.* London: Oxford University Press, 1933.

Noffke, Suzanne. "Soul." In *The New Dictionary of Catholic Spirituality*, edited by Michael Downey, 908–10. Collegeville, MN: Liturgical Press, 1993.

Nygren, Anders. *Agape and Eros.* Philadelphia: Muhlenberg, 1953.

O'Dwyer, Peter. "Celtic Monks and the Culdee Reform." In *An Introduction to Celtic Christianity*, edited by James P. Mackey, 140–71. Edinburgh: T and T Clark, 1995.

Oatley, Keith, and P. N. Johnson-Laird. "Toward a Cognitive Theory of Emotions." *Cognition and Emotion* 1, no. 1 (1987): 29–50.

Oden, Thomas C. *Life in the Spirit.* Peabody, MA: Prince, 1998.

———. *The Living God.* Peabody, MA: Prince, 1998.

———. *The Word of Life.* Peabody, MA: Prince, 1998.

Orange, Donna. *Emotional Understanding: Studies in Psychoanalytic Epistemology.* New York: Guilford, 1995.

Origen. *Against Celsus.* In *The Ante-Nicene Fathers*, Vol. 4. Edited by A. Roberts and J. Donaldson. Albany, OR: Ages Software, 2000.

———. *On First Principles.* Translated by G. W. Butterworth. Gloucester, MA: Peter Smith, 1973.

———. *Origen: An Exhortation to Martyrdom; Prayer; First Principles: Book IV; Prologue to the Commentary on the Song of Songs; Homily XXVII on Numbers.* Translated by Rowan A. Greer. Classics of Western Spirituality. New York: Paulist Press, 1979.

———. *The Song of Songs: Commentary and Homilies.* Translated by R. P. Lawson. Ancient Christian Writers. London: Longmans, Green, 1957.

Orr, J. Edwin. *Campus Aflame: Evangelical Awakenings in Collegiate Communities.* Glendale, CA: Regal Books, 1971.

———. *The Eager Feet: Evangelical Awakenings, 1790–1830.* Chicago: Moody, 1975.

———. *The Event of the Century: The 1857–1858 Awakening.* Wheaton: International Awakening Press, 1989.

———. *The Fervent Prayer: The Worldwide Impact of the Great Awakening of 1858.* Chicago: Moody, 1974.

———. *The Flaming Tongue: The Impact of Twentieth Century Revivals.* Chicago: Moody, 1973.

———. *The Light of the Nations: Evangelical Renewal and Advance in the Nineteenth Century.* Grand Rapids: Eerdmans, 1965.

———. "The Outpouring of the Spirit in Revival and Awakening and Its Issue in Church Growth." Pasadena, CA: Privately distributed paper, 1984.

———. *The Re-Study of Revival and Revivalism.* Pasadena, CA: School of World Mission, 1981.

———. *The Second Evangelical Awakening in America.* London: Marshall, Morgon, and Scott, 1952.

Orsy, Ladislas. *Probing the Spirit: A Theological Evaluation of Communal Discernment.* Denville, NJ: Dimension Books, 1976.

Ortony, Andrew, and T. J. Turner. "What's So Basic about Basic Emotions." *Psychological Review* 97, no. 3 (1990): 315–31.

Otto, Rudolf. *The Idea of the Holy: An Inquiry into the Non-Rational Factor in the Idea of the Divine and Its Relation to the Rational.* Translated by John W. Harvey. 2nd ed. New York: Oxford University Press, 1958.

Ouspensky, Leonid, and Vladimir Lossky. *The Meaning of Icons.* Translated by G. E. H. Palmer and E. Kadloubovsky. Crestwood, NY: St. Vladimir's Press, 1999.

Owen, John. *The Work of the Spirit.* Vol. 3 of *The Works of John Owen.* Edited by William Goold. 16 Vols. Edinburgh: The Banner of Truth Trust, 1967.

Packer, J. I. *Knowing God.* Twentieth Anniversary Edition. Downers Grove, IL: InterVarsity Press, 1993.

Padberg, John W., ed. *The Constitutions of the Society of Jesus and Their Complementary Norms.* St. Louis: Institute of Jesuit Sources, 1996.

Painter, John. "World." In *Dictionary of Jesus and the Gospels*, edited by Joel Green and Scott McKnight. Downers Grove, IL: InterVarsity Press, 1992.

Palmer, G. E. H., Philip Sherrard, and Kallistos Ware, trans. *The Philokalia: The Complete Text.* Compiled by Saint Nikodimos of the Holy Mountain and Saint Makarios of Corinth. London: Faber and Faber, 1979–1995.

Palmer, Parker. *The Active Life: A Spirituality of Work, Creativity, and Caring.* San Francisco: Jossey-Bass, 1990.

Palmer, Stephen. *Vision Science: Photons to Phenomenology.* Cambridge, MA: MIT Press, 1999.

Park, Robert E. *Society.* New York: Free Press, 1955.

Parker, Kelly A. *The Continuity of Peirce's Thought.* Nashville: Vanderbilt University Press, 1998.

Pascal, Blaise. *Pascal's Pensees.* Translated by H. F. Stewart. New York: Modern Library, 1947.

Pasely, Ben. *Enter the Worship Circle.* Lake Mary, FL: Relevant Books, 2001.

Paulsell, Stephanie. *Honoring the Body: Meditations on a Christian Practice.* San Francisco: Jossey-Bass, 2002.

Payne, Leanne. *Restoring the Christian Soul: Overcoming Barriers to Completion in Christ through Healing Prayer.* A Hamewith Book, 1991.

Peace, Richard. *Conversion in the New Testament: Paul and the Twelve.* Grand Rapids: Eerdmans, 1999.

Peck, M. Scott. *People of the Lie: The Hope for Healing Human Evil.* New York: Touchstone, 1983.

Pennington, Basil, with Simon Chan. "Spirituality, Christian." In *A Dictionary of Asian Christianity*, edited by Scott W. Sundquist, 790–94. Grand Rapids: Eerdmans, 2001.

———. *Lectio Divina: Renewing the Ancient Practice of Praying the Scriptures.* New York: Crossroad, 1998.

Peperzak, Adriaan. *To the Other: An Introduction to the Philosophy of Emmanuel Levinas.* Purdue Series in the History of Philosophy. West Lafayette, IN: Purdue University Press, 1993.

Peterson, Eugene. *Answering God: The Psalms as Tools for Prayer.* San Francisco: HarperSanFrancisco, 1989.

Phillips, Susan S., and Patricia Benner, eds. *The Crisis of Care: Affirming and Restoring Caring Practices in the Helping Professions.* Washington, DC: Georgetown University Press, 1994.

Piaget, Jean. *The Construction of Reality in the Child.* New York: Basic, 1954.

———. *The Origins of Intelligence in Children.* New York: Norton, 1952.

Piaget, Jean, and B. Inhelder. *The Psychology of the Child.* New York: Basic, 1969.

Pinnock, Clark H. *Flame of Love: A Theology of the Holy Spirit.* Downers Grove, IL: InterVarsity Press, 1996.

Pinnock, Clark, Richard Rice, John Sanders, William Hasker, and David Basinger. *The Openness of God: A Biblical Challenge to the Traditional Understanding of God.* Downers Grove, IL: InterVarsity Press, 1994.

Piper, John. *Desiring God: Meditations of a Christian Hedonist.* Tenth Anniversary expanded edition. Sisters, OR: Multnomah Press, 1996.

———. *Future Grace: The Purifying Power of Living by Faith in Future Grace.* Sisters, OR: Multnomah Press, 1995.

Plantinga, Alvin. *Warrant and Proper Function.* New York: Oxford University Press, 1993.

Plato. *The Collected Dialogues of Plato.* Edited by Edith Hamilton and Huntington Cairns. Bollingen Series. Princeton: Princeton University Press, 1989.

Polkinghorne, John. *The Faith of a Physicist: Reflections of a Bottom-Up Thinker.* Minneapolis: Fortress, 1996.

———. *Science and Providence.* London: SPCK, 1989.

Pourrat, Pierre. *Christian Spirituality.* 4 Vols. Translated by S. P. Jacques. Westminster, MD: Newman Press, 1927–55.

Powell, Samuel M. *A Theology of Christian Spirituality.* Nashville: Abingdon, 2005.

Principe, Walter. "Spirituality, Christian." In *The New Dictionary of Catholic Spirituality*, edited by Michael Downey, 931–38. Collegeville, MI: Liturgical Press, 1993.

———. "Toward Defining Spirituality." *Studies in Religion* 12, no. 2 (1983): 127–41.

Prior Peter and Master Peter. "The Life of Blessed Birgitta." In *Birgitta of Sweden: Life and Selected Revelations*, translated by Albert Ryle Kezel. Classics of Western Spirituality. New York: Paulist Press, 1990.

Proterra, Michael. *Homo Spiritualis Nititur Fide: Martin Luther and Ignatius of Loyola; An Analytical and Comparative Study of a Hermeneutic Based on the Heuristic Structure of Discretio.* Washington, DC: University Press of America, 1983.

Pruyser, Paul W. *A Dynamic Psychology of Religion.* New York: Harper and Row, 1968.

Pseudo-Dionysius. *The Divine Names.* In *Pseudo-Dionysius: The Complete Works*, translated by Colm Luibheid. Classics of Western Spirituality, 47–132. New York: Paulist Press, 1987.

———. *The Mystical Theology.* In *Pseudo-Dionysius: The Complete Works*, translated by Colm Luibheid. Classics of Western Spirituality, 133–42. New York: Paulist Press, 1987.

Pullinger, Jackie, with Andrew Quicke. *Chasing the Dragon.* Ann Arbor, MI: Servant Books, 1980.

Rahner, Karl. "Concerning the Relationship of Nature and Grace." In *Theological Investigations*, 23 vols. 1:297–318. Baltimore, MD: Helicon, 1961.

———. *Foundations of Christian Faith: An Introduction to the Idea of Christianity.* Translated by William V. Dych. New York: Crossroad, 1987.

———. *The Need and Blessing of Prayer.* Translated by Bruce W. Gillette. Collegeville, MN: Liturgical Press, 1997.

———. *The Practice of Faith: A Handbook of Contemporary Spirituality.* Edited by Karl Lehmann and Albert Raffelt. New York: Crossroad, 1992.

Rakoczy, Susan. "The Structures of Discernment Processes and the Meaning of Discernment Language in Published U.S. Catholic Literature, 1965–1978."

PhD dissertation. Catholic University of America, 1980.

Rambo, Lewis R. *Understanding Religious Conversion.* New Haven: Yale University Press, 1993.

Ramsey, Boniface. "Martyrdom." In *The New Dictionary of Catholic Spirituality*, edited by Michael Downey, 632–35. Collegeville, MN: Liturgical Press, 1993.

Rensberger, David. "Asceticism in the Gospel of John." In *Asceticism and the New Testament*, edited by Leif E. Vaage and Vincent L. Wimbush, 127–48. New York: Routledge, 1999.

Rice, Howard L. *Reformed Spirituality: An Introduction for Believers.* Louisville: Westminster John Knox, 1991.

Richards, Kent Harold. "Bless/Blessing." In *The Anchor Bible Dictionary*, edited by David Noel Freedman, 6 vols., 1:753–55. New York: Doubleday, 1992.

Rinker, Rosalind. *How to Have Family Prayers.* Grand Rapids: Zondervan Publishers, 1977.

Riss, Richard M. *A Survey of 20th-Century Revival Movements in North America.* Peabody, MA: Hendrickson, 1988.

Rizzuto, Ana-Maria. *Birth of the Living God: A Psychoanalytic Study.* Chicago: University of Chicago Press, 1979.

Roberts, A. and J. Donaldson, eds. *The Ante-Nicene Fathers.* 10 vols. Distributed by the Master Christian Library. Albany, OR: Ages Software, 2000.

Robison, David. *The Christian Family Toolbox: 52 Benedictine Activities for the Home.* New York: Crossroad, 2001.

———. *The Family Cloister: Benedictine Wisdom for the Home.* New York: Crossroad, 2000.

Robison, N. F. *Monasticism in the Orthodox Churches: Being an Introduction to the Study of Modern Hellenic and Slavonic Monachism.* London: Cope and Fenwick, 1916.

Roeder, Antoinette Voûte. "The Witness." *Presence: An International Journal of Spiritual Direction* 11, no. 1 (February 2005): 56.

Rohr, Richard, and Joseph Martos. *The Wild Man's Journey: Reflections on Male Spirituality.* Cincinnati: St. Anthony's Messenger Press, 1996.

Rolheiser, Ronald. *The Shattered Lantern: Rediscovering a Felt Presence of God.* New York: Crossroad, 2001.

Rosch, Eleanor. "The Environment of Minds: Toward a Noetic and Hedonic Ecology." In *Cognitive Ecology*, edited by Morton P. Friedman and Edward C. Carterette, 3–27. San Diego: Academic Press, 1996.

Ross, Virginia. "The Transcendent Function of the Bilateral Brain." *Zygon* 21, no. 2 (June 1986): 233–46.

Royce, Josiah. *The Problem of Christianity*. Washington, DC: Catholic University Press of America, 2001.

———. *The Sources of Religious Insight*. Washington, DC: Catholic University of America Press, 2001.

Rummel, R. J. *The Conflict Helix*. Beverly Hills: Sage, 1976.

Russell, Anthony. "Sociology and the Study of Christian Spirituality." In *The Study of Spirituality*, edited by Cheslyn Jones, Geoffrey Wainwright, and Edward Yarnold, 33–38. New York: Oxford University Press, 1986.

Russell, Kenneth C. "Asceticism." In *The New Dictionary of Catholic Spirituality*, edited by Michael Downey, 63–65. Collegeville, MN: Liturgical Press, 1993.

The Rutba House. *School(s) for Conversion: Twelve Marks of a New Monasticism*. Eugene, OR: Cascade, 2005.

Ruusbroec, John. *John Ruusbroec: The Spiritual Espousals and Other Works*. Translated by James A. Wiseman. Classics of Western Spirituality. New York: Paulist Press, 1985.

Ryle, James. *Hippo in the Garden: A Non-Religious Approach to Having a Conversation with God*. Orlando, FL: Creation House, 1993.

Sacks, Oliver. *The Man Who Mistook His Wife for a Hat and Other Clinical Tales*. New York: HarperPerennial, 1987.

Saldarini, Anthony J. "Asceticism in the Gospel of Matthew." In *Asceticism and the New Testament*, edited by Leif E. Vaage and Vincent L. Wimbush, 11–28. New York: Routledge, 1999.

Savan, David. *An Introduction to C. S. Peirce's Full System of Semeiotic*. Monograph Series of the Toronto Semeiotic Circle, Monograph number 1. Toronto: Toronto Semiotic Circle/ Victoria College in the University of Toronto, 1989.

Schaeffer, Edith. *What Is a Family?* Old Tappan, NJ: Fleming Revell, 1975.

Schneiders, Sandra M. "Biblical Spirituality: Life, Literature, and Learning." In *Doors of Understanding: Conversations in Global Spirituality in Honor of Ewert Cousins*, edited by Steven Chase, 51–76. Quincy, IL: Franciscan, 1997.

———. "The Letter and the Spirit: Spirituality as an Academic Discipline." *Christian Spirituality Bulletin* 1, no. 2 (Fall 1993): 10–15.

———. *The Revelatory Text: Interpreting the New Testament as Sacred Scripture*. 2nd ed. Collegeville, MN: Liturgical Press, 1999.

———. "Scripture and Spirituality." In *Christian Spirituality: Origins to the Twelfth Century*, edited by Bernard McGinn, John Meyendorff, and Jean Leclercq. Vol. 16, World Spirituality: An Encyclopedic History of the Religious Quest, 1–20. New York: Crossroad, 1985.

———. "Spirituality in the Academy." In *Exploring Christian Spirituality: An Ecumenical Reader*, edited by Ken Collins, 249–69. Grand Rapids: Baker, 2000.

———. "Theology and Spirituality: Strangers, Rivals, or Partners?" *Horizons* 13 (Fall 1986): 253–74.

Schrag, Calvin O. *The Self after Postmodernity*. New Haven: Yale University Press, 1997.

Schweitzer, Friedrich L. *The Postmodern Life Cycle: Challenges for Church and Theology*. St. Louis: Chalice, 2004.

Scupoli, Lorenzo. *Unseen Warfare: The Spiritual Combat and Path to Paradise of Lorenzo Scupoli, Edited by Nicodemus of the Holy Mountain and Revised by Theophan the Recluse*. Translated by E. Kadloubovsky and G. E. H. Palmer. Crestwood, NY: St. Vladimir's Seminary Press, 1987.

Searle, Mark. "Ritual." In *The Study of Liturgy*, edited by Cheslyn Jones, Geoffrey Wainwright, Edward Yarnold, and Paul Bradshaw, rev. ed., 51–58. New York: Oxford University Press, 1992.

Senn, Frank C., ed. *Protestant Spiritual Traditions*. New York: Paulist Press, 1986.

Sheehan, Mary Ellen. "Mystical Experience and the Grounds for Religious Belief." In *Christian Spirituality Bulletin* 2, no. 1 (Spring 1994): 27–30.

Sheeran, Michael. *Beyond Majority Rule: Voteless Decisions in the Religious Society of Friends*. Philadelphia: Philadelphia Yearly Meeting, 1983.

Sheikh, Anees A., ed. *Imagery: Current Theory, Research, Application*. New York: John Wiley and Sons, 1983.

Sheldrake, Philip. *Spirituality and History: Questions of Interpretation and Method*. Maryknoll, NY: Orbis, 1998.

———. *Spirituality and Theology: Christian Living and the Doctrine of God*. Maryknoll, NY: Orbis, 1998.

Short, T. L. "The Development of Peirce's Theory of Signs." In *The Cambridge Companion to Peirce*, edited by C. J. Misak, 214–40. New York: Cambridge University Press, 2004.

Sider, Ronald J. *Andreas Bodenstein von Karlstadt: The Development of His Thought 1517–1525*. Studies in Medieval and Reformation Thought. Leiden, Netherlands: Brill, 1974.

———. *Rich Christians in an Age of Hunger: Moving from Affluence to Generosity*. 20th anniv. ed. Nashville: Word, 1997.

Sisters of the Holy Names of Jesus and Mary. *Momentum*. St. Anthony-on-Husdon, Rensselaer, NY: Privately printed, 1991.

Smart, Ninian. *The Religious Experience of Mankind*. New York: Scribner, 1984.

Smith, Gordon. *Beginning Well: Christian Conversion and Authentic Transformation*. Downers Grove, IL: InterVarsity Press, 2001.

———. *Listening to God in Times of Choice*. Downers Grove, IL: InterVarsity Press, 1997.

Smith, Hannah Whitall. *The Christian's Secret of a Holy Life*. The Master Christian Library. Albany, OR: Ages Software, 2000.

Smith, James Bryan, and Linda Graybeal. *A Spiritual Formation Workbook: Small-Group Resources for Nurturing Spiritual Growth*. San Francisco: HarperSanFrancisco, 1999.

Smith, John E. *America's Philosophical Vision*. Chicago: University of Chicago Press, 1992.

Smith, Theophus H. "The Spirituality of Afro-American Traditions." In *Christian Spirituality: Post-Reformation and Modern*, edited by Louis Dupré and Don E. Saliers. Vol. 18, World Spirituality: An Encyclopedic History of the Religious Quest, 372–414. New York: Crossroad, 1989.

Snyder, Howard A. *The Community of the King*. Downers Grove, IL: InterVarsity Press, 1977.

Sobrino, Jon. "Following Jesus as Discernment." In *Discernment of the Spirit and of Spirits*, edited by Casiano Floristan and Christian Duquoc, 14–22. New York: Seabury, 1979.

Solzhenitsyn, Alexander. *From Under the Rubble*. Translated by Michael Scammel. New York: Bantam, 1976.

Sommerfeldt, John R. *Abba: Guides to Holiness East and West*. Kalamazoo, MI: Cistercian Publications, 1982.

Spears, Larry. "A Rule for Families of Faith." *American Benedictine Review* 40, no. 2 (June 1989): 142–69.

Spohn, William C. "Charismatic Communal Discernment and Ignatian Communities." *The Way: Supplement* 20 (Autumn 1973): 38–54.

Spong, John Shelby. *Why Christianity Must Change or Die: A Bishop Speaks to Believers in Exile*. San Francisco: HarperSanFrancisco, 1998.

Springsted, Eric O., ed. *Spirituality and Theology: Essays in Honor of Diogenes Allen*. Louisville: Westminster John Knox, 1998.

Staniloae, Dumitru. *The Experience of God: Orthodox Dogmatic Theology.* Translated by Ioan Ionita and Robert Barringer. 2 vols. to date. Brookline, MA: Holy Cross Orthodox Press, 1994–2000.

———. *Revelation and the Knowledge of the Triune God.* Translated by Ioan Ionita and Robert Barringer. Vol 1, The Experience of God: Orthodox Dogmatic Theology. Brookline, MA: Holy Cross Orthodox Press, 1994.

———. *The World: Creation and Deification.* Translated by Ioan Ionita and Robert Barringer. Vol. 2, The Experience of God: Orthodox Dogmatic Theology. Brookline, MA: Holy Cross Orthodox Press, 2000.

Stanley, Paul D., and J. Robert Clinton. *Connecting: The Mentoring Relationships You Need to Succeed in Life.* Colorado Springs: NavPress, 1992.

Steere, Douglas V., ed. *Quaker Spirituality: Selected Writings.* Classics of Western Spirituality. New York: Paulist Press, 1984.

Steinmetz, David. "The Superiority of Pre-Critical Exegesis." *Theology Today* 37 (April 1980–January 1981): 27–38.

Stewart, Carlyle Fielding, III. *Black Spirituality, Black Consciousness: Soul Force, Culture, and Freedom and the African-American Experience.* Trenton: Africa World Press, 1999.

Stewart, John. "Interpersonal Communication: A Meeting between Persons." In *Understanding Relationships: Selected Readings in Interpersonal Communication,* edited by Benjamin J. Broome, 5–21. Dubuque, IA: Kendall/Hunt, 1986.

Studzinski, Raymond. *Spiritual Direction and Midlife Development.* Chicago: Loyola University Press, 1985.

Stylianopoulos, Theodore G. *The Way of Christ: Gospel, Spiritual Life and Renewal in Orthodoxy.* Brookline, MA: Holy Cross Orthodox Press, 2002.

Sweet, Leonard, ed. *The Church in Emerging Culture.* Grand Rapids: Zondervan, 2003.

Symeon the New Theologian. *Symeon the New Theologian: The Discourses.* C. J. deCatanzaro. Classics of Western Spirituality. New York: Paulist Press, 1980.

Synan, Vinson. *The Holiness-Pentecostal Tradition: Charismatic Movements in the Twentieth Century.* 2nd ed. Grand Rapids: Eerdmans, 1997.

Tamburello, Dennis E. *Union with Christ: John Calvin and the Mysticism of St. Bernard.* Columbia Series in Reformed Theology. Louisville: Westminster John Knox, 1994.

Tanquerey, Adolphe. *The Spiritual Life: A Treatise on Ascetical and Mystical Theology.* Translated by Herman Branderis. 2nd and rev. ed. Tournai, Belgium: Desclée, 1930.

Tarango, Yolanda, Consuelo Covarrubias, and Ada-Maria Isasi-Diaz, editors. *Así Es: Stories of Hispanic Spirituality.* Collegeville, MN: Liturgical Press, 1994.

Tauler, Johannes. *Johannes Tauler: Sermons.* Translated by Maria Shrady. Classics of Western Spirituality. New York: Paulist Press, 1985.

Taylor, Charles. *The Sources of the Self: The Making of Modern Identity.* Cambridge: Harvard University Press, 1989.

Taylor, Jeremy. *Holy Living and Holy Dying.* In *Jeremy Taylor: Selected Works,* edited by Thomas K. Carroll. Classics of Western Spirituality, 427–504. New York: Paulist Press, 1990.

Teresa of Avila. *The Book of Her Life.* In vol. 1 of *The Collected Works of St. Teresa of Avila,* translated by Kieran Kavanaugh and Otilio Rodriguez, 1–308. Washington, DC: Institute of Carmelite Studies, 1976.

———. *The Interior Castle.* In vol. 2 of *The Collected Works of St. Teresa of Avila,* translated by Kieran Kavanaugh and Otilio Rodriguez, 260–452. Washington, DC: Institute of Carmelite Studies 1976.

Tertullian. *On Prayer* and *Against Marcion.* In *The Ante-Nicene Fathers,* vol. 3. Edited by A. Roberts and J. Donaldson. Albany, OR: Ages Software, 2000.

TeSelle, Eugene. *Augustine the Theologian.* London: Burns and Oates, 1970.

The Theologia Germanica of Martin Luther. Edited by Bengt Hoffman. Classics of Western Spirituality. New York: Paulist Press, 1980.

Theophan the Recluse. *The Heart of Salvation: The Life and Teachings of Russia's Saint Theophan the Recluse.* Translated by Esther Williams. Newbury, MA: Praxis Institute Press, n.d.

———. *The Path to Salvation: A Manual of Spiritual Transformation.* Translated by Fr. Seraphim Rose. Platina, CA: St. Herman Press, 1998.

Thomas À Kempis. *The Imitation of Christ.* Translated by William Creasy. Notre Dame, IN: Ave Maria Press, 1989.

Thomas, Gary. *Sacred Pathways: Discover Your Soul's Path to God.* Nashville: Thomas, Nelson, 1996.

Thompson, Marjorie J. *Soul Feast: An Invitation to the Christian Spiritual Life.* Louisville: Westminster John Knox, 1995.

Thompson, William. "Evangelization of Whole Families Report." In *Let the Earth Hear His Voice: International Congress on World Evangelization. Lausanne, Switzerland,* edited by J. D. Douglas, 974–76. Minneapolis: World Wide Publications, 1975.

Thornton, Martin. *English Spirituality: An Outline of Ascetical Theology According to the English Pastoral Tradition.* Cambridge, MA: Cowley Publications, 1986.

Thunberg, Lars. "The Human Person as Image of God: Eastern Christianity." In *Christian Spirituality: Origins to the Twelfth Century,* edited by Bernard McGinn, John Meyendorff, and Jean Leclercq. Vol. 16, World Spirituality: An Encyclopedic History of the Religious Quest, 291–312. New York: Crossroad, 1985.

———. *Man and the Cosmos: The Vision of St. Maximus the Confessor.* Crestwood, NY: St. Vladimir's Seminary Press, 1885.

———. *Microcosm and Mediator: The Theological Anthropology of Maximus the Confessor.* Second edition. Chicago: Open Court Publishing Company, 1995.

Tiessen, Terrance. *Providence and Prayer: How Does God Work in the World?* Downers Grove, IL: InterVarsity Press, 2000.

Tikhon of Zadonsk. *Journey to Heaven: Counsels on the Particular Duties of Every Christian.* Translated by George D. Lardas. Jordanville, NY: Holy Trinity Monastery, 1991.

Toner, Jules J. *A Commentary on Saint Ignatius' Rules for the Discernment of Spirits.* St. Louis: Institute of Jesuit Sources, 1982.

———. *Discerning God's Will: Ignatius of Loyola's Teaching on Christian Decision Making.* St. Louis: Institute of Jesuit Sources, 1991.

———. "A Method for Communal Discernment of God's Will." *Studies in the Spirituality of Jesuits* 3, no. 4 (September 1971): 121–52.

———. *Spirit of Light or Darkness? A Casebook for Studying Discernment of Spirits.* St. Louis: Institute of Jesuit Sources, 1995.

Torrance, James B. "Contemplating the Trinitarian Mystery of Christ." In *Exploring Christian Spirituality: An Ecumenical Reader,* edited by Kenneth J. Collins. 296–307. Grand Rapids: Baker, 2000.

Tozer, A. W. *The Pursuit of God.* Harrisburg, PA: Christian Publications, 1948.

Transformations. Video Directed by George Otis Jr. Lynwood, WA: Sentinel Group, 2001.

Travarthen, Colwyn. "Brain Science and the Human Spirit." *Zygon* 21, no. 2 (June 1986): 161–200.

Tugwell, Simon. "A Dominican Theology of Prayer." *Dominican Ashram* 1, no. 3 (September 1982): 128–44.

Turner, M. M. B. "Spirit Endowment in Luke-Acts: Some Linguistic Considerations." *Vox Evangelica* 12 (1981): 45–63.

Tyrrell, Bernard J. *Christotherapy II: The Fasting and the Feasting Heart*. New York: Paulist Press, 1982.

Ulanov, Ann, and Barry Ulanov. *Primary Speech: A Psychology of Prayer*. Louisville: Westminster John Knox, 1982.

Underhill, Evelyn. *Mysticism: A Study in the Nature and Development of Man's Spiritual Consciousness*. New York: Meridian Books, 1955.

Upkong, J. S. "Pluralism and the Discernment of Spirits." *The Ecumenical Review* 41 (1989): 416–25.

Vaage, Leif E., and Vincent L. Wimbush. *Asceticism and the New Testament*. New York: Routledge, 1999.

Valantasis, Richard. "Constructions of Power in Asceticism." *Journal of the American Academy of Religion* 63, no. 4 (Winter 1995): 775–821.

van Huyssteen, J. Wentzel. *The Shaping of Rationality: Toward Interdisciplinarity in Theology and Science*. Grand Rapids: Eerdmans, 1999.

Van Ness, Peter H. "Introduction: Spirituality and the Secular Quest." In *Spirituality and the Secular Quest*, edited by Peter H. Van Ness. Vol. 22, World Spirituality: An Encyclopedic History of the Religious Quest, 1–17. New York: Crossroad, 1996.

———. "Philosophy as Spiritual Catalyst: Spirituality in a Secular Age." *Christian Spirituality Bulletin* 5, no. 1 (Spring 1997):16–18.

———. *Spirituality, Diversion and Decadence: The Contemporary Predicament*. Albany, NY: State University of New York Press, 1992.

Vande Kemp, Hendrika. "Psychology and Christian Spirituality: Explorations of the Inner World." *Journal of Psychology and Christianity* 15, no. 2 (1996): 161–74.

Vanier, Jean. *Community and Growth*. New York: Paulist Press, 1982.

Varela, Francisco J., Evan Thompson, and Eleanor Rosch. *The Embodied Mind: Cognitive Science and Human Experience*. Cambridge, MA: MIT Press, 1991.

Vennard, Jane E. *Praying with Body and Soul: A Way to Intimacy with God*. Minneapolis: Fortress, 1998.

Viswanathan, Gauri. *Outside the Fold: Conversion, Modernity, and Belief*.

Princeton: Princeton University Press, 1998.

Voaden, Rosalynn. *God's Words, Women's Voices: The Discernment of Spirits in the Writing of Late-Medieval Women Visionaries*. Woodbridge, UK: York University Press, 1999.

Volf, Miroslav. *Exclusion and Embrace: A Theological Exploration of Identity, Otherness, and Reconciliation*. Nashville: Abingdon, 1996.

von Hügel, Baron Friedrich. *The Mystical Element of Religion as Studied in Saint Catherine of Genoa and Her Friends*. London: James Clarke, 1961.

Waaijman, Kees. *Spirituality: Forms, Foundations, Methods*. Translated by John Vriend. Leuven, Belgium: Peeters, 2002.

Wagner, C. Peter. "Territorial Spirits." In *Wrestling with Dark Angels: Toward a Deeper Understanding of the Supernatural Forces in Spiritual Warfare*, edited by C. Peter Wagner and F. Douglas Pennoyer, 73–92. Ventura, CA: Regal Books, 1990.

Wagner, C. Peter, and F. Douglas Pennoyer, eds. *Wrestling with Dark Angels: Toward a Deeper Understanding of the Supernatural Forces in Spiritual Warfare*. Ventura, CA: Regal Books, 1990.

Wainwright, Geoffrey. "Types of Spirituality." In *The Study of Spirituality*, edited by Cheslyn Jones, Geoffrey Wainwright, and Edward Yarnold, 592–605. New York: Oxford University Press, 1986.

Wakefield, Gordon S., ed. *The Westminster Dictionary of Christian Spirituality*. Atlanta: The Westminster Press, 1983.

Wallis, Arthur. *China Miracle: A Silent Explosion*. Columbia, MO: Cityhill, 1986.

Wallis, Jim. *God's Politics: Why the Right Gets It Wrong and the Left Doesn't Get It*. San Francisco: HarperSanFrancisco, 2005.

Walls, Andrew. "Christianity." In *A New Handbook of Living Religions*, edited by John R. Hinnells, 55–161. Oxford: Blackwell, 1997.

Walpot, Peter. "True Yieldedness and the Christian Community of Goods." In *Early Anabaptist Spirituality*, edited by Daniel Liechty. Classics of Western Spirituality, 138–96. New York: Paulist Press, 1994.

Ward, Benedicta, trans. *The Sayings of the Desert Fathers: The Alphabetical Collection*. Kalamazoo, MI: Cistercian Publications, 1975.

Ware, Bruce A. *God's Lesser Glory: The Diminished God of Open Theism*. Wheaton: Crossway, 2000.

Ware, Kallistos. *How Are We Saved? The Understanding of Salvation in the Orthodox Tradition*. Minneapolis: Light and Life, 1996.

———. *The Orthodox Way*. Crestwood, NY: St. Vladimir's Seminary Press, 1995.

———. *The Power of the Name: The Jesus Prayer in Orthodox Spirituality*. Oxford: SLG Press, 1986.

———. "The Spiritual Father in Orthodox Christianity." In *Spiritual Direction: Contemporary Readings*, edited by Kevin G. Culligan, 20–40. Locust Valley, NY: Living Flame Press, 1983.

———. "The Way of the Ascetics: Negative or Affirmative." In *Asceticism*, edited by Vincent L. Wimbush and Richard Valantasis, 3–15. New York: Oxford University Press, 1995.

Warren, Rick. *The Purpose-Driven Church: Growth without Compromising Your Message and Mission*. Grand Rapids: Zondervan, 1995.

Watson, David Lowes. "Methodist Spirituality." In *Exploring Christian Spirituality: An Ecumenical Reader*, edited by Kenneth J. Collins, 172–213. Grand Rapids: Baker, 2000.

Webber, Robert E. *The Younger Evangelicals: Facing the Challenges of the New World*. Grand Rapids: Baker, 2002.

Weigel, George. *God's Choice: Pope Benedict XVI and the Future of the Catholic Church*. New York: HarperCollins, 2005.

Wenham, Gordon. *Genesis 1–15*. Word Biblical Commentary. Dallas: Word, 1987.

Wesley, John. *The Works of John Wesley*. 14 vols. Peabody, MA: Hendrickson, 1984.

White, Charles Edward. *Beauty of Holiness: Phoebe Palmer as Theologian, Revivalist, Feminist, and Humanitarian*. Grand Rapids: Zondervan, 1986.

White, John. *When the Spirit Comes in Power: Signs and Wonders among God's People*. Downers Grove, IL: InterVarsity Press, 1988.

White, Thomas B. *The Believer's Guide to Spiritual Warfare*. Ann Arbor, MI: Servant, 1990.

Whitehead, Alfred North. *Process and Reality: An Essay in Cosmology*. New York: Free Press, 1929.

Whitehead, James D., and Evelyn Eaton Whitehead. *Shadows of the Heart: A Spirituality of the Painful Emotions*. New York: Crossroad, 1996.

Wilberforce, William. *Real Christianity Contrasted with the Prevailing Religious System*. Classics of Faith and Devotion. Portland, OR: Clarendon, 1982.

Wilhoit, James, ed. *Nelson's Personal Handbook on Prayer*. Nashville: Thomas Nelson, 2002.

Willard, Dallas. *The Divine Conspiracy: Rediscovering Our Hidden Life in God*. San Francisco: HarperSanFrancisco, 1998.

———. *Hearing God: Developing a Conversational Relationship with God*. Downers Grove, IL: InterVarsity Press, 1999.

———. *Renovation of the Heart: Putting on the Character of Christ*. Colorado Springs: NavPress, 2002.

———. *The Spirit of the Disciplines: Understanding How God Changes Lives*. San Francisco: Harper and Row, 1988.

Williams, Robert R. "Sin and Evil." In *Christian Theology: An Introduction to Its Traditions and Tasks*, edited by Peter C. Hodgson and Robert H. King, 194–221. Minneapolis: Fortress, 1994.

Williams, Rowan. *The Wound of Knowledge: A Theological History from the New Testament to Luther and St. John of the Cross*. Eugene, OR: Wipf and Stock, 1998.

Wimber, John. *Power Evangelism*. San Francisco: Harper and Row, 1986.

Wimbush, Vincent L., ed. *Ascetic Behavior in Graeco-Roman Antiquity: A Sourcebook*. Minneapolis: Fortress, 1990.

Wimbush, Vincent L., and Richard Valantasis, eds. *Asceticism*. New York: Oxford University Press, 1995.

Wink, Walter. *The Bible in Human Transformation: Toward a New Paradigm for Biblical Study*. Philadelphia: Fortress, 1973.

———. *Engaging the Powers: Discernment and Resistance in a World of Domination*. Philadelphia: Fortress, 1992.

———. *Naming the Powers: The Language of Power in the New Testament*. Philadelphia: Fortress, 1984.

———. "The Powers Behind the Throne." *Sojourners*, September 1984, 22–25.

———. *Unmasking the Powers: The Invisible Forces that Determine Human Existence*. Philadelphia: Fortress, 1986.

Winter, Ralph D. "The Two Structures of God's Redemptive Mission." In *Perspectives on the World Christian Movement: A Reader*, edited by Ralph D. Winter and Steven C. Hawthorne, rev. ed., B-45–57. Pasadena, CA: William Carey Library, 1992.

Witherspoon, Gary. *Language and Art in the Navajo Universe*. Ann Arbor: University of Michigan Press, 1977.

Wolfson, Harry Austryn. "St. Thomas on Divine Attributes." In *Studies in Maimonides and St. Thomas Aquinas*, edited by Jacob I. Dienstag, 29–49. Jersey City, NJ: KTAV Publishing House, 1975.

Wolpert, Daniel. *Creating a Life with God: The Call of Ancient Prayer Practices*. Nashville: Upper Room Books, 2003.

Wolterstorff, Nicholas. *Reason within the Bounds of Religion*. Grand Rapids: Eerdmans, 1976.

Woods, Richard. *Christian Spirituality: God's Presence through the Ages*. Chicago: Thomas Moore Press, 1989.

Woolever, Cynthia, and Deborah Bruce. *Beyond the Ordinary: Ten Strengths of U.S. Congregations*. Louisville: Westminster John Knox, 2004.

Woolman, John. *The Journal of John Woolman*. In *Quaker Spirituality*, edited by Douglas V. Steere. Classics of Western Spirituality, 159–239. New York: Paulist, 1984.

———. *The Journal of John Woolman and a Plea for the Poor*. New York: Corinth Books, 1961.

———. "On the Slave Trade." http://www.qhpress.org/texts/oldqwhp/wool-496.htm.

Wright, N. T. *The Climax of the Covenant: Christ and the Law in Pauline Theology*. Minneapolis: Fortress, 1993.

———. *Jesus and the Victory of God*. Vol. 2, Christian Origins and the Question of God. Philadelphia: Fortress, 1996.

———. *The New Testament and the People of God*. Vol. 1, Christian Origins and the Question of God. Minneapolis: Fortress, 1992.

———. *The Resurrection of the Son of God*. Vol. 3, Christian Origins and the Question of God. Philadelphia: Fortress, 2003.

Wright, Wendy M. *Sacred Dwelling: A Spirituality of Family Life*. Leavenworth, KS: Forest of Peace Publishing, 1994.

———. "Woman-Body, Man-Body: Knowing God." In *Women's Spirituality: Resources for Christian Development*, edited by Joann Wolski Conn, 2nd ed. New York: Paulist Press, 1996.

Wuthnow, Robert. *After Heaven: Spirituality in America Since the 1950s*. Berkeley and Los Angeles: University of California Press, 1998.

———. *Saving America?: Faith-Based Services and the Future of Civil Society*. Princeton: Princeton University Press, 2004.

Wyschogrod, Edith. "The Howl of Oedipus, the Cry of Héloïse: From Asceticism to Postmodern Ethics." In *Asceticism*, edited by Vincent L. Wimbush and Richard Valantasis, 16–30. New York: Oxford University Press, 1995.

Yancey, Philip. *The Jesus I Never Knew*. Grand Rapids: Zondervan, 1995.

———. *Reaching for the Invisible God*. Grand Rapids: Zondervan, 2000.

———. *Where Is God When It Hurts?* Grand Rapids: Zondervan, 1990.

Yarbrough, O. Larry. "Canons from the Council of Gangra." In *Ascetic Behavior in Graeco-Roman Antiquity: A Sourcebook*, edited by Vincent L. Wimbush, 448–55. Minneapolis: Fortress, 1990.

Zaleski, Irma. *Living the Jesus Prayer*. New York: Novalis Continuum, 2003.

Zimmer, Heinrich. *Philosophies of India*. Edited by Joseph Campbell. Bollingen Series 26. Princeton: Princeton University Press, 1951.

Zizioulas, John D. *Being as Communion: Studies in Personhood and the Church*. Crestwood, NY: St. Vladimir's Seminary Press, 1985.

Zuercher, Suzanne. *Enneagram Spirituality: From Compulsion to Contemplation*. Notre Dame, IN: Ave Maria Press, 1992.

Index